DIVINE MIRRORS

Divine Mirrors

The Virgin Mary in the Visual Arts

MELISSA R. KATZ, EDITOR

WITH ESSAYS BY
MELISSA R. KATZ AND ROBERT A. ORSI

OXFORD
UNIVERSITY PRESS
2001

OXFORD
UNIVERSITY PRESS

Oxford   New York
Athens   Auckland   Bangkok
Bogotá   Buenos Aires   Cape Town
Chennai   Dar es Salaam   Delhi   Florence
Hong Kong   Istanbul   Karachi
Kolkata   Kuala Lumpur   Madrid
Melbourne   Mexico City   Mumbai
Nairobi   Paris   São Paulo   Shanghai
Singapore   Taipei   Tokyo   Toronto   Warsaw

and associated companies in
Berlin   Ibadan

Library of Congress Cataloging-in-Publication Data
Katz, Melissa R.
Divine mirrors : the Virgin Mary in the visual arts /
Melissa R. Katz and Robert A. Orsi.
     p. cm.
Catalog of an exhibition held at
the Davis Museum and Cultural Center, Wellesley
College, Wellesley, Mass.
Includes bibliographical references and index.
ISBN 0-19-514557-7 (cloth) — ISBN 0-19-514558-5 (pbk.)
1. Mary, Blessed Virgin, Saint—Art—Exhibitions.
2. Art—Massachusetts—Wellesley—Exhibitions.
3. Davis Museum and Cultural Center—Exhibitions.
I. Orsi, Robert A. II. Davis Museum and Cultural Center.
III. Title.

N8070.K3 2001
704.9'4855'0747447   00-051478

Front cover: Pintoricchio, *Virgin and Child with Saints
Andrew and Francis and the Infant Saint John the Baptist,*
1495–1500, oil on panel, collection of the Davis Museum
and Cultural Center, Wellesley College.

Frontispiece: Ubaldo Gandolfi, *Virgin, Children, and God the
Father with Saint Joseph,* circa 1775, ink and wash with black
chalk underdrawing, collection of the Davis Museum and
Cultural Center, Wellesley College.

9 8 7 6 5 4 3 2 1
Printed in Hong Kong
on acid-free paper

This publication has been produced by the Davis Museum and
Cultural Center, Wellesley College, to accompany *Divine Mirrors: The Virgin Mary in the Visual Arts,* a multiphase project to
research, exhibit, and interpret the museum's permanent collection. Funding from the Samuel H. Kress Foundation, Phyllis
Anina Nitze Moriarty (Class of 1969), Andrew W. Mellon
Foundation, Sandra Cohen and David Bakalar Fund for Art,
Judith Blough Wentz (Class of 1957) Museum Programs Fund,
and Wellesley College Friends of Art supported the exhibition,
publication, symposium, and accompanying programs.

For Astrid,
   who knew how God worked,
and Emilia,
   who knew why.

Mary the Dawn, Christ the perfect Day;
Mary the Gate, Christ the heavenly Way.

Mary the Root, Christ the mystic Vine;
Mary the Grape; Christ the sacred Wine.

Mary the Wheat-sheaf, Christ the living Bread;
Mary the Rose tree, Christ the Rose blood-red.

Mary the Font, Christ the cleansing Flood;
Mary the Chalice, Christ the saving Blood.

Mary the Temple, Christ the temple's Lord;
Mary the Shrine, Christ the God adored.

Mary the Beacon, Christ the Haven's Rest;
Mary the Mirror, Christ the Vision blest.

—MEDIEVAL HYMN

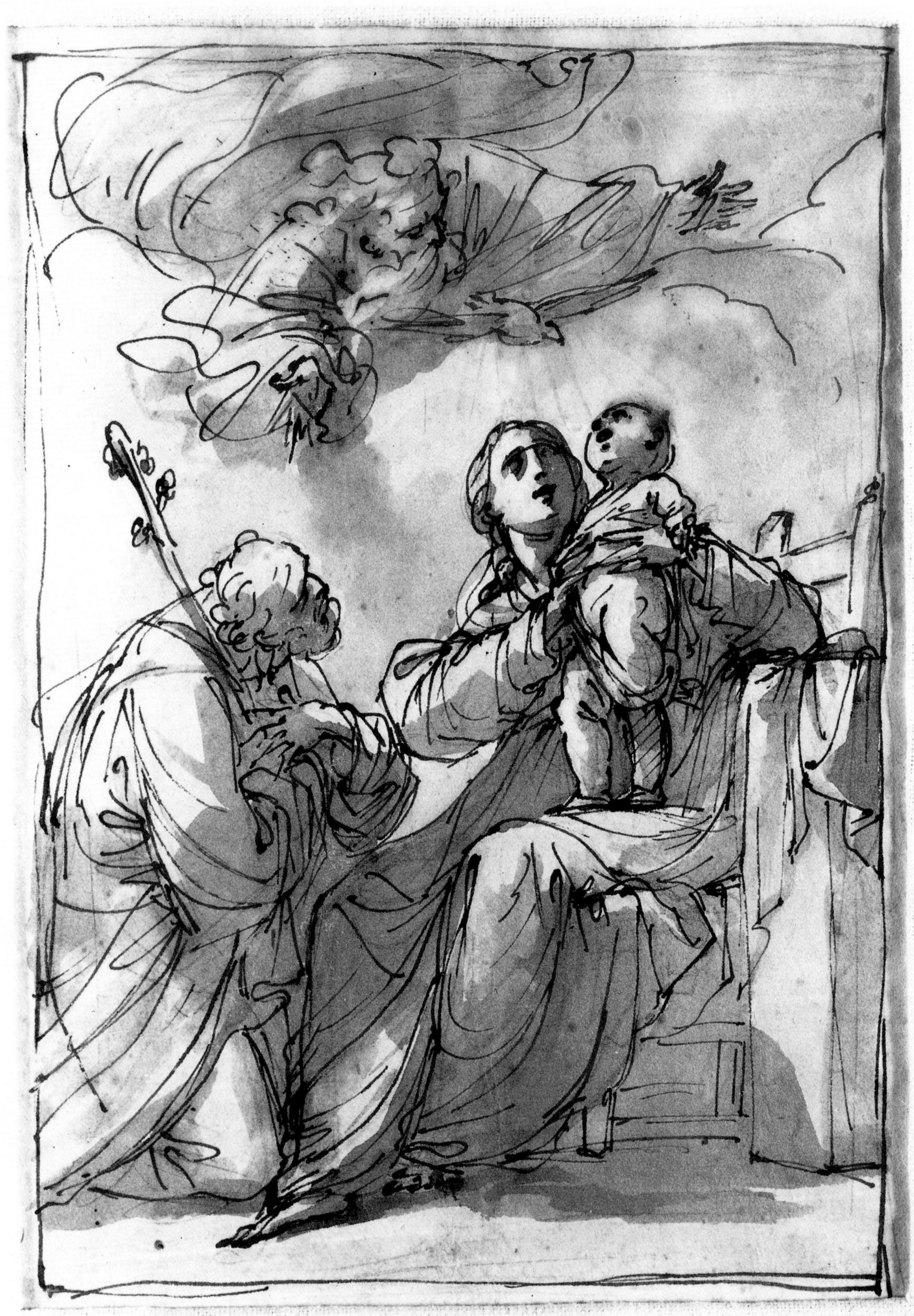

Symbol or energy, the Virgin had acted as the
greatest force the Western world ever felt, and had
drawn man's activities to herself more strongly
than any other power, natural or supernatural,
had ever done; the historian's business was to
follow the track of the energy; to find where it
came from and where it went to; its complex
source and shifting channels; its values, equiva-
lents, conversions.

—HENRY ADAMS,
"The Dynamo and the Virgin (1900)"
in *The Education of Henry Adams*

CONTENTS

List of Contributors to the Catalogue   x

List of Figures   xi

Acknowledgments   xvii

Preface   xix

Part I: Essays

The Many Names of the Mother of God   3
    ROBERT A. ORSI

Regarding Mary: Women's Lives Reflected in the Virgin's Image   19
    MELISSA R. KATZ

Part II: Other Voices

Mary and the Ancient Goddesses   133
    MARY R. LEFKOWITZ

Mary in the Christian Tradition   136
    SHARON K. ELKINS

The Virgin's Voice: Representations of Mary in Seventeenth-Century Italian Song   139
    CLAIRE FONTIJN-HARRIS

In a Corner of Africa: Reflections on the Virgin Mary   142
    IFEANYI ANTHONY MENKITI

Part III: The Catalogue

List of Catalogue Entries   148

Part IV: Checklist

Works of Art with Marian Themes in the Collection
    of the Davis Museum and Cultural Center, Wellesley College   265

Index   289

Photography Credits   298

CONTRIBUTORS

HILLARY L. ANDERSON
Wellesley College Class of 2000
(Cat. nos. 21, 22, 27, 29, 33)

LILIAN ARMSTRONG
(Wellesley College Class of
1958)
Mildred Lane Kemper Professor
of Art
Wellesley College
(Cat. nos. 1, 2, 4, 6, 8, 10, 11, 12,
13)

PATRICIA GRAY BERMAN
Barbara Morris Caspersen Asso-
ciate Professor of Art
Wellesley College
(Cat. nos. 38, 39, 45)

BLAIR A. BROOKS
Wellesley College Class of 2002
(Cat. nos. 15, 21, 29, 42)

MARIA MAGADALENA
CAMPOS-PONS
Artist
(Cat. no. 50)

MARGARET D. CARROLL
Professor of Art
Wellesley College
(Cat. nos. 5, 18, 24, 25)

SHARON K. ELKINS
Professor of Religion
Wellesley College
(Essay, pages 136-38)

CLAIRE FONTIJN-HARRIS
Associate Professor of Music
Wellesley College
(Essay, pages 139-41)

JEREMY J. FOWLER
Assistant Curator of Education
Davis Museum and Cultural
Center
(Cat. nos. 43, 46)

MEG HENSON SCALES
Artist
(Cat. no. 49)

ANNE HIGONNET
Associate Professor of Art
Wellesley College
(Cat. nos. 37, 40, 41)

MELISSA R. KATZ
Assistant Curator
Davis Museum and Cultural
Center
(Essay, pages 19-129; Cat. nos. 7,
14, 18, 20, 23, 32, 36)

MARLENE KUHN
Wellesley College Class of 2000
(Cat. no. 47)

MARY R. LEFKOWITZ
Andrew W. Mellon Professor in
the Humanities
Department of Classical Studies
Wellesley College
(Essay, pages 133-35)

ELIZABETH LOSADA
Wellesley College Class of 2000
(Cat. no. 35)

LISA MCDERMOTT
former Museum Registrar/Assis-
tant Curator for the Permanent Collection
Davis Museum and Cultural
Center
(Cat. nos. 16, 26, 33)

IFEANYI ANTHONY MENKITI
Professor of Philosophy
Wellesley College
(Essay, pages 142-44)

REBECCA MONGEON
(Wellesley College Class of 1997)
Liliane Pingoud Soriano Class of
1949 Curatorial Assistant
Davis Museum and Cultural
Center
(Cat. nos. 34, 44)

JAMES OLES
Assistant Professor of Art
Wellesley College
(Cat. no. 48)

ROBERT A. ORSI
Warren Professor of American
Religious History
Harvard Divinity School
(Essay, pages 3-18)

JENNIFER SORRA PARK
Wellesley College Class of 2001
(Cat. no. 3)

MARGARET A. SAMU
Davis Scholar
Wellesley College Class of 2001
(Cat. nos. 17, 19)

CURTIS H. SHELL
former Professor of Art
Wellesley College
(Cat. nos. 9, 30)

JOAN C. SIEGFRIED
former Professor of Art
Skidmore College
(Cat. no. 31)

RICHARD W. WALLACE
Professor of Art
Wellesley College
(Cat. no. 28)

LIST OF FIGURES

ORSI ESSAY

1. Replica of the Grotto at Lourdes, University of Notre Dame campus, South Bend, Indiana

2. Apparition of the Virgin Mary on the windows of an office building in Clearwater, Florida, mid-1990s

3. Devotees improvise a shrine to the Weeping Madonna of Siracusa, Sicily, ca. 1954

4. Basilica of the National Shrine of the Immaculate Conception, Washington, DC

5. View of the *Divine Mirrors* exhibition at the Davis Museum

6. Scene from Roberto Rossellini's 1948 film *The Miracle*

KATZ ESSAY

7. Albrecht Dürer, *Joachim and St. Anne Meet at the Golden Gate*, 1504, Davis Museum and Cultural Center (DMCC)

8. John Baptist Jackson, *Presentation of the Virgin in the Temple*, 1742, DMCC

9. French from Amiens, *Saint Luke the Evangelist*, ca. 1480, DMCC

10. Bartholomeus Breenbergh, *Abraham Dismissing Hagar*, 1630s, DMCC

11. Marc Chagall, *Moses Dies in View of the Promised Land*, 1931–1939, DMCC

12. Rembrandt van Rijn, *Jews in the Synagogue*, 1648, DMCC

13. Roman, *Orant Virgin and Child*, 4th century, Coementerium Maius catacomb

14. Roman, *Virgin and Child with Prophet*, early 3rd century, Catacomb of Priscilla

15. James Anderson, *Temple of Antonius and Faustina*, ca. 1858, DMCC

16. Pieter Neefs the Younger, *Interior of Antwerp Cathedral*, 1657, DMCC

17. Spanish, *Monk Purchasing a Painting*, ca. 1280, Library of the Monastery of Él Escorial

18. French from Amiens, *Franciscan Saint before Seated Virgin*, ca. 1480, DMCC

19. German, *Pietà*, 16th century, DMCC

20. Italian, *Visitation, Adoration of the Magi, Flight into Egypt, Christ among the Doctors, and Raising of Lazarus*, 15th century, DMCC

21. Jacopo Vignali, *Abraham Entertaining the Three Angels*, ca. 1620, DMCC

22. German from Middle Rhineland, *Annunciation with Sts. Barbara and Catherine of Alexandria*, ca. 1460, DMCC

23. Albrecht Dürer, *Annunciation*, ca. 1503, DMCC

24. Hendrik Goltzius, *The Annunciation*, 1594, DMCC

25. Albrecht Dürer, *Visitation*, ca. 1504, DMCC

26. French and/or Flemish, *Visitation*, ca. 1450, Wellesley College Library

27. French from Amiens, *Lamentation*, ca. 1480, DMCC

28. Albrecht Dürer, *Betrothal of the Virgin*, ca. 1504, DMCC

29. School of Fontainebleau, *Holy Family with Saints*, 16th century, DMCC

30. German from Ulm, *Virgin and Child*, ca. 1500–1515, DMCC

31. Hans Sebald Beham, *Virgin and Child with a Pear*, 1520, DMCC

32. French from Amiens, *Visitation*, ca. 1480, DMCC

33. German from Strasbourg, *Pentecost*, 1483, DMCC

34. French from Brittany, *Virgin, Child, and Saint Anne*, ca. 1470, Wellesley College Library

35. German from Alsace, *Virgin and Child*, ca. 1490, DMCC

36. Italian, *Half-length Figure of the Virgin*, 17th/18th century, DMCC

37. Albrecht Dürer, *Adoration of the Shepherds*, ca. 1503, DMCC

38. French from Amiens, *Nativity*, ca. 1480, DMCC

39. Francesco Furini, *Adam and Eve*, 1630, DMCC

40. Auguste Rodin, *Eve (after the Fall)*, 1899, DMCC

41. Gaudenzio Ferrari, *God the Father*, ca. 1540, DMCC

42. French from Amiens, *Annunciation to the Shepherds*, ca. 1480, DMCC

43. Bonifazio Veronese, *Adoration of the Shepherds*, mid-16th century, DMCC

44. French from Amiens, *Virgin and Child Enthroned*, ca. 1480, DMCC

45. Pintoricchio, *Madonna and Child with Saints*, 1495–1500, DMCC

46. French from Paris or Northeastern France, *Mary Presents the Infant Jesus to the Men and Women who Serve Her*, ca. 1290–1300, Wellesley College Library

47. Cristofano Robetta, *Adoration of the Magi*, 1496–1500, DMCC

48. Lucas van Leyden, *Virgin and Child with Two Angels*, 1523, DMCC

49. Ferê Seyon, *Our Lady Mary with Her Beloved Son*, 1445–1480, Institute of Ethiopian Studies

50. French from Paris or Northeastern France, *Mary as the City of God*, ca. 1290–1300, Wellesley College Library

51. Master of the Tucher altarpiece, *Circumcision*, ca. 1450, Suermondt-Ludwig-Museum, Aachen

52. Michael Wohlgemut, *Circumcision*, 1491, DMCC

53. Ubaldo Gandolfi, *Holy Family with God the Father*, ca. 1775, DMCC

54. GianDomenico Tiepolo, *Mary Holding the Child in her Arms . . .* , 1753, DMCC

55. Michael Wohlgemut, *Holy Kinship*, 1493, DMCC

56. Anton Wierix, *The Garden*, late 16th century, DMCC

57. Giuseppe Ma. Crespi, *Sacrament of Ordination*, pre-1712, DMCC

58. Italian after Raphael, *Alba Madonna* cartoon, 16th/17th century, DMCC

59. Albrecht Dürer, *Birth of the Virgin*, ca. 1503–1504, DMCC

60. Wenzel Coebergher, *Virgin and Child with St. Stephen*, ca. 1600, DMCC

61. Albrecht Dürer, *Holy Family in Egypt*, ca. 1502, DMCC

62. Giorgio Vasari and workshop, *Holy Family with Saints*, post-1544, DMCC

63. French from Amiens, *Elevation of the Host*, ca. 1480, DMCC

64. Emanuel de Witte, *Interior of a Renaissance Church*, 1660s, DMCC

65. Johann Franz van Helmont, *Study for an Altarpiece of the Assumption*, mid-18th century, DMCC

66. Pierre Hubert Subleyras, *Pope Benedict XIV Presents St. Catherine dei Ricci to the Virgin*, 1745, DMCC

67. Mexican from Guanajuato, *Ex-Voto Commissioned by José María Ramírez*, 1798, DMCC

68. Italian from North, *Transfiguration*, ca. 1575, DMCC

69. Claudine Bouzonnet Stella, *Crucifixion*, 1674, DMCC

70. Matthaus Merian, *This is My Dear Son, Whom You Shall Hear!*, 1630, Private Collection

71. Gregorio Martínez, *Lamentation with Saints*, 1590s, DMCC

72. Alessandro Magnasco, *Monastic Saint in Ecstasy*, 1720s, DMCC

73. Axel Herman Haig, *Church Interior with Worshipers at a Pietà*, 1891, DMCC

74. Italian, *Lamentation* pax, mid-16th century, DMCC

75. Hans von Aachen, *Crucifixion*, late 16th/early 17th century, DMCC

76. Francesco Trevisani, *Deposition*, ca. 1698, DMCC

77. Italian from Umbria or Tuscany, *Christ Mounting the Cross* (detail), 1290s, DMCC

78. Tyrolese, *Madonna and Child*, ca. 1430, Harvard University Art Museums

79. Austrian, *Pietà*, ca. 1420, Harvard University Art Museums

80. Albrecht Dürer, *Crucifixion*, ca. 1520, DMCC

81. French from Paris or Northeastern France, *Virgo Lactans*, 1290–1300, Wellesley College Library

82. Giovita Garavaglia, *Angels Adoring the Christ Child*, early 19th century, DMCC

83. Cavaliere d'Arpino, *Holy Family with a Male Saint*, ca. 1600, DMCC

84. German, *Shepherdess Kneeling at a Rural Shrine*, 19th century, DMCC

85. Spanish, *Virgin Rescuing a Painter from the Devil*, ca. 1280, Library of the Monastery of Él Escorial

86. Spanish, *Our Lady of Montserrat*, 12th century, Abbey and Sanctuary of Montserrat

87. German, *Virgin and Child with Saint Bridget of Sweden*, late 17th century, DMCC

88. Italian from Umbria or Tuscany, *Funeral of Saint Clare* (detail), 1290s, DMCC

89. French from Amiens, *Coronation of the Virgin*, ca. 1480, DMCC

90. French from Amiens, *Pentecost*, ca. 1480, DMCC

91. French from Amiens, *Mary as the Woman Clothed with the Sun*, ca. 1480, DMCC

92. Albrecht Dürer, *Death of the Virgin*, 1510, DMCC

93. German from Augsburg, *Burial of the Virgin*, 1482, DMCC

94. French from Île de France, *Dormition of the Virgin*, 14th century, DMCC

95. Pedro Berruguete, *Assumption of the Virgin*, ca. 1485, DMCC

96. Italian (after Agostino Carracci), *Assumption of the Virgin*, 17th/18th century, DMCC

97. Mexican, *La Inmaculada (Immaculate Conception)*, 1870, San Antonio Museum of Art

98. Giuseppe Nasini, *Apotheosis of a Male Saint*, late 17th/18th century, DMCC

99. German from Strasbourg, *King Ortnit Christens the Heathens*, 1483, DMCC

100. Erich Heckel, *Geschwister (Siblings)*, 1913, DMCC

101. Otto Müller, *Zigeunermadonna (Gypsy Madonna)*, 1927, DMCC

102. Julia Margaret Cameron, *La Santa Julia*, 1867, DMCC

103. Gertrude Käsebier, *Heritage of Motherhood*, 1904, DMCC

104. Gertrude Käsebier, *Heritage of Motherhood*, 1900/1904, Detroit Institute of Art

105. Marcel-Lenoir, *La Madone aux yeux d'Onyx Vert (Madonna with Green-Onyx Eyes)*, ca. 1897, DMCC

106. Religious medal known as the "Miraculous Medal of Paris," late 20th century, Private Collection of Henry and Patricia Schwarz

107. J. Michael Walker, *Planchando, Pensando (Ironing, Thinking)*, 1995, Collection of Henry and Patricia Schwarz

108. Danny Lyon, *Showers, Diagnostic Unit, Texas*, 1969/70, DMCC

109. *Our Lady of Guadalupe* spray, late 20th century, Private Collection

110. Ethiopian, *Mary Enthroned with Christ*, 2nd half of 17th century, Dabra Warq, Gojjam

CATALOGUE ENTRIES

111. Cat. no. 1. Italian from Umbria or Tuscany, *Christ Mounting the Cross and the Funeral of Saint Clare*, 1290s, DMCC

112. Cat. no. 2. French from Paris or Northeastern France, *Dominican Monk Envisioning the Virgin*, 1290–1300, Wellesley College Library

113. Cat. no. 3. French from Île de France, *Dormition of the Virgin*, 14th century, DMCC

114. Cat. no. 4. French from Paris, *Coronation of the Virgin*, 1400–1410, Wellesley College Library

115. Cat. no. 5. Martin Schongauer, *Rest on the Flight into Egypt*, 3rd quarter 15th century, DMCC

116. Cat. no. 6. Circle of Willem Backer van Vrelant, *Annunciation*, ca. 1470, Wellesley College Library

117. Cat. no. 7. Pedro Berruguete, *Assumption of the Virgin*, ca. 1485, DMCC

118. Pedro Berruguete, *Birth of the Virgin*, ca. 1485, Abbey and Sanctuary of Montserrat

119. Pedro Berruguete, *Death of the Virgin*, ca. 1485, Abbey and Sanctuary of Montserrat

120. Cat. no. 8. Andrea Mantegna, *Entombment of Christ*, ca. 1470 or 1490, DMCC

121. Cat. no. 9. German from Alsace, *Virgin and Child*, ca. 1490, DMCC

122. Cat. no. 10. Pintoricchio, *Virgin and Child with Saints*, 1495–1500, DMCC

123. Cat. no. 11. Cristofano Robetta, *Adoration of the Magi*, 1496–1500, DMCC

124. Cat. no. 12. Silvestro dell'Aquila, *Bust of the Virgin*, 1495–1500, DMCC

125. Silvestro dell'Aquila, *Virgin Adoring the Child*, 1495–1500, Church of San Francesco, Aquila

126. Cat. no. 13. French from Paris, *Annunciation*, 1507–1515, DMCC

127. Cat. no. 14. Albrecht Dürer, *Christ Taking Leave of His Mother*, ca. 1504–1505, DMCC

128. Cat. no. 15. Lucas van Leyden, *Virgin and Child in a Niche*, 1518, DMCC

129. Cat. no. 16. Marcantonio Raimondi, *Madonna with the Long Thigh*, ca. 1520–1525, DMCC

130. Cat. no. 17. Giorgio Vasari, *Holy Family with St. Francis and the Infant St. John*, post-1544, DMCC

131. Cat. no. 18. Flemish, *Judith with the Head of Holofernes*, third–quarter 16th century, DMCC

132. Infrared reflectograph of *Judith with the Head of Holofernes* underdrawing, overall

133. Infrared reflectograph of *Judith with the Head of Holofernes* underdrawing, detail of Judith's head

134. Cat. no. 19. Lavinia Fontana, *Holy Family with Saints Margaret and Francis*, 1578, Postar Collection of Selma Postar

135. Cat. no. 20. Gregorio Martínez, *Lamentation with Saints Augustine and Nicholas of Tolentino*, 1590s, DMCC

136. Cat. no. 21. Pietro Faccini, *St. Francis of Assisi Holding the Infant Christ in the Presence of the Virgin*, 1590s, DMCC

137. Cat. no. 22. Hendrik Goltzius, *Annunciation*, 1594, DMCC

138. Cat. no. 23. Francesco Furini, *Adam and Eve*, ca. 1630, DMCC

139. Francesco Furini, *Adamo ed Eva nel Paradiso Terrestre*, early 1630s, Galleria Palatina, Palazzo Pitti

140. Cat. no. 24. Rembrandt van Rijn, *Flight into Egypt* (small plate), 1633, DMCC

141. Cat. no. 25. Bartholomeus Breenbergh, *Abraham Dismissing Hagar*, 1630s, DMCC

142. Cat. no. 26. Stefano della Bella, *Rest on the Flight into Egypt*, pre-1642, DMCC

143. Cat. no. 27. Carlo Sacchi, *Adoration of the Shepherds*, 1649, DMCC

144. Cat. no. 28. Salvator Rosa, *Three Marys at the Sepulchre*, ca. 1665, DMCC

145. Cat. no. 29. Claudine Bouzonnet Stella, *Crucifixion*, 1674, DMCC

146. Cat. no. 30. Giuseppe Maria Crespi, *Sacrament of Ordination*, pre-1712, DMCC

147. Cat. no. 31. Alessandro Magnasco, *Monastic Saint in Meditation*, 1720s, DMCC

148. Cat. no. 32. François Boucher, *Sacrifice of Isaac*, 1720s, DMCC

149. Cat. no. 33. John Baptist Jackson, *Presentation of the Virgin in the Temple*, 1742, DMCC

150. Cat. no. 34. Pierre Hubert Subleyras, *Pope Benedict XIV Presents St. Catherine dei Ricci to the Virgin*, 1745, DMCC

151. Pierre Hubert Subleyras, *Mystic Marriage of St. Catherine dei Ricci*, 1746–1748, Sacchetti Collection of Marchese Giovanni Sacchetti, Rome

152. Cat. no. 35. GianDomenico Tiepolo, *Holy Family Leaving by a City Gate*, ca. 1750–1753, DMCC

153. Cat. no. 36. Mexican, *Ex-Voto Commissioned by José María Ramírez*, 1798, DMCC

154. Mexican, *Ex-Voto Commissioned by Anita Pacheco*, 1955, Collection of James Oles

155. Cat. no. 37. Julia Margaret Cameron, *La Santa Julia*, 1867, DMCC

156. Cat. no. 38. Émile Bernard, *Confirmand's Procession*, 1891, DMCC

157. Cat. no. 39. Edvard Munch, *Madonna (Conception)*, 1902, DMCC

158. Cat. no. Edvard Munch, *Madonna*, 1895, Harvard University Art Museums

159. Cat. no. 40. Gertrude Käsebier, *Adoration (Mother and Child)*, 1897, DMCC

160. Cat. no. 41. Gertrude Käsebier, *Heritage of Motherhood*, 1904, DMCC

161. Cat. no. 42. Auguste Rodin, *Eve (after the Fall)*, 1899, DMCC

162. Auguste Rodin, letter to Julia Richardson, 1899, DMCC

163. Cat. no. 43. Erich Heckel, *Geschwister (Siblings)*, 1913, DMCC

164. Cat. no. 44. Gertrude Fiske, *Mary*, 1920, DMCC

165. Cat. no. 45. Fernand Léger, *Woman and Child*, 1921, DMCC

166. Cat. no. 46. Otto Müller, *Zigeunermadonna (Gypsy Madonna)*, 1927, DMCC

167. Cat. no. 47. Marc Chagall, *Abraham Sacrificing Isaac*, 1952, DMCC

168. Cat. no. 48a. Lola Álvarez Bravo, *La Patrona*, 1960s, DMCC

169. Cat. no. 48b. Danny Lyon, *Showers, Diagnostic Unit, Texas*, 1969/1970, DMCC

170. Cat. no. 49. Meg Henson Scales, *Mary Loves Jesus Bartlet Prayers*, 1997, DMCC

171. Cat. no. 50. María Magdalena Campos-Pons, *Sagrada Familia/Holy Family*, 2000, DMCC

ACKNOWLEDGMENTS

When I was in college, I came upon a musty volume in a secondhand bookstore entitled *The Complete Knowledge of the Universe in One Volume*. Something told me it might come in handy one day, but being a penny-pinching undergrad, I passed it up. How I have regretted that decision! Lacking the complete knowledge of the universe, I have had to rely instead on the generous collaboration of numerous colleagues, who have joined together in this project, both as catalogue contributors and behind-the-scenes aids. Religion professor Sharon Elkins saved me from a multitude of sins, venial and mortal, while history professor Margaret Mc-Glynn, with much tolerance and guidance, watched me reduce her fine discipline to a series of sound-bites. Dean of Religious Life Victor Kazanjian convinced both doubters and dissenters that delicate issues of faith can and should be dealt with openly and honestly, while philosophy professor Ifeanyi Menkiti persuaded many they were not nearly as delicate as they'd thought.

Art professors Lilian Armstrong and Margaret Carroll asked all the right questions, probed all the sloppy arguments, and dissected early drafts of sections of this text. They did their best—any errors that slipped into the final manuscript were on my watch, not theirs. In addition, they brought their considerable expertise to the study and interpretation of individual works in the exhibition. Their art department colleagues Pat Berman, Anne Higonnet, James Oles, and Richard Wallace matched their dedication in the preparation of catalogue entries that make great scholarship accessible to the general reader. My thanks also to past and present staff members of the Davis Museum and Cultural Center (DMCC) Jeremy Fowler, Lisa McDermott, and Rebecca Mongeon for their entry contributions, and to our brave student authors—Hillary L. Anderson, Blair A. Brooks, Marlene Kuhn, Elizabeth Losada, Jennifer S. Park, and Margaret A. Samu—who dared to make their debut in such imposing company. Outstanding entries by former professors Curtis H. Shell and Joan C. Siegfried produced originally for the 1958 *Catalogue of European and American Sculpture and Paintings at Wellesley College* have also been included here, rounding out our total catalogue entries to an even fifty.

The "Other Voices" contributed by professors Elkins, Fontijn-Harris, Lefkowitz, and Menkiti were conceived initially to provide exhibition viewers with a broader context for the art on view. Each has graciously allowed me to reprint here thoughts and comments that remind us how broadly the image of the Virgin Mary extends into other disciplines and cultures. There is grace in their brevity and wisdom in their arguments. Not all contributors to this volume appear in print, however. Special Collections librarian Ruth Rogers once again proved willing to share not only her rich treasury of rare books and manuscripts but also her deep knowledge of their history and use. The museum is continually enriched by her collaborative efforts. Ruth also assisted with the selection of works for the exhibition and publication, as did art department colleagues Judy Black, James Oles, and Richard Wallace, and museum friends Lisa McDermott and John Rossetti.

In the conception and development of this project, I have benefited immensely from conversations with Colin Eisler of the Institute of Fine Arts, New York University; Patricia Johnston of the Bunting Institute, Radcliffe College and Salem State College; and Joanna Ziegler of the College of the Holy Cross, as well as with my colleagues in the museum, Laura DeNormandie, Lucy Flint-Gohlke, Jeremy J. Fowler Judith Hoos Fox, Gretchen Sinnett, and Susan M. Taylor. I also owe much to the advice and encouragement of Fr. J. Bryan Hehir of the Harvard Divinity School; Fr. Ted Stylianopoulos of the Holy Cross Greek Orthodox School of Theology; Kathleen Harleman of the Fort Lauderdale Museum of Art; and to Marina Warner of London, whose early enthusiasm for this project was critical to its ultimate acceptance and success. Robert Orsi of Indiana University, Bloomington provided not only a brilliant essay but also a well-timed confirmation of the project's worthiness; much of my stamina through the summer of 2000 was fueled by his faith and commitment.

All the knowledge in the universe would have been for naught had it not been for the help of my coworkers in giving physical form to my ideas. The Davis Museum is blessed with a remarkably talented and dedicated staff. Former DMCC director Susan M. Taylor, now at the helm of the Princeton Museum of Art, lent full institutional support to an untraditional approach to collection research and publication. She and director of museum development Nancy Gunn were valuable allies in the rallying of institutional resources and support; acting director Dennis McFadden continues on the path of enlightened leadership. A special debt is owed to the "Monday meeting" veterans Sandy Hachey, Lisa McDermott, Rebecca Mongeon, Melissa Organek Dupree, Janet Saad, and above all John Rossetti, whose instinctive understanding of art brings meaning to light throughout the museum's galleries. If I am still alive today, it is because these good friends were so tired by their efforts on my behalf that they hadn't the strength left to kill me, no matter how great the urge.

Still, I'd like to imagine that my magnificent interns would have come to my defense with the same staggering energy and dedication they gave to their work. Jennet Zerbe and Jennifer Kirchmyer Dobe were my *alpha* and *omega*; they are dearly missed, as is Hillary Anderson, my *beta* through *psi*, whose detective skills, hunter-gatherer instincts, and research talents brought many an obscure artist to light and to life. A special debt is owed to my DMCC colleague, curator Lucy Flint-Gohlke, who carefully critiqued my manuscript(s) with the same level of critical inquiry and keen insight that she brings to curatorial matters. Joyce Berry, my editor at Oxford University Press, has steered this publication through rough waters with dedication and determination for which I am truly grateful. It may have been business-as-usual for her, but it was professionalism-in-action to me. Publication designer Adam Bohannon rose to the challenge to shape our ideas into a volume that I hope truly delights the minds and eyes of its readers.

Divine Mirrors reflects questions I have had about art and its intersection with larger issues of cultural determination. Answers were found among the stacks of the Wellesley College Art Library; Harvard University Fine Arts Library; Andover-Harvard Theological Library; St. Paul Parish Library; and my beloved Somerville Public Library. I thank these institutions for access, as I thank the Samuel K. Kress Foundation, Andrew W. Mellon Foundation, and Wellesley College Friends of Art for their vision and their vital funding. As one former Wellesley College student put it, it takes a village, and I am proud and pleased that so many fine institutions and individuals came together in this one.

MELISSA R. KATZ
SEPTEMBER 2000

PREFACE

Divine Mirrors: The Virgin Mary in the Visual Arts examines the convergence of the secular world with the sacred, demonstrating how donors, patrons, artists, and congregations fulfilled (and thwarted) social roles and expectations through the rubric of religious art. It grew out of a multi-year project that included a museum exhibition, publication, scholarly symposium, and reinstallation of a segment of the permanent collection of the Davis Museum, Wellesley College around the theme of the Madonna in art across seven centuries. This publication is designed to serve as a record of an exhibition, a guide to a significant portion of the museum's permanent collection, and an interdisciplinary consideration of the ability of visual art to inform historical, social, geographic, and cultural inquiries.

The number and variety of contributors to this publication reflect an experiment in community-building through the arts. Robert Orsi brings to his essay an expertise in twentieth-century American religious practices arising from the unique confluence of immigrant traditions. My essay attempts to place works of art with a Christian theme (or more accurately, a Marian theme) within the broad context of European and world history, culture, and religion. In the section headed "Other Voices," professors of religion, philosophy, classics, music, and art history respond to issues raised by these artworks from the perspectives of their individual disciplines. Finally, the catalogue entries place individual works in art histori-cal context, while also revealing the shift in interpretive strategies brought about by the displacement of religious art from a devotional setting to the secular shrine of the art museum. These entries present a multitude of voices, from seasoned professor to museum professional to gifted undergraduate, all members of the Wellesley College community whose collaboration has made this project possible.

Divine Mirrors does not propose to be a thorough examination of the religious, social, and cultural origins of the Virgin Mary, for many admirable studies already in print address that topic—most notably Marina Warner's *Alone of All Her Sex: The Myth and Cult of the Virgin Mary*, and Jaroslav Pelikan's *Mary through the Centuries: Her Place in the History of Culture*. Drawing on the abundant scholarship in print, I have selected elements felt to be most relevant to the study of art history and woven them together to provide a guide for modern audiences to engage with the religious origins of many works of art. No particular knowledge of art history, Christianity, or the Bible is assumed on the part of the reader—only a great desire to learn and explore. No particular faith is endorsed or disparaged, nor is any fully represented, for again, the focus is works of art that draw on and reflect religious faith.

Divine Mirrors had its origins in 1995 when one of my first tasks as a museum curator was to research the potential acquisition of a *Madonna and Child with Saints* by Pintoricchio. [fig. 45, cat.

no. 9] Before any major purchase, museums prepare and circulate a brief to external review com-
mittees stating why this particular acquisition is
important. The document falls halfway between a
scholarly argument and a sales pitch, and if all suc-
ceeds, the expenditure is approved. I prepared a
solid essay on this painting—well within the norms
of art historical writing, and well received by the
review committee. It began with a description of
the painting and its place within the artist's *oeuvre*,
then reviewed recent scholarship on Pintoricchio,
surveyed other works in area collections, and elaborated on the role the painting would play within
the museum's collection and academic
curriculum.

Two factors nagged at my conscience, however.
I had made no reference to the fact that this painting had served a religious purpose, that it had
once been intended to stimulate devotion among
the faithful within an environment of Christian
worship. Nor had I made more than a passing reference to its Marian theme, much less asserted
why any museum needed one more painting of
Mary in its collection. Religion was an essential
component of the painting's early history and its
meaning to earlier audiences, yet in the late twentieth century, addressing this dimension of the
work's earlier history was no longer necessary. In
fact, for me to have drawn attention to these origins would have seemed rather odd. Religion in
the 1490s, like religion in the 1990s, was not a
matter the museum world felt comfortable dis-
cussing in public.

In the midst of the manufactured hysteria surrounding the Brooklyn Museum's fall 1999 presentation of *Sensation: Young British Artists from the
Saatchi Collection*, I heard the clever remark that no
member of the New York art world public would
be shocked by the material on view. No one would
raise an eyebrow over formaldehyde shark tanks or
scattered limbs, much less a Madonna collage
daubed with elephant dung.[1] The only thing that
could shock a real New Yorker was the sincere
expression of religious belief. There again, in a
milieu noted for its tolerance and broad-minded-
ness, was the one taboo that not only had the
power to shock, but to render us silent.

In retrospect, what seems strange to me is not
how reluctant people were to engage in an open
discussion of the religious content of much
museum art, but how long we managed to avoid
the discussion. I marvel at how much art history I
had learned without having to confront the purposes for which many works were made and the
context in which they were meant to be seen. As
to why, I can but speculate. In part, it reflects the
evolution of art history as a discipline, and a
desire to elevate religious art above the realm of
biblical illustration. In part, it reflects the temper
of the times. For a certain segment of the population wishing to demonstrate tolerance and open-
ness, differences (religious, racial, sexual, social)
were anticipated and accepted, but not mentioned. Freedom of expression was supported by
simply not expressing what might be controversial, or offensive, or merely private. This pre-
vented conflict and discomfort, but also true
engagement.

Divine Mirrors breaks this taboo by directly con-
fronting the problematic role of religious art in a
secular culture with growing non-Christian con-
stituents. Rather than skirt these integral elements
on the pretext of avoiding offense, I have
addressed the role of the visual arts as a means of
shaping belief, stimulating devotion, and teaching
faith in order to allow women and men of all cultural and religious backgrounds to draw meaning
and relevance from traditional European art. Religion need not be a barrier to the enjoyment of
art, nor a requirement to its understanding. "We
can admire a cathedral," wrote Henry Adams,
"without comprehending the force of the Cross
that produced it."[2] Yet museums do a disservice if
we keep our knowledge veiled, and alienate viewers more by deciding for them whether they can
find meaning in faiths they may not share. *Divine*

Mirrors seeks to provide a bridge for visitors of all ethnic and religious backgrounds to engage with a common artistic legacy, and reinforce the museum's role as a cultural nexus for the entire community.

MELISSA R. KATZ

NOTES

1. See Damien Hirst, *The Physical Impossibility of Death in the Mind of Someone Living* (1991); Jake and Dinos Chapman, *Great Deeds against the Dead* (1994); and Chris Ofili, *The Holy Virgin Mary* (1996) in *Sensation: Young British Artists from the Saatchi Collection*, exhibition catalogue (London: Thames & Hudson, 1998).

2. Henry Adams, *Mont-Saint-Michel and Chartres* (New York: Penguin Books, 1986).

Part I

Essays

The Many Names
of the Mother of God

ROBERT A. ORSI

WARREN PROFESSOR
OF AMERICAN RELIGIOUS HISTORY
HARVARD DIVINITY SCHOOL

One of the most common images of Mary in the United States in this century was the dashboard Madonna, slender statuettes of the Virgin set under the curved glass of automobile windshields. The Blessed Mother protected drivers and passengers from the hazards of the highways that were taking the children and grandchildren of immigrants away from the old ethnic enclaves out to the new suburbs ringing the industrial cities of the northeast and midwest and rising up in the western deserts. These were usually glow-in-the-dark figurines: late at night, in cars parked on city streets or suburban driveways, Mary shone with the light she captured during the day from street lamps and from the sun.[1]

*   *   *

It is impossible to tell a simple story about the Virgin Mary. She cannot be held in place by a single attribute—sorrow or delight, purity or compassion—or held accountable for a single social consequence—liberation or oppression, solidarity or fracture. She is not innocent. Her sorrow, for example, has been a source of great consolation to women in their own grief but also a means of disciplining them to understand pain and self-abnegation as their destinies. Mary stands for peace and for divisiveness. She is not solely the creation of theologians or of the masses; she belongs completely neither to her devout nor to culture. The Virgin averts her eyes in most images, a conventional sign of her modesty and virginity but also an indication that she has very serious things on her mind; her poise is inseparable from her power. She is always refracted through the prism of the needs and fears of the people who approach her and so she is a protean and unstable figure. Because of this instability of meaning, Mary can be the occasion of serious cultural and psychological distress, which in turn provokes more determined efforts to fix her in place. But she continually frustrates these agendas.

The Madonna cannot be fixed to museums' walls, either. It is impossible to stand back and simply look at images of the Virgin Mary, for most Catholics certainly, but for others too. She subverts the distance that museums enjoin on viewers and alters the practice of looking itself. "When we see a painting," art historian David Freedberg writes about contemporary orientations to art in *The Power of Images: Studies in the History and Theory of Response*, "we speak of it in terms of color, composition, expression, and the means of conveying things like space and movement . . . . We refuse, or refuse to admit, those elements of response that are more openly evinced by people who are less schooled" in this way of seeing. We do not try to stroke art or kiss it; if we did, museum guards would rush over to reimpose the obligatory distance (and escort us out the door). We can look at paintings and sculptures in the formal way Freedberg describes because we do not mistake—as some see it—the representation of a thing with the thing itself; the thing is not *there*, the sign of it is. Icons of Mary, on the other hand, which Freed-

berg introduces as paradigmatic instances of another experience of the visual, fuse "image and prototype"; responses to them are "predicated on the perception that what is represented on an image is actually present, or present in it."[2]

Media of presence, devotional images and objects are used to act upon the world, upon others and oneself. "Unlike objects created for disinterested or 'aesthetic' contemplation," historian and theorist of religious art, David Morgan, writes, "popular iconography is thoroughly 'interested,' 'engaged,' functional and extrinsically purposive."[3] Pilgrims travel great distances to representations of Mary that are believed to heal, and then they plead, bargain, and argue with them, bring them gifts, make them promises. Haitian Vodou practitioners write their requests for help in thick pencil strokes on the plaster robes of the Madonna (who is the Catholic face of powerful African female spirits) in churches in Miami and New York City. Mary is taken out onto the waves by fishermen to bring them good catches and protect them from shipwreck, and by farmers into dry fields so that the Mother of God can see the cracked earth and send soaking rain. Frustrated petitioners sometimes inflict their disappointment on the images of uncooperative or dilatory holy figures, turning the face of a statue toward the wall, for instance, or moving it to a lesser position in a home shrine. No one treats the Blessed Mother this way, however, because she is so beloved, and so feared. Encounters with images of the Virgin are encounters with presence and they are characterized by the whole range of emotion and behavior that is possible when persons are present to each other in one place.[4]

So whatever artists, patrons, and curators intend—and I recognize that they intend many things, including, in some cases, devotion—Mary is *there* in representations of her. Responses to images and three-dimensional objects that are motivated by desire, need, love, or fear are neither premodern or postmodern: although the precise relationship between this way of experiencing objects and the one described by Freedberg is a matter of historical and cultural study, they exist together and inflect each other. They are not as distinct as those on either side who are dedicated to maintaining the boundaries between them hope they are. It is also a question for local and historical analysis how these divergent ways of see-ing—one formal and aesthetic, premised on the absence of the thing represented; the other devo-tional and instrumental, predicated on pres-ence—are implicated in patterns of social power and domination. Eruptions of iconoclastic vio-lence, for instance, are efforts to foreclose the power of presence in things or to limit the access of particular communities or individuals to that power. Political regimes may obliterate presence in one set of objects and images in order to trans-pose it, often by force, censorship, and torture, onto others. Ecclesiastical institutions try to con-trol the traffic in presence-bearing objects. Devo-tional experience, including the intimate han-dling of sacred objects, may be discounted and pushed to the social and psychological margins, branded infantile or even insane, especially when it is associated with women. At the same time, the devotional or instrumental experience of images and objects is commonly appropriated by elites, as in the European and North American vogue for "primitivism" in the nineteenth and twentieth cen-turies; artifacts of African or Native American cul-ture—costumes, for instance, ritual implements, or weapons—were believed to have the power to endow Westerners with virility, spiritual wisdom, and magical powers.[5] The nomenclature itself (*primitivism* as a term simultaneously of desire and denigration) articulates the dual colonialist pro-ject of domination and spiritual repossession; it also hides one way of seeing (the devotional) inside another (the aesthetic).

The Virgin Mary transforms looking into a devotional activity. The carefully monitored space between the wall and the viewer becomes an imag-inative opening for need, fantasy, desire, like the space between the faces and bodies of children and their caregivers. Devotional space is consti-tuted by the presence of the Madonna and her devout to each other, by the desires of the devout, and by Mary's invitation to them to come to her and her recognition of their needs. One visitor to the *Divine Mirrors* exhibition painstakingly wrote out the Hail Mary on a page in the book set out for comments; in this case, looking became pray-ing. Another, drawing on the iconographic tradi-tion associated with Marian apparitions in the nineteenth and twentieth centuries, sketched out in ink an image of Mary standing forth in a halo of bright light. In the experience of this visitor, all representations of Mary—including the (appar-ently) static and aesthetic ones in the exhibition— are apparitional. Someone else left a white, glow-in-the-dark rosary, made from the same material as the dashboard Madonnas, on a bench in the cur-tained area set aside as a "chapel" in the center of the exhibition, further marking this area as sacred space (and perhaps issuing a warning to anyone who failed to treat it as such; rosaries, as we will see, can be distinctly mean implements too). The fact is, images of Mary will be venerated. Roman women seeking assistance with difficult pregnan-cies, for example, have surrounded Jacopo Sanso-vino's *Madonna del Parto* in the church of Sant'-Agostino with burning candles and they have worn away her foot by their kisses and touch.

There are different ways of seeing and different reasons for wanting and having things. Cultural critic Walter Benjamin speculated in a famous essay that the advance of the technology of the mechanical reproduction of works of art would dissipate the powerful and compelling aura that attached to originals. The diffusion of Mary's image does not follow this logic. She is as present everywhere as she is anywhere. American Catholics seek cures at "reproductions" of the Lourdes grotto built on church grounds across the United States, confident that the Virgin is as pres-

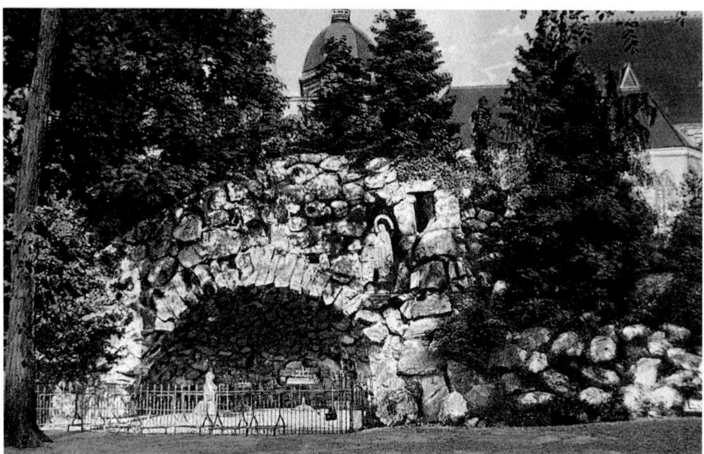

Fig. 1. Replica of the Grotto at Lourdes, University of Notre Dame campus, South Bend, Indiana

ent in these reproductions as she is in southern France [fig. 1]. They take from these sites healing "Lourdes water" that comes from city reservoirs, not from the spring that miraculously bubbled up at Bernadette's feet. This experience of presence in the reproduction occurs even when the resemblance between the "original" and the "copy" is utterly attenuated. Images of Guadalupe on refrigerator magnets, t-shirts, and holy cards—and on the skins of *cholos* (gang members)—can be bearers of the presence of the *Virgencita* (as Guadalupe is affectionately known) as much as the miraculous imprint on Juan Diego's *tilma*. There is still special merit in journeying to the sites where Mary visited. But her presence is not exhausted at them; rather, she is repetitively present, generously and lovingly so, as her devout see it.[6] The Blessed Mother does not have strong feelings about what constitutes appropriate or inappropriate venues for her visits, either: In the mid–1990s, for example, she began appearing on the glassy side of an office building in Florida [fig. 2].

In the interplay of persons and things, one thing is sometimes used to displace another, in which case the presence of the one may become the sign of the absence of the other. This is how philosopher and critic Susan Stewart understands souvenirs: as the mere "traces of authentic experience" that gesture elsewhere, to what is not there. By definition, Stewart says, souvenirs are objects taken out of their original contexts and away from the sites of their production, and they come to stand for otherwise inaccessible places, times, experiences. She writes, "The possession of the metonymic object is a kind of dispossession in that the presence of the object all the more radically speaks to its status as a mere substitution and to its subsequent distance from the self."[7]

The Blessed Mother's devout take things away with them from Marian shrines; there is a huge international market in Marian souvenirs. The devout display these objects, cherish them, and give them to people they love or care about (or into whose lives they wish to insert themselves). But these are not souvenirs in the way that Stewart defines them, and, again, like the Madonna's presence in works of art, the use of Marian souvenirs challenges us to reconsider fundamental notions—in this case, how we understand people's relationships with objects taken from one place and brought to another. More broadly, we are asked to reconsider the modernist imposition of absence everywhere, and the insistence on absence, or lack, as the necessary origin of desire. Marian souvenirs connect moments and sites of experience—here and there, the place of Mary's special presence and here, at home. They establish bonds of reciprocity, affection, and responsibility, and they are used to achieve effects (healing, for example, or reconciliation). They are conduits of power. Such objects cannot be understood apart from the phenomenology of presence; what makes them desirable and valued is the experience, in and through them, of presence.

But what is presence? What accounts for Mary's thereness?

One response is that presence is a psychological effect. The Virgin Mary exists in relationships: in the relationships of men, women, and children with her, and in her involvement in complicated relational triangles among people—between husbands and wives, for example, or parents and children, among the members of religious orders, between clergy and laity, between believers and nonbelievers (as was the case in France in the early nineteenth century, for example). In many of her appearances over the past two centuries, Mary has complained bitterly to visionaries about the character of the local clergy in the apparition areas, to the chagrin of regional hierarchies. She is called on to mediate family disputes, judge behavior, listen to the most intimate sorrows and fears. In individuals' experience of her, the Virgin draws deeply on the whole history of a person's relationships, real and imagined, living, dead, present and absent; she borrows from and contributes to memories, needs, fantasies, hopes, desires, and fears. To tell the story of any man's or woman's bond with Mary, it is necessary to recount the story of all his or her relationships, from childhood to adulthood. The Marian devotional world is an interpersonally crowded one.[8]

Relationships with Mary are never lived apart from the circumstances of particular times and places, however. There is a debate among scholars of Marian apparitions—those occasions when humans claim to have been visited and directly addressed by the Virgin—about the relative worth of social or psychological approaches to the phenomena. The distinction has more to do with academic boundaries and anxieties than with Mary's place in people's experience. Mary cannot be found solely in psychological analyses of any single believer's (or even community's) experience of her, because Mary and her devout alike find their being in culture. How her devout approach the Blessed Mother, the languages that give shape and limit to the prayers they bring to her and the fantasies they have of her, the memories she evokes, the patterns of family dynamics into which she enters, the disciplinary uses to which she is put, the desires that are thinkable and not in her sight, the emergence of new needs and possibilities—all of this is constituted and constrained by culture and history. Mary is a cultural figure not simply in the sense that she "reflects" cultural idioms or social

dynamics (although she does) or that the idioms and lineaments of Marian piety are inherited generationally. She is a cultural figure in that she enters the intricacies of a culture, becomes part of its webs of meanings, limitations, structures, and possibilities. She contributes to making and sustaining culture, and reinventing it, at the same time that she herself is made and sustained by culture, in dynamic exchanges with her devout.[9]

This is not a matter of culture *or* self, cultural implication *or* cultural transcendence. Mary arises on the ground of the imagination, that point where people take hold of the world around

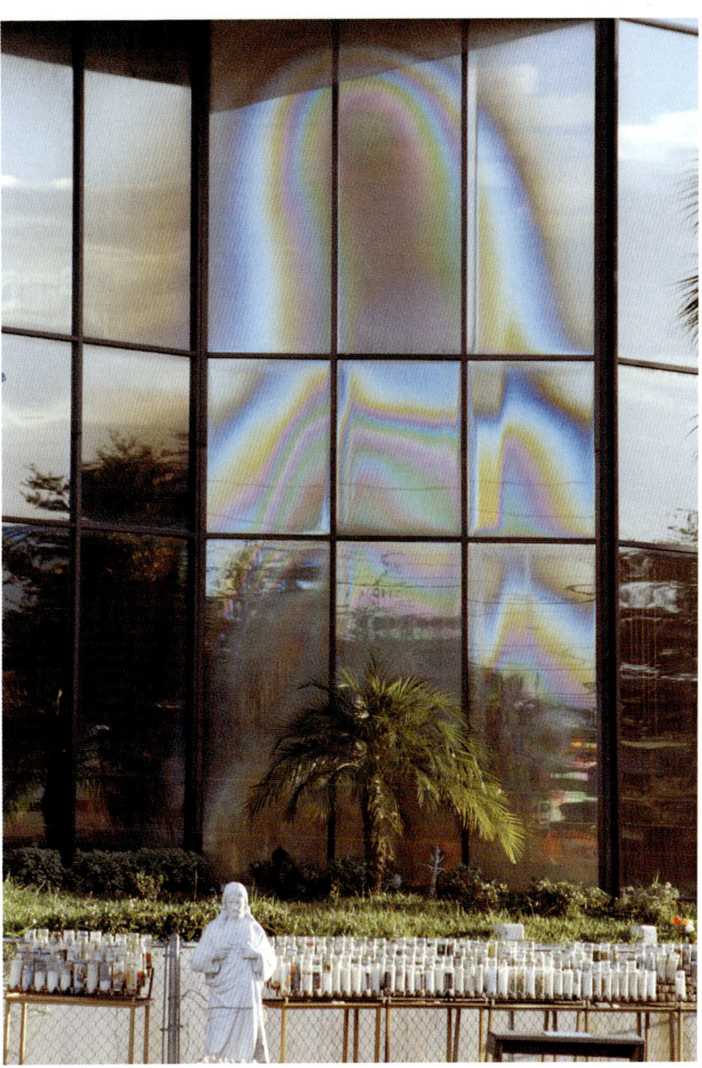

Fig. 2. Apparition of the Virgin Mary on the side of an office building in Clearwater, Florida, mid–1990s

them, in the idioms they have inherited, found, and invented. She does not belong completely either to culture or to self, but to the spaces where the two are most intimately entangled. The Blessed Mother tends to make her most dramatic, public appearances—in southern France in 1858, for example, the Saarland in 1876, Portugal in 1917, in the Basque country in 1931—when social, political, and economic transformations disrupt the customary ways people have been connected to each other and to the social world. Analogous to Mary's relationship to culture is the case of the languages she speaks when she appears: she always uses local dialects, which ensures that her visionaries understand and respond to her, but it also means that the Virgin is necessarily constrained by the syntactic limits of these languages. She may assist men and women accept the circumstances of their lives, resist them, or, most often, find some way of living between the desirable and the ordained, within the possibilities of the given.[10]

Given the complex social and psychological etiology of Mary's presence, she is not always a benign figure. She may touch the most primitive fears in her devout, of abandonment, for example, or rejection. Her children bring the most insistent needs to her—and there is always the threat that Mary will refuse or ignore them. Or they may fail to satisfy her. The danger of the Blessed Mother surfaces in certain features of Marian lore and in aspects of her apparitional messages. There is a Southern Italian tradition, for example, which holds that the Madonna will wound those who do not respond adequately to her demands for attention. Mary often warns visionaries of dire consequences to humankind if her calls to repentance are not heeded. Apparitional sites are psychological playgrounds, where the most intense desires, needs, and fears are put in play; inevitably, this kind of complicated imaginative activity provokes uncertainty, dread, confusion, and panic [fig. 3]. "The Devil . . . comes to Oliveto almost as often as the Madonna," anthropologist Paolo Apolito writes of a contemporary apparition site outside Naples, Italy—Oliveto Citra, where the Madonna began appearing in 1985. "The two figures sometimes seem to alternate on the stage of the transcendent in a kind of two-sided game." On a visit to Ireland in 1975, I was told by a gas station attendant in the town of Knock, where Mary appeared in 1879, that "here is where the transcendent broke into time." Such tectonic shifts in the relationship of the planes of the natural and the supernatural are eruptive and destabilizing. There is, says Apolito, "a kind of vertigo from the temptation of the transcendent." Describing an incident in which visionaries suddenly lost any interpretive grip on what they were seeing, Apolito writes, "All was left suspended between ordinary perception and the possibility that all of a sudden something might emerge from the depths of the unspoken, breaking out of the accustomed surface of things, creating an opening that might suck the everyday order into metahistorical reality."[11]

Because Mary exists relationally—and only relationally—it is impossible to read out from theology or iconography the quality of people's experience of her or to anticipate its social implications. Devotional writers may have evoked a sorrowing, submissive Mary against the desires and aspirations of young women; indeed, there is such a disciplinary literature of Marian piety and poetry, written by men and women, lay and religious, clearly intended to constrain women's imaginations, desires, and behavior. But all this tells us very little about Mary's place in real women's lives. Mary's perpetual virginity may have been intended to authorize an ideal of sexless and obedient womanhood and to shame living women for their desires, but the American adolescents who belonged to the Children of Mary and other devotional sodalities in the middle years of this century dated each other's brothers and called on the Blessed Mother to help them find work, regardless of what devotional literature stipulated. Praying to Mary is not an activity that is easily controlled by others, or ever completely controlled.[12]

While the meanings of Mary are not exhausted by theology or ecclesiastical iconography and while there are often serious discrepancies between the moralizing intentions of clerical proponents of Mary's cult and the prayers of her female devout, it is not the case that there are two completely distinct worlds of Marian devotion, official and popular, one disciplinary, the other emancipatory. Contemporary theologians in the United States, Latin America, and Africa have developed a doctrine of Mary as champion of the oppressed; on the other hand, "popular" expressions of Marian piety in the United States today include harsh and abusive tactics by self-declared soldiers in Mary's armies against young women and their families entering or leaving abortion clinics, such as aggressively brandishing rosaries in women's faces. (Not since the Reformation has the rosary been so regularly implicated in vicious social conflict as it has been in the American struggle over abortion.) Priests and nuns participate in all forms of Marian devotionalism, including ones not officially sanctioned by the church; theological discussions about Mary build on and authorize popular understanding and practice. It was the decision of the "Queen of the Castle Committee," which represented the concerns and authority of the church in Oliveto Citra, to accept the claim of local boys to have seen the Madonna that unleashed the popular imagination there, which soon enough was seeing, in addition to the Madonna, bleeding stones and "strange and inexplicable fiery snakes in the shape of the number six." It is another dimension of Mary's protean nature that she completely confounds any attempt to stabilize the categories of popular and elite.[13]

*   *   *

Mary was the clearest sign of Catholic difference in the United States. One of the reasons that Ameri-

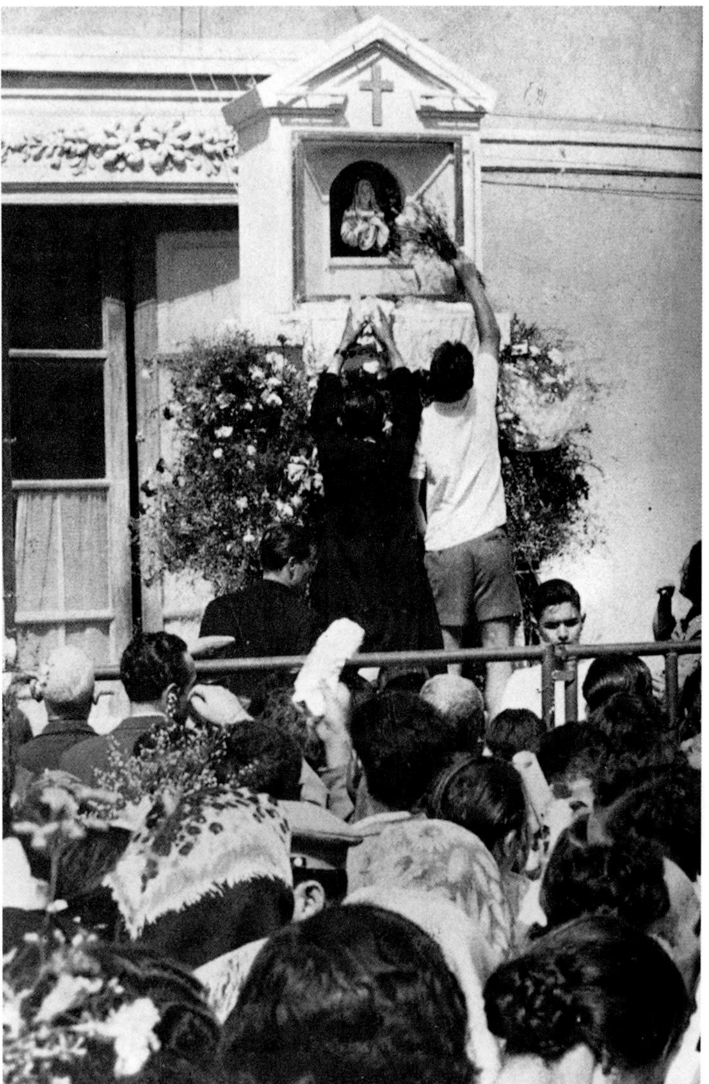

Fig. 3. Devotees improvise a shrine to the Weeping Madonna of Siracusa, Sicily, ca. 1954

can Catholics carried rosaries in their pockets until recently was so that in the event of an accident their religious identities would be immediately recognized and a priest (not a minister) called for them. But Mary's relationship to Catholic identity and difference—between Catholics and other Americans, as well as among the various Catholic ethnic communities—is complicated. Mary is enthroned in the Basilica of the National Shrine of the Immaculate Conception in Washington, DC, as the patroness of the United States [fig. 4]. The cornerstone of this immense temple, which integrates elements of Byzantine tradition with American architecture,

The Many Names of the Mother of God   9

was blessed in 1920 by James Cardinal Gibbons, the Archbishop of Baltimore. Some years earlier, in 1887, Gibbons, who was one of the leading figures in late nineteenth-century American Catholicism, had delivered a powerful sermon in another Marian temple, the Roman church of Santa Maria in Trastevere, in which he proclaimed his love of the United States and its political institutions, especially for the separation of church and state. "Our country has liberty without license," Gibbons proudly declared, "authority without despotism . . . . [O]ur nation is strong, and her strength lies, under Providence, in the majesty and supremacy of the law, in the loyalty of her citizens to that law, and in the affection of our people for their free institu-

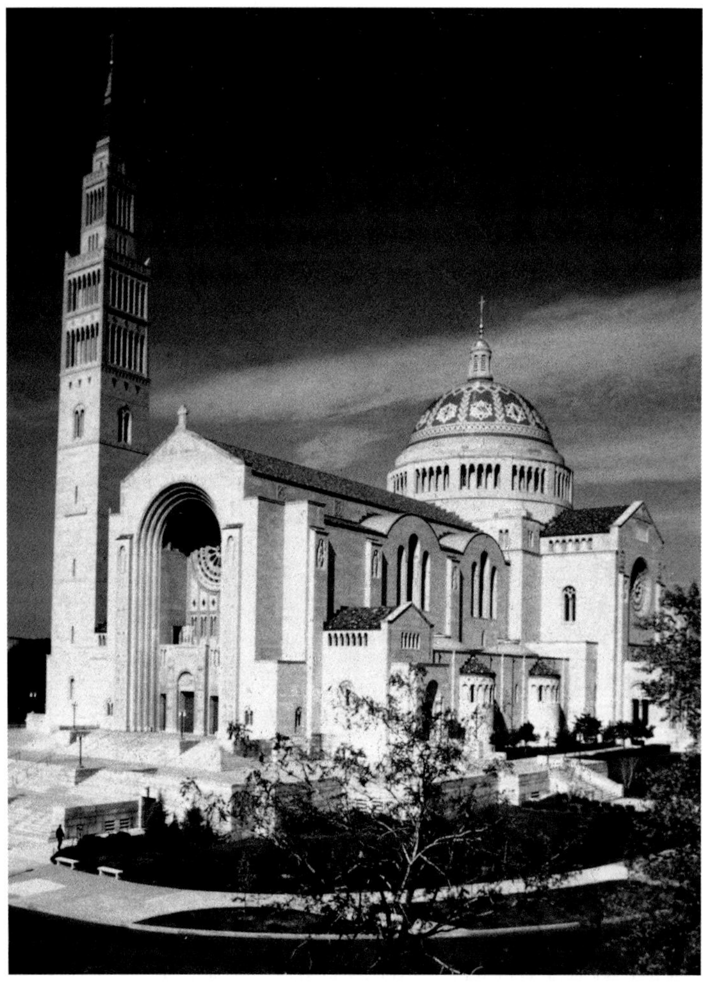

Fig. 4. Basilica of the National Shrine of the Immaculate Conception, Washington, DC

tions." Mary's presence in the capital city represented the unity of *American* Catholics, sanctioning their patriotism and loyalty to the nation. This is Mary as an American citizen.[14]

Among earlier generations of American Protestants, however, fearful that Catholic immigrants were plotting to take over the country, Catholic devotion to the Blessed Mother provoked great bitterness and alarm. The Virgin was the sign of what was threatening and inassimilable in Catholicism, of what was most profoundly un-American (although, ironically, it was precisely as the avatar of Catholic otherness, evoking ancient times and distant places, that the Virgin also became the object of desire among elite critics of industrialism, consumerism, and modernity). From the perspective of this fear, Mary was the anti-citizen, a decadent European queen out of place in the New World democracy. Catholicism was perversely feminized, anti-Catholics maintained, dominated by a woman who had usurped Jesus' prominence. Pornographic anti-Catholic literature offered Americans fascinated by the Catholic Other a compelling terrain of dark, wet interiors (convents, monasteries, crypts, and ruins) presided over by obscene, lascivious priests who ravished innocent virgins—just as the Pope threatened to ravish the innocent United States. The bitter taste of this is still with older Catholics.[15]

"Thank you," a visitor who identified herself as "an Active Legion of Mary Member" wrote in the exhibition comment book, "to Wellesley College (a bastion of WASP Boston civility) for recognizing the contributions of a poor young ethnic minority (pretty much single mother)." This begins a long communication with a number of interleaved messages. With whose contribution is this woman concerned: Mary's? her own? Perhaps she is thinking about the contributions of Catholics—"a poor young ethnic minority"—to democracy in the United States (an important theme in a tradition of American Catholic political thought to which Gibbons belonged). The writer's own vulnerability becomes clear in the next sentence. "By showing this exhibit you are validating the existence of the Blessed Mother . . ." But why does Mary require validation by Wellesley College? Even to imagine this is to disclose the deepest uncertainty about the value of one's own culture in the eyes of others who are believed to hold the authority to validate and invalidate it. It is not surprising that such a disturbing revelation should be followed immediately by a protective hostility. "Perhaps this will assist to bridge the class gap between the students of your fine (real or perceived) institution and the members of surrounding communities who haven't had the same types of privileges. Thank you." *Real or perceived.* Things are not always as they seem. Fine institutions like Wellesley may not really be as good as they are held to be; groups as mistrusted as Catholics may not be as bad as others say they are. I cannot imagine a Catholic writing such a note in the Midwest, where immigrants did not have to confront entrenched prejudices, but in New England, Mary stands at the intersection of Catholics' desire for membership in American society and their fear of exclusion from it, of their longing and their outrage. This woman's Madonna glows with the captured light of three centuries of anti-Catholicism.[16]

Mary has not been an uncomplicated symbol of unity among Catholics either, however. Different immigrant and migrant groups brought regional and national representations of the Virgin with them to the ethnic enclaves of American cities, including Southern Italy's Madonna del Carmine; Mexicans' Nuestra Señora Santa María de Guadalupe; la Caridad, who is the patroness of Cuba; and the Polish Black Madonna of Czestochowa. These dark-skinned Madonnas existed alongside "American" images of the Blessed Mother—"American" here meaning those either not associated with any particular ethnic group (such as the Sorrowful Mother or Our Lady of Perpetual Help, both of whom had hugely popular novenas in their honor in the twentieth century)

or those who attracted universal devotion (Our Lady of Lourdes, for instance). Nationally and regionally identified Madonnas contributed to sustaining immigrant and migrant affective ties to the old countries, serving, in some cases, as pivots of enduring political and social aspirations for the homelands. Annual feast day celebrations in honor of these Madonnas were occasions for making the worlds their respective devout had come from present again in the American environment: in the gaze of the Madonna, the familiar sense of the world of the old countries—smells, the taste of remembered food and drink on the tongue, the music of childhood, and so on—were recreated, or created anew according to the exigencies of immigrant memories. The ethnic Madonnas evoked absent relatives (just as shrines in their honor recalled absent places), especially absent women (which was particularly important, and complicated, in those periods of immigration when men preceded their female kin to the new country, sometimes by years). By their faithfulness to the Madonna, immigrants and migrants could demonstrate to the community—and to themselves—their enduring compliance with the expectations and norms of the old societies, even as the circumstances of their lives made such faithfulness extremely difficult, if not impossible. At the same time, Marian devotions assisted (and continue to assist) migrants in coming to terms with the facts of their departures and its implications. Our Lady of the Americas, for example, who has been appearing to the visionary Estela Ruiz in South Phoenix, Arizona, since the early 1980s, has helped the Ruiz family, and many of their neighbors, negotiate the tension between the values with which they were raised in Mexican households (and which they are eager to pass on to their children and grandchildren, in some fashion) and their success and ambitions in the American economy (which depended on other qualities).[17]

The immigrant and migrant Madonnas also stood at the intersection of generations. Men and women whose lives were shaped in one place (or in the movement from one place to another) took their children, born or raised in the United States, into the shrines of the ethnic Madonnas, on pilgrimages to ideal visions of the moral and religious worlds of their childhoods. Such moments were usually tense and uncomfortable for young people, because the cultures of European and Latin American villages were most often recast in such a way as to chastise them for their lives in the new country. Calling on the Madonna to be their witness, members of the first generation held their offspring accountable to ways of living that were not only irrelevant to them but that had been abandoned by the immigrants themselves. Younger people were asked to assume roles in their parents' inner struggles, and, not surprisingly, many of them came to despise such devotions, ridiculed them, or resisted participating in them until they were older. Then the Madonna would assist them, in turn, in demonstrating their own faithfulness and dedication to

their aging parents and grandparents and then they could make pilgrimages of memory themselves, with their own children, to the Madonnas in the old neighborhoods.

*   *   *

At the end of novenas in honor of the Virgin, in October or May or on her major feast days, people knelt to chant her litany. On the altar, priests dressed in the heavy robes used for the service of Benediction and flanked by altar boys swinging smoking censers, intoned a long list of Mary's titles; in response to each the congregation sang, "pray for us." Mary's names unfolded—Mother Most Pure (*pray for us*) . . . Mother Most Chaste (*pray for us*) . . . Mother inviolate (*pray for us*) . . . Mother most amiable . . . Virgin most prudent . . . Gate of Heaven . . . Morning star . . . Health of the sick . . . Queen of Angels, Queen of Patriarchs, Queen of Prophets . . . on and on and on. There were litanies for other figures too, but the Marian

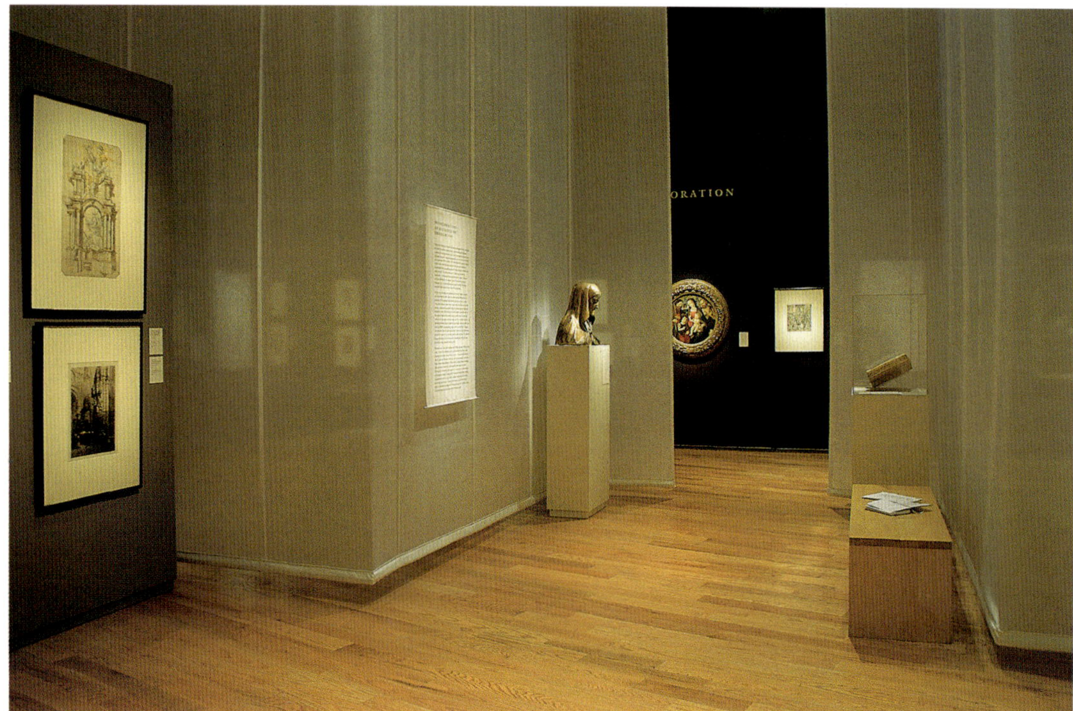

Fig. 5. View of the *Divine Mirrors* exhibition gallery

litany expressed social and psychological realities. Mary is not easily named. She requires long lists of names and attributes—pure, chaste, inviolate, undefiled, amiable, admirable, prudent, venerable, renowned, powerful, merciful, faithful—succeeding each other, in many voices, accumulating.[18]

There was also a Marian prayer called the *Memorare*, which read in part, "Remember, O most gracious Virgin Mary, that never was it known that any one who fled to thy protection, sought thy intercession, was left unaided. Inspired by this confidence, I fly unto thee, O Virgin of Virgins, my mother."[19] The Mother of God denied no one her compassion.

*   *   *

Catholics were once taught, in their religious formation (as Catholics call instruction in the faith), imaginatively to conjure up scenes from the lives of Mary and Jesus, in great detail, while they tolled the beads of the rosary. These were called "mysteries," in the sense of signs of God's truth in history, and there were fifteen of them: five Joyful Mysteries (the Annunciation, the Visitation, the Nativity, the Presentation, and Finding in the Temple); five Sorrowful Mysteries (Agony in the Garden; Scourging at the Pillar; Crowning with Thorns; Carrying of the Cross; and the Crucifixion); and five Glorious Mysteries (Resurrection of Christ, Ascension of Christ, Descent of the Holy Ghost, Assumption of the Virgin Mary, and Crowning of the Blessed Virgin Mary). These moments constitute as well a catalogue of the subjects of Western religious art: such imagery was there to assist people in the work of imagining their way into the narrative of salvation history, aiding "the inner eye," as Melissa R. Katz wrote in her introduction to the *Divine Mirrors* exhibition, "to mentally recreate sacred experience" [fig. 5]. This was one juncture of art and devotion.[20]

These imaginings were meant to be emotionally vivid: one of the attitudes to be developed by this practice was empathy, and the route to this posture toward Mary was meditation on how she felt as the mysteries unfolded. So Catholics imagined the Blessed Mother's delight in her infant boy, although they appreciated that this joy was shadowed from the start by the Virgin's foreknowledge of Jesus' necessary fate. (What parent cannot identify with this sorrow?) They rushed into the temple with her when she finds the boy Jesus who had wandered away, to be, mysteriously, about his father's business, recognizing that, like any parent, Mary would have been feeling simultaneously relief and annoyance. They were encouraged especially to imagine and sympathize with Mary's great sorrow on Calvary. The murmuring of the repetitive prayers, the presence of others praying alongside oneself, and the feel of the beads across one's fingers rendered the interior processes of the imagination corporal and moved Mary into the body.

So Mary became everyone's contemporary. Her kinship with Elizabeth located the Blessed Mother in the recognizable context of family ties. The Mysteries told the story of Mary's movement through the life course, subject to all the vicissitudes and sorrows of human finitude. She aged, she knew loss and loneliness, her hair whitened. Mary has never been held, at least not in popular experience (or in artistic representation) to a single life moment; she was not always, only, the young, slender, beautiful mother. Rather, the Blessed Mother accompanied her devout through the succession of the mysteries, joyful and sorrowful, of their own lives. By imagining Mary's history with the emotional discernment born of their own experience, her devout understood and affirmed that Mary recognized the anxiety, loss, and promise of what was happening to them. She had experienced all of them herself. Through the recitation of the Mysteries, the Blessed Mother and her devout became recognizable to each other. This was their shared book of years, the popular equivalent of the monastic Book of Hours.

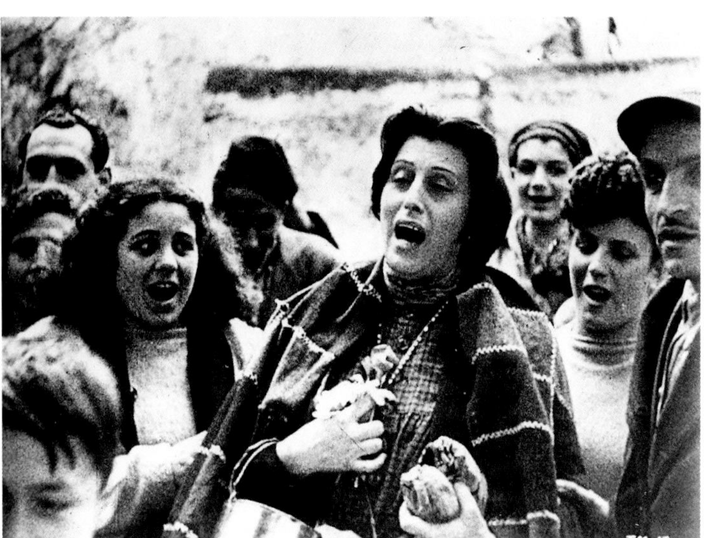

Fig. 6. Scene from
Roberto Rossellini's
1948 film *The Miracle*

Her devout know what Mary looked like, therefore. She was familiar from contemplative practice and from the conventions of devotional art. The Madonna's image has taken shape, again and again, in the ongoing interplay of art, devotion, and experience, in the everyday lives and practice of Catholics. One consequence of this is that among the criteria the devout use in assessing different representations of her is whether or not they know her as she is depicted. Some images of Mary are disappointing; this is not what she looks like, the devout think. All Marian art is, in this sense, realistic, more like photography than painting. The image on the wall is inevitably viewed through the lens of the image within.[21]

*　　　*　　　*

On several occasions over the last century in the United States a portrayal of the Blessed Mother in art has offended and outraged some of her devout, who have vigorously protested what they saw as sacrilege. Sometimes Mary's defenders have demanded that the troubling image be banned or censored. An example of such controversy at the time of this writing was the tumult over the painting titled *Holy Virgin Mary*, by Nigerian artist Chris Ofili, which appeared in the *Sensations* exhibition organized by London's Royal Academy and presented at the Brooklyn Museum in 1999. Ofili's use of small quantities of elephant dung in the preparation of the work incensed some Catholics, who considered the proximity of the Blessed Mother to little piles of animal feces to be a defilement of her.[22] (But as other, more earthbound, Catholics might point out, what about the oxen and asses in the Bethlehem stable? I will return to this alternative perspective in a moment.)

This was not the first time New York Catholics—or, more accurately, some of them—were convulsed by outrage on Mary's behalf. An even more intense furor greeted the 1950 American premiere of Roberto Rossellini's film, *The Miracle* [fig. 6].[23] The movie told the story of an unstable young Italian woman who believes that the child she bears after a liaison with a stranger, whom she takes to be Saint Joseph, is the infant Jesus. Catholic activists denounced the film as blasphemy. They threatened distributors with boycotts (a strategy that had served Catholic censors well in the previous decades). New York's Cardinal Francis Spellman angrily asserted, in a letter read from the city's pulpits on 7 January 1951, that Rossellini had offered "a vicious insult to Italian womanhood."

Any number of social and cultural issues came into play in this incident, including the eagerness of American Catholics to display themselves, in the early years of the Cold War, as the last dependable defenders of morality against the threatening onslaught of world Communism. (Other Catholics, such as the editors of the liberal journal *Commonweal*, defended both the artistic merit of the movie and people's right to come to their own judgments about it.) The religious source of the scandal (although this can never be completely separated out from other factors) was outrage at what was seen as the degradation of the Madonna by her association with human sinfulness, madness, and shame. Such offense seems completely out of place, however, in relation to a holy figure who is regularly begged, in the prayer addressed to her daily by millions of Catholics, to "pray for us sinners/now and at the hour of our death." Many people die in their beds; many others die in truly awful places. Catholics believed that Mary would be present even in the most dreadful of them. This was affirmed, described, and elaborated in fiction, pious literature, poetry, and prayer, and especially in the legends and tales Catholics told each other about the Blessed Mother. There was no place, no circumstance, so degraded that Mary would not enter it to comfort the lost and afflicted, especially if they had once loved her and had, in some way, even the most secret, remained faithful to her.[24]

When the transcendent breaks into time, as Mary repeatedly does in the belief of her followers, the transcendent is bound to get dirty. Mary may have been free of sin, but her robes got stained with the mud and blood of Calvary. This is not a theological affirmation; this is how Catholics imagined and talked about the Blessed Mother. Devotional practice had elaborated a story of the Blessed Mother as knowing shame, humiliation, and suffering. As the Legion of Mary visitor puts it, reflecting such popular traditions about the Blessed Mother, Mary was "pretty much [a] single mother," stunned (as Catholics were encouraged to imagine devotionally) by the enormity of what had happened to her and feeling at least a transitory disgrace at an unexpected pregnancy of uncertain paternity.[25] Stories are told today that Our Lady of Guadalupe comes in the middle of the night to distract guards along the border between the United States and Mexico, allowing migrants to slip past them. How does she capture the attention of these rough men so late at night?[26]

*   *   *

Of all the images of the Virgin in the *Divine Mirrors* exhibition, the one that touched me most deeply, in part because it was the one that seemed truest to the popular history of Marian devotion, was the tattoo of Our Lady of Guadalupe on the showering prisoner's naked back in Danny Lyon's *Showers, Diagnostic Unit, Texas* [fig. 108, cat. no. 48b]. Guadalupe is a national symbol, but her presence is more intimate here. It is a common practice among Latino gang members to put Guadalupe on their skins to protect them from violence, and common also for their mothers to grieve to *la Morencita* when their sons die. We cannot assume anything about this man's experience, but it would be good to know if Guadalupe's touch on his back comforted him, whether it reminded him of his mother or of the skin of his lovers, whether Guadalupe indeed kept harm away, and what he made of the moments when she failed him.

The excitement caused by the Virgin's apparitions may distract from the fact that, among her devout, the Blessed Mother is always there, amid the daily circumstances of their lives. This is not a benign reality; presence, however it is understood, is not easily or finally located on one side, the positive side, of a set of discrete moral categories—helpful/hurtful, reassuring/frightening, good/bad, and so on. Recall here the rosary held in the faces of shaken young women outside of abortion clinics or the proliferation of mischievous devils at Oliveto Citra. Presence changes things, alters experience, reconfigures relationships, necessitates new maps for familiar landscapes; it is known by what happens, what becomes possible, what is foreclosed, in the space between the faces of the devout and the face of the Virgin, present to each other, in art and experience.

NOTES

1. Hindu goddesses also ride dashboards. See, for example, the sad description of the unnamed narrator's taxi ride to retrieve his recently deceased sister's infant from a hospital in Calcutta, in Raj Kamal Jha, *The Blue Bedspread* (New York: Random House, 1999), pp. 12–13. Jha writes, "There's a black earthen idol of a goddess above his dashboard, two incense sticks burn, their heap

of ash tremble when he changes gears" (p. 13). For general discussions of this transitional period in American Catholic history, see Andrew M. Greeley, *The American Catholic: A Social Portrait* (New York: Basic Books, 1977); Jay P. Dolan, *The American Catholic Experience: A History from the Colonial Times to the Present* (Garden City, NY: Doubleday, 1985), pp. 349–454; Charles R. Morris, *American Catholic: The Saints and Sinners Who Built America's Most Powerful Church* (New York: Random House/Times Books, 1997); and Mark S. Massa, *Catholics and American Culture: Fulton Sheen, Dorothy Day, and the Notre Dame Football Team* (New York: Crossroad Publishing, 1999).

2. David Freedberg, *The Power of Images: Studies in the History and Theory of Response* (Chicago: University of Chicago Press, 1989), pp. 17–18, 30.

3. David Morgan, *Visual Piety: A History and Theory of Popular Religious Images* (Berkeley: University of California Press, 1998), p. 25. Morgan points out that negative critical assessments of popular art forms—indeed, the denial of the very possibility of a popular aesthetic—is the outcome of "the history of aesthetics since the eighteenth century" which imposed "disinterestedness as the basis for judgments of taste and artistic quality" (Morgan, *Visual Piety*, 26).

4. On Vodou practitioners in relation to the Madonna of Mount Carmel, see Elizabeth McAlister, "The Madonna of 115th Street Revisited: Vodou and Haitian Catholicism in the Age of Transnationalism," in *Gatherings in Diaspora: Religious Communities and the New Immigration* eds. R. Stephen Warner and Judith G. Wittner (Philadelphia: Temple University Press, 1998), pp. 123–60. A superb introduction to the relationships between Vodou practitioners and the spirits is Karen McCarthy Brown, *Mama Lola: A Vodou Priestess in Brooklyn* (Berkeley: University of California Press, 1991).

5. The literature on primitivism is huge. I have been helped by Marianna Torgovnick, *Gone Primitive: Savage Intellects, Modern Lives* (Chicago: University of Chicago Press, 1990); Torgovnick, *Primitive Passions: Men, Women, and the Quest for Ecstasy* (Chicago: University of Chicago Press, 1996); David Chidester, *Savage Systems: Colonialism and Comparative Religion in Southern Africa* (Charlottesville: University Press of Virginia, 1996); and Elazar Barkan and Ronald Bush, eds., *Prehistories of the Future: The Primitivist Project and the Culture of Modernism* (Stanford, CA: Stanford University Press, 1995).

6. Walter Benjamin, *Illuminations: Essays and Reflections* (New York: Schocken Books, 1968), pp. 217–51. Benjamin introduces devotional idioms as an art form distinct from art in the more modern sense; he calls these "two polar types" (p. 224) The cult value of art, he suggests, demands that such objects be hidden, whereas "with the emancipation of the various art practices from ritual go increasing opportunities for the exhibition of their products. It is easier to exhibit a portrait bust that can be sent here and there than to exhibit the statue of a divinity that has its fixed place in the interior of a temple" (p. 225). Clearly, images of the Virgin Mary do not fit this typology. Benjamin sees the shift from one art form to the other as a process of historical development; following Freedberg, I am suggesting that there is an interplay between the two forms of experiencing objects. Certainly, Marx's theory of fetishism taught us that there is a presence in consumer objects; on this subject, I have been helped by Michael T. Taussig, *The Devil and Commodity Fetishism in South America* (Chapel Hill: University of North Carolina Press, 1980). For a discussion of the history of American Protestant approaches to religious imagery, see David Morgan, *Protestants and Pictures: Religion, Visual Culture, and the Age of American Mass Production* (New York: Oxford University Press, 1999). On the reproduction of Lourdes grottoes in the United States, see Colleen McDannell, *Material Christianity: Religion and Popular Culture in America* (New Haven, CT: Yale University Press, 1995), pp. 132–62. McDannell writes, "The production of religious replicas was, curiously enough, the production of authenticity" (p. 161) She points out that the Vatican has often granted the same tally of indulgences (units of merit) at reproductions that it makes available to the faithful at the originals, thus further erasing the distinction between them.

7. Susan Stewart, *On Longing: Narratives of the Miniature, the Gigantic, the Souvenir, the Collection* (Durham, NC: Duke University Press, 1993), pp. 132–69; the phrases quoted in the text come from p. 135.

8. This emphasis on the intersubjective nature of devotional experience was influenced by Ana-Maria Rizzuto, M.D., *The Birth of the Living God: A Psychoanalytic Study* (Chicago: University of Chicago Press, 1979). For a fuller discussion of my understanding of devotional relationships see Robert A. Orsi, *Thank You, Saint Jude: Women's Devotion to the Patron Saint of Hopeless Causes* (New Haven, CT: Yale University Press, 1996).

9. For a discussion of the methodological debates over Marian apparitions, see Paolo Apolito, *Apparitions of the Madonna at Oliveto Citra: Local Visions and Cosmic Drama*, translated by William A. Christian, Jr. (University Park: Pennsylvania State University

Press, 1998), pp. 19–26; see also Sandra I.. Zimdars-Swartz, *Encountering Mary: From LaSalette to Medjugorje* (Princeton, NJ: Princeton University Press, 1991). The exemplary practitioner of the psychoanalytical approach to Marian devotions is Michael P. Carroll; see, for example, *The Cult of the Virgin Mary: Psychological Origins* (Princeton, NJ: Princeton University Press, 1986).

10. The apparitions referred to in this paragraph are Lourdes (see, most recently, the superb study by Ruth Harris, *Lourdes: Body and Spirit in the Secular Age* [New York: Viking, 1999]); Marpingen (see David Blackbourn, *Marpingen: Apparitions of the Virgin Mary in Nineteenth-Century Germany* [New York: Alfred A. Knopf, 1994]); Fatima (see Zimdars-Swartz, *Encountering Mary*, pp. 67–91); and Ezkioga (see William A. Christian, Jr., *Visionaries: The Spanish Republic and the Reign of Christ* [Berkeley: University of California Press, 1996]).

11. Michael P. Carroll, *Madonnas That Maim: Popular Catholicism in Italy since the Fifteenth Century* (Baltimore: Johns Hopkins University Press, 1992); Apolito, *Apparitions of the Madonna at Oliveto Citra*, pp. 109–10, 170.

12. On the history of Marian clubs in the early twentieth century, see Sister Mary Florence, S. L. (Bernice Wolff), *The Sodality Movement in the United States, 1926–1936* (St. Louis, MO: The Queen's Work, 1939). Marina Warner emphasizes the disciplinary nature of Mary's identity in *Alone of All Her Sex: The Myth and the Cult of the Virgin Mary* (New York: Knopf, 1976).

13. Apolito, *Apparitions of the Madonna at Oliveto Citra*, p. 171, also pp. 165–79, 178, 191, 205, 210–11. Of the Queen of the Castle Committee, Apolito writes, "The installation of the Queen of the Castle Committee is perhaps the most decisive of the acts that constituted the apparitions. . . . Without the Committee, and in particular without the parish priest Don Giovanni, it is possible that the apparitions would not have existed, and it is certain that they would quickly have faded away" (pp. 44–45) For an example of the reinterpretation of Mary by liberation theologians, see Leonardo Boff, *The Maternal Face of God: The Feminine and Its Religious Expressions* (San Francisco: Harper & Row, 1987).

14. "The Roman Sermon of the American Cardinal on Church and State in the United States," in John Tracy Ellis, ed., *Documents of American Catholic History* (Milwaukee: Bruce, 1956), pp. 476–79. On Gibbons, see John Tracy Ellis, *The Life of James Cardinal Gibbons, Archbishop of Baltimore, 1834–1921*, vols. 1–2, (Milwaukee: Publishing, 1952), and James Hennesey, S.J., *American Catholics: A History of the Roman Catholic Community in the United States* (New York and Oxford: Oxford University Press, 1981), pp. 172–233. On the Washington basilica, see Thomas A. Tweed, "Proclaiming Catholic Inclusiveness: Ethnic Diversity and Ecclesiastical Unity at the National Shrine of the Immaculate Conception," *U.S. Catholic Historian*, 18, no. 1 (Winter 2000).

15. The best study of this literature is Jenny Franchot, *Roads to Rome: The Antebellum Protestant Encounter with Catholicism* (Berkeley: University of California Press, 1994); see also Ellis Hanson, *Decadence and Catholicism* (Cambridge, MA: Harvard University Press, 1997). For a provocative introduction to the Virgin's place in the imagination of cultural critics of the United States, see T. Jackson Lears, *No Place of Grace: Antimodernism and the Transformation of American Culture, 1880–1920* (Chicago: University of Chicago Press, 1981), pp. 248–49, 279–86, 294.

16. The great American Catholic sociologist, Paul Hanley Furfey, opened one of his last works, *Love and the Urban Ghetto*, with this autobiographical reflection: "I grew up an Irish lad in Boston. To be such at the turn of the century was to be a member of a minority group. The WASPs were in control. They were the doctors, the judges, the mayors, the bank presidents, the intellectuals. The Irish were struggling upward from the level of pick-and-shovel men or housemaids. But we Irish had one big compensation. We were Catholics. On Judgment Day, the WASPs would be humiliated and we would be triumphant" (p. vii).

17. The apparitions of the Lady of the Americas is the subject of Kristy Nabhan-Warren's dissertation, tentatively titled "Religion in El Barrio: The Virgin of the Americas and Evangelical Catholicism in South Phoenix," currently in progress in the Department of Religious Studies, Indiana University. A recent study of the Virgin's place in the context of contemporary transnationalism is Thomas A. Tweed, *Our Lady of the Exile: Diasporic Religion at a Cuban Catholic Shrine in Miami* (New York and Oxford: Oxford University Press, 1997).

18. This is taken from *The Catholic Family Book of Novenas* (New York: John J. Crawley, 1956), pp. 329–30.

19. *The Catholic Family Book of Novenas*, p. 328.

20. *The Catholic Family Book of Novenas*, p. 336. On the medieval origins of this practice, see Anne Winston-Allen, *Stories of the Rose: The Making of the Rosary in the Middle Ages* (University Park: Pennsylvania State University Press, 1997), esp. pp. 111–52, and Eugène Honée, "Image and Imagination in the Medieval Culture of Prayer: A Historical Perspective," in *The Art of Devotion in the Late Middle Ages in Europe, 1300–1500* (Princeton, NJ: Princeton

University Press, 1994). For an example of a meditation on the mysteries in light of present-day concerns, see Rosemary Haughton, *Feminine Spirituality: Reflections on the Mysteries of the Rosary* (New York: Paulist Press, 1976).

21. David Morgan identifies this dimension of the viewing of sacred images as the "psychology of recognition" and finds it to be especially present in popular attitudes toward the widely distributed image of Jesus by the American artist, Warner Sallman. See Morgan, *Visual Piety*, pp. 34–50, for a discussion of devotional recognition. Morgan considers as well how believers manage to see many different images of a holy figure all as corroborative of this figure's "real likeness." As he writes, "Believers purport to see through the local features and apprehend the transcendent Jesus who stands behind every instantiation of his image" (p. 39).

22. I did not have the opportunity to see Ofili's work, so I cannot comment on it (a scruple that any number of Catholic protesters and the Mayor of New York, Rudolph Giuliani, did not share with me). Paula Kane's discussion of this incident, in "American Madonnas: Perspectives on Mary since the 1940s" (unpublished paper, Cushwa Center for the Study of American Catholicism, University of Notre Dame, March, 2000), pp. 2–4, was helpful in preparing these few sentences of my text.

23. *Il Miracolo* (*The Miracle*), second vignette of the 1948 film *L'Amore*, starred Anna Magnani as the shepherdess, Federico Fellini as the vagabond, and the inhabitants of Amalfi and Maiori as the villagers. Roberto Rossellini directed, and Fellini wrote the screenplay (after a short story by Ramon del Valle-Inclan). This was the "half" film Fellini referred to in his famous movie *8 1/2*.

24. In a theological reflection on the *Ave Maria*, Nicholas Ayo, C.S.C., writes, "Sinners know they cannot attract love in their wounded condition, unless that love be unconditional. They must be loved in their sinfulness as a mother loves a child in his or her woundedness. Something of that gratuitous quality of love that goes beyond one's deserts and gives life where there is no claim to life captures the tone of this petition in the Ave Maria." *The Hail Mary: A Verbal Icon of Mary* (Notre Dame, IN: University of Notre Dame Press, 1994), pp. 110–11. For a study of the mood and self-perception of Catholics in the United States in the early, post-World War II days of the Cold War, see James T. Fisher, *Dr. America: The Lives of Thomas A. Dooley, 1927–1961* (Amherst: University of Massachusetts Press, 1997).

25. For a discussion of this controversy, see Frank Walsh, *Sin and Censorship: The Catholic Church and the Motion Picture Industry* (New Haven, CT: Yale University Press, 1996), pp. 241–61.

26. Ruben Martinez reports this in "The Undocumented Virgin," in *Goddess of the Americas/La Diosa de las Americas: Writings on the Virgin of Guadalupe* ed. Ana Castillo (New York: Riverhead Books, 1996), p. 100.

Regarding Mary
Women's Lives Reflected in the Virgin's Image

MELISSA R. KATZ

INTRODUCTION

The following essay explores the intersection of secular culture and sacred art in the portrayal of the Virgin Mary through twenty centuries. It is arranged chronologically, beginning with first-century Gospel accounts, second-century apocrypha, and third-century images, then moving forward through the artistic, theological, and social elements that combine to form our image of the Virgin Mary. Simultaneously, it moves through the story of Mary's life, from the annunciation through her death and coronation in heaven, with a modest (but by no means perfect) attempt to observe a parallel chronology in her artistic representation. In short, the ANNUNCIATION section considers early Christian sources, the NATIVITY section is informed by Medieval perspectives, the HOLY FAMILY section takes the Renaissance as its reference point, and the CORONATION section concerns itself with post-Reformation themes.

Through the unifying theme of the Virgin Mary in art, three elements of artistic intent are considered: For whom and for what purpose were these objects made (initial context); how were their meanings shaped and interpreted by contemporary viewers (original intent); and how may we use them today to try to understand past cultures (historical content). These collected images of a single, extraordinary woman function as a two-way mirror, allowing a glimpse of past lives and attitudes, and reflecting back an image of ourselves that, while very different from the image in the mirror, bears some family resemblance. It is this shared membership in the human family that allows us to see in Mary a shifting icon of society's concerns. The forces that have shaped her devotion and nuanced her representation by artists are the same forces that moved Western culture through its curious route to the present.

The evaluation of past images through the filter of present experience is a challenging endeavor, fraught with pitfalls. Care has been taken to anticipate conflicts in interpretation and to distinguish our own preconceptions and contemporary biases from the assumptions that original viewers brought to these works of art. We are mindful, however, that no matter how skillful the artist and how pure one's intentions, the barrier of history can never be completely overcome. Looking into these "divine mirrors," one encounters knowledge lost as well as gained, belief systems formed and still in formation, and a journey that cannot be completely retraced, but is well worth undertaking. With Mary as our guide, let us investigate the legacy of Western culture that accompanies us all into the twenty-first century.

A Note on the Style

Ordinarily, the first letter of the title of "saint" appears capitalized in a text. However, I have chosen in this essay to emphasize sainthood as a matter of individual belief by having it remain lowercase. To be fair, I have also left worldly titles such as "king" or "emperor" uncapitalized. On the other hand, wherever possible, I have provided years of birth and death, to emphasize that no matter one's personal views regarding their dignity or sanctity, these men and women were historical figures.

Titles of works of art and literature appear in italics. References to a body of art associated with a religious narrative appear in upper-case letters, to distinguish them from an event or an artwork depicting that event. Hence, when I refer to Gabriel's annunciation to Mary as depicted by Hendrick Goltzius, I refer to Goltzius's *Annunciation*, yet when I refer to images of Gabriel and Mary shown together, I speak of scenes of the ANNUNCIATION.

MARIAN ORIGINS IN THE GOSPELS AND CHRISTIAN TRADITION

Mary's place in art combines image and imagination. Her visual identity is a compilation of scripture, tradition, faith, and interpretation. So frequently is she depicted in art that many are surprised to learn how little the Bible tells us of Mary's life. Rarely is she mentioned in the four Gospels that form the Christian New Testament.[1] Indeed, the confusing accounts have led to what Marina Warner termed "a muddle of Marys."[2] Cruden's *Concordance to the Old and New Testaments* lists twenty-eight references to "Mary," but these include Mary of Bethany, of Magdala, wife of Cleophas, mother(s) of James, of Joses, and of the sons of Zebedee—Marys whose ambiguous identity can and has been interpreted by a variety of Bible commentators according to their various needs and preferences.[3] Our goal is not to probe the New Testament in search of truth or duplicity, but rather to demonstrate that while it provides a beginning for Mary's story, it leaves adequate room for artists, clergy, and the faithful to explore that story without fear of contradicting biblical accounts.

Let us look at a few examples. Despite the prominence of the Virgin and Child in the visual arts, two of the four Gospels—those of the evangelists Mark and John—begin their narratives with an adult Jesus. The evangelists Matthew and Luke narrate his birth, with variations.[4] Take the case of the Annunciation, for example. In Matthew's Gospel, an angel appears to Joseph (in a dream) to foretell Jesus' birth (Matt. 1: 20–21); in Luke the angel appears to Mary (Luke 1: 26–38). Neither event contradicts the other, yet the latter scene has been more frequently depicted by artists than the former, and hence more firmly fixed in our visual memories. There are also two separate adoration narratives. In Matthew a star guides wise men to the newborn child (Matt. 2: 1–12; commonly known as the ADORATION OF THE MAGI); in Luke, an angel guides shepherds to the manger (Luke 2: 8–20; referred to as the ADORATION OF or ANNUNCIATION TO THE SHEPHERDS); Luke tells of the VISITATION, Mary's sojourn with her cousin Elizabeth (Luke 1: 39–56); Matthew narrates Herod's census (2: 16–18). Luke relates Jesus' CIRCUMCISION AND PRESENTATION IN THE TEMPLE eight days after birth (Luke 2: 21–40); Matthew continues the timeline with his account of Holy Family's FLIGHT INTO EGYPT (Matt. 2: 13–21).[5]

Read together, the Gospels of Matthew and Luke form a basis for depictions of Christ's infancy but tell us little of Mary's early history. Her own birth and childhood are not discussed in the New Testament, though they are frequently depicted in art. In the Gospels we are told the names of Mary's cousin Elizabeth and her husband Zechariah, who are to become parents of John the Baptist, but never hear of Mary's parents, much less learn their names. Yet other sources exist, some composed during the same period as the canonical scriptures, that include not only the names of Mary's parents—Anne and Joachim in the Christian tradition, Anna and Imran in the Muslim tradition—but details of their lives [fig. 7]. These sources tell of Anne and Joachim's long and barren marriage, their joy and disbelief at Mary's conception, and their decision at her birth to dedicate her to God's service in the synagogue at Jerusalem, where Mary would live from the age of three until reaching the marriageable age of twelve.[6] (Sharon Elkins' commentary on pages 136–38 discusses the inconsistencies of these traditions with actual Jewish practice.) John Baptist Jackson's embossed chiaroscuro woodcut after Titian's great painting of the *Presentation of the Virgin in the Temple* [fig. 8] depicts Mary mounting the temple steps to meet the High Priest, who wears a breastplate consisting of twelve engraved gemstones arranged in four rows of three. The High Priest's attire is described in Exodus 28 in the Hebrew Bible, but Mary's presentation is not to be found within the scriptures.

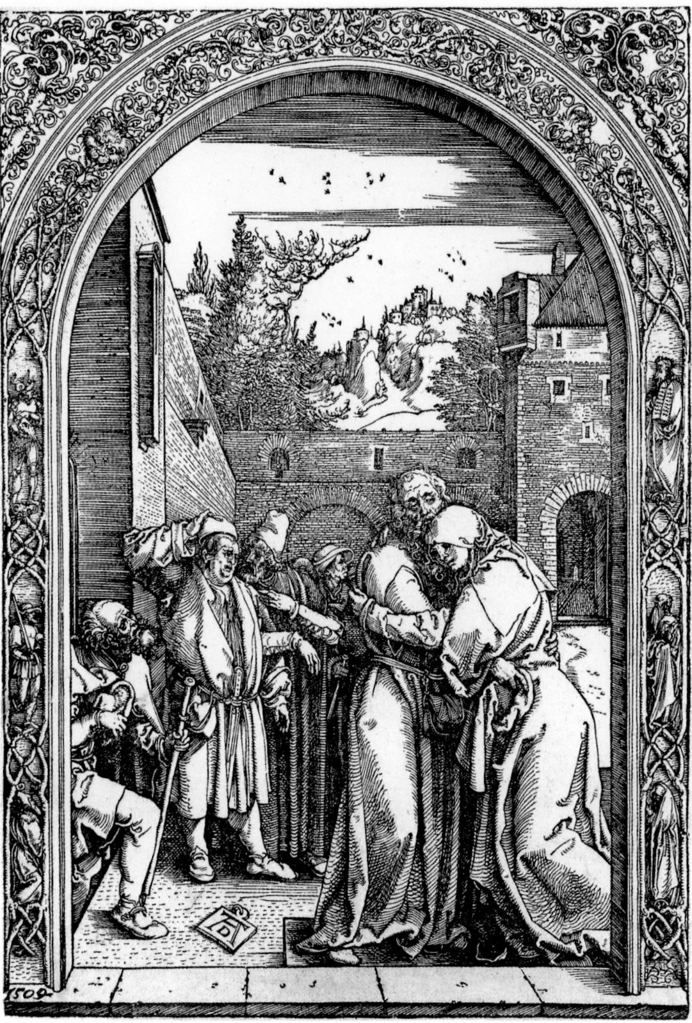

Fig. 7. Albrecht Dürer, *Joachim and St. Anne Meet at the Golden Gate*, 1504, woodcut from the *Life of the Virgin* series

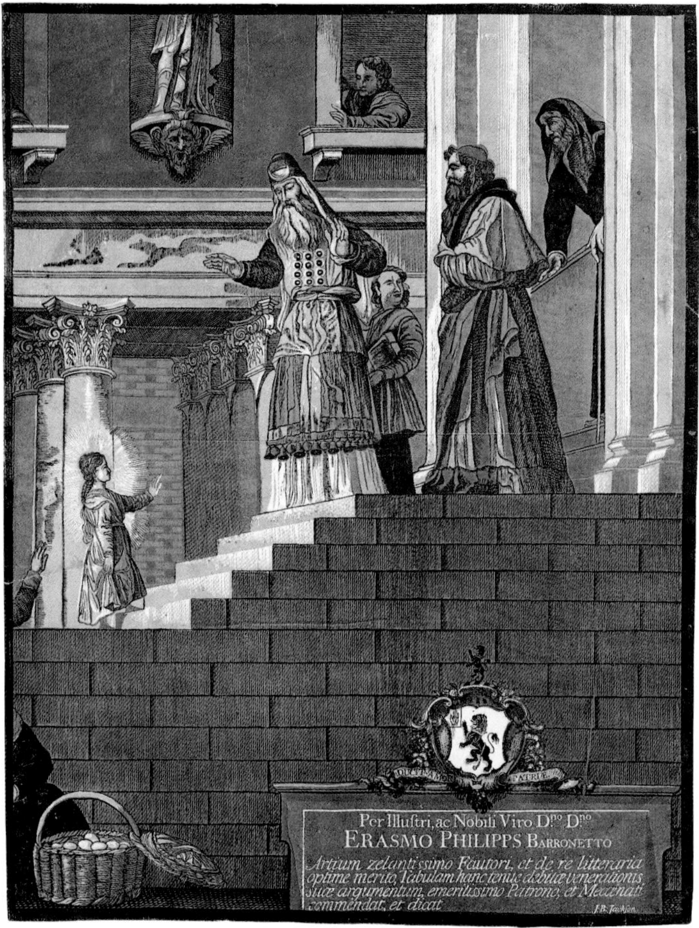

Fig. 8. John Baptist Jackson, *Presentation of the Virgin in the Temple (after Titian)*, 1742, chiaroscuro woodcut

Catholic churches include ten books (known as the Deutero-Canonical books) in their authorized version of the Bible that most Protestants classify as apocryphal.[7] The Hebrew canon omits the Books of Judith, the Maccabees, and parts of Esther but includes their content within Jewish tradition (particularly regarding the important feasts of Purim and Chanukah). Texts accepted by early Christians but unlikely to be found in today's New Testaments include the Infancy Gospels of James and of Thomas, the Gospel of Peter, and the Gospel of Mary—a reference to Mary Magdalene, not the Virgin Mary [cf. cat. no. 49].[8]

The New Testament should not be regarded as an historical record, nor should one expect consistency from its various authors, though one can gain insight from what is included and what is omitted. The evangelists wrote for specific communities, not to record Jesus' biography (or why would Mark and John omit his birth and first thirty years?), and certainly not Mary's (or why would she appear only in conjunction with her son's life?). Nevertheless, they provide insight into an emerging faith still in the process of defining its origins. Scholars agree that the four Gospels date from after Jesus' lifetime and were probably composed between 70 and 150 CE. The earliest, Mark's Gospel, was written during the tumultuous period following the destruction of the Synagogue in Jerusalem during a war between the Roman Empire and the Jews of Palestine. Mark wrote in Greek, probably for one specific Christian group; his language is stark, his Jesus a messiah, his Mary a cipher.[9]

Luke was a Gentile, who wrote for his fellow non-Jews living outside of Palestine [fig. 9]. His language is eloquent, his Jesus is a compassionate teacher, and his Mary is an enigmatic woman who keeps "all these things, pondering them in her heart" (Luke 2: 19).[10] Mary's only sustained speech—the 18–line *Magnificat*, addressed to Elizabeth—is included in Luke's Gospel (Luke 1: 46–55). Luke is also the patron saint of artists and

Later writings appeared to satisfy audiences eager for anecdotes about the early lives of Mary and Jesus. The above summary of Mary's birth and girlhood is drawn from a second-century CE (Common Era) manuscript known as the Protevangelium (or Infancy Gospel) of James, probably written not long after the Gospel of John. These nonbiblical sources are known as the Apocrypha (from the Greek for 'obscure' or 'hidden') This word designates works not included among the canonical books that make up the Bible due to questions of authenticity. Many stories familiar to art historians are drawn from apocryphal sources, including Tobias and the Angel, and Susannah and the Elders. The shaping of the biblical canon was a slow process and its present form differs among religions. The Eastern Orthodox and

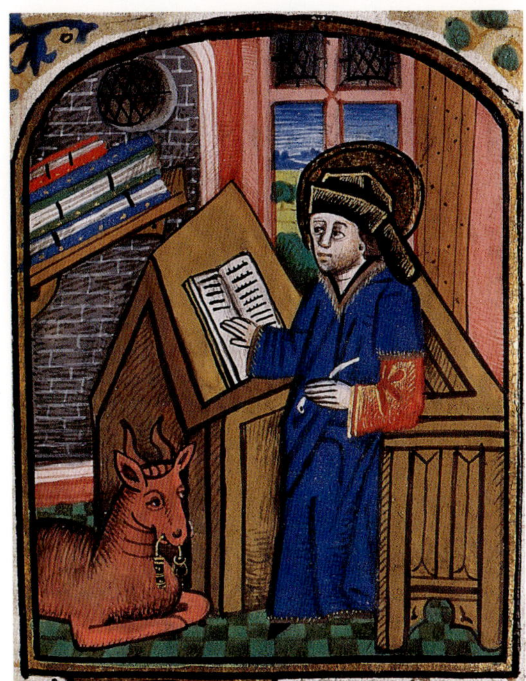

is said to have been a physician and a painter. According to tradition, Luke painted the earliest portraits of Mary, which served as sources for Byzantine icons; similar icons can still be found in Eastern Orthodox churches today. The somewhat archaic appearance of many icons is due to a deliberate attempt to remain consistent with the earlier "authorized" portraits.[11]

*　　　*　　　*

Matthew, a Jew, wrote for Jewish- and Gentile-Christians in Antioch of Syria (now part of Turkey). Pharisees figure prominently in Matthew's Gospel, though the sect was of little importance during Jesus' time.[12] Matthew's language is expressive, his Jesus humane, his Mary human. John's Gospel was the last to be written, probably emerging a generation after the three synoptic (linked) Gospels; it is the hardest to place, though it was probably written outside of Palestine. John's language is dramatic, his Jesus serene, his Mary in command, initiating Jesus' first public miracle at the wedding feast at Cana (John

2: 5). Only John clearly states Mary's presence at Jesus' crucifixion, referring to her not by name, but as "his mother" (John 19: 25); the remaining Gospels refer to that "muddle of Marys," mother(s) of James, Joseph, and the sons of Zebedee—ambiguous references that tantalize both scholars and skeptics.

MARIAN PARALLELS IN THE QUR'AN AND HEBREW BIBLE

Those surprised by the evangelists' silence regarding much of Mary's life most likely will be equally amazed to find the Qur'an voluble on the subject. No doubt, many are unaware that the Moslem holy book, the Qur'an, includes a detailed account of Mary's life, and that Mary is included among Islam's "four perfect women."[1] The Qur'an praises her as "Mary, Imran's daughter, who preserved her chastity and into whose womb We [Allah] Breathed of Our Spirit; who put her trust in the words of her Lord and His scriptures, and was truly devout" (66: 12).[2] Her son Jesus is considered a great prophet, but fully mortal like his mother. As the Qur'an's *Table* chapter explains, "The Messiah, the son of Mary, was no more than a prophet: other prophets passed away before him. His mother was a saintly woman. They both ate earthly food" (5: 75).

To Muslims, the Qur'an (Arabic for "the recital") is the infallible word of God revealed to the prophet Muhammad (died 629) by the angel Gabriel, the same divine messenger who informs Mary of her pregnancy in Luke's Gospel. It contains elements of Mary's story from the four Gospels (the ANNUNCIATION, the VIRGIN BIRTH) and the Christian apocrypha (her dedication at birth to the Lord, her childhood in the Temple). Their incorporation into the Qur'an, written circa 600 CE, shows how integrated these details were in Middle-Eastern lore by the seventh century.[3] Some aspects of the Qur'anic story, however, vary from the standard

Regarding Mary　23

Christian telling. The *Mary* chapter tells of how she "left her people and betook herself to a solitary place in the east" (19:14) to give birth alone and in great pain. Consistent with Muslim thought, her physical suffering emphasizes her humanity.

Mary's isolation in the Muslim account is also striking: there is no Joseph in the Qur'anic version, no husband for Mary or earthly father for Jesus. She faces the wilderness armed only with God's support, in a manner reminiscent of Hagar, another woman whose story is central to Islam. Hagar, the Egyptian servant of the patriarch Abraham (Ibrahim to Muslims), was the mother of Abraham's first-born son Ishmael, from whom the Arab race, and its great prophet Muhammad, is said to descend. Genesis 21: 9–21 tells how Hagar and Ishmael were cast out into the wilderness by Abraham at his wife Sarah's insistence [fig. 10].

God provided Hagar and her child with a source of fresh water, key to desert survival, just as in the Qur'an he provided Mary and her newborn with a stream and a date tree for nourishment.

Mary is the only woman to have a chapter in the Qur'an named after her. A chapter also bears the name of Mary's father—Imran in the Muslim tradition, Joachim in the Christian tradition—and others are named after Jonah, Joseph, Noah, and Abraham, figures who appear in both the Hebrew Bible and the Qur'an. The patriarch Abraham is the common ancestor of the three major monotheistic religions: Islam through Ishmael, his child with Hagar; Judaism and Christianity through Sarah's child Isaac, his second son. Many parallels can be drawn between Mary and Abraham. Both are told by angels that they have found favor with God. Both are destined to engender great nations. Both obey God's commands without fully understanding—Mary at the ANNUNCIATION, and Abraham when asked to sacrifice his son.[4]

Many have pointed to Mary's humility as a sign of Christian patriarchal thought, yet failed to observe its parallels in the Hebrew scriptures, perhaps because of the unexpected inversion of gender roles (as understood today). Mary shares the unquestioning faith of Old Testament males rather than the heroic characteristics of Old Testament women. Whereas the Hebrew Bible offers leaders like Esther, Deborah, and Judith—powerful women who saved their people from destruction—the Christian Bible celebrates its holiest woman as a mother, not a leader.[5] Though current Catholic spirituality emphasizes Mary's free will and voluntary assent, hers is essentially a passive act.[6] Mary was obedient to God's word, as was Moses before the burning bush or when told he would die without entering the Promised Land [fig. 11]. Once again, scriptural precedent aligns her with male behavior in the Hebrew Bible and underlines the peril of applying twentieth-century stereotypes (i.e., "male" activity vs. "female" passivity) to biblical exegesis.

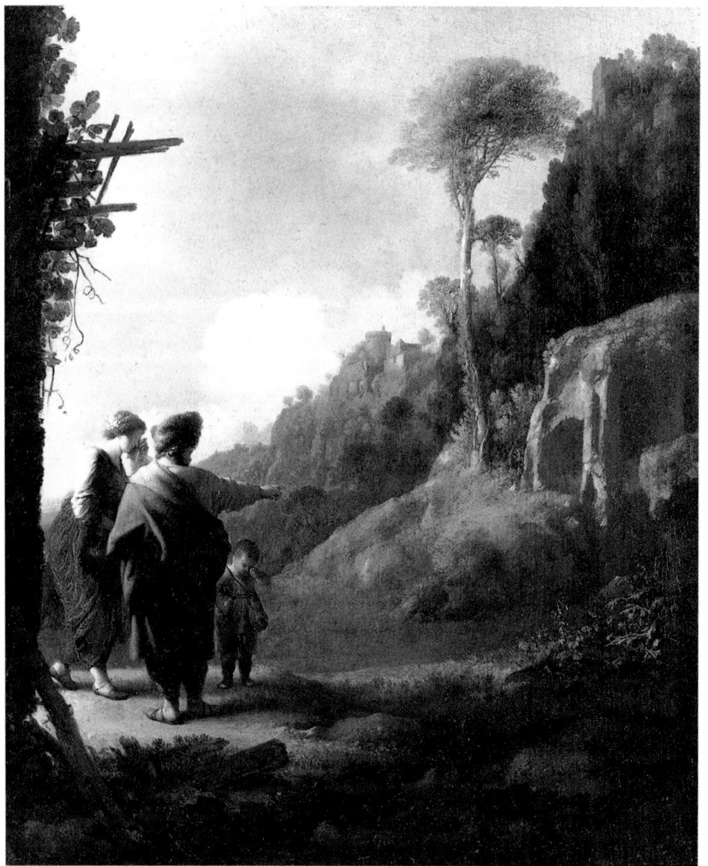

Fig. 10. Bartholomeus Breenbergh, *Abraham Dismissing Hagar*, 1630s, oil on panel

Mary is shared by all three of the monotheistic
religions to arise in the Middle East. Judaism is the
faith into which Mary was born and whose practices she followed; Christianity and Islam are the
religions that celebrate her life [fig. 12]. Unlike
earlier religions, Judaism, Christianity, and Islam
are linked by the absence of a female deity; despite
Mary's elevation, she is not accorded divine status.
Mary's humanity is essential to the Christian doctrine of Jesus' dual nature, in which God contributes the divine aspect and Mary the human.

As Mary Lefkowitz explains in her commentary
(pages 135–36), pagan audiences in late antiquity
would not have confused Mary with their fertility
goddesses, who were shown alone, not with infants,
wearing elaborate costumes. Isis, the Egyptian deity
often shown suckling her child Horus, wore a large
formal headdress, not the *maphorion*, or simple veil
of an ordinary woman, which Mary wears in early
Christian portraits.[7] (In the sixth century, a heavy
mantle began to replace the long maphorion.)
With her single child and her reputation of perpetual virginity, she was hardly a model of fertility.[8]
Nor did Mary embody the destructive powers of
the pagan divinities, many of whom, including Isis,
were sexually promiscuous. Converted pagans may
have transferred to Mary the esteem once held for

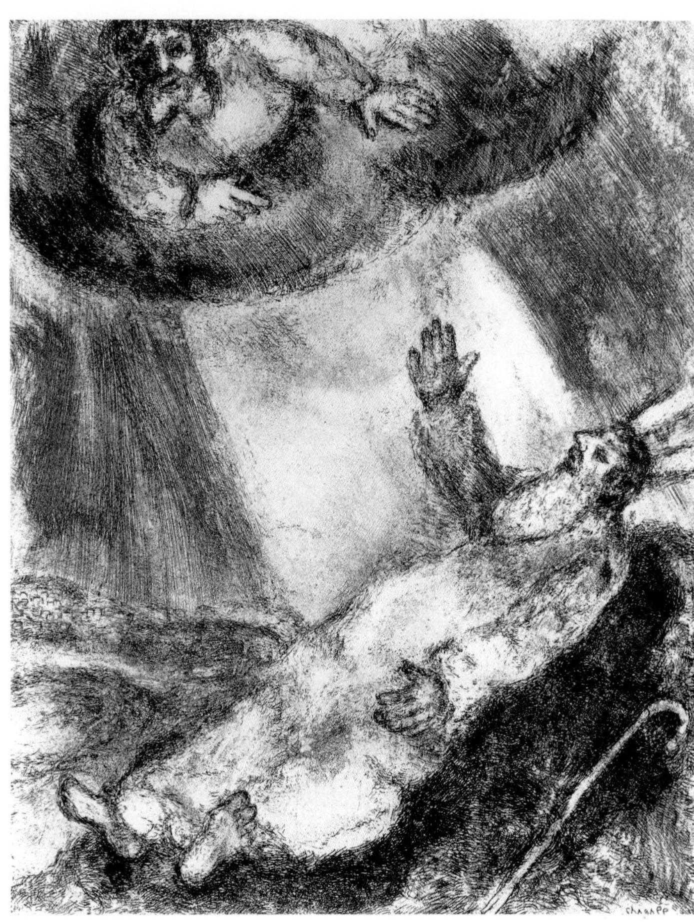

Fig. 11 (above). Marc Chagall, *Moses Dies in View of the Promised Land*, 1931-39, etching from
the *Bible* series

Fig. 12 (below). Rembrandt, *Jews in the Synagogue*, 1648, etching (shown actual size)

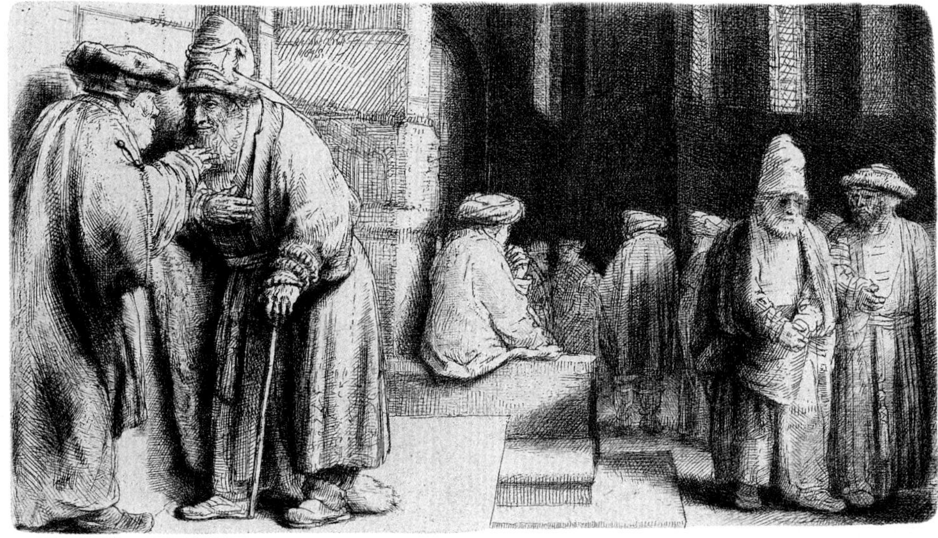

their goddesses, but they would not have seen her as a substitute or equivalent.[9] Pagan goddesses kept apart from humans, but Mary was accessible to Christians. Through her they could approach her powerful son and his austere father, much as the mothers and wives of the remote and all-powerful Roman emperors served as intercessors for their subjects.[10]

Early Christians argued about Mary's role in Christ's duality, finally accepting her as human yet with special status, and honoring her at the Council of Ephesus (in Asia Minor, now part of Turkey) in 431 with the title *Theotokos*, God Bearer.[11] The last centuries of the Roman Empire and first centuries of the Christian era witnessed the debate over Mary's status and formulation of doctrine for which the Bible did not fully provide guidance. Chief among these were the doctrine of the VIRGIN BIRTH (indicating Mary both conceived of and gave birth to Jesus while remaining a virgin), Mary's perpetual virginity throughout her marriage (a belief widely held during the Middle Ages but no longer endorsed by many Protestant Christians), and Mary's birth free of sin (the doctrine of the IMMACULATE CONCEPTION). The Christian religion passed down to the twenty-first century did not originate fully formed in the first century; it developed and changed over many centuries, as did its artistic representation.

THE MAKING OF MARY: ART IN THE EARLY CHURCH

The young Christian faith grew increasingly more organized and consistent in worship during the third through fifth centuries of the first millennium, thanks in part to a series of councils, including those of Nicaea (held in the year 325), Constantinople (381), Ephesus (431), and Chalcedon (451), convened to achieve consensus among varying groups scattered around the Mediterranean basin. Simultaneously, Christian art was emerging and assembling a coherent structure of its own, giving visual form to the beliefs and writings of the nascent church. Our earliest glimpses of New Testament art come from the gravesites of early Christians who, like their Pagan and Jewish neighbors, were buried in underground catacombs. Heavily influenced by contemporary styles and practices, the decoration of catacomb sarcophagi (stone coffins) and wall paintings reflected the artistic traditions of the Roman Empire.

A true Christian art did not begin to emerge until the end of the second century. The Ten Commandments' warning against graven images initially dissuaded early Christians from portraying biblical personages, and early representations were often symbolic, with fish being a favorite emblem, along with doves, anchors, ships, and lyres.[1] Fish played a role in several Gospel miracles—the feeding of 5,000 with five loaves and two fishes (Matt. 14, Mark 6, Luke 9, John 6), Simon Peter's miraculous catch of fish (Luke 5), the tax money found in the mouth of a fish (Matt. 17), and Jesus' appearance to his disciples after his resurrection (John 21)—and were also associated with Christ's purity, baptism, and charge to the apostles to be "fishers of men" (Mark 1:17, Matt. 4:19). A tradition arose that fish were consumed at the Last Supper, so fish in early Christian art symbolized the Eucharist.[2] Audiences of the first centuries of the common era also interpreted ΙΧΘΥΣ/*ichthys*, the Greek word for fish, as an acrostic for the phrase *Iesus Christos Theou Yios Soster* (Jesus Christ, Son of God, Saviour).[3]

When Christians began to portray humans, they usually represented the faithful—either the deceased or living mourners—rather than specific biblical personages. Orants, figures in prayer shown standing with arms raised, decorated many catacombs. The allegorical figure of the Good Shepherd—a standing male with a sheep around his shoulders, based on the Roman representation of Philanthropy—helped bridge the transformation from portraiture of early believers to portrayal of biblical figures and narratives.[4] Narrative scenes frequently illustrated Old Testament tales. DANIEL IN THE LION'S DEN, MOSES STRIKING THE ROCK, and NOAH'S ARK were especially popular.

Around the year 200, images of Jesus, Mary, and other biblical figures began to appear in frescos decorating passageways and tomb walls. Catacomb artists borrowed Greco-Roman conventions of prestige used for monarchs and deities, such as crowns, jewels, thrones, and frontal portrayal. It was prudent for a new religion to express unfamiliar ideas by using an artistic vocabulary already in place and understood by the public. To show the Virgin Mary seated and robed in the manner of an empress conveyed her high status and encouraged viewers to hold her in equal or higher regard than secular rulers. Early portraits, such as a fourth-century fresco in Rome's *Coemeterium Maius* [fig. 13], show Mary with arms upraised in orant posture and the infant Jesus on her lap. Both face forward, staring straight ahead, wide-eyed and somber.

A frescoed archway in Rome's Catacomb of Priscilla (late second/early third century) shows a seated mother gazing at her child beside a man who points to a star—a scene many scholars identify as the earliest portrayal of the Madonna and Child, and a nascent depiction of the ANNUNCIATION, because it deals with the foretelling of Jesus' birth [fig. 14].[5] The man is often identified as Hebrew sage Balaam, who prophesied that "a star shall come out of Jacob, and a scepter shall rise out of Israel" (Numbers 24:17) or Isaiah, whose writings also are said to prefigure the VIRGIN BIRTH.[6] At this early stage, Christians placed emphasis on typological affinities between Old Testament prophecies and New Testament events that validated for them Jesus' role as messiah. As Christians grew in numbers and confidence, artistic consensus coalesced around the scriptural account. Balaam would be replaced by the archangel Gabriel, and Mary would be shown alone, without the infant Jesus (who, of course, had yet to be born).

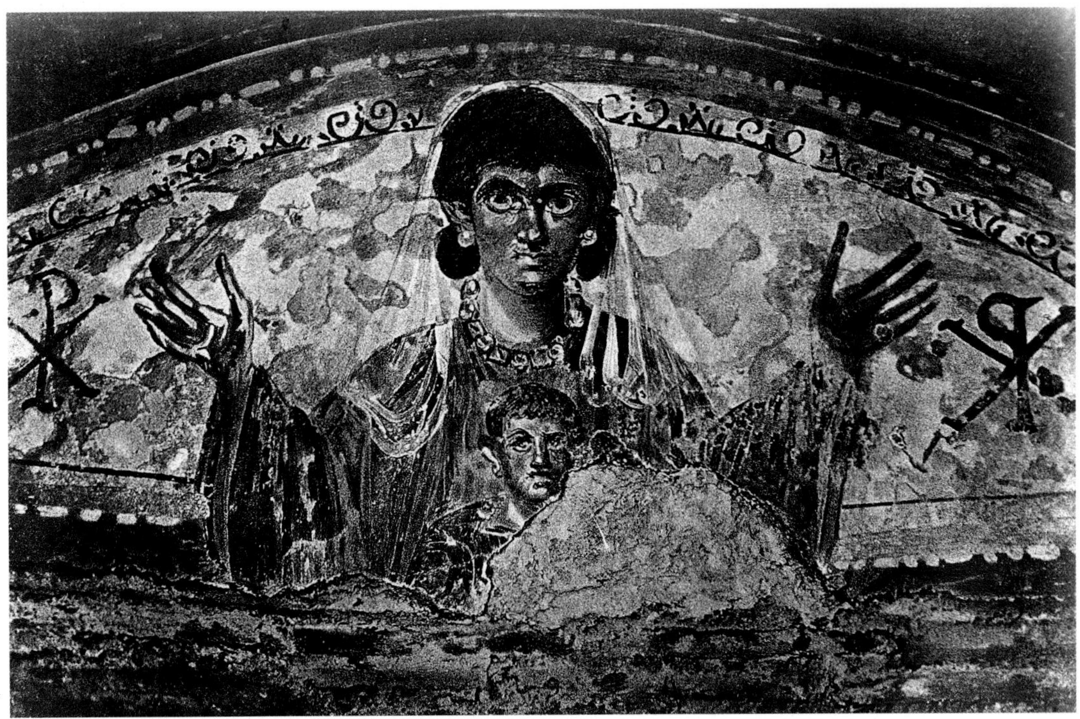

Fig. 13. Roman, *Orant Virgin and Child*, 4th c., Coementerium Maius catacomb, fresco

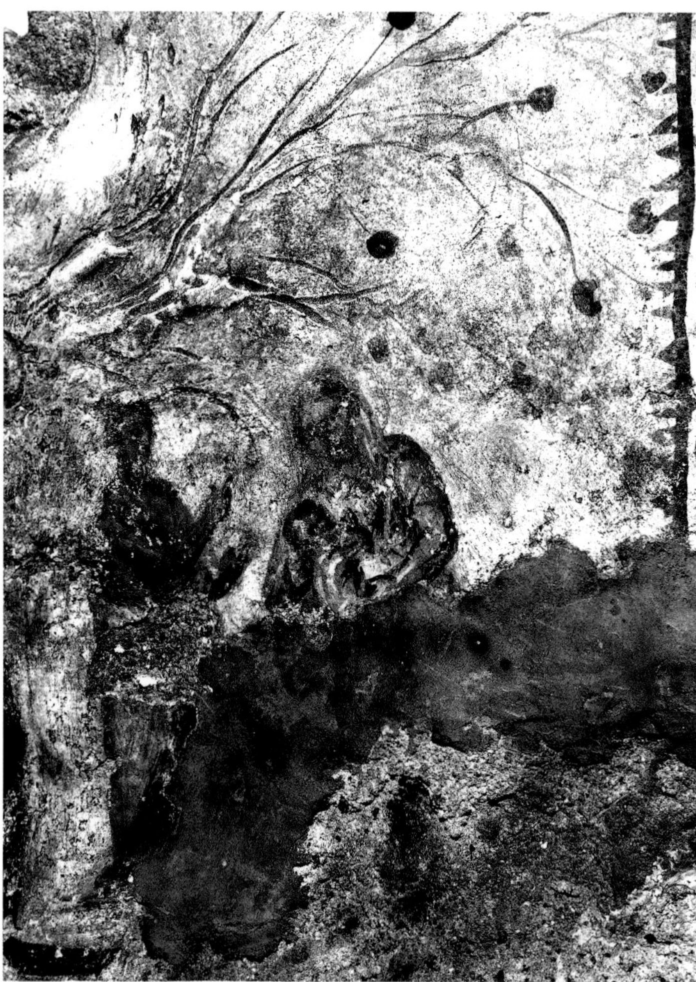

Fig. 14. Roman, *Virgin and Child with Prophet*, early 3rd c., Catacomb of Priscilla, fresco

supplying the details omitted in scriptural accounts.

New Testament art moved above ground in the year 313, when Constantine issued the Edicts of Tolerance, allowing freedom of worship in the Roman Empire. Christians were now permitted to build churches for public assembly and worship, and art became a means of linking the Bible and liturgy. The declarations of the council of Ephesus in 431, confirming Mary's status as Mother of God, led to an explosion of Marian devotional imagery. In 432, in celebration of Mary's confirmed status as God-bearer, a fourth-century Roman basilica was renamed Santa Maria Maggiore, the first church to be dedicated to Mary.[8] By the sixth century, catacombs were no longer in use, but Christian art was well established and already beginning to spread from the churches into private homes. In addition to icons of the Mother and Child, and the narrative cycles of frescos and mosaics adorning early Christian basilicas, we find domestic objects, including oil ampullae, embossed pendants, and small plaquettes indicating that Christian art had come to be owned, and in all probability used in worship, by individuals as well as congregations.[9]

Not long after, a famous icon—*Theotokos Hodegetria* (Greek for "mother of God who leads the way")—was placed on public display in Constantinople, and countless copies were made and disseminated throughout the Byzantine empire.[10] The icon showed Mary holding the infant Jesus in her left arm, pointing to her son in acknowledgment of his status. This Byzantine composition—Mary regal, distant, solemn, her young son extending his hand in blessing—became a standard format for portraying the Virgin and Child, and a familiar visual expression of the Christian faith. Over the next centuries, a more loving, less formal relationship unfolded. By the ninth century, *Hodegetria* images were joined by those of the *Eleousa* or Compassionate Virgin, whose head is inclined toward her son, their cheeks touching, their gazes meeting. Soon

It is significant to find images of an infant Jesus emerging simultaneously with those of an adult Jesus, as it gives Mary as mother a central role in the new religious faith. The *Conceptio Christi* (feast of the Conception), has been celebrated since the first century and may be the earliest official feast to be established by the Church. It revolves as much around Mary as mother-conceiver, as around Jesus, the future saviour-messiah.[7] In another niche of the early third-century Catacomb of Priscilla, the seated mother and child receive visitors holding out their gifts: the wise men, or Magi, already numbering three, though the Gospel gives no number. Within two centuries of the completion of the four Gospels, standards of iconography were being shaped, with artists

after the infant began to twist in his mother's arms, the somber child now a squirming baby, and Mary a tender mother. *Glykophilousa* or Loving icons showed the child embracing his mother, while in *Galaktotrophousa* (Milk-Giving) icons, he nursed at her breast.[11] These Eastern compositions would have great influence over Western depictions of the Virgin and Child, particularly after the sack of Constantinople on 13 April 1204, during the Fourth Crusade. Although the original *Theotokos Hodegetria* was not captured, enough images of the *"Madonna di Constantinopoli"* were brought back by crusaders to establish a major shift in Western iconography, particularly in Italian *duecento* painting, toward Byzantine paradigms.[12]

RELIGIOUS USES OF DEVOTIONAL ART TO 1500

The use of images to stimulate worship did not originate with the Christian church, nor did the strategy of superimposing elements of one cult onto another. It is no accident that in 354 pope Liberius fixed the date of the feast of Jesus' birth on December 25th, the feast day of the Persian god Mithras, whose cult flourished in Rome during the early centuries of Christianity.[1] His gesture need not be seen as a concession to assimilation but rather as an assertion of the dominance of his faith over an earlier one. The conversion of pagan temples to Christian sanctuaries was undertaken deliberately, not to dupe gullible peasants into switching loyalties but to demonstrate the authority and power of the Christian faith. As pope Gregory I the Great (ca. 540–604) wrote to an abbot engaged in converting English pagans to Christianity:

I have decided after long deliberation about the English people, namely that the idol temples of that race should by no means be destroyed, but only the idols in them. Take holy water and sprinkle it in these shrines, build

altars and place relics in them. For if the shrines are well built, it is essential that they should be changed from the worship of devils to the service of the true God. When this people see that their shrines are not destroyed they will be able to banish error from their hearts and be more ready to come to the places they are familiar with, but now recognizing and worshipping the true God.[2]

The name of the Roman church Santa Maria sopra Minerva indicates its erection over the remains of a temple dedicated to Minerva, the Roman goddess of wisdom; wisdom also became an attribute of Mary in her role as *Sede Sapientiae,* or Throne of Wisdom. Nor were the temples of the Roman forum spared: the columns and steps of the Temple of Antonius and Faustina, built in 141 CE, now form part of the church of San Lorenzo in Miranda, dating from 1602 [fig. 15].

Visual art served many functions within the church, not the least of which was its use in teaching Bible stories to the young and the illiterate. "Pictures and ornaments in churches are the lessons and the scriptures of the laity," wrote bishop William Durandus (ca. 1220–1296). "Because they who are uninstructed thus see what they ought to follow: and *things* are read, though letters be unknown."[3] Art also became a means of honoring the saintly, and a tool for recalling points in the salvation story during periods of private and collective prayer. Giovanni Balbi of Genoa (d. 1298), in his late thirteenth-century dictionary *Catholicon,* stated this clearly:

Know that there were three reasons for the institution of images in churches. *First,* for the instruction of simple people, because they are instructed by them as if by books. *Second,* so that the mystery of the incarnation and the examples of the saints may be the more active in our memory through being daily presented in our eyes. *Third,* to excite feelings of devo-

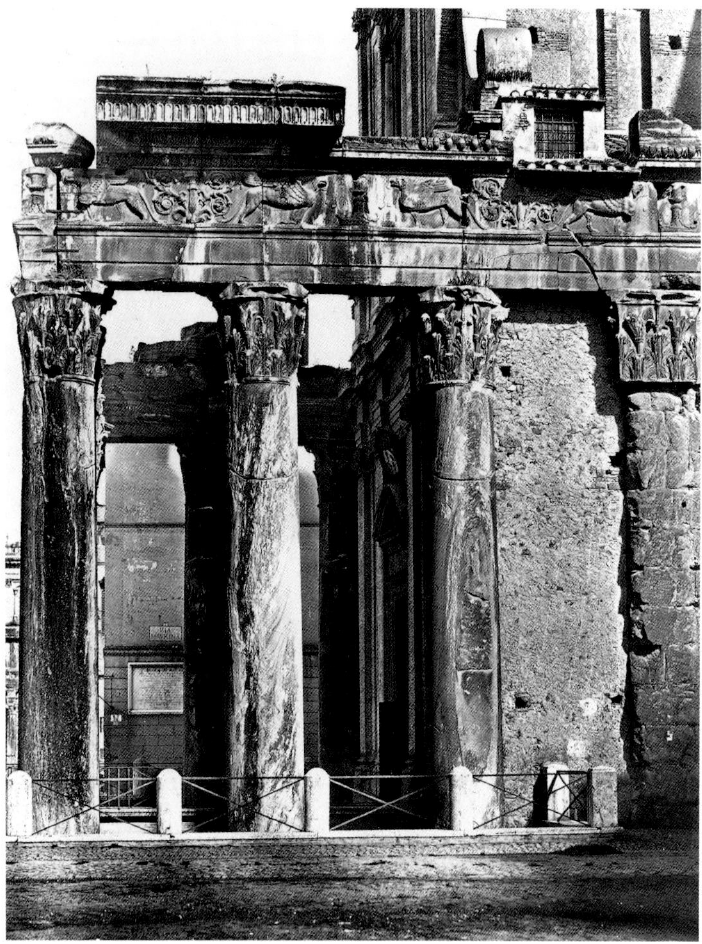

in it at one time without interfering with each other."[5] In addition to the mass being conducted in a side chapel at left and the clergyman preaching from the pulpit at right, Neefs has included glimpses of the various secular activities—strolling, child-minding, gossiping, and business negotiation—that took place in great churches. Neefs also shows the long aisle lined with paintings hung above small altars, donated by various trade guilds and individual patrons, that leads to the choir (or rood) screen dividing the nave from the chancel. The main altar of the cathedral, visible through the screen's arched opening, is as difficult to see in Neefs's painting as it would have been for the majority of Antwerp's worshippers. Indeed, the entire area behind the rood screen—choir stalls, presbytery (or sanctuary), and high altar—could be accessed only by members of the clergy.

From its inception, the Church took pains to distinguish the use of religious art in devotional practices from the worship of idols. Periodically debate arose concerning whether the presence of devotional images violated the prohibitions of the first or second commandment, "you shall not make for yourself a graven image, or any likeness of anything that is in heaven above, or that is in the earth beneath, or that is in the water under the earth; you shall not bow down to them or serve them" (Exodus 20:4–5, Deuteronomy 5:8–9).[6] Iconodules (supporters of the use of images) drew attention to the distinction between the veneration of a holy person and the use of an image of that holy person as an aid to veneration. The debate over the veneration of icons (from the Greek *eikon*, image) grew particularly heated during the eighth century, punctuated by periodic outbursts of iconoclasm, the intentional destruction of images. The second Council of Nicaea, convened in 787, reaffirmed the veneration of icons, ruling that "the honour paid to the image passes to the original, and he that adores an image adores in it the person depicted."[7] This subtle but important distinction between adoration, reserved

tion, these being aroused more effectively by things seen than by things heard.[4]

To these functions—instruction, veneration, and remembrance—we may add the role of adornment. What enriched God's house enhanced his glory, providing an appropriate environment in which to encounter the divine. Liturgical vessels were made of precious materials, altar cloths and vestments of embellished fabrics, and altars adorned with devotional images initially placed in front of altar tables, and later behind.

Pieter Neefs's 1657 painting, *Interior of Antwerp Cathedral* [fig. 16], shows the lively space described by the German artist Albrecht Dürer during his 1520 visit to Antwerp: "The Church of Our Lady at Antwerp is so very large that many masses are sung

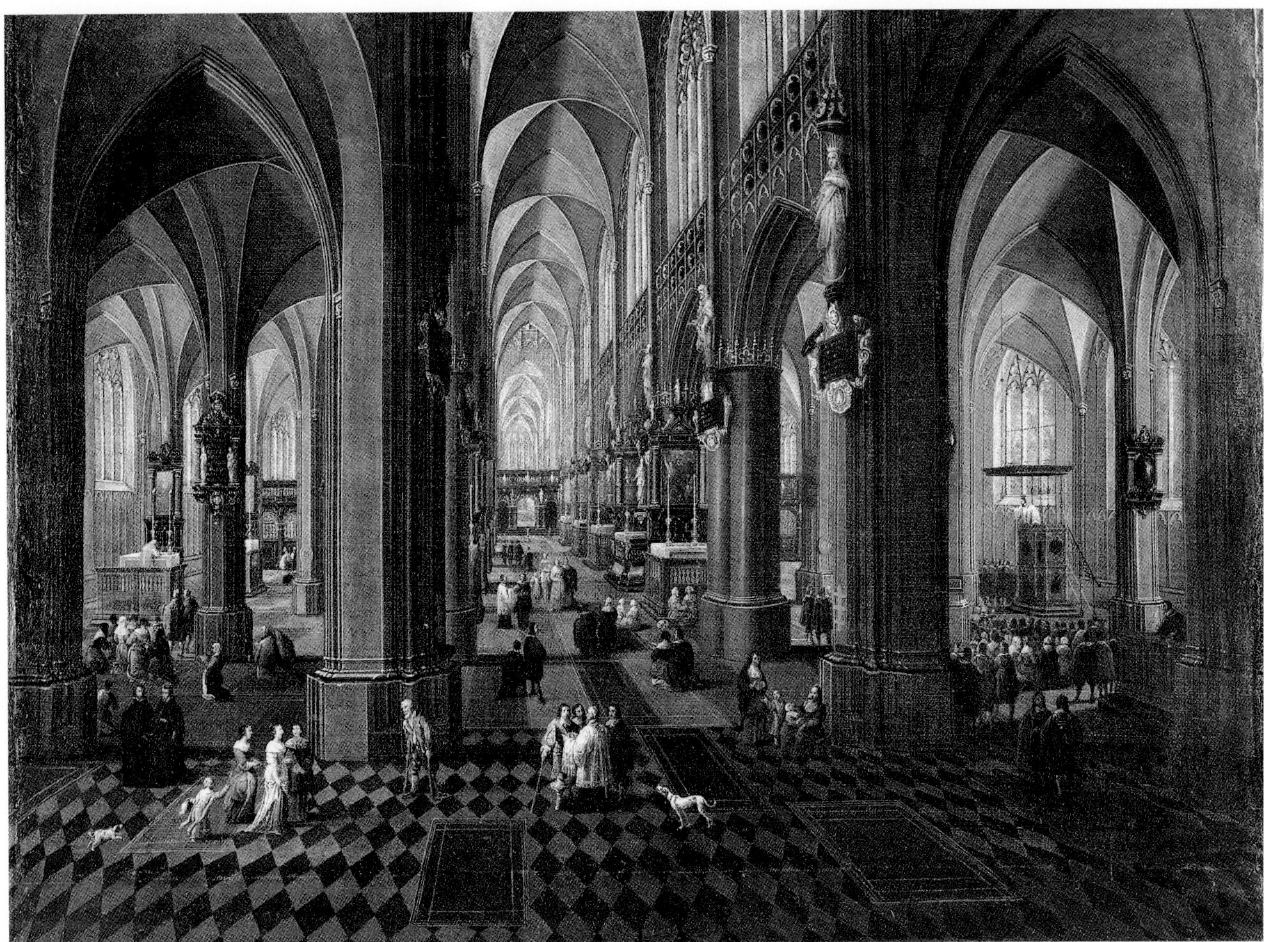

for God, and veneration, permitted for the saints, was formally adopted.

Controversy resurfaced during the Reformation, the religious upheaval of the sixteenth century, when reforms and counter-reforms of an institution grown corrupt resulted in the division of the Western church into Protestant and Catholic churches. Protestant leaders once again compared the presence of art in the churches to the practice of idolatry.[8] The teachings of Martin Luther (1483–1546), the Augustinian monk whose actions initiated the Reformation, did not directly preclude a role for art in the reformed church, so long as it did not compete with the hearing of God's word, the primary route to salvation. The 95 theses that Luther posted onto the door of Wittenberg's castle church on the eve of All Saints' Day (October 31), 1517—a standard procedure (and location) for giving notice of one's dispute with university positions and not the dramatic gesture that has been supposed—strongly condemned the pope, indulgences, sale of pardons, and pompous ritual, but they made no mention of the veneration of images or the devotional use of art.[9] In a 1525 tract, Luther criticized those reformers who dramatically removed images from people's sight instead of instructing them to discard false assumptions regarding religious art, "for when they [i.e., images] are no longer in the heart, they can do no harm when seen with the eyes."[10]

Luther himself befriended artists such as Lucas Cranach (1472–1553), who painted his portrait, and his writings strongly influenced his contemporary, Albrecht Dürer (1471–1528).[11] Nevertheless,

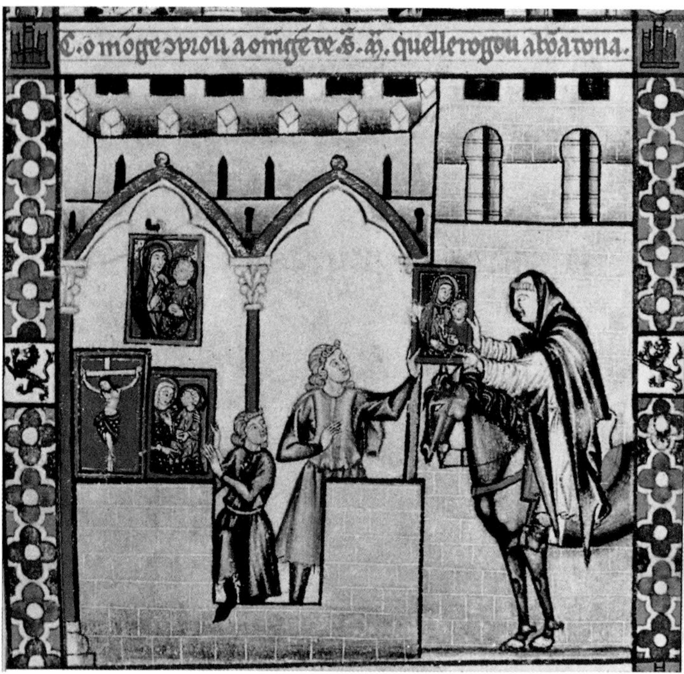

Fig. 17. Spanish, *Monk Purchasing a Painting*, ca. 1280, detail of an illumination from the *Cantigas de Santa María*, Library of the Monastery of Él Escorial, Spain, fol. 17

Dürer's hopes to create a monumental art embodying Lutheran doctrine were met with indifference or open hostility from more conservative reformers—including Andreas Bodenstein von Karlstadt (ca. 1480–1541) of Wittenberg; Guillaume Farel (1489–1565) and Jean Calvin (1509–1564) of Geneva; and Huldrych Zwingli (1484–1531) of Zurich—who took a restrictive view of the visual arts.[12] Works of art from cathedrals where they preached were stripped from the altars and aisles to be smashed or burned, and austere coats of whitewash applied to cover painted walls and polychrome decorations.[13] Other congregations followed their example, removing and destroying works of art in parish churches throughout the region.

DEVOTIONAL USES OF RELIGIOUS ART TO 1500

Roughly halfway between these two iconoclastic eras (those of the eighth and sixteenth centuries), an important shift took place, moving devotional art from the realm of the "religious professional" to the sphere of the layperson, or ordinary believer. For much of the Middle Ages, the intellectual life of the church resided not with secular clergy (who officiated in parish churches) but with the monastic elite, whose renunciation of the material world was considered a holier and more worthy lifestyle. During the early and central Middle Ages, devotional images (often referred to by the German term *andachtsbilder*) developed as a means to enhance liturgy and aid the spiritual growth within religious communities. Thus, the greatest demand for Christian art came from monasteries, where nuns and monks devoted themselves to the discovery of God through individual and group prayer.[1] An illumination accompanying a circa. 1280 Spanish manuscript shows a monk purchasing a devotional painting from a shop whose inventory includes three *Virgin and Child* paintings and one *Crucifixion* [fig. 17].

In the 1200s, new monastic orders were founded that had more contact with lay parishioners than did the strictly cloistered orders such as the Benedictines and Augustinians. The Franciscan followers of the Italian saint Francis of Assisi (born Giovanni Francesco da Bernardone, 1181–1226) and Dominican followers of the Spanish saint Domingo de Gúzman (1170–1221) formed mendicant orders—dependent on alms and public charity rather than revenues from land and real estate holdings—and sought to remain in contact with the secular world rather than remove themselves from daily life. Franciscans and Dominicans deliberately built their friaries in towns to minister to lay people, who in turn were able to observe directly certain aspects of cloistered life and could adopt such traditionally monastic activities as daily prayer and silent meditation on the lives of Jesus, Mary, and the saints.

The laity also embraced the monastic practice of using visual art as devotional aids. Late medieval prayer combined oral recitation, spiritual readings, and silent meditation to stimulate piety and enhance concentration. Artworks provided focus

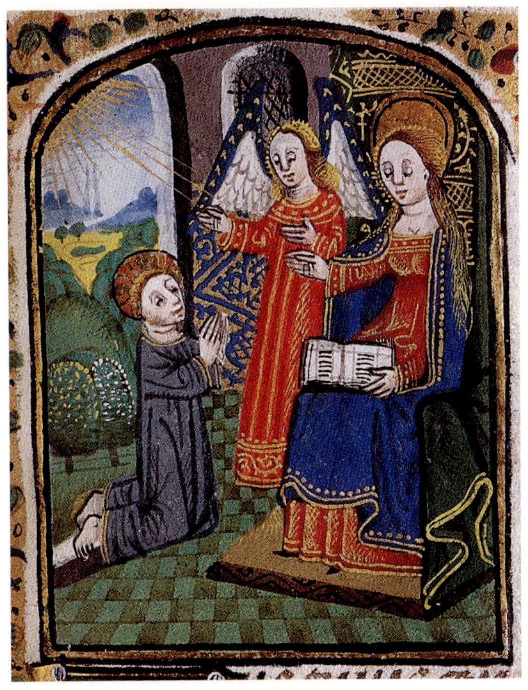

long ago . . . . But blame there is none in a moderate use of pictures, to teach how ill is to be avoided, and good followed . . . . For paintings appear to move the mind more than descriptions: for deeds are placed before the eyes in paintings, and so appear to be actually carrying on . . . . Hence, also, is it that in churches we pay less reverence to books than to images and pictures.[3]

Like any good attorney, bishop Durand diligently cited precedents, most notably the writings of Moses, the prophet Ezekiel, and saint Gregory the Great's sixth-century discourse (quoted on page 29).

During the thirteenth and fourteenth centuries, Franciscans, Dominicans, and clergy influenced by the practices of these orders helped ordinary people learn to pray (in their own languages). Since few people outside of the clergy or cloister understood Latin, lay people were often disengaged from the celebration of the mass (which, from the twelfth century until the reforms of Vatican II (1962–1965), was conducted entirely in Latin by a priest who faced the altar, not the congregation). All the medieval church required of the faithful was that they learn by heart the twelve articles of faith (the Apostle's Creed), the Lord's prayer (Our Father), and the Hail Mary prayer.[4] Left unfulfilled by formal liturgy, the laity embraced the practice of vernacular prayer to help strengthen their faith and enrich their spiritual lives.

Out of these practices a religious movement arose in the 1300s known as *Devotio moderna*. "Modern devotion" encouraged believers to identify personally with Mary and Jesus through intense meditation on their lives and internalization of their experiences, aided by the stimulus of visual art. Many citizens were inspired to adopt semimonastic lifestyles, observing regular prayer cycles and devotional exercises without withdrawing from the secular world. Some joined "third

for one's prayers and encouraged a personal identification with God that helped one achieve a higher state. While contemplating images, viewers would strive to imagine and internalize Christ's sufferings and Mary's sorrows [fig. 18]. Devotional art aided the inner eye to mentally recreate sacred experience. Art served only as an exterior stimulus to interior prayer, and the images summoned up in the minds of believers gazing at these works were considered far richer and more powerful than any artwork their eyes could behold.[2]

Again, adherents of this form of prayer distinguished their practices from those of idolatry by stressing that they revered not the wooden statue or painted scene but rather the holy person(s) represented in these works. The French-born William Durandus of Mende (ca. 1220–1296), professor of canon law at the University of Modena in Italy, prepared this 1286 rationale:

We worship not images, nor account them to be gods, nor put any hope of salvation in them; for that were idolatry. Yet we adore them for the memory and remembrance of things done

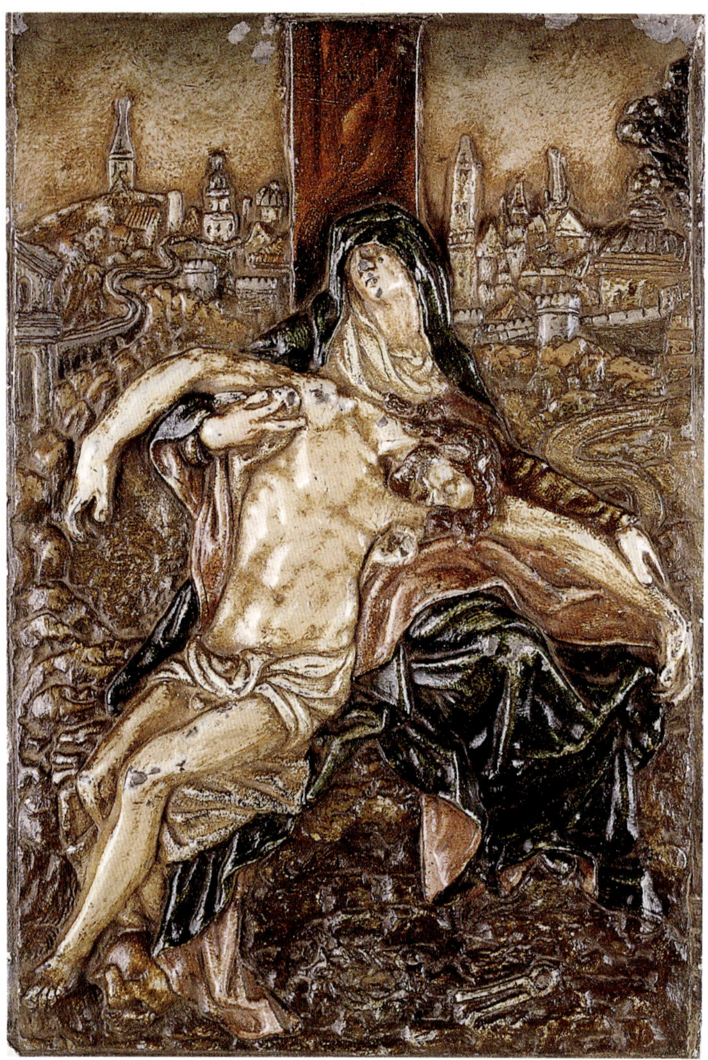

Fig. 19. German, *Pietà*, 16th c., polychromed lead bas-relief

were summarized in a book by the Augustinian monk Thomas à Kempis (1380–1471), who had studied with the Brethren of the Common Life in Germany. His book, *On the Imitation of Christ*, written in 1418 for his fellow Augustinian monks, was quickly adopted by lay people and became a bestseller second only to the Bible. After the introduction of the printing press in 1453, it was translated into all European languages, spreading the influence of *Devotio moderna* beyond the northern regions where it had developed.[5]

While large altarpieces were generally commissioned by specific donors, artists also produced for the open market and shipped them throughout Europe. Artwork meant for personal use tended to be smaller than works made for church display so as to fit within a bedchamber or an alcove fitted up as a private chapel. A sixteenth-century polychromed lead *Pietà* in the museum's collection, approximately 7 inches high and 5 inches wide, is perfectly scaled for domestic use, as is the palm-sized fourteenth-century ivory *Dormition* [figs. 19, 94]. Originally one wing of a diptych hinged to close like a book, the ivory could also be brought along on travel, as both a comforting token of home and an accessory to prayer.[6] Yet size is not always a clue to an object's original use. A small painting such as the Martínez *Lamentation* [fig. 71] might have been destined by its creator for private devotional use by a monk, nun, or layperson, or it might have been joined with other images to form part of a *banco* or predella, a sequence of images along the bottom of a larger altarpiece.

Church and home were not the only possible destinations for such images. One could envision paintings of moderate size, such as Pintoricchio's *tondo* (or circular painting) [fig. 45], in the private chapel of a wealthy family, the type of semiliturgical, semidomestic chamber described by thirteenth-century authors as having just become fashionable among Roman noblewomen.[7] Mid-sized paintings such as the *tondo* or the Mid-Rhenish *Annunciation* triptych [fig. 24] might also have

orders" of monastic communities (so named because they came after the first order of monks and the second of nuns), or formed independent brother- and sisterhoods not affiliated with an established religious community. These groups did not require permanent vows of their members and thus provided an alternative to those unwilling or unable to make lifelong commitments.

One such lay spiritual community, the Brethren of the Common Life, was founded in the Netherlands by Geert Grote (1340–1384), who had also formulated the principles of *Devotio moderna*. Its principles, and endorsement of the use of devotional images as memory aids during silent prayer,

been commissioned for the semiprivate chapel of a trade guild, located within a guild hall or along the side aisles of a church. Artworks were also commissioned by the members of confraternities (lay brotherhoods), whose middle-class members pooled resources to outfit chapels for the use of their members.[8] Organized by neighborhood or along professional lines, like a guild, religious confraternities served the purpose of today's insurance companies. In exchange for annual dues, confraternities covered burial fees, looked after widows and orphans, aided workers in times of illness, and otherwise provided social services for their community.[9]

Illustrated books formed another category of prayer aids accessible to less wealthy citizens. *Biblia pauperum* ("Bibles of the poor")—picture collections of Bible stories—helped the illiterate learn and remember the salvation story. Literate citizens made use of Books of Hours—illustrated collections of prayers, psalms, Gospel readings, calendars, and devotional cycles. The prayer cycles in these books, meant to be recited at set hours, helped the laity emulate the monastic model of prayer at eight daily intervals.[10] Owners could personalize their purchases by requesting the inclusion of certain saints' litanies and psalms within their texts, but almost all Books of Hours featured the Hours of the Virgin, a series of readings on Mary's life. Other services that might be included were the Hours of the Cross (readings on Christ's passion), Hours of the Holy Spirit, the Office of the Dead, penitential psalms, and prayers to individual saints. Illustrations introduced main sections, and elaborate borders adorned texts.

Like the artworks used in religious devotion, the illuminations in Books of Hours served the functions of instruction, veneration, and remembrance. In the fourteenth century, these devotional manuals were favored possessions of nobles, royals, and wealthy urbanites. By the fifteenth century, inexpensive versions were being produced, allowing people of modest means to own them.

Vernacular texts helped ordinary parishioners follow the Latin liturgies, a particular help for women who were unlikely to be taught Latin. Many women owned and cherished these volumes, often receiving them as wedding gifts and passing them on to their daughters and daughters-in-law, as surviving wills attest.[11] By the sixteenth century, however, the popularity of Books of Hours had diminished. Protestant reformers organized worship around readings from the Bible rather than emotional prayer, while Catholic clergy sought to end irregular practices of private piety by promoting a return to formal church liturgy.

THE MADONNA UNVEILED: PART I

The following eight numbered sections investigate the manner in which artists represented Mary's life and the ways contemporary audiences might have interpreted them. Each section reviews the scriptural origins of the scene and its significance in Christian thought, and explores the iconography employed to allow viewers to readily identify a scene and recognize its significance. These images are then evaluated regarding what they reveal (intentionally and accidentally) about the cultures that made them and first used them. Artworks designed to meet ecclesiastic objectives also reflect aspects of secular culture which, when placed in a proper frame of reference, help bridge the historical divide and achieve a more accurate understanding of past societies.

By attempting to identify the preconceptions that original viewers brought to these works of art and to distinguish them from our own, we can place their lives in perspective, and temper the tendency of our own beliefs and expectations to distort interpretations of the art and cultures of the past. For example, viewers of NATIVITY scenes in earlier centuries interpreted doctrines such as the VIRGIN BIRTH through an understanding of conception and childbirth that differs greatly from

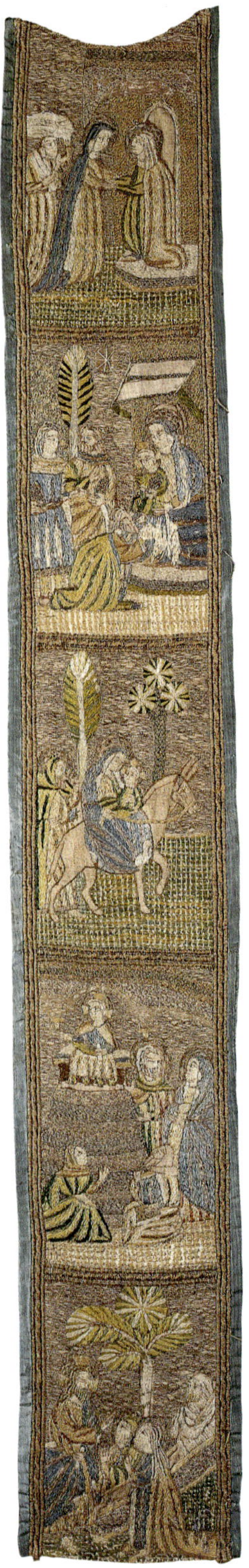

modern thinking. Similarly, our perception of a CRUCIFIXION created in an earlier century is influenced by our current attitudes toward death and mortality. Sacred imagery is infused with worldly assumptions, illuminating both Marian theology and secular ideology regarding ideal womanhood and appropriate social behavior.

This is by no means a celebration of how much we have learned in a half-dozen centuries. Much of the content of the next eight sections concerns knowledge lost rather than gained. Aspects of Christian art that would have been readily apparent to original viewers are no longer well understood and may even go unnoticed by modern viewers who are trained to approach art of the past from an aesthetic standpoint. Indeed, the displacement of religious art from

church settings to museum galleries, and their subsequent shift from objects of cult to objects of beauty, renders even more difficult the task of restoring context, observing content, and exploring intent within these various works.

The sequence of these eight sections is inspired by the eight Hours of the Virgin, once recited by monastic and lay users of Books of Hours. The Hours of the Virgin followed Mary's adult life, divided into joys and sorrows. A typical Infancy (or Joyous) cycle might include the ANNUNCIATION, VISITATION, NATIVITY, ANNUNCIATION TO THE SHEPHERDS, ADORATION OF THE MAGI, PRESENTATION (OF THE INFANT JESUS) IN THE TEMPLE, FLIGHT INTO EGYPT (OR MASSACRE OF THE INNOCENTS), and CORONATION OF THE VIRGIN (OR ASSUMPTION, OR DEATH OF THE VIRGIN). Paired with these would be the Hours of the Cross, a Passion (Sorrowful) cycle that might include the AGONY IN THE GARDEN, JUDAS' BETRAYAL, CHRIST BEFORE PILATE, FLAGELLATION (OR CROWNING WITH THORNS), CHRIST CARRYING THE CROSS,

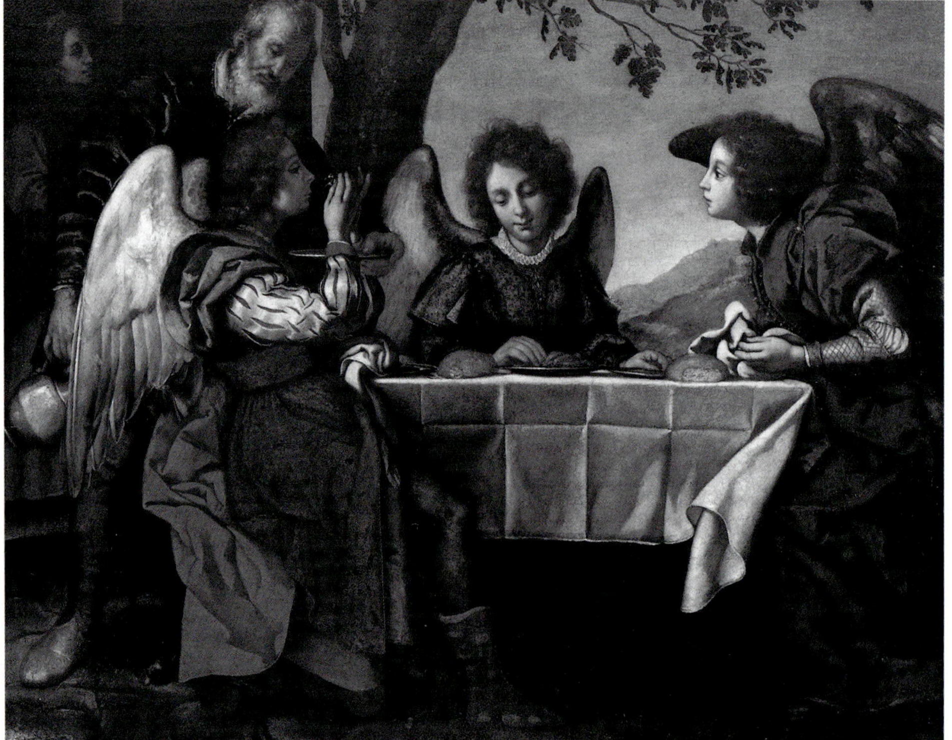

CRUCIFIXION, DEPOSITION, and ENTOMBMENT (or
LAMENTATION).[1] Taking liberties, I have con-
densed these two cycles into the following sec-
tions: the Annunciation, the Visitation, the Nativ-
ity, the Adoration(s), the Holy Family
(PRESENTATION, CIRCUMCISION, FLIGHT INTO
EGYPT), the Passion (CRUCIFIXION, DEPOSITION,
LAMENTATION, and ENTOMBMENT), Veneration (an
exploration of sainthood), and Coronation (DOR-
MITION, DEATH, and ASSUMPTION).

While there is no such thing as an "average
viewer" of religious art, whether in today's museums or in churches centuries ago, the establish-
ment of certain general characteristics gives both
relevance and consistency to this comparative portrait. When I speak of "past audiences" I refer to
people living and viewing the art in the decades
directly after it was made. When the discussion is
broader, featuring many works of art, I imagine
these viewers as women and men living roughly
500 years ago, a period termed by some the late
Middle Ages, by others the Renaissance, and still
others the nascent moments of the Early Modern
period. Like most Americans today, they live in a
town, not a rural outpost, and belong to the middle class, rather than the peasantry or the aristoc-
racy. Their steady lives revolve around work and
family, and there is still one Christian church in
the West (the Eastern branch having split away in
the schism of 1054), which will soon be splintered
apart by the Reformation. Several Protestant
churches will emerge from the original hierarchic
church, which will itself continue, though diminished in number, as the Catholic church.

1. The Annunciation

In Luke's Gospel, the archangel Gabriel
announces to Mary that God has chosen her to
bear his son. Her initial response is guarded. "She
was greatly troubled" we are told, but Gabriel
assures her not to be afraid. Her final reply, "Let it
be to me according to your word," affirms Mary's
central role in the new religion (Luke 1:28–38).

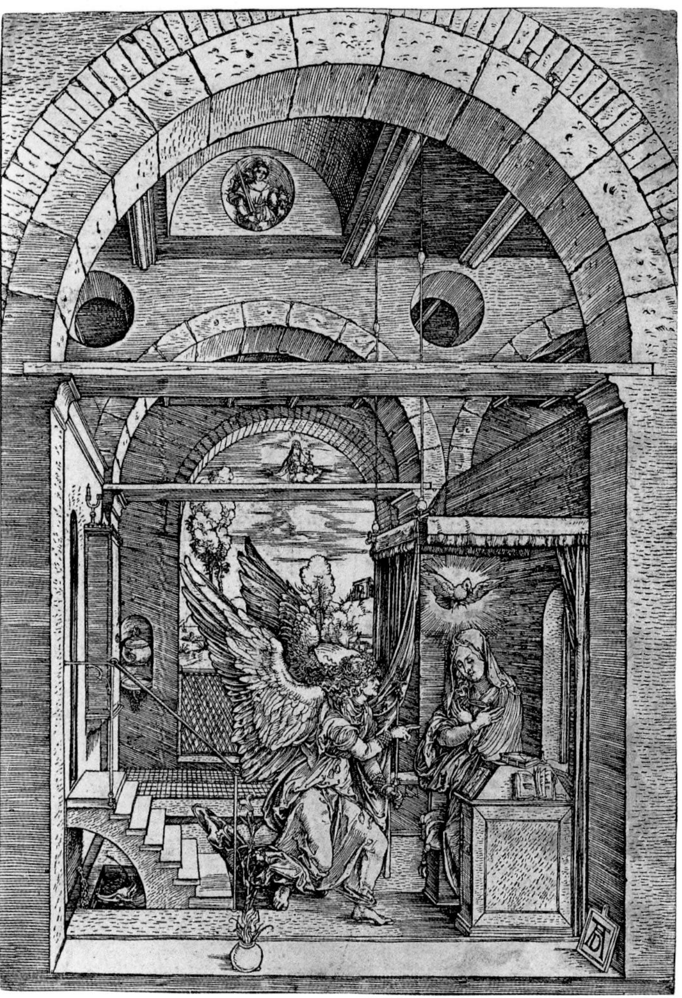

Fear, doubt, apprehension, and assent are com-
pactly conveyed in this brief exchange. Although
the word "annunciation" is most closely associated
with Mary, angels bring news to numerous figures
in the New Testament. In Matthew's Gospel, Jesus'
birth is announced to Joseph, not Mary (Matt
1:20–21). An angel announces John the Baptist's
imminent birth to his father Zechariah with the
same preface used for Mary, "Do not be afraid"
(Luke 1:11–13). In the Protevangelium of James,
annunciations of Mary's conception are received
by both Anna (4:1) and Joachim (4:4). There is an
Old Testament precedent as well for the ANNUNCI-
ATION, when three angels come to Abraham's
home to announce that his wife Sarah is pregnant

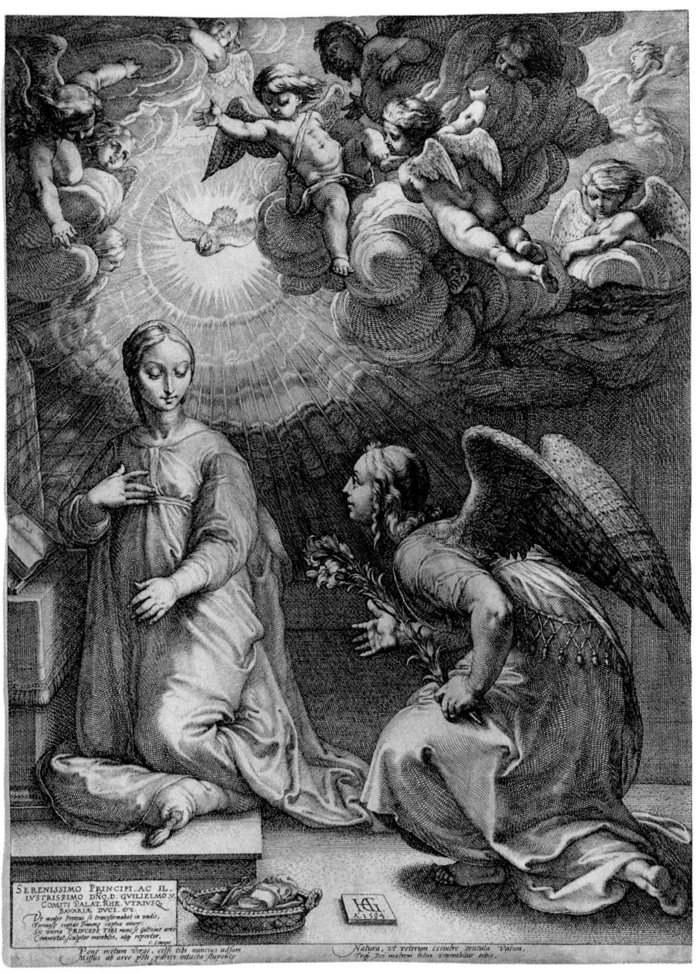

Fig. 23. Hendrik Goltzius, *The Annunciation*, 1594, engraving

seated at a four-sided lectern, while in an early six-teenth-century French Book of Hours the volume rests in her lap [fig. 126]. A single lily, symbolizing purity, is a symbol frequently found in ANNUNCIA-TIONS, whether in a vase, as in the two German works, or held by Gabriel in Goltzius's 1594 engraving [fig. 23]. A single stem with three blos-soms (as in the figure 24) was understood as a ref-erence to Mary's virginity before, during, and after giving birth, as well as to the holy trinity of God the Father, Christ the Son, and the Holy Spirit.[3]

Another common (but not obligatory) icono-graphic element is a dove, ray of light, or miniature infant, which signifies the Holy Spirit implanting the child in Mary's womb. Rays of light emanate from a dove hovering above Mary's head in Dürer's woodcut and Goltzius's engraving, while in the French manuscript, the dove travels along a beam of light. As with all Christian art, symbolic conven-tions developed to allow viewers to recognize the events being narrated, eventually coalescing into a visual shorthand of familiar signs. While subse-quent sections do not go into this same level of detail, the discussion of the development of ANNUNCIATION iconography serves as a case study of the evolutionary process undergone in the for-mation of a symbolic vocabulary.

The reading motif was a late development in Christian art, as was Mary's posture of prayer. Early Christian ANNUNCIATIONS portrayed Mary enthroned in queenly fashion, though by the year 700, both Mary and Gabriel were often shown standing. By 900, Gabriel began to find Mary at home, seated and spinning. Spindle and thread referred not only to female domestic activity but also to an apocryphal story of Mary's childhood, in which she spins a new veil for the Ark of the Covenant (the veil that would rend at the moment of Jesus' death on the cross).[4] By the start of the next millennium, Western artists began to show Mary reading rather than spinning at the angel's arrival, perhaps in response to efforts by clergy to reduce the influence of apocryphal stories, or per-

with his son Isaac (Genesis 18:10). Vignali's canvas of circa 1620 [fig. 21] shows the patriarch gra-ciously receiving the strangers, unaware of their heavenly origin.

ANNUNCIATIONS in Christian art usually portray the Virgin Mary, seated or kneeling, and the archangel Gabriel, standing or kneeling. In West-ern art, Gabriel usually stands to Mary's left, while in Byzantine and modern Orthodox icons, he is on her right.[2] Mary is often shown reading a book, in postures at times prayerful, at times restful. In a circa 1460 German panel [fig. 24], she kneels at a *prie-dieu*, or prayer stool, while in a circa 1470 Dutch Book of Hours she kneels before a modi-fied altar [fig. 116]. A circa 1503 woodcut by Albrecht Dürer (1471–1528) [fig. 22] shows her

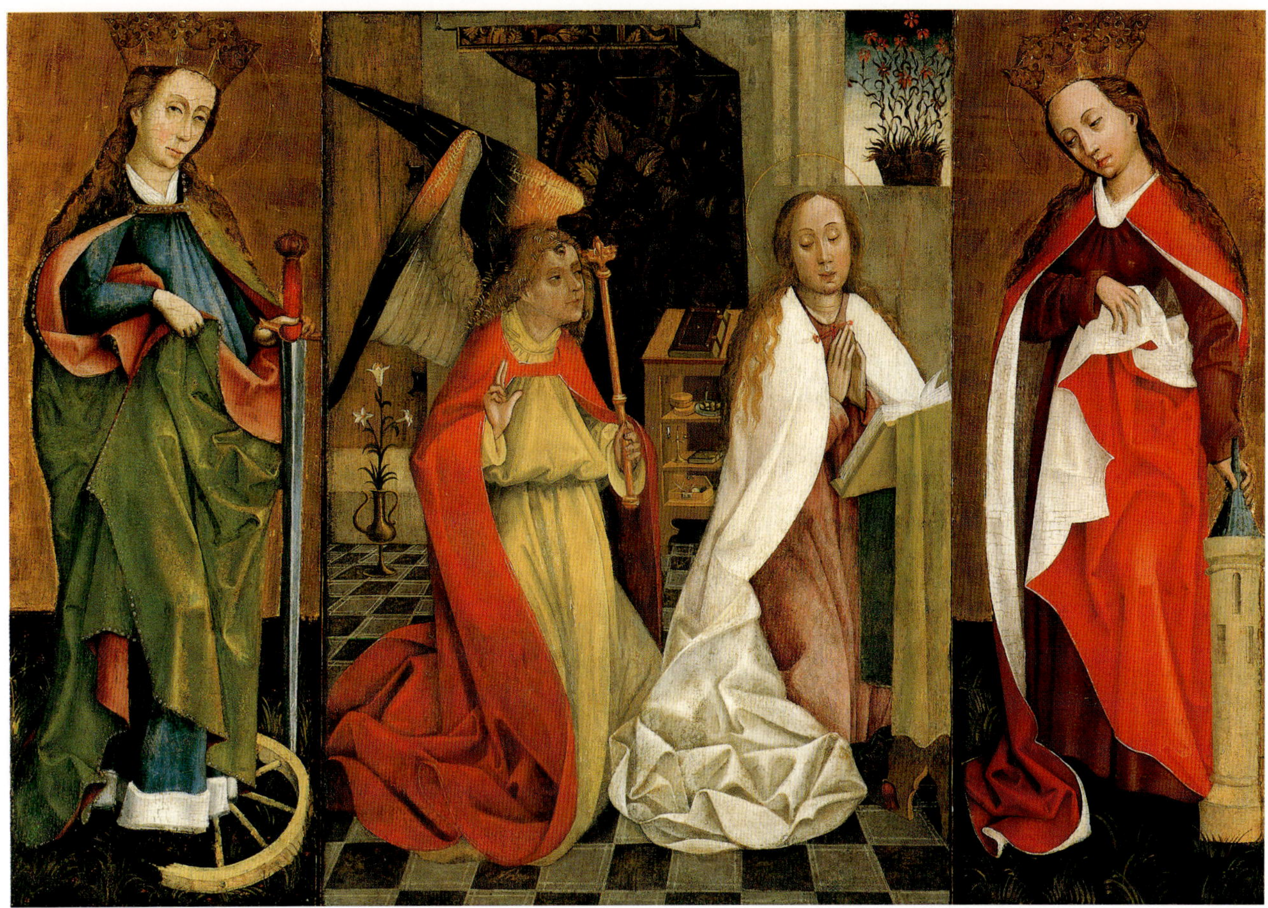

haps in reflection of the monastic emphasis on reading.[5] The scroll she was initially shown reading in the eleventh century became a book by the twelfth century, and by the thirteenth century a Bible,[6] namely the Book of Isaiah, whose messianic prophecies and allusions to a virgin (or young woman) giving birth were considered by Christians to prefigure their holy story.[7]

Occasionally artists set the ANNUNCIATION inside a church rather than a domestic setting, as in van Eyck's celebrated panel in Washington's National Gallery and Wellesley's Book of Hours from the circle of the Flemish illuminator Willem Backer van Vrelant.[8] In these renditions, Mary symbolizes *Ecclesia* (the Church), or the Bride of the Church, allusions to the words of the Hebrew Bible's Song of Solomon (or Song of Songs). In the circa 1470 manuscript illumination, Mary is shown inside a church in contemplative prayer aided by the reading of a book, thereby serving as a model to be emulated in the pious conduct of the book's owner [cat. no. 6, fig. 116].

Just as the representation of Mary's physical posture evolved over time, so did the emphasis on her mental activity during the ANNUNCIATION. Images of the seventh and eighth centuries stressed Mary's listening to the word of God, whereas ninth- and tenth-century scenes emphasized her reaction, and in twelfth-century works her active conversation with Gabriel. In scenes privileging the hearing of God's word, Mary was often depicted with a phylactery or symbolic stream connecting her ear to the heavenly source; on a side portal of Würzburg Cathedral (eleventh century), a rope dangles into her ear. Occasionally a baby was shown traveling down this band, a visual shorthand for *conceptio per aurem*: conception through hearing or, literally, through the ear. In the twelfth century, we begin to see the more familiar dove presented as the agent of the incarnation, traveling on rays of light to areas on Mary's body meant to represent her womb (either belly or genital area), her soul (forehead, heart, or mouth), or at times both.[9]

The interaction between Mary and Gabriel also formed part of an elaborate symbolic language, whose meaning is largely invisible to us today. ANNUNCIATION scenes often depict Gabriel with his hand raised in an ancient gesture denoting speech. Mary does not raise her hand in reply, but reacts with awe, by holding her hand to her breast; with welcoming gestures, by extending her hand in greeting; or with fear, by drawing her veil around her (as in Simone Martini's Uffizi *Annunciation* of 1333). Medieval and Renaissance viewers familiar with devotional art could recognize five specific moments in the ANNUNCIATION—reading the visual cues that signified Gabriel's arrival, Mary's reaction, their conversation, her contemplation, and final assent. In his sermons published in 1489, the Italian priest Fra Roberto Caracciolo da Lecce (1425–1495) termed this the "Angelic Colloquy," defining the five stages as *Conturbatio* (disquiet), *Cogitatio* (reflection), *Interrogatio* (inquiry), *Humiliatio* (submission), and *Meritatio* (merit).[10]

Having become familiar with some of the iconographic conventions of ANNUNCIATION scenes, our attention turns to the possible significance of these images in the everyday lives of earlier audiences. Following the metaphor of reading and the frequent depiction of this act in these images, let us begin with a consideration of literacy, as reflected by Christian art. How would the presentation of a woman in her home calmly reading a book have resonated with female viewers in the late medieval and early modern periods? Was it common for women of the late medieval and early modern periods to conduct themselves in

the manner of the woman shown in these ANNUNCIATION scenes?

The extent of women's literacy cannot be determined with complete accuracy, but recent scholarship suggests that it was greater than previously thought; in late medieval courtly circles, women's literacy appears to have been higher than men's.[11] Twelfth- and thirteenth-century troubadours frequently dedicated their poetry to women patrons, for whom the vernacular language of this type of verse was accessible.[12] Giovanni Boccaccio (1313–1375) in his preface to the *Decameron* addresses his audience of "gracious Ladies" whom he hoped would "further proceed in reading" his tales.[13] The women envisioned by these writers were aristocratic ladies of noble birth who belonged to privileged classes and courtly circles who might have interpreted Mary's quiet contemplation of an opened book as a reflection of their own activity of leisured reading.

Between the elite and the illiterate came another important class of women readers. Few members of the rural population could read, but this condition was independent of gender, encompassing parish priests and other authority figures as well as peasant laborers. In cities, towns, and larger villages, however, trade and commerce called for certain basic skills. By the late Middle Ages, quite a number of urban upper- and middle-class women were functionally literate in their native tongue. Merchants' wives and daughters would be taught enough math and writing to help in family businesses and to teach these same skills to young children at home, boys as well as girls.[14] The popularity of Books of Hours among middle-class audiences in the fifteenth century—with their vernacular prayers as well as Latin liturgies, and pictures to help orient readers and explain the written components—argues for the adaptation of the practice of prayerful reading by the semiliterate classes.[15]

Iconography associated with saint Anne, Mary's

mother, often showed her teaching the young virgin to read as well as to sew, knit, spin, or perform other domestic tasks. In pre-Reformation images of the Holy Kinship (see HOLY FAMILY section), education of children is presented as a task assigned to mothers, who imparted lessons equally to male and female offspring. After the Reformation, men were likely to be shown in the role of educators, both within scenes of Anne and Mary's extended family and in secular art.[16] Both before and after the Reformation, girls were less likely than boys to receive extensive schooling outside the home or to be instructed in Latin, the language of the church and of the learned, unless they entered a convent to prepare for a life of religious service. However, this does not preclude the possibility of limited schooling. The Florentine banker Giovanni Villani (ca. 1275–1348), in his mid-fourteenth-century chronicle of the city of Florence, estimated that in a population of 90,000 men, women, and children, between 8,000 and 10,000 boys *and* girls were learning to read Italian, while 1,000 to 1,200 boys were learning calculations, and 550 to 600 boys were learning Latin and logic.[17]

In northern Europe, the Brethren of the Common Life promoted education for girls as well as boys. Founder Geert Grote (1340–1384) translated medieval prayers into the vernacular to use in teaching; the Vrelant *Annunciation* folio comes from a Dutch Book of Hours based on Grote's translation[18] [fig. 116]. Renaissance humanists argued in favor of education for both sexes, deeming knowledge an incremental means to virtue: the more learned a person, the more virtuous. Spanish humanist Juan Luís Vives (1492–1540), tutor to Mary (1516–1558), daughter of Henry VIII, wrote that it was a husband's duty to teach an illiterate wife to read, noting "all lewd and evil women are unlearned and . . . they which be learned are most desirous of honesty."[19] The impact of female literacy can be gauged indirectly by the ban imposed in 1543 by England's Henry VIII (1491–1547) on women reading the Bible, an indication both that women were literate and that men viewed this as dangerous.[20] Hence, one cannot conclude that Mary's presentation as a woman reading would have seemed exotic or inappropriate to early audiences (particularly as Mary was meant to represent the ideal woman).

While these depictions of female literacy were less provocative in previous centuries than we might have assumed, another aspect of her ANNUNCIATION demeanor, which goes unnoticed today, would have probably struck earlier audiences as unusual. In truth, Mary's education would have surprised early viewers less than her independence. ANNUNCIATIONS placed in domestic settings depict Mary alone and engaged in solitary tasks in her chamber. Few women would have found opportunities for privacy within an active household, and unmarried women would have been closely controlled and chaperoned by their families. Women's sex drives were considered stronger than men's in the fifteenth and sixteenth centuries, and unmarried women—who had to fight against these natural drives until they could be safely married off—were considered perilously "masterless."[21] Florentine chronicles also record that very few children were born before the eighth month of a recent marriage, indicating couples abstained from premarital sex, thanks in part, no doubt, to the vigilance of family members over the whereabouts of betrothed maidens in the household.[22]

2. *Visitation*

The ANNUNCIATION marks God's incarnation, or entrance into the world as Mary's child; the VISITATION signifies the first earthly recognition of the incarnation. It is during this interim period—the nine months of pregnancy following the ANNUNCIATION —in which Mary is most literally the *Theotokos/* God-bearer, and it is Elizabeth's recognition of the incarnate God within Mary's womb that gives purpose and meaning to Luke's VISITATION narrative. Luke tells how Mary, shortly after the ANNUNCIA-

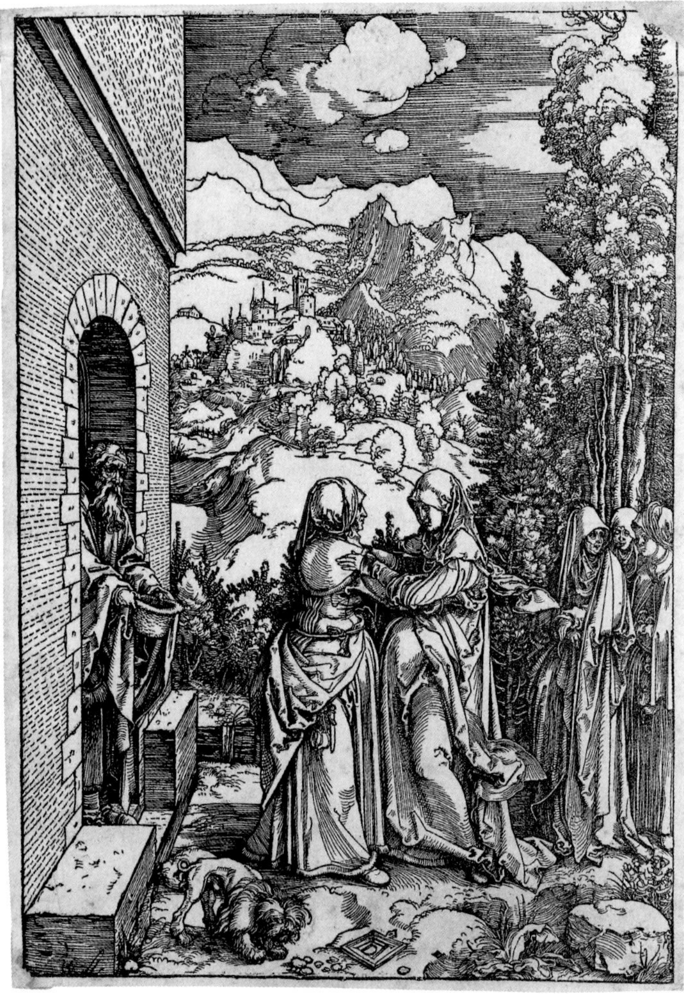

its way into the Little Office of the Virgin Mary.[23] Along with the *Lord's Prayer* (Our Father), found in Matthew 6:9–13 and Luke 11:2–4, it was one of two prayers medieval Christians were expected to know by heart.[24] The mendicant friars who taught the laity their basic prayers encouraged the illiterate to recite the *Ave Maria* over and over in substitution for more elaborate prayers. With the development of the rosary (adapted from Muslim prayer beads brought back by crusaders), serial recitation of up to 150 *Ave Marias* was incorporated.[25]

Mary replied to Elizabeth's greeting with her only sustained speech in the Bible. These eighteen lines of praise—written in the style of a Hebrew psalm and echoing the words of Hannah, a once-barren woman giving thanks for her son (I Samuel 2:1–10)—became incorporated into the liturgy as the *Magnificat* (Luke 1:46–55). Mary, of course, was not a barren elderly woman, but a youth who, in the words of the Qur'an, had "neither been touched by any man nor ever been unchaste" (Mary 19:18). Yet her conception was as remark-able and unexpected as those of Sarah, Hannah, and Elizabeth. Saint Bernard of Clairvaux (1090–1153) compared the child in Mary's womb to the eucharistic wafer consecrated during the mass, as two earthly containers of divine force.[26] "Offer your son, sacred Virgin, and present the blessed fruit of your womb to God," he wrote in a sermon, "Offer the blessed host, pleasing to God, for the reconciliation of us all."[27]

Mary's virginal conception is a fundamental element of Christian doctrine. Saint Augustine's analogy of light passing through glass without breaking it was used by clergy to explain to the faithful how a child entered Mary's womb without puncturing her hymen.[28] Windows feature promi-nently in the ANNUNCIATION scenes discussed ear-lier (though the artists have not attempted to ren-der glass). The metaphor took on greater power once churches became embellished with stained glass; not only could one observe how the light did not break the glass, but also how the glass trans-

TION, goes to visit for three months with her cousin Elizabeth. Elizabeth, who is also pregnant with the future John the Baptist, recognizes Mary's pregnancy and immediately apprehends its special nature and momentous import [fig. 25]. The words of Elizabeth's greeting to Mary, "Blessed are you among women, and blessed is the fruit of your womb" (Luke 1:42), became part of the *Ave Maria* (Hail Mary) prayer, still in use by Catholics today.

In the seventh century, the words of Elizabeth's greeting from the VISITATION became linked with Gabriel's greeting from the ANNUNCIATION—*Ave [Maria], gratia plena, Dominus tecum* ("Hail, O favored one, the Lord is with you," Luke 1:28)—in a prayer which by the eleventh century had found

formed the light into richly colored patterns without breaking the ray. Mary's hymen was also believed to remain unbroken after giving birth, though the scriptures do not comment on this.[29] According to the second-century Protevangelium of James, a midwife attending at the birth of Jesus confirmed Mary's enduring virginity—an implausible anecdote, yet one regularly included in dramatic reenactments of the NATIVITY.[30]

Mary's postpartum virginity was an essential step on the way to the concept of her perpetual virginity, a belief widely held among Western Christians until the Reformation, and Catholics afterward (though in recent decades Vatican theologians have allowed certain debate on this topic).[31] Many Protestant churches currently teach that Mary went on to give birth normally afterward, reserving the importance of the VIRGIN BIRTH for her first child, Jesus. The Orthodox church continues to teach the doctrine of Mary's perpetual virginity, regarding Jesus' brethren as Mary's stepchildren (see HOLY FAMILY section) and honoring Mary as *Aeiparthenos*, "Ever-Virgin," the title bestowed upon her in 553 by the Council of Constantinople.[32] All Christian sects agree, however, that at the time of the VISITATION, Mary

was a pregnant young woman who had conceived a child without sexual contact.

Youth and purity are two key elements of Mary's character translated into visual form in Marian art. In a circa 1450 Book of Hours from northern France (or Flanders), Elizabeth's matronly appearance contrasts with her cousin's youthful demeanor [fig. 26]. Artists, including the anonymous illuminator of a circa 1480 Book of Hours from Amiens, portrayed Mary as a young woman not only when conceiving and delivering the infant Jesus, but also while mourning his crucifixion [fig. 27]. This artistic depiction—arrested, as it were, in an eternally youthful VISITATION phase between conception and parenthood— merely made visible a generalized cultural attitude toward Mary's identity and ever-youthful appearance. Theologians also concerned themselves with Mary's looks. The Dominican preacher Gabriele de Barletta (d. ca. 1480) gave a sermon on Mary's beauty (a fairly common theme) in which he asked, "Was the Virgin dark or fair? Albertus Magnus says that she was not simply dark, nor simply red-headed, nor just fair-haired . . . . Mary was a

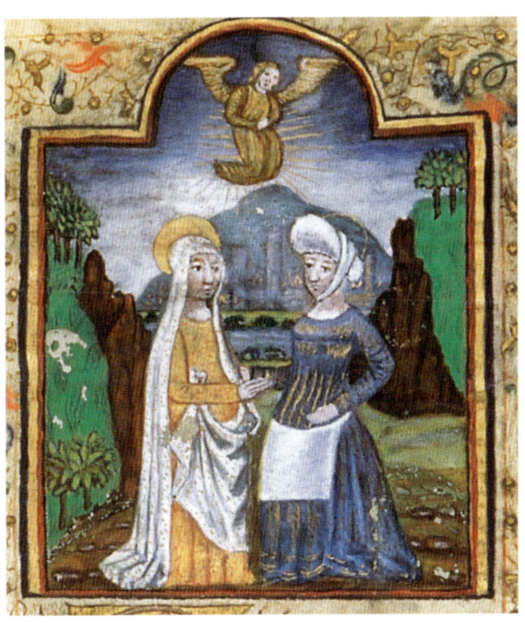

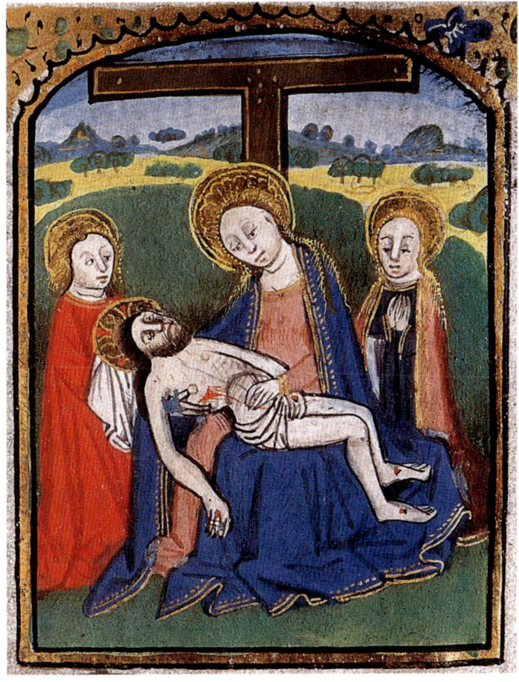

blend of complexions, partaking of all of them, because a face partaking of all of them is a beautiful one."[33] Hers was, after all, as Dante (1265–1321) wrote, "the face that most resembles Christ." As an anonymous medieval hymn phrased it, "Mary the mirror, Christ the vision blest."[34]

The physical aspects that artists bestowed on Mary record contemporary historical standards of beauty and also convey nuances whose significance is not immediately apparent to modern viewers. Particularly revealing is the way artists treated Mary's hair. When the renowned German artist Albrecht Dürer (1471–1528) published his nineteen-scene *Life of the Virgin* series (produced between 1502 and 1511, and issued together with a frontispiece in 1511), he placed a scene of the VISITATION at its midpoint, immediately following a scene of her BETROTHAL.[35] At the time these woodcuts were made, the period of betrothal was a significant interval in a woman's life, marking her transformation from youth to adulthood, and maidenhood to matrimony; it was distinguished (indeed, celebrated) by a shift from loose hair to covered hair.

Images such as Dürer's *Betrothal of the Virgin* [fig. 28], which portrayed Mary and Joseph in the synagogue in a ceremony at which a Jewish high priest officiated, supported clerical efforts to bring the sacrament of marriage under church control. Religious ceremonies were encouraged but not required until the Council of Trent (1545–1563); prior to then, one could be married in the eyes of the church if consent were given freely before witnesses in public. Wedding customs varied throughout Europe, but usually two ceremonies took place: betrothals and nuptials. Betrothal ceremonies were held in public, often outside or in front of churches rather than before an altar. Dowry contracts were exchanged and a veil placed on the bride, which she wore until her nuptials.[36] The Orthodox church retains to this day the two-part format of the medieval wedding ceremony, the preliminary Office of Betrothal and exchange of rings, followed by the sacramental Office of Crowning. Nowadays, these two ceremonies are celebrated simultaneously, rather than weeks apart.[37]

By tradition, married women wore their hair up and/or their heads covered—a custom observed in much of Europe and North America until the twentieth century.[38] The official *Homily on Matrimony*, preached at Elizabethan Church of England marriage ceremonies, reminded the congregation that the cap worn on a woman's head symbolized that "she is under covert or obedience of her husband."[39] In contrast to Mary's delicate veil, the large starched headdress of the woman on the

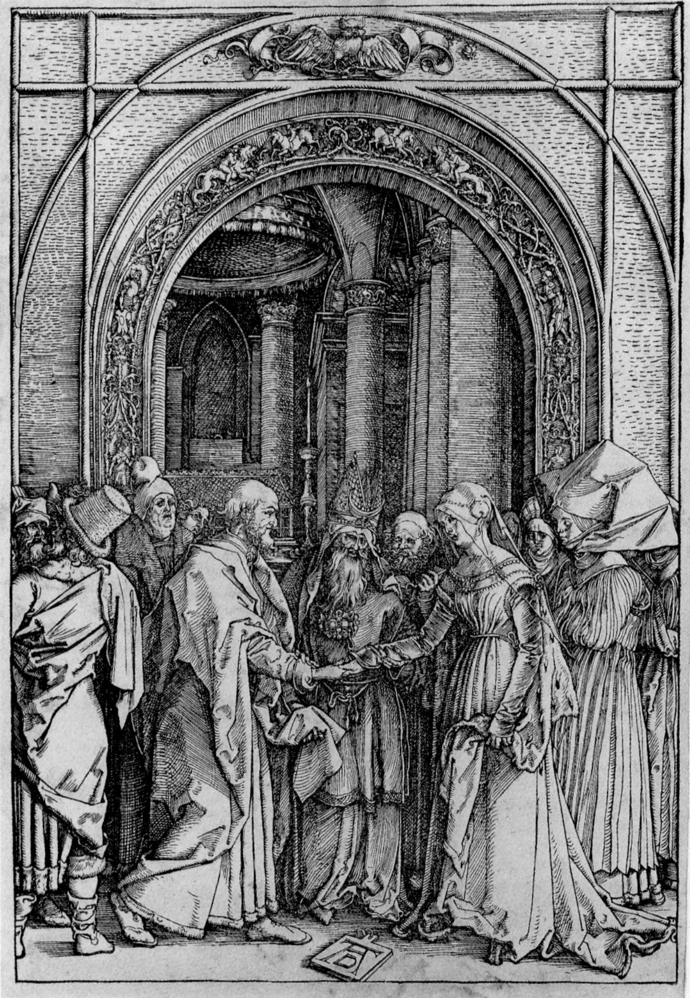

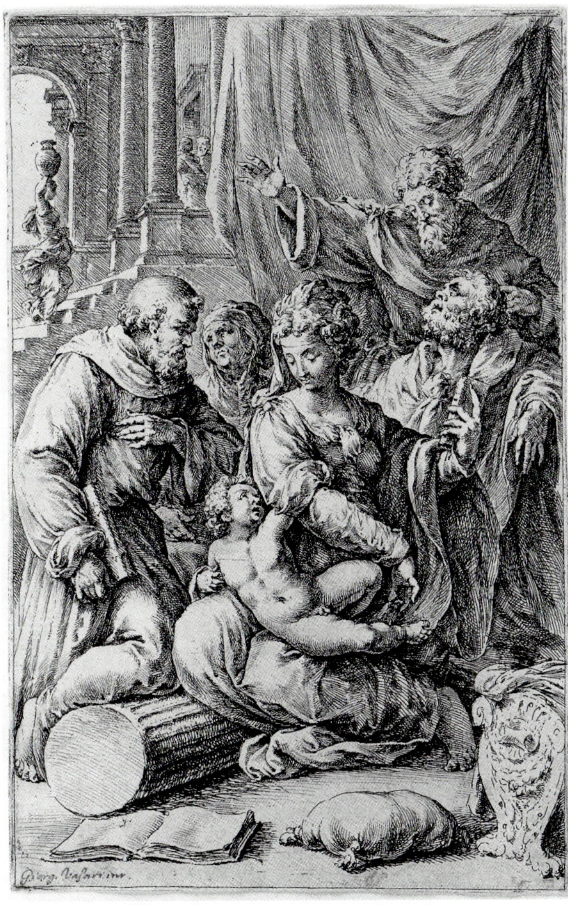

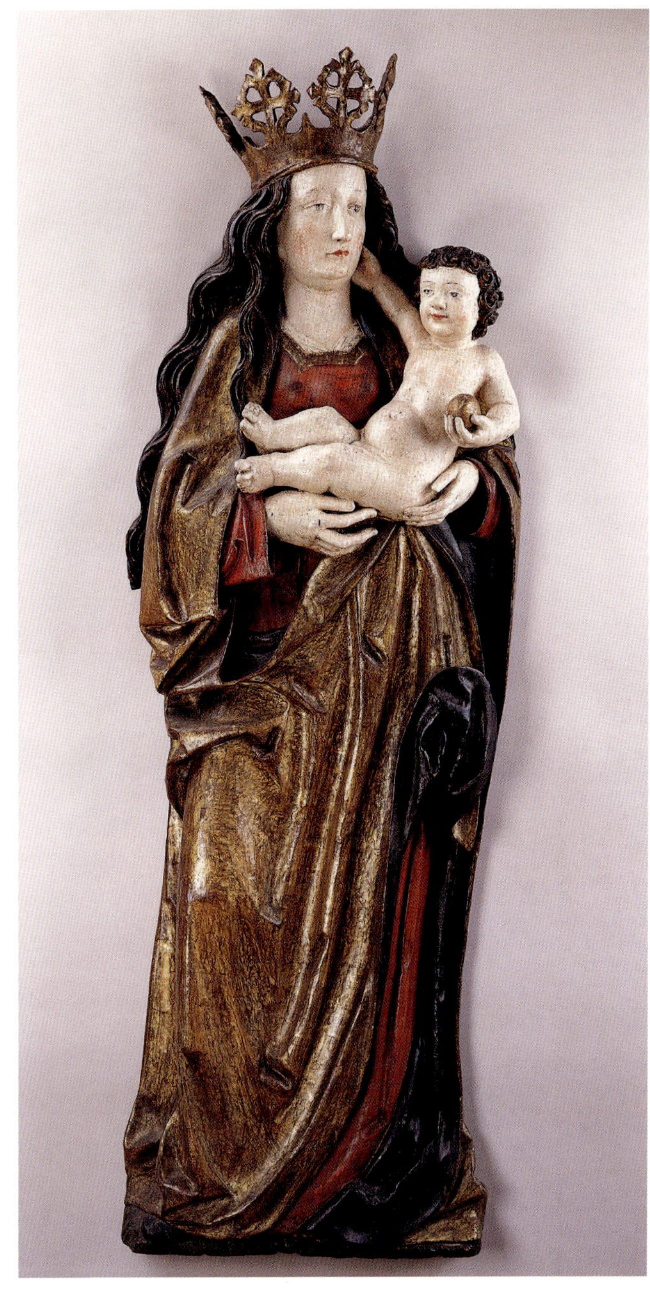

right in Dürer's *Betrothal of the Virgin* denotes her as a married woman. While its elaborate structure might strike us today as an artist's fanciful creation, on a watercolor sketch of this figure made in 1500 Dürer wrote, "So does one dress for church in Nuremberg."[40] When married women encountered artistic depictions of Mary, most of the time they saw not a matron like themselves—wimpled, coiffed, bonneted, or hatted—but an adult girl with hair at times confined by a modest veil [figs. 29, 56], and at times adorned with nothing more constraining than a halo or a crown [figs. 30, 31]. Of the thirteen images of Mary found within a circa 1480 Book of Hours from Amiens, only one image—a CRUCIFIXION scene—portrays her with a covered head. In the remaining miniatures, long blonde hair streams over her shoulder, painted in ocher with gilded highlights [fig. 32].

Artists continued to portray Mary with loose hair, even when inappropriate for her age according to their own conventions. The PENTECOST illustrations from a 1483 German and Latin *Plenarium* (compilation of epistles and evangel readings for the liturgical year) [fig. 33] and a circa 1480 French Book of Hours [fig. 90] show Mary seated among the apostles, with the light from the

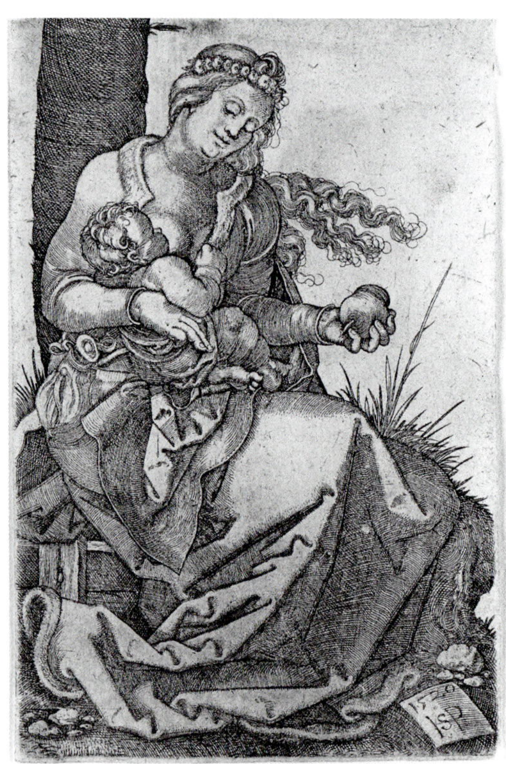

Holy Spirit streaming down her long blonde hair.
The PENTECOST, narrated in Acts 1:14 and the last
direct reference to Mary in the New Testament,

takes place forty days after Jesus' crucifixion. At
this time in her life, Mary was probably widowed
and certainly old enough to have a 33–year-old
son; she should have been shown in the
respectable matronly garb worn by saint Anne in a
fifteenth-century Parisian Book of Hours [fig. 34].
Nevertheless, the artist presents Mary with long
flowing hair. For both artists and audiences, the
styling of Mary's hair was an indication of her perpetual virginity, which they believed persisted
throughout her married life and exempted her, in
their minds, from the social conventions practiced
in their own society.[41]

Paradoxically, in secular culture, long hair also
conveyed notions of attractiveness and desirability,
indicating a woman's availability for marriage and
presumably conjugal relations.[42] Just as Mary's
identity embraced the contradictory elements of
virginity and maternity, so was her purity and physical restraint conveyed by artists through attributes
of carnality and physical beauty. In the circa 1490
polychromed sculpture of the *Virgin and Child*
from the Alsace region of the Upper Rhine valley
[fig. 35], for example, we see the delicate arms,

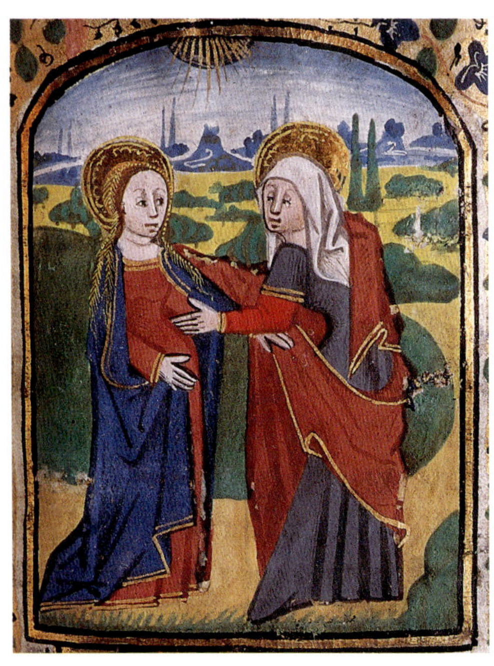

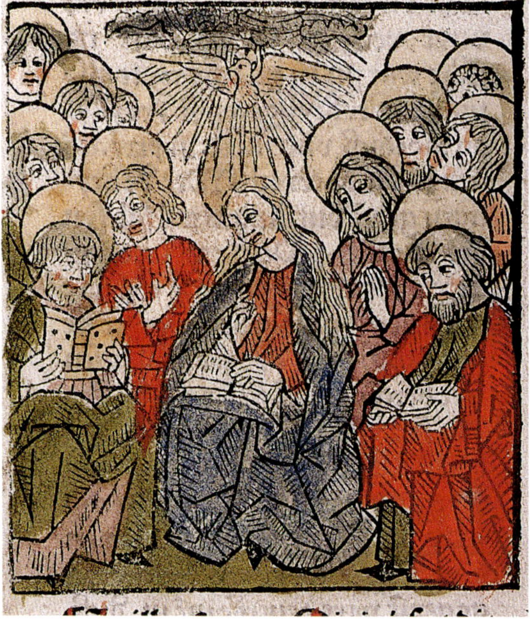

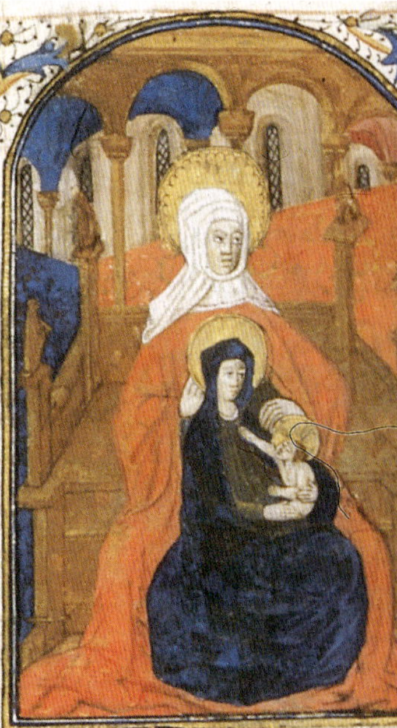

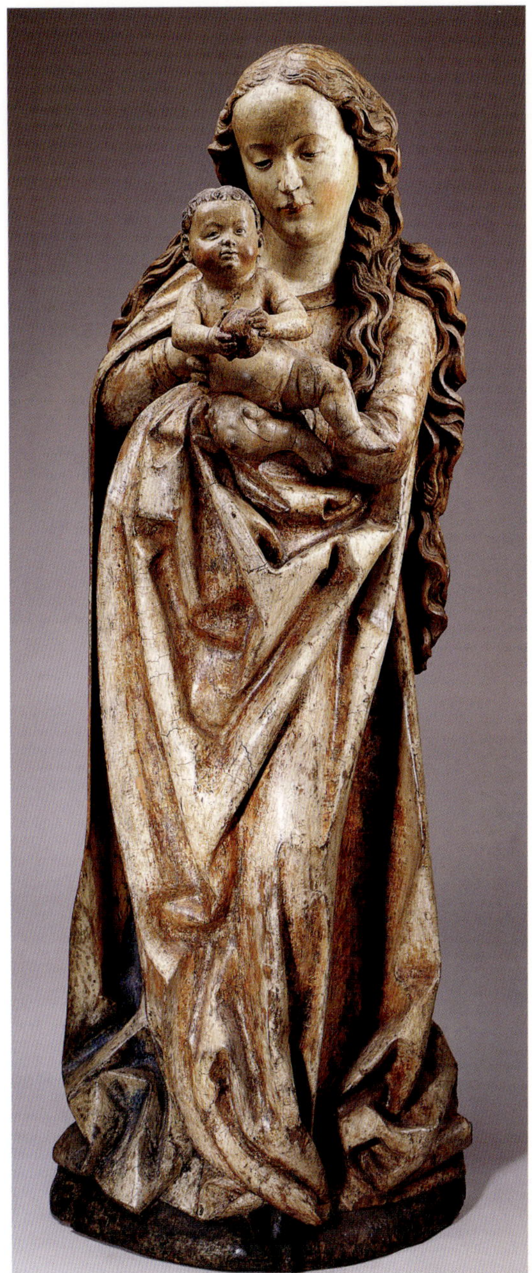

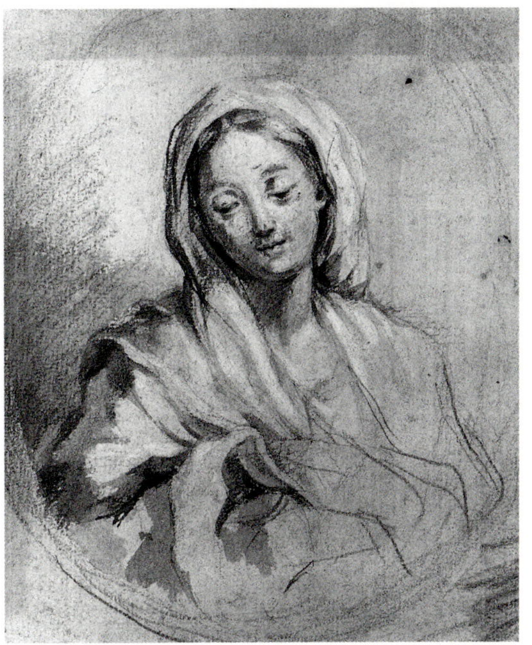

youthfulness, as blonde hair often darkens with age.[44]

Another feature that draws comment is the tendency to depict Mary with closed lips, or a half-smile in which the teeth do not show [fig. 36]. As Mary's comely demeanor at times seemed inconsistent with concepts such as chastity or modesty, artists neutralized her sensual appeal via a decorous downward glance, submissive expression, and sealed mouth. Theologians linked Mary's sad expression to a presentiment of her infant son's future suffering, just as additional pictorial elements alluded to his future crucifixion and death (e.g., the grasping of the cross-topped staff in Pintoricchio's *tondo* and the sleeping pose in Vasari's work) [figs. 45, 62]. Mary's subdued appearance, however, also draws upon a standard of female behavior that found there is "nothing more pleasant [in a woman] than a fair countenance and a quiet demeanor."[45]

Marian imagery was crafted to represent not only what were considered to be the ideal physical characteristics of the period but also perfect moral and social qualities. For societies living around 1500, a good woman would be seen as one who

clear skin, narrow waist, high breasts, rounded belly, full hips, and dainty feet that characterized not only feminine beauty at the time, but also suitability for childbearing.[43] Modern viewers also remark upon the tendency to portray Mary as blonde, even by artists from Mediterranean cultures. Blondeness was not only part of the idealized feminine image but also an indicator of

spoke little; obeyed first her father and then her husband; practiced modesty and restraint in conduct, speech, and dress; and emulated Mary's example of chastity, virtue, humility, and honorability. A fourteenth-century conduct book written for the three daughters of a knight and reprinted twice in the fifteenth century included chapters outlining "How the wymmen ought to be charytable after the exemplary of Our Lady" and "How men oughte to sette and put theyr children to scole" so that their daughters might read about the elevating lives of Mary, the saints, and the virgin martyrs, and model their own behavior accordingly.[46] Christine de Pisan (ca. 1364–ca. 1431), who accurately described fifteenth-century French manners and social mores (though she may have meant to be critical of their limiting role on women's lives), wrote that "virgins who are waiting for the state of marriage ought to be in their countenances, conduct, and speech, moderate and chaste, and, especially in church, quiet, looking at their books or with their eyes lowered."[47] Were they to slip, and look up in church, their eyes would no doubt soon rest on an image of Mary, whose model behavior would remind them of their own.

3. Nativity

With the delivery of her son, Mary's role as instrument of God's incarnation or presence on earth in human form entered a new phase. In many ways, Mary's motherhood brought her closer to ordinary female experience and allowed women to identify more closely with her; yet in other ways it drew attention to elements of Mary's experience that set her apart from the rest of humanity. The first Council of Nicaea, convened in 325, left no doubt that Mary was the ideal woman, declaring: "The Lord looked upon the whole of creation, and he saw no-one equal to Mary. Therefore he chose her for his mother."[48]

Luke's description of Jesus' birth in a manger (the travelers' inn having no spare rooms) gave artists a basis on which to build NATIVITY scenes. Some envisioned the manger (literally a feeding trough) within a crumbling hovel, others in a multilevel barn bustling with human and animal life [fig. 37]. Sometimes the company grew quite exotic; Tintoretto's animal population included a peacock [fig. 143]. From the mid-fourteenth century on, many artists shaped their NATIVITIES in accord with the mystical visions of saint Birgitta (or Bridget) of Sweden (1303–1373). Birgitta's *Revelations* recorded a lifetime of conversations with Mary, during which specific details of the NATIVITY were described. The circa 1500 illumination from a Rouen Book of Hours accords with Birgitta's description of a stable filled with light radiating from the newborn infant, who lies on the ground beside a kneeling Mary [fig. 38]. Seemingly lacking in tenderness, this scene represents not a quiet contemplation of the newborn infant but the actual moment of birth. The peculiar placement of the child on the hard uncushioned floor was drawn from Birgitta's description of Mary's delivery, which occurred abruptly, as she stood in prayer, facing east. Without pain or forewarning, Birgitta explained, the baby appeared at her feet and cried out with cold, and Mary kneeled and took him in her arms.[49]

The event that transformed Mary from Virgin Maiden to Virgin Mother is summarily treated in the Gospels, yet expansively rendered in Christian art, dramatic as well as visual. The Byzantine church (ca. 800) had introduced theatre into the liturgy as a tool for teaching the mysteries of faith. Out of these dramatized sermons and performed texts grew the medieval mystery plays, popular entertainments that recreated Bible stories and complemented the liturgical cycle.[50] In England, trade guilds and religious confraternities staged comedies and dramatic plays at Christmas, Easter, Corpus Christi (a feast celebrating the Eucharist), and Whitsun (or Pentecost, a feast marking the descent of the Holy Spirit on Mary and the apostles).

The NATIVITY—Jesus' birth (also known as the

Christmas story)—was frequently enacted on the
medieval stage, always with an emphasis on the
painless nature of Mary's labor. During dramatic
reenactments, characters would often point to
Mary's "blissful" delivery as proof she had borne
the son of God and retained her virginity in the
process.[51] Though thoroughly apocryphal, Mary's
childbirth free of discomfort was a staple of nativity plays and theology as well. Mary "conceived
without pleasure and therefore gave birth without
pain," concluded saint Augustine (354–430), for
whom pleasure was anathema.[52] The Dominican
priest Jacopo da Varazze (known as Jacobus de
Voragine, ca. 1228–1298), archbishop of Genoa
and author of the *Legenda aurea (Golden Legend*, a
compilation of hagiographical tales, or saints' stories), listed a painless birth "above the human condition" as one of his criteria proving that "the
birth of Christ was miraculous, as regards the
mother, the child born of her, and the mode of
the birth."[53]

The Qur'an also provides an explicit account of
the NATIVITY, but one that differs significantly
from the Christian account. Upon receiving word
of God's plan for her, the *Mary* chapter tells us,
Mary entered a voluntary exile. "Thereupon she
conceived him," we are told, "and retired to a far-
off place. And when she felt the throes of childbirth, she lay down by the trunk of a palm-tree,
crying: 'Oh, would that I had died and passed into
oblivion!' " (19:22–23). The Lord provides a running brook and ripe dates to nourish her until she
can return to her people, much as Hagar and Ishmael had been sustained in their desert sojourn.
Mary's very human suffering in the Islamic
account accords with its theology of Jesus' nondi-
vine status. In the Christian tradition, however, to
be spared the pains of childbirth is to be free from
the stain of original sin, the inheritance of all
mankind since the expulsion from the Garden of
Eden.

The Book of Genesis in the Hebrew Bible tells
how Eve, tempted by the serpent, gave to Adam

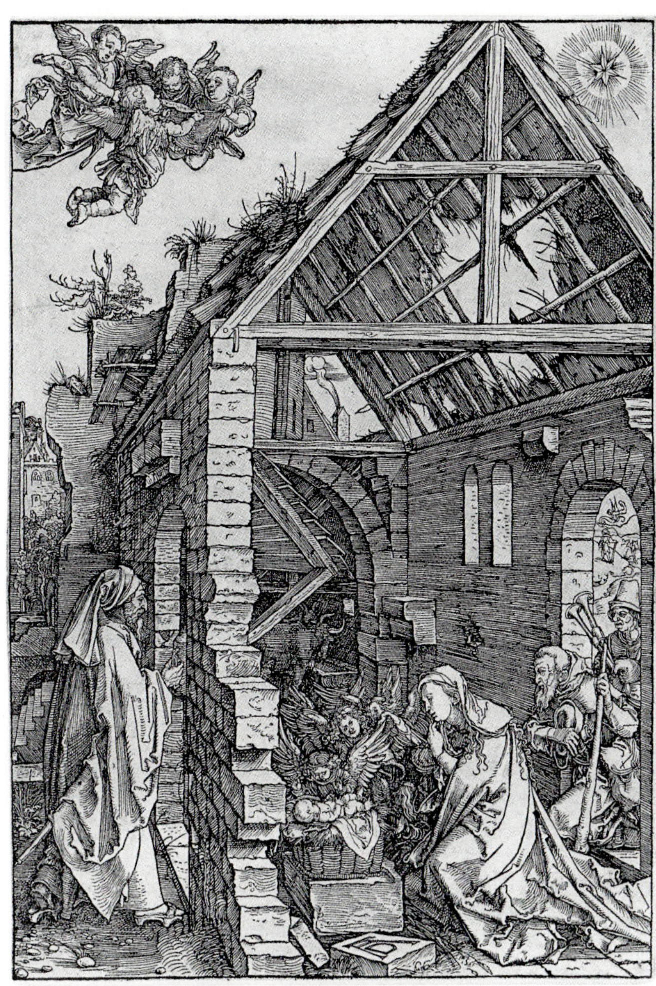

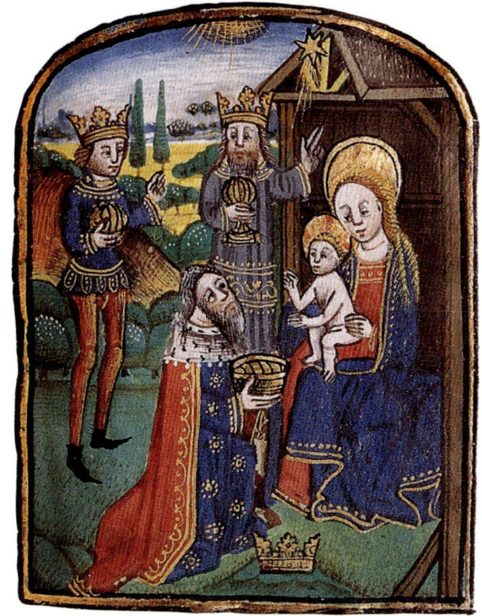

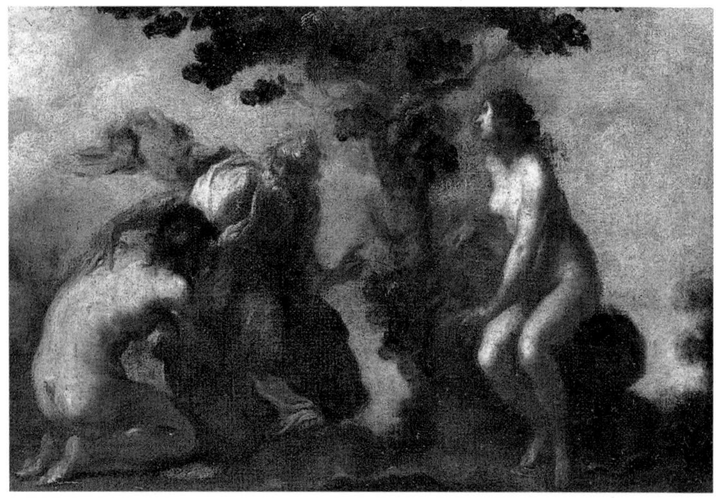

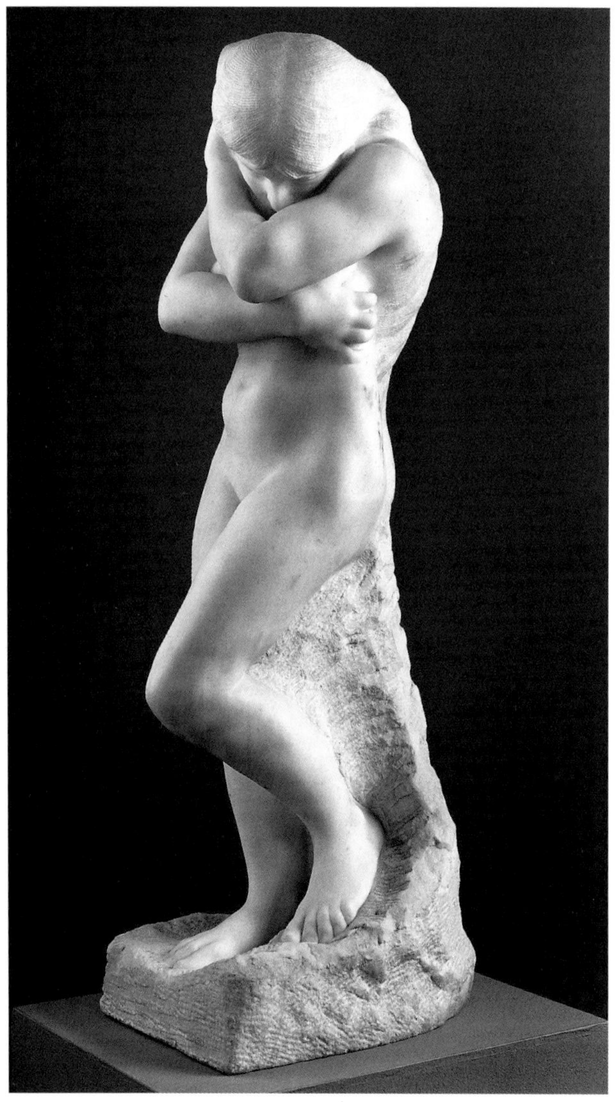

the fruit of the tree of the knowledge of good and evil, which they had been warned not to eat. After both have eaten the forbidden fruit (the ORIGINAL SIN) and realized their nakedness, God confronts them. Adam blames Eve for giving him the fruit, which he ate; Eve blames the serpent for having beguiled her; and God punishes both. Because of their disobedience, Adam and Eve are expelled from paradise and must, like all humans after them, toil for food, live by their own labor, and eventually die. For women, an additional injunction was added: "In pain you shall bring forth children, yet your desire shall be for your husband, and he shall rule over you" (Gen. 3:16). These words were often used to justify the general presumption of women's natural subservience to men and the legal condition of a wife's subjugation to her husband. Francesco Furini's sketch [fig. 39] for a larger composition (now in the Palazzo Pitti, Florence) shows the moment of confrontation, while Rodin's marble reveals a sorrowing Eve after the fall [fig. 40].

From the beginning, Christian writers compared Mary to Eve, playing with the resemblance between *Ave* and *Eva* to stress their interrelated state, with one woman the mirror image of the other. As early as the second century Mary was spoken of as the New Eve or Second Eve, whose obedience to God atoned for Eve's sinful disobedience.[54] In Christian thought, Mary and Eve made a fitting pair. Eve was the mother of all humankind, and Mary the mother of its saviour. Whereas Eve brought death into the world, Mary, through her son Jesus, brought eternal life. "Eve is pardoned through her daughter [Mary], and the complaint of men against women is put to rest" wrote the Cistercian abbot saint Bernard of Clairvaux (1090–1153), who became the great champion of Marian devotion in the twelfth century.[55]

Unfortunately, Mary's redemption brought only partial compensation for Eve's "crime." Women continued to be blamed for bringing sin into the world and to be identified as secondary, if not inferior, beings. Confessor's manuals, penitential handbooks (catalogues of sins and penance), and recorded sermons demonstrated a tendency to exalt Mary while simultaneously disparaging contemporary women. The openly misogynist Tertullian (155/60–post-220) preached in *On the Apparel of Women* that a Christian woman should "affect meanness of appearance, walking about as Eve mourning and repentant . . . [that] she might the more fully expiate that which she derives from Eve, [blame for] the first sin."[56] Fourteen centuries later, women were still judged to be "lewde, idle, [and] inconstant" like Eve, not "milde, yielding, and vertuous" like Mary.[57] Saint Thomas Aquinas (1225–1274) viewed this as part of the natural order, writing that "this kind of subjection [of women to men] existed even before [original] sin. For the good of order would have been wanting in the human family if some were not governed by others wiser than themselves. So, by such a kind of subjection woman is naturally subject to man, because in man the discernment of reason predominates."[58]

Secular writings, whether fiction, fables, or conduct and household manuals, show an equal tendency *not* to put the complaint to rest. Thomas Becon (1512–1567), in a manual for the behavior of unmarried girls (daughters or maidservants), instructs, "Let her kepe silence for there is nothing that doth so much commend . . . a maid, as silence," reminding all that it was a woman's tongue that led Adam astray.[59] Women writers aligned themselves with the obedient Mary, even to the point of excusing Eve's weakness. Poet Aemilia Lanyer (d. circa 1640) observed that Eve sinned "for knowledge sake" while Adam succumbed because "the fruit was faire."[60] The feisty Ester Sowernam, in a 1617 defense of women, argued that Eve's trouble stemmed from a "Serpent of masculine gender" and that if God commanded women to obey men (as was taught), "the cause is, the more to encrease her [women's] glorie . . . for nothing is more acceptable before God

than to obey," an attribute that linked all women to the "blessed mother and mirrour of al womanhood, the Virgin *Marie*."[61] Nevertheless, the Mary/Eve comparison encouraged the classification of women as either wholly good or wholly bad, and none could ever meet Mary's high standard. She was the model of ideal female behavior, but not a standard any woman could hope to attain.

*   *   *

To fully comprehend how men and women in the past interpreted the NATIVITY—the virgin birth of a divine saviour in human form—one must consider how these same people would have viewed the birth of any child by any woman. Rather than record naïve superstitions regarding biological functions or crude simplifications of human physiology, late medieval and early modern writings show a surprisingly sophisticated understanding of reproduction, especially as the female ova or "seed," unlike male semen, would not be observable until the development of the microscope.[62] What the writings also reveal, however, is a growing unease as patriarchal theories were displaced by more accurate models of human reproduction—unease that emerges in relation to the high degree of women's involvement in both conception and childbearing—and anxiety about men's dependence on women for the survival of the species.

Two forms of medical writing influenced both scholarly and popular understanding of human reproduction in the Middle Ages and Renaissance. Ancient Greek texts by Hippocrates, Aristotle, and Galen—rediscovered and translated into Latin in the twelfth and thirteenth centuries—circulated among scholars alongside more practical treatises drawn from and aimed at midwives, physicians, and other health care providers. Examples of the latter include a gynecological handbook by the second-century physician Soranus of Ephesus (translated into Latin in the fifth century and still

Regarding Mary   51

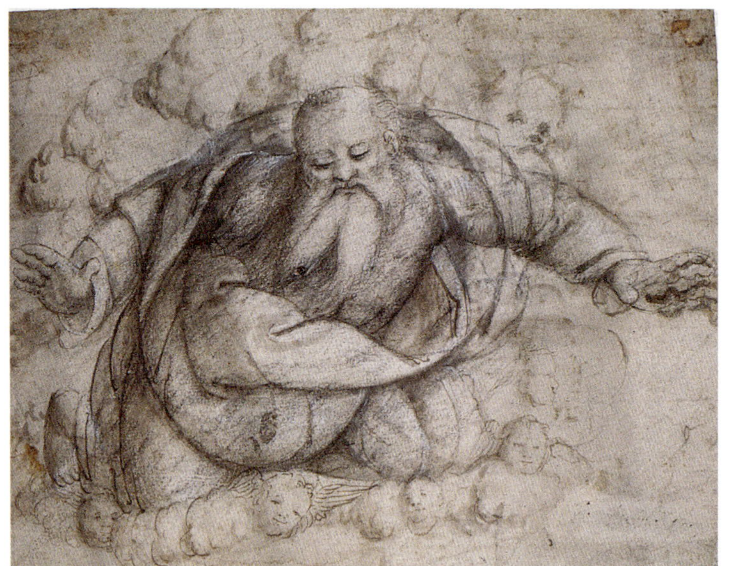

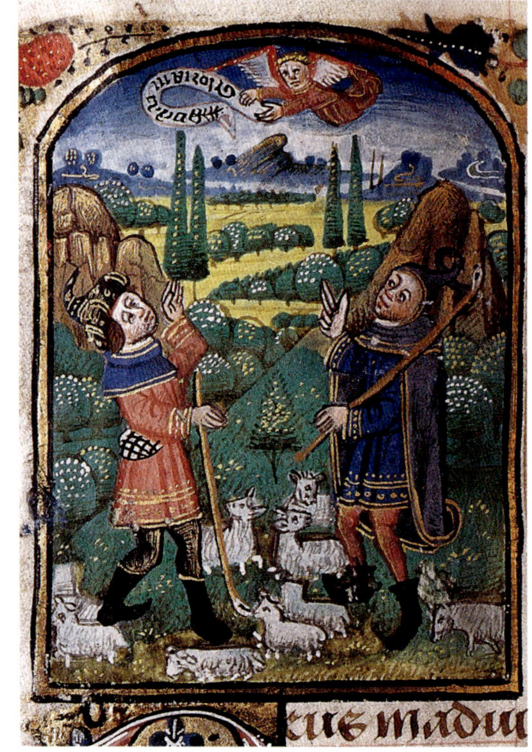

The ancient Greek sources offered various scenarios for human reproduction. Hippocrates (circa 460–370 BCE), in writings such as *The Seed* and *On the Nature of the Child*, proposed a model in which both parents released sperm that mingled to form a child. Aristotle (384–322 BCE), in the *Generation of Animals*, endorsed what was known as the "seed-and-soil" model, maintaining that the mother provided the inert matter for the fetus, and the father generated the life-form that gave it substance, shape, and spirit. Galen of Pergamos (circa 130–200 CE), writing four centuries later, attempted to reconcile Hippocrates and Aristotle with a "two-seed" model in which both father and mother contributed matter and "movement." He presented no challenge, however, to the Aristotelian theory that male children resulted from perfect embryos, and females from defective couplings.[64] The presumption that women were morally, physically, and biologically inferior to men extended from Greek and Roman times well into the second millennium.

The Dominican provincial Albertus Magnus (saint Albert the Great, circa 1200–1280), university professor and influential author of scientific as well as theological tracts, continued to advance the view that females were imperfect males. Nature intended to reproduce males, he theorized, but embryo defects or excess heat during conception led to the development of a female. Yet nature's "failure" had a purpose, he reasoned, as both male and females were required for the continuance of the species.[65] Though Galen's argument eventually prevailed in medical science, the medieval church was reluctant to relinquish Aristotle's paradigm. Far more was at stake in this chauvinistic battle than the superiority of one sex

in use through the eighteenth); the eleventh-century *Diseases of Women* by Trotula of Salerno (rumored to be by a woman though this now seems unlikely); and a fifteenth-century manual catalogued in the British Library as the *Medieval Woman's Guide to Health*.[63]

over the other: issues of conception influenced contemporary understanding of Christ's dual natures. According to Christian dogma, Jesus was born both fully human and fully divine. The Aristotelian model of reproduction, though less accurate, was more consistent with this doctrine. Mary, it could be reasoned, provided the material in her womb to form Jesus' human aspect, while God the Father was fully responsible for the contribution of his soul[66] [fig. 41].

Women's perceived lesser involvement in human reproduction was also used by reformers to disparage Mary's role in the incarnation (and by extension, within the Christian faith). Rebellious Protestants would use Albert's theory that God provided the seed and Mary "fermented" it to argue that she was no more than a passive vessel into which God placed his son, rather than an active agent in a miraculous birth. As Jean Calvin (1509–1564) wrote, "His [Christ's] divine glory must not be obscured by excessive honor paid to His mother."[67] Claiming that Mary's importance to the faith ended once she had given birth, reformers sought to diminish (if not eliminate entirely) her presence in their churches. The *Widdowes Mite,* a devotional treatise published in 1619 during the religious debates preceding the English Civil Wars (1642–1651), attacked the view that Mary was enlarged—literally and figuratively—while the Christ Child was within her womb, but once Jesus left her body, became as "useless as a saffron bagge."[68]

4. Adoration

The monastic prayer cycles reflected in the Hours of the Virgin Mary dedicated three devotional units to the adoration of Mary's newborn infant: the NATIVITY, the ANNUNCIATION TO THE SHEPHERDS [fig. 42], and the ADORATION OF THE MAGI. Artists frequently compressed these three events into a single scene, in which parents, angels, noble visitors, and humble neighbors all gathered to revere Mary's infant son [fig. 43]. Dürer's *Adoration of the Shepherds* [fig. 37] from his *Life of the Virgin* cycle combined in one image a NATIVITY scene (with Mary and Joseph in the manger), an ANNUNCIATION TO THE SHEPHERDS (depicting an angel bringing word to shepherds guarding their flocks in the background at right) and an ADORATION OF THE SHEPHERDS (who, having been alerted by the angel, join the holy family in their worship of the newborn child). Mental prayer

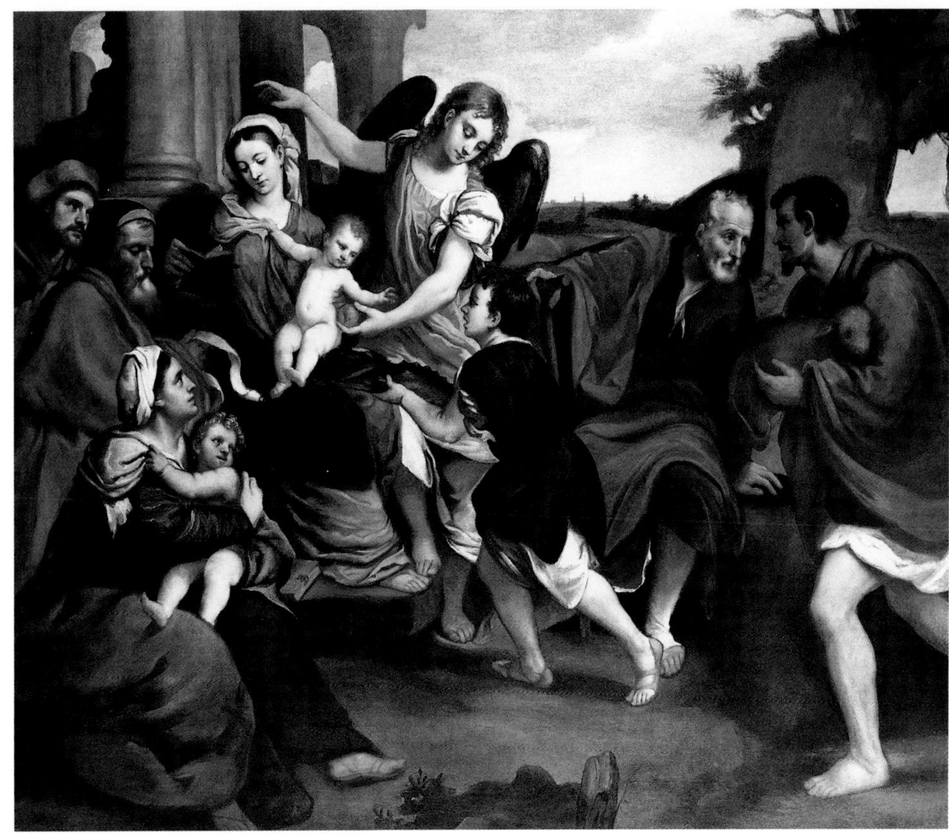

Fig. 43. Bonifazio Veronese, *Adoration of the Shepherds,* mid-16th c., oil on canvas

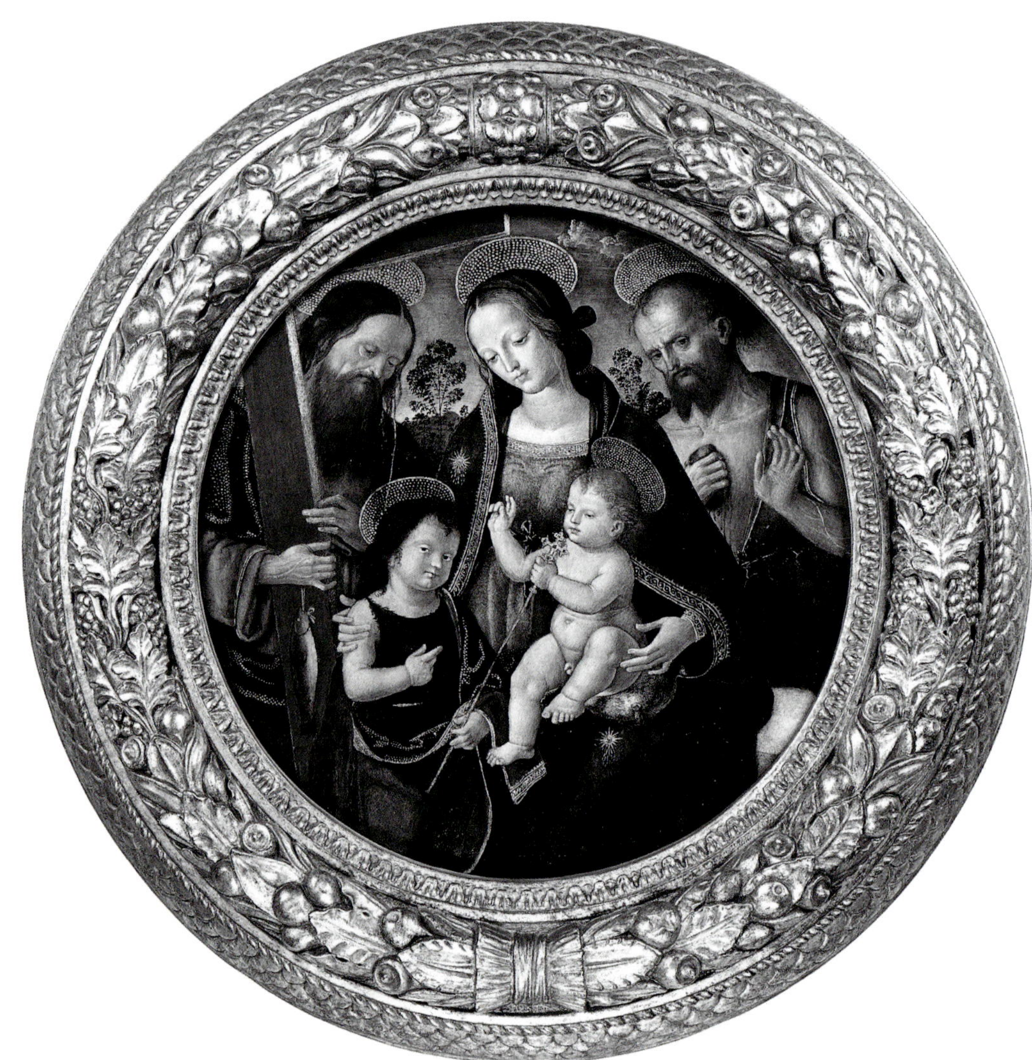

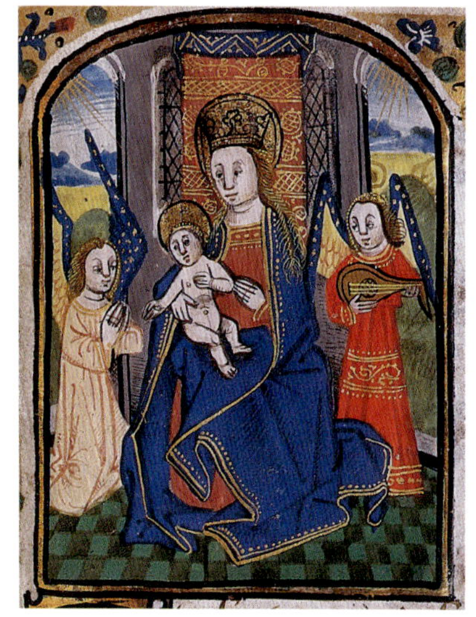

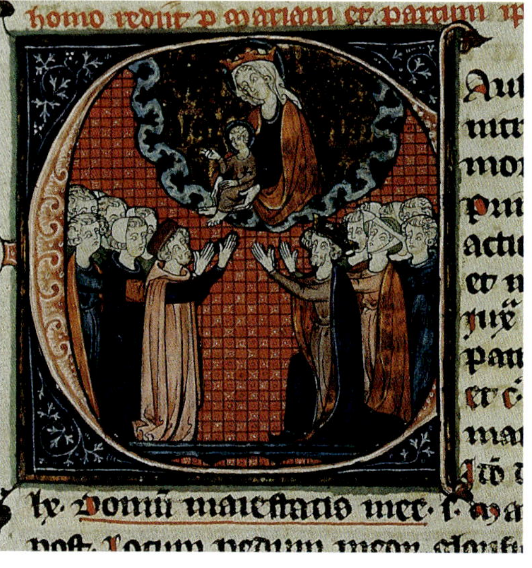

Fig. 44 (bottom left). French from Amiens, *Virgin and Child Enthroned*, half-page illumination from a ca. 1480 Book of Hours, folio 41r

Fig. 45 (above). Pintoricchio, *Madonna and Child with Saints*, 1495-1500, oil on panel

Fig. 46 (bottom right). French from Paris or Northeastern France, *Mary presents the infant Jesus to the Men and Women who Serve Her*, ca. 1290-1300, historiated initial accompanying *De laudibus* Book II, folio 36v (shown actual size)

allowed each moment to be examined separately, whereas visual art, if employed for narrative purposes, could treat the historical sequence as a single group.

ADORATION narratives thus condensed also bring together two separate Gospel accounts, Luke's tale of the shepherds, who spread news of the events beyond Bethlehem, and Matthew's account of the wise men who journey to see Mary's newborn son. These scenes of strangers gathering to look at mother and child replicated contemporary behavior: people in prayer or in passing gazing at images of the VIRGIN AND CHILD, whether in the church or on its architecture. Images abound of Mary holding out her infant for public inspection and regard; generally she is seated, and often enthroned, her lap forming its own throne on which the divine child sits[69] [fig. 44]. Often Mary appears to be not so much mothering the infant Jesus as displaying him to the faithful; in the Pintoricchio *tondo* [fig. 45], her fingers retract making sure none of the precious body is hidden from view, while in an historiated capital from a late thirteenth-century manuscript, she emerges from the clouds holding him before a large crowd [fig. 46]. This sense of display is heightened in works in which mother and child gaze not at each other but at those assembled before them, as in Robetta's engraving of the *Adoration of the Magi* [fig. 47], or directly outward, at the worshiper(s) presumably engaged in prayer before sacred images such as the twelfth-century sculpture of Our Lady of Montserrat [fig. 86].

The very concept of adoration is linked with notions of Christ's divinity.[70] Saint John of Damascus (circa 675–749), in his defense of the veneration of images against charges of idolatry (*eidolatreia* in Greek), recalled Augustine's distinction between adoration (*latreia*), reserved for God alone (as Creator, Son, or Holy Ghost), and reverence (*douleia*), shown to saintly humans. Medieval theologians, including saint Thomas Aquinas (1225–1274), would add a third category of ven-

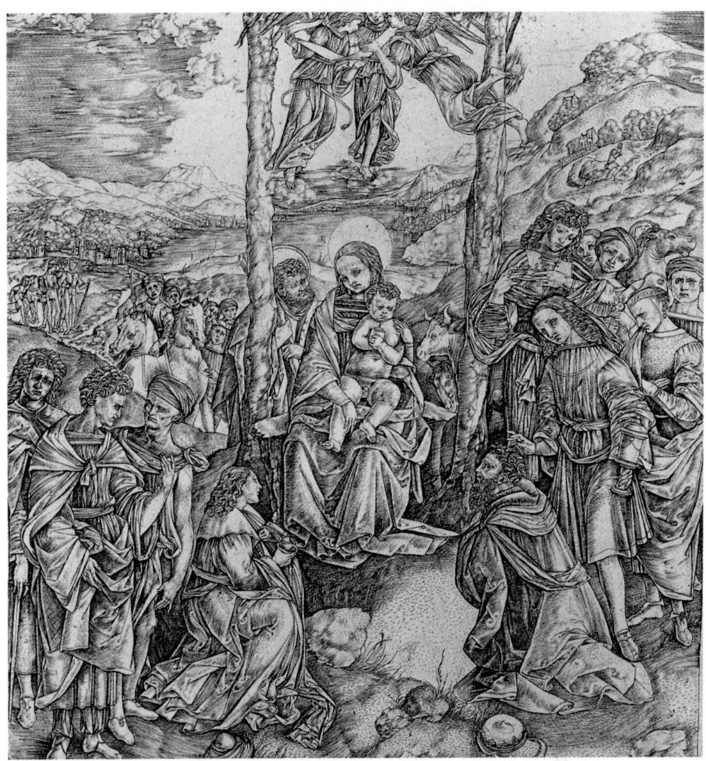

Fig. 47. Cristofano Robetta, *Adoration of the Magi*, 1496–1500, engraving

eration reserved for Mary, which they termed *hyperdouleia*;[71] this acknowledged her special status as less than divine but more than human. The presentation of an infant (rather than an adult) as an object of worship implied Jesus' divine status. At the same time, Mary's presentation of her son, through her simple act of holding him up for us to see, emphasized two elements of his human aspect: the maternal bond, and Jesus' carnality.

The popular appeal of the maternal image, with its implications of unrestricted love and benevolence, requires no explanation to modern audiences. Yet the significance of Jesus' corporeality—conveyed through any scene featuring touch—is less apparent to audiences today, as is the implicit allusion to Jesus as the word made flesh (John 1:14). To theologians of the medieval and early modern period, scenes of Mary touching the infant Jesus signified and communicated the complex doctrine known as the hypostatic union: the simultaneous divinity and humanity of Christ. Thus, any of the innumerable scenes of Mary holding her infant child, whether in maternal solicitude, loving playfulness, or solemn regard, could be applied to the teaching of this doctrine [fig. 48].

Given the natural pairing of mother and child in devotional art, worshipers had difficulty separating adoration of the divine son from admiration for his gracious mother. Popular devotion to the cult of the Virgin Mary bears out this spillover. Eventually charges would be launched that Mary was being accorded too much status and her child not enough. Radical Protestants condemned Mary's cult, accusing the church of "Mariolatry"—absolute idolatry. The more moderate leader Mar-

tin Luther (1463–1546) deplored the excesses of popular devotion, yet acknowledged Mary's holiness and approved of her veneration.[72] Seeking balance, Luther wrote:

> Mary does take it amiss that the vain characters preach and write so many things about her merits. In proportion as we ascribe merit and worthiness to her, we lower the grace of God and diminish the truth of the Magnificat. All those who heap such great praise and honor upon her head are not far from making an idol of her, as though she were concerned that men should honor her and look to her for good things, when in truth she thrusts this from her and would have us honor God in her and come through her to a confidence in his grace.[73]

Ruefully, Luther did admit that while devotions to the mother were curbed, they did not automatically transfer to the son. "Once we said so many rosaries to Mary; now we are so sleepy in prayer to Christ that we do not pray even once in a whole year," Luther wrote in 1532. "Is it not a shame to have once elevated the Mother so highly and now completely to forget the Son?"[74]

Artists' renditions of ADORATION scenes tend to embrace all levels of the social strata, emphasizing Jesus' prestige among and appeal to both the lowly and humble—represented by the shepherds—and the high and mighty—represented by the Magi. The ADORATION OF THE MAGI, in Christian theology, also marked the first acknowledgment of Jesus' special status by outsiders. The shepherds were thought to be Jews, members of Mary and Joseph's community, and the Magi Gentiles (non-Jews, or pagans). This concept was translated into visual form by clothing the Magi in exotic costumes with turbans, furs, and oriental robes. Artists found descriptions of foreign dress in the accounts of traveling merchants. The Catalan Atlas of circa 1375–1385, attributed to the Majorcan mapmaker Abraham Cresques (1325–1387),

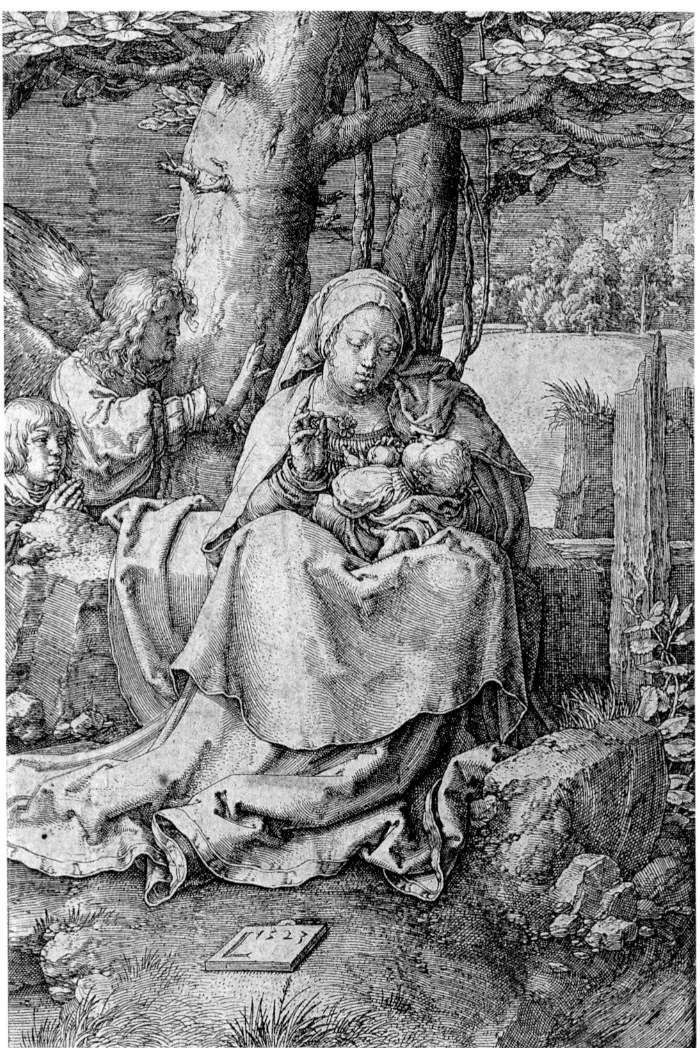

Fig. 48. Lucas van Leyden, *Virgin and Child with Two Angels*, 1523, engraving

depicted African and Asian monarchs, including Mansa Musa (ruled 1312–1337) of Mali, with whom the Catalans traded.[75]

The "wise men from the East" (Matt. 2:1) of Matthew's gospel rapidly developed consistent traditions and forms of depiction. Matthew supplied no number, but three men have been shown since antiquity. The first identification of the Magi as kings came circa 200 in the writings of the Carthaginian scholar, Tertullian (155/60–post-220), while Origen (circa 185–254), the Alexandrian theologian, was the first to refer to them as Gaspar, Balthasar, and Melchior.[76] Both traditions were widespread by the sixth century, though until the tenth century, the Magi were more commonly depicted as sages than sovereigns. From the sixth century on, age was used to distinguish the three journeyers: one young, one old, one middle-aged.[77] Beginning in the ninth century, these kings began to be depicted as members of three distinct races; Gaspar became a European, Balthasar Asian, and Melchior an African. This became a way to emphasize visually as well as metaphorically the universality of Christ's realm.[78]

*   *   *

The depiction of the Magi as rulers of three continents—Africa, Asia, and Europe—became especially frequent during the late fifteenth and sixteenth centuries, the period of the European voyages of exploration. Depictions of the Magi as non-Europeans, in ADORATION scenes in which Mary, Joseph, and others in attendance wore distinctly Western dress, reveal Christian attitudes toward outsiders. They also reflect a certain degree of anxiety, based in part on a belief that the second coming of Christ (when all will be judged—living and dead—and the faithful rewarded) could not take place until the perfect age of peace had arrived on earth, a state that could not be achieved until all humanity became Christian.[79] Universality, though more a metaphor than reflection of reality, had long been asserted as a goal of the faith. The word "catholic" comes from the Greek for *katholikos*, "according to the whole," and when spelled with a lower-case "c" means universal, or comprehensive.[80] Yet the Christian church, whether headquartered in Constantinople or Rome, was aware that it could not truly claim a universal following.

Missionary zeal within Christianity's first centuries had established Christian communities around the Mediterranean basin. During the second half of the first millennium, great strides were made in converting the pagan tribes of Europe, generally by securing the conversion of local sovereigns [fig. 99]; at the same time the original Holy Land strongholds were being lost to the new religion of Islam.[81] The twelfth century is often referred to as the apex of Marian devotion in Christian Europe, as evidenced by the sermons of Bernard of Clairvaux, the rapid rise of cathedrals, and the popularity of troubadour songs, which gave Mary her courtly title of Our Lady.[82] Yet even within this great Marian century, parts of Europe were still actively pagan. Scandinavian tribes were not fully converted until the twelfth century and various Baltic territories remained pagan through the fourteenth century.[83] (Of course, converting pantheists to a monotheistic cause proved far easier than convincing fellow monotheists—namely Jews and Muslims—to abandon one monotheistic faith for another.) Then there was the matter of soul-saving among non-Europeans.

When the Franciscan friar Giovanni da Monte Corvino, the first papal legate to China, arrived in Beijing in 1292/93, he found several Christian communities already in place, established in the seventh century by Nestorian Christians (followers of Nestorius, patriarch of Constantinople [d. circa 451].[84] Though Giovanni built a large church at Cambalec (as Beijing was then known) and baptized 6,000 Chinese, according to his diary of 1303, his greatest opposition came not from the

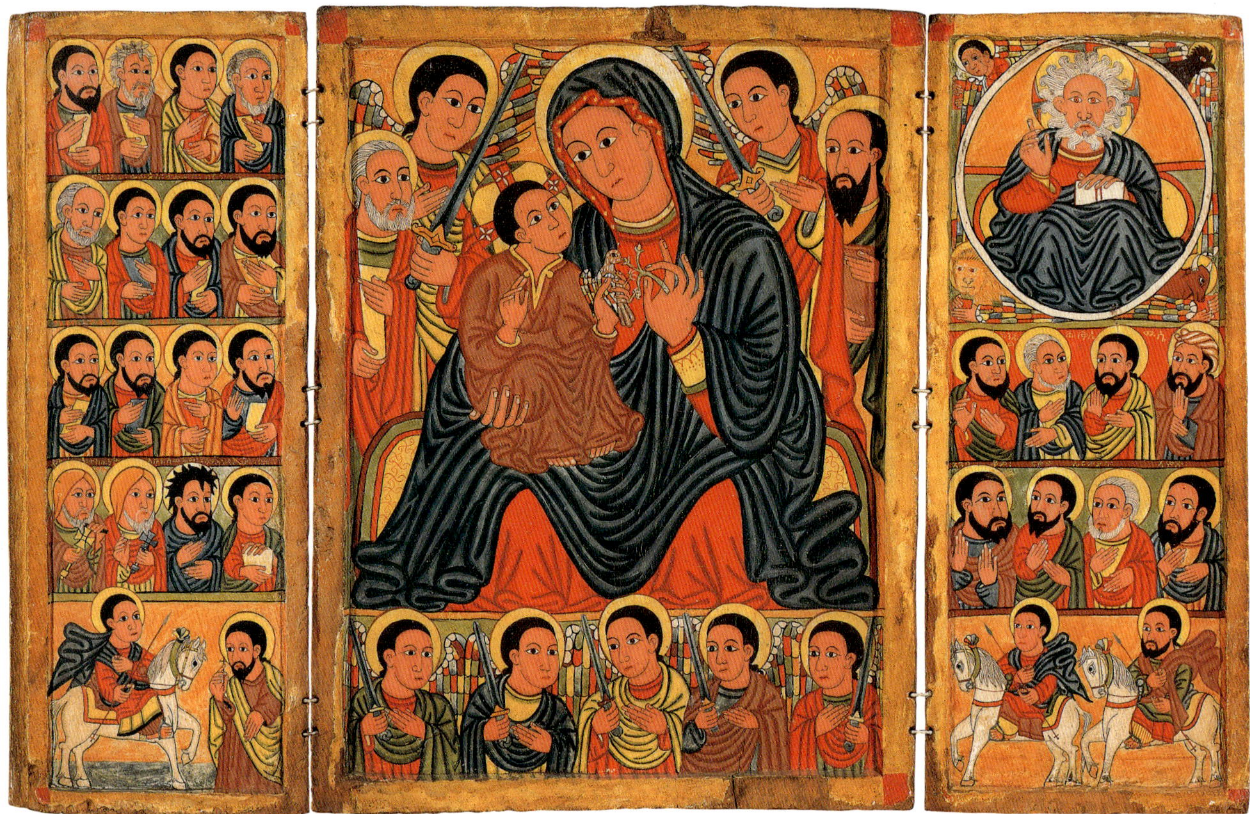

local population but from the Nestorians.[85] Chinese Christian communities disappeared with the fall of the Mongol empire in 1368, and missionary activity in Asia was suspended until the arrival of the Jesuits in the sixteenth century. The Jesuits established academies to train native painters to produce images for Asian converts. Clients of Namban studios (where Japanese artists imitating European styles) overwhelmingly requested images of the Virgin and Child, often enclosed in tabernacles decorated with traditional Japanese lacquerwork.[86]

Christians seeking to spread their faith through Africa encountered similar reversals. By the year 600 much of Roman Africa (mostly north of the Sahara) had converted from paganism to Christianity; a century later, these territories had reconverted to Islam. Not until the arrival of Portuguese traders in the 1480s would Christians again attempt to convert the natives of sub-Saharan

Africa. Two communities on the African continent did resist Islamic inroads—the Coptic Christians of Egypt, and the Ethiopian kingdom, where Christianity had been the state religion since the fourth century.[87] The Ethiopian church has a uniquely rich tradition of Marian devotion, spurred in the mid-fifteenth century by emperor Zar'a Ya'eqob's institution of 33 new feast days dedicated to Mary within the Ethiopian liturgical calendar.[88] Ethiopian devotional art [fig. 49] in manuscript and icon form reflects a merging of Coptic art and European traditions, learned from Italian painters imported by Zar'a Ya'eqob (ruled 1434–1468) and Renaissance artworks brought back by Ethiopians who attended the church's Council of Florence in 1439.[89]

Pre-Renaissance acquaintance with communities beyond Europe also included Arab populations, called Saracens by the Europeans . In the seventh century, Arab and Berber settlers had conquered most of the Iberian peninsula and crossed the Pyrenees into southern France. During the eleventh through thirteenth centuries, it was the Europeans' turn to be considered invaders, in a series of Crusades launched to gain control of Christian holy sites in Muslim hands. These quasi-religious military campaigns were concerned more with conquest than conversion. "Enter upon the road to the Holy Sepulchre," declared Pope Urban II (circa 1035–1099) as he launched the first Crusade (1095–1099) from a shrine dedicated to Mary in Clermont-Ferrand; "wrest that land from the wicked race, and subject it to yourselves."[90] Crusaders regularly marched into battle under banners painted with the Madonna and Child, and various references were made to her role as protector in battle, perhaps inspiring imagery such as a circa 1290 miniature illumination identifying Mary as the City of God and depicting her above a fortified gateway [fig. 50].[91]

Literary sources record Mary's place within crusaders' lives. The Italian knight, Ricoldo da Monte-Croce (1242/43–1320), wrote letters from his post in Jerusalem addressed to the "most blessed Virgin Mary, mother of God, queen of heaven and the world's advocate, that joy and gladness which the afflicted soul lacks."[92] In battle and in the jousts that helped to promote (and romanticize) the Crusades, Mary was frequently invoked as a military aid. A legend recorded in both *Les Miracles de Notre Dame* by Gautier de Coinci (1171–1236) and the *Dialogus miraculorum* of Caesarius of Heisterbach (ca. 1180–1240) told of Mary donning armor and assuming a knight's place while he remained in prayer to her, oblivious of the passing time.[93] Yet, it is surprising that visual representations of Mary in armor were few (or have failed to survive). Nor did the depiction of Mary as the Tower of David, with the attributes of armor, chain-mail, and the sword of strength, become more than a rare occurrence in her iconography.[94]

Despite the capture of Jerusalem in 1096–1099, the only lasting effect of the Crusades in the East was to eradicate all hope of repairing the 1054 schism between the Eastern and Western churches.[95] The Crusades also had an enduring legacy in the West of a far more chilling nature. At the onset of each Crusade, knights in arms marched across the Rhinelands, killing Jews along the way. These enthusiastic massacres of German Jewry inaugurated a millennium of violent anti-Semitism and periodic pogroms.[96] Christian antipathy toward Jews flourished in spite of (or perhaps because of) Mary and Jesus' Jewish origins. For much of the year, this could be overlooked, but on January 1st, the Feast of the Circumcision, it became painfully clear. Luke related that eight days after giving birth, Mary had Jesus circumcised according to Jewish law. Theologians interpreted this as this first occasion on which Jesus shed blood, offering proof of his humanity and foreshadowing his future death by crucifixion.[97] Yet when compelled to illustrate CIRCUMCISION scenes, artists tempered their approbation, perhaps unconsciously, with anti-Semitic overtones.

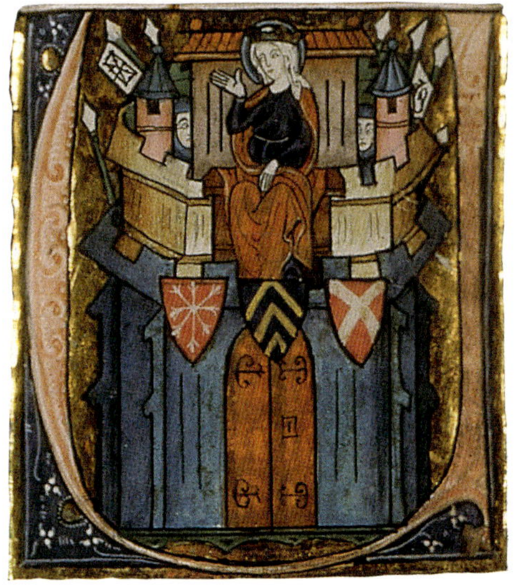

Fig. 50. French from Paris or Northeastern France, *Mary as the City of God*, ca. 1290-1300, historiated initial accompanying *De laudibus* Book XI, folio 319r (actual size)

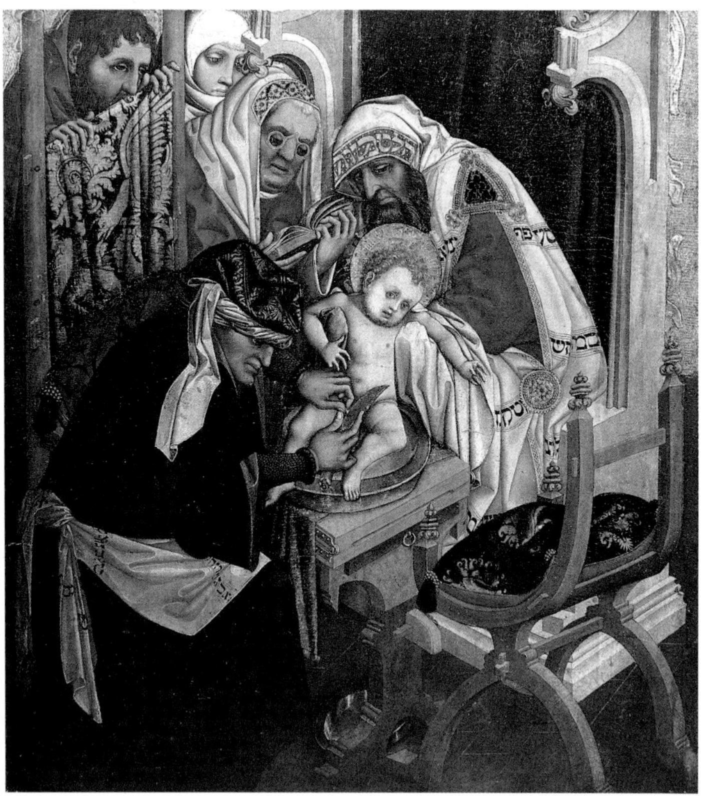

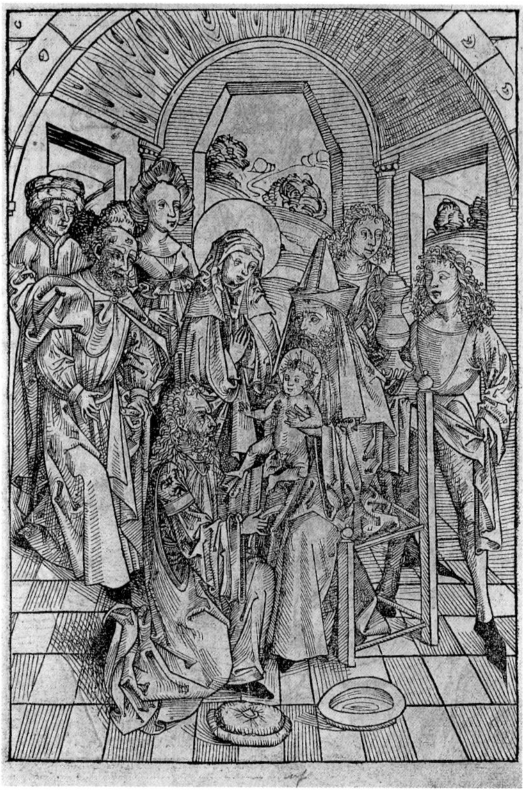

Modern viewers hardly find Michael Wohlge-mut's *Circumcision* [fig. 52] offensive, particu-larly when compared to openly hostile scenes, such as the circa 1450 panel from the *Frauenkirche* (Church of Our Lady) in Nurem-berg, where the oversized knife, child's awkward pose, and expression of the anxious parents crowded away by three menacing men turn the CIRCUMCISION into ritual torture [fig. 51]. Nev-ertheless, late fifteenth-century viewers of Wohlgemut's woodcut would have recognized emblems of Jewish identity easily overlooked today, and associated them with unfavorable portrayals of Jews in art, drama, sermons, and literature.[98] These attributes include the flat rounded hats, hooded capes, and yellow arm-bands worn by the hawk-nosed rabbi holding the infant Jesus and the *mohel* with the knife, and which German Jews were legally obliged to wear so as always to be identifiable.[99]

5. *Holy Family*

The FLIGHT INTO EGYPT, according to theologians, marked the introduction of Mary, Joseph, and Jesus as a nuclear family [figs. 53, 129]. According to Matthew's Gospel, the Roman governor Herod (73 BCE–4 BCE), angered that the wise men have not returned to tell him of the newborn's where-abouts, ordered all infants in Bethlehem to be killed. An angel, however, warned Joseph to flee to Egypt with Mary and her child; after Herod's death, Joseph is notified by an angel to return to Israel with his family, settling in Nazareth. The flight narrative proved popular artistically; Gian-Domenico Tiepolo actually managed to stretch it into 27 separate scenes in his 1754 etching series [fig. 54]. Artists generally preferred the pastoral REST ON THE FLIGHT INTO EGYPT to the actual FLIGHT, often dwelling more on landscape than figures [figs. 115, 140, 142].

The concept of the Holy Family as nuclear fam-ily was not readily embraced by the church, as it

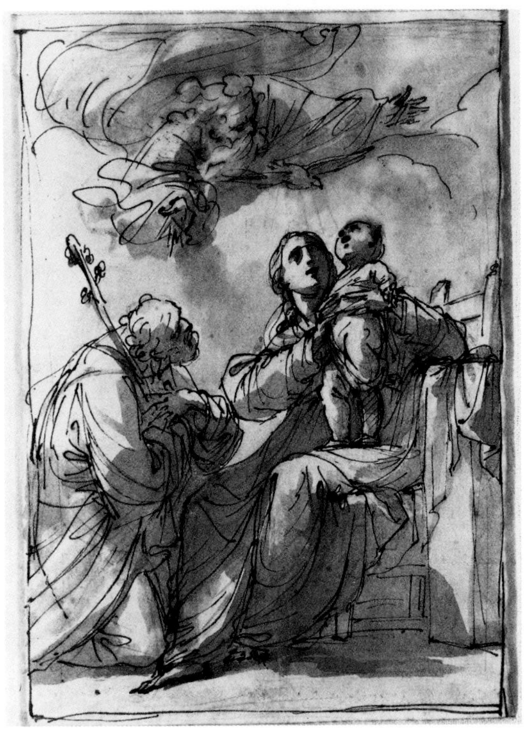

Fig. 53. Ubaldo Gandolfi, *Holy Family with God the Father*, ca. 1775, ink, and wash with black chalk

raised the issue of how to enfold Mary's married life within the cult of her perpetual virginity. Today, Catholics and most Orthodox Christians are taught that both before and after Jesus' birth, Mary and Joseph had a celibate marriage. This doctrine prevailed in pre-Reformation Christianity, obliging clergy to patly explain the numerous New Testament references to Jesus' brothers and sisters. Often congregations were told these were cousins, who by ancient custom were included within the term *brethren*.[100] Sometimes (as in the Protevangelium) they were described as half-siblings, Joseph's children from a previous marriage, but this too openly implied sexual activity on Joseph's part, so they became foster children.[101] The fourth explanation, popularly known as the KINSHIP OF CHRIST or the HOLY KINSHIP, was the most complicated and least plausible, yet had the broadest appeal, despite the fact that it con-

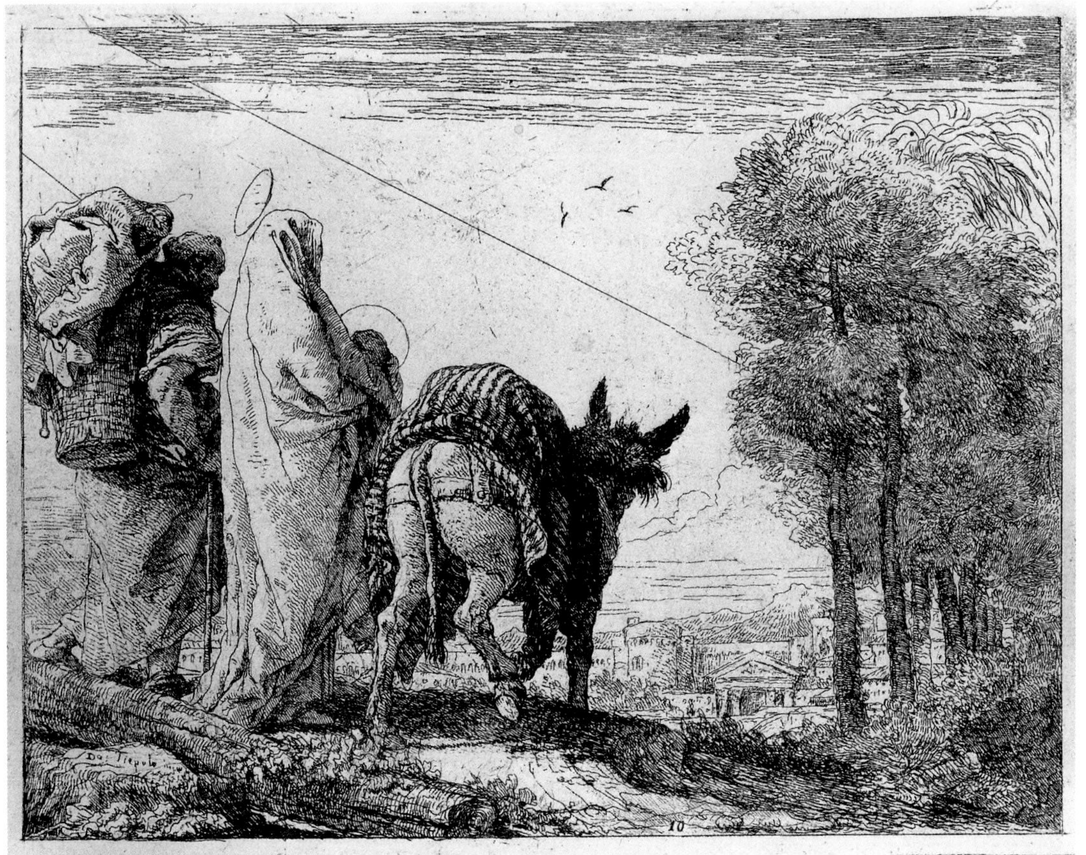

Fig. 54. Gian-Domenico Tiepolo, *Mary holding the Child in her Arms...*, 1753, etching from the *Flight into Egypt* series

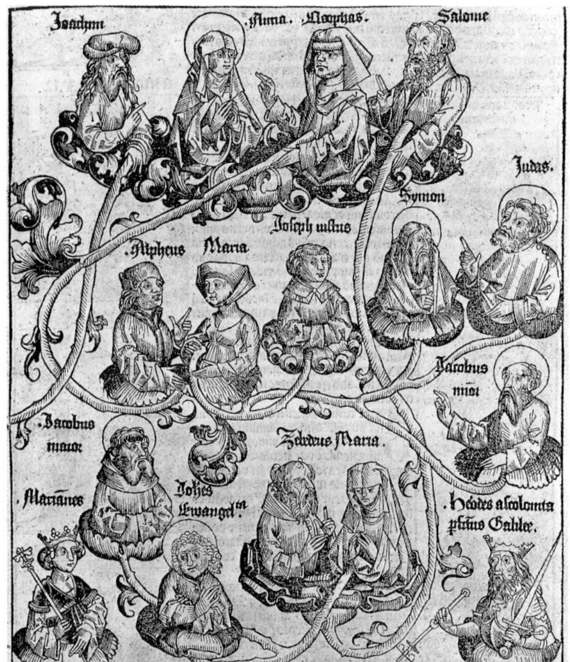

Fig. 55. Michael Wohlgemut, *Holy Kinship*, 1493, woodcut from the *Nuremberg Chronicle*, folio 95r

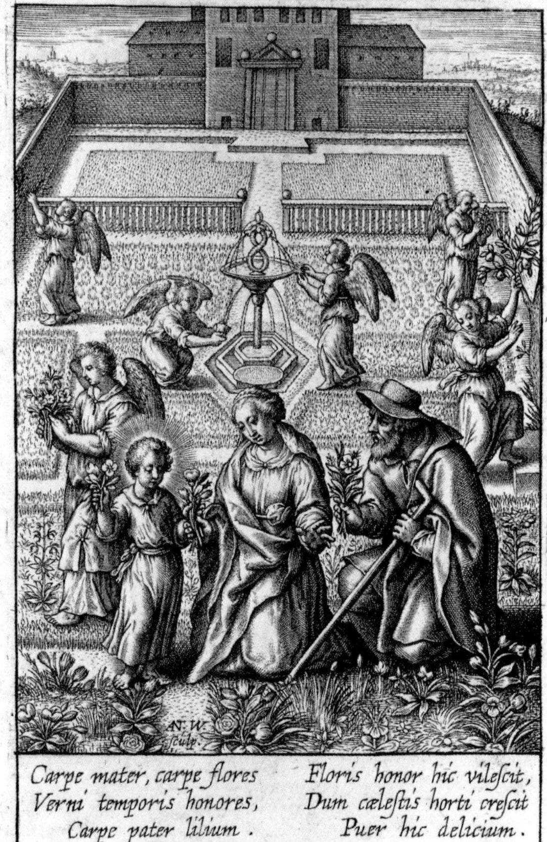

Fig. 56. Anton Wierix, *The Garden*, late 16th c., engraving from the *Life of the Virgin* series

flicted with equally popular legends of the elderly saint Anne's barrenness.

According to the legend of the HOLY KINSHIP, recounted by Jacobus de Voragine (circa 1228–1298) in his *Legenda aurea* (*Golden Legend*) of 1255–1266, and illustrated in Hartmann Schedel's (1440–1514) *Liber chronicarum* (*Nuremberg Chronicle*) of 1493, Mary's mother saint Anne had been married and widowed three times [fig. 55]. With each husband she gave birth to a daughter whom she named Mary—Mary Salome, Mary Cleophas, and the Virgin Mary. Mary, her eldest, married Joseph and gave birth to Jesus; Mary Salome, the middle daughter, married Alpheus and gave birth to James Alpheus (the lesser), Simon, Jude, and Joseph (or Joses); and Mary Cleophas, her youngest, married Zebedee, and gave birth to the apostles James (the great) and John. Hence, when the New Testament referred to a son of Mary other than Jesus, the Golden Legend explained, another of Anne's three Marys was his mother.[102] These three Marys (daughters of Anne and Joachim, Anne and Cleophas, and Anne and Salomas) were also frequently represented together at the crucifixion and at the empty tomb after the resurrection [fig. 144].

If Mary represented the ideal woman, then her marriage would have to be the ideal union. Early Christians such as saints Ambrose (339–397) and Jerome (circa 347–419/20), who privileged virginity over matrimony, urged married couples to emulate Mary and Joseph and practice voluntary celibacy. By the late middle ages, a more tolerant church advocated a model of chastity, while acknowledging the difficulty of resisting temptation.[103] In either case, Mary's marriage could be used as an example and her abstinence a paradigm to emulate. Clergy emphasized visual metaphors for Mary's virginity that expressed both purity and fecundity. Anton Wierix's small print of Mary in an enclosed garden included the symbolic elements of the garden as fruitfulness, the shut door as perpetual virginity, and the fountain as the sealed spring of eternal life—imagery drawn from the text of the Song of Solomon in the Hebrew Bible [fig. 56]. Also known as the Song of Songs, this passionate declaration of love between bride and bridegroom was interpreted from the Middle Ages on as a love song between Christ as the bridegroom and Mary as his bride (with no apparent oedipal concerns), or a metaphorical marriage of Christ and the church (again with Mary often portrayed as *Ecclesia*).[104]

The realities of secular marriage placed most of the lay population at odds with the religious example of Mary and Joseph's ideal union. The minority who did heed the priestly call to celibacy lived not as married couples but rather as nuns and monks, religious professionals whose lives were dedicated to the discovery of God through individual and group prayer. Monastic communities—born in third-century Eastern desert hermitages and codified by the sixth-century Western Rule of saint Benedict of Nursia (circa 480–547)—had become an ecclesiastical elite, eclipsing the needs of the laity until the Franciscan and Dominican orders began their program of outreach and education of the lay public in the ways of monastic prayer. (See "Devotional Uses of Religious Art to 1500," pp. 32–35.)

The popularity of these new religious orders, formed in the early thirteenth century and fully ensconced by the early fourteenth, influenced not only secular behavior but also the church's attitudes toward the spiritual needs of the laity. Whereas monastic life presumed that holiness was best obtained by removing oneself from secular life, clergy now acknowledged marriage as a viable path to holiness. Emphasizing Mary and Joseph's marriage as a model for married Christians, clergy became more focused on the needs of lay parishioners. Ordinary citizens could now better identify with a religion that reflected their lifestyle, and clergy could now meddle in the intimate affairs of family life.[105] One demonstration of this new attitude was the inclusion of marriage as one of the sacraments (along with baptism, receipt of the Eucharist, taking holy orders, etc.) [fig. 57]. Although the seven sacraments were not universally defined until the Council of Trent (1545–1563), marriage was first accorded sacramental status in the twelfth century.[106] It retains this status in the Catholic and Orthodox churches, though Protestants restored its secular status after the Reformation, at first allowing only civil marriages, then permitting church weddings but retaining municipal control over the marriage registry.[107]

Premodern marriages were social contracts between families rather than romantic unions of individuals. Families that might otherwise compete formed alliances for mutual benefit; they broadened kinship circles through married daughters and ensured a continued lineage

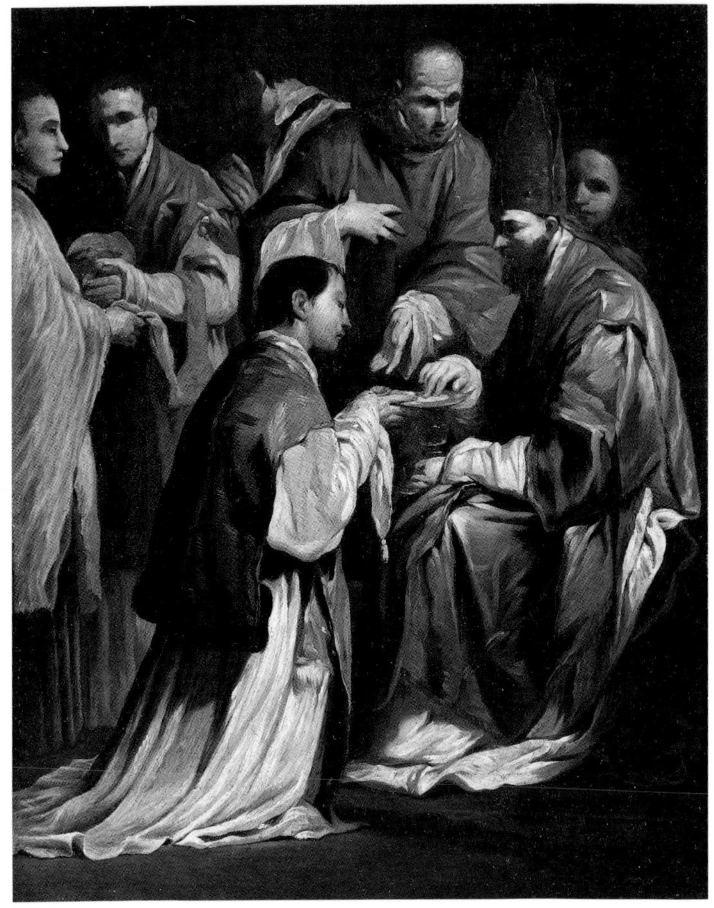

Fig. 57. Giuseppe Ma. Crespi, *Sacrament of Ordination*, pre-1712, oil on canvas

through married sons.[108] Despite the church's insistence that for a Christian marriage to be valid, both parties had to consent freely, families still chose marriage partners. Ideally, the bride's parents would heed her wishes, but the number of instances in which young women chose to enter convents rather than accept marriage partners selected by their parents leaves doubt about the options open to dissenting daughters. Saint Catherine of Siena (1347–1380), for example, underwent her conversion to radical holiness at the moment when her older sister, Bonaventura, died in childbirth, and her mother, eager to keep property within their family, proposed marrying her to the young widower. Other ploys Catherine used to compromise her chances on the marriage market included cutting off her long hair (bleached blonde by her mother), and living on nothing more than bread, water, and raw vegetables.[109]

The purpose of marriage, as understood by church and society, was to produce offspring. Saint Raymond of Peñafort (circa 1185–1275), a canon lawyer, determined that clergy "have the power to excuse [people] from sin if, respecting the fidelity of the marriage bed, spouses come together for the sake of children," noting, "conjugal union for the sake of generation is without fault."[110] Motherhood was not particularly revered, but it was considered a woman's duty and destiny. Hence, women were historically defined by reproductive status: as either mothers, potential mothers, nonmothers or, in the case of nuns, spiritual mothers.[111] The production of children—whether to work fields, perform trades, inherit wealth, or nurse aging parents—was essential to society's well-being, and it was in this realm that women's contributions were perceived.

As the church became more attentive to married life, issuing guides to a Christian union and handbooks for the raising of children, Mary underwent a similar domestication. The regal, dignified, yet distant Madonnas of early Gothic art evolved into tender, nurturing figures. Popular plays of virgin martyrs calling upon Mary to protect them from harm gave way to dramas of noble wives calling upon Mary to protect them from sin.[112] Though as the mother of only one child, Mary was hardly a fertility figure, she was a model mother and thus a model of motherhood. Women in particular could draw upon their experiences of pregnancy, birth, and nurturing to deepen their spiritual empathy with Mary's joys and sorrows, and suggest an intimate bond between their experiences and those of the Holy Family.[113] Images of the Virgin Mary as a gentle, caring young mother gave comfort and a sense of purpose to women who were fulfilling their Christian and civic duty through motherhood [fig. 58].

In an age when pregnancy and childbirth were closely associated with death and distress, Mary provided comfort to women about to give birth, as this French prayer of 1655 reveals:

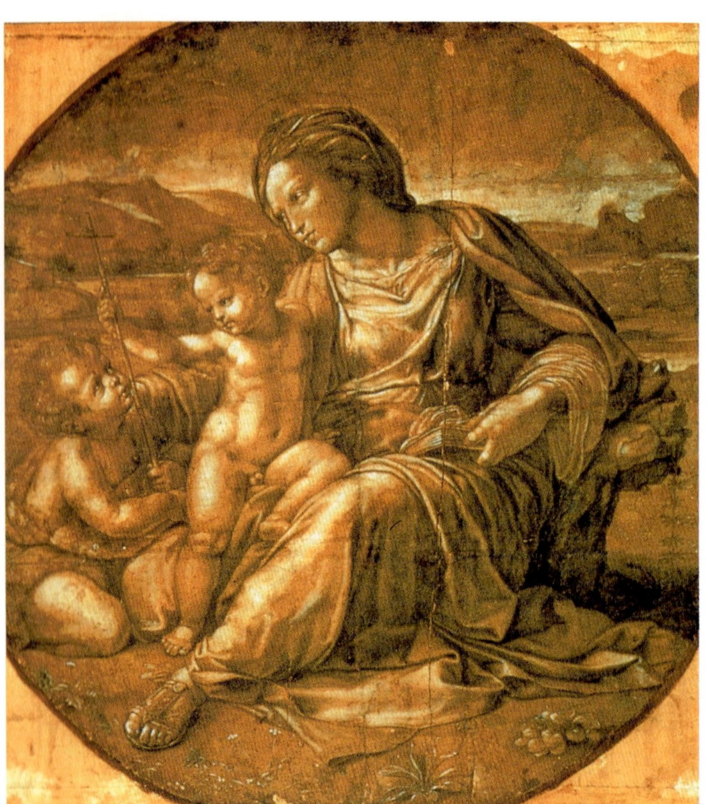

Fig. 58. Italian, *Alba Madonna* cartoon (after Raphael), 16th/17th c., ink, graphite, and white chalk

Oh Mother of the holiest one of
holies who approached nearest to his
divine perfection and so became
mother to such a son, obtain for me
by your Grace . . . the favour to let me
suffer with patience the pain which
overwhelms me and let me be delivered from this ill. Have compassion
upon me. I cannot hold out without
your help.[114]

Mary was not the only one to aid the
imminent birth. Female relatives, friends,
and neighbors also gathered in the birth-
chamber to provide solace, as illustrated
in Dürer's *Birth of the Virgin Mary* [fig. 59].
Dürer's scene of 1503–04, set in a contemporary chamber, gives us a glimpse of
sixteenth-century domestic life and
allowed Renaissance women to see their
lives reflected in those of Mary and saint
Anne, to whom many women addressed
prayers for a successful birth. Saint Margaret of Antioch (supposedly third or
fourth century) was the most popular
patron of childbirth in Renaissance Italy,
owing to her legendary escape intact from
the belly of a dragon.[115] One edition of
her legend advised women in labor to
place the text on their stomachs, a fitting
companion to the Marian girdles
(inscribed with prayers to Mary for a safe
delivery) worn around their bodies.[116]

Lavinia Fontana (1552–1614) depicted Mary,
Joseph, and Saint Margaret in her *Holy Family*
painting of 1574 [fig. 134], along with saint Francis of Assisi (1181–1226), who originated the
Christmas *crèche* (or crib). In a manner far subtler
than Dürer's woodcut, Fontana's painting has secular childbirth as an underlying theme. A successful artist who received major commissions from
influential people such as pope Gregory XIII
(1502–85), Fontana was the mother of eleven

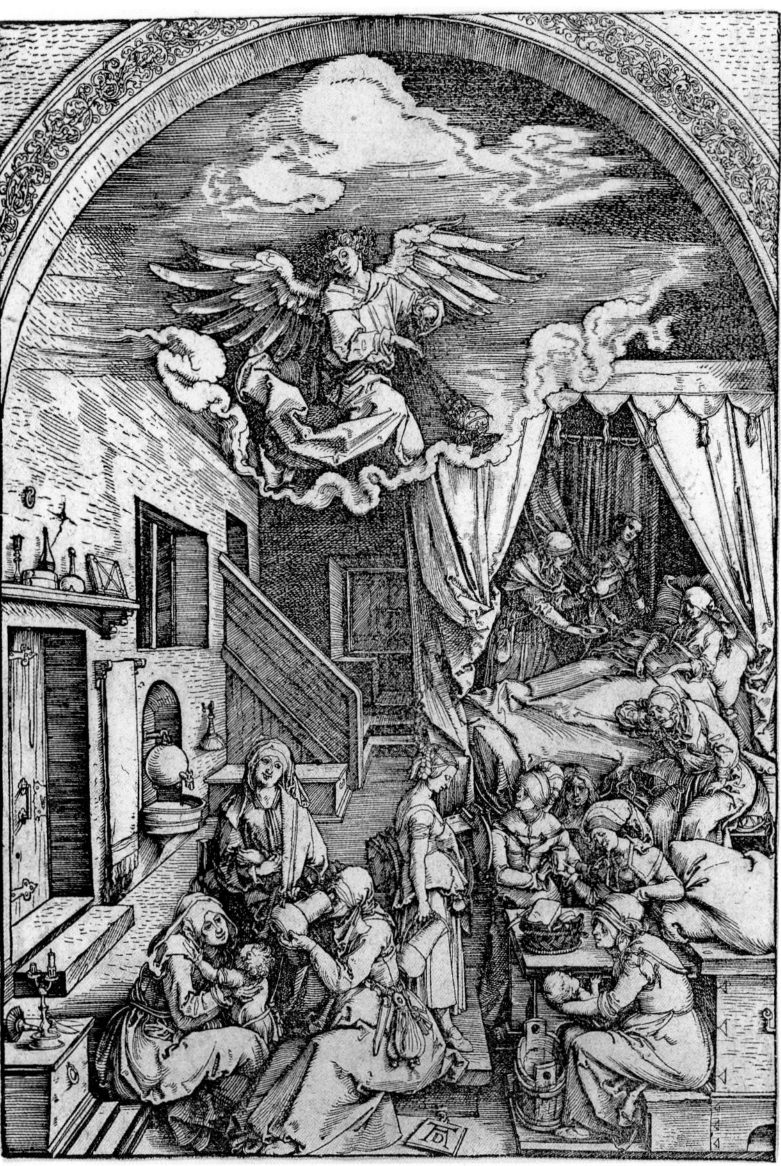

Fig. 59. Albrecht
Dürer, *Birth of the
Virgin*, ca. 1503-04,
woodcut from the
Life of the Virgin
series

children. This early work, however, was painted
shortly after the death of her first-born child, a
daughter who lived only a few days. In addition,
the infant Jesus' crib is a Roman sarcophagus,
alluding to mortal and divine realms, to Jesus'
fate, and perhaps to Fontana's recent bereave-
ment as well.[117]

One can easily imagine pregnant women draw-
ing comfort from this *Holy Family* with its sweet
Margaret and Mary, and envision the conflict
Protestant women felt when asked to turn away

from traditional saints and seek comfort instead from a remote masculine God. Luther instructed his followers:

This is also how to comfort and encourage a woman in the pangs of childbirth, not by repeating St. Margaret legends and other silly old wives' tales but by speaking thus, "Dear Grete, remember that you are a woman, and that this work of God in you is pleasing to him. Trust joyfully in his will and let him have his way with you. Work with all your might to bring forth the child. Should it

mean your death, then depart happily, for you will die in a noble deed and in subservience to God."[118]

No doubt the midwives and attendants in the birth chamber helped mothers in childbirth keep their minds off unacceptable saints and discouraging words as well.

The cult of the Holy Family brought another male role model to the fore of Christian art and thought.[119] Prior to the fifteenth century, Joseph of Nazareth had been very much a background figure, with theological emphasis placed on Jesus' having no earthly father. Artists would portray Joseph as an elderly man, often asleep, to imply a diminished potency and no possible threat to Mary's miraculous conception. In medieval dramas he had been a clownish figure, an occasion for sexual jokes, as bystanders would hint that if Mary were pregnant, Joseph had either broken his own vow of chastity or been cuckolded.[120] Now this status was revised, and Joseph converted into a responsible husband and father (tending to the stable animals in Coebergher's drawing) and a vigorous worker (earning a living and supporting his family in Dürer's woodcut) [figs. 60, 61]. Jean Gerson (1363–1429), chancellor of the University of Paris, was a great advocate of Joseph's cause, proposing at the Council of Constance (1414–1418) that a feast day be established in his honor.[121] Marriage to an impotent old man, he reasoned, detracted from Mary's virginity, as she would not be tempted, whereas marriage to a virile husband glorified Mary's choice to remain a virgin.[122]

Along with Joseph's rehabilitation and Mary's shift from Virgin Queen to Ideal Mother, children also gained in status. Around the year 1400 children began to be shown new affection, in both art and in life. As Jacques Le Goff put it, parents loved their offspring, but valued the adults they were to become.[123] As children's status was revised, youth became appreciated on its

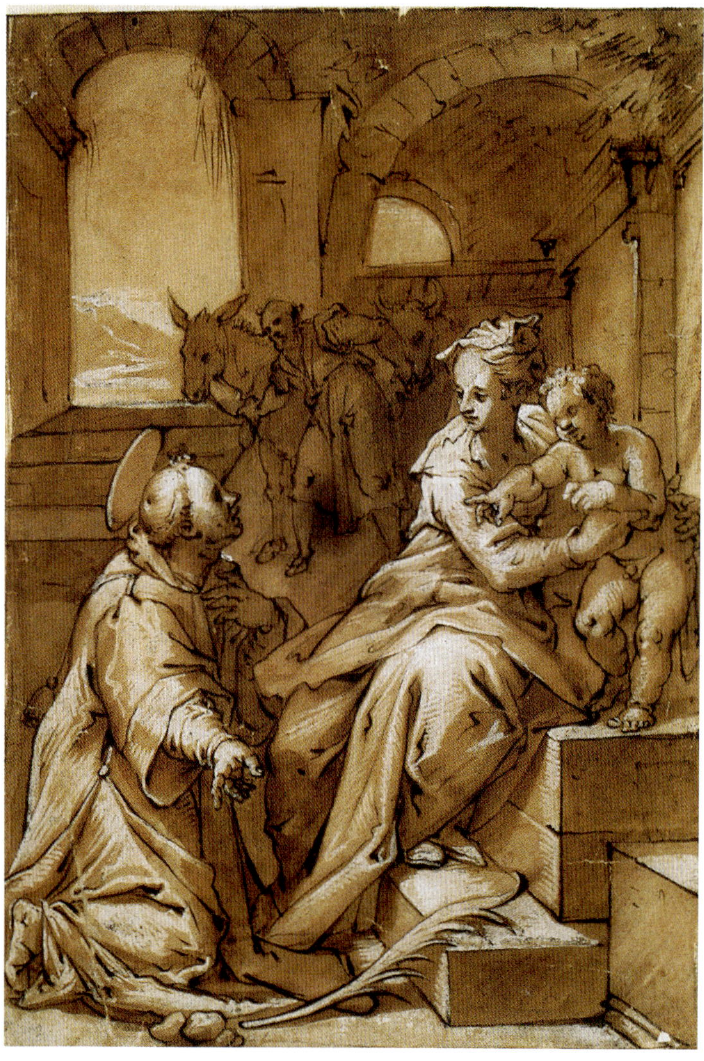

Fig. 60. Wenzel Coebergher, *Virgin and Child with St. Stephen*, ca. 1600, ink and wash with white highlights

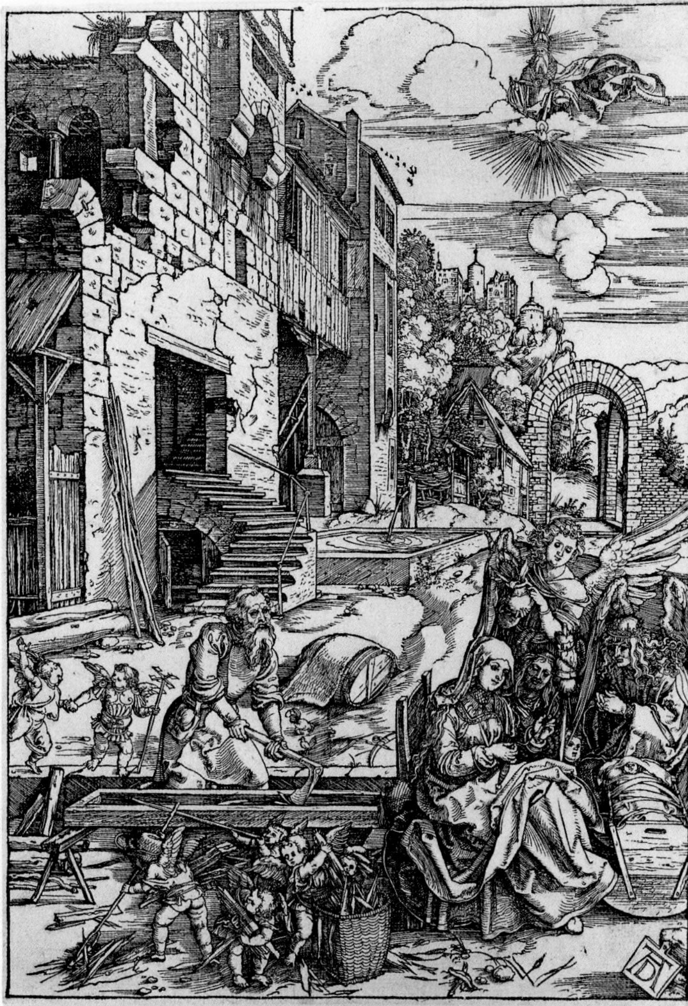

whole, seeking to recover from the devastating effects of plague.

The wealthy celebrated successful births with great feasting, the poor with great relief. The city of Florence, which lost three-quarters of its citizens between 1330 and 1430, enacted sumptuary laws restricting the amount that could be spent on birth and baptism feasts, fearing citizens were bankrupting themselves in an orgy of celebration. The Florentine *signoria* (or municipal council) declared in 1433 that "women were made to replenish this free city and to observe chastity in marriage; they were not made to spend money on silver, gold, clothing, and gems. For did not God Himself, the master of nature, say this: 'Increase and multiply and replenish the earth and conquer it.' "[126] In response to the same demographic pressures, theologians now placed greater emphasis on Christ's humanity than on his divinity, which in turn elevated Mary's prominence as instrument of the divine incarnation. Artists, influenced by the same forces affecting popular and ecclesiastical culture, also developed greater interest in human life and natural occurrences.

own merits. Adorable *putti* (the souls of dead children) sprouted in Renaissance art [fig. 61]; tender scenes of an infant Jesus far surpassed images of an adult Christ; and domestic wares featuring children and childbirth became a feature of Italian homes.[124] This change arose partly in response to the plague of 1348–1351 that killed more than a third of Europe's population and returned a dozen times over the next two centuries.[125] A sobering austerity initially followed this purge, during which both art and society grew increasingly mystic and introspective. This was followed by a sense of recovery and rebirth; young life had great value now, both to individual families and to the community as a

The shift in attitude is quite visible when comparing traditional work to Giorgio Vasari's (1511–1574) *Holy Family* of 1544 [fig. 62]. Mary's traditional heavy gown and mantle have been exchanged for contemporary fashions and her traditional colors of blue (for heaven and spiritual love) and red (for passion and true love) have morphed into teal and rose.[127] Though to our

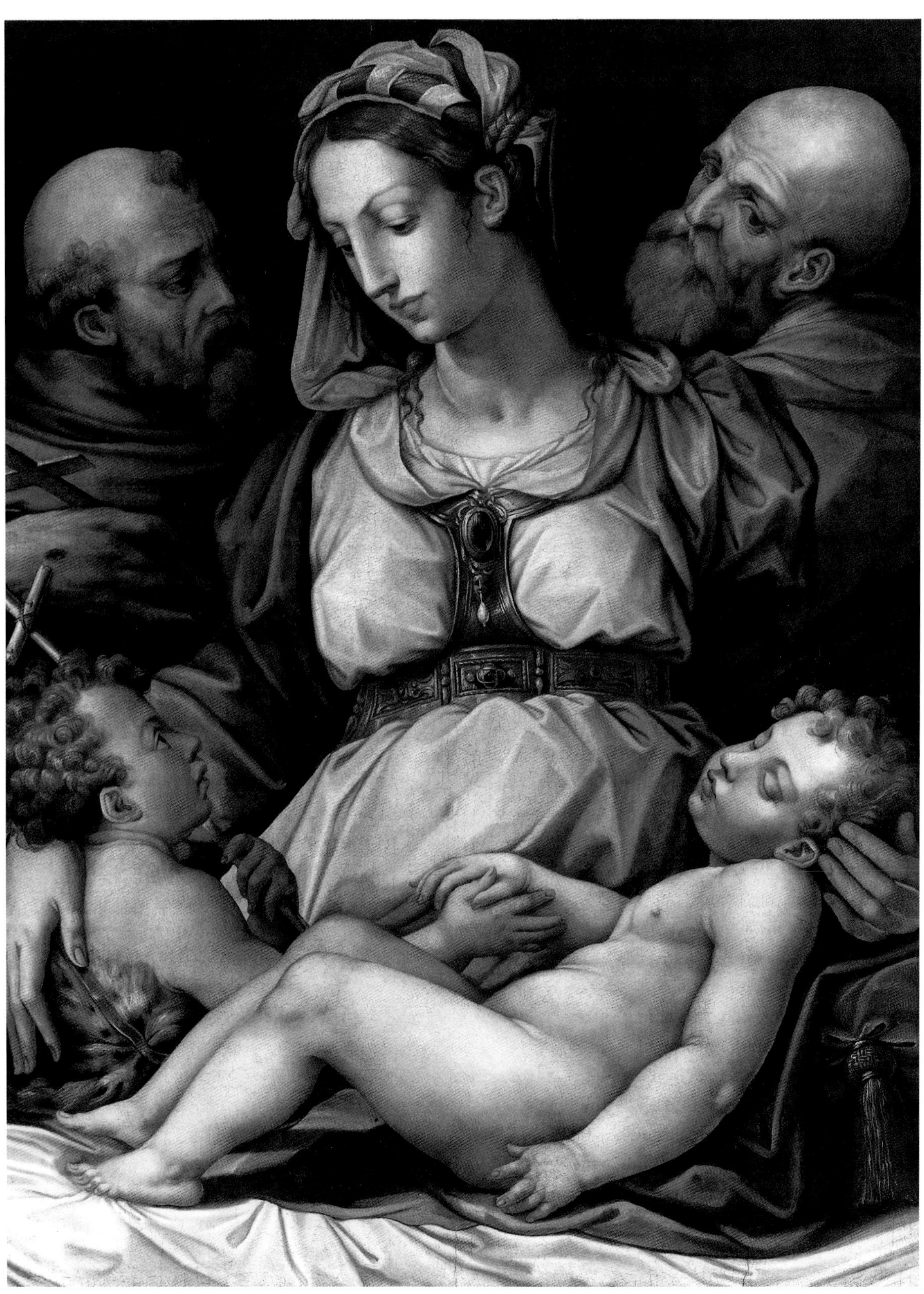

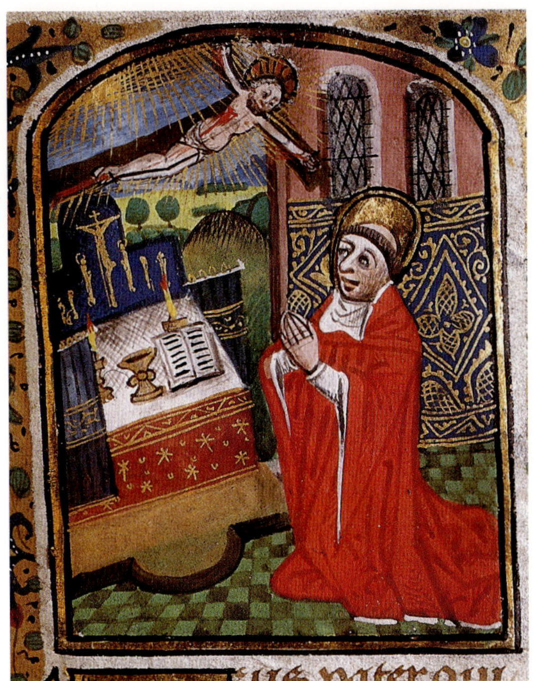

eyes this may look like a secular portrait dressed in the guise of religious art, Vasari's Madonna alludes to sophisticated elements of faith. To early viewers, the sleeping child laid on a table could have suggested not only Jesus laid in the tomb but also laid upon the altar, an indirect but not uncommon reference to the moment during mass when Christ's body is said to appear on the altar in the form of the eucharistic wafer (known as transubstantiation) [fig. 63]. This places Mary in the position occupied by the priest, making her the agent of transubstantiation (a provocative idea, given that dressed as a secular woman of the mid-sixteenth century she metaphorically enacts a role reserved for an all-male clergy).[128] For audiences schooled in the language of devotional art, Vasari's *Holy Family* celebrated Jesus' birth, foreshadowed his adult life and death, and reflected forms of worship acted out daily in churches consecrated to his teachings, all in the naturalistic style favored by Renaissance artists, and with a delicate tinge of daring as well.

RELIGIOUS USES OF DEVOTIONAL ART FROM 1500

The Reformation acted as a wake-up call for a negligent church whose bureaucracy had failed to root out corrupt officials, and many of whose clergy conducted themselves in a manner inconsistent with church teachings. In circa 1500 Nuremberg (which was to was to embrace the Protestant cause in 1520), religious observances and feasts occupied fully one-third of the annual calendar, and priests dictated secular as well as spiritual policy, often levying taxes from which they were exempted. Clergy and religious made up 6 to 10 percent of the total population, and some flaunted mistresses and illegitimate children, gladly paying penitential fines while continuing sinful practices. By 1550, most of Nuremberg's monasteries and nunneries had been shut down, the number of clergy and their powers greatly reduced; also the number of religious holidays on which a business had to close had shrunk to twenty days annually.[1]

Protestants adapted medieval churches designed for daily pre-Reformation services to the needs of new forms of worship focused on Sunday services. Much was removed—devotional images, ornamentation, rood-screens, and permanent altars—but additions were made as well, in the way of moveable table-altars, central pulpits, and the introduction of pews, to provide comfort to congregations expected to listen attentively to lengthy sermons explicating Bible passages. Through selection and distribution of furnishings, Protestant churches embodied the new religion's greater appreciation of the word over the sacraments.[2] In Emanuel de Witte's 1660s painting of a Protestant church interior, the pulpit lies directly under the domed crossing, and the baptismal font and crucifix abut the public spaces, while the altar-painting of a *Crucifixion* is hidden at the rear [fig. 64].

The church hierarchy in Rome initiated its own series of reforms as counterparts to those under-

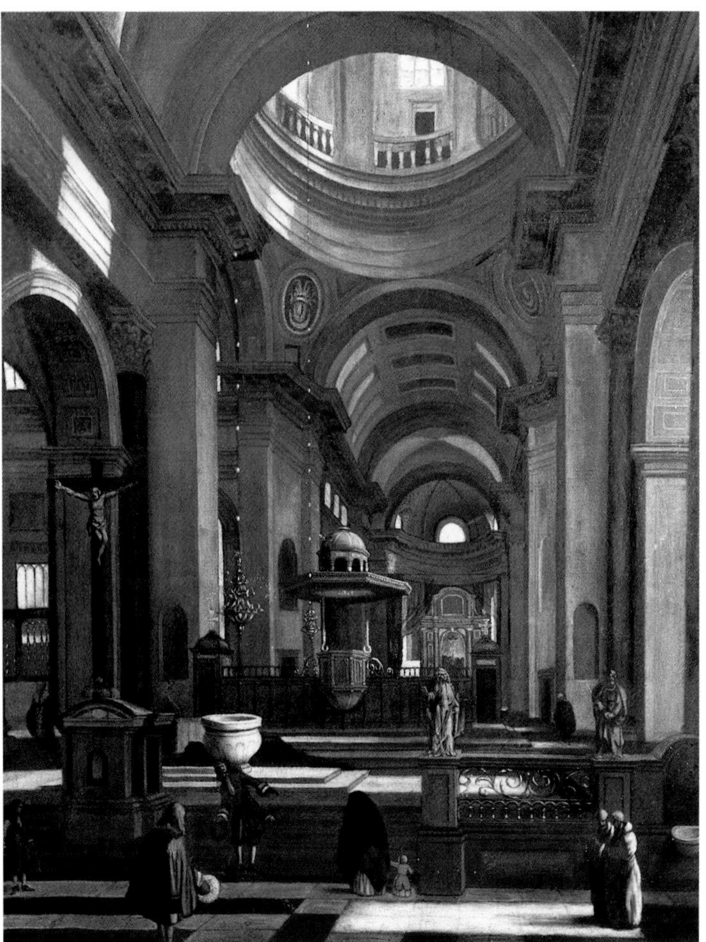

Fig. 64. Emanuel de Witte, *Interior of a Renaissance Church*, 1660s, oil on canvas

taken by Protestants; this was known as the Counter-Reformation movement or the Catholic Reform. In terms of visual art, church officials took steps to ensure that works produced for devotional use accurately reflected official church teachings and interpretations. Pope Pius IV (1499–1565) called on all bishops to profess, "I firmly assert that the images of Christ and of the ever Virgin Mother of God, as also those of other Saints, are to be kept and retained, and that due honour and veneration is to be accorded them."[3] The Council of Trent (1545–1563), convened to solidify the Catholic church in the wake of Protestant dissent, further decreed that "the Holy Council forbids any image to be exhibited in churches which represents false doctrines and might be the occasion of grave error to the uneducated."[4]

The prohibition of false doctrine was not very meaningful (after all, it had never been officially favored), but the definition of what constituted true doctrine was another matter, and did influence artistic production. During the Counter-Reformation period, church leaders strongly disapproved of art drawn from postbiblical sources, which included cycles of the life of the Virgin prior to the ANNUNCIATION, featuring stories of her parents, Anne and Joachim. Similarly, saints' lives embroidered with elements of legend or outright fiction—a staple of medieval art—no longer met with theological approval. In some localities, the Inquisition (founded in the twelfth century to combat heresy and revived in Italy and Spain after the Reformation) established overseers to vet the fidelity of sacred imagery to approved sources. Velásquez's teacher and father-in-law, Francisco Pacheco (1564–1654), was appointed to Seville's overseer post in 1618.[5]

Though the Catholic church disapproved of certain artistic subjects, they staunchly supported the use of the visual arts to express elements of faith. Many scholars equate Counter-Reformation art with the Baroque style that emerged in the seventeenth century. Baroque art was as popular in Protestant territories as Catholic, however, and evoked a sense of worldly splendor as much as piety [fig. 65]. Counter-Reformation art, while often executed in the Baroque style, was the visual counterpoint of a movement of dynamic renewal within the Catholic church. Art was construed in genuinely idealistic terms, intended not only to consolidate Catholic territories and form a visual vocabulary for the new theology, but also to serve the higher moral purpose of leading people to God.[6] Post-Reformation faith also found music a powerful medium for spiritual enlightenment, as Claire Fontijn-Harris discusses on pages 139–41.

Mary's vital presence in Counter-Reformation art helped to counter anti-Marian Protestant propaganda. Much of the debate among Catholics and Protestants revolved around Mary's stature in the

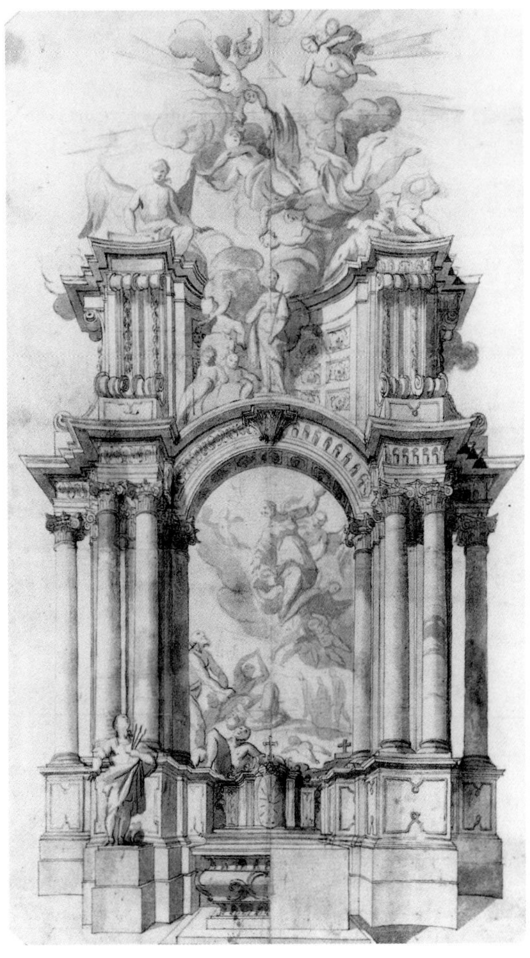

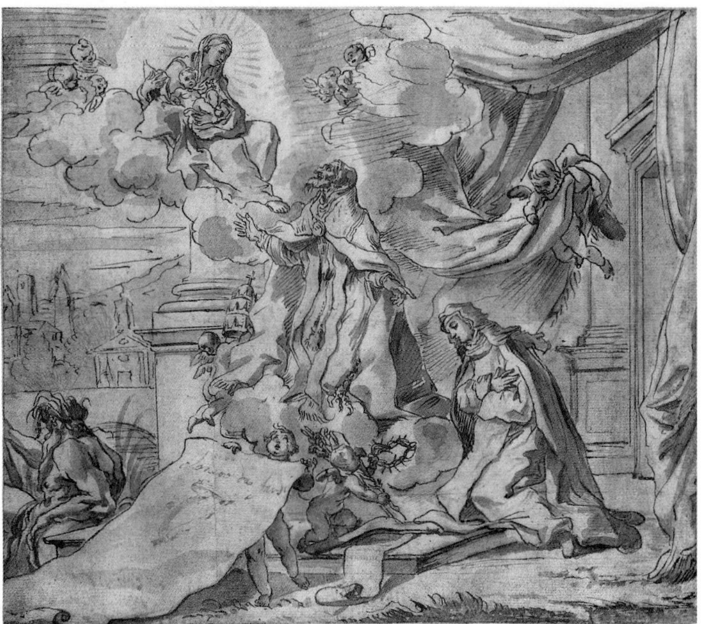

semihistorical saints, such as Barbara, Margaret, and George—martyrs of remote times and places whose *acta* (lives) could not be proven and whose achievements (while admirable) could not be imitated.[7] Hence, saint Catherine of Alexandria (a supposed fourth-century virgin martyr whose cult was unknown before the ninth century) was joined by the historically secure saints Catherine of Siena (1347–1380), Catherine of Bologna (1413–1463), and Catherine dei Ricci (1522–1590). In honor of the latter's canonization in 1746, the Dominican order commissioned Pierre Subleyras to execute an artwork of this nun celebrated not as a martyr but as a mystic [fig. 66].[8] Even the cult of saint Francis of Assisi (1181–1226), a popular medieval and Renaissance saint endorsed by Counter-Reformation authorities, took on new iconographical forms suited to the theology of the renewed church. The Capuchin monks of Bologna commissioned images promoting the ecstatic and mystical side of Franciscan spirituality. Pietro Faccini complied with his circa 1590 painting, *St. Francis Adoring the Christ Child* [fig. 136], a subject not found in earlier biographies or images of the saint, but one

Fig. 65 (left). Johann Franz van Helmont, *Study for an Altarpiece of the Assumption*, mid-18th c., ink, wash, and watercolor with incising

Fig. 66 (above). Pierre Hubert Subleyras, *Pope Benedict XIV Presents St. Catherine dei Ricci to the Virgin*, 1745, ink, wash, and graphite with incising

church and whether honor and reverence shown to the mother detracted from that due to her son. On the artistic battlefront, papal forces defended Mary's place within Christian art, giving prominence to her visual presence in Catholic territories to counter her diminished status in the Protestant north. New artistic themes filled the void of religious iconography created by the redefinition of Christianity being carried out across western and central Europe. Emphasis on Bible reading created a demand for Old Testament scenes among Protestants, whereas Catholics commissioned art depicting beliefs rejected by Protestants, such as Mary's ASSUMPTION INTO HEAVEN and IMMACULATE CONCEPTION.

Cults of recently deceased and newly canonized saints were promoted to expand the circle beyond

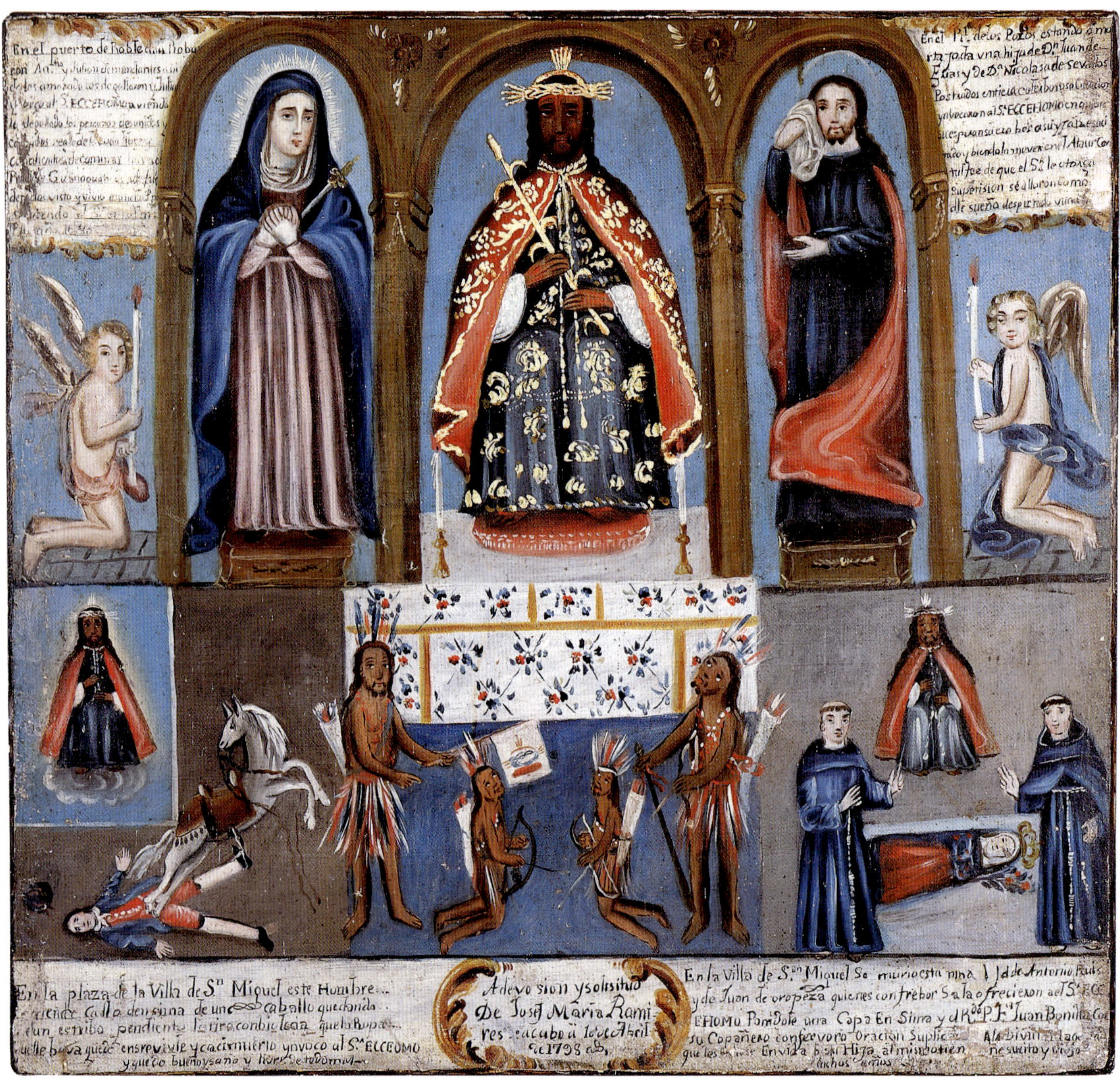

Fig. 67. Mexican from Guanajuato, *Ex-Voto commissioned by José María Ramírez*, 1798, oil on canvas

well-suited to the spiritual mysticism popular in post-Reformation Italy.[9]

Simultaneously, new markets for post-Reformation art were being created in the Spanish and Portuguese New World colonies, whose military conquerors were accompanied by religious missionaries who placed a high priority on converting rather than eliminating the native population. Just as sixth-century missionaries had appropriated pagan sanctuaries, so did colonizing Christians graft European religious practices onto native American traditions. Europe had a long tradition of wonder-working Marian shrines, many of which were associated with black Madonnas; these include shrines in Austria, Belgium, England, France, Italy, Poland, Spain, and Switzerland.[10] Yet when they tried to import this tradition to the American colonies, Europeans found that natives associated the miraculous powers of blackness with male deities. Hence, in Latin America, one finds a

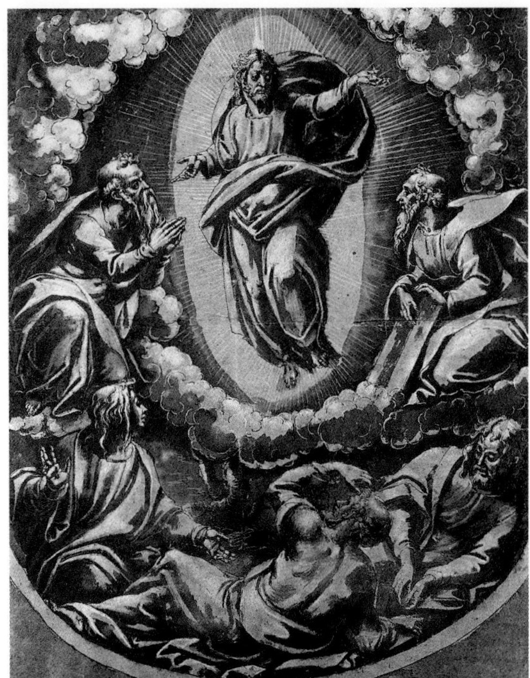

comparable tradition of wonder-working black Christs [fig. 67]. The Mexican patroness Our Lady of Guadalupe, known affectionately as *La Morenita* ("little brown one"), is actually a paler version of the original black figure worshipped at the shrine of Our Lady of Guadalupe in Guadalupe, Spain. To win over the indigenous population, a black Madonna was lightened rather than a Caucasian Madonna darkened.[11]

This rare early votive painting from the state of Guanajuato in Mexico commemorates four miracles attributed to a black Christ shown on an altar between statues of Mary and saint John (or Joseph) [fig. 67]. Images and text recount how this miraculous figure revived two dead girls (upper and lower right), and saved men from robbers (upper left) and a bad fall. Significantly, when this painting was made, indigenous Mexicans wore Western clothes, not traditional costumes; nor had Guanajuato natives ever worn feathered garments and headdresses of the type shown, which are more representative of Plains tribes such as the Comanche and Apache. Their presence here can be interpreted as a late eighteenth-century short-

hand for "indigenous Indian" rather than an appropriate illustration of the same.

This reference to an indigenous past is an allusion to Mexico's pre-Colonial identity and a means of asserting national identity in a country still ruled by Europeans. Nevertheless, a Colonial hierarchy remains: the bounties of the Christian God, while displayed to Amerindians, are bestowed on Caucasians. The Mexican struggle for independence would break out only twelve years later, when Father Miguel Hidalgo y Costilla (1753–1811) and his followers marched on Guanajuato city under the banner of the Virgin of Guadalupe. Though designed in thanksgiving to Jesus and his mother Mary, this ex-voto reflects premonitions of political disorder, and the subtle anxieties of the *criollo* populations—Mexican-born descendents of European settlers—regarding their place in a society ordered by race, class, and birthplace.

DEVOTIONAL USES
OF RELIGIOUS ART FROM 1500

The *Devotio moderna* movement (discussed on pp. 33–34) has been interpreted as a predecessor of Protestantism within the still-unified Western church. With its emphasis on individual experience with God, and deemphasis of clergy and church ritual, this fourteenth-century spiritual movement shared many common principles with the sixteenth-century reform movements introduced by Martin Luther and his colleagues. On the matter of art, however, the two movements diverged; fourteenth-century mystics approved of and relied on devotional images (and readings) to stimulate interior prayer, while sixteenth-century reformers dispensed with the visual arts (often violently), anchoring their worship in bibliocentric prayer. This attitude has often been linked to the rise in production of secular subject matter in northern European art; namely portraiture, landscape, still life, mythological, and genre scenes

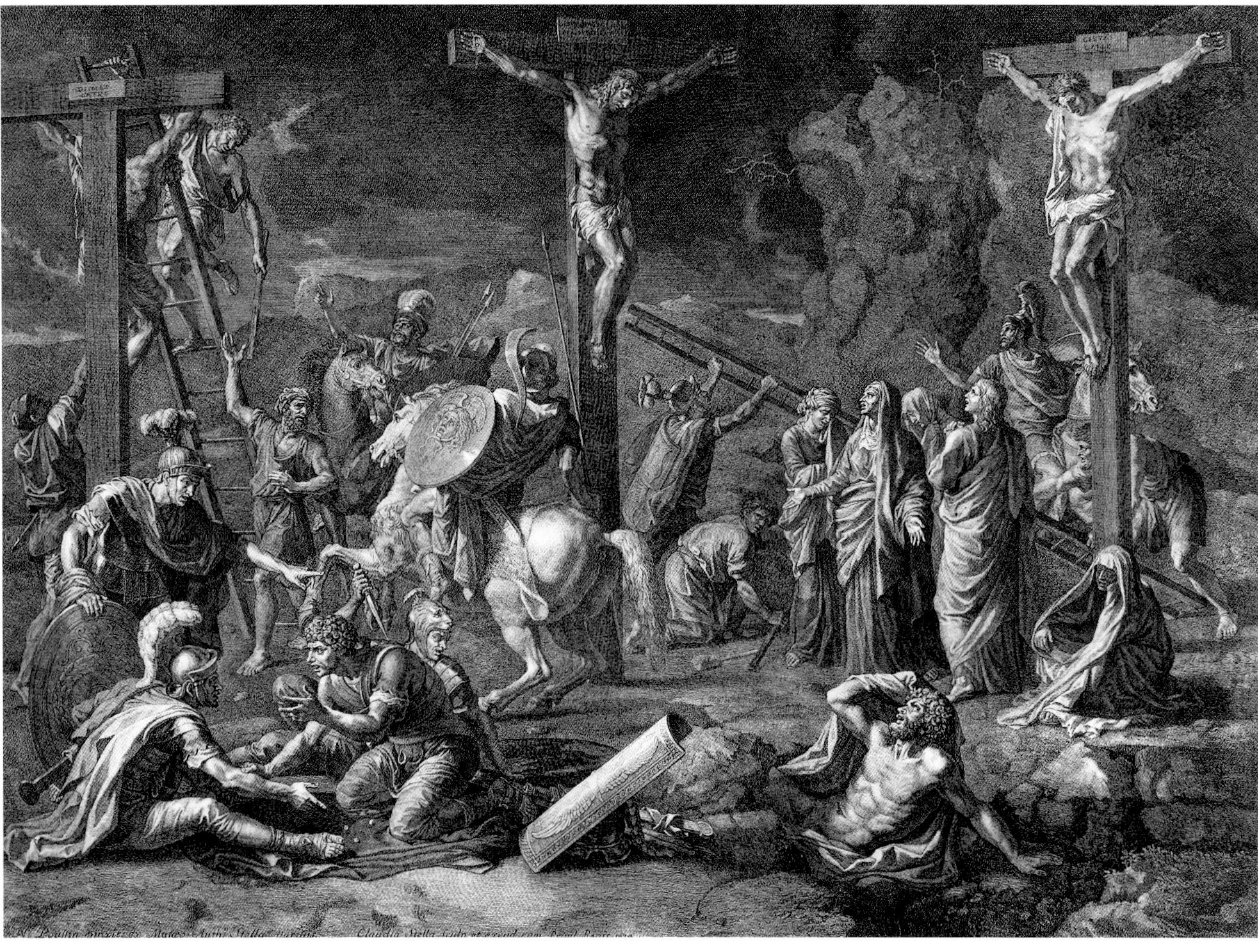

Fig. 69. Claudine Bouzonnet Stella, *Crucifixion* (after Poussin), 1674, etching with engraving

produced by artists to enlarge the market for non-religious art and supplant revenue once obtained through church patronage.

As the new Protestant sects became more established, many became less austere and less stringent in their opposition to visual art which, after all, could be an effective tool for education, dissemination of faith, and propaganda. By 1600, religious art was again being produced in Protestant territories for Protestant clientèle (private citizens as well as church congregations), with several adjustments to fit the tastes of new audiences. Though sixteenth- and seventeenth-century Protestants did not hold Mary in the same regard as she was held by Catholics, she was still acclaimed as the mother of God's only son and appeared in ANNUNCIATION and CRUCIFIXION scenes [figs. 23, 69]. Scenes from the Hebrew Bible were popular in Protestant art [fig. 10], as were images depicting a powerful, adult male Christ [fig. 68].

A survey of altarpieces commissioned in eastern Germany between 1560 and 1660 found the LAST SUPPER to be the most popular theme for a Protestant church, and the CRUCIFIXION next in popularity.[1] Not common prior to the Reformation, scenes of the LAST SUPPER linked the congregation's communion to that of the apostles through the sacrament of the Eucharist. CRUCIFIXION scenes illustrated the climactic moment of each of the four Gospels, while emphasizing themes of Christ's sacrifice and resurrection. When a full scene of CALVARY was depicted, showing Jesus crucified alongside two thieves, additional spiritual interpretations were possible [fig. 69]. Pastors could cite the example of the fate of the thieves—one who acknowledges Christ's divinity and enters heaven and one who dies unconverted and descends to hell—as confirmation of the Protestant belief that Christian salvation depended on faith alone (vs. the Catholic belief in faith combined with good works).[2]

Protestants did remain suspicious of the visual arts and were admittedly judicious in their application. Emmanuel de Witte's Protestant church interior [fig. 64] is notably sparser than Neefs's interior of Antwerp's Catholic cathedral [fig. 16]. Matthaus Merian (1593–1650) of Basel, printmaker and author of the three-part *Iconum Biblicarum (Biblical Illustrations)* of 1625–1630, assumed a defensive posture in the presentation of his work, justifying to his Frankfurt patron the utility of art applied to religious ends. He asserted that "those gifted by God with talent" should be allowed to exercise their talents without shame. He alluded to the period of iconoclasm as the "cold winter of the forgotten" that has finally given way to "this new spring" in which Protestant artists could join their predecessors, Dürer, Cranach, and Holbein.[3]

Each of the *Iconum Biblicarum*'s 233 engravings is accompanied by a didactic quatrain translated into Latin, German and French [fig. 70]. Merian also felt the need to defend his motives and actions to his readers, writing in his first volume:

Dear Reader: I come to the end of the Biblical figures, printed by copperplates, hoping they have not only been amusing to you but also enlightening to your soul, namely by making you refer back to the holy scriptures themselves from which [the engravings] were taken. The *carmina* rhymes or verses are intended to explain or interpret the picture, for your pleasure. This work not only goes out to all art lovers but, hopefully, reaches people of many levels.[4]

Today, nearly five centuries after Luther posted his 95 principles to the door of Wittenberg's *Schlosskirche* (castle church) in 1517 and Zwingli methodically stripped Zurich's churches of Christian art (20 June–2 July 1524), the Protestant

Fig. 70. Matthaus Merian, *This is My Dear Son, Whom You Shall Hear!*, 1630, engraving from *Iconum Biblicarum*, plate 57

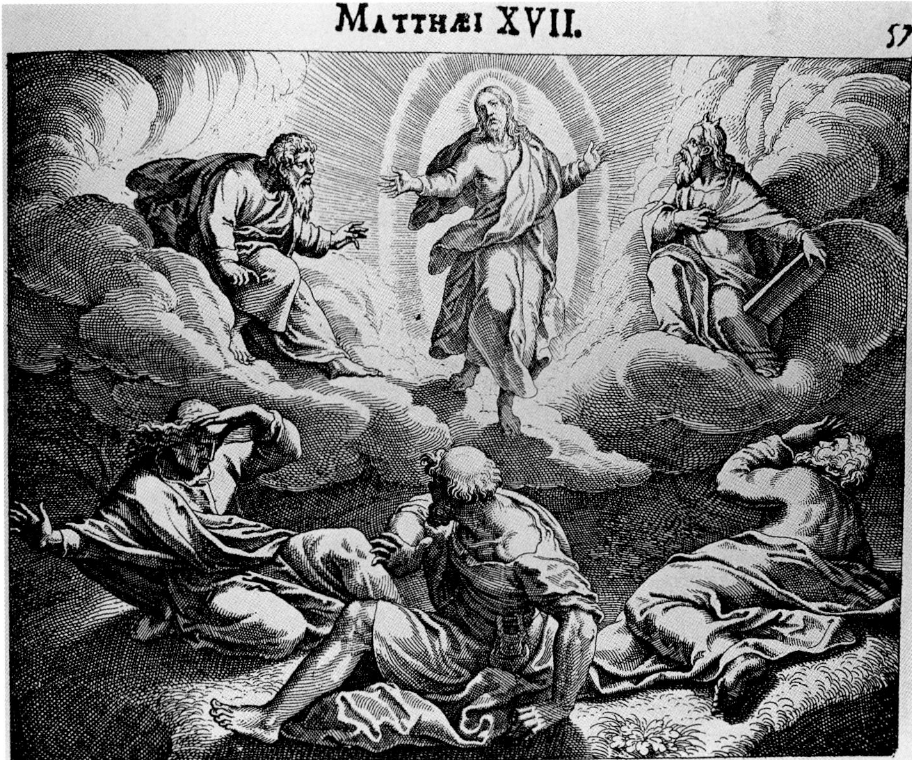

church still is more at ease with verbal than visual expression of religious sentiment. For a Protestant artist a mere century after these dramatic events, there was just cause to tread gently.

*   *   *

It could equally be argued that *Devotio moderna* served as a precedent for the Catholic post-Reformation worship, which revived the medieval tradition of mysticism as a means of personal engagement with divine creation. Counter-Reformation spirituality emphasized the pursuit of excellence, acquisition of virtues, and performance of works of mercy and charity. The simultaneous practice of mental prayer aided earnest Catholics in these intense activities. The writings of mystic intellectuals such as saint Ignatius of Loyola (1491–1556), saint Teresa of Ávila (1515–1582), and saint Francis de Sales (1567–1622) guided individuals through a "science of meditation" aimed to develop and strengthen a profound interior life of prayer and faith.[5] Unlike *Devotio moderna*, an extra-ecclesiastical movement based in lay piety, Catholic reform created channels for individual emotional experience within the institutional church. While none of *Devotio moderna*'s founding members or leading proponents were singled out for sainthood, the leaders of the sixteenth-century mystic fellowship were canonized within a century of their death.[6]

As with the fourteenth-century movement, visualization and projection were again favored spiritual tools, and once again a book—the *Spiritual Exercises* of saint Ignatius (Iñigo de Reclade de Loyola, 1491–1556)—introduced laymen to practices developed among professional religious. The *Spiritual Exercises*, compiled in 1520 and 1530 by the founder of the Society of Jesus (known as the Jesuits), were based on the lessons of Ignatius's own conversion. Number eight of his "Rules for Thinking with the Church" endorsed "the construction of churches, and ornaments; also images, to be venerated with the fullest right, for the sake of what they represent."[7] In his meditation on the mystery of the incarnation, saint Ignatius instructed followers to visualize three scenes: Mary's acquiescence to Gabriel (and God's plan) at the moment of the annunciation, a vision of sinful humanity, and a compassionate saviour awaiting Mary's voluntary cooperation to facilitate human redemption.[8]

These visualizations were not necessarily dependent on outward models (for it was assumed one could imagine a scene without needing to have an artist's rendering at hand on which to meditate), yet it did reinforce the relation between Christian art and Christian prayer. On occasion, artists would produce works that reflected the acts of devotion the image was intended to stimulate. In the 1590s *Lamentation with Saints Augustine and Nicholas of Tolentino* by the Spanish painter Gregorio Martínez y Espinosa (1547–1598), neither Mary nor the two saints seem aware of any presence other than Jesus' [fig. 71]. Each is focused in deep reverence of the martyred body, an act of devotion presumably replicated by the viewer). By replacing the biblical personages Joseph of Arimathæa and Nicodemus (who by tradition were said to remove Jesus' body from the cross) with two Augustinian saints—Augustine of Hippo (354–430) and Nicholas of Tolentino (1245–1305)—who lived nine centuries apart, Martínez turned a traditional deposition scene rooted in biblical time into a timeless meditation on Christ's passion, facilitating the viewer's ability to enter into the scene and emulate its examples.

Painted in a mannerist style combining polished realism with emotional fervor, Martínez's *Lamentation* reflected Counter-Reformation piety as well as actual devotional practices carried out in Spain at this time. On feast days life-size, realistically polychromed sculptures, known as *pasos*, were carried through the streets in processional *tableaux* recreating the story of Christ's passion, just as live actors had done in medieval mystery

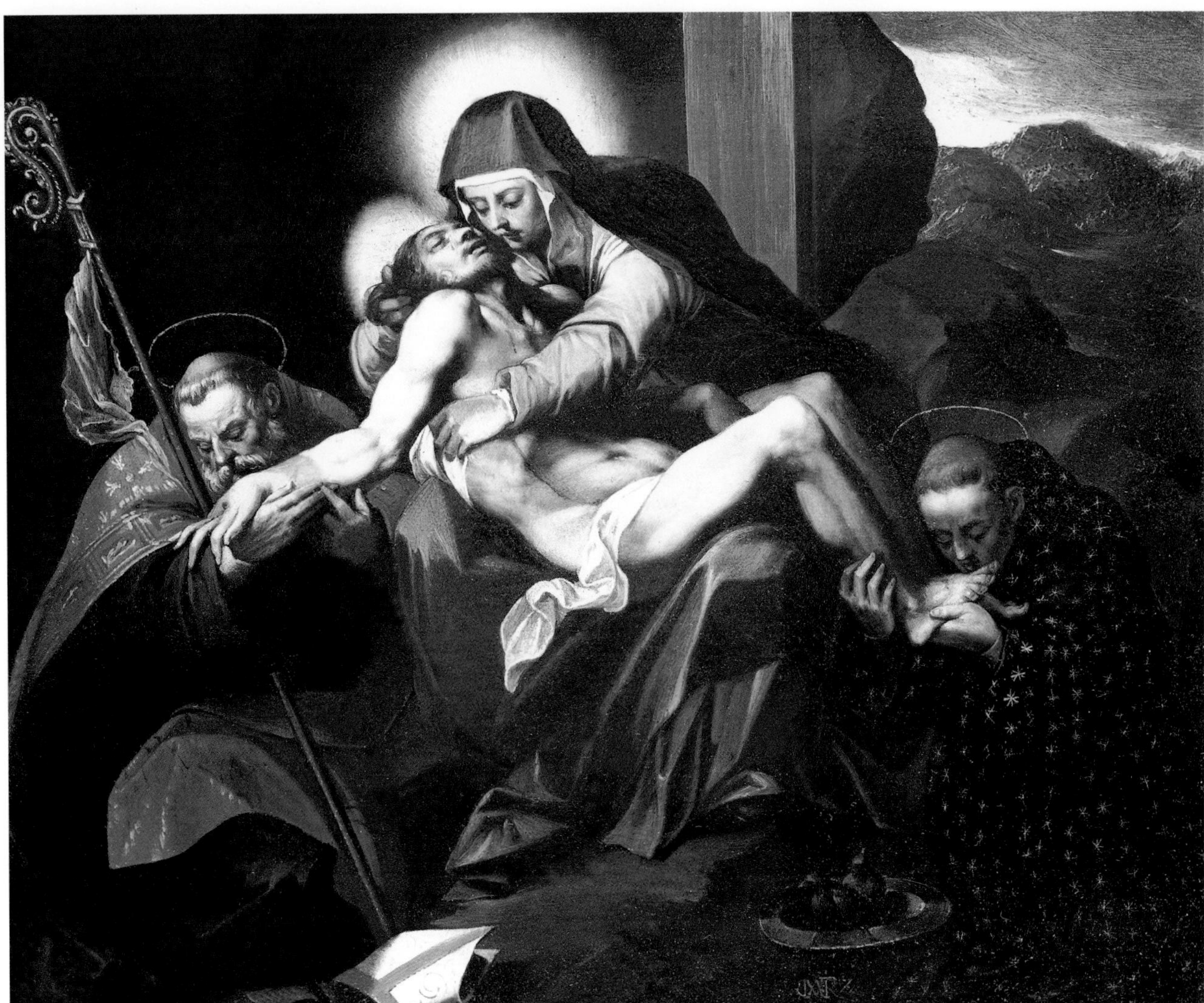

plays. Between processions, the sculptures were often displayed within churches, where worshipers could touch the figures and imagine themselves in physical contact with Jesus' body, kissing his wounds via the intermediary of sculpture.[9] This is the form of piety, style of worship, and type of imagery that the Spaniards brought with them to their American colonies, and which natives adapted and infused with indigenous traditions to produce the unique Catholic culture of Hispanic America [fig. 67].

Mysticism itself became a popular artistic subject; often saints were portrayed using a cross (a symbol of the crucifixion) or skull (a symbol of mortality) as a visual cue and focal point to stimulate meditation [fig. 72]. The focus on the interior experience, rather than external cause, reflects two other facets of art (and society) in the sixteenth and seventeenth centuries—increasing appreciation of individual consciousness (a prelude to psychology) and growing emphasis on naturalism.[10] Much of the devotional literature of the Catholic Reform is autobiographical in nature, and many artists of the Catholic south depicted Mary as an earthy peasant rather than an ethereal creature. Caravaggio's Madonnas, dressed in contemporary costume of the lower classes yet infused with great dignity, are emblematic of this shift in attitude.

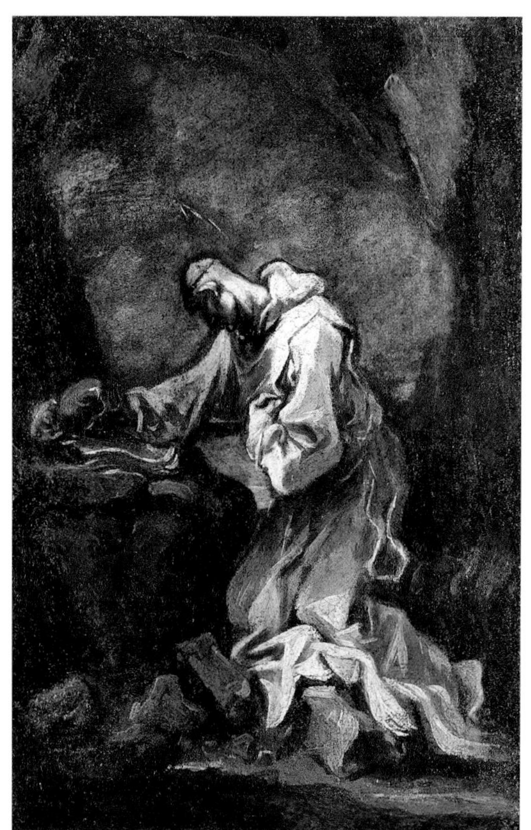

Fig. 72. Alessandro Magnasco, *Monastic Saint in Ecstasy*, 1720s, oil on canvas

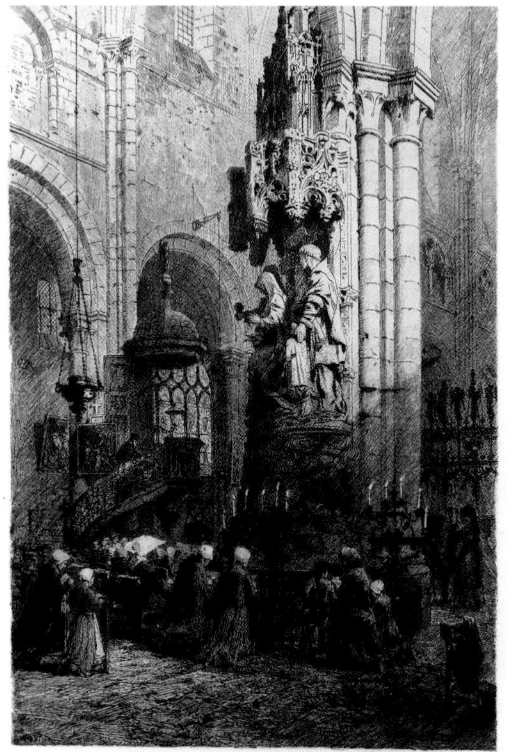

Fig. 73. Axel Herman Haig, *Church Interior with Worshipers at a Pietà*, 1891, etching

Catholic worship today is far more influenced by practices introduced after the Council of Trent (1545–1563) than by medieval customs [fig. 73]. One enduring legacy was the adoption of frequent church attendance, communion, and confession (though the latter was deemphasized following the reforms of Vatican II in 1962–1965). Prior to the mid-fifteenth century, lay people attended church sporadically, participating on festivals and feast days but not every Sunday. Sins might be confessed once a year and communion taken once or twice (probably Easter and Christmas); emphasis was placed on seeing the host elevated during mass rather than receiving it.[11] The main communal ritual for the congregation was not the shared Eucharist but rather the *pax*, or kiss of peace, celebrated before communion. Nowadays, greetings are exchanged among the congregation in the form of handshakes accompanied by the phrase "peace be with you." The pre-Tridentine (i.e., Trent) kiss of peace, however, involved the passing around the congregation of a small object known as a *pax*, to which parishioners would lightly touch their lips before passing it on to their neighbors.[12] Paxes ranged from simple boards pasted with a woodcut image of the CRUCIFIXION, to refined objects of more durable materials, such as the mid-sixteenth century *Lamentation* pax made of brass coated with silver [fig. 74].

Nor would devout Christians, including nuns and monks, participate with great frequency in the sacrament of the Eucharist. According to the 1253 Rule of Saint Clare, Franciscan nuns were instructed to "receive communion seven times [a year], that is, on Christmas, Thursday of Holy Week, Easter, Pentecost, the Assumption of the Blessed Virgin [August 15th], the Feast of St. Francis [October 4th], and the Feast of All Saints [November 1st]."[13] During the 1431 trial of Joan of Arc, carefully recorded by multiple notaries, far more surprise and suspicion is aroused by her urgent desire for daily communion than by her claim to hear the voices of archangels and saints.[14] Only in the post-Tridentine period did the Catholic church institute daily mass and encourage frequent attendance, ensuring a regular audience for its newly acquired artworks.[15]

THE MADONNA UNVEILED: PART II

6. Passion

Although the Gospels deal primarily with Jesus' adult mission of teaching, miracles, and activism (when Mary's role is minimal and presence, if at all, is implicit), Christian art focuses on the beginning and end of his life.[1] The final week of Jesus' life—beginning with his entry into Jerusalem on the day now known as Palm Sunday—is a drama of betrayal, arrest, torture, crucifixion, death, burial, and resurrection, known as the PASSION cycle. Marian imagery created in association with depictions of Christ's passion contrasts sharply with the limited range of expression allowed to her otherwise. Artists could draw upon a variety of interpretations, convictions, doctrines, and gesticulations, to depict Mary either swooning, as in Hans von Aachen's mid-sixteenth-century *Crucifixion* [fig. 75]; collapsing, as in Francesco Trevisani's 1698 *Deposition* [fig. 76]; actively protesting, as in a rare Italian thirteenth-century panel [fig. 77]; or suffering nobly, as in the magnificent unreversed engraving of Nicolas Poussin's *Calvary* by Claudine Bouzonnet Stella (1636–1697), niece and disciple of the master printmaker Jacques Stella (1596–1657) [fig. 69].

The upper scene of the *duecento* panel, in which Christ voluntarily ascends the cross, derives

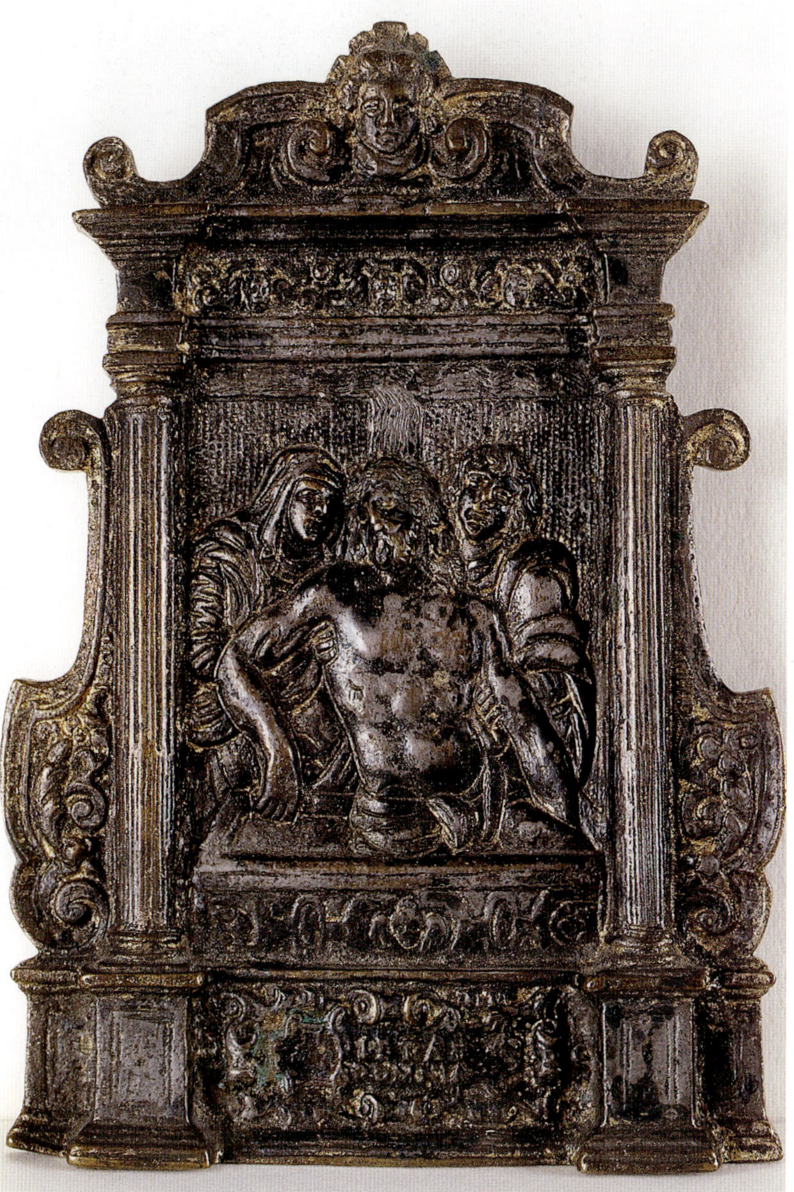

from Byzantine precedents and became closely associated with Franciscan piety in Italy.[2] Mary's posture cannot as easily be classified. The pairing with the lower scene of the funeral of saint Clare (1194–1253) confirms the panel's affiliation with the Franciscan order, whose devotional writings alluded to Mary's sorrow at the sight of her son's naked body on the cross.[3] One could interpret Mary's left arm placed around Jesus' waist as an attempt to cover her son's exposed body, yet its

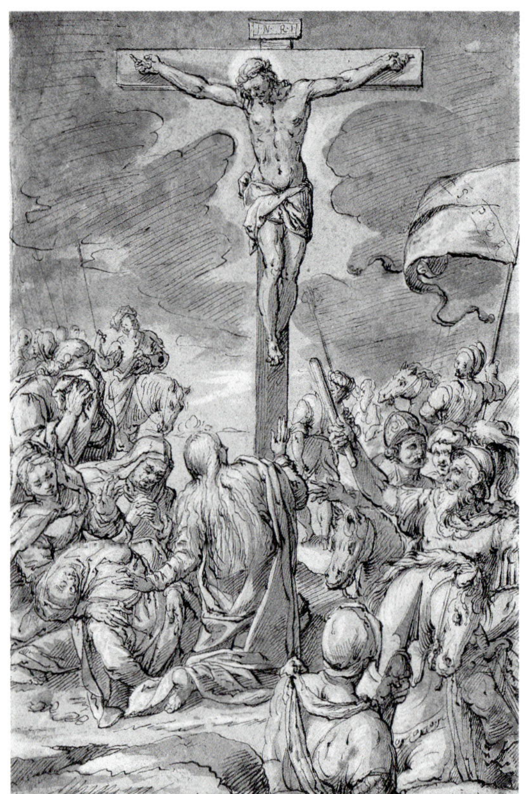

Fig. 75. Hans von Aachen, *Crucifixion*, late 16th/early 17th c., ink and wash with white highlights

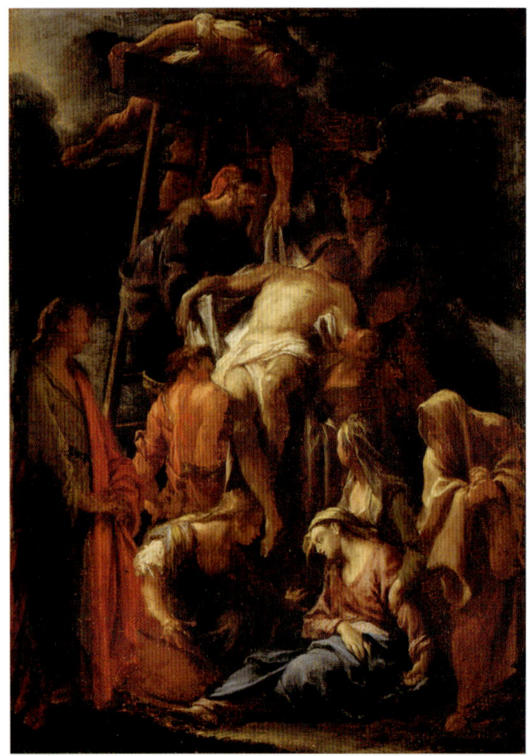

Fig. 76. Francesco Trevisani, *Deposition*, ca. 1698, oil on canvas

meaning is complicated by the position of her right arm, which restrains a belligerent onlooker. To us, Mary's gesture appears an impulsive attempt to stop her son from mounting the cross. Such a gesture is contrary to orthodox (accepted) theology, which declared that Mary had to be, if not a willing spectator, then a passive participant at Jesus' crucifixion, because of both her obedience to God's will and foreknowledge of the sacrifice her son would be called to make. Mary's spontaneous resistance, though theologically incorrect, might have appealed to the public, as a natural sign of motherly distress that heightened the emotional impact of the scene and enabled viewers to identify with Mary's suffering. Indeed, a Byzantine verse poem from the sixth century describes Mary's resolute attempt to intervene at the crucifixion; clergy immediately condemned it as heresy inconsistent with church teachings, yet could not suppress its popular appeal and endurance among lay Christians.[4] Nevertheless, this thirteenth-century altarpiece was probably destined for viewing by Franciscan nuns, not a susceptible public. In any event, Mary's ambiguous gesture faded from art, replaced by postures evocative of interpretations more consistent with church teachings.

Two contrasting figure types emerged in northern Europe and Spain in the late fourteenth century: images of Mary as the loving young mother of a healthy baby (associated with events at the beginning of her son's life) and as the sorrowing mother associated with events at the end of his life. Art historians often speak of the *Schönemadonna* (or Beautiful Lady, using the German term) [fig. 78], the *Schmerzenmutter* (or Mother of Sorrows in German) [fig. 76], and the *Vesperbild* (image accompanying evening vespers in the Book of Hours' passion cycle, which featured Christ's DEPOSITION from the cross and ENTOMBMENT).[5] One *Vesperbild* image, a depiction of Mary holding her dead son's body, is more widely known as by the Italian term *Pietà* (Lady of Pity or Compassion)

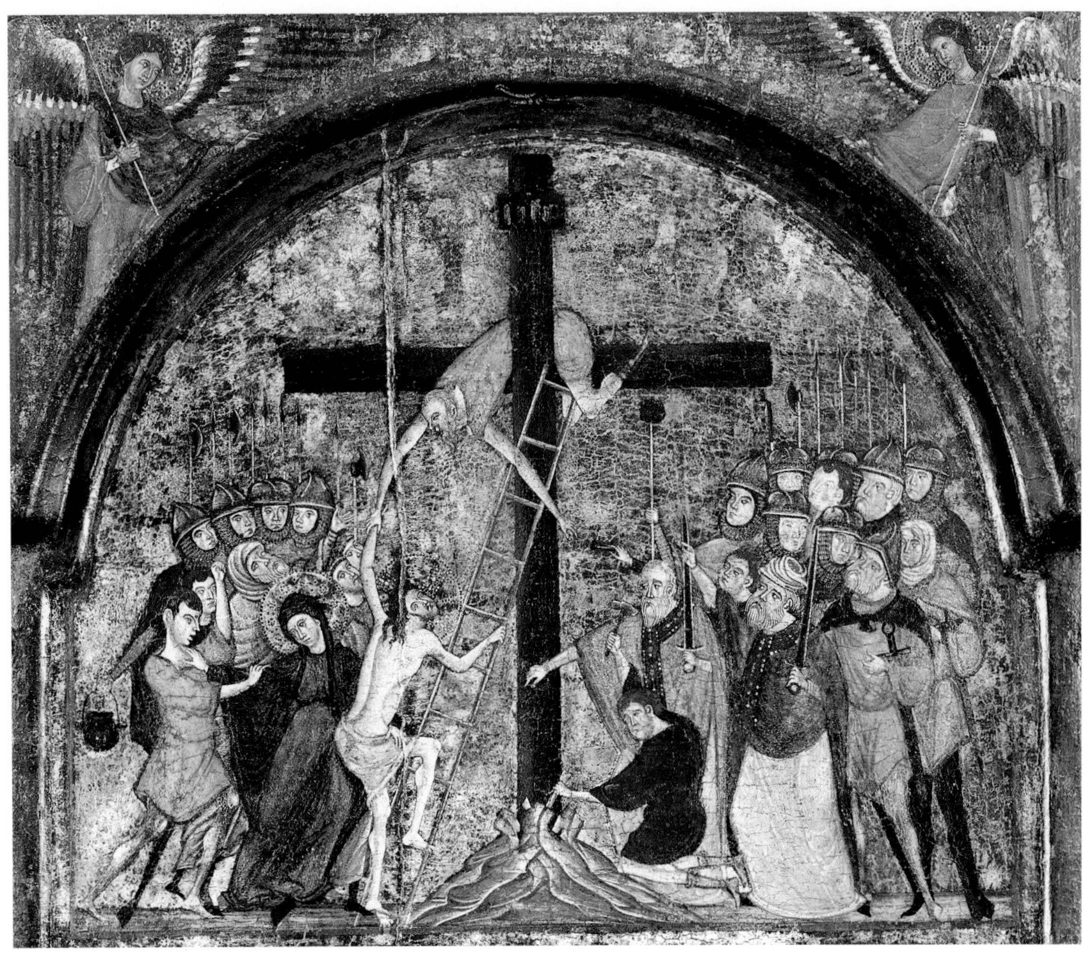

Fig. 77. Italian from Umbria or Tuscany, *Christ Mounting the Cross* (upper half of altarpiece), 1290s, tempera on panel

[fig. 79], although this figure-type was widespread in northern Europe a century before Michelangelo created his famous *pietà* statue of 1498–1499. One cannot judge which Marian prototype earlier artists and audiences preferred based on what remains today. The shift of artwork from a religious to an aesthetic function and from church setting to museum has favored the preservation of works depicting beautiful Madonnas. This is especially true in the United States, whose museum collections were formed largely by Protestant benefactors in the mid-nineteenth century; these donors, though drawn to Renaissance art, avoided collecting images of disturbing content and overt Catholic overtones.[6]

Images of Mary's suffering helped viewers achieve the heightened emotional state thought to bring one closer to God in prayer. Texts like saint Bonaventure's (circa 1217–1274) *Meditations on the Life of Christ* encouraged believers to visualize the Passion, entreating:

> Oh, if you could see [Our] Lady weeping between these words, but moderately and softly, and the Magdalen frantic about her Master and crying with deep sobs, perhaps you too would not restrain your tears. Meditate on their condition as they spoke of these things. Feel for them, for they are in great affliction.[7]

Women could particularly identify with Mary's maternal anguish, seeing reflected in her pain the grief and loss associated with motherhood during these centuries of high child mortality, when mis-

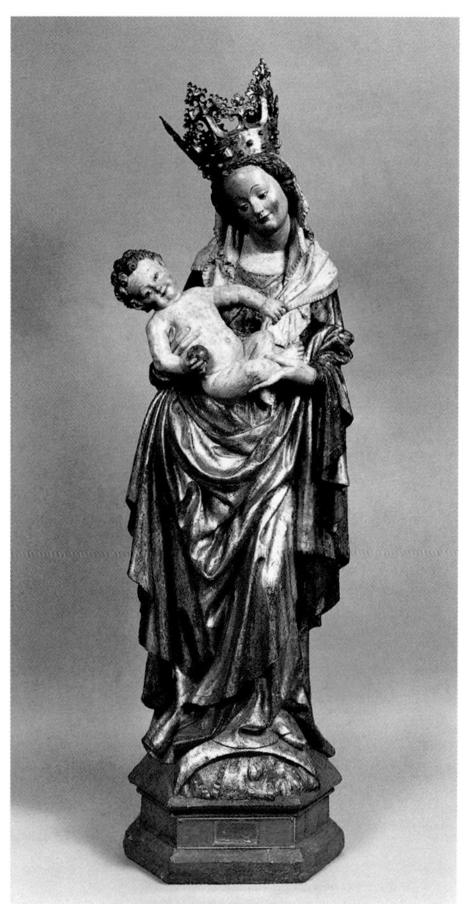

Fig. 78. Tyrolese, *Madonna and Child*, ca. 1430, polychromed wood, Harvard University Art Museums, Cambridge, MA

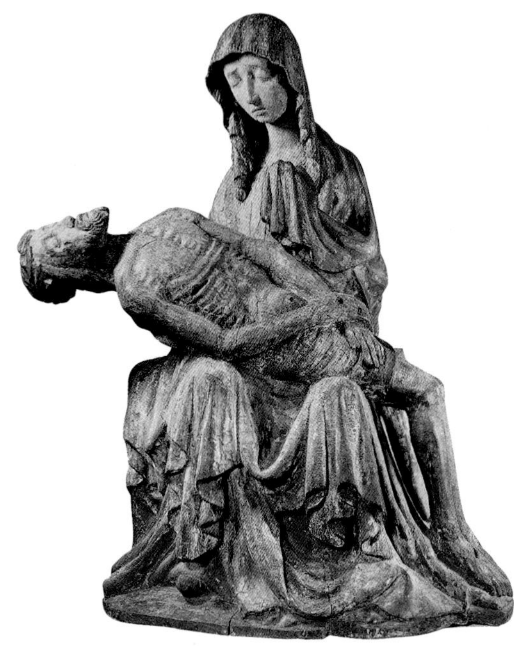

Fig. 79. Austrian, *Pietà*, ca. 1420, polychromed wood, Harvard University Art Museums, Cambridge, MA

carriages were carefully recorded and the risks of losing one's offspring before one's own death touched every stratum of society.[8] Even nuns, who had broken all family bonds to enter the convent, identified with Mary's grief at the loss of her son, viewing themselves as "spiritual mothers" entirely devoted to their child.[9]

The cult of Mary as sorrowing mother, the *Mater dolorosa*, extended from Spain and Italy to England, arising in the eleventh century and burgeoning during the plague- and famine-stricken fourteenth century, coinciding with the cult of the Holy Family.[10] Women were known not only to identify strongly with images of Mary's suffering but also to be patrons of this type of imagery. PIETÀ sculptures or lamentation images were often commissioned by women and for women, for private chapels, convent use, and lay communities such as the Beguines. Beguines were an order of religious women who lived together without taking formal vows. Claiming Mary as their foundress, they flourished in northern Europe from circa 1210 through the Reformation. Southern counterparts included the Beata communities of Spain, the Mantellati of Tuscany, and the Humilitati of Lombardy.[11] Beguines allowed married and widowed women to join their ranks, requiring that members be celibate but not virginal. Hence many Beguines were both spiritual and physiological mothers, and they were great promoters of PIETÀ figures.[12]

Though three of the four scriptural accounts do not clearly indicate Mary's presence at the crucifixion, the evangelist John is unambiguous about her presence, though he refers to her only as "Jesus' mother" and not as Mary.[13] In this fourth gospel, a dying Jesus entrusts his mother's care to his beloved disciple: "And from that hour the disciple took her to his own home" (John 19:27). For this reason, Mary and the apostle John (traditionally identified as the "beloved disciple") are paired at the foot of the cross, as in Dürer's *Crucifixion* miniature of circa 1520, printed from a gold

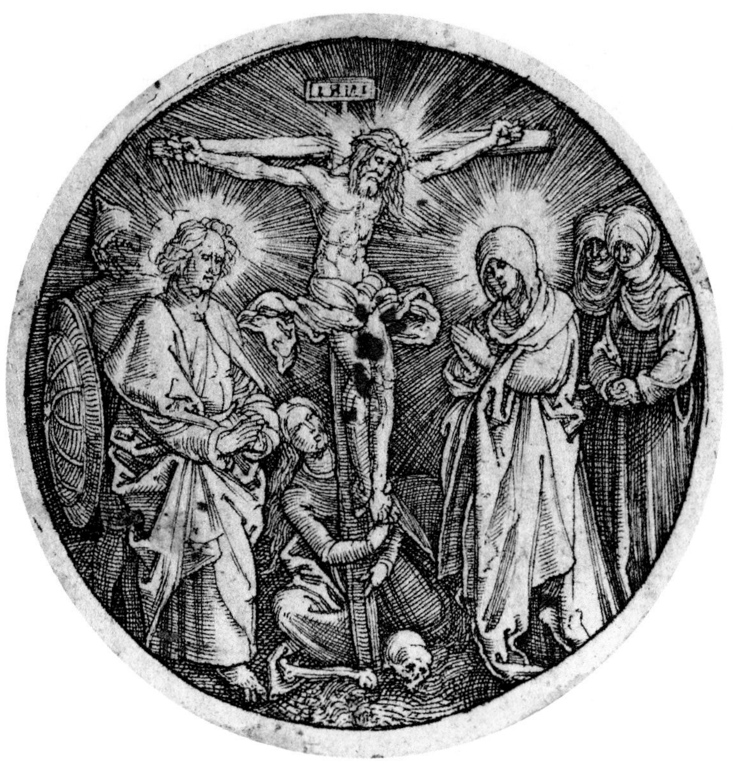

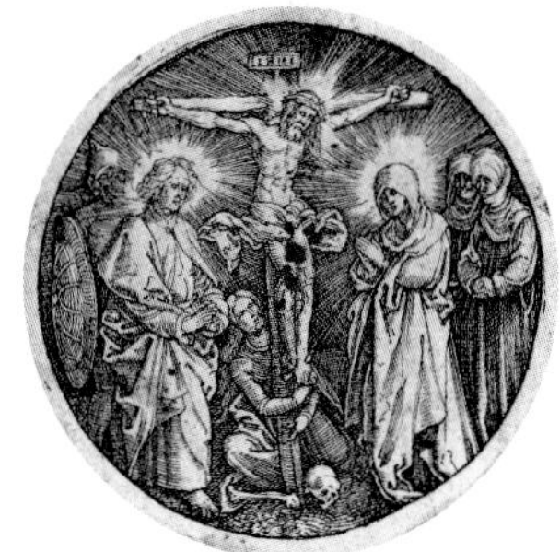

Fig. 80. Albrecht Dürer, *Crucifixion*, ca. 1520, woodcut (shown actual size, above)

medallion engraved for Holy Roman emperor Maximilian (1459–1519) [fig. 80]. This act of a dying child arranging for the care of the living would have resonated powerfully with societies who depended on relatives (especially children) to support the elderly. In extreme destitution, one could always turn to the parish for support, though one found little comfort in the poorhouse, whether run by Catholic nuns who made a virtue of poverty or by Protestant municipalities who equated poverty with vice.[14] Most children heeded Jesus' example, accepting responsibility for the welfare of their aged parents.

While poor and rural widows faced dire economic straits without male support, middle-class town widows fared better, particularly if their husbands' confraternity or trade guild helped with burial expenses and if they were legally entitled to have their dowry returned. Laws varied from region to region, but if the property and assets a woman brought into the marriage were returned to her upon her husband's death, widows could enjoy greater social, legal, and economic freedom than married women. Such was the case in medieval and Renaissance France, Italy, and England.[15] According to the 1261 municipal laws of Magdeburg, Saxony, most of a deceased husband's assets passed to the male heirs, but the widow received

> her dower and all that belongs to her; that is, all the sheep, geese, chests, yarn, beds, pillows, cushions, table [and] bed linen, towels, cups, candlesticks, linen, women's clothing, finger rings, bracelets, headdress, psalters, and all prayer-books, chairs, drawers, bureaus, carpets, curtains, etc.... But uncut cloth, and unworked gold and silver do not belong to her.[16]

The list emphasizes women's association with the home and significantly notes that psalters and prayer-books are considered women's property.

In sixteenth-century Germany, widows could pass membership in their husband's guild on to their new husbands—an enticement to younger men seeking advancement—while in fifteenth-century England, women could become guild members themselves and take over their husband's trade.[17] Women in sixteenth- and seventeenth-century Holland enjoyed significant legal rights, including the ability to own property, testify in court, and file lawsuits without having to append a male relative's name; hence Dutch widows remarried less often than widows in other European countries, enjoying independent status without need of male protection.[18] Most widows did remarry, however, a situation that brought secular society into conflict with church opinion.[19] Many women had no choice; wealthy women might have to remarry to protect their assets, inheritances, and family alliances, while poor and middle-class women, especially mothers of minor children, might be unable to survive otherwise. (Note the widow with her long black veil and young child in de Witte's 1660s *Church Interior* [fig. 64].)

The existence of widows who did not remarry also placed the clergy in a difficult bind: on the one hand, the church welcomed the return to chastity, brought by widowhood, believing a woman should "belong" sexually to only one man during her life.[20] On the other hand, this left widows as unmastered by male authority as young single women, with the added dangers of maturity and perhaps economic independence. Still, from Ambrose of Milan's (339–397) treatise *Concerning Widows*, to Juan Luís Vives's *De institutione foeminae christianae* (*Education of a Christian Woman*) of 1529, and Francis de Sale's *Introduction a la Vie Dévote* (*Introduction to the Devout Life*) of 1609, widows were advised not to remarry.[21] To distance her from implications of sexuality, the church did not hold Mary up as exemplar of widowhood. Nevertheless, saint Birgitta of Sweden (1303–1373), whose *Revelations* chronicle her recurring visions of Mary, recorded a conversation in which Mary stated that she was at once maiden, mother, and widow, as her child had had no earthly father.[22] Instead of Mary,

the church offered as a model the apocryphal heroine Judith, a chaste widow who only ended her mourning for her husband Manasseh to save the Israelites from destruction by slaying the Assyrian general Holofernes [fig. 131].[23] Judith was also considered a typological forebear of Mary as Second Eve—Judith's beheading the general compared to Mary's trampling the serpent as symbols of conquered evil; for this reason Dürer depicted a bust of Judith in the arched roof of Mary's chamber in his *Annunciation* woodcut from the *Life of the Virgin* series [fig. 22]. (The badger under the staircase, a symbol of sloth and thus of Satan, also refers to Mary's triumph over evil.)[24]

Secular society had no such hesitation in encouraging women to remarry and reenter the safety of the patriarchal structure. Women needed to be brought as quickly as possible back within a family structure and removed from the ambiguous state of sexual availability created by their once again being unmarried.[25] Accusations of witchcraft—often focused on elderly, widowed, or otherwise independent women—reflect these attitudes. Protestant clergy, faced with no ambivalence over celibate status, urged widows to remarry on moral grounds, fearing the effects of their ungoverned energies. "A woman does not have complete mastery over herself," Luther wrote; "God so created her body that she should be with a man and bear and raise children. The words of Gen[esis], ch. 1, clearly state this, and the members of her body sufficiently show that God himself formed her for this purpose."[26]

Secular Protestants and Catholics of the sixteenth and seventeenth centuries saw additional virtues in a widow's remarriage. Both sides competed for women's allegiance during the Reformation period, acknowledging that the entire household—husband, wife, children, servants, apprentices—generally followed the woman's choice of faith. Frequent widowhood meant women could remarry and convert yet another household to the Protestant or Catholic cause.[27]

Of course, whether a woman *could* remarry was often questionable, especially as women tended to outnumber and outlive men. In fifteenth-century Florence, only 1.8 percent of women under 38 were widows, but the figures rose to 46 percent of women age 60, 53 percent of women age 65, and 75 percent of those age 70.[28] Statistics available from seventeenth-century Germany show that 80 percent of widowed men remarried within a year, but only 40 percent of widowed women found new husbands; for women over 40, the number dropped to 20 percent.[29]

*   *   *

From the number and status of living children, medieval and Renaissance communities could deduce not only the likely condition and comfort of widowed and elderly parents but also a family's economic status. Looking at images of the CRUCI-FIXION, contemporary audiences would have associated Mary, the mother of only one child, not only with the vulnerable members of its society but also with the poor. While in these days of reliable contraception and family planning, we tend to associate small families with industrialized nations and the upper-middle class, and larger families with developing nations and the underclass, the reverse was true in the past: smaller families were associated with poverty, and larger families with wealth.[30]

Though childhood diseases claimed victims of all classes, poor diet and nutrition made lower-class children more vulnerable to illness. Wealthy and middle-class families could afford to send their infants to professional wet nurses, a practice parents from the Middle Ages through the eighteenth century thought was better for children (though only aristocrats and the urban middle class could afford to do so). Poor mothers nursed their own children (often for two or three years) and experienced the natural contraceptive effects of breast-feeding, reinforced by social customs dic-tating that nursing women should refrain from sexual activity.[31] Mothers who employed wet nurses might give birth every year or two, whereas poor mothers would give birth less frequently, to children less likely to live into adulthood.

The choice of a wet nurse was considered one of the most important decisions a family would make for the well-being of their offspring, as breast milk was thought to provide mental and moral as well as physical characteristics to the infant. (This is why women would seek a qualified professional to breast-feed the child rather than undertake such a task themselves.) Saint Bernardino of Siena (1380–1444) reflected predominant views when he preached that "the child acquires certain of the customs of the one who suckles him."[32] Few fifteenth-century Tuscans heeded his condemnation of commercial wet nursing; for most, he only confirmed their need to hire with care. Trotula of Salerno (eleventh century) advised that a wet nurse "ought to be young and have a pink and white complexion . . . and she should be moderately fat," exercise regularly, and avoid garlic.[33] Soranus of Ephesus (second century), whose advice was still being taken in Renaissance Italy,

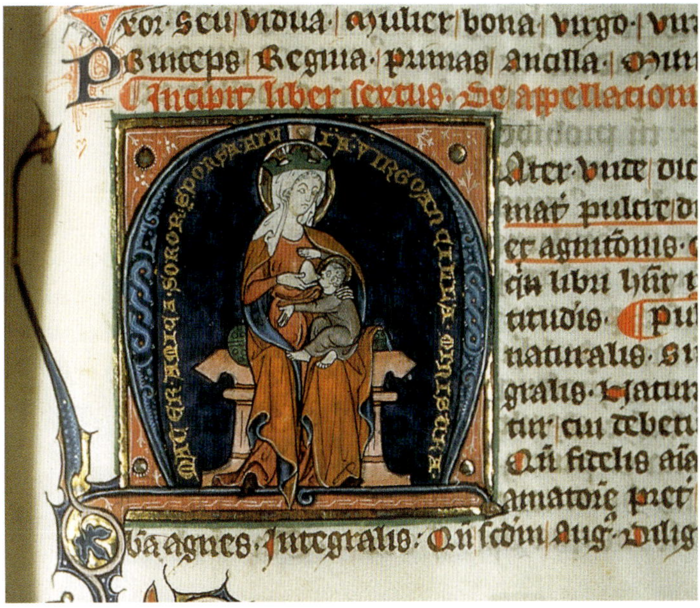

Fig. 81. French from Paris or Northeastern France, *Virgo Lactans*, 1290-1300, historiated initial accompanying *De laudibus* Book VI, folio 192r (actual size)

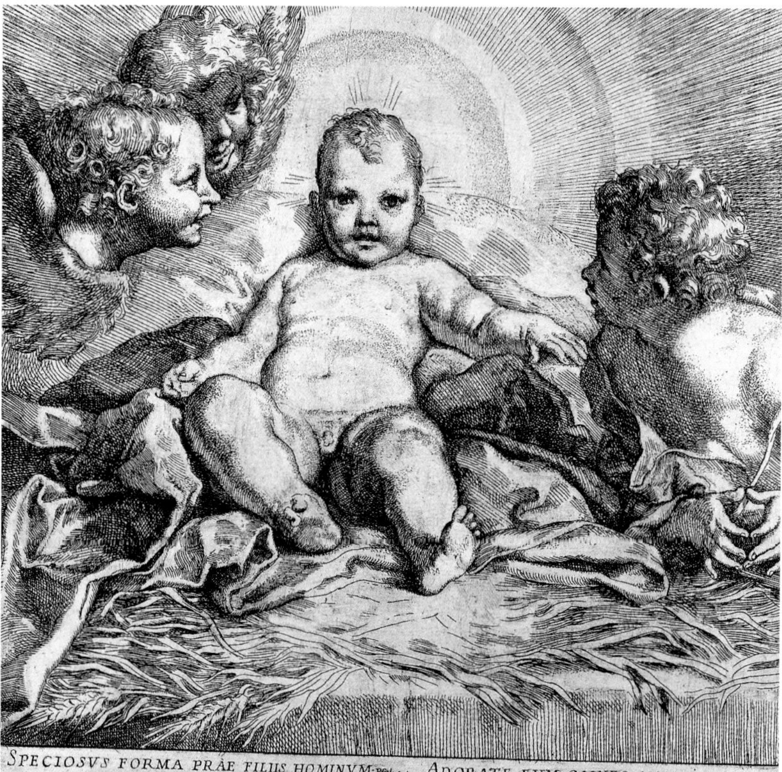

recommended choosing a healthy woman between 20 and 40 who had more than one child of her own and was "self-controlled, sympathetic and not ill-tempered, a Greek, and tidy."[34]

Mary was often shown nursing the infant Jesus, from her earliest known representation in Rome's Catacomb of Priscilla, to sumptuous manuscripts intended for monastic use, to moderately priced and widely circulating woodcuts [figs. 14, 31, 81].[35] While no one could doubt the superior efficacy of Mary's breast milk on moral or intellectual grounds, to see her nursing her own child conveyed her poor and humble status to earlier viewers as much as a crumbling manger does to viewers today. Clergy pointed to these depictions of the *Virgo lactans*, the Virgin nursing her own child, and urged all women to do the same. Jean Gerson (1363–1429) of Paris preached that mother's milk was not only natural infant's food but the beginning of a Christian education.[36] Erasmus of Rotterdam (1469–1536), who had been educated by the Brethren of the Common Life, reasoned in his colloquy *The New Mother* that "there is no class of living creatures that does not nurse its own young" and that if sent to a wet nurse the child's affection will be "divided, as it were, between two mothers."[37] While humanists argued on grounds of maternal bonds, the church cited sexual promiscuity, contending that mothers were unwilling to abstain from sex as nursing required. (The church attributed no such motives to the fathers, presuming that women already facing a lifetime of risky pregnancy and childbirth couldn't wait to resume that perilous condition again.)[38]

Protestant opponents of Mary's cult approved neither of commercial wet nurses (because no mother should shirk her duties) nor images of Mary nursing her child (because these emphasized Mary's power over Jesus and his dependency on her for nourishment). Agitators almost wished he had no mother. To the English Puritan minister, William Crashaw (1572–1626), it was degrading to depict Jesus as a small baby subservient to a woman. Catholic imagery, he complained, wouldn't let Christ grow up into a miracle-working male, equal in size and stature to God the Father. Crashaw fumed that Jesus must be a "suckling child in his mothers armes" and Mary "must still bee a commanding Mother, and must shew *her authority over him*, and he *must receive our prayers by her means*, and still she must beare him in her armes; or lead him in her hand, and her Picture must work all the miracles, but his none; and she must be saluted as a Lady, a Queene, a Goddesse, and he as a Child."[39]

The intriguing etching *Angels Adoring the Christ Child*, ascribed to Carlo Maratti (1625–1713), a prolific Roman artist, seems to literally embody these thoughts, displaying the infant alone without his "interfering" mother, not as an adult, but large and powerful nonetheless [fig. 82]. There is one troubling element: Maratti was an able master of Catholic Reformation themes, not a Protestant sympathizer. Needless to say, the print (and its signature) turned out to be the invention of Giovita Garavaglia (1790–1835), professor at the Florentine *Accademia,* who, in addition to copying Titian's portrait of Charles V, Raphael's *Madonna della Sedia,* and works by Reni, Ferrari, and Luini in etched form, created this hitherto unknown work inscribed "Carolus Marattus Inuen."[40] Perhaps Garavaglia's work was intended only as an homage to and not a forgery of Maratti's work. Nevertheless, by isolating the infant Jesus as the sole subject of the print, aggrandizing him to the scale of over ten inches squared, he failed to grasp the nuances of religious allegiance implicit in Christian art-as-propaganda in the sixteenth and seventeenth centuries, that would have made such an image unthinkable in Maratti's *oeuvre.*

7. *Veneration*

No one particular Hour of the Virgin deals specifically with Mary's sanctity, yet one cannot consider Mary's presence in art without exploring this aspect of her identity. Though fully aware of the power of Mary's cult and extent of her devotion, the Catholic and Orthodox faiths have always taught that Mary is human, not divine, but do acknowledge her to be a saint. Sainthood varies among Christian sects, but most confer sanctity on people who demonstrate exemplary holiness and virtue. In the Catholic and Orthodox churches, saints serve two purposes: as models of holy lives (for which they are venerated), and as intercessors before God on behalf of those on earth (for which

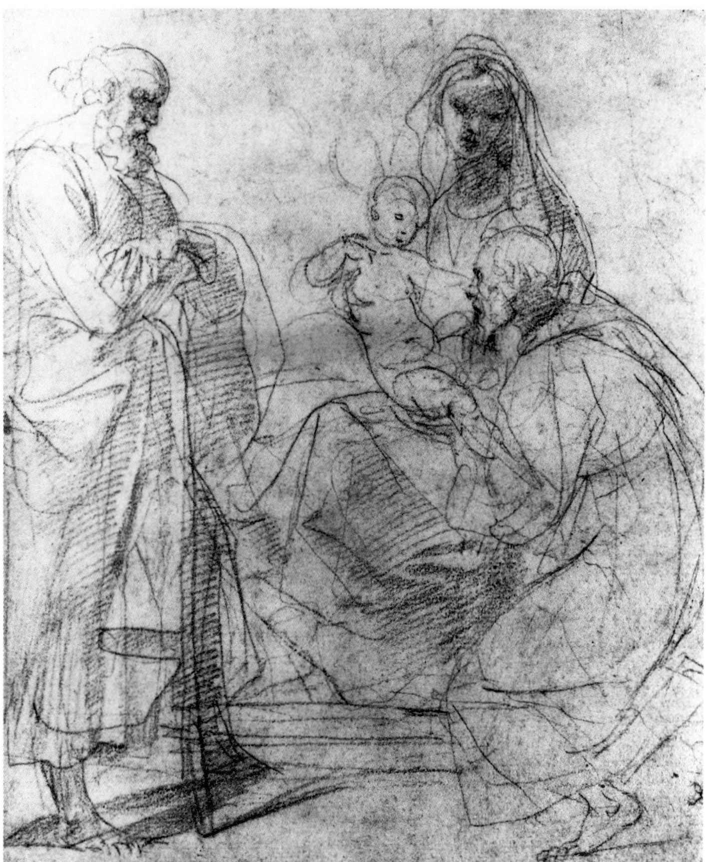

prayers are directed to them). Historically, as well as today, devotion to a particular saint might stem from a shared name or date, or connection with a place, profession, or affliction under that saint's protection. The cult of saints had broad popular appeal, and devotion to local saints was often combined with appeals for Mary's special intercession [fig. 83].

For the faithful, Mary was a two-way street, bringing people's petitions to God, and bringing God (through the less intimidating son) to the believers. Thomas à Kempis (1380–1471) wrote in his *Meditations on Mary* of the rewards one could expect from devotion to Mary. "Happy was that religious who condemned all the solaces of the world choosing Our Lady Saint Mary to be a mother of consolation to him and a guardian to protect him all the days of his life," he wrote, for on his behalf Mary will say to her son,

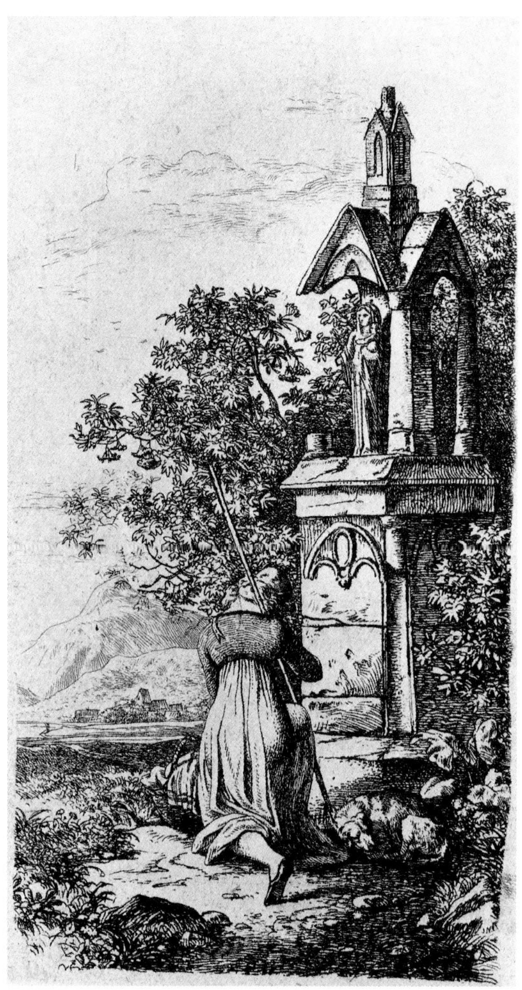

*My most loving son, have mercy on the soul of this
thy lover and my praiser . . . from whose mouth the
holy Angels have oft-times brought unto me the
delights of that devout salutation [Ave Maria]. . . .
When he saw at church or anywhere my picture
painted, or thee lying in my bosom or sitting, or
hanging as it were dead within my arms, straightway
he wept and prayed, bowed the knee and worshipped.
. . . Grant that he may now find mercy before thee
when I with all the saints and angels plead for him
exceeding earnestly.*[41]

Note that images, too, have a role to play in intercession.

Mary was revered as both a healing saint, whose
relics had powers to cure, and a helping saint, to
whom one could pray for aid [fig. 84]. Because of
Mary's assumption into heaven (see discussion
below), no physical relics of her body (such as a
bone or finger) were available. Nevertheless, artifacts that once supposedly belonged to Mary were
housed in many shrines, where miraculous healing
was reported to have taken place. The English
shrine at Walsingham claimed to have a replica of
her house at Nazareth, and the Italian shrine of
Loreto, her actual house. The churches of
Chartres kept the tunic worn by Mary at the
Annunciation; St. John Lateran and Sta. Maria
sopra Minerva locks of her hair; and Poitou her
nail-parings in a red silk purse.[42]

Relic ownership was so extensive that saint
Bernadino of Siena (1380–1444) proudly concluded, "there is not a church without a relic of
our blessed Virgin."[43] Calvin concurred, with less
enthusiasm, writing, "there is no town so small,
nor convent . . . so mean that it does not display
some of the Virgin's milk . . . . There is so much
that if the holy Virgin had been a cow, or a wet
nurse all her life she would have been hard put to
yield such a great quantity."[44] (Frankly, medieval
audiences were neither as gullible as we might
believe nor bothered by the excessive numbers of
relics, because of their belief in secondary relics—
a form of relic multiplication in which new relics
were created by touching a similar substance to
the primary relic.)[45]

Numerous collections of miracles attributed to
Mary's intervention circulated around Europe,
often with similar stories set in diverse locations,
attesting to the popularity and influence of texts
such as the *Miracula sancte dei genitricis Virginis
Marie* by Nigel of Canterbury (Nigellus Wireker,
circa 1130–1200), *Les miracles de Notre Dame* by
Gautier de Coinci (1177–1236), *Cantigas de loor
de Sancta Maria* by Alfonso X (King of Castile and
León and Holy Roman emperor, 1221–1284),
Milagros de Nuestra Señora by Gonzalo de Berceo
(circa 1198–1264), and *Miraculis beate Marie virginis* by Johannes Herolt (called Discipulus, writ-

ten 1435–1440). Often the miracle was attributed to an image of Mary that came to life in aid of needy humans, leading to popular belief in the miraculous abilities of particular works of art, and pilgrimages to the locations of these celebrated statues and icons. A circa 1280 illumination accompanied Alfonso's tale of a devil who, jealous of a painter's skill at rendering sacred subjects, literally pulled the scaffolding out from underneath him. Fortunately, the image of Mary that he was painting came to life and rescued him[46] [fig. 85].

Many of these miracle-working Madonnas were accompanied by traditions of their sudden discovery. The statue might be drifting alone in a boat (Our Lady of Boulogne, France), found in a tree (Our Lady of Mount Aigu, Belgium; Our Lady of Faith, Namur, France; Our Lady of Telgte, Germany), or discovered near a stream (Our Lady of the Sand, Roermond, Holland; Our Lady of Chapi, Peru). Variations on the miraculous discovery include tales of oxen refusing to move a statue any farther causing a church to be built on that site (Our Lady of Flores, Indonesia; Our Lady of Luján, Argentina), and stories of statues that cannot be moved from their sites of discovery (Our Lady of Avioth, France; Our Lady of the Angels, Costa Rica; Our Lady of Montserrat, Spain).[47] These "origin stories" enhanced the wondrous reputations of these images and distanced them in people's minds from the artistic process and mundane origins associated with sculptures commissioned for church display.

There may be a grain of truth to these legends, for as Christianity spread during the early Middle Ages, evidence suggests that pagans buried cult figures to prevent Christians from desecrating their idols. These female figures, identified on discovery as Marian images, were often unearthed in locations near ancient goddess shrines.[48] Christian images might also have been protected by burial. The statue of Our Lady of Guadalupe housed in a thirteenth-century monastery in Spain (as

opposed to the painted image enshrined in Mexico City) was said to have been given by pope Gregory the Great (circa 540–604) to saint Leandro, Archbishop of Seville (circa 534–600/01) who, after the Arab conquest of Seville in 711, had the statue buried alongside the remote Guadalupe River to protect it from Muslim desecration. Five centuries later, according to tradition, cowherd Gil Cordero (thirteenth century) encountered a dead animal along the river's bank. When he began cutting up the carcass, the cow resuscitated and Mary appeared. Returning to the site with others, Cordero unearthed a statue on the same spot, and a church was erected that soon became a major pilgrimage site.[49] Traditions aside, the monks who now reside in the shrine at Guadalupe describe

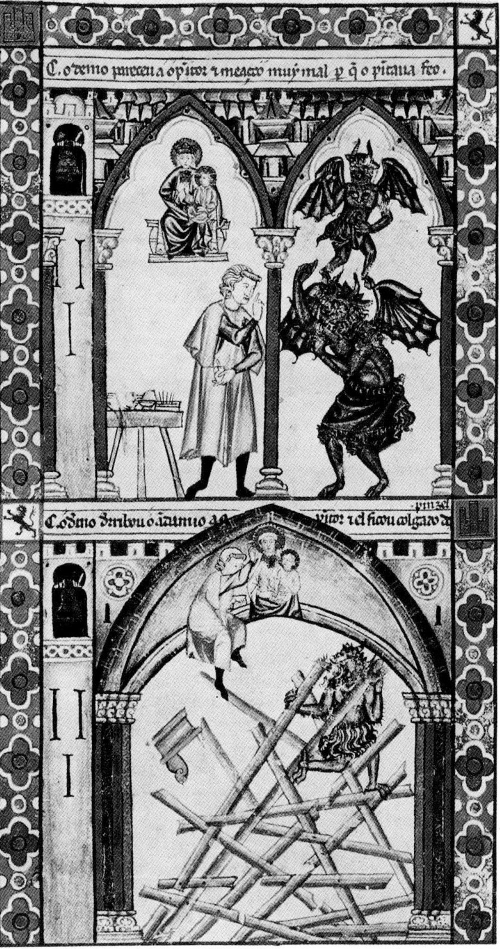

Fig. 85. Spanish, *Virgin Rescuing a Painter from the Devil*, ca. 1280, detail of an illumination from the *Cantigas de Santa María*, Library of the Monastery of Él Escorial

the image as a seated Virgin and Child by a late twelfth-century anonymous artist.[50]

The black Madonna of Montserrat [fig. 86], housed in a tenth-century Benedictine monastery near Barcelona, was said to have been brought from Jerusalem, where it had been carved by saint Nicodemus and painted by saint Luke, hidden during the Moorish conquest in the remote saw-toothed mountains from which it derives its name, then miraculously rediscovered by shepherds guided to the spot by an unnatural light. Far from timeless, the popular legend of Our Lady of Montserrat can be dated as having emerged in the late seventeenth century. Accounts prior to the seventeenth century were less concerned with the origin of the image than with its powers; and

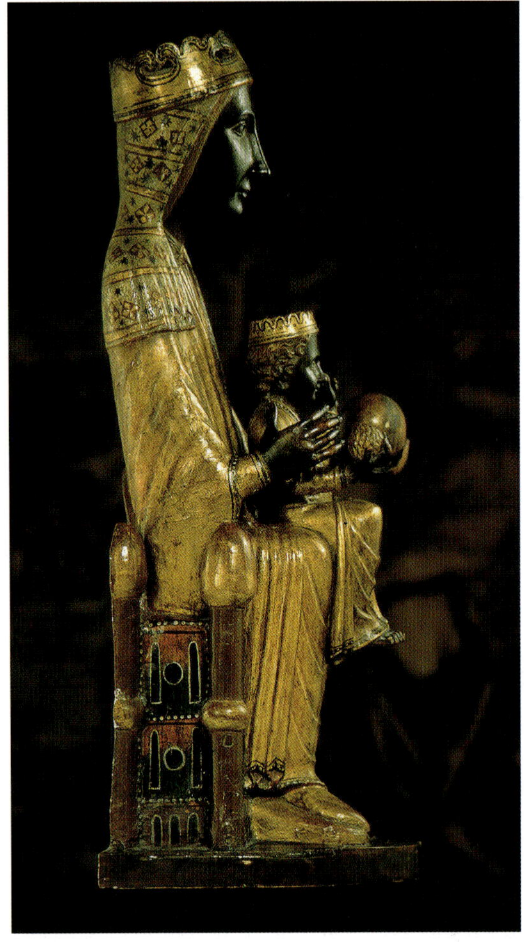

Fig. 86. Spanish, *Our Lady of Montserrat*, 12th c., polychromed wood, Abbey and Sanctuary of Montserrat, Spain

before the sixteenth century, little mention was made of its darkened skin—indicating less a change in the statue's appearance than in the way medieval and Renaissance authors viewed the external world.

Late twelfth- and thirteenth-century pilgrim manuscripts did not refer directly to the statue at all but rather to the miraculous altar where prayers were answered and needs addressed, thanks to the intervention of Mary, whose painted wooden image sat on the altar.[51] The early identification of the cult of Our Lady of Montserrat with the altar not the figure indicates the ability of medieval Catalonians to distinguish between the Madonna and her statue. Such discrimination is also demonstrated by the endurance of a cult (or, ritual devotion) beyond the physical life of a particular object. When the wooden statue of Our Lady of Einsiedeln, Switzerland burned in 1465, a new sculpture was made, and the cult continued as before.[52]

Conversely, the later history of the cult of Montserrat demonstrates that over time the image did come to dominate pilgrims' accounts. Prior to 1500, gifts from the devout consisted primarily of silver lamps to light the shrine; after 1500, gifts of jewelry and cloth were given to adorn the statue. In the sixteenth and seventeenth centuries, the cult expanded throughout Europe and the Americas, accompanied by replicas of the original image.[53] It was this attachment to representations of Mary as Our Lady of this and Our Lady of that—to which particular local favor and preferential patronage were attributed—and the excessive regard many believers held for specific Marian figures that led Protestants to equate the worship of images with idolatry and describe the popular cult of Mary as "Mariolatry."

Though many believers probably did esteem Mary too highly, their feelings contradicted the teachings of their faith. In church teachings, only God may be worshipped, but saints may be venerated (paid homage) and asked to intercede on

behalf of the faithful. Special status was (and is)
accorded to Mary, who ranked above all other
saints, though below Jesus and God the Father.[54]
Such status is implicit in the numerous artworks
depicting saints venerating Mary, in which the
artist portrays her in an elevated position, whether
in heaven (as in the devotions of Catherine dei
Ricci and Francis of Assisi) [figs. 66, 136] or on
earth (as in the kneeling posture adopted by saint
Stephen) [fig. 60]. In the delicate watercolor, *Virgin and Child with Saints Hugh of Lincoln and Bridget of Sweden* [fig. 87], this hierarchy becomes explicit;
one could imagine the owner in prayer to the two
patron saints (shown standing on the ground),
asking them to intercede with Mary (shown floating above), to mediate on his or her behalf with
(an undepicted) God.

*　　*　　*

Mary's presence might also be said to underlie or
be implicit in one's devotion to local or patron
saints whose own holiness was modeled on Mary's.
Throughout Christian history, pious women were
urged to emulate Mary's behavior and that of the
female saints. A review of the women saints whose
stories were collected in Jacobus de Voragine's *Legenda aurea* (*Golden Legend*) of 1255–1266 reveals
chastity as the principal virtue women were meant
to learn. Although some of the earliest female martyr-saints were not virgins, including the Carthaginian noblewoman Perpetua (circa 182–203),
mother of a small child, and her slave Felicity (died
203), who gave birth while in prison, the majority
of female saints popular in the Middle Ages seem
as eager to preserve their virginity as their faith.

These virtuous women, almost always of noble
birth (i.e., with much to renounce), admirably
chose religion and chastity over the comforts and
pleasures of secular life and thus were seen as fit
role models and followers of Mary. Yet to protect
their virginity, they also defied their parents, disobeyed local customs, and asserted their wills—

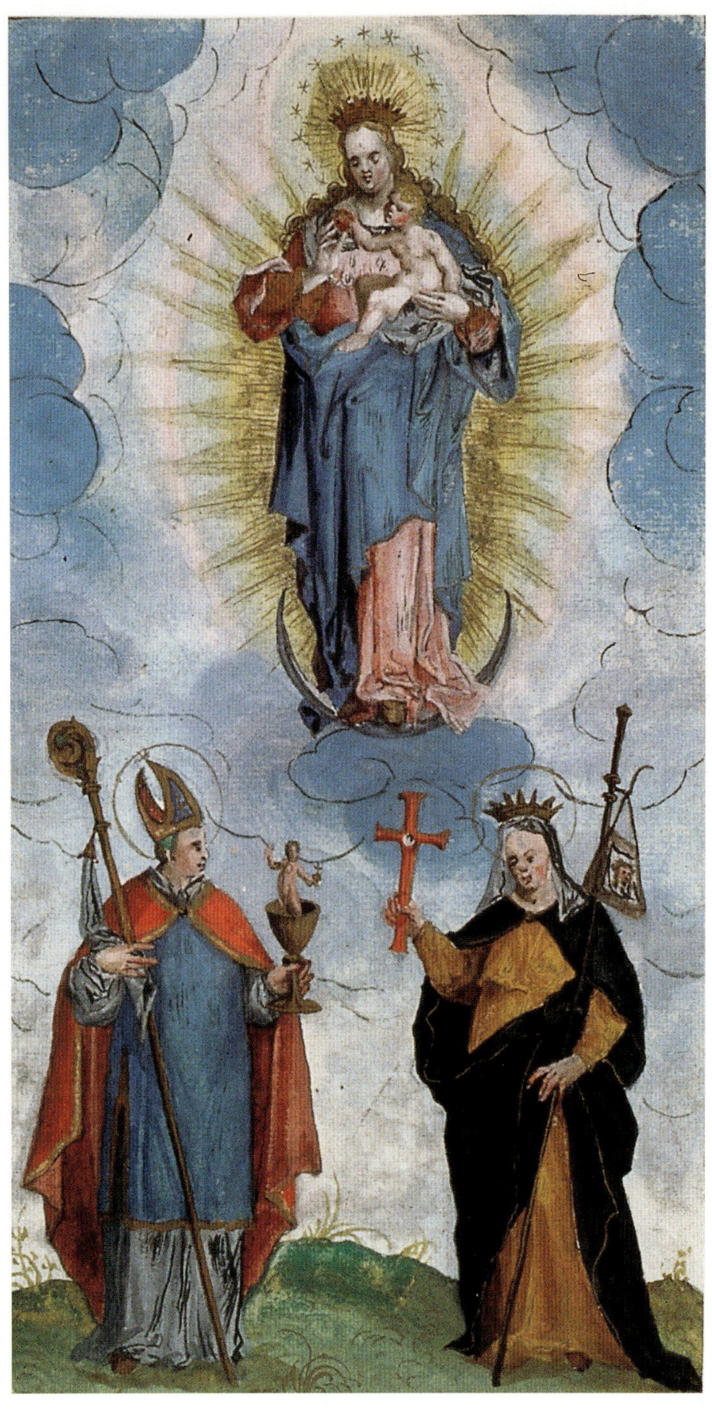

Fig. 87. German, *Virgin and Child with Saint Bridget of Sweden and Hugh of Lincoln*, late 17th c., watercolor, gouache, and ink

Regarding Mary　　91

conduct considered inappropriate for women, contrary to patriarchal values, and inconsistent with Mary's model of obedience.[55] In the name of chastity, saintly women were defiant, deviant, and anything but meek. One wonders if the hearers of these tales perceived this double message. Judging from contemporary behavior, one message seemed to penetrate: if a woman did not wish to marry or have children, she could pledge herself to emulate Mary's example of chastity, poverty, and holiness, and enter a convent.[56]

In exchange for obedience to the church, women gained independence from their families and control over their bodies. The Jesuits, a new order in the sixteenth century, openly encouraged young women to avoid arranged marriages by entering convents (but as they had no female branch, did not directly bear the brunt of the defied parents' anger).[57] In a society in which single women had few opportunities and little status, convents offered opportunities for education and spiritual development. Women monastics pursued within religious life paths otherwise closed to women: running hospitals and charities, electing officers to rotated terms of leadership, and exercising internal authority over community and property.[58] Exceptional nuns like saints Clare of Assisi (1194–1253) and Catherine dei Ricci (1522–1590) corresponded with high church officials and were consulted by popes [fig. 66]. The attendance of pope Innocent IV (d. 1254) at the funeral of saint Clare is

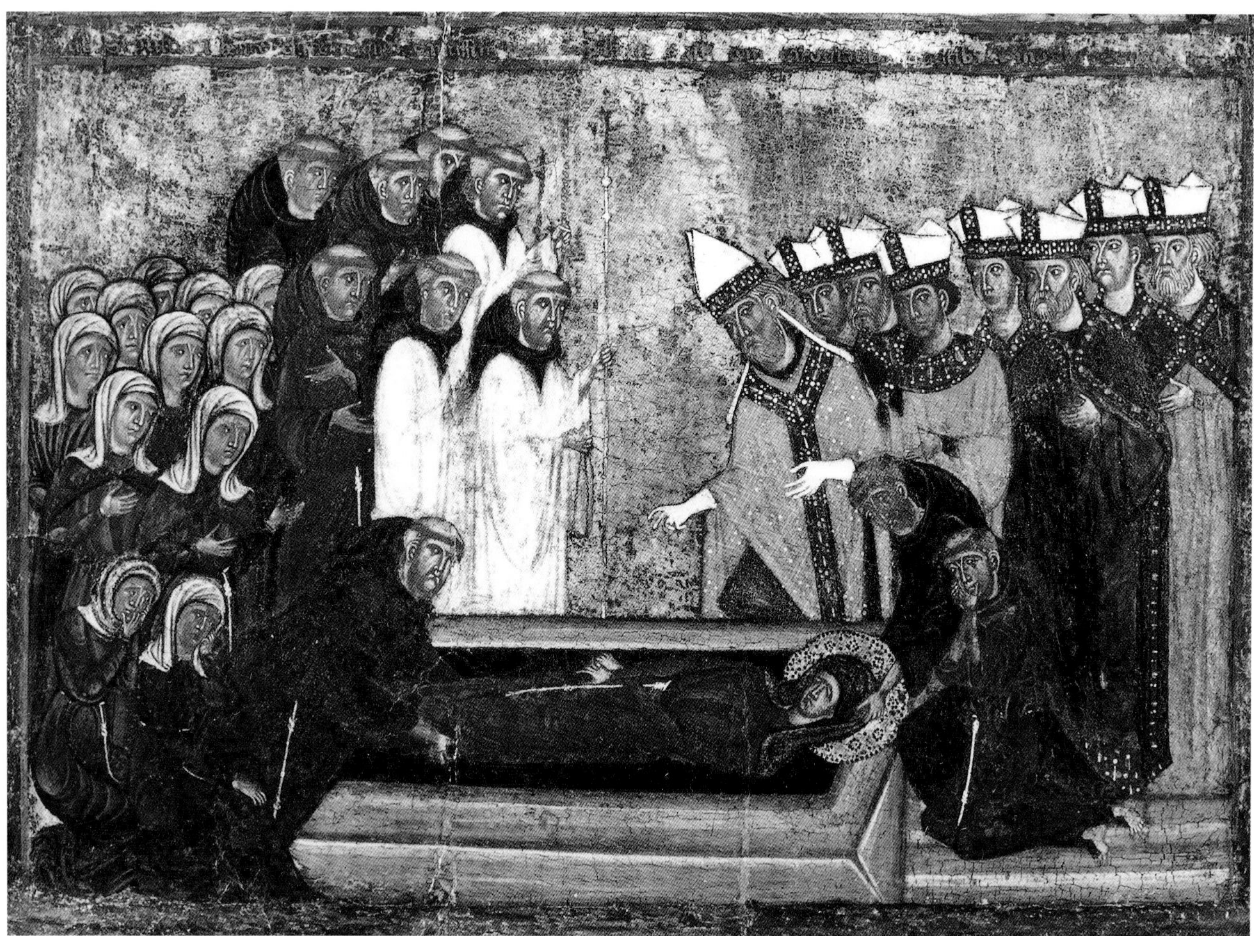

Fig. 88. Italian from Umbria, *Funeral of Saint Clare* (lower half of altarpiece), 1290s, tempera on panel

recorded in the lower scene of the *duecento* panel [fig. 88].

Convent life provided a reasonable alternative to marriage with a partner not of one's choosing, a way to evade the very real possibility of an early death in childbirth, and was, in the church's view, the best way a Christian woman could emulate Mary. As Francis of Assisi (1181–1226) wrote to saint Clare, founder of a female branch of the Franciscan order, of the noble path chosen by Clare and her convent sisters, "Each one [of you] will be crowned queen in heaven with the Virgin Mary."[59] Influenced by nineteenth-century anti-Catholicism, Romanticism, and a soft-porn literary genre fashioned around convent escapes, many today view monasteries as places where unwanted daughters were imprisoned against their will.[60] Geert Grote (1340–1384), the anticlerical founder of the lay Brethren of the Common Life and *Devotio moderna* practice, also complained that dowry inflation created economic motives for families to place daughters in religious orders. Nevertheless, fourteenth- and fifteenth-century postplague demographics were such that women were in great demand, and only the "most undesirable" might be obliged to enter a convent against her inclination.[61]

In reality, and for whatever motive, religious or worldly, there was no shortage of women wishing to enter religious life. In Cologne, only two decades after its 1229 founding as a refuge for prostitutes, the Penitential Convent of Mary Magdalene was completely occupied by middle-class nuns. The excessive demand by ordinary middle-class women for places within city convents led to the displacement of the more-marginalized clientèle the new order had hoped to attract.[62] Having a daughter enter a convent was less expensive than having her marry, for no elaborate wedding feasts were necessary, but it was not the economic boon some have imagined it to be. Families provided nuns as well as brides with dowries to support them in their new life. While rules varied widely among orders and across centuries, in general, a postulant's property and capital were made over to the convent *mense*, or communal funds, while she received the *prebend*, or income generated by her dowry, to pay for her upkeep and needs of food, clothing, charity contributions, masses, and even maidservants.[63]

The economic inequalities of secular life followed women into religious life, where dowry provisions imposed an internal class structure. Scholarships were available to provide poor women (or disobedient daughters preferring religious vows to marriage vows) with the dowries required to enter religious orders, to educate young girls, and to help support the many women—especially widows and *malmaritate* (the "badly married," or battered wives)—who opted to live in convents without taking formal vows.[64] Distinctions were drawn, though, between choir nuns, whose dowries freed them to devote their lives to prayer, and lay nuns, who earned their keep through kitchen and housework. The lay sisters also recited simple prayers rather than the full monastic offices that (along with income-generating activities such as needlework and manuscript copying) occupied much of the choir nuns' days.[65]

As far as women were concerned, their economic freedom was greater in religious life, where they managed the income of their dowries, than in secular life, where husbands controlled both principal and income, and widows received back only a portion of their inheritance, the bulk passing to male heirs. (Of course, the dowries of most individual nuns went directly to the community; only the most powerful or wealthiest—conditions that often went hand in hand—retained an active role in their own financial management. Nevertheless, ordinary women had an indirect sense of ownership through their stake in communal welfare.) For single women living five or six centuries ago, their loss by not marrying (not only sexual expression but also family life) was balanced by gains in the convent. Through convent life, they obtained not only education, economic independence, and

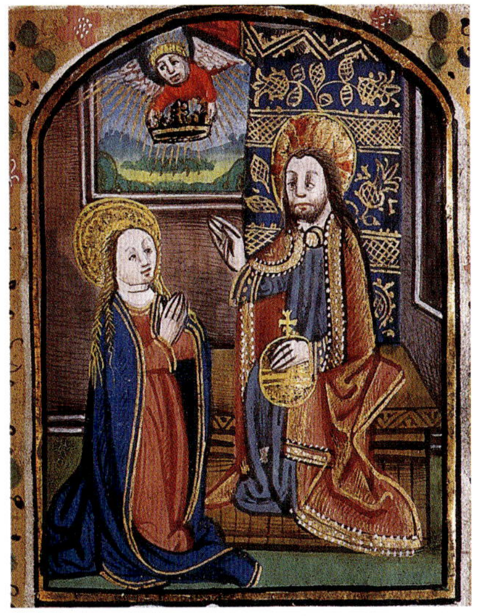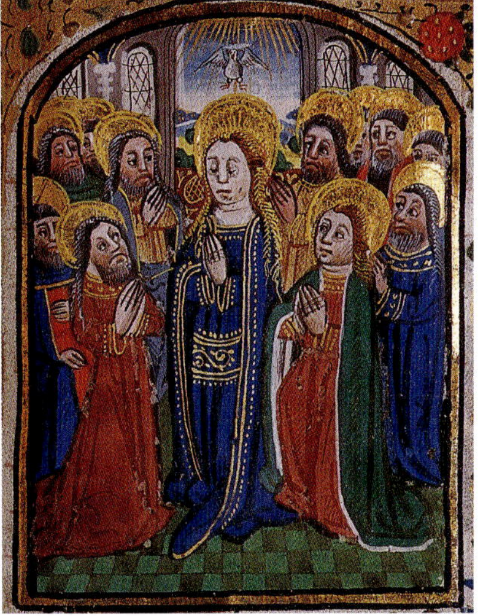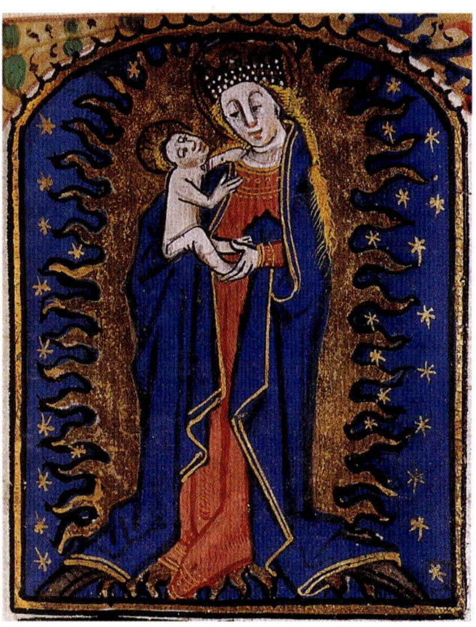

From left to right:
Fig. 89. French from Amiens, *Coronation of the Virgin*, from a ca. 1480 Book of Hours, half-page illumination accompanying Compline, folio 110r
Fig. 90. French from Amiens, *Pentecost*, from a ca. 1480 Book of Hours, half-page illumination accompanying the Hours of the Holy Spirit, folio 121r
Fig. 91. French from Amiens, *Mary as the Woman Clothed with the Sun*, half-page illumination from a ca. 1480 Book of Hours, folio 23r

self-determination, but also the means to secure eternal salvation. After all, "what would it profit a [wo]man if [s]he gains the whole world and forfeits [her] soul?" (Matt. 16:26); salvation, then as now, was the primary reason to take religious vows.

8. Coronation

Compline was the final office read at the close of day by those reciting the Hours of the Blessed Virgin. Its readings centered around (and were accompanied by illustrations of) the CORONATION OF THE VIRGIN, a reference to the moment when Mary rises into heaven and is crowned its queen by her son Jesus [figs. 5, 89, 114]. There, according to the pre-Reformation church and post-Reformation Catholic church, she acted not as Jesus' equal but as a mediator for those on earth hoping to gain his sympathy through her intercession.

In art, and in life, the link between Mary's queenship and secular monarchy could be drawn either to support or to challenge earthly authority. In early Christian art, Jesus and Mary were portrayed crowned and robed like emperors to indicate that their power was greater than the power of the temporal rulers of Rome and Byzantium. Among pagan regimes, this borrowing of conventions reminded Christians that their ultimate loyalty was owed to a higher force than secular king-

ship.[66] Later, when Christianity became the official state religion of much of Europe, the same regal elements of Christian art were employed to justify the divine right of kings and queens to rule and serve as God's surrogates on earth [fig. 30].

Court records leave no doubt that royalty wished to link the roles of the secular and heavenly queens. Royal women styled themselves as intermediaries between their ruling husbands and their subjects, just as Mary acted as intercessor between Jesus and humanity. At their coronations and in their official portraits, English queens wore their hair loose, invoking comparison with the Virgin Mary and the ideal state of maidenhood.[67] A pageant held in Coventry welcomed queen Margaret of Anjou (1430–1482), wife of England's Henry VI (1421–1471), with hopes for a fertile reign and marriage so that "like as mankynde was gladdid by the birght of Jhesus, so shall this empyre [j]ioy the birthe of your bodye."[68]

Within the scriptures one finds no reference to Mary's CORONATION IN HEAVEN, nor her means of arriving there. All four Gospels give full attention to Jesus' death on the cross, resurrection from the dead, and ascent into heaven, but they say little of Mary's later life. Neither the New Testament nor the Qur'an mentions her death. In the 23 books that make up the the New Testament beyond the four gospels and come next both in sequence and historic reference, Mary appears only once—in the first chapter of the first book to follow the Gospels. Luke, in the book of Acts, notes the presence of the (now) eleven apostles "together with the women and Mary the mother of Jesus, and with his brothers" (Acts 1:14). Though Mary is not mentioned again in the next chapter's narration of the Pentecost, when the Holy Spirit descends onto the gathered disciples, artists frequently placed her at the center of this nascent congregation of believers [figs. 33, 90].

Few current biblical scholars support the identification of Mary as "the woman clothed with the sun, with the moon under her feet, and on her head a crown of twelve stars" described in the Book of Revelations (12:1). Nevertheless, Mary's association with the woman of the Book of Revelations was common in medieval and early modern times, even though the passage continues, "she was with child and she cried out in her pangs of birth, in anguish for delivery" (Rev. 12:2), a form of childbirth more in keeping with Eve than Mary, or with the Qur'an's portrayal of Mary's delivery.[69] Artists often depicted Mary within an almond-shaped *mandorla* to represent the solar cloth; the moon was often entwined with a serpent or dragon to represent Christianity's triumph over paganism through Mary's triumph over evil [fig. 91]. Yet the golden aureole, silver crescent moon, and crown of stars of the Woman Clothed with the Sun became features of the iconography of Mary in representations of both the ASSUMPTION and her IMMACULATE CONCEPTION, events that follow her death and precede her birth.

Few elements of Mary's story have raised as much controversy as these events said to have preceded and followed her life on earth. In early apocryphal texts such as the fourth-century *Transitus Mariae* (*Transition of Mary*), which dates from the period of a unified church, the scattered apostles return from their missions to mourn Mary's passing, then lay her body in a tomb, which three

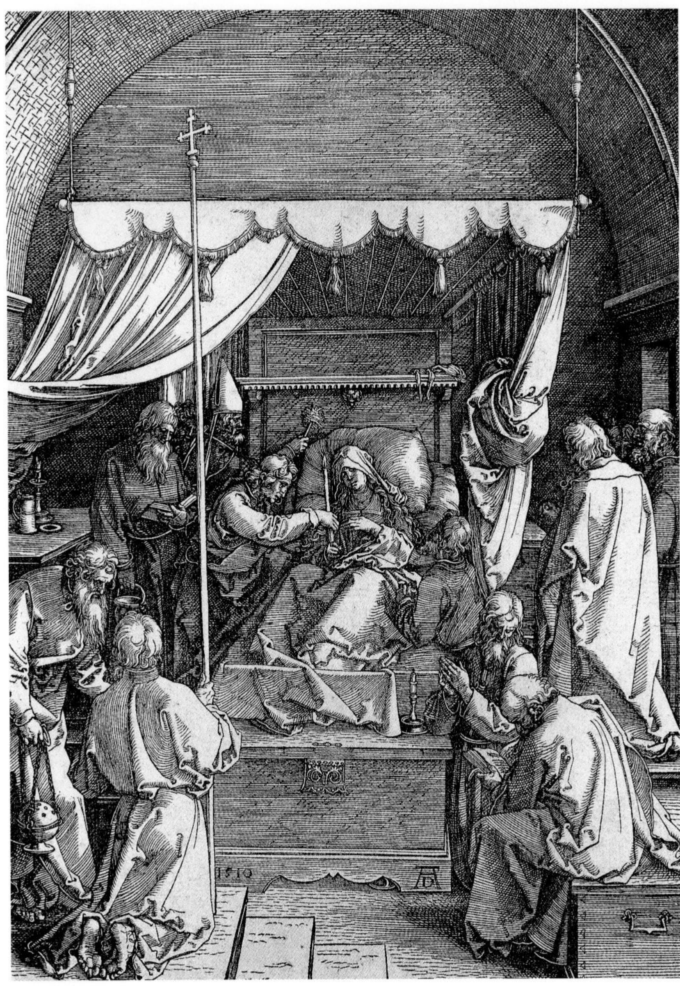

Fig. 92 (above). Albrecht Dürer, *Death of the Virgin*, 1510, woodcut from the *Life of the Virgin* series

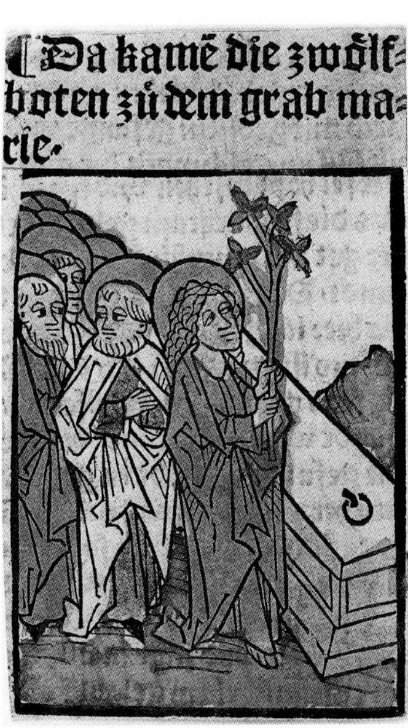

Fig. 93 (left). German from Augsburg, *Burial of the Virgin*, 1482, hand-colored woodcut from the *New Marriage and Passion of Jesus*, plate 67

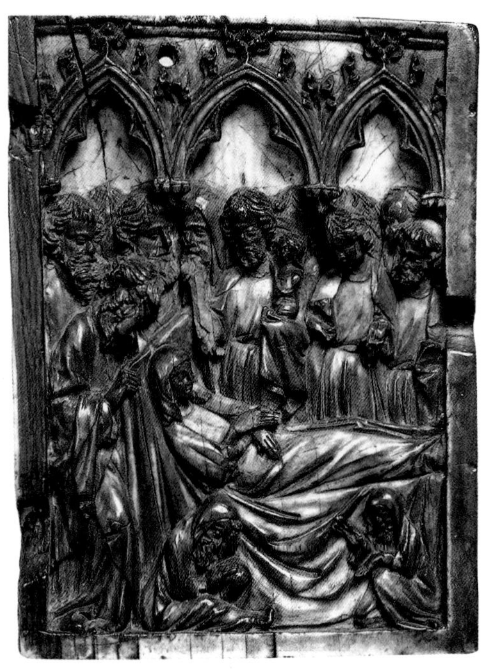

Fig. 94. French from Île de France, *Dormition of the Virgin*, 14th c., one wing of an ivory diptych (shown actual size)

days later is found empty [figs. 92, 93].[70] Even this bare-bones account raised controversy, with theologians disputing the state of Mary's body during the interval in her tomb. According to Orthodox teaching, Mary's soul, upon her death, was carried immediately to heaven; her death is referred to as *koimesis*, her DORMITION or falling asleep.[71] Days later, according to Orthodox tradition, Mary's body was found missing from her grave, giving rise to the teaching of her bodily assumption to heaven.[72] A miniature *Dormition* in ivory [fig. 94], dating from early fourteenth-century France but employing imagery developed in eleventh-century Byzantium, depicts the apostles gathered at Mary's bedside, while her soul, portrayed as a small child, rests at center in Jesus' arm, a touching reversal of the traditional VIRGIN AND CHILD posture.

Circa 600, the Eastern church fixed August 15th as the date of the Feast of the Dormition, and the Western church followed within half a century. By the ninth century, the Western name was changed to the Feast of the Assumption to emphasize the subsequent discovery of Mary's empty tomb (traditionally recorded to have taken place three days later, in echo of the scriptural account of Christ's resurrection), and the ASSUMPTION (or raising) of her body into heaven. Early Christian and medieval art primarily represented the end of Mary's life by depicting a prone horizontal body; but following a series of visions by saint Elisabeth of Schönau (1126–1164), Mary's body began to be shown rising vertically.[73] Nevertheless the Catholic religion did not define its teaching of Mary's ASSUMPTION as dogma (a required truth of faith) until 1950, and the Orthodox faith, while affirming the tradition of her bodily assumption, has never declared it a doctrine of faith.

Early Protestants, not surprisingly, rejected the nonscriptural teachings of Mary's ASSUMPTION, CORONATION, and HEAVENLY QUEENSHIP, as well as the doctrine of her IMMACULATE CONCEPTION. When Martin Luther (1463–1546) removed the ASSUMPTION from the Lutheran calendar in 1544, he declared, "The feast of the Assumption is totally papist, full of idolatry and without foundation in the Scriptures. But we, even though Mary has gone to heaven, should not bother about how she went there."[74] It is worth noting, however, that Luther waited over 25 years after his 1517 break with the official church before taking this definitive step, and that he did retain the feast days of the Annunciation (March 25th), the Purification (February 2nd), Visitation (July 2nd), and Christ's Ascension (celebrated forty days after Easter).[75]

The IMMACULATE CONCEPTION, a far more controversial teaching, was formally defined as Catholic dogma in 1854, a full century earlier than the less-contested ASSUMPTION. This doctrine, often confused with the VIRGIN BIRTH, refers to Mary's birth free of original sin, not to Mary's giving birth to Jesus. It asserts that when Mary was conceived by her mother, saint Anne, she was already in a state of absolute purity, making her fit to later become the chosen vehicle for Jesus' conception by the Holy Spirit. Equally confusing is the visual representation of the IMMACULATE CONCEP-

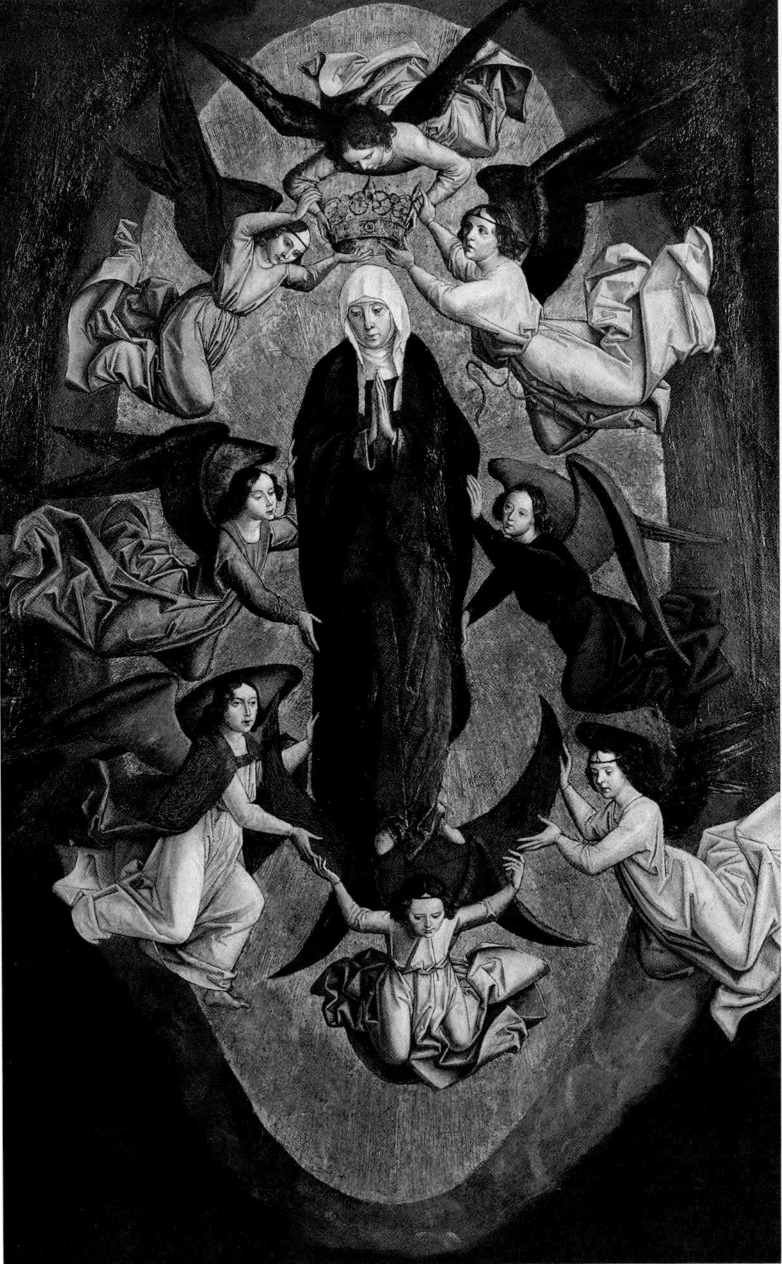

In Pedro Ber-
ruguete's circa 1485
painting of the *Assump-
tion*, Mary is isolated
against a gilded *mandorla*
guided by seven angels,
with no visual cue to
establish whether she
gazes downward in
farewell to her earthly
existence or out of habit-
ual modesty [fig. 95].
The work is powerful in
its gravity and abstract in
its simplicity—doctrine
reduced to an elemental
core. Context may have
made the subject more
readily identifiable to
early viewers, as the
Assumption originally
formed the central panel
of a now-dispersed polyp-
tych, which also featured
panels of the *Birth of
Mary, Annunciation, Visi-
tation*, and *Death of Mary*,
above a *banco* (lower tier)
of the Old Testament fig-
ures of *David, Solomon,
Isaiah*, and *Jeremiah*[76]
[figs. 118, 119]. Mary's
head covering in this
painting also indicates a
mature woman rather
than an adolescent, though one finds many
ASSUMPTION images in which a youthful Mary is
shown, including Agostino Carracci's *Assumption
of the Virgin*, seen in a drawing made after the
1592/93 painting [fig. 96].

Perhaps the greatest clue to the painting's subject is its date. This panel was executed at some
point between Berruguete's circa 1483 return

TION, which can easily be mistaken for the
ASSUMPTION, as both feature Mary in mid-air moving down to earth or up to heaven. (Many of us
faced with art history exams were told to judge by
her gaze—does Mary look downward to her terres-
trial home or upward to a crowd of welcoming
angels?—but apparently not all artists followed
our professors' advice.)

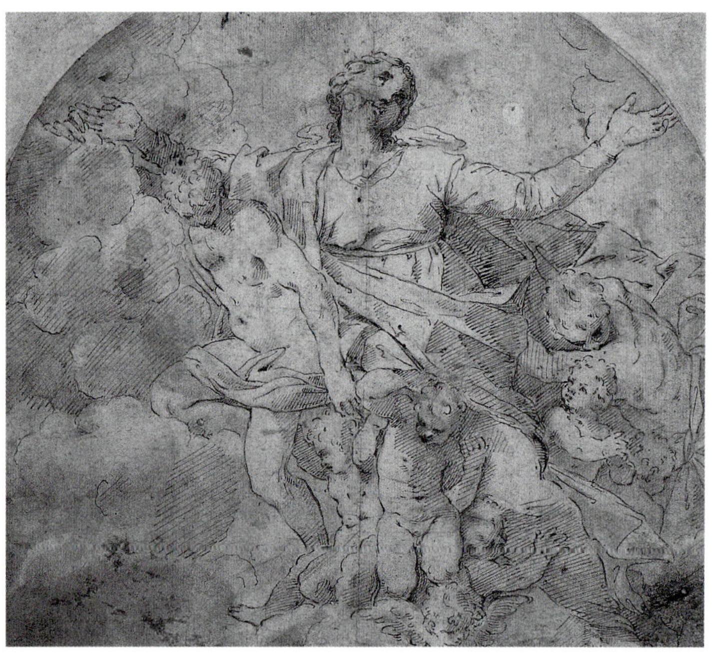

from Italy (where he had served as painter to duke Federigo da Montefeltro in Urbino) and his death in 1503.[77] Few visual representations of the IMMACULATE CONCEPTION are known before 1500, though they became a staple of Catholic Reformation art, featuring prominently in Spanish art of the sixteenth and seventeenth centuries and in the art of their New World colonies [fig. 97].[78] Rare early IMMACULATE CONCEPTION images that survive do not conform to Counter-Reformation iconography, which Spanish painter and art theorist Francisco Pacheco (1564–1654) described in his 1649 *El arte de la pintura (Art of Painting)* as follows:

> In this loveliest of mysteries, Our Lady should be painted as a beautiful young girl, 12 or 13 years old, in the flower of her youth. . . . She is surrounded by the sun, an oval sun of white and ochre [colored pigments], which sweetly blends into the sky. Rays of light emanate from her head, around which is a ring of twelve stars. An imperial crown adorns her head. . . . Under her feet is the moon.[79]

Many aspects of IMMACULATE CONCEPTION iconography—including the oval sunburst, shining rays, crown, and moon—are prefigured in Berruguete's rendering of the *Assumption*. The golden *mandorla* and silver crescent at her feet link this Mary to the unnamed woman of Revelations, and would become in the sixteenth century common attributes of Mary in the IMMACULATE CONCEPTION, but not regular features of ASSUMPTIONS (in which Mary rested more frequently on clouds rather than a moon [figs. 65, 96]. Given its unusual treatment and pivotal date, Berruguete's panel may well be an important prototype of IMMACULATE CONCEPTION imagery still in a developmental phase.

Whether moving toward heaven or descending from it, Mary operates under the control of outside forces. Language is not innocent; we speak of

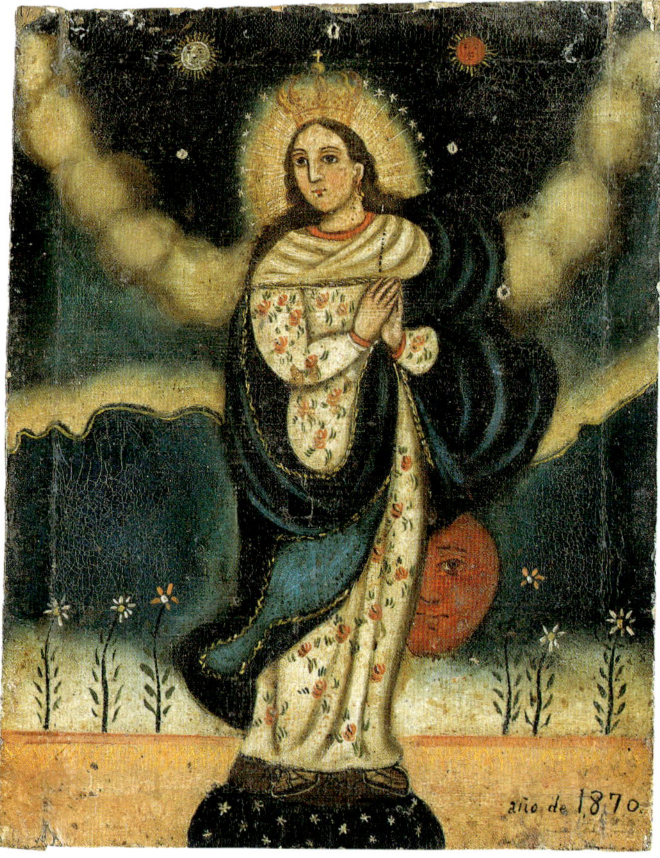

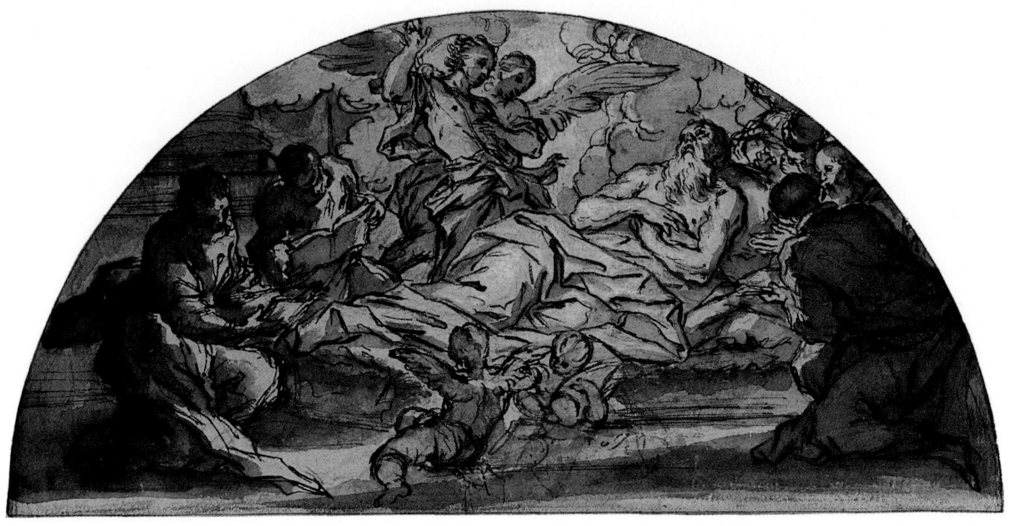

Mary's body being *assumed* into heaven, whereas Jesus *ascends* after the Resurrection, implying his reliance on his own powers, and Mary's dependency on God's actions. Muhammad also ascended to heaven from a site in Jerusalem, now occupied by the beautiful tile-covered mosque known as the Dome of the Rock. In the Hebrew Bible, the prophets Moses, Enoch, and Elijah are said to have ascended to heaven—Elijah in a fiery chariot—while an apocryphal first-century text describes the ascension of the prophet Isaiah [fig. 98].[80] As for women, Mary, and occasionally Mary Magdalene, have been shown by artists being transported heavenward, usually with an escort of *putti* and angels. Rarely does Mary travel under her own agency; at her ASSUMPTION, as at the ANNUNCIATION, she is the passive recipient of God's grace.

Mary's ASSUMPTION and IMMACULATE CONCEPTION, like her freedom from sin, sex, and bodily decay, further distanced her from human experience and, in some minds, from all humanity. Many Christians supported one doctrine but not the other, believing in her ASSUMPTION and QUEENSHIP as the just reward of an extraordinary life, but arguing that no human save Jesus could be born free of sin. The two great medieval mendicant (nonmonastic, alms-dependent) orders—the Franciscans and the Dominicans—both supported the ASSUMPTION but took opposing stances on the IMMACULATE CONCEPTION. Dominican theologian Thomas Aquinas (1225–1274) argued that every act of sexual intercourse carried "pollution" to the womb, and since Mary had been conceived by conventional methods, she could not be free of the taint of original sin.[81] Franciscan friars, by contrast, began to observe the Feast of the Immaculate Conception in 1263.[82]

The Council of Trent (1545–1563), convened in response to the upheavals of the Protestant Reformation, sidestepped the controversy entirely. In 1054, the Christian church had formally divided into Eastern (Orthodox) and Western branches, and after 1517 the Western portion had undergone a violent separation into Protestant and Catholic allegiances. To rule on contested points of Marian theology risked further fracturing the Catholic church at its most vulnerable point in history.[83] Doctrinal disputes had been only one cause of the sixteenth-century rupture, however; resentment over religious practices were as much to blame as irreconcilable beliefs. While dissenting priests fought over questions of salvation by faith alone, the laity fumed over moral depravity among allegedly celibate clergy, and the

Regarding Mary   99

costs imposed by the church to maintain elaborate rituals.[84]

In Rostock, Mecklenburg, a town of 10,000 inhabitants, there were 182 functioning altars, each requiring furnishings and donations to finance liturgical services.[85] The practice of granting indulgences—documents officially remitting time that would be spent in purgatory after death in punishment of sins on earth—to those who made charitable contributions to the church (as well as those who performed other penances such as helping the poor, making pilgrimages, and fighting crusades) came to be viewed as religion for sale and evidence of a corrupt Roman hierarchy. A circa 1530 anti-Catholic broadsheet from Vienna bore the satirical title *The Pope Fleeces His Sheep*.[86]

As far as the average sixteenth-century citizen was concerned, which form of Christianity one ended up practicing at the end of the Reformation period was determined as much by geography as by theology. Even before Constantine converted to Christianity taking his subjects along with him, religion had been largely a matter of nationality [fig. 99] (save for Jews, who were thus doubly outsiders).[87] As the assembled princes of the Holy Roman empire ruled at the Peace of Augsburg in 1555: *cuius regio, eius religio* (whose region, his religion). Each ruler was thus free to decide whether his region remained Catholic or became Protestant, a decision that depended in part on whether individuals felt it would be to their advantage to break off relations with Rome.[88] Hence, while Protestant preachers launched attacks on the supposed arrogance and over-aggrandizement of Mary's celestial queenship, local sovereigns assessed how a shift to the new noncentralized religion might advance the interests of worldly kingship.

Women were active participants in the upheavals of the Reformation period, not only maintaining families and businesses while their husbands were away fighting, but also joining street mobs, leading riots, and defending their towns. Some of their names are known to us, including two women from the Netherlands: Kenau Hasselaar Simonsdr, a Protestant sympathizer (and middle-age widow) who led a rebellion of 300 women in Haarlem in 1573, and Magdalena Moon, a young unmarried Catholic credited with saving the city of Leiden in 1574.[89] Municipal unrest and street fighting in the northern Netherlands were particularly vehement, as religious reform was equated with national liberation from their Spanish rulers who were staunchly Catholic. Many of the social restraints placed on women were suspended during these decades of crisis. In the name of religion, women escaped the strictures of accepted female behavior and demonstrated strength, competence, and leadership. Some men did object to this loud, disobedient, and highly unfeminine behavior, claiming such "impure" conduct constituted a threat to the social order. Other men—realizing that women were less likely to be arrested for civic unrest and less likely to be convicted if brought to trial—put them at the heads of the protests.[90]

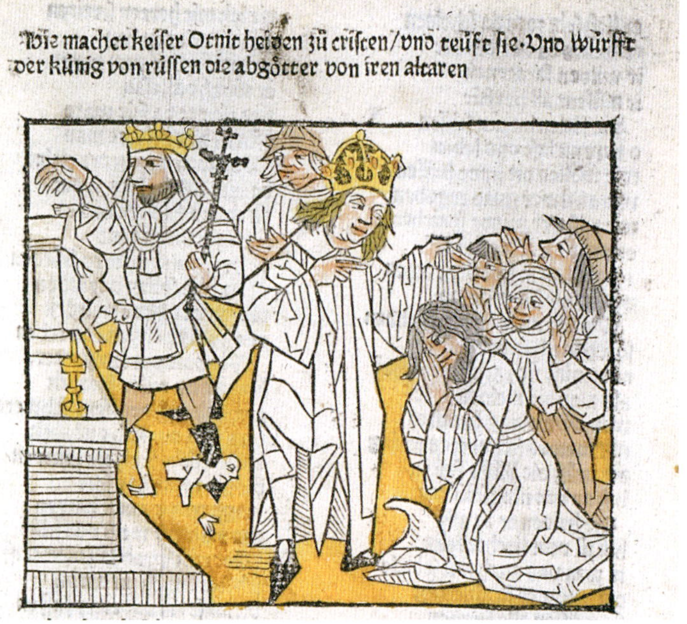

Fig. 99. German from Strasbourg, *King Ortnit Christens the Heathens*, 1483, hand-colored woodcut from the *Book of Heroes*

Despite the many changes the Reformation brought to European society, the sobering truth is that little changed for women, though many had expected the religious revolution to improve their lot. The two religions differed somewhat on policies that affected women's lives—Protestants demoting marriage to a civil rather than a sacramental act, Catholics promoting religious life over marriage—but they agreed on women's status, expecting them to be "silent, chaste, and obedient" to husbands, pastors, and communities. Some Protestant women hoped to become preachers and leaders of new congregations, but they soon learned that Luther's call for a "priesthood of all believers" did not apply to them. The new Protestant sects had no official role for the strong, competent women who helped bring about reform. Former priests and monks were given the option to become pastors; former nuns were advised to become wives and mothers.[91]

Indeed, with the closing of convents in the Protestant territories, and the imposition of strict cloistering by church reformers in Catholic territories, women lost the one sphere where they had experienced both autonomy and purpose. The philanthropic network formerly run by nuns—shelters, hospitals, orphanages, schools, and other social service agencies—was turned over to municipal control; women might be employed in these institutions, but they were no longer in charge. Protestant women were told that the proper place to serve their church was in their home, by overseeing a Christian household and tending to the moral and religious instruction of children and servants.[92] Catholic women were encouraged to enclose themselves in convents or submerge themselves in family service. Suppression of Marian devotion left Protestant women with neither a religious role nor a role model. Mary remained present in the lives of Catholic women, but at a greater distance; the church's increasing focus on issues of her purity, and its promotion of ASSUMPTION and IMMACULATE CONCEPTION imagery, stressed ways

in which Mary transcended the human condition and emphasized the impossibility of any human being living up to her ideal standard.

LEGACY

Ostensibly Mary's story ends here, with her death or her passing, and her entry into heaven, where she may or may not have a role to play in the salvation story, depending on which religious interpretation one follows. For some people, she is a palpable living presence in their lives, guiding them from grace to grace and intervening when they falter and require pardon. For others, she is a vestige of an institution that once held great sway over society but now continues greatly diminished in power and impact. For still others, she is a symbol of the beliefs of families into which they were not born and cultures among whom they have yet to feel totally included. For almost everyone, she is a quiet, beautiful lady who arrives on Christmas cards, looks out from frames on museum visits, and occasionally shows up on book jackets or in foreign travelogues.

On the surface, nineteenth- and twentieth-century art seems to have little place for Mary, who had featured so prominently in the art of earlier centuries. It is all too easy to see Mary as an image of the past, particularly given the proliferation of Marian imagery in traditional Western art of the twelfth through eighteenth centuries, and thus all the more important not to let her story end at this juncture without addressing her impact on the visual arts beyond this period. A quick trip through the galleries of most museums can easily give one the sense that Mary faded away after the French Revolution, which (as was also said of the Reformation) freed artists and audiences to focus on themes other than religion, to explore secular life and daily experience, and eventually to invent Realism, Impressionism, Modernism, Expressionism,

Fig. 100 (below). Erich Heckel, *Geschwister (Siblings)*, 1913, woodcut

Fig. 101 (right). Otto Müller, *Zigeunermadonna (Gypsy Madonna)*, 1927, hand-colored lithograph from the *Gypsy Portfolio*

and other "isms." A closer look corrects this supposition.

Many artists of the nineteenth century—including the Pre-Raphaelites in England, the Nazarenes in Germany, and the Symbolists in France—deliberately chose Christian themes as their subject matter, while other artists, such as Eugène Delacroix, Gustave Doré, and Edouard Manet—better known for treating "modern" subjects—occasionally painted religious works.[1] The Cleveland Museum of Art owns a *Madonna and Child* painted by the surrealist Man Ray, while the Davis Museum collection includes a painting by Fernand Léger that turns the familiar woman-child pairing reminiscent of early Christian orant portraits into a fractured Cubist composition[2] [fig. 165]. Even had artists wished to change their focus completely, one cannot simply erase eighteen centuries of art built around the image of a single, extraordinary woman. Indeed, it is far from clear that anyone did wish to erase Mary, even those artists considered avant-garde.

For example, works by two German artists of the early twentieth century use familiar VIRGIN AND CHILD imagery—mother seated with child in her lap—for two distinct purposes. Erich Heckel (1883–1970) appropriated the traditional religious pose in his 1913 woodcut *Geschwister (Siblings)* [fig. 100] to demonstrate his break with artistic precedence, and to contrast the psychologically ambiguous relation between his two figures (whose intimacy is more apparent in the title than in the print) with the loving parental bond conveyed by images of the Madonna and Child.[3] Heckel's arrangement of the two figures in front of a window whose mullions form a cross further strengthens his allusion to and contrast with earlier works of art. Otto Müller (1874–1930), by

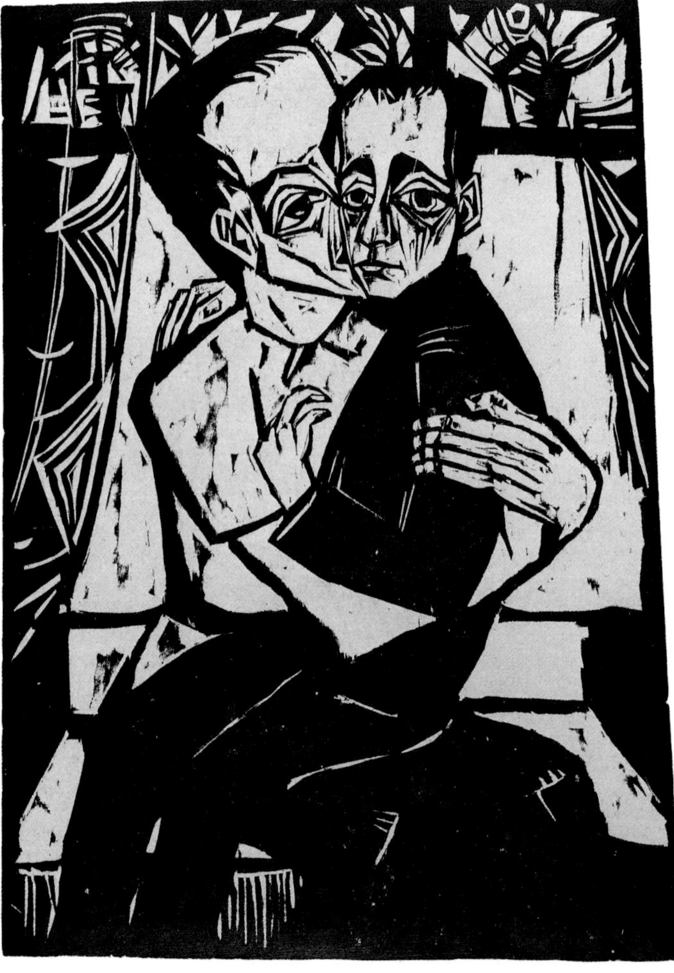

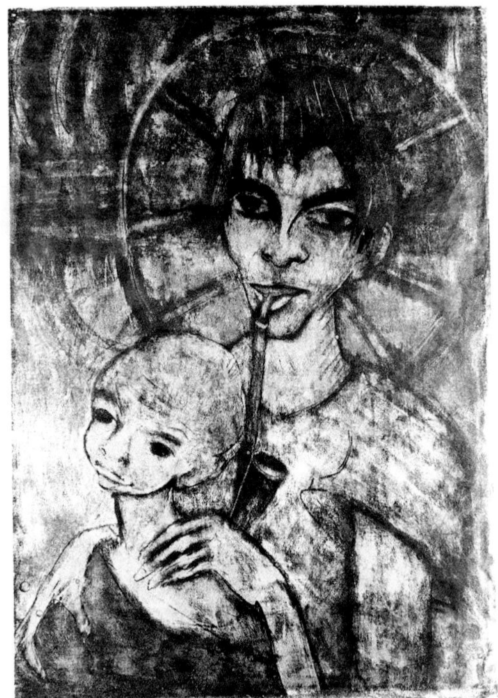

contrast, in his *Zigeunermadonna* (*Gypsy Madonna*) of 1927 [fig. 101], employed a pose associated with Mary and the infant Jesus to arouse sympathy for the Romany people among whom he had lived in Eastern Europe.[4] His choice of title acknowledges his debt to Christian art, while his placement of a wagon wheel behind the woman's head to simulate a halo confirms his respect for the marginalized mother. With Müller, as with Heckel, a modern work was designed with earlier artworks in mind, and its meaning deepened by its comparison to Marian antecedents.

For practitioners of the new art of photography, the adaptation of religious subject matter supported their argument that the camera was as much an artist's tool as the brush or burin (tool of the engraver). Early photographers such as Julia Margaret Cameron (1815–1879) helped gain acceptance for their work by designing photographs that reflected the style and subjects of the accepted media of painting, sculpting, and graphic art. Cameron's niece, Julia Jackson (1846–1895), posed as the Madonna on numerous occasions, as did Cameron's maid, Mary Hillier (1847–1936), and other family acquaintances. Though Wellesley's portrait does not bear the name *Madonna*, it is evocative of other images of Jackson by that title. *La Santa Julia* [fig. 102] was made in early 1867, shortly before Jackson's May wedding to Herbert Duckworth. During her marriage (which ended abruptly with Duckworth's sudden death in 1870), Julia Jackson did not pose for her aunt. Victorian society considered it unsuitable for married women to model for artists, and so, ironically, when Julia Jackson ceased to be a virgin, she ceased to pose as the Virgin Mary.[5]

The next generation of photographers continued to produce works that invited comparison with the religious art of earlier periods. Gertrude Käsebier (1852–1934) created her *Adoration* negative in 1897, manipulating it in the developing bath to approximate the appearance of a charcoal drawing [fig. 159]. While any depiction of woman and child

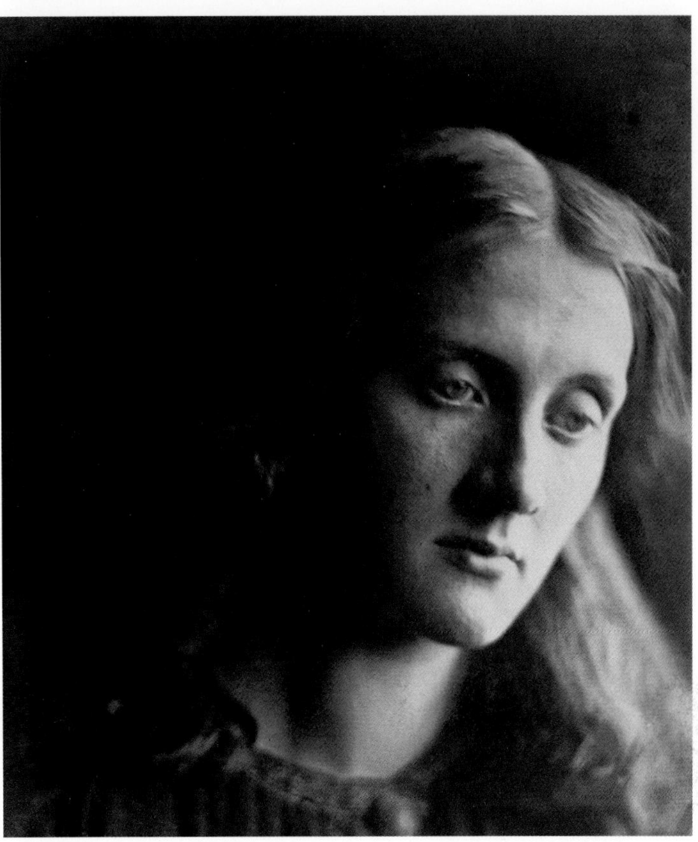

Fig. 102. Julia Margaret Cameron, *La Santa Julia*, 1867, albumen print

can be said to evoke to the gentle maternal qualities of Mary, Käsebier's title as well as image alludes to traditional imagery of the Virgin Mary.[6]

Käsebier and other pictorialist (or symbolist) photographers altered their negatives and/or varied their developing process to produce unique photographic prints, strengthening their argument that photography was more than a method of mechanical reproduction. The museum's collection includes two prints of the *Heritage of Motherhood* made by Käsebier from the same circa 1904 negative, one cropped and shaded to emphasize the figure rather than the landscape, the other more tonal in appearance and moody in nature [figs. 103, 160]. There is little doubt that Käsebier drew on Marian imagery to compose this image of maternal suffering.[7] A version in the collection of the Detroit Institute of Arts [fig. 104] shows three crosses etched in the background to the left of the sitter (the poet Agnes

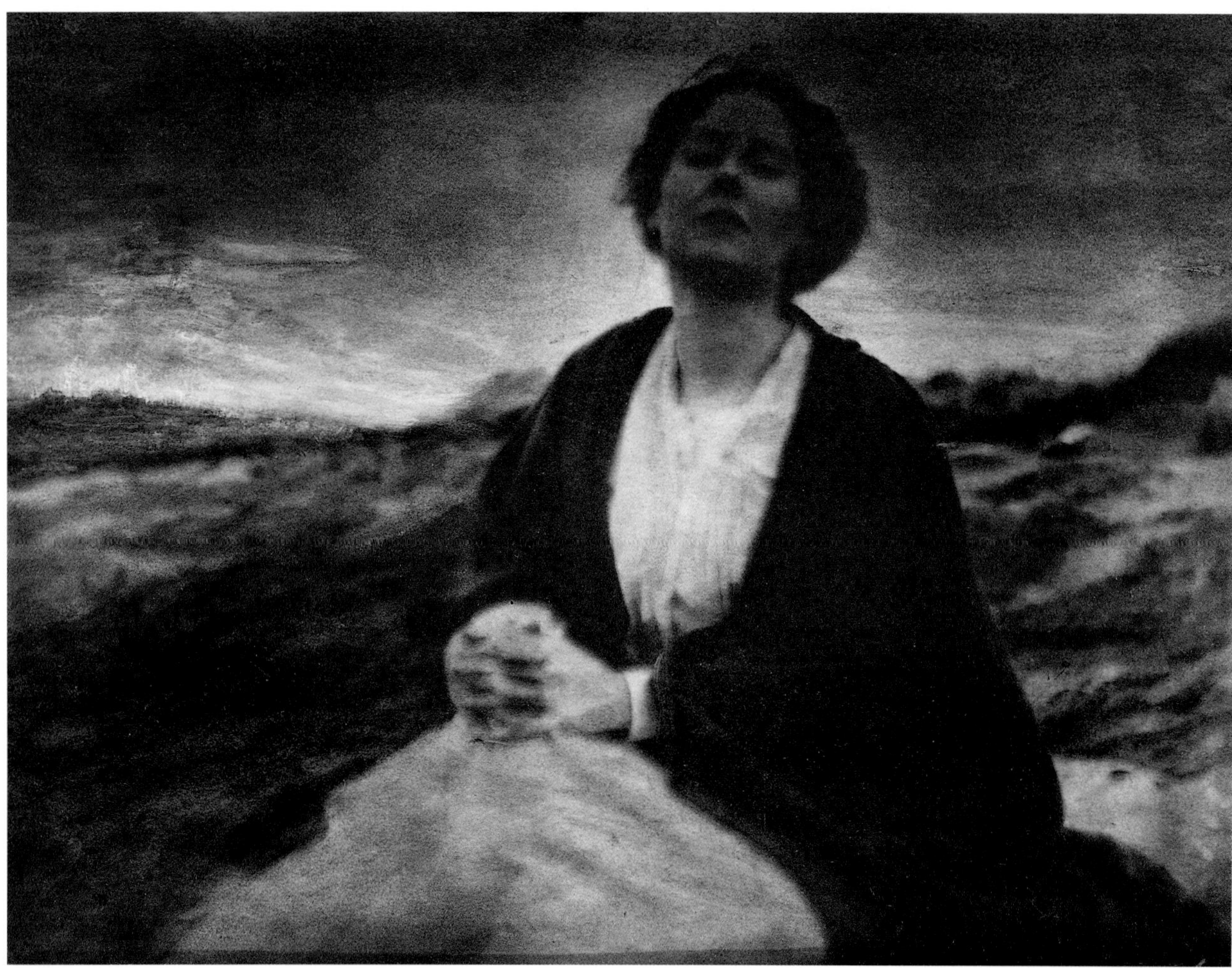

Lee), in reference to the hill of Calvary, site of the crucifixion. Previously it had been thought that Käsebier experimented with the Calvary allusion in only one example.[8] Comparison of the Detroit background [fig. 104] with one of Wellesley's two prints [fig. 103] show ghostly outlines above the hillside corresponding to the location of the crosses in the Detroit photograph. This strongly suggests that Käsebier drew the crosses directly onto the negative, then covered them over, rather than adding them to the surface of the Detroit print.[9] The alteration of the actual negative, and not just an individual print, indicates the degree to which Marian imagery inspired the *Heritage of Motherhood*, suggesting that the dilemma lay not in whether to invoke compar-

ison between Agnes Lee and the Virgin Mary but whether to make the reference so overt.[10]

Victorian audiences found confirmation of their values in images such as those produced by Cameron and Käsebier, which transformed the docile, unselfish aspects of Mary's persona into the essence of womanhood. Not all of the nineteenth century's "secular Madonnas" were so comforting. Few artists relied now on official church patronage, and religious works such as Émile Bernard's 1891 *Confirmand's Procession*[fig. 156] were products of artistic motivation and not market demand. Artists found Mary a useful foil for expressing universal notions of female identity and appropriated her image to suit pictorial needs independent of historic precedent. Representa-

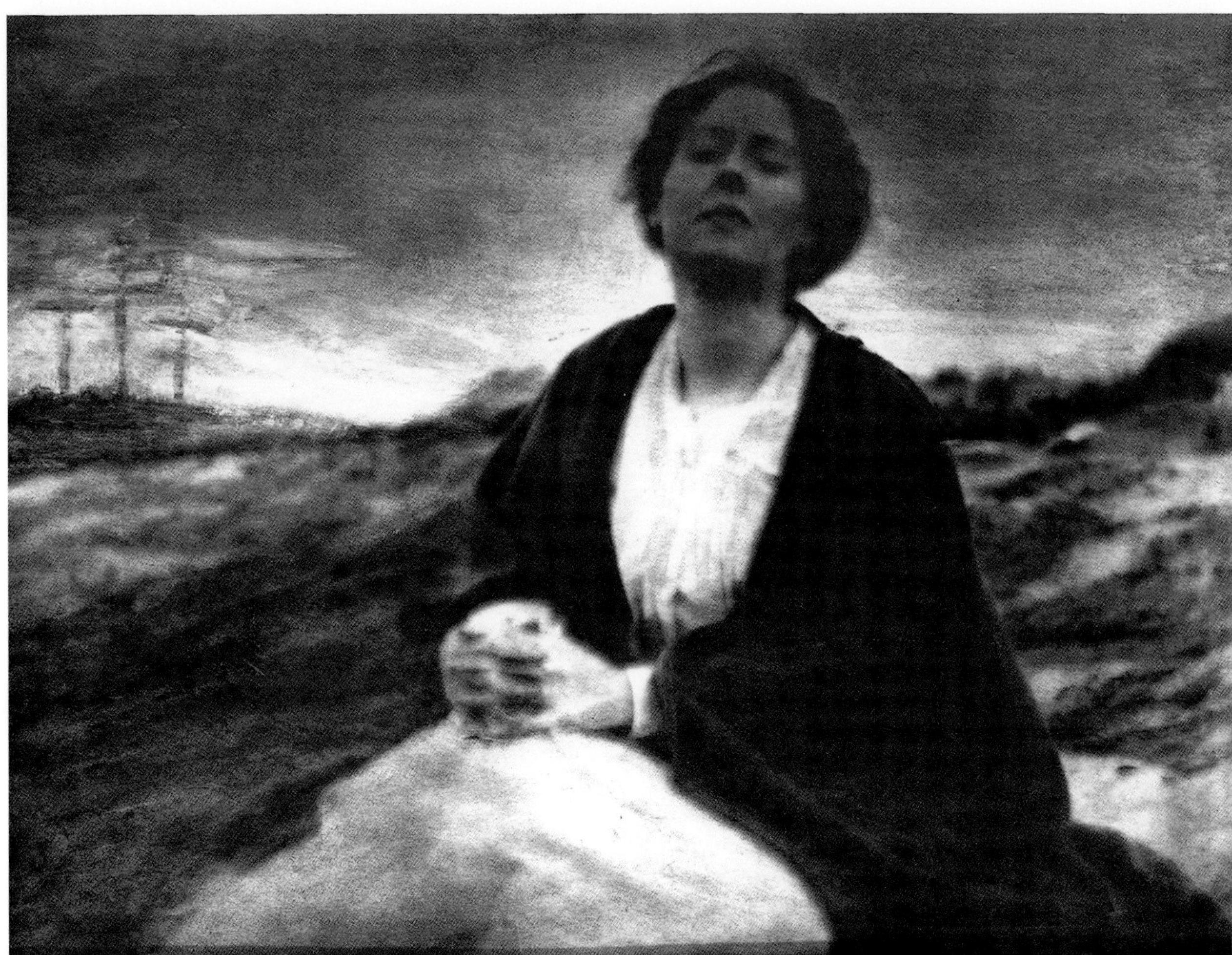

tions such as the haunting *Madonna* by Edvard Munch (1863–1944) [fig. 157] and *Invocation à la Madonne d'Onyx Vert* by Marcel-Lenoir (1872–1931) [fig. 105] blend sacred and profane elements into troubling, sexualized images of Mary that draw not on artistic traditions but on aesthetic perceptions of the *femme fatale* .

*   *   *

Mary's legacy in the nineteenth and twentieth centuries intertwines history, politics, and national identity with religion and art. The rise of secular governments in Europe and the Americas diminished religion's political role, while scientific advances from Darwin to Freud weakened its intellectual

hold. Prior to the French Revolution (1789–1795), the Catholic church rather than the French state controlled formal education, provided social welfare, and registered births, deaths, and marriages.[11] During the revolutionary period, whose impact spread throughout Europe and its colonies, Church properties were nationalized, monasteries emptied, and the pope taken prisoner. Events settled down after the Congress of Vienna (1814–1815), but many church buildings and art remained state property; works seized by Napoleon in his European campaigns went on view in the Louvre, which had been opened to the public in 1793.

As official Church influence faded from European politics, reported encounters with Mary began to increase. The 1830s to 1930s are known

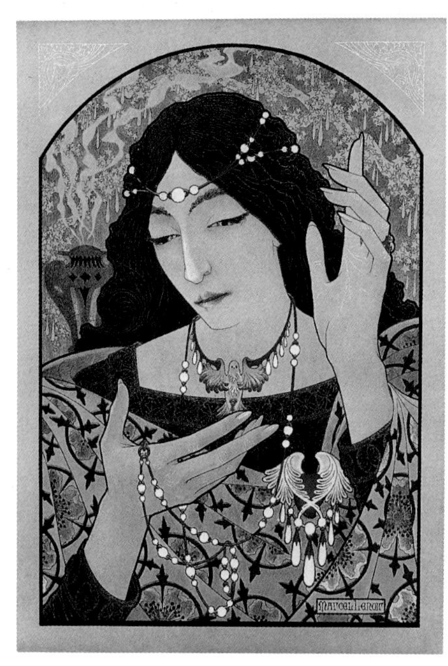

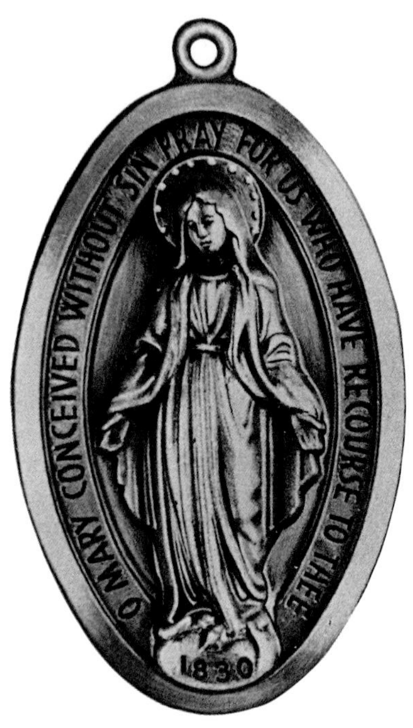

as the century of apparitions. Numerous encounters with Mary were reported; of these, the Catholic church authenticated eight sightings—in Paris (1830), La Salette (1846), Lourdes (1858), and Pontmain (1871) in France; Knock, Ireland (1879); Fátima, Portugal (1917); and Beauraing (1932–1933), and Banneaux (1933) in Belgium.[12] Claims of repeated visits from Mary were more frequent in the nineteenth century than during the Middle Ages and were associated with an entirely distinct populace.[13]

Earlier apparitions were said to have occurred to men and women who came from respected aristocratic families, had received privileged educations, and occupied a certain respected status within the church. The first Marian apparition was reported by Gregory Thaumaturgus (circa 213–270), saint Gregory "the Wonder-Worker," bishop of Neocaesarea.[14] Later visionaries, usually monks, nuns, and clergy of noble birth, such as saints Birgitta of Sweden (1303–1373) [fig. 87] and Bernard of Clairvaux (1090–1153), were perceived as having been honored for their piety and holiness by personal communication from Mary.

Those who reported having seen and/or heard Mary in the nineteenth and earlier twentieth centuries, by contrast, were young children and illiterate peasants, and this singular honor was attributed to their innocence and purity rather than to any deed or demonstrated merit.[15]

The century of apparitions began with a vision whose visual properties have been widely reproduced as the Miraculous Medal of Paris [fig. 106]. Provincial-born Catherine Labouré (1806–1875), a 24–year-old novitiate in a Parisian convent, received a vision of Mary standing within an oval, her feet on a globe and trampling a snake, dressed in white with a blue mantle, with jeweled rings on her fingers from which rays of light radiated. The woman in the vision told Labouré to have a medal struck with the text, *Ô Marie conçue sans péché priez pour nous qui avons recours à vous* ("Oh, Mary, conceived without sin, pray for us who have recourse to thee").[16] The image described by Labouré and the medal produced by the diocese closely follow Francisco Pacheco's 1649 description of the iconography of the IMMACULATE CONCEPTION (see quote on page 98). Pacheco's young girl on a

globe with a snake at her feet was also clothed in
blue and white, the colors of purity and innocence
and of the French royalists [fig. 97].[17] Tellingly,
one aspect of the vision was omitted from the
medal. Labouré described Mary as holding a
golden ball topped by a small gold cross, but the
official version shows her empty-handed, with
arms reaching down, a posture more in keeping
with IMMACULATE CONCEPTION imagery.[18]

Marian appearances in nineteenth-century
France transcended class boundaries and were
interpreted as a sign of particular favor toward the
French people. Along with a resurgence of pilgrimage activity came a renewed wave of French
nationalism, which was employed by right-wing
politicians and clergy as a unifying force for a
divided postrevolutionary nation.[19] In the United
States, however, Mary was a symbol of national dis-
unity. Viewed as a specifically Catholic, and not
Protestant, symbol, Mary became identified with
class and ethnicity via the working-class immigrants whose arrival brought diversity, not unity, to
the national identity and unease to many established residents. Coherence was lacking even
among American Catholics; European religious
allegiance had been broadly geographical, but in
New World parishes, Irish, Polish, German, and
Italian Catholics felt as distinct from each other as
from their Protestant neighbors.[20] The mostly
Irish-Catholic New York archdiocese, accustomed
to a more austere liturgy, found the fervent traditions of Italian immigrants startling. The diocese's
efforts to suppress ethnic processions and "Ameri-
canize" parish behavior—while in keeping with
turn-of-the-century attitudes toward successful
integration of immigrant populations—brought
the nation's hierarchy into conflict with the
papacy, who did not appreciate hearing Italo-
American devotion to the Madonna described as
semipagan behavior.[21]

Following the first World War, the group identification fostered by nineteenth-century nationalism gave way to a twentieth-century emphasis on

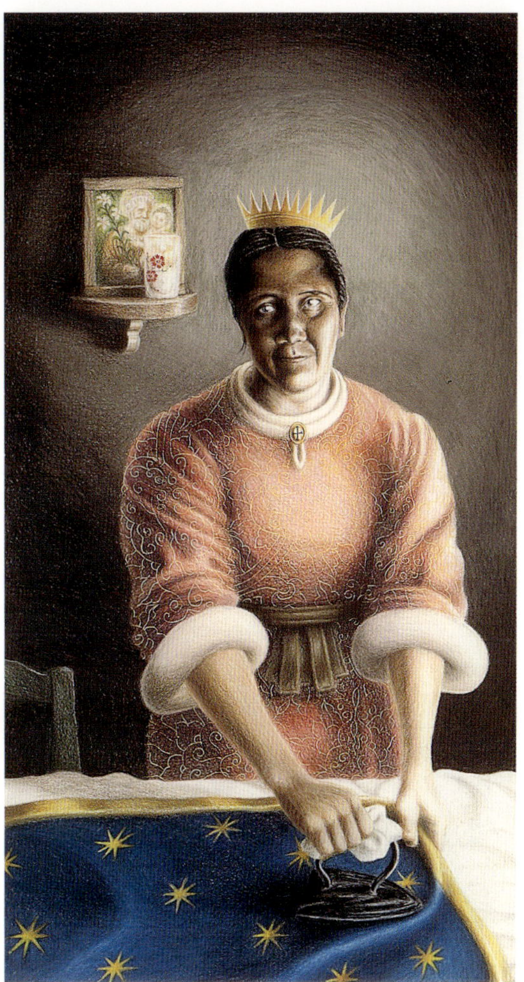

Fig. 107. J. Michael
Walker, *Planchando,
Pensando (Ironing,
Thinking)*, 1995,
color pencil drawing
from the *Life of the
Virgin of Guadalupe*
series, Collection of
Henry and Patricia
Schwarz, Los Ange-
les

the individual, whose search for meaning, aware-
ness, or instant gratification became the subject of
intellectual debate. Mary retained her affiliation
with immigrant classes, her identity now allied
with recent arrivals from Spanish-speaking
nations. The image of Our Lady of Guadalupe,
who appeared in 1531 to the 55-year-old native
Mexican convert Juan Diego, has become a familiar symbol on both sides of the U.S.-Mexican border, evoking ethnic pride and cultural identity as
well as Marian devotion. Picking up where Dürer's
Life of the Virgin series left off, artist J. Michael
Walker (b. 1952) has created a series known as the
Daily Life of the Virgin of Guadalupe, which depicts
Mary as a rural indigenous woman ironing her
cloak before bed, or eating *Maria*-brand cookies

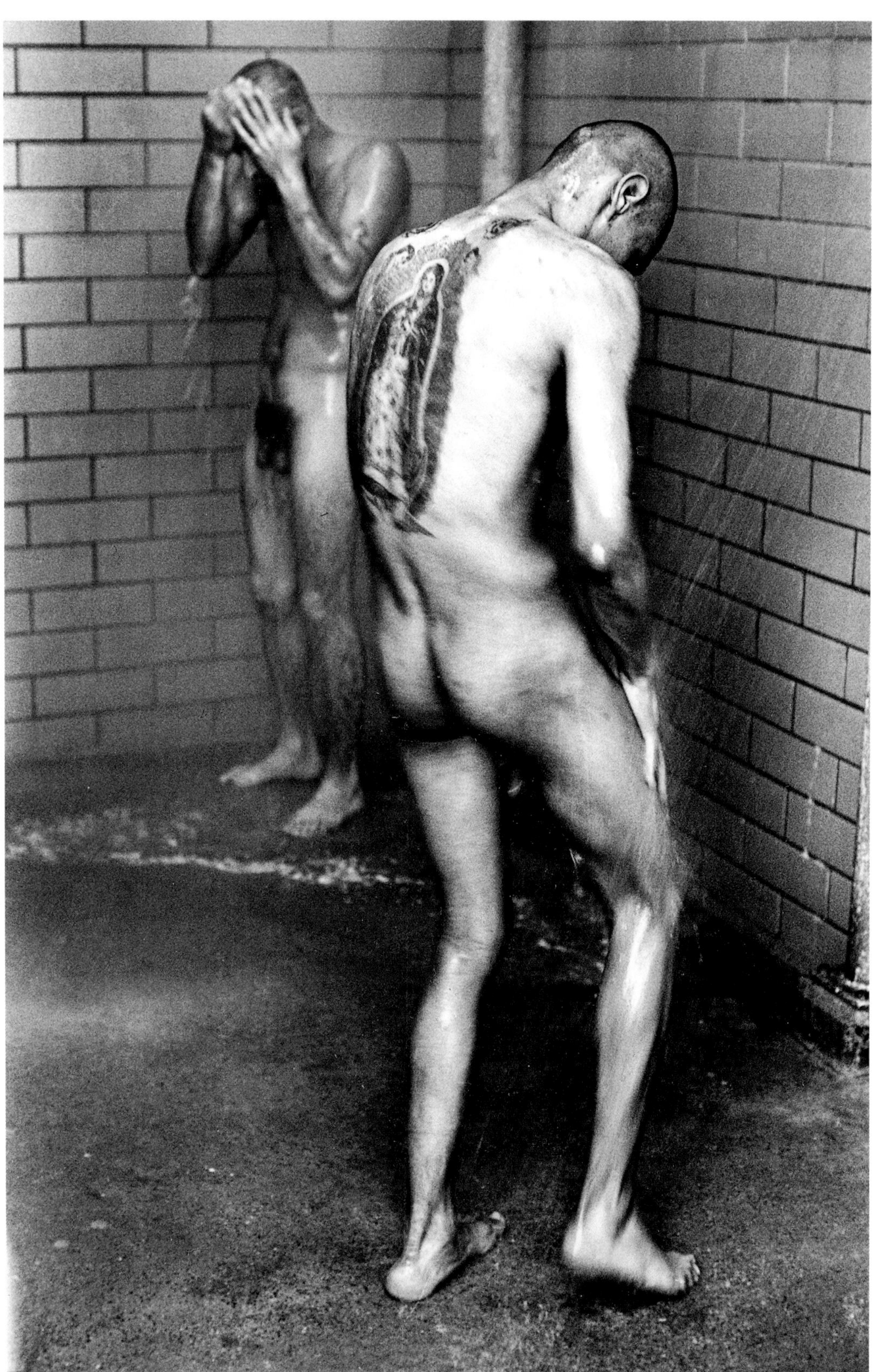

Fig. 108. Danny
Lyon, *Showers, Diag-*
nostic Unit, Texas,
1969/70, gelatin sil-
ver print from the
Conversations with
the Dead series

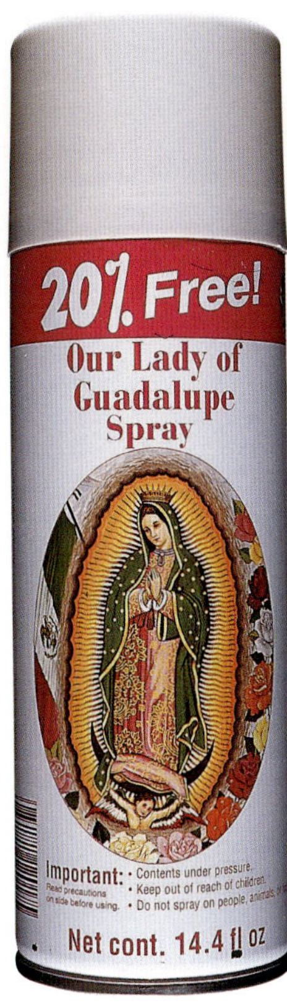

Fig. 109 (left). *Our Lady of Guadalupe* spray can, late 20th c., enamel paint on metal

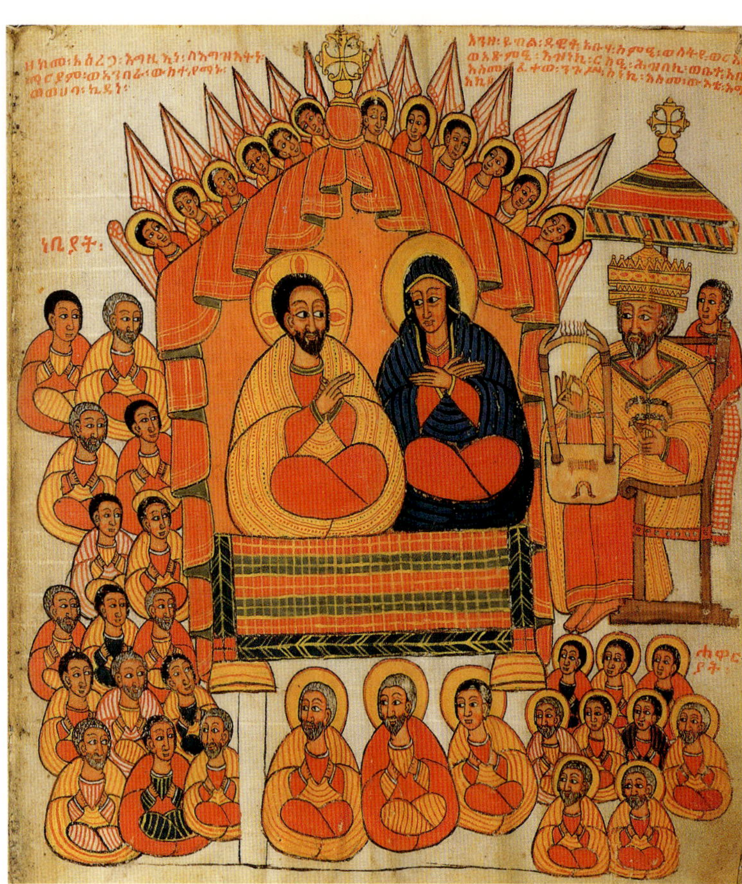

Fig. 110 . Ethiopian, *Mary Enthroned with Christ*, 2nd half 17th c., manuscript illumination from the *Miracles of Mary*, Dabra Warq, Gojjam, Ethiopia

while reading letters from her son Jesus, who sends money orders from abroad [fig. 107].[22]

The decorative functions of Christian imagery, always an undercurrent in popular devotion, have become increasingly apparent as mass production has facilitated the merging of religion and retail.[23] The luminous scarves captured by Lola Ávarez Bravo (1907–1993) for sale in a Mexican market commodify Mary as well as honor her; she is a desirable ally to have on one's side or, in the case of a prisoner in a Texas jail, on one's back [fig. 108]. Mary's appearance on a spray can [fig. 109], and as a tattoo, epitomizes her journey from aloof and perfect queen to all-forgiving mother and underscores another aspect of her American identity: defender of the vulnerable, refuge of the marginal, and champion of the lowly. Rather than insult her, these appropriations demonstrate Mary's adaptability to the needs of those who need her most. The faith of the man in the Danny Lyon (b. 1942) photograph [fig. 108] is heartbreaking; in a realm where no one can be trusted, he asks Mary to guard him from what he most fears when his back is turned.

While each generation discovers Mary anew, hardly anything in Marian devotion is truly novel. A recent movement among American Catholics has called for Mary to be officially declared *co-redemptrix*, or partner with Jesus in the redemption of humanity. Mary has enjoyed a similar status in the Ethiopian church since the fifteenth century, through the COVENANT OF MERCY. According to this tradition, which attributes broad powers to Mary as intercessor and as co-ruler of heaven, Jesus promises to pardon all sinners who invoke the name of his mother.[24] The COVENANT OF MERCY is expressed by the depiction of Mary and Jesus sitting side by side with joined hands [fig.

Regarding Mary   109

110]. While many of the faithful who currently advocate bestowal of the title of co-redemptrix believe it will recognize Mary's contribution to salvation and acknowledge a role she already plays on behalf of the faithful, others believe this movement to be undertaken by conservative partisans, to appease those factions who call for a priesthood open to both women and men.

Perhaps the greatest irony is Mary's enduring fascination to modern audiences, despite centuries of patriarchy, colonialism, and religious ambivalence. The last Marian apparition to be authenticated by the Catholic church occurred in Belgium in 1933, but sightings continue to be reported in locales as diverse as Montichiari, Italy (1947 and 1966); Lipa, Philippines (1948–49); Necedah, Wisconsin (1949); Jerusalem, Israel (1954); Garabandal, Spain (1961); Zeitoun, Egypt (1968–71); Bayside, Queens, New York (1970); Akita, Japan (1973); Kibeho, Rwanda (1981); Medjugorje, Herzegovina (1981–ongoing); Cameroon, West Africa (1986); and Conyers, Georgia (1990–ongoing). The United States enters the twenty-first century with a greater population of Muslims than Episcopalians, and a generation for whom icons are found not in churches but on computer screens. Mary enters the twenty-first century as the woman whose face has appeared most often on the cover of *Time* magazine—an ambiguous commentary on women's achievement, recognition, and historical visibility.

NOTES

Marian Origins
in the Gospels and Christian Tradition

1. Raymond E. Brown, Karl P. Donfried, Joseph A. Fitzmyer, and John Reumann, eds., *Mary in the New Testament: A Collaborative Assessment by Protestant and Roman Catholic Scholars.* (Philadelphia: Fortress Press, 1978).

2. Marina Warner, *Alone of All Her Sex: The Myth and Cult of the Virgin Mary* (London: Weidenfeld and Nicolson, 1976), Appendix B, pp. 344–45. Page numbers refer to the Picador edition, 1985.

3. Alexander Cruden, *Cruden's Complete Concordance*, 1737, repr. A. D. Adams, C. H. Irwin, and S. A. Waters, eds. (Grand Rapids, MI: Zondervan Publishing House, 1949).

4. Specially printed scripture editions, such as *Gospel Parallels*, ed. Burton H. Throckmorton, Jr. (Toronto/New York: Thomas Nelson & Sons, 1949), allow comparative simultaneous reading of the three synoptic (interlinked) Gospels.

5. For an extensive comparison of Gospel narratives and analysis of Old and New Testament parallels, see Warner, *Alone*, chapter 1: "Mary in the Gospels," pp. 3–24.

6. "The Infancy Gospel of James," in Robert J. Miller, ed., *The Complete Gospels* (San Francisco: HarperSanFrancisco, 1992), pp. 369–79.

7. 3 Esdras; Tobit; 1, 2, and 3 Maccabees; Wisdom of Solomon; Ecclesiasticus; Baruch; and Letter of Jeremias comprise the Deutero-Canonical books. Timothy Ware, *The Orthodox Church* (Harmondsworth, UK: Penguin Books, 1963), pp. 207–08.

8. Miller, pp. 369–79. Later Christian texts that record apocryphal beliefs include the eighth- or ninth-century Latin text, the *Gospel of the Pseudo-Matthew*, and the ninth century *Story of the Birth of Mary*, attributed to the scholar Paschasius Radbertus (786–ca. 860).

9. Gospel précis drawn from R. Brown et al., *Mary in the New Testament*; Raymond E. Brown, *An Introduction to the New Testament* (New York: Doubleday, 1997); and Bruce M. Metzger and Michael D. Coogan, eds., *The Oxford Companion to the Bible* (New York: Oxford University Press, 1993).

10. Translations are from the Revised Standard Version of the New Testament, a revision based on the American Standard Version of 1901 and the King James Version of 1611 (New York: Thomas Nelson & Sons, 1946).

11. Our Lady of Czestochowa, the widely venerated Polish icon, traditionally has been considered by many faithful to be a painting by saint Luke, made from a table carved by saint Joseph for the Holy Family. Alberto Rum, in Bernard Billet, Alphonse Bossard, et al., *Dictionary of Mary* (New York: Catholic Book Publishing, 1985), pp. 63–67.

12. R. Brown et al., *Mary in the New Testament*, pp. 74–75, and Metzger and Coogan, pp. 502–06.

Marian Parallels
in the Qur'an and Hebrew Bible

1. The other three perfect women are Khadijah, Muhammad's

wife; Fatima, his daughter; and Asiyah, wife of the Pharaoh drowned while pursuing the Israelites across the Red Sea in Exodus. Diane Apostolos-Cappadona, *Dictionary of Women in Religious Art* (New York: Oxford University Press, 1998), "Fatima," pp. 130–31.

2. Qur'an extracts from the translation by N. J. Dawood (London: Penguin Books, 1956, rev. 1995).

3. Jaroslav Pelikan, *Mary through the Centuries: Her Place in the History of Culture* (New Haven, CT: Yale University Press, 1996), chapter 5: "The Heroine of the Qur'an and the Black Madonna," pp. 67–80. From a Muslim perspective, Gabriel's recitation to Muhammad of Christian history would naturally have included all relevant details from the lives of Mary and Jesus.

4. Sally Cunneen, *In Search of Mary: The Woman and the Symbol* (New York: Ballantine Books, 1996), pp. 37–38, 51. Noah, Jacob, his son Joseph, and Esther are also told they have found favor with God.

5. Medieval Christians did draw parallels between Mary and Judith. The *Speculum Humanae Salvationis* (*Mirror of Man's Salvation*) compared Judith conquering Holofernes to Mary's victory over Satan. See Warner, *Alone*, p. 55.

6. For contemporary spiritual approaches, see Rosemary Radford Ruether, *Mary—The Feminine Face of the Church* (Philadelphia: The Westminster Press, 1977), p. 33; and Els Maeckelberghe, *Desperately Seeking Mary: A Feminist Appropriation of a Traditional Religious Symbol* (The Hague, Netherlands: Pharos, 1994).

7. Gertrud Schiller, *Iconography of Christian Art*, trans. Janet Seligman (Greenwich, CT: New York Graphic Society, 1971/72), vol. 1, p. 36.

8. Pamela Berger, *The Goddess Obscured: Transformation of the Grain Protectoress from Goddess to Saint* (Boston: Beacon Press, 1986), pp. 45–46. There are pagan goddesses who give birth without intercourse (Danaë), virgin goddesses (Diana/Artemis), and celibate goddesses (Cybele), but there is no parallel tradition of virgin birth combined with perpetual virginity. Even the maidens of the Temples of Vesta, the so-called Vestal Virgins, served five-year celibate terms, after which they could then pursue normal lives. See Geoffrey Ashe, *The Virgin: Mary's Cult and the Re-emergence of the Goddess* (London and New York: Arkana, 1976).

9. Michael P. Carroll, *The Cult of the Virgin Mary: Psychological Origins* (Princeton, NJ: Princeton University Press, 1986), pp. 32–48, 110–12.

10. Mary R. Lefkowitz, *Women in Greek Myth* (Baltimore: Johns Hopkins University Press, 1986), p. 94.

11. Thomas Bokenkotter, *A Concise History of the Catholic Church* (Garden City, NY: Doubleday & Co., 1979).

The Making of Mary: Art in the Early Church

1. Robin Margaret Jensen, *Understanding Early Christian Art* (London: Routledge, 2000), pp. 46–51.

2. Linda Murray and Peter Murray, "Communion" and "Last Supper" in *The Oxford Companion to Christian Art and Architecture* (Oxford, UK: Oxford University Press, 1996), pp. 115, 269.

3. Walter Lowrie, *Art in the Early Church* (New York: Harper & Row, 1947), pp. 55–57.

4. André Grabar, *Christian Iconography: A Study of its Origins* (Princeton, NJ: Princeton University Press, 1968), p. 11; and Jensen, p. 37. The metaphor of Jesus as the good shepherd is found in John 10:1–6.

5. Lowrie, p. 43; and Robert Milburn, *Early Christian Art and Architecture* (Berkeley: University of California Press, 1988), p. 29.

6. The scholarly debate surrounding this image is fascinating. Lowrie identifies the subject as the Annunciation and the prophet as Balaam, and dates the fresco from the mid-second century; Lowrie, p. 43 and plate 18. Duchet-Suchaux and Pastoureau identify the male figure as Balaam but date the painting from the fourth century; Gaston Duchet-Suchaux and Michel Pastoureau, *The Bible and the Saints* (Paris and New York: Flammarion, 1994), pp. 54–55. Trens identifies the scene as Mary nursing the infant Jesus, and the male figure as the prophet Isaiah; Manuel Trens, *María: Iconografía de la Virgen en el Arte Español* (Madrid: Editorial Plus Ultra, 1946), p. 33. Milburn dates the scene as mid-third century, stresses the importance of the (unidentified) prophet's gesture, and links it to Balaam's oracle; Milburn, p. 29. Grabar identifies the figure as either Balaam pointing to the star or Isaiah prophesying the Messiah's birth; André Grabar, *The Beginnings of Christian Art 200–395* (London: Thames & Hudson, 1967), pp. 98–99. The Murrays identify the man as either Balaam or Isaiah; they date the scene as third century and the earliest known depiction of the Madonna and Child; Murray and Murray, pp. 43, 245–46. Warner identifies the figure as an angel or prophet, and the image as second century; *Alone*, fig. 3, unpaginated.

7. Andrew Greeley, *The Mary Myth: On the Femininity of God* (New York: Seabury Press, 1977), p. 98.

8. Lowrie, pp. 107–08; and Schiller, vol. 1, p. 27.

9. Schiller, vol. 1, pp. 7, 25, 26, et al.

10. Hans Belting, *Likeness and Presence: A History of the Image before the Era of Art,* trans. Edmund Jephcott (Chicago: University of Chicago Press, 1994), pp. 73–77. Despite its poetry, the name derives from the icon's location in the Hodegon monastery, a building that once housed *hodegoi,* guides for the blind.

11. Helen C. Evans and William D. Wixom, eds., *The Glory of Byzantium: Art and Culture of the Middle Byzantine Era,* A.D. 843–1261 (New York: Metropolitan Museum of Art, 1997); and Belting, *Likeness and Presence,* pp. 281–96.

12. Hans Belting, *The Image and Its Public in the Middle Ages: Form and Function of Early Paintings of the Passion,* trans Mark Bartusis and Raymond Meyer (New Rochelle, NY: Aristide D. Caratzas: 1990), pp. 114–16, 213–18.

Religious Uses of Devotional Art to 1500

1. Schiller, vol. 1, p. 5. This date also coincided with the pagan feast *Sol Invictus,* a celebration of the invincible sun held at the time of the winter solstice; Berger, p. 154, fn. 17.

2. Venerable Bede (ca. 673–735), *The Ecclesiastical History of the English People,* book I, chapter 30 (Oxford, UK: Oxford University Press, 1969), pp. 56–57.

3. William Durandus, "Of Pictures and Images, and Curtains, and the Ornaments of Churches," *Rationale divinorum officiorum,* 1285–1291, repr. in Elizabeth Gilmore Holt, ed., *A Documentary History of Art,* vol. 1: *The Middle Ages and the Renaissance* (Princeton, NJ: Princeton University Press, 1947), pp. 120–29.

4. John of Genoa, *Catholicon,* thirteenth century, quoted in Michael Baxandall, *Painting and Experience in Fifteenth-Century Italy* (Oxford, UK: Oxford University Press, 1988), pp. 41, 161.

5. Albrecht Dürer, Netherlandish Journal, 1520, in Wolfgang Stechow, *Northern Renaissance Art 1400–1600: Sources and Documents* (Evanston, IL: Northwestern University Press, 1966), pp. 96–100.

6. Numbering of the Ten Commandments varies among religions. The prohibition against images is the second commandment in the Jewish, Eastern Orthodox, and Reformed Protestant traditions. In Medieval Christian and Lutheran traditions, it forms part of the first commandment.

7. Act VII, *Decree of the Second Council of Nicaea,* 787, in Henry Bettenson, ed., *Documents of the Christian Church* (London: Oxford University Press, 1963), p. 98; cf. Belting, *Likeness and Presence* pp. 505–07.

8. For an extensive discussion of Reformation and Counter-Reformation attitudes toward visual art, see Margaret R. Miles, *Image as Insight: Visual Understanding in Western Christianity and Secular Culture* (Boston: Beacon Press, 1985), chapter 5: "Vision and the Sixteenth-Century Protestant and Roman Catholic Reforms," pp. 95–126.

9. Martin Luther, *The Ninety-Five Theses,* 1517, in Bettenson, pp. 185–91.

10. Martin Luther, "Against the Heavenly Prophets in the Matter of Images and Sacraments," 1525, in Stechow, pp. 129–30, and Belting, *Likeness and Presence,* p. 546.

11. See, for example, Dürer's letters of 1520 regarding Luther, Netherlandish diary excepts (17 May 1521), and text presenting his *Four Apostles* to the Nuremberg Council (6 October 1526), in Stechow, pp. 94–108.

12. Felipe Fernández-Armesto and Derek Wilson, *Reformations: A Radical Interpretation of Christianity and the World 1500–2000* (New York: Scribner, 1996), pp. 97–121. See also Belting, *Likeness and Presence,* pp. 458–65, 545–51; and Stechow, p. 129.

13. Anne Cuenod, et al., *Saint-Pierre, cathédrale de Genève, un monument, une exposition* (Geneva: Musée Rath, 1982) recreates the pre-Reformation appearance of Calvin's principal church.

Devotional Uses of Religious Art to 1500

1. Henk van Os, et al., *The Art of Devotion in the Late Middle Ages in Europe: 1300–1500* (London: Merrell Holberton, 1994), p. 62.

2. For an extensive discussion, see van Os, et al., and Belting, *The Image and Its Public,* esp. pp. 41–64.

3. Durandus, in Holt, pp. 121–23.

4. Eugène Honée, "Image and Imagination in the Medieval Culture of Prayer," in van Os, p. 162.

5. Edward J. Klein, "Introduction" to Thomas Hemerken, known as Thomas à Kempis, *On the Imitation of Christ: a modern version based on the English translation made by Richard Whitford around the year 1530* (New York: Harper & Brothers, 1955). Thomas à Kempis also authored the less well-known *On the Imitation of Mary.*

6. Peter Barnet, ed., *Images in Ivory: Precious Objects of the Gothic Age* (Detroit, MI: Detroit Institute of Arts, 1997).

7. *Tractatus de Miraculis Beatae Francisci,* quoted by Honée in van Os, p. 173, fn. 10.

8. While size can be a guide, Belting cautions that it cannot be a

rule. For example, the largest panel painting produced in thirteenth-century Italy, Duccio's Ruccelai Madonna of 1285–450 cm x 290 cm (14 ft. 12 in. x 9 ft. 6 in., now in the Uffizi)—was made not for a high altar, but for the side altar of the Laudesi confraternity chapel in S. Maria Novella, Florence; *Likeness and Presence*, pp. 384–97.

9. Antonio Rumeu de Armas, *Historia de la Previsión Social en España: Cofradías, Gremios, Hermandades, Montepíos* (Barcelona: El Albir, 1944, repr. 1981), pp. 40–77.

10. These "hours" were Matins (2:00 A.M.), Lauds (3:00 A.M.), Prime (6:00 A.M.), Terce (9:00 A.M.), Sext (noon), Nones (3:00 P.M.), Vespers (5:00 P.M.) and Compline (6:00 P.M.). At 7:00 P.M. one retired for bed.

10. Sandra Penketh, "Women and Books of Hours," in Jane H. M. Taylor and Lesley Smith, eds., *Women and the Book* (London: The British Library, 1996), pp. 266–81. See also the 1261 laws of Magdeburg, quoted on page 83, which state that widows are entitled to keep the family psalter and prayer-books along with other goods associated with the household.

The Madonna Unveiled I

1. Roger S. Wieck, *The Book of Hours in Medieval Art and Life* (London: Sotheby's Publications, 1988). Some cycles ended with a triumphant meditation on the Resurrection; James Snyder, *Northern Renaissance Art* (Englewood, Cliffs, NJ: Prentice-Hall, 1985), p. 21.

2. Murray and Murray, "Annunciation," pp. 23–24.

3. Josep de C. Laplana and Teresa Macià, *Nigra Sum: Iconografía de Santa María de Montserrat* (Barcelona: Publicaciones Abadia de Montserrat, 1995), p. 11.

4. The rending of the veil of the Ark of the Covenant is found in Mark 15:38, Matt. 27:51, and Luke 23:45. According to the Infancy Gospel of James and subsequent texts, virgins were assembled to weave the temple veil. Lots were drawn to assign colors, with the colors purple and scarlet, the most expensive dyes, and hence most precious colors, falling to Mary (Inf Jas. 10:1–10); Miller, p. 388.

5. The motif of Mary spinning continues to be featured in many icons of the Annunciation used in Orthodox worship. I am grateful to Sharon Elkins for her observations on iconographic developments in the Eastern and Western churches.

6. Schiller, vol. 1, pp. 42–44.

7. The evangelist Matthew based his reference to the Book of Isaiah (Matt. 1:23) on a Greek version of the Bible, which translated the Hebrew *almah* (young woman) as *parthenos* (virgin) (see Warner, *Alone*, p. 19, and Pelikan, p. 29). The passage most often cited, Isaiah 7:14, appeared in the Latin vulgate as *Ecce virgo concipiet et pariet filium* and was translated in the King James version as "Behold, a virgin shall conceive and bear a son." The Revised Standard version of Isaiah translates this phrase as "Behold, a young woman shall conceive and bear a son."

8. Variations include Petrus Christus's outdoor *Annunciation* in the Metropolitan Museum, which takes place on the church threshold, with Gabriel outside and Mary emerging.

9. Schiller. vol. 1, pp. 42–44.

10. Baxandall, pp. 36, 48–56, 164–65. Sermons greatly influenced popular religious thought in the Italian Renaissance because they were delivered in the vernacular, rather than in Latin, and because they were often entertaining as well as enlightening. Large crowds would gather to hear famous preachers like saint Bernardino of Siena (1380–1444), who traveled from town to town spreading their message (and earning their living).

11. Olwen Hufton, *The Prospect Before Her: A History of Women in Western Europe 1500–1800* (New York: Alfred A. Knopf, 1996), p. 35. Bear in mind that the ability to read is separate from the ability to write, and far fewer people developed the latter skill.

12. Susan Groag Bell, "Humanism and the Renaissance Education of Women," in Susan Groag Bell, ed., *Women from the Greeks to the French Revolution* (Stanford, CA: Stanford University Press, 1973), pp. 178–79; and Warner, *Alone*, pp. 134–39.

13. Giovanni Boccaccio, *Il Decamerone* (Harmondsworth, UK: Penguin Books, 1972), *Prima Giornata: Introduzione.*

14. Martha W. Driver, "Mirrors of a Collective Past: Re-considering Images of Medieval Women," in Jane H. M. Taylor and Lesley Smith, eds., *Women and the Book* (London: The British Library, 1996), pp. 75–93.

15. Penketh, in Taylor and Smith.

16. Pamela Sheingorn, "Appropriating the Holy Kinship: Gender and Family History," in Kathleen Ashley and Pamela Sheingorn, *Interpreting Cultural Symbols: Saint Anne in Late Medieval Society* (Athens: University of Georgia Press, 1990), pp. 188–91.

17. Giovanni Villani, "Chronicle of Florence," ca. 1308–48, in Norman F. Cantor, ed., *The Medieval Reader* (New York: HarperCollins, 1994), pp. 70–72.

18. Apostolos-Cappadona, "Devotio Moderna," p. 103, and S.

Bell, ed., pp. 181–90.

19. Juan Luís de Vives, *De institutione feminae christianae (Instruction of a Christian Woman)*, 1523, quoted in S. Bell, p. 188. Though written for royalty, Vives's text circulated in many languages and was reprinted several times over the next two centuries.

20. Merry E. Wiesner, "Nuns, Wives, and Mothers: Women and the Reformation in Germany" in Sherrin Marshall, ed., *Women in Reformation and Counter-Reformation Europe: Public and Private Worlds* (Bloomington: Indiana University Press, 1989), p. 15. Bible literacy in women was perceived as perilously close to having women assume official roles within religious observance.

21. Wiesner, in Marshall, p. 13.

22. Christiane Klapisch-Zuber, "Women and the Family," in Jacques Le Goff, ed., *The Medieval World* (London: Parkgate Books, 1979), p. 298.

23. Anne Winston-Allen, *Stories of the Rose: The Making of the Rosary in the Middle Ages* (University Park: Pennsylvania State University Press, 1997), pp. 13–14. The second verse, used today— "Holy Mary, mother of God, pray for us sinners, now and at the hour of our death"—was not adopted until 1568; Warner, *Alone*, pp. 305–09, 359.

24. Honée, in van Os, pp. 157–74.

25. Warner, *Alone*, and Winston-Allen. Social historian Michael Carroll believes the rosary to be a devotional practice that developed in the late fifteenth century independently of Muslim contact. See Michael P. Carroll, *Catholic Cults and Devotions: A Psychological Inquiry* (Kingston, ON; Montreal: McGill-Queen's University Press, 1989), pp. 10–14.

26. Carolyn Walker Bynum, *Holy Feast and Holy Fast: The Religious Significance of Food to Medieval Women* (Berkeley: University of California Press, 1987), pp. 268–69.

27. Bernard of Clairvaux (1090–1153), quoted in Bynum, *Holy Feast*, p. 268.

28. Murray and Murray, "Virgin Birth of Christ," p. 561.

29. R. Brown et al., *Mary in the New Testament*, pp. 65–72 and 267–78; and Thomas A. O'Meara, *Mary in Protestant and Catholic Theology* (New York: Sheed and Ward, 1966), p. 157–59, 306–12. Indeed, Luke's comment regarding Jesus' ritual presentation in the Synagogue in Jerusalem—for "as it is written in the law of the Lord 'Every male that opens the womb shall be called holy to the Lord' " (Luke 2:23)—can be interpreted to argue against Mary's postpartum virginity.

30. Rosemary Woolf, *The English Mystery Plays* (Berkeley: University of California Press, 1972), pp. 178–80.

31. In 1966, Dutch bishops issued a catechism that made no reference to Mary's virginity. After pope Paul VI objected, a compromise was reached allowing it to remain out of the catechism, as long as an appendix stating the Vatican position was attached. Bokenkotter, pp. 443–46.

32. Ware, pp. 261–65.

33. Gabriele de Barletta, mid-fifteenth century, quoted in Baxandall, pp. 57, 166.

34. Dante Alighieri, 'Paradiso' canto 32:85–87, *La Divina Commedia*, C. H. Grandgent, ed. (Boston: D. C. Heath, 1933), p. 960. For the full text of the hymn, see pg. v.

35. Dürer's *Visitation* follows the *Betrothal of the Virgin* and the *Annunciation*, and precedes the *Nativity*. As his source, Dürer used Matthew's Gospel, which states that Mary was betrothed to Joseph at the time she was found to be with child. Matthew refers to Joseph as her husband who considers divorcing her, presuming she has been unfaithful by conceiving before he has consummated the marriage. However, an angel assures Joseph of Mary's innocence and reveals that she conceived her child by the Holy Spirit (Matt. 1:18–25).

36. "Christian Marriage" in Georges Duby, ed., *A History of Private Life: Revelations of the Medieval World*, vol. 2 (Cambridge, MA: Belknap Press, 1988), pp. 124–36.

37. Ware, pp. 300–02.

38. The custom predates Christianity; in the Roman Empire, unmarried women (i.e., virgins) wore their hair loose, and married women wound theirs in chignons. See Margaret R. Miles, *Carnal Knowing: Female Nakedness and Religious Meaning in the Christian West* (Boston: Beacon Press, 1989), pp. 49–50.

39. Doris Stenton, "On the *Homily on Matrimony*," in S. Bell, p. 219.

40. Charles W. Talbot, *Dürer in America: His Graphic Work* (Washington, DC: National Gallery of Art, 1971. The watercolor sketch is in the collection of the Graphische Sammlung Albertina, Vienna.

41. Kim M. Phillips, "Maidenhood as the Perfect Age of Woman's Life," in Katherine J. Lewis, Noël James Menuge, and Kim M. Phillips, eds., *Young Medieval Women* (New York: St. Martin's Press, 1999), pp. 8–15.

42. Phillips, in Lewis et al., pp. 8–9.

43. Description of a beautiful woman drawn from Geoffrey of

Vinsauf, *The Poetria Nova*, ca. 1200, quoted by Phillips, in Lewis et al., p. 7. See also Miles, *Carnal Knowing*, pp. 135–36.

44. Marina Warner, *From the Beast to the Blonde: On Fairy Tales and their Tellers* (London: Vintage Books, 1995), pp. 367–68. Robert Orsi has observed in his essay (pages 3–18) that in the popular imagination of her devotees, Mary ages, sharing their troubles at all stages of life. Artistic depictions of an elderly Mary are known (see PASSION section), but this is by no means consistent. In the visual arts, Mary's aging process is often arrested.

45. Christine de Pisan, *The Treasure of the City of Ladies, or the Book of the Three Virtues*, Sarah Lawson, trans. (Harmondsworth, UK: Penguin Books, 1985), p. 150

46. William Caxton's 1484 version of *The Book of the Knight of the Tour Landry*. See Katherine J. Lewis, "Model Girls? Virgin-Martyrs and the Training of Young Women in Late Medieval England," in Lewis et al., *Young Medieval Women*, pp. 25–46.

47. Christine de Pisan, "Treasure," pp. 160–62. De Pisan continues, "They should have a humble manner and not be too talkative. . . . A maiden must not be in any way forward, outspoken, or loose, especially in the presence of men. . . . A young girl should also especially venerate Our Lady, St. Catherine, and all virgins, and if she can read, eagerly read their biographies. . . . Young girls taught and brought up in this way are much sought after by men looking for wives."

48. *Decree of the First Council of Nicaea*, 351, quoted in Warner, *Alone*, p. 68.

49. Clarissa W. Atkinson, *The Oldest Vocation: Christian Motherhood in the Middle Ages* (Ithaca, NY: Cornell University Press, 1991), pp. 112–13, 182.

50. Belting, *Likeness and Presence*, p. 300, and Murray and Murray, "Mystery (or Miracle) Plays," pp. 340–42.

51. Cindy L. Carlson, "Like a Virgin: Mary and her Doubters in the N-Town Cycle," in Cindy L. Carlson and Angela Jane Weisl, eds., *Constructions of Widowhood and Virginity in the Middle Ages* (New York: St. Martin's Press, 1999), p. 201. The character who utters such proofs is often a midwife named Salome, a figure claimed to be present at Mary's delivery in the second-century Protevangelium as well as in fourteenth- and fifteenth-century mystery plays.

52. Augustine of Hippo, quoted in Uta Ranke-Heinemann, *Eunuchs for the Kingdom of Heaven: Women, Sexuality, and the Catholic Church* (New York: Doubleday, 1990), p. 343.

53. Jacopo da Varazze, known as Jacobus de Voragine, "The Birth of Our Lord Jesus Christ According to the Flesh," in *The Golden Legend: Readings on the Saints*, trans. William Granger Ryan (Princeton, NJ: Princeton University Press, 1993), vol. 1, pp. 38–39.

54. Cf. the writings of Saints Irenaeus (ca. 130–200 AD) and Justin (ca. 100–165 AD).

55. St. Bernard of Clairvaux, *Sermon on the Nativity of the Blessed Virgin Mary*, quoted in Atkinson, p. 120.

56. Tertullian, *On the Apparel of Women*, circa. 200, quoted in Katherine M. Rogers, "The Troublesome Helpmate: A History of Misogyny in Literature," in S. Bell, p. 95. Tertullian continues: "*You* are the devil's gateway . . . *you* are the first deserter of the divine law; *you* are she who persuaded him the devil was not valiant enough to attack. . . . *You* destroyed so easily God's image, man. On account of *your* desert—that is, death—even the Son of God had to die."

57. Ester Souwerman, *Ester hath hang'd Haman . . .* 1617, quoted in Elaine V. Beilin, *Redeeming Eve: Women Writers of the English Renaissance* (Princeton, NJ: Princeton University Press, 1987), pp. 258, 262.

58. St. Thomas Aquinas (1225–1274), *Summa Theologica*, thirteenth century, quoted in S. Bell, p. 122.

59. Thomas Becon, *Catechism*, mid-sixteenth century, quoted in Hufton, p. 39. Becon was also the author of the ca. 1543 *Golde Boke of Christen Matrimonye*, a Protestant variation on Catholic marriage handbooks, and other conduct manuals and religious guides.

60. Aemilia Lanyer, *Salve Deus Rex Judæorum*, 1611, quoted in Beilin, p. 196.

61. Sowerman, quoted in Beilin, pp. 260–61. Her name is a pseudonym, playing sour (*sower*) off of sweet (*swet*), as her pamphlet, subtitled *An Answere to a lewd Pamphlet, entituled, The Araignment of Women*, responds to a work by Joseph Swetman.

62. The Italian astronomer and botanist Giovanni Battista Amici (1796–1863) made major improvements to the compound microscope circa 1823 (ironically, for his study of the reproductive process of plants). The Estonian embryologist Karl Ernst von Baer (1792–1896) in 1827 was the first to identify the mammalian *ovum* and establish its role in human as well as animal reproduction. "Baer, Karl Ernst, Ritter von (knight of), Edler (lord) Von Huthorn" and "Biology," *Encyclopædia Britannica Online*.

63. For an extensive discussion, see Atkinson, and Jacqueline Marie Musacchio, *The Art and Ritual of Childbirth in Renaissance Italy* (New Haven, CT: Yale University Press, 1999). Current scholarship on Trotula casts doubt on both her dates and gender, and writings signed with her name are believed to originate from male practitioner(s) of the thirteenth century.

64. Atkinson, pp. 46–49.

65. Atkinson, pp. 35–36.

66. Atkinson, p. 113.

67. Jean Calvin, *Commentary on John*, 1550s, quoted in O'Meara, p. 133. Calvin paraphrases saint Bonaventure (1217–1274) as do the seventeenth-century Englishmen quoted below. English Protestants stated the case more firmly, charging that Mary "sinned by exceeding her boundes, and by intruding her selfe so far, as that she might chance to have obscured the glory of Christ thereby"; to which English Catholics countered, "We must take heede we so inlarge not the excellencie of the Mother, that wee diminish the glorie of the sonne." See Frances E. Dolan, *Whores of Babylon: Catholicism, Gender and Seventeenth-Century Print Culture* (Ithaca: Cornell University Press, 1999), p. 108.

68. A. G., *The Widdowes Mite. Cast into the Treasure-house of the Prerogatives, and Prayses of our B. Lady* (St. Omer, France: 1619), quoted in Dolan, *Whores of Babylon*, p. 108.

69. See Ilene Forsyth, *The Throne of Wisdom: Wood Sculptures of the Madonna in Romanesque France* (Princeton, NJ: Princeton University Press, 1972).

70. Louis Réau, *Iconographie de l'Art Chrétien* (Paris: Presses Universitaires de France, 1957), vol. 2, part 2, pp. 224–29.

71. Pelikan, pp. 100–02.

72. For discussions of Luther's Marian theology, see Hilda Graef, *Mary: A History of Doctrine and Devotion*, vol. 2: *From the Reformation to the Present Day* (New York: Sheed and Ward, 1965), pp. 6–12; O'Meara, pp. 109–46; and Pelikan, pp. 153–64.

73. Martin Luther, quoted in O'Meara, p. 111.

74. Martin Luther, quoted in Graef, vol 2, p. 12.

75. Felipe Fernández-Armesto, *Millennium: A History of the Last Thousand Years* (New York: Charles Scribner's Sons, 1995), pp. 159–60 and 195–96.

76. Murray, and Murray, "Magi," in *The Oxford Companion*, pp. 293–95.

77. Thomas F. Mathews, *The Clash of the Gods: A Reinterpretation of Early Christian Art* (Princeton, NJ: Princeton University Press, 1993), p. 83.

78. Murray and Murray, "Magi," pp. 293–95.

79. Bernard McGinn, "Apocalypticism and Church Reform: 1100–1500" in McGinn, ed., *Encyclopedia of Apocalypticisim*, vol. 2: *Apocalypticism in Western History and Culture* (New York: Continuum Press, 1998), pp. 74–109.

80. William Morris, ed., *American Heritage Dictionary of the English Language* (Boston: Houghton Mifflin Company, 1975).

81. The Visigothic, Frankish, Lombard, and Anglo-Saxon kingdoms converted to Christianity in the sixth and seventh centuries; the Frisian, Hessian, and continental Saxon tribes followed in the seventh and eighth centuries, while Christianity spread among Germans and Slavs in the ninth through eleventh centuries. Bokenkotter, pp. 151–52.

82. See for example, Penny Schine Gold, *The Lady & the Virgin: Image, Attitude, and Experience in Twelfth-Century France* (Chicago: University of Chicago Press, 1985); and Cunneen, chapter 5: "Mary, Her Son, and Their Extended Family: Twelfth-Century Europe," pp. 141–82. The title "Our Lady" had occurred infrequently in preceding centuries, but became widespread in the twelfth through fourteenth centuries.

83. Bokenkotter.

84. Albert J. Nevins, ed., *The Maryknoll Catholic Dictionary* (New York: Grosset & Dunlap, 1965), "China," p. 121. Nestorians were considered heretical Christians because they did not accept the hypostatic union of Christ's full humanity and divinity, believing instead that Jesus was partly divine and partly human.

85. John of Monte Corvino, *The Labors of a Friar in Cathay*, 1305, in James Bruce Ross and Mary Martin McLaughlin, eds., *The Portable Medieval Reader* (New York: Viking Press, 1949), pp. 476–81.

86. Jerrilynn D. Dodds and Edward J. Sullivan, eds., *Crowning Glory: Images of the Virgin in the Arts of Portugal* (Newark, NJ: Newark Museum, 1997), pp. 32–33. For an extensive discussion of Jesuit influences on non-Western art, see Gauvin A. Bailey, *Art on the Jesuit Missions in Asia and Latin America 1542–1773* (Toronto, ON/Buffalo, NY: University of Toronto Press, 1999).

87. Taddesse Tamrat, "Church and State in Ethiopia: The Early Centuries," in Marilyn E. Heldman, ed., *African Zion: The Sacred Art of Ethiopia* (New Haven, CT: Yale University Press, 1993), pp. 33–42.

88. Marilyn E. Heldman, *The Marian Icons of the Painter Frê Seyon: A Study in Fifteenth Century Ethiopian Art, Patronage, and Spirituality* (Wiesbaden, Germany: Harrassowitz Verlag, 1994), p. 196; and

"Maryam Seyon: Mary of Zion," in Heldman, *African Zion*, pp. 71–75.

89. Stanley Chojnacki, *Major Themes in Ethiopian Painting: Indigenous Developments, the Influence of Foreign Models, and their Adaptation from the 13th to the 19th Century* (Wiesbaden, Germany: Franz Steiner Verlag, 1983), pp. 376–78; and Ephraim Isaac, *The Ethiopian Church* (Boston: Henry N. Sawyer Company, 1967), p. 26. The Council of Florence was held 1438–1445.

90. Speech of pope Urban II to the Council of Clermont, 1095, in Cantor, pp. 91–93.

91. For a discussion of the metaphorical tradition of Mary as military general, and the use of icons as protection in battle, see Belting, *The Image and Its Public*, pp. 203–21; and Bissera V. Pentcheva, "Images behind the Veil of Texts: The Byzantine Paradox of the Virgin as Invincible General," paper delivered at *There's Something about Mary: The Virgin Mary in the Visual Arts* symposium, DMCC/Wellesley College, 11 November 2000.

92. Ricoldo di Monte-Croce, "Letter to Blessed Queen Mary," ca. 1280–1305, in Carolly Erickson, ed., *The Records of Medieval Europe* (Garden City, NY: Anchor Books, 1971), pp. 325–37. In this letter he invoked Mary's protection, chided her for not replying to his earlier missives, and informed her of Saracen attacks against her honor.

93. Franco Cardini, "The Warrior and the Knight," in Le Goff, p. 100.

94. Marina Warner, *Joan of Arc: The Image of Female Heroism* (London: Vintage Books, 1981), p. 235.

95. Ware, pp. 67–69.

96. John Morris Roberts, *A History of Europe* (New York: Allen Lane/The Penguin Press, 1996), pp. 148–51.

97. A degree of popular devotion to the CIRCUMCISION existed, particularly regarding relics of the foreskin of Christ, as this was the one bodily part believed to have remained on earth, given that Jesus ascended bodily to heaven; Leo Steinberg, *The Sexuality of Christ in Renaissance Art and in Modern Oblivion* (New York: Pantheon, 1983), pp. 50–65, 158–59.

98. E.g. Woolf, p. 253. For an extensive discussion see, Ruth Mellinkoff, *Outcasts: Signs of Otherness in Northern European Art of the late Middle Ages* (Berkeley: University of California Press, 1993); and Heinz Schreckenberg, *The Jews in Christian Art: An Illustrated History* (New York: Continuum, 1996).

99. Henry Royston Loyn, ed., *The Middle Ages: A Concise Encyclopaedia*, (London: Thames & Hudson, 1989), "Jews," pp. 190–93. The rabbi's tall ceremonial hat is probably imaginative, but there is an extra rounded shallow cap on the floor which presumably he will put on before leaving the synagogue.

100. The Greek term *adelphos* means a blood brother, but was on occasion used in New Testament times to describe kinsmen; R. Brown et al., *Mary in the New Testament*, pp. 65–72. St. Jerome (ca. 341–420) vehemently promoted Mary's perpetual virginity via the "cousin" interpretation. See Cunneen, p. 74.

101. Warner, *Alone*, pp. 366–67, fn. 30.

102. De Voragine, "The Birth of the Blessed Virgin Mary," in Ryan, vol. 2, pp. 149–57.

103. Pierre J. Payer, *The Bridling of Desire: Ideas of Sex in the Later Middle Ages* (Toronto: University of Toronto Press, 1993), pp. 6–9.

104. Warner, *Alone*, pp. 121–33. From 1135 until his death in 1153, saint Bernard preached 86 sermons on the Christian symbolism of the Song of Songs; Bernard of Clairvaux, "Sermon of the Song of Songs," *Selected Works*, trans. G. R. Evans (New York: Paulist Press, 1987), pp. 207–78.

105. Atkinson, pp. 149–54.

106. Duby, pp. 124–36, and Atkinson, p. 152. The Christian sacraments as defined at Trent are Baptism, Confirmation, Holy Eucharist, Penance (often called Confession or Reconciliation), Matrimony, Holy Orders, and Anointing the Sick.

107. Wiesner, in Marshall, p. 14.

108. Klapisch-Zuber, p. 287; and Musacchio, p. 21.

109. Bynum, *Holy Feast*, pp. 165–67; and Rudolph M. Bell, *Holy Anorexia* (Chicago: University of Chicago Press, 1985), pp. 29–40.

110. Raymond of Peñafort, *Summa de casibus*, 1235, in Payer, pp. 84–86. Raymond, who from 1238 on was master-general of the Dominican order, is citing Augustine's precedent.

111. Atkinson, pp. 6, 66. Barren women were greatly pitied and at times scorned, and their lives seen as almost meaningless. See, for example, Monna Margherita's treatment by her (fertile) sister-in-law, recorded in Iris Origo's *Merchant of Prato: Francesco di Marco Datini* (London: Jonathan Cape, 1957).

112. Wiesner, in Marshall, p. 12.

113. Musacchio, p. 10.

114. *Dévotions particuliéres pour les femmes enceintes*, 1665, quoted in Hufton, p. 187.

115. Hufton, p. 179; and Musacchio, pp. 141–42. In the previous century, St. Anne was favored in prayers for an easy birth. Saint

Nicholas was also popular in northern Europe at times of birth.

116. Hufton, pp. 186–87; and Musacchio, p. 142.

117. Liana Cheney, "Lavinia Fontana: Boston *Holy Family*," *Woman's Art Journal*, Spring/Summer 1989, pp. 12–15; and Liana Cheney, "Holy Family with Saints," in Vera Fortunati, *Lavinia Fontana of Bologna 1552–1614* (Washington, DC: National Museum of Women in the Arts, 1998), cat. no. 3, p. 54.

118. Martin Luther, "Estate of Marriage," mid-sixteenth century, quoted in Atkinson, p. 210.

119. For an extensive discussion, see Cynthia Hahn, " 'Joseph will perfect, Mary enlighten and Jesus save thee': The Holy Family as Marriage Model in the Mérode Triptych," *Art Bulletin*, 68, no. 1 (March 1986), pp. 54–66.

120. Woolf, pp. 162–64.

121. Warner, *Alone*, pp. 188–90. The feast of St. Joseph was not inserted into the liturgical calendar until 1479, and then at the lowest rank; Michael J. Walsh, *Dictionary of Catholic Devotions* (New York: HarperCollins, 1993), "Joseph," p. 147.

122. Atkinson, p. 159.

123. Le Goff, p. 16.

124. Atkinson, p. 149–56; and Musacchio, p. 25. See Musacchio for an extensive discussion of the material culture surrounding childbirth.

125. Florence's population of 120,000 in the late 1330s had dropped to 37,000 by 1427, and by 1552 had reached only 60,000. Steady population growth began only around 1600, and by the nineteenth century, the city still had not expanded to fill the circumference of its 1333 (pre-plague) walls. Musacchio, pp. 32–33, 155.

126. Sumptuary legislation; quoted in Musacchio, p. 54. Female chastity was essential if heirs were to be legitimate. The biblical quote is from Genesis 1:28. Ironically, the *signoria* chastises women's spending on goods for the birthing chamber, when documents indicate that fathers were quite keen to show off wealth and a new heir through lavish banquets.

127. Apostolos-Cappadona, "blue" and "red," pp. 50, 313.

128. The interpretation is the author's. Iconography of Mary as priest is generally associated with scenes of the PRESENTATION OF CHRIST IN THE TEMPLE; Bynum, pp. 268–69 and 409, fn. 41. Jean-Auguste-Dominique Ingres's 1841 painting of *The Virgin of the Host* (now in the Pushkin Museum, Moscow, with an 1854 variant in the Louvre, Paris) places Mary behind an altar adoring the host, the consecrated eucharistic wafer, in the priest's posi-tion, a theme accepted by the clergy of the time; Michael Paul Driskel, *Representing Belief: Religion, Art, and Society in Nineteenth-Century France* (University Park: Pennsylvania State University Press, 1992), pp. 101–04.

Religious Uses of Devoltional Art from 1500

1. Steven Ozment, *Protestants: The Birth of a Revolution* (New York: Doubleday Image Books, 1991), pp. 24–28.

2. Fernández-Armesto and Wilson, pp. 99–103.

3. Pius IV, *Injunctum nobis*, papal bull of 1564, in Bettenson, pp. 266–68.

4. "On the Invocation, Veneration, and Relics of Saints and on Sacred Images," December 1563, in H. J. Schroeder, ed., *Canon and Decrees of the Council of Trent* (St. Louis, MO: B. Herder, 1950), pp. 215–17. See also Belting, *Likeness and Presence*, pp. 554–55.

5. Bokenkotter, p. 255; and Jonathan Brown, *Golden Age Painting in Spain* (New Haven, CT: Yale University Press, 1991), p. 121.

6. J. Brown, p. 96.

7. In 1969–70 the Catholic church removed such popular but ahistorical medieval saints as Catherine of Alexandria, Margaret of Antioch, Barbara, Ursula, and Valentine from its official calendar and limited Christopher, George, Appolonia, and other doubtful saints to local cults; Walsh, Appendix, pp. 289–315.

8. Olivier Michel and Pierre Rosenberg, *Subleyras: 1699–1749* (Paris: Editorial de la Réunion des Musées Nationaux, 1987), pp. 317–19.

9. Diane De Grazia, *Correggio and His Legacy: Sixteenth Century Emilian Drawings* (Washington, DC: National Gallery of Art, 1984), p. 387.

10. Sites of Black Madonnas include Mariazell in Styria, Austria; Brussels, Hal, and Tongeren in Belgium; Walsingham in England; Arles, Auvergne, Chartres, Clermont, Corrèze, Le Puy, Liesse, Limousin, Lyons, Marsat, Montpellier, Neuilly, Orléans, and Rocamadour in France; Alltöting in Germany; Loreto, Rome, and Tindari in Italy; Czestochowska in Poland; Atocha (Madrid), Montserrat, Guadalupe, and Zaragoza in Spain; and Einsiedeln in Switzerland. See Cunneen, pp. 172–78; Réau, p. 95; Peg Streep, *Mary, Queen of Heaven: Miracles, Manifestations, and Meditations on Mary* (New York: QPBC, 1997), pp. 90–93, 111–20, 130–35, 146–47; and Warner, *Alone*, pp. 273–74. All are three-dimensional, save for Our Lady of Czestochowska, which is a painted icon. Cunneen outlines the parallels between the cults

of Cybele, Demeter, and Isis, whose idols were frequently black, and other pagan goddesses associated with blackness.

11. Jeanette Favrot Peterson, "Shades of Blackness: The Virgin of Guadalupe in Spain and the Americas," the Bakwin Lecture, Wellesley College, 15 February 2000; and Peterson, "*Nigra sum sed Formosa*: The Señor de Chalma and the Virgin of Guadalupe in Mexico," in *Black Christs of the Americas*, Arturo Lindsay, ed. (pending publication). The affectionate term "La Morenita" was used in reference to the images of Our Lady of Montserrat and Our Lady of Guadalupe in Spain, prior to the Spanish settlement of Central and South America.

Devotional Uses of Religious Art from 1500

1. Carl C. Christensen, *Art and the Reformation in Germany* (Athens: Ohio University Press, 1979, pp. 147–48.

2. Mitchell B. Merback, *The Thief, the Cross, and the Wheel: Pain and the Spectacle of Punishment in Medieval and Renaissance Europe* (Chicago: University of Chicago Press, 1999), pp. 293–95. I am grateful to Joseph L. Koerner for bringing this work to my attention. All four evangelists state that Jesus is crucified along with other men, but only Luke includes the story of one's spontaneous conversion, contradicting Mark and Matthew, who specify that "those who were crucified with him also reviled him" (Mark 15:32). Luke's story is repeated in the apocryphal Gospel of Nicodemus, where the good thief is named Dysmas, the bad thief Gestas, and the centurion Longinus. Luke's story is contradicted in the apocryphal Gospel of Peter (pre-ninth century, rediscovered 1886), where the two criminals ask that the Romans prolong Jesus' death so that he suffer more.

3. Matthaus Merian, *Iconum Biblicarum (Biblical Illustrations)*, 1625–27, reissued as one volume in 1630 by Lazari Zetzner of Strasbourg; anonymous translation (Wenatchee, WA: AVB Press, 1981), pp. 18–21. Merian is also defensive about printmaking, which he refers to as "monochromatic painting," an artform equal to pure painting, with the added advantage of allowing for multiple reproductions (p. 134).

4. Merian, p. 24.

5. Bokenkotter, pp. 255–60.

6. Benedictine Monks of St. Augustine's Abbey, Ramsgate, *The Book of Saints: A Dictionary of Servants of God* (Wilton, CT: Morehouse Publishing, 1989). Of the many handbooks on saints, this is the most accurate and extensive, with over 225 entries for the name "John" alone. Those seeking a reference guide applicable to the study of art will find Duchet-Suchaux and Pastoureau a more suitable iconographic guide.

7. Ignatius of Loyola, "Rules for Thinking with the Church," *Spiritual Exercises*, part II, in Bettenson, pp. 258–61.

8. Cunneen, p. 212–14.

9. Marie-France Boyer, *The Cult of the Virgin: Offerings, Ornaments, and Festivals* (London: Thames & Hudson, 2000), pp. 70–79. Belting traces the origin of the devotional practice of kissing Christ's wounds to a ninth-century Good Friday sermon by bishop George of Nicomedia (in office before 866 and after 877); Belting, *The Image and Its Public*, pp. 94–96

10. Horst W. Janson, *History of Art* (New York: Harry N. Abrams, 1984), pp. 483–84.

11. Bokenkotter, p. 156; and Sherrin Marshall, "Protestant, Catholic, and Jewish Women in the Early Modern Netherlands," in Marshall, *Women in Reformation and Counter-Reformation Europe*, pp. 125–26.

12. Patricia DeLeeuw, "Fragments of Ritual: The Liturgical Use of Objects in the Collection of Alexander Schn.tgen," *Fragmented Devotion: Medieval Objects from the Schnütgen Museum, Cologne*, Nancy Netzer and Virginia Reinburg, eds. (Boston: McMullen Museum of Art, 2000), p. 37.

13. Rule of Saint Claire, 1253, in Emilie Amt, ed., *Women's Lives in Medieval Europe: A Source Book* (New York: Routledge, 1993), pp. 235–38.

14. Warner, *Joan of Arc*, pp. 114–16.

15. Bokenkotter, p. 258.

The Madonna Unveiled II

1. See R. Brown et al., *Mary in the New Testament*, pp. 51–218; and O'Meara, pp. 147–202.

2. Anne Derbes, "Images East and West: The Ascent of the Cross," in *The Sacred Image East and West*, Robert Ousterhout and Leslie Brubaker, eds. (Chicago: University of Illinois Press, 1995), pp. 110–31.

3. See Lilian Armstrong's catalogue entry for this work, pp. 150–52; and Steinberg, p. 32. Mary covering Christ's nakedness was also a theme in medieval dramas; Woolf, p. 262

4. Margaret Alexiou, "Romanos Melodos, Kontakion 19: Mary at the Cross," *The Ritual Lament in Greek Tradition* (Cambridge, UK: Cambridge University Press, 1974), pp. 142–45. I am grateful to Bissera V. Pentcheva for bringing this work to my attention.

5. van Os, p. 104; Snyder, p. 21; and Wieck, pp. 60–90.

6. This becomes apparent when one encounters a wider range of narrative works in European churches, convents, and galleries, many of which emphasize bodily pain, mental suffering, and gory realism in contrast with the blandly maternal content of much religious art imported to this country. For a discussion of American art collecting in an anti-Catholic milieu, see Patricia Johnston, *'Imminent Dangers': Nativist Thought in Nineteenth-Century American Visual Culture*, pending publication (chapters presented at the Warren Center, Harvard University, 4 April, 2000.

7. St. Bonaventure (ca. 1217–1274), *Meditations on the Life of Christ*, fourteenth-century manuscript version, quoted in Miles, *Image as Insight*, p. 69. The passage concludes, "Here one may interpolate a very beautiful meditation of which the Scripture does not speak."

8. Musacchio, pp. 17–34.

9. Atkinson, pp. 64–100.

10. Warner, *Alone*, pp. 210–12.

11. Joann Kay McNamara, *Sisters in Arms: Catholic Nuns through Two Millennia* (Cambridge, MA: Harvard University Press, 1996), pp. 327, 391–93.

12. Joanna E. Ziegler, *Sculpture of Compassion: The Pietà and the Beguines in the Southern Low Countries c. 1300–c. 1600* (Brussels: Institut Historique Belge de Rome, 1992).

13. Warner, *Alone*, pp. 210–12; and Cunneen, pp. 47–48. John also speaks of "the mother of Jesus" in his account of the miracle at the Marriage of Cana (John 2:1–12).

14. Ozment, pp. 72–77.

15. Rebecca Hayward, "Between the Living and the Dead: Widows as Heroines of Medieval Romances," in Carlson and Weisl, p. 229.

16. *Magdeburg Recht (Laws of Magdeburg)*, 1261, in Amt, pp. 70–72.

17. Hufton, p. 66; and A. Abrams, "Women Traders in Medieval London," in S. Bell, pp. 152–58. Nevertheless, medieval tradeswomen had difficulty supporting themselves.

18. Marshall, in Marshall, pp. 121–34.

19. Hufton, p. 223.

20. Hayward, in Carlson and Weisl, p. 229.

21. Hufton, pp. 33–38.

22. Atkinson, pp. 172–73. Birgitta was an unusual figure and one of the few historic medieval saints not to be a virgin. She was a Swedish noblewoman who married and bore eight children (one of whom, Catherine, also became a saint). Widowed at the age of 41, she entered a convent and eventually founded the Brigittine order of nuns. Her mystic visions had occurred from childhood onward, long before she adopted a celibate lifestyle.

23. Apostolos-Cappadona, "Judith," p. 203. See also fn. 5, page 111, in this text. Archaeologists and biblical scholars find no evidence of an Assyrian siege of a city named Bethulia nor battle anywhere in Palestine within this time frame; if Judith's story is entirely imagined, it is wonderful to speculate why the need was felt to invent such a heroine.

24. Walter L. Strauss, ed., *Albrecht Dürer: Woodcuts and Wood Blocks* (New York: Abaris Books, 1980), cat. no. 94, pp. 259–61.

25. Hayward, in Carlson and Weisl, pp. 225–26.

26. Atkinson, pp. 230–34; and Martin Luther, *Letters of Spiritual Council*, mid-sixteenth century, quoted in Atkinson, p. 213.

27. Wiesner, in Marshall, p. 18.

28. Charles de la Roncière, "Tuscan Notables on the Eve of the Renaissance," in Duby, p. 229.

29. Hufton, pp. 221–22. Christine de Pisan (1364–ca. 1430) was a rare exception; widowed at 25 with three young children, she chose not to remarry but to earn her living through her writing. Still, she complained of her widowed and exiled state in a poem: "alone am I without friends who live nearby;" Klapisch-Zuber, p. 308.

30. Dolan, *Whores of Babylon*, pp. 149–50; and Frances E. Dolan, "Command of Mary: Marion Devotion, Henrietta Maria's Intercessions, and Catholic Motherhood," paper delivered at the Humanities Center, Harvard University, 13 May 1999.

31. Atkinson, pp. 24–25, 60–61; Hufton, pp. 182, 197–203; and Musacchio, p. 52. Hufton observes that fifteenth-and sixteenth-century urban women were encouraged not to nurse because city "milk" was thought to be unhealthy compared to that of country women, and that upper-class women were thought to produce inferior breast milk, which, due to the tight lacing of their bodices, may have had some basis in truth; Hufton, p. 198.

32. St. Bernardino of Siena, fifteenth-century sermon, quoted in Atkinson, p. 60

33. Trotula, "Diseases of Women," eleventh through thirteenth centuries, in Amt, p. 105.

34. Soranus of Ephesus, *Gynecology*, second century, quoted in Atkinson, p. 60.

35. For a review of the cult surrounding the Virgin's milk, see Warner, *Alone*, chapter 13, pp. 192–205; and Margaret R. Miles, "The Virgin's One Bare Breast: Nudity, Gender, and

Religious Meaning in Tuscan Early Renaissance Culture" in *Expanding Discourse: Feminism and Art History,* Norma Broude and Mary D. Garrard, eds. (New York: HarperCollins, 1992), pp. 26–37. Carolyn Walker Bynum draws attention to parallels between images of Mary nursing the infant Jesus and images of Jesus displaying his wounds; Bynum, *Holy Feast,* pp. 260–76.

36. Atkinson, pp. 156–59.

37. Desiderius Erasmus, "The New Mother," *Colloquia,* 1522–1533, quoted in Atkinson, pp. 201–04.

38. Atkinson, pp. 80–81.

39. William Crashaw, *Jesuites Gospell,* 1610, quoted in Dolan, *Whores of Babylon,* p. 113.

40. Paolo Bellini, *L'Opera Incisa di Carlo Maratti* (Pavia: Museo Civico-Castello Visconteo, 1977), cat. no. 22, p. 86; and Ulrich Thieme and Felix Becker, "Giovita Garavaglia," *Allgemeines Lexikon der bildenden Künstler von der Antike bis zur Gegenwart* (Leipzig, W. Engelmann, 1907–1950), vol. 13, p. 167.

41. Thomas à Kempis, *Meditations on Our Lady,* mid-fifteenth century, trans. W.H.F.S. (Ditchling, Sussex, UK: St. Dominic's Press, 1929), pp. 24–25.

42. Warner, *Alone,* pp. 285–98.

43. Réau, p. 61.

44. Jean Calvin, *Treatise on Relics,* mid-sixteenth century quoted in Warner, *Alone,* p. 200.

45. Catholic University of America, *New Catholic Encyclopedia* (New York: McGraw-Hill, 1967), "Relics;" and Réau, p. 61.

46. The same tale is found in the Smithfield Decretals (mid-fourteenth century, England).

47. Walsh, various.

48. Berger, pp. 37–38. Burial may also partially explain the blackened surfaces of many European cult Madonnas, and why some feature Mary alone without the infant Jesus, or with the child added later to the ensemble.

49. Sebastián García, *Guadalupe: Cita de Fe y Arte* (Barcelona: Comunidad Franciscana, 1985). While residing in Spain during the 1980s and early 1990s, I had occasion to be called in to advise workmen who, while renovating a fourteenth-century church, had unearthed an eleventh-century statue of CHRIST PANTOCRATOR (Christ in Majesty with hand raised in blessing), and was able to witness its disinterring.

50. The Benedictines of Guadalupe discount the pre-thirteenth century account as legend, but accept most of the mid-thirteenth story of Gil Cordero's unearthing a statue from the twelfth century that for some reason had been buried in this remote mountainous region, a region which to this day remains largely uninhabited; García.

51. Laplana and Macià, pp. 19–23.

52. Walsh, "Einsiedeln," p. 93.

53. Laplana and Macià, pp. 41–48. Curiously, though Montserrat is one of the most famed Black Madonnas, artists' replicas from the fifteenth through the eighteenth century colored her skin anywhere from marble white to coal black, and every shade of brown in between. It is not until the late eighteenth century that we find visitors speculating on why her face is dark (or rather, whether it was darkened accidentally by candle smoke and incense or was intended to be dark).

54. Pelikan, pp. 100–02; and Ware, pp. 260–62. Once again, the distinction is made between *latreia* (adoration, reserved for God), *douleia* (reverence, shown for saints and holy figures), and *hyperdouleia* (extreme reverence, allowed to Mary).

55. The *Golden Legend*'s virgin-martyrs, for example, chose death over marriage and in many cases were tortured by their fathers (Juliana, Barbara, Margaret, Christina) or fiancés (Lucy, Anastasia, Catherine, Agnes, Agatha, and Justina) for refusing to obey their families' wishes.

56. For a discussion of women's motivations in joining religious orders, see Bynum, *Holy Feast,* esp. pp. 13–30.

57. Wiesner, in Marshall, p. 11.

58. Sherrill Cohen, "Asylums for Women in Counter-Reformation Italy," in Sherrin Marshall, ed., *Women in Reformation and Counter-Reformation Europe,* pp. 166–88; and Marshall, in Marshall, pp. 128–33.

59. Jeryldene M. Wood, *Women, Art, and Spirituality: The Poor Clares of Early Modern Italy* (New York: Cambridge University Press, 1996), p. 14.

60. See, for example, "Maria Monk," *The Awful Disclosures of Maria Monk* (New York: Howe and Bates, 1836); and Rebecca Reed, *Six Months in a Convent* (Boston: Russell, Odiorne & Metcalf, 1835), reprinted in Nancy Lusignan Schultz, *Veils of Fear: Nineteenth Century Convent Tales* (West Lafayette, IN: NotaBell Books, 1999). A centuries-old misogynism, which cannot comprehend women willingly giving up sexual activity, also influences historic and contemporary attitudes toward nuns. Sixteenth-century Protestant reformers, living in an age when the female sex drive was considered stronger than the male, consid-

ered female celibacy contrary to natural and divine order; Wiesner, in Marshall, p. 13.

61. McNamara, pp. 353–56.

62. McNamara, p. 375.

63. McNamara, pp. 186, 385–400. Jeryldene Wood notes that dowries brought in to Franciscan convents by young postulants were used for their support, but those brought by widows (whose days in the convent were numbered, so to speak), would be dedicated in part to the purchasing of artworks and liturgical objects, as would legacies left to the nuns; Wood, pp. 103–04.

64. McNamara, pp. 385–400; and Cohen, pp. 168–72.

65. McNamara, pp. 395–96.

66. Grabar, 1968, pp. 31–51. Thomas Mathews in his intriguing book *The Clash of the Gods* disagrees with what he terms "the Emperor mystique," arguing that early Christians did not depict Jesus as a ruler. However, he has yet to comment extensively on Mary's presentation.

67. Joanna L. Chamberlayne, "Crowns and Virgins: Queenmaking during the Wars of the Roses," in Lewis et al., *Young Medieval Women*, pp. 47–68.

68. Lines spoken by the character of Isaiah in the Coventry pageant, 1456, quoted by Chamberlayne, in Lewis et al. p. 53.

69. R. Brown et al., *Mary in the New Testament*, pp. 219–39.

70. Warner, *Alone*, pp. 81–89.

71. Gertrud Schiller, *Ikonographie der christlichen Kunst* (Gutersloh, Germany: Gutersloher Verlagshaus G. Mohn, 1968–1980), vol. 4, part 2, pp. 83–95.

72. I am grateful to Fr. Ted Stylianopoulos for clarifying my understanding of Orthodox doctrine, teaching, and tradition.

73. Schiller, vol. 4, part 2, p. 405, plates 709–12 (works dated ca. 1235, 1225–1280/90, 1270–80, and third-quarter thirteenth century; and Warner, *Alone*, pp. 81–89. The Feast of the Dormition, marking Mary's *transitus* and assumption, was widely celebrated by the fourth century, and Emperor Maurice (582–602) made official its August date; O'Meara, p. 76.

74. O'Meara, p. 118.

75. O'Meara, pp. 118–22. The Ascension, traditionally celebrated on a Thursday, represents the end of the period in which (according to Matthew, Mark, and Luke) the resurrected Jesus reappears to his followers before making his final ascent into heaven (described by Mark and Luke).

76. Eric Young, "A Rediscovered Painting by Pedro Berruguete and Its Companion Panels," *Art Bulletin*, 57, no. 4 (December 1975), pp. 473–75. Despite the complexity of this polyptych, it is smaller than most *retablos mayores* of this period and was probably designed for a side chapel rather than a main altar.

77. Judith Berg Sobré, *The Artistic Splendors of the Spanish Kingdoms: The Art of Fifteenth-Century Spain* (Boston: Isabella Stewart Gardner Museum, 1996), cat. no. 10, pp. 46–48; and María Pilar Silva Maroto, *Pedro Berruguete* (Valladolid: Junta de Castilla y León, Conserjería de Educación y Cultura, 1998). The upturned crescent moon may also be a clue to dating. The crescent moon was often turned downward in Spanish compositions (shortly) after 1492 to signify victory over Islam at the 1492 Battle of Granada; Apostolos-Cappadona, "Moon," p. 258. Nevertheless, in all known examples, Berrugeute's Madonnas stand on a moon facing upward (see cat. no. 7 in this volume).

78. Schiller, vol. 4, part 2, pp. 169–78; and Suzanne L. Stratton, *The Immaculate Conception in Spanish Art* (New York: Cambridge University Press, 1994).

79. Francisco Pacheco, *El arte de la pintura*, 1649, quoted in Murray and Murray "Immaculate Conception," pp. 239–40. Details supplied by Pacheco and omitted from the above quote include the clothing of Mary in a white tunic and blue mantle, and the inclusion of the text *tota pulchra es amica mea* ("ah, you are beautiful, my love," Song of Solomon 1:16).

80. Murray and Murray, "Ascension," pp. 34–35 and "Isaiah," pp. 245–46.

81. Ranke-Heinemann, p. 193. Augustine also opposed the doctrine of the Immaculate Conception, for reasons of sexual contamination, while Bernard of Clairvaux opposed it due to lack of scriptural precedent; Pelikan, pp. 192–95.

82. Walsh, "Immaculate Conception," p. 136.

83. Graef, vol. 2, p. 16.

84. Ozment, pp. 11–31; and Marshall, pp. 125–26.

85. Ozment, p. 17.

86. Ozment, pp. 4–7, 50–51; and Walsh, "Indulgences," pp. 138–41.

87. Fernández-Armesto and Wilson, p. 205–06.

88. Ozment, pp. ix-xiv. The principle of *cuius regio, eius religio* also brought a modicum of tolerance to Catholic-Protestant coexistence; Merback, p. 293.

89. Marshall, pp. 122–23.

90. Marshall, pp. 120–26.

91. Wiesner, in Marshall, pp. 9–10, 15–16.

92. Wiesner, in Marshall, pp. 18–26.

Legacy

1. See, for example, Driskel; Leslie Parris, ed., *The Pre-Raphaelites* (London: Tate Gallery, 1984); and Pierre Theeberge, ed., *Lost Paradise: Symbolist Europe* (Montréal: Montréal Museum of Fine Arts, 1995).

2. The Léger painting *Woman and Child*, entered the collection with the title *Mother and Child*, although nothing in the painting implies any relation between the two sitters save for visual association with several centuries of VIRGIN AND CHILD imagery.

3. Erich Heckel, *Holzschnitte, Radierungen, Lithographien aus den Jahren 1905 bis 1968* (Bonn: 1968).

4. Otto Müller, *Zigeunermappe* (Dresden: Verlag der Kunst, 1958).

5. Once widowed, Jackson would resume posing for her aunt; Sylvia Wolf, *Julia Margaret Cameron's Women* (Chicago: Art Institute of Chicago, 1998). Julia Prinsep Jackson was named after her aunt Julia Margaret Cameron. She was the daughter of Cameron's sister Maria (known as Mia); the wife first of publisher Herbert Duckworth, then scholar Lesley Stephen; and the mother of author Virginia Woolf and artist Vanessa Bell. Like so many Victorian women, her identity was defined by her relation to others.

6. Barbara L. Michaels, *Gertrude Käsebier: The Photographer and her Photographs* (New York: Harry N. Abrams, 1992), pp. 17–18, 45–53, 76–83.

7. The photograph's alternate title is *Mrs. Lee Mourning Her Child*; its sitter was Agnes Rand Lee (1868–1939), a poet and friend of Käsebier's whose only child had died five years earlier.

8. Michaels, pp. 51–52.

9. Author's observation. The original negative has not been examined.

10. Michaels comes to the same conclusion, citing LAMENTATION imagery as a source for the *Heritage of Motherhood*, modified to make the allusion more subtle; p. 52. However, the alteration of the negative (vs. the inking of one image) indicates a greater commitment initially on Käsebier's part to this theme.

11. Bokenkotter, p. 287.

12. Streep, pp. 176–209. The church has not officially ruled on the Knock apparition, but papal visits suggest approval is likely.

13. Medieval traditions record Mary's one-time miraculous intervention—often via the media of painted or sculpted images— among common people, but few people of this class reported recurring visions.

14. Streep, p. 176; and Benedictine Monks of St. Augustine's Abbey, p. 255. While medieval tales of wondrous interventions by visions of Mary or images coming to life are plentiful, the Marian apparitions under consideration, both prior to and during the nineteenth century, involve sustained appearances and direct communications. Also, during the Middle Ages, appearances of saints and the infant Jesus were common, whereas post-medieval apparitions are overwhelmingly of Marian; Carroll, *Cult of the Virgin Mary*, p. 115.

15. Carroll, *Cult of the Virgin Mary*, pp. 132–34. Catherine Labouré (1806–1875) of Paris was a novice nun when she experienced her apparition, while Mélanie Calvat dit Mathieu (1831–1904) of La Salette, Bernadette Soubirous (1844–1879) of Lourdes, and María Lucia Irma dos Santos (b. 1907) of Fátima became nuns after their visions. Labouré and Soubirous were later canonized; Streep, pp. 176–209.

16. Barbara Corrado Pope, "Immaculate and Powerful: The Marian Revival in the Nineteenth Century," in Clarissa W. Atkinson, Constance H. Buchanan, and Margaret R. Miles, eds., *Immaculate and Powerful: The Female in Sacred Image and Social Reality* (Boston: Beacon Press, 1985), p. 176.

17. Pacheco, quoted in Murray and Murray, "Immaculate Conception," pp. 239–40. See fn. 281.

18. Carroll, *Cult of the Virgin Mary*, pp. 166–68. Released in 1832, the medal was originally known as the "Medal of the Immaculate Conception" and its popularity contributed to the papal decision to proclaim the dogma of the IMMACULATE CONCEPTION in 1854.

19. Pope, in Atkinson et al., pp. 173–200.

20. Robert A. Orsi, *The Madonna of 115th Street: Faith and Community in Italian Harlem, 1880–1950* (New Haven, CT: Yale University Press, 1985), pp. 55–58.

21. Orsi, pp. 61–63.

22. Margarita Zires, "Our Undocumented Lady of Guadalupe," *Voices of Mexico*, no. 45 (Oct/Dec 1998), pp. 42–50.

23. For further discussion, see Colleen McDannell, *Material Christianity: Religion and Popular Culture in America* (New Haven: Yale University Press, 1995); and David Morgan, *Visual Piety: A History and Theory of Popular Religious Images* (Berkeley: University of California Press, 1998).

24. Heldman, *Marian Icons*, p. 196; and Heldman, *African Zion*, pp. 71–75.

BIBLIOGRAPHY

Amt, Emilie, ed. *Women's Lives in Medieval Europe: A Source Book.*
New York: Routledge, 1993.

Andersson, Christiane, and Charles Talbot. *From a Mighty Fortress:
Prints, Drawings, and Books in the Age of Luther 1483–1546,*
exhibition catalogue. Detroit, MI: Detroit Institute of Arts,
1983.

Apostolos-Cappadona, Diane. *Dictionary of Women in Religious Art.*
New York: Oxford University Press, 1998.

Ashe, Geoffrey. *The Virgin: Mary's Cult and the Re-emergence of the
Goddess.* London and New York: Arkana, 1976.

Ashley, Kathleen, and Pamela Sheingorn. *Interpreting Cultural
Symbols: Saint Anne in Late Medieval Society.* Athens: University
of Georgia Press, 1990.

Atkinson, Clarissa W. *The Oldest Vocation: Christian Motherhood in
the Middle Ages.* Ithaca, NY: Cornell University Press, 1991.

Atkinson, Clarissa W., Constance H. Buchanan, and Margaret R.
Miles, eds. *Immaculate and Powerful: The Female in Sacred Image
and Social Reality.* Boston: Beacon Press, 1985.

Bailey, Gauvin A. *Art on the Jesuit Missions in Asia and Latin America 1542–1773.* Toronto, ON/Buffalo, NY: University of
Toronto Press, 1999.

Baxandall, Michael. *Painting and Experience in Fifteenth-Century
Italy.* Oxford, UK: Oxford University Press, 1988.

Bede, the Venerable. *The Ecclesiastical History of the English People.*
Oxford, UK: Oxford University Press, 1969.

Begg, Ean C. M. *The Cult of the Black Virgin.* London: Arkana,
1985.

Beilen, Elaine V. *Redeeming Eve: Women Writers of the English Renaissance.* Princeton, NJ: Princeton University Press, 1987.

Bell, Rudolph M. *Holy Anorexia.* Chicago: University of Chicago
Press, 1985.

Bell, Susan Groag, ed. *Women From the Greeks to the French Revolution.* Stanford, CA: Stanford University Press, 1973.

Bellini, Paolo, *L'Opera Incisa di Carlo Maratti.* Pavia, Italy: Musco
Civico-Castello Visconteo, 1997.

Belting, Hans. *The Image and its Public in the Middle Ages: Form and
Function of Early Paintings of the Passion,* trans. Mark Bartusis and
Raymond Meyer. New Rochelle, NY: Aristide D. Caratzas, 1990.

Belting, Hans. *Likeness and Presence: A History of the Image before the
Era of Art,* trans. Edmund Jephcott. Chicago: University of
Chicago Press, 1994.

Benedictine Monks of St. Augustine's Abbey, Ramsgate. *The Book
of Saints: A Dictionary of Servants of God.* Wilton, CT: Morehouse Publishing, 1989.

Berger, Pamela. *The Goddess Obscured: Transformation of the Grain
Protectoress from Goddess to Saint.* Boston: Beacon Press, 1986.

Bernard of Clairvaux. *Selected Works,* trans. G. R. Evans. New York:
Paulist Press, 1987.

Bettenson, Henry, ed. *Documents of the Christian Church.* London:
Oxford University Press, 1963.

Billet, Bernard, and Alphonse Bossard, et al. *Dictionary of Mary.*
New York: Catholic Book Publishing, 1985.

Bokenkotter, Thomas. *A Concise History of the Catholic Church.* Garden City, NY: Doubleday, 1979.

Boyer, Marie-France. *The Cult of the Virgin: Offerings, Ornaments,
and Festivals.* London: Thames & Hudson, 2000.

Broude, Norma, and Mary D. Garrard, eds. *Expanding Discourse:
Feminism and Art History.* New York: HarperCollins, 1992.

Brown, Jonathan. *Golden Age Painting in Spain.* New Haven, CT:
Yale University Press, 1991.

Brown, Raymond E. *An Introduction to the New Testament.* New
York: Doubleday, 1997.

Brown, Raymond E., Karl P. Donfried, Joseph A. Fitzmyer, and
John Reumann, eds. *Mary in the New Testament: A Collaborative
Assessment by Protestant and Roman Catholic Scholars.* Philadel-
phia: Fortress Press, 1978.

Bynum, Caroline Walker. *Fragmentation and Redemption: Essays on
Gender and the Human Body in Medieval Religion.* New York:
Zone Books, 1992.

Bynum, Carolyn Walker. *Holy Feast and Holy Fast: The Religious Significance of Food to Medieval Women.* Berkeley: University of
California Press, 1987.

Bynum, Caroline Walker. *Jesus as Mother: Studies in the Spirituality
of the High Middle Ages.* Berkeley: University of California
Press, 1982.

Cantor, Norman F., ed. *The Medieval Reader.* New York: Harper-
Collins, 1994.

Carlson, Cindy L., and Angela Jane Weisl, eds. *Constructions of
Widowhood and Virginity in the Middle Ages.* New York: St. Martin's Press, 1999.

Carroll, Michael P. *Catholic Cults and Devotions: A Psychological
Inquiry.* Kingston, ON/Montréal, QB: McGill-Queen's University Press, 1989.

Carroll, Michael P. *The Cult of the Virgin Mary: Psychological
Origins.* Princeton, NJ: Princeton University Press, 1986.

Carroll, Michael P. *Madonnas That Maim: Popular Catholicism in Italy since the Fifteenth Century.* Baltimore, MD: Johns Hopkins University Press, 1992.

Catholic University of America. *New Catholic Encyclopedia.* New York: McGraw-Hill, 1967.

Chojnacki, Stanley. *Major Themes in Ethiopian Painting: Indigenous Developments, the Influence of Foreign Models, and their Adaptation from the 13th to the 19th Century.* Wiesbaden, Germany: Franz Steiner Verlag, 1983.

Chorpenning, Joseph F. *The Holy Family as Prototype of the Civilization of Love: Images from the Viceregal Americas.* Philadelphia: Saint Joseph's University Press, 1996.

Christensen, Carl C. *Art and Reformation in Germany.* Athens: Ohio University Press, 1979.

Christian, William A., Jr. *Apparitions in Late Medieval and Renaissance Spain.* Princeton, NJ: Princeton University Press, 1981.

Christian, William A., Jr. *Person and God in a Spanish Valley.* New York: Seminar Press, 1972.

Christine de Pisan. *The Treasure of the City of Ladies, or the Book of the Three Virtues,* Sarah Lawson, trans. Harmondsworth, UK: Penguin Books, 1985.

Cruden, Alexander. *Cruden's Complete Concordance,* A. D. Adams, C. H. Irwin, and S. A. Waters, eds. Grand Rapids, MI: Zondervan Publishing House, 1949.

Cuenod, Anne et al. *Saint-Pierre, cathédrale de Genève, un monument, une exposition,* exhibition catalogue. Geneva, Switzerland: Musée Rath, 1982.

Cunneen, Sally. *In Search of Mary: The Woman and the Symbol.* New York: Ballantine Books, 1996.

Devotio Moderna: Basic Writings. John van Engen, trans. New York: Paulist Press, 1988.

Dodds, Jerrilynn D., and Edward J. Sullivan, eds. *Crowning Glory: Images of the Virgin in the Arts of Portugal,* exhibition catalogue. Newark, NJ: Newark Museum, 1997.

Dolan, Frances E. "Command of Mary: Marion Devotion, Henrietta Maria's Intercessions, and Catholic Motherhood," paper delivered at the Humanities Center, Harvard University, 13 May 1999.

Dolan, Frances E. *Whores of Babylon: Catholicism, Gender and Seventeenth-Century Print Culture.* Ithaca, NY: Cornell University Press, 1999.

Driskel, Michael Paul. *Representing Belief: Religion, Art, and Society in Nineteenth-Century France.* University Park: Pennsylvania State University Press, 1992.

Duby, Georges, ed. *A History of Private Life: Revelations of the Medieval World,* vol. 2. Cambridge, MA: Belknap Press, 1988.

Duchet-Suchaux, Gaston, and Michel Pastoureau. *The Bible and the Saints.* Paris and New York: Flammarion, 1994.

Durham, Michael S. *Miracles of Mary: Apparitions, Legends, and Miraculous Works of the Blessed Virgin Mary.* San Francisco: HarperSanFrancisco, 1995.

Eck, Diana. *On Common Ground: World Religions in America.* New York: Columbia University Press, 1997.

Erickson, Carolly, ed. *The Records of Medieval Europe.* Garden City, NY: Anchor Books, 1971.

Evans, Helen C., and William D. Wixom, eds. *The Glory of Byzantium: Art and Culture of the Middle Byzantine Era,* A.D. *843–1261,* exhibition catalogue. New York: Metropolitan Museum of Art, 1997.

Fernández-Armesto, Felipe. *Millennium: A History of the Last Thousand Years.* New York: Charles Scribner's Sons, 1995.

Fernández-Armesto, Felipe, and Derek Wilson. *Reformations: A Radical Interpretation of Christianity and the World 1500–2000.* New York: Scribner, 1996.

Forsyth, Ilene. *The Throne of Wisdom: Wood Sculptures of the Madonna in Romanesque France.* Princeton, NJ: Princeton University Press, 1972.

Foster, Marjory Bolger. *The Iconography of St. Joseph in Netherlandish Art, 1400–1500.* Ph.D. diss., University of Kansas, 1978. Ann Arbor, MI: University Microfilms International, 1979.

García, Sebastián. *Guadalupe: Cita de Fe y Arte.* Barcelona: Comunidad Franciscana, 1985.

Gold, Penny Schine. *The Lady & the Virgin: Image, Attitude, and Experience in Twelfth-Century France.* Chicago: University of Chicago Press, 1985.

Grabar, André. *The Beginnings of Christian Art 200–395.* London: Thames and Hudson, 1967.

Grabar, André. *Christian Iconography: A Study of its Origins.* Princeton, NJ: Princeton University Press, 1968.

Graef, Hilda. *Mary: A History of Doctrine and Devotion,* vol. 1: *From the Beginning to the Eve of the Reformation.* New York: Sheed and Ward, 1963.

Graef, Hilda. *Mary: A History of Doctrine and Devotion,* vol. 2 *From the Reformation to the Present Day.* New York: Sheed and Ward, 1965.

Greeley, Andrew. *The Mary Myth: On the Femininity of God.* New York: Seabury Press, 1977.

Guerrero Lovillo, José. *Las Cántigas: Estudio Arqueológico de sus Miniaturas.* Madrid: Instituto Diego Velásquez, 1949.

Hahn, Cynthia. " 'Joseph will perfect, Mary enlighten and Jesus save thee': The Holy Family as Marriage Model in the Mérode Triptych." *Art Bulletin*, 68, no. 1 (March 1986), pp. 54–66.

Hamington, Maurice. *Hail Mary?: The Struggle for Ultimate Womanhood in Catholicism.* New York: Routledge, 1995.

Harbison, Craig. *The Last Judgment in sixteenth-century Northern Europe: a Study of the Relation between Art and the Reformation.* New York: Garland Publishers, 1976.

Heldman, Marilyn E., ed. *African Zion: The Sacred Art of Ethiopia,* exhibition catalogue. New Haven, CT: Yale University Press, 1993.

Heldman, Marilyn E. *The Marian Icons of the Painter Frê Seyon: A Study in Fifteenth-Century Ethiopian Art, Patronage, and Spirituality.* Wiesbaden, Germany: Harrassowitz Verlag, 1994.

Henry, Avril, ed. *The Mirour of Mans Saluacioune: A Middle English translation of Speculum humanae salvationis.* Philadelphia: University of Pennsylvania Press, 1987.

Holt, Elizabeth Gilmore, ed. *A Documentary History of Art*, vol. 1: *The Middle Ages and the Renaissance.* Princeton, NJ: Princeton University Press, 1947.

Hufton, Olwen. *The Prospect Before Her: A History of Women in Western Europe 1500–1800.* New York: Alfred A. Knopf, 1996.

Jacobus de Voragine. *The Golden Legend: Readings on the Saints,* trans. William Granger Ryan. Princeton, NJ: Princeton University Press, 1993.

Jameson, Mrs. (Anna). *Legends of the Madonna as Represented in the Fine Arts.* Boston: Houghton Mifflin, ca. 1895.

Jensen, Robin Margaret. *Understanding Early Christian Art.* London: Routledge, 2000.

Johnston, Patricia. *'Imminent Dangers': Nativist Thought in Nineteenth-Century American Visual Culture,* pending publication; chapters presented at the Warren Center, Harvard University, 4 April 2000.

Jones, Pamela M., ed. "The Reception of Christian Art." *Art Journal*, 57, no. 1 (Spring 1998).

Kirschbaum, Engelbert. *Lexicon der Christlichen Ikonographie.* Rome: Herder, 1968–76.

Klapisch-Zuber, Christiane. "Women and the Family," in Jacques Le Goff, ed., *The Medieval World.* London: Parkgate Books, 1979, pp. 285–312.

Kloek, Els, Nicole Teeuwen, and Marijke Huisman, eds. *Women of the Golden Age: An International Debate on Women in seventeenth-century Holland, England and Italy.* Hilversum, Netherlands: Verloren, 1994.

Koran, trans. N. J. Dawood. London: Penguin Books, 1956.

Landau, David, and Peter Parshall. *The Renaissance Print 1470–1550.* New Haven, CT: Yale University Press, 1994.

Laplana, Josep de C., and Teresa Macià. *Nigra Sum: Iconografía de Santa María de Montserrat,* exhibition catalogue. Barcelona: Publicaciones Abadia de Montserrat, 1995.

Lefkowitz, Mary R. *Women in Greek Myth.* Baltimore: Johns Hopkins University Press, 1986.

Le Goff, Jacques, ed. *The Medieval World.* London: Parkgate Books, 1979.

Levi D'Ancona, Mirella. *The Iconography of the Immaculate Conception in the Middle Ages and Early Renaissance.* New York: College Art Association of America/Art Bulletin, 1957.

Lewis, Katherine J., Noël James Menuge, and Kim M. Phillips, eds. *Young Medieval Women.* New York: St. Martin's Press, 1999.

Lowrie, Walter. *Art in the Early Church.* New York: Harper & Row, 1947.

Loyn, H. R., ed. *The Middle Ages: A Concise Encyclopaedia.* London: Thames & Hudson, 1989.

MacGregor, Neil with Erika Langmuir. *Seeing Salvation: Images of Christ in Art.* New Haven, CT: Yale University Press, 2000.

Maeckelberghe, Els. *Desperately Seeking Mary: A Feminist Appropriation of a Traditional Religious Symbol.* The Hague, Netherlands: Pharos, 1994.

Mancinelli, Fabrizio, et al. *The Life of the Madonna in Art.* Boston: Daughters of St. Paul, 1985.

Marshall, Sherrin, ed. *Women in Reformation and Counter-Reformation Europe: Public and Private Worlds.* Bloomington: Indiana University Press, 1989.

Mathews, Thomas F. *The Clash of the Gods: A Reinterpretation of Early Christian Art.* Princeton, NJ: Princeton University Press, 1993.

McAndrew, John, and Curtis H. Shell. *Catalogue of European and American Sculpture and Paintings at Wellesley College.* Wellesley, MA: Jewett Arts Center Wellesley College, 1958, repr. 1964.

McDannell, Colleen. *Material Christianity: Religion and Popular*

Culture in America. New Haven, CT: Yale University Press, 1995.

McGinn, Bernard, ed. *Encyclopedia of Apocalypticisim*, vol 2: *Apocalypticism in Western History and Culture.* New York: Continuum Press, 1998.

McNamara, Joann Kay. *Sisters in Arms: Catholic Nuns through Two Millennia.* Cambridge, MA: Harvard University Press, 1996.

Mellinkoff, Ruth. *Outcasts: Signs of Otherness in Northern European Art of the late Middle Ages.* Berkeley: University of California Press, 1993.

Merback, Mitchell B. *The Thief, the Cross, and the Wheel: Pain and the Spectacle of Punishment in Medieval and Renaissance Europe.* Chicago: University of Chicago Press, 1998.

Merian, Matthaus. *Iconum Biblicarum.* Wenatchee, WA: AVB Press, 1981.

Metzger, Bruce M., and Michael D. Coogan, eds. *The Oxford Companion to the Bible.* New York: Oxford University Press, 1993.

Milburn, Robert. *Early Christian Art and Architecture.* Berkeley: University of California Press, 1988.

Miles, Margaret R. *Carnal Knowing: Female Nakedness and Religious Meaning in the Christian West.* Boston: Beacon Press, 1989.

Miles, Margaret R. *Image as Insight: Visual Understanding in Western Christianity and Secular Culture.* Boston: Beacon Press, 1985.

Miller, Robert J., ed. *The Complete Gospels.* San Francisco: HarperSanFrancisco, 1992.

Morgan, David. *Visual Piety: A History and Theory of Popular Religious Images.* Berkeley: University of California Press, 1998.

Murray, Linda, and Peter Murray. *The Oxford Companion to Christian Art and Architecture.* Oxford, UK: Oxford University Press, 1996.

Musacchio, Jacqueline Marie. *The Art and Ritual of Childbirth in Renaissance Italy.* New Haven, CT: Yale University Press, 1999.

Netzer, Nancy, and Virginia Reinburg, eds. *Fragmented Devotion: Medieval Objects from the Schnütgen Museum, Cologne,* exhibition catalogue. Boston: McMullen Museum of Art, 2000.

Nevins, Albert J., ed. *The Maryknoll Catholic Dictionary.* New York: Grosset & Dunlap, 1965.

Newton, Eric, and William Neil. *2000 Years of Christian Art.* London: Thames & Hudson, 1966.

Norman, Diana. *Siena and the Virgin: Art and Politics in a late Medieval City State.* New Haven, CT: Yale University Press, 1999

Oettinger, Marion, Jr., ed. *Folk Art of Spain and the Americas: El Alma del Pueblo,* exhibition catalogue. San Antonio, TX: San Antonio Museum of Art, 1997.

O'Meara, Thomas A. *Mary in Protestant and Catholic Theology.* New York: Sheed and Ward, 1966.

Orsi, Robert Anthony. *The Madonna of 115th Street: Faith and Community in Italian Harlem, 1880–1950.* New Haven, CT: Yale University Press, 1985.

Orsi, Robert A. *Thank You Saint Jude: Women's Devotion to the Patron Saint of Hopeless Causes.* New Haven, CT: Yale University Press, 1996.

van Os, Henk, et al. *The Art of Devotion in the Late Middle Ages in Europe: 1300–1500,* exhibition catalogue. London: Merrell Holberton, 1994.

Ostrow, Steven F. *Art and Spirituality in Counter-Reformation Rome: The Sistine and Pauline Chapels in S. Maria Maggiore.* Cambridge, UK: Cambridge University Press, 1996.

Ousterhout, Robert, and Leslie Brubaker, eds. *The Sacred Image East and West.* Chicago: University of Illinois Press, 1995.

Ozment, Steven. *Protestants: The Birth of a Revolution.* New York: Doubleday, 1991.

Payer, Pierre J. *The Bridling of Desire: Ideas of Sex in the Later Middle Ages.* Toronto: University of Toronto Press, 1993.

Pelikan, Jaroslav. *Mary through the Centuries: Her Place in the History of Culture.* New Haven: Yale University Press, 1996.

Pentcheva, Bissera V. "Images behind the Veil of Texts: The Byzantine Paradox of the Virgin as Invincible General," paper presented at *There's Something about Mary: The Virgin Mary in the Visual Arts* symposium, Davis Museum, Wellesley College, 11 November 2000.

Peterson, Jeanette Favrot. "*Nigra sum sed Formosa*: The Señor de Chalma and the Virgin of Guadalupe in Mexico." In *Black Christs of the Americas,* edited by Arturo Lindsay, Spelman College, pending publication.

Peterson, Jeanette Favrot. "Shades of Blackness: The Virgin of Guadalupe in Spain and the Americas." The Bakwin Lecture, Wellesley College, 15 February 2000.

Peterson, Jeanette Favrot. "The Virgin of Guadalupe: Symbol of Conquest or Liberation?" *Art Journal,* 51, no. 4 (Winter, 1992), pp. 39–47.

Pinder, Wilhelm. *Die Pieta.* Leipzig, Germany: E. A. Seemann, 1922.

Ranke-Heinemann, Uta. *Eunuchs for the Kingdom of Heaven:*

Women, Sexuality, and the Catholic Church. New York: Doubleday, 1990.

Réau, Louis. *Iconographie de l'Art Chrétien.* Paris: Presses Universitaires de France, 1957.

Revised Standard Version of the New Testament. New York: Thomas Nelson & Sons, 1946.

Roberts, J. M. *A History of Europe.* New York: Allen Lane/The Penguin Press, 1996.

Ross, James Bruce, and Mary Martin McLaughlin, eds. *The Portable Medieval Reader.* New York: Viking Press, 1949.

Ruether, Rosemary Radford. *Mary—The Feminine Face of the Church.* Philadelphia: The Westminster Press, 1977.

Rumeu de Armas, Antonio. *Historia de la Previsión Social en España: Cofradías, Gremios, Hermandades, Montepíos.* Barcelona: El Albir, 1944.

Russell, H. Diane. *Eva/Ave: Woman in Renaissance and Baroque Prints.* Washington, DC: National Gallery of Art, 1990.

Schaberg, Jane. *The Illegitimacy of Jesus: A Feminist Theological Interpretation of the Infancy Narratives.* San Francisco: Harper & Row, 1987.

Schiller, Gertrud. *Iconography of Christian Art,* vols. 1 and 2, trans. Janet Seligman. Greenwich, CT: New York Graphic Society, 1971/72.

Schiller, Gertrud. *Ikonographie der christlichen Kunst,* vols. 3 to 6. Gutersloh, Germany: Gutersloher Verlagshaus G. Mohn, 1968–80.

Schreckenberg, Heinz. *The Jews in Christian Art: An Illustrated History.* New York: Continuum, 1996.

Schroeder, H. J., ed. *Canon and Decrees of the Council of Trent.* St. Louis, MO: B. Herder, 1950.

Schultz, Nancy Lusignan. *Veils of Fear: Nineteenth Century Convent Tales.* West Lafayette, IN: NotaBell Books, 1999.

Snyder, James. *Northern Renaissance Art.* Englewood Cliffs, NJ: Prentice-Hall, 1985.

Sobré, Judith Berg. *The Artistic Splendors of the Spanish Kingdoms: The Art of Fifteenth-Century Spain,* exhibition catalogue. Boston: Isabella Stewart Gardner Museum, 1996.

Stechow, Wolfgang. *Northern Renaissance Art 1400–1600: Sources and Documents.* Evanston, IL: Northwestern University Press, 1966.

Steinberg, Leo. *The Sexuality of Christ in Renaissance Art and in Modern Oblivion.* New York: Pantheon, 1983.

Stratton, Suzanne L. *The Immaculate Conception in Spanish Art.* New York: Cambridge University Press, 1994.

Streep, Peg. *Mary, Queen of Heaven: Miracles, Manifestations, and Meditations on Mary.* New York: QPBC, 1997.

Swann, Ingo. *The Great Apparitions of Mary: An Examination of Twenty-two Supranormal Appearances.* New York: Crossroad, 1996.

Taylor, Jane H. M., and Lesley Smith, eds. *Women and the Book.* London: The British Library, 1996.

Thieme, Ulrich, and Felix Becker. *Allgemeines Lexikon der bildenden Künstler von der Antike bis zur Gegenwart.* Leipzig, Germany: W. Engelmann, 1907–50; and revised edition, Gunter Meissner, ed. Munich: K. G. Saur Verlag, 1992–2000.

Thomas à Kempis. *Meditations on Our Lady.* Ditchling, Sussex, UK: St. Dominic's Press, 1929.

Thomas à Kempis. *On the Imitation of Christ,* Edward J. Klein, ed. New York, NY: Harper & Brothers, 1941.

Throckmorton, Burton H., Jr., ed. *Gospel Parallels.* Toronto/New York: Thomas Nelson & Sons, 1949.

Toal, M. F., ed. and trans. *The Sunday Sermons of the Great Fathers.* Chicago: Henry Regnery Company, 1958.

Todini, Filippo. *La pittura umbra: dal Duecento al primo Cinquecento.* Milan: Longanesi, 1989.

Trens, Manuel. *María: Iconografía de la Virgen en el Arte Español.* Madrid: Editorial Plus Ultra, 1946.

Turner, Jane, ed. *Dictionary of Art.* New York: Grove's Dictionaries, 1996.

Verdier, Philippe. *Le Couronnement de la Vierge: les origines et les premiers développements d'un Thème iconographique.* Montréal: Institut d'études médiévales, 1980.

Walsh, Michael J. *Dictionary of Catholic Devotions.* New York: HarperCollins, 1993.

Ware, Timothy. *The Orthodox Church.* Harmondsworth, UK: Penguin Books, 1963.

Warner, Marina. *Alone of All Her Sex: The Myth and Cult of the Virgin Mary.* London: Weidenfeld and Nicolson, 1976.

Warner, Marina. *From the Beast to the Blonde: On Fairy Tales and their Tellers.* London: Vintage Books, 1995.

Warner, Marina. *Joan of Arc: The Image of Female Heroism.* London: Vintage Books, 1981.

Wellen, G. A. *Theotokos: eine ikonographische Abhandlung Über das Gottesmutterbild in fruhchristlicher Zeit.* Utrecht, Netherlands: Het Spectrum, 1961.

Wheeler, Marion Michael. *Her Face: Images of the Virgin Mary in Art.* Cobb, CA: First Glance Books, 1998.

Wieck, Roger S. *The Book of Hours in Medieval Art and Life.* London: Sotheby's Publications, 1988.

Wieck, Roger S. *Painted Prayers: The Book of Hours in Medieval and Renaissance Art,* exhibition catalogue. New York: George Braziller, 1997.

Winston-Allen, Anne. *Stories of the Rose: The Making of the Rosary in the Middle Ages.* University Park: Pennsylvania State University Press.

Wood, Jeryldene M. *Women, Art, and Spirituality: The Poor Clares of Early Modern Italy.* New York: Cambridge University Press, 1996.

Woodward, Kenneth L. "Hail, Mary," *Newsweek,* 130, no. 8 (25 August 1997), pp. 43–56.

Woolf, Rosemary. *The English Mystery Plays.* Berkeley: University of California Press, 1972.

Ziegler, Joanna E. "The Medieval Virgin as Object: Art or Anthropology?" *Historical Reflections/Réflexions Historiques,* 16, nos. 2 and 3 (1989), pp. 251–64.

Ziegler, Joanna E. *Sculpture of Compassion: the Pietà and the Beguines in the Southern Low Countries c. 1300–c. 1600.* Brussels: Institut Historique Belge de Rome, 1992.

Zires, Margarita. "Los Mitos de la Virgen de Guadalupe. Su proceso de construcción y reinterpretacieón en el México pasado y contemporáneo." *Mexican Studies/Estudios Mexicanos,* 10, no. 2 (Summer 1994), pp. 281–315.

Zires, Margarita. "Reina de México, Patrona de los Chicanos, y Emperatríz de las Américas: Los mitos de la Virgen de Guadalupe—Estrategias de producción de identidades." *Iberoamericana,* 3/4 (nos. 51/52) 1993, pp. 76–91.

Zires, Margarita. "Our Undocumented Lady of Guadalupe," *Voices of Mexico,* 45 (Oct./Dec. 1998), pp. 42–50.

Part II

Other Voices

Mary and the Ancient Goddesses

MARY R. LEFKOWITZ

ANDREW W. MELLON PROFESSOR IN THE HUMANITIES

DEPARTMENT OF CLASSICAL STUDIES

WELLESLEY COLLEGE

The Virgin Mary first appears in Western art in a grave site, a Roman catacomb of the second century of the common era (CE). She is nursing the infant Jesus while a male figure next to her points to a star [fig. 14].[1] The painting tells the story of Jesus' birth as told in the Gospel according to Matthew (1:9–12). It suggests that the dead shall eventually be reborn, because Jesus was the Messiah who has come to save people from their sins (Matt. 1: 20–21).

To ordinary Romans, who believed in the old gods and had not read the Gospels or other Christian literature, an image of a mother nursing her baby would not have suggested rebirth or resurrection. They would have seen it as a representation of a woman who had died in childbirth, perhaps along with her child. It would not have reminded them of goddesses like Demeter/Ceres or Hera/Juno, because in Greek and Roman art mother goddesses are not shown with infant children. And in Greek myth, the most powerful goddesses, Athena and Artemis, have no children at all.

The closest analogy in ancient religion to the image of Mary as mother comes from the Egyptian goddess Isis, whose cult was popular in Rome in the early centuries of the common era. In Egyptian art, Isis is shown holding or suckling her infant son Horus. His father, Osiris, had been murdered by his enemy Seth; but Isis found Osiris, breathed life into him, and in the process conceived Horus. So the image of Isis with Horus is meant to remind the onlooker of the existence of life after death. But Isis could never be mistaken for Mary. Isis is an imposing figure, with a formal wig and large headdress. Mary wears an ordinary woman's veil. Jesus is a baby. Isis' divine child, Horus, looks like a miniature man.

The emphasis on Mary's humanity in early representations suggests that her cult did not originate in Near Eastern or Greco-Roman religion. Rather, the notion that she was superior to other women developed only gradually, within the Christian community. Christians needed to show that she was different from other women, free from the bodily pollution that was their legacy from their ancestor Eve. As the antithesis of Eve, Mary was portrayed in the early literature of the church as obedient to God's will, especially at the moment of the Annunciation, when the angel Gabriel announced to her that she was to bear his son (Luke 1:38).

Later Christians put even greater emphasis on the notion of Mary's purity. Writers in the East told how Mary remained a virgin *after* Jesus was born (Protevangelium of James 19:3), and that she herself was conceived without sin (Prot. 4: 1–5). She acquired some of the feminine aspects that had been attributed to God in Hellenistic Judaism: God as Midwife (Psalm 22: 9–10), as a comforting mother (Isaiah 49: 15), as a mother in labor (Isaiah 42:14b) (Harvey, p. 289). Words that originally described Sophia, the spirit of divine Wisdom, were incorporated into her liturgy (Ecclesiasticus 24:19–22) (Warner, p. 195; Harvey, p. 290). After the fourth century, Christians

began to believe that Mary did not die. Unlike Eve, who was deprived of immortality by God because of her disobedience, Mary was taken from her deathbed and brought to heaven by her son.[2]

Meanwhile, as Christianity spread out into the pagan world, Mary also began to bear a closer resemblance to Isis and the Eastern mother goddess known to the Greeks as Artemis of Ephesus. She became the central figure in paintings of her and her infant son. In the fifth century, prayers were addressed to her, and pictures of her were carried into battle by the soldiers on their chariots. In a Greek hymn of thanksgiving, it is Mary rather than Demeter who is praised for bringing the harvest (Baring and Cashford, pp. 574–76). The Parthenon, the temple of Athena the war goddess in Athens, was consecrated to Mary's name (Baring and Cashford, pp. 550–51). In a Roman painting of the sixth century, Mary is shown seated on a throne, wearing a crown and dressed in a gown covered with jewels, like the eastern goddess Cybele (Warner, p. 104).

But even when she wore the trappings and sat in the temples of these now forgotten goddesses, Mary never acquired their destructive powers. Unlike the pagan goddesses, who kept apart from humans, Mary was always directly accessible to her worshipers and in sympathy with them. Through her they were able to approach her powerful and distant son, and his even more remote father, much as the mothers and wives of the remote and all-powerful Roman emperors had served as intercessors for their subjects.[3] Thus the cult of the Virgin Mary was a replacement for, rather than a continuation of, the ancient cults of the goddesses

NOTES

1. Catacomb of Saint Priscilla, Rome; see figure 14 and footnote 6, page 111 in "Regarding Mary: Women's Lives Reflected in the Virgin's Image" in this volume.

2. "Mary, the Blessed Virgin," *The Oxford Dictionary of the Christian Church*, ed. F. L. Cross and E. A. Livingstone, 3rd ed. (Oxford, UK: Oxford University Press, 1997), p. 1047.

3. Mary R. Lefkowitz, *Women in Greek Myth* (Baltimore: Johns Hopkins University Press, 1986), p. 94.

SUGGESTED READING

Baring, Anne, and Jules Cashford. *The Myth of the Goddess.* London: Viking, 1991, especially pp. 547–608.

Harvey, Susan Ashbrook. "Women in Early Syrian Christianity." In *Images of Women in Antiquity*, ed. Averil Cameron and Amélie Kuhrt. London: Croom Helm, 1983.

Pelikan, Jaroslav. *Mary through the Centuries: Her Place in the History of Culture.* New Haven: Yale University Press, 1996.

Warner, Marina. *Alone of All Her Sex: The Myth and Cult of the Virgin Mary.* London: Weidenfeld and Nicolson, 1976.

Mary in the Christian Tradition

SHARON K. ELKINS

PROFESSOR OF RELIGION

WELLESLEY COLLEGE

Artistic representations of Mary—like most of those in this publication—usually focus on the biblical stories about her. Yet in Scripture Mary's activities are fairly limited: primarily she prepares for Jesus' birth, holds him as an infant, and stays with him at his death. Seeing these representations of her, one can wonder about the reasons for Mary's preeminence in Christian history. Indeed, Protestants who rely on Scripture alone as the basis for their faith typically devote little attention to Mary. However, in Catholic and Orthodox Christianity, tradition has greatly amplified Mary's role.

The exhibition opened with prints illustrating scenes from the earliest postbiblical document about Mary, The Protevangelium of James. Claiming to provide information about Mary's life before the first events recorded in the canonical Gospels of Matthew and Luke, this pre-Gospel, or *proto-evangelium,* was attributed to James "the brother" of Jesus. Although most Christian writers disputed this authorship, the document had a lasting influence. For instance, the story that an angel told the elderly Joachim and Anna that they would have a child comes from this text, as does the portrayal of Joseph as an old man [fig. 7].

The Protevangelium is a curious document for many reasons. In the first place, it is surprisingly early to contain so many stories about Mary, for the text probably dates to the mid-second century. Also, for an such early text, it is filled with numerous historical inaccuracies about Jewish practices. It erroneously claims that the temple priests in Jerusalem refused the sacrificial offerings of childless men like Joachim and that they agreed to raise the three-year-old Mary [fig. 8]. Many of the Protevangelium's stories were so distasteful that they soon disappeared from common parlance—such as the episode in which a woman tested Mary's hymen with her finger in order to ascertain whether Mary had remained a virgin after the birth of Jesus.

However, the developing traditions about Mary did not depend primarily on apocryphal documents like the Protevangelium. Rather, traditions grew through a complex, rich interplay of legendary narratives, theological arguments, dogmatic assertions, artistic representations, and devotional prayers. Indeed, the Protevangelium put in narrative form what second-century Church leaders were also saying, that Mary is a New Eve. The story that Mary was born to an elderly barren couple and given to the temple as a young girl emphasized that Mary was pure and sinless before her espousal to Joseph. By insisting that Mary never had sexual intercourse with her elderly husband-protector Joseph and gave birth to Jesus without breaking her hymen, the Protevangelium was stating in a dramatic way that Mary overcame the penalties imposed on the first Eve in Genesis 3: Mary had no desire for her husband, he did not dominate her, and she had no pain in childbearing. Hence, the Protevangelium expressed in story form the developing theological dictum that Mary is a New Eve.

The belief that Mary overcame the penalties imposed on Eve led to additional legendary

accounts, such as the stories about Mary's dormition, which indicated that her body was not subject to the corruption of death. In 1950, after almost two millennia of stories, feasts, prayers, artistic representations, and theological debates, Pope Pius XII declared it officially to be Catholic dogma that Mary, after her life on earth ended, was assumed body and soul into heaven [figs. 95, 96]. The process of tradition formation could be reversed, for a dogmatic pronouncement might precede visual representations and narrative accounts. For instance, after the Ecumenical Council of Ephesus in 431 declared that Mary is the *Theotokos*, the Mother of God, she began to be portrayed as a regal figure, and stories were told of her activities as Queen of Heaven.

Increasingly during the second millennium of Christian history, visions and apparitions of Mary have enriched Catholic traditions about her. The account of her appearance to Juan Diego in 1531, manifested in the picture of herself she left on his mantle, led to widespread devotion to her as Our Lady of Guadalupe, Protectress of the Innocent, Patroness of the Americas [figs. 67, 107, 108, 109, 168]. Other revered "dark madonnas" are also said to have miraculous origins [fig. 86]. Many of the most popular Catholic images of Mary today— Our Lady of Lourdes, Our Lady of Fatima, the Queen of Peace (Medjugorje)—are based on descriptions that seers gave of the Mary they saw in visions.

When viewed in the context of this elaborate tradition, the Biblical scenes involving Mary have deeper significance. For Christians who accept the developed traditions about Mary, the woman displaying Jesus to the Magi [fig. 123] and standing by him at his crucifixion [fig. 69] is the Mother of God and became the Queen of Heaven. For believers, the Mary who fled to Egypt [figs. 115, 152] is the same woman who appeared to Juan Diego 1500 years later [fig. 168] and is still appearing to visionaries today. Hence, informed by the growing traditions about her, viewers of images of Mary find additional meaning even in the seemingly simple biblical stories.

SUGGESTED READING

Pelikan, Jarolsav. *Imago Dei: The Byzantine Apologia for Icons.* Princeton, NJ: Princeton University Press, 1990.

Pelikan, Jarolsav. *Mary through the Centuries: Her Place in the History of Culture.* New Haven and London: Yale University Press, 1996.

"The Protevangelium of James." *New Testament Apocrypha*, ed. Edgard Hennecke, vol. 1. Philadelphia: Westminster Press, 1963, pp. 370–88.

The Virgin's Voice

Representations of Mary in Seventeenth–Century Italian Song

CLAIRE FONTIJN–HARRIS

ASSOCIATE PROFESSOR OF MUSIC

WELLESLEY COLLEGE

Just as artists painted vivid depictions of the Madonna and Child, and Mary at the Cross, composers evoked the same scenes through music. Seventeenth-century Italy offered up a particularly striking group of works that portrayed the events of Christ's birth and crucifixion through the voice of Mary herself: lullabies sung around Christmastime by the young nursing mother, and laments for Holy Week and Easter sung by the weeping mother mourning the death of her son on the cross. If the especially strong traditions of Marian devotion in southern Europe no doubt did much to prompt the creation of these songs, so, too, did the growing attention given the solo soprano voice during this period. Through vocal performance of first-person narratives, the Blessed Virgin Mary could come to life, whether characterized as *Maria lactans*—the young nursing mother who feels unsure of herself, who feels pride, who enjoys an intimate bond with her child—or as *Mater dolorosa*, the older mother who embodies sadness or indignation.

What might the composers have had in mind as a general vocal concept for the voice of the Virgin

Mary? Purity had to be foremost, given that she had been selected as the pure vessel to bear the Christ child, the archetypal mother to whom so many—literate and illiterate alike—could pray in times of need. What does "pure" correspond to in music? Beatless intervals are pure and so are the proportions that determine them; the very notion of purity invokes music's physical nature, prior to the application of the artifice of culture. Linda Austern has recently explored the rich topic of nature and culture in music-making of the early modern period, noting that Mary serves as a nexus between the two realms. In *Parthenia sacra*, the seventeenth-century writer Henry Hawkins compared Mary's voice to that of the nightingale, but cleverly stated that her voice exceeds that of the bird, thereby enjoying the gift of pure nature while simultaneously elevated to a divine level; indeed, Austern comments that "Hawkins positions Mary's pure, spiritual voice not only above this little avian's, but far beyond the merely mortal musics of Orpheus, Amphion, Arion, and even the no less legendary Orlando di Lasso and Luca Marenzio."[1]

If the notion of Mary's pure, spiritual voice had some grounding in contemporary European thought, then it would suggest a point of departure for the composers' concept of a naturally beautiful as well as supremely virtuosic instrument. A belief in Mary as the intercessor to Christ for the people could also include one of Mary the singer mediating between nature and culture, between pure physicality and spiritual expression. The humanizing element of the divine, an extension of Mary's long-held associations with the people, prompted the need for the direct quality that the first-person voice provides.

What type of voice might the composers have sought for their portrayal of Mary? A soprano voice in the period could be either male or female. It cannot be ascertained for which gender the pieces were intended, but a consideration of the possibility that several were meant for a woman to sing raises questions about performance venues, about where women's voices could and could not be heard. Women's voices were particularly prized; ducal patronage and the theater in effect prepared the way for them to enter formalized spectacle with solo singing.[2] These voices lent themselves to roles in early opera and in *sacre rappresentazioni* alike. The spawning of first-person Marian narratives may have arisen from a general fascination with the woman's solo voice as well as from the particularly powerful effects obtained through the direct expression of Mary's character. The Church excluded female voices—only in the convents could women participate in sacred musical production; thus boys or *castrati* were required to represent a female character. If a woman was to interpret the role of Mary, her voice by necessity had to be heard in an extraliturgical context.[3]

The newfound appearance of women on stage in the seventeenth century makes one wonder whether these pieces might have been part of their repertory. The freely conceived poetry and musical venue for the works belonged neither to church music nor to opera proper, allowing musical performance by sopranos of either gender. Depending on the context, composers found in Mary's subjective depiction the vehicle for highly expressive vocal writing that could link the power of a naturally talented singer with the cultivated *maniere* of the period.

NOTES

1. Linda Phyllis Austern, "Nature, Culture, Myth, and the Musician in Early Modern England," *Journal of the American Musicological Society*, 51 (Spring 1998), p. 37.

2. During Monteverdi's period of service to the Mantuan court, female *virtuose* were especially treasured and well-rewarded for their singing. The lead singer for *L'Arianna* was to have been Caterina Martinelli, had she not prematurely died before the production. See Edmond Strainchamps, "The Life and Death of Caterina Martinelli: New Light on Monteverdi's 'Arianna,' " pp. 155–86 in *Early Music History*, 5 (Cambridge, UK: Cambridge University Press, 1985).

3. There were also settings for men to sing. In his preface to an

edition of Maurizio Cazzati's *In Calvaria rupe*—a motet for bass voice that contains within it a *Lamento di Maria*—Rudolf Ewerhart noted the preponderance of pieces representing Mary in the basso-continuo period and situated the practice as an extraliturgical one that was based on freely conceived poetry. See *Cantio Sacra—Geistliche Solokantaten,* 19 (Cologne: Verlag Edmund Bieler, n.d.).

This commentary is adapted from Claire Fontijn's essay "The Virgin's Voice: Representations of Mary in Seventeenth-Century Italian Song" in *Maternal Measures: Caregiver Figures in Early Modern Europe,* edited by Naomi J. Miller and Naomi Yavneh (Brookfield, VT: Ashgate, 2000). Reproduced with permission from Ashgate Publishing, Ltd.

In a Corner of Africa

Reflections on the Virgin Mary

IFEANYI ANTHONY MENKITI

PROFESSOR OF PHILOSOPHY

WELLESLEY COLLEGE

Three women slain by the spirit
holding tears in their hands;
the mango leaves of St. Mary's, Inland;
Onitsha darkening now at year's end.[1]

I began my academic career at St. Mary's Elementary School in Onitsha, Nigeria—a Catholic school in a mid-size town in a country in Africa, a continent where Christianity, as a matter of history, did not originate. Later, during the secondary school years, it was Christ the King College where the Irish missionaries ran things with a sure hand; where the sounds of names like Flannagan, Heery, and McCabe filled the air; and where, as boarders, we were allowed to go into town on St. Patrick's Day. We sang songs to the patron saint of Ireland asking that he look kindly "on Erin's green valley." And Erin, for us, was not just an isle across the sea from Cromwell's England, but also British-ruled Nigeria which we hoped someday to liberate.

But I must acknowledge that this habit of song just mentioned was not primarily centered around a beloved Irish bishop turned saint, a man who drove the snakes out of someone else's living space and made them stay out for good. Rather, it was centered around Mary, the blessed mother. One song that I remember, in Igbo, went like this:

Maria eze nwanyi nke May
Welu nwayo nolu anyi
Eze nwanyi nke May
Welu nwayo nolu anyi

which can be translated into English this way:

O Mary, queen of May,
Gently abide with us.
O thou queen of May,
Gently now abide with us.

For many of us in those days, Mary came through most clearly as an acknowledged mother of sadness (*Mater dolorosa*). Her other prominent image in Christianity, as a nurturing (nursing) mother (*Maria lactans*), did not hold as much evocative power for young African lads. We knew from the Catechism that she herself was purely birthed, that as a young girl she had responded affirmatively to the startling message of the Angel of Gabriel that she would conceive a child named Jesus, even though she knew no man. We knew these things, and got to draw the appropriate conclusion that Mary was no ordinary woman. But it was Mary's power to deliver protection and solace to those who were burdened that resonated with many. She became a hoped-for source of efficacious release from sadness and suffering; and people came to believe that, whatever difficulties they faced, Mary would make things right in the end.

This was especially the case during the devastations of the Nigerian Civil War (1967–70), a war in which Britain strongly supported the federal side and most of which was fought on Igbo soil. It was a war in which the southeastern area had tried to secede from Nigeria, under the name of Biafra, and failed, following massacres in the Muslim north of the country. For a great number of the adults in the area, who earlier had attended the Catholic schools under the tutelage of the Irish missionaries, there was the belief that just as Mary had stood behind the Irish in their struggle to survive the brutal hand of the Iron Chancellor and the devastations of the Great Famine, so likewise the Igbos, with the Mother of Sorrow behind them, would survive their own travails and survive, also, the kwashiorkor-driven distended bellies of the starving children.[2]

And so there were these lines from a poem of that war period:

that a bomber flew low over Owerrinta
the loss of that hour, how
it could not be counted—

Anna, not really *belle*, but *ebele*.[3]

Here, *Anna* refers to a Relief Services jungle airstrip known by the name of "Annabelle," an airport hewn out of deep bush, and providing at one point Biafra's only link to the outside world. And *ebele* in Igbo stands for "mercy." For, at Annabelle, the remote African airport, in addition to some charms and amulets worn by her defenders for protection, there were also icons to be found of the Virgin Mother of Mercy.

But leaving aside for now the Mary supplications of the war years, and what one may call the "Irish connection" of the years preceding, it ought also to be noted that traditional society was well familiar with images of female power, and this familiarity, most likely, was what prepared the ground for the reception of the image of Mary as *doer*, more so than the reception of her image as an unblemished mother of the child Jesus.

For one thing, the most powerful deity in the traditional Igbo pantheon was Ani, the earth goddess. And what was most interesting about this goddess is that in her we find not just a divinity responsible for the usual female qualities of fecundity and nurturance, but also a divinity responsible for the assuredly male quality of defender of justice in the land—a goddess, in other words, who functions both as male and female and who lets the sword of righteousness fall without partiality, and sometimes without mercy, if ever the need arose to cleanse the land of an abomination.

For another thing, when one considers the force of the female name found within the Igbo culture, names such as *Nneka* ("mother is supreme") and *Ezidimma* (which is difficult to translate in a straightforward way, but which carries the sense of strength of lineage, and also the sense of a charged protective presence in the open spaces, the open road), one begins to understand the power of female enactments within the culture's grid of meanings.

I suggest that without these facts being already in place on the ground in this part of Africa, the reception of the idea and person of Mary within the population would have been quite different from what actually occurred.

NOTES

1. The lines of poetry appearing in this essay are from a work in progress by Ifeanyi Menkiti tentatively titled "No Ordinary Matter, This Dark Matter."

2. Kwashiorkor is a condition caused by severe protein deficiency that results in a swollen abdomen. It principally affects young children in regions where the diet is high in starch and low in protein.

SUGGESTED READING

Victor Uchendu, *The Igbos of Southeast Nigeria* (New York: Holt, Rinehart, and Winston, 1965).

Elizabeth Allo Isichei, *A History of Christianity in Africa: From Antiquity to the Present* (Lawrenceville, NJ: Africa World Press, 1995).

Lamin O. Sanneh, *Encountering the West: Christianity and the Global Cultural Process: The African Dimension* (Maryknoll, NY: Orbis Books, 1993).

Part III

The Catalogue

Catalogue Entries

Works are listed chronologically, with cataloguing information provided in the following order, and identified by the following symbols:

A Artist's Name
Place of birth/Year of birth—Year of death/Place of death
Place(s) of activity during the artist's career

T *Title of work*

D date of work (if known)

M medium and support

X dimensions (height x width x depth)

S signature (if present)

I inscriptions, collectors marks, stamps, labels, et al.

W watermark(s)

C Credit line
accession number

1. Italian from Umbria or Tuscany, *Christ Mounting the Cross and the Funeral of Saint Clare*, 1290s (Lilian Armstrong)

2. French from Paris or northeastern France, *De laudibus beatae Mariae* (*In Praise of the Blessed Mary*), 1290s (Lilian Armstrong)

3. French from Île de France, *The Dormition of the Virgin*, 14th century (Jennifer S. Park)

4. French from Paris for Nantes, *Officium Beatae Mariae Virginis* (Latin and French *Book of Hours*), 1400–1410 (Lilian Armstrong)

5. Martin Schongauer, *Rest on Flight into Egypt*, third-quarter 15th century (Margaret D. Carroll)

6. Circle of Willem Backer van Vrelant, *Gebeden Boek* (Dutch *Book of Hours*), ca. 1470 (Lilian Armstrong)

7. Pedro Berruguete, *Assumption of the Virgin*, circa 1485 (Melissa R. Katz)

8. Andrea Mantegna, *Entombment of Christ*, ca. 1470 or 1490 (Lilian Armstrong)

9. German from Alsace, *Virgin and Child*, ca. 1490 (Curtis H. Shell)

10. Pintoricchio, *Virgin and Child with the Infant Saint John the Baptist and Saints Andrew and Jerome*, 1495–1500 (Lilian Armstrong)

11. Cristofano Robetta, *Adoration of the Magi*, 1496–1500 (Lilian Armstrong)

12. Silvestro dell'Aquila, *Bust of the Virgin*, 1495–1500 (Lilian Armstrong)

13. French from Paris, *Annunciation* folio from a *Book of Hours*, 1507–1515 (Lilian Armstrong)

14. Albrecht Dürer, *Life of the Virgin* series, circa 1502–1511 (Melissa R. Katz)

15. Lucas van Leyden, *Virgin and Child in a Niche*, 1518 (Blair A. Brooks)

16. Marcantonio Raimondi, *Madonna with the Long Thigh*, circa 1520–1525 (Lisa McDermott)

17. Giorgio Vasari and workshop, *Holy Family with St. Francis and the Infant St. John*, post-1544 (Margaret A. Samu)

18. Flemish *Judith with the Head of Holofernes*, 3rd quarter 16th century (Margaret D. Carroll and Melissa R. Katz)

19. Lavinia Fontana, *Holy Family with Saints Margaret and Francis*, 1578 (Margaret A. Samu)

20. Gregorio Martínez, *Lamentation with Saints Augustine and Nicholas of Tolentino*, 1590s (Melissa R. Katz)

21. Pietro Faccini, *St. Francis of Assisi Holding the the Infant Christ in the Presence of the Virgin*, 1590s (Hillary L. Anderson and Blair A. Brooks)

22. Hendrik Goltzius, *Annunciation*, 1594 (Hillary L. Anderson)

23. Francesco Furini, *Adam and Eve*, circa 1630 (Melissa R. Katz)

24. Rembrandt van Rijn, *Flight into Egypt* (small plate), 1633 (Margaret D. Carroll)

25. Bartholomeus Breenbergh, *Abraham Dismissing Hagar*, 1630s (Margaret D. Carroll)

26. Stefano della Bella, *Rest on the Flight into Egypt*, before 1642 (Lisa McDermott)

27. Carlo Sacchi, *Adoration of the Shepherds*, 1649 (Hillary L. Anderson)

28. Salvator Rosa, *Three Marys at the Sepulchre*, circa 1665 (Richard W. Wallace)

29. Claudine Bouzonnet Stella, *Crucifixion*, 1674 (Hillary L. Anderson and Blair A. Brooks)

30. Giuseppe Maria Crespi, *Sacrament of Ordination*, before 1712 (Curtis H. Shell)

31. Alessandro Magnasco, *Monastic Saint in Meditation*, 1720s (Joan C. Siegfried)

32. François Boucher, *Sacrifice of Isaac*, 1720s (Melissa R. Katz)

33. John Baptist Jackson, *Presentation of the Virgin in the Temple*, 1742 (Hillary L. Anderson and Lisa McDermott)

34. Pierre Hubert Subleyras, *Pope Benedict XIV Presents St. Catherine dei Ricci to the Virgin*, 1745 (Rebecca Mongeon)

35. GianDomenico Tiepolo, *Flight into Egypt* series, circa 1750–1753 (Elizabeth Losada)

36. Mexican *Ex-Voto commissioned by José María Ramírez*, 1798 (Melissa R. Katz)

37. Julia Margaret Cameron, *La Santa Julia*, 1867 (Anne Higonnet)

38. Émile Bernard, *Confirmand's Procession*, 1891 (Patricia Gray Berman)

39. Edvard Munch, *Madonna (Conception)*, 1902 (Patricia Gray Berman)

40. Gertrude Käsebier, *Adoration (Mother and Child)*, 1897 (Anne Higonnet)

41. Gertrude Käsebier, *Heritage of Motherhood*, 1904 (Anne Higonnet)

42. Auguste Rodin, *Eve (after the Fall)*, 1899 (Blair A. Brooks)

43. Erich Heckel, *Geschwister (Siblings)*, 1913 (Jeremy J. Fowler)

44. Gertrude Fiske, *Mary*, 1920 (Rebecca Mongeon)

45. Fernand Léger, *Woman and Child*, 1921 (Patricia Gray Berman)

46. Otto Müller, *Zigeunermadonna (Gypsy Madonna)*, 1927 (Jeremy J. Fowler)

47. Marc Chagall, *Abraham Sacrificing Isaac*, 1952 (Marlene Kuhn)

48. Lola Álvarez Bravo, *La Patrona (The Patroness)*, 1960s and Danny Lyon, *Showers, Diagnostic Unit, Texas*, 1969–1970 (James Oles)

49. Meg Henson Scales, *Mary Loves Jesus Bartlet Prayers*, 1997 (artist's statement)

50. María Magdalena Campos-Pons, *Sagrada Familia/Holy Family*, 2000 (artist's statement)

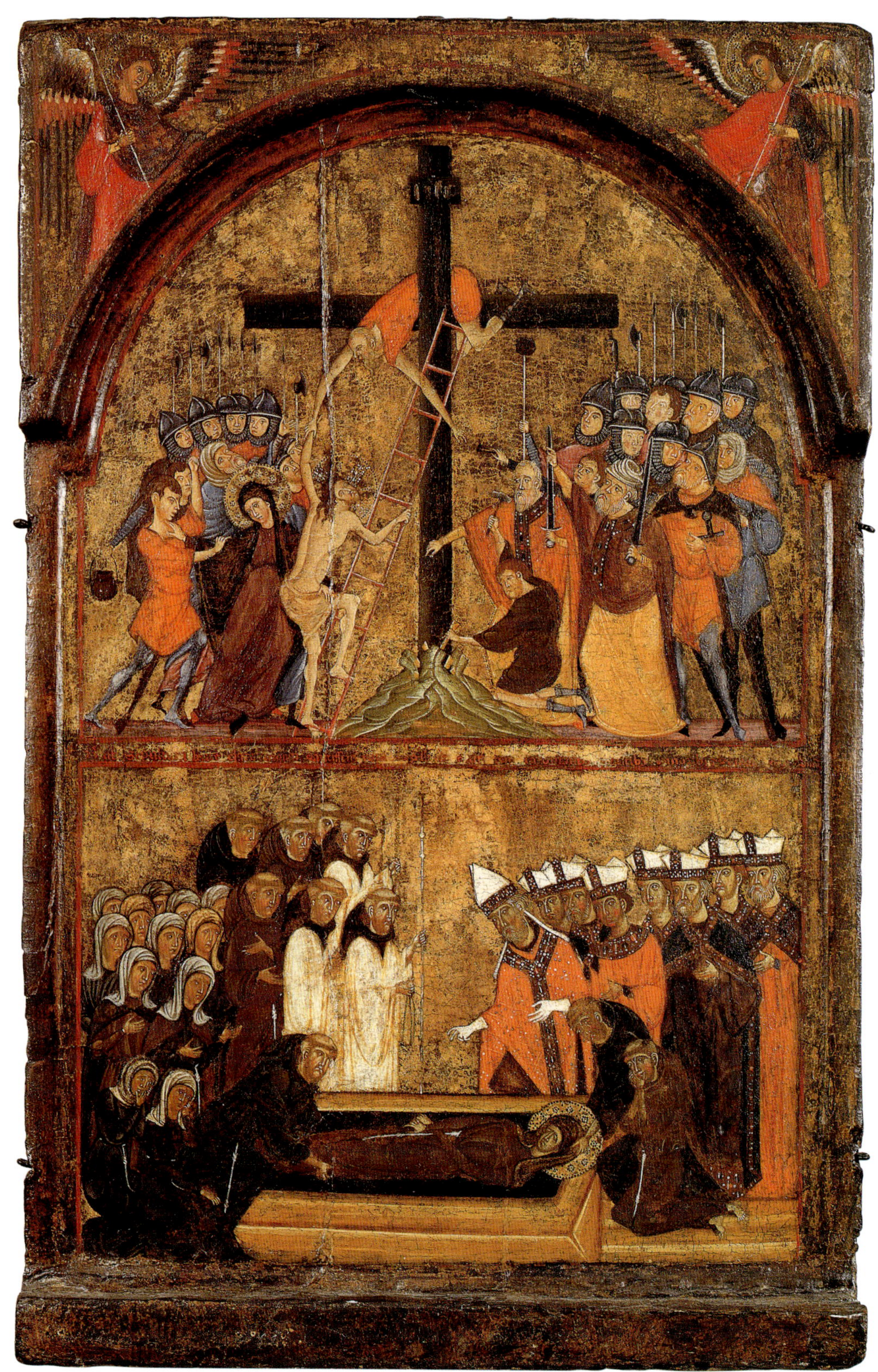

Fig. 111. Italian from
Umbria or Tuscany,
*Christ Mounting the
Cross and the Funeral
of Saint Clare*, 1290s,
tempera on panel

A Italian, from Umbria or Tuscany

T *Christ Mounting the Cross and the Funeral of Saint Clare* (central panel of an altarpiece)

D 1290s

M tempera and silver leaf on panel

X 31 1/4 in. x 20 3/8 in. (79.4 cm x 51.8 cm)

C Museum purchase from a fund given by President Caroline Hazard

1905.2

Doubtless the most important Italian painting in the Wellesley College collections is the late thirteenth-century panel depicting *Christ Mounting the Cross and the Funeral of St. Clare* [fig. 111]. Its subjects are rare and uniquely combined; its style incorporates Byzantine and Italian Romanesque characteristics. The Wellesley panel was earlier attributed to the circle of the Tuscan painter Guido da Siena (active circa 1260–80) (Shell and McAndrew; Stubblebine), but more recently it has been called Umbrian (Gardner, 1973; Maginnis, 1996; see verbal opinions in DMCC files). One scholar has hazarded the possibility that it was painted for the church of Santa Chiara in Assisi (Boskovits).

The Wellesley painting was originally the central panel of a portable altarpiece with two wings, hinged to fold over the central images. Complete, it would have resembled the triptychs by Duccio di Buoninsegna (documented 1278–1319) in the Museum of Fine Arts, Boston, and in the National Gallery, London, both dated circa 1300 (White). Evidence for this arrangement is both the raised arch above the narrative scenes under which the wings would have fitted and the hinge marks at the sides of the extant panel.

In the upper half of the Wellesley panel is depicted the tragic scene of *Christ Mounting the Cross*. A ladder leans diagonally against the centrally placed cross; Christ steps onto its first rung, assisted by an executioner awkwardly twisted around the horizontal bar of the cross. At the left, the Virgin Mary appears to restrain Christ while simultaneously pushing away another executioner threatening to strike her. At the right a third member of the execution team pounds wedges into the base of the cross and Jewish priests brandish weapons. Behind the principal figures on both sides are ranged soldiers in helmets, one of whom holds aloft a wand with the sponge filled with sour wine (Matthew 27:48). The figures are fragile but move and gesture vigorously. Tunics of the executioners and of one priest form a triangle of brilliant orange contrasting with the somber purple of the Virgin's robe and the pale flesh of Christ. The repetitious soldiers' helmets are conservative Byzantine features, but the active grouping of Christ, the Virgin, and the lunging executioner indicate the artist's command of new naturalistic trends in Central Italian art of the late thirteenth century.

The scene represented below *Christ Mounting the Cross* is the *Funeral of St. Clare*. The image was explained by a formerly legible inscription on the band between the two narratives: *(Hic) est sepultura beatae clarae inquae sanctissim(us) papa (Innocentus) (a)s (ti)tit cum cardinalibus (et) fratribus minoribus (et) sororibus hui(us) ordini(s) [q(ue)].* (Here is buried the Blessed Clare with the most holy Pope Innocent standing with cardinals and friars and sisters of the Order) (Shell and McAndrew; Stubblebine, [*tertius*] for *hui(us)*). Again the composition is divided between two groups of figures. In the center, friars lower the body of St. Clare into a coffin. To the right stand the Pope and other ecclesiastics dressed in bright orange or purple vestments and wearing white miters. On the left can be distinguished three friars in white surplices officiating at the service, others dressed in their brown Franciscan habits, and a crowd of kneeling women in brown with white veils over their heads—either members of the Order of the Poor Clares or lay sisters of the Third Order of St. Francis. Altogether the colors are more somber than those of *Christ*

Mounting the Cross, enlivened only by the orange and white of the papal entourage.

Both narrative scenes are significant for an exhibition of the roles of the Virgin Mary. St. Clare of Assisi (1194–1253), an early follower of St. Francis of Assisi (1181–1226), founded the Order of the Poor Clares, also known as the Second Order of St. Francis. When Clare was dying at San Damiano outside of Assisi, where she had been abbess since 1215, Pope Innocent IV and his court were at Perugia. As depicted in the Wellesley panel, the pope and his entourage attended her funeral, and she was canonized as a saint two years later in 1255. Thus the Wellesley panel is an unusual documentation of an historical event, painted only some 40 years after its occurrence.

Like St. Francis, St. Clare was fervid in her devotion to the Crucified Christ and to the Virgin. She was also a passionate defender of the vow of absolute poverty, the distinctive and controversial feature of Francis's teaching that papal authority intermittently tried to modify later in the thirteenth century. The iconography of Christ's Ascent of the Cross is probably Byzantine in origin, but its earliest appearances in Italy are almost exclusively in paintings for the Franciscans and are marked by innovations deriving from Franciscan writings (Derbes, 1995, 1996). In the 1270s, Guido da Siena had already expanded earlier Byzantine models by adding a crowd of agitated figures to intensify the drama. Like the closely related Wellesley panel, Guido accentuated Christ's willing ascent and Mary's passionate intervention, amplified by the activities of the brutal execution team (Derbes, 1996, fig. 89). The gesture of Mary placing her arm around Christ's waist in both paintings is related to other images in which she attempts to cover his nudity. In Franciscan writings by St. Bonaventure and others, Mary agonizes over the shame of Christ's nudity as well as suffering at the sight of his body bloodied by the flagellation. Franciscan theologians also developed elaborate parallels between the Life of Christ and the Life of Francis, the *alter christus*. The Stripping of Christ prefigures Francis's disrobing to espouse absolute poverty, his nudity hastily covered by the bishop of Assisi as Mary had covered the nudity of Christ. Thus, for the Poor Clares and Franciscans, Christ's willingness to suffer the Crucifixion and Mary's desire to protect him had immediate relevance to their spiritual devotion and to the charged issue of absolute poverty.

LILIAN ARMSTRONG

BIBLIOGRAPHY

Boskovits, Miklos. "Un'opera probabile di Giovanni di Bartolomeo Cristiani e l'iconografia della 'Preparazione alla crocifissione'." *Acta Historiae Artium: Academiae Scientiarum Hungaricae* II (1965): 69–94, esp. fig. 17.

Derbes, Anne. "Images East and West: The Ascent of the Cross." In *The Sacred Image East and West*, Robert Ousterhout and Leslie Brubaker, eds. Chicago: University of Illinois Press, 1995 (Illinois Byzantine Studies IV): pp. 110–31 and figs. on 270–79, esp. 116, 126 note 40, and fig. 66 on 277.

Derbes, Anne. *Picturing the Passion in Late Medieval Italy: Narrative Painting, Franciscan Ideologies, and the Levant.* Cambridge, UK: Cambridge University Press, 1996, p. 153 and p. 190, note 52.

Edgerton, Samuel Y. *Pictures and Punishment: Art in the Service of Criminal Prosecution during the Florentine Renaissance.* Ithaca, NY: Cornell University Press, 1984, p. 188 and fig. 52 on p. 189.

Shell, Curtis, and John McAndrew. *Catalogue of the European and American Sculpture and Paintings at Wellesley College*, Wellesley, MA: Jewett Arts Center, 1958, pp. 64–67 (with previous biography).

Stubblebine, James. *Guido da Siena.* Princeton, NJ: Princeton University Press, 1964, pp. 16, 102–04.

White, John. *Duccio: Tuscan Art and the Medieval Workshop.* London: Thames and Hudson, 1979, pp. 46–61.

A   French, from Paris or Northeastern France

T   *De laudibus beatae virginis Mariae (In Praise of
the Blessed Virgin Mary)* by Richard de Saint-Laurent

D   circa 1290–1300

M   manuscript with black, red, and blue inks, glair,
and gold leaf on vellum

   503 folios, with 13 historiated initials, and 21
additional initials illuminated in colored inks
and gold

X   folios: 11 3/4 in. x 8 1/4 in. (300 mm x 200 mm)

I   inscribed in ink, folio 2r: 'Auctor eſt fr Orɖinis
Prædicatorum erraſ si Sic putaſ'

C   Wellesley College Library, Special Collections,
Gift of Caroline Hazard

   MS 19

The most prestigious manuscript in the Special
Collections of the Margaret Clapp Library is
a copy of Richard de Saint-Laurant (d. 1174), *De
laudibus beatae Mariae virginis*, a treatise on the
many roles of the Virgin Mary, illuminated either
in Paris or in Northeastern France around 1300.
Its exquisite historiated initials and superb condition rival the finest illuminated books of the
Gothic period in Europe.

A gift to Wellesley by one of her most generous
presidents, Miss Caroline Hazard, the *De laudibus
beatae Mariae virginis* has also benefited from the
research of two Wellesley alumnae, Emily Trevor,
Class of 1969, and Ann Sievers, Class of 1969.
Much of the information given below draws on
their knowledge and insights. The *De laudibus* was
a popular didactic text, virtually "an encyclopedia
of Mariology" (Sievers). Its compilation paralleled
that of other twelfth- and thirteenth-century treatises that were eagerly copied for use in the newly
established universities, especially at the University
of Paris for use by Dominican and Franciscan
preachers and teachers.

Organized into a preface and twelve chapters

or books, the Wellesley *De laudibus* is illustrated
with thirteen historiated initials whose images
relate to the text below. A full listing of the titles
and images suggests the originality of both the
twelfth-century author and the thirteenth-century
artist who illustrated the Wellesley manuscript:

- Preface *(Prefatio)*: V*ision of the Virgin to a Domini-
can Friar* (fol. 1r);
- Book I, *The Salutation of Gabriel (Ave Maria gra-
tia plena)* and other salutations: Annunciation;
Visitation; Christ greeting the Apostles after the
Resurrection (fol. 2v) (Miner, p1. XXXII);
- Book II, *On the Ways of Serving the Virgin (Quare
Mariae serviend[um] . . .* : Virgin presents the
Christ Child to men and women who serve her
(fol. 36v) [fig. 46];
- Book III, *The Twelve Privileges of Mary (De privi-
legiis Mariae)*: Mary as the Apocalyptic Woman,
surrounded by twelve stars (fol. 90v);
- Book IV, *The Innumerable Virtues of Mary (14
Beatitudes) (De Virtutibus Mariae)*: Virgin stand-
ing between 14 crowned heads adored by a
kneeling Dominican (fol. 102r; Sievers, illus.);
- Book V, *On the Beauty of Mary (De pulchritudine)*:
Mary blesses kneeling Dominicans (fol. 161v);
- Book VI, *On the Names of Mary (De appellationibus)*: Virgin enthroned, suckling the Christ
child; around the letter "M" the names of Mary
are inscribed in gold: MATER. AMICA. SOROR.
SPONSA. FILIA. VIRGO. ANCILLA. MINISURA (fol. 192
recto) [fig. 81];
- Book VII, *Mary as the Heavens, Sun, Moon, and
Stars (Mariae c[a]elum, Mariae firmamentum,
Maria sol, Maria luna*, etc.): Mary standing surrounded by stars, the sun and the moon (fol.
216r);
- Book VIII, *Mary as the Earth (Maria terra)*: Mary
standing by a flowering lawn addressing a
seated Dominican (fol. 239r) [fig. 112];
- Book IX, *Mary as Every Kind of Water (Maria
mare, Maria fons, Maria flumen)*: Mary bends
down from a circle of clouds to direct the

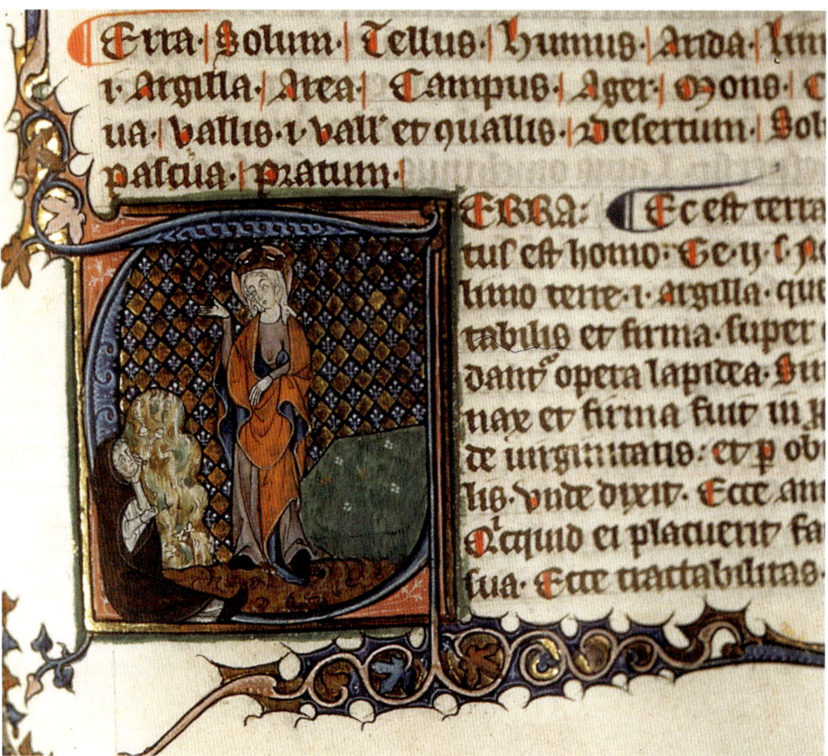

Fig. 112. *Mary addressing a Domini-can Friar,* historiated initial accompanying Book VIII, 2 1/4 in. x 2 1/4 in., folio 239r (shown actual size)

waters of a spring that symbolize Christ (fol. 251v);

- Book X, *Mary as the Ark (Maria archa)*: Mary enthroned between a chair and a chest, observed by an astonished Dominican (fol. 264r);
- Book XI, *Mary as the City of God (Maria civitas dei)*: Mary seated above the gate of a walled city, three coats of arms hang on the wall (fol. 319r) [fig. 50];
- Book XII, *Mary as the Closed Garden (Maria ortus conclusus)*: Virgin (half-length) enclosed by a woven fence before a landscape (fol. 358r).

The images of Mary show her seated or standing in a swaying "hip-shot" pose; her draperies fall in complex linear patterns typical of French late thirteenth-century Gothic art. The faces, curly hair, and delicate hands are white and the features are expressively delineated by fine penwork. In several initials, Mary's cloak is a brilliant orange-red, contrasting with her dress of pale mauve or pink. In other examples the Virgin wears blue over pink (Book IV: Virtues of Mary: illus. in Sievers), and when she appears as a vision to those who serve her (Book II) [fig. 46], she is robed in gold. The background colors vary to contrast with Mary's garments, sometimes solid blue with gold stars (Books III, VII), in other cases red checked, or blue and gold in diamond shapes that form a so-called diaper pattern. If Mary appears as a heavenly vision, she is set against a gold-leaf background, edged by wavy blue and white clouds [fig. 46]. Blue, pink, and gold leaf are also used to form the large initials and the baguettes (bars) and ivy leaves of the marginal decoration. The technical quality of the execution is extremely fine throughout.

Perhaps the most moving image initiates Book VI on the names of the Virgin which begins with the word *Mater (Mother)*. Appropriately, Mary is seated suckling the Christ child who actively reaches for her breast [fig. 81]. As Ann Sievers noted, "The *Virgo lactans* . . . expressed all the power and virtue which accrues to the Virgin in her role as mother of God; . . . she embodies both charity and mercifulness; she is mother and nurse not only of God, but of us all" (p. 131). In addition, Mary is Queen of Heaven, her green (!) crown emphasizing this elevated role while the action of offering her breast demonstrates her humanity and humility.

Earlier scholars associated the style of Wellesley's *De laudibus* with northeast France or French Flanders, based in part on the tentative identification of a coat of arms on the city gate illustrating Book XI as those of the Count of Cleves (Trevor, pp. 4–5; Sievers) [fig. 50]. More recently the prominence of scholarly Dominicans and the strong resemblances to the style associated with Master Honoré has pointed to Paris as the possible origin of the manuscript. Master Honoré was documented in Paris as the illuminator of a Gratian *Decretals* (1288) and a *Breviary for Philip le Bel* (1296), the latter linked to a magnificent copy of Frère Laurent, *La Somme le Roi* (ca. 1290–1295) (Millar; De Winter). The elegant Parisian style, with Honoré as its most famous exponent, has recently been reevaluated by François Avril in the 1998 exhibition *L'Art au temps des rois maudits: Philippe le Bel et ses fils 1285–1328*. Among the manuscripts catalogued by Avril, similarities to the Wellesley *De laudibus* figures may be seen not only in the Master Honoré Gratian (No. 184) but also in the crowned figure of Ecclesia in a *Breviary-Missal of Saint-Étienne of Châlons-sur-Marne* and the queens of the miniature beginning the *Oeuvres* of Adenet, both illuminated in Paris circa 1290 (nos. 185, 176). The *De laudibus* more than holds its own when compared to the finest of these Gothic treasures, whether executed in Paris or in northeast France under the influence of the capital.

Wellesley's *De laudibus* merits an historical postscript. As early as the fifteenth century, the manuscript had left France for Italy. Somewhere in its travels, part of Book XII was damaged and replaced. The script and especially the historiated initial of this section is in a characteristic mid-fifteenth-century Florentine style. It could have rested in one of the great Florentine Dominican monasteries until their suppression and the dispersal of their possessions in the nineteenth century.

LILIAN ARMSTRONG

BIBLIOGRAPHY

Avril, François. "Manuscrits." In *L'Art au temps des rois maudits: Philippe le Bel et ses fils 1285–1328*, exhibition catalogue. Paris: Galeries Nationales du Grand Palais (17 March–29 June 1998), pp. 256–334.

De Ricci, Seymour. *Census of Medieval and Renaissance Manuscripts in the United States and Canada*. New York: Bibliographical Society of America, 1935 (repr. Kraus, 1961), vol. 2, p. 2308, no. 19; and Supplement, 1962, p. 285, no. 19.

De Winter, Patrick. "Honoré, Master." In *Dictionary of Art*, ed. Jane Turner. London: Grove's Dictionaries, 1996, vol. 3, pp. 724–26.

Millar, Eric G. *The Parisian Miniaturist Honoré*. London: Faber and Faber, 1959.

Miner, Dorothy E. *Illuminated Books of the Middle Ages and Renaissance*, exhibition catalogue. Baltimore, MD: Trustees of the Walters Art Gallery, 1949, p. 27, no. 68 and pl. 32 (illustration misnumbered 67).

Sievers, Ann. *"De laudibus Beatae Mariae Virginis."* In Brown University Department of Art. *Transformations of the Court Style: Gothic Art in Europe 1270 to 1330*, exhibition catalogue, Museum of Art, Rhode Island School of Design. Providence, RI: The Department of Art, 1977, pp. 103–31, no. 49 (with prior bibliography).

Trevor, Emily. "The *De Laudibus beatae mariae* at Wellesley College: The Role of the Artist." Independent research paper, Wellesley College, 1969.

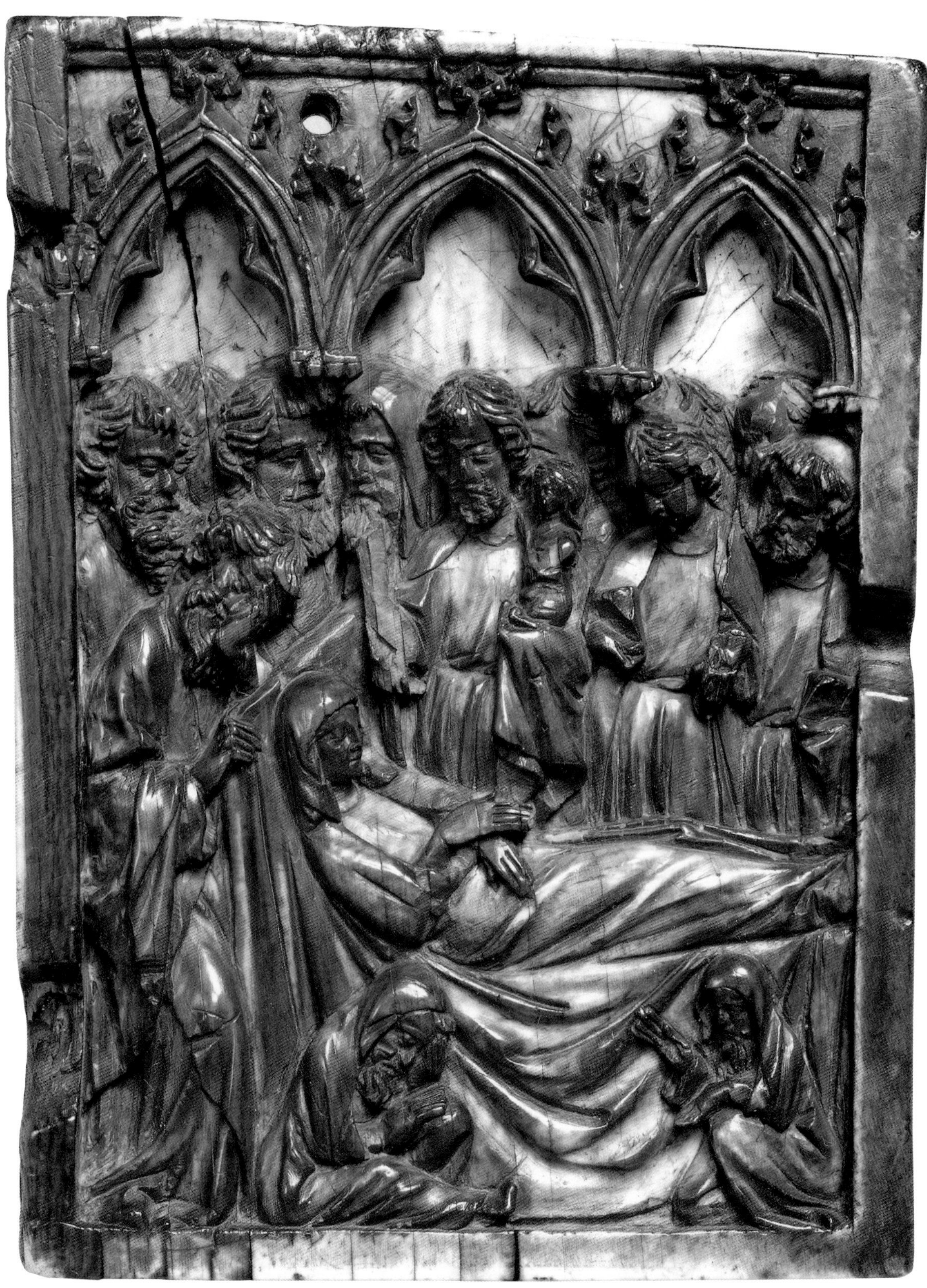

A   French, from Île de France

T   *Dormition of the Virgin* (right wing of diptych)

D   14th century

M   ivory

X   3 3/8 in. x 2 1/2 in. (8.6 cm x 6.4 cm)

C   Museum purchase in honor of Professor Agnes
A. Abbot

1964.35

This small ivory plaque is the right wing of a fourteenth-century diptych from France. The Virgin Mary lies in a bed surrounded by the twelve apostles and Christ, who holds Mary's infant soul in his left hand. Many ivories were painted and gilded, though it was much less common for plaquettes, diptychs, and polyptychs. The dark brown appearance of this ivory is due to a clear coating that was applied and has darkened with age.[1]

Placing a date on ivory plaques is difficult because the style varies only slightly between centuries. This relative stagnancy may be linked to the eighth-century Nicene Council, which attempted to curb artistic freedom of expression: "The composition of the figures is not the invention of the painter, but the law of tradition of the Catholic Church" (Cust, p. 94). At the end of the fourteenth century, however, a loose, delicate style emerged in an attempt at realism; and as the centuries passed, ivory carvings, whether stylized icons or precious secular objects, became a self-conscious art, often being attributed to a particular artist.

In the thirteenth and fourteenth centuries, ivories enjoyed popularity and commonly featured religious subject matter, in particular the lives of Christ and of Mary. The tremendous impulse of religious enthusiasm that began in the thirteenth century is evidenced by the mass multiplication of Mary's images for public and private devotion. Ivory, viewed as a symbol of purity and chastity, was a preferred medium for depictions of the Virgin.

France, the center of major ivory work, attracted artists from other countries who wanted to learn the technique of ivory carving. As a result, the style of ivories tends to be similar from region to region, making it difficult to distinguish an ivory's origin. However, as the individual countries nurtured the ivory craft, differing characteristics did emerge: for example, in the thirteenth and fourteenth centuries, German ivories—in contrast to those of the French—tended to include quite elaborately carved architecture.

Ivories, classed with precious metals, were originally sought after for ecclesiastical purposes. Later on, ivories became objects of exchange, being bought and sold by wealthy patrons. Considering the high price for ivory and the complicated process of carving, ivory carvers were most likely well off and highly skilled. Indeed, despite the difficulty posed by the otherwise implacable nature of ivory, the talented ivory carver had remarkable flexibility with his medium. Because ivories are necessarily limited in size and lack any sparkle or brilliance to compel the eye, they are best appreciated at close range.

The Virgin came to occupy a central role in late medieval spirituality and was increasingly seen as an accessible figure, to whom the faithful could appeal for help.[2] The Dormition, one of the scenes in the life of the Virgin, illustrates Mary's passing; theologians still dispute, however, whether Mary truly died or merely fell asleep and entered heaven. According to tradition, three days after Mary was laid in the tomb, it was found empty, her body having been assumed into heaven to be crowned Queen. The Dormition is depicted on the right leaf of this ivory diptych, which is highly unusual since the Dormition is usually paired with the Coronation, left leaf and right leaf, respectively (Randall, p. 75). It is possible that the missing left leaf contained a scene of the angel announcing the Virgin's death, as that scene would be subordinate to the scene of the Dormition, and traditionally the most important leaf of a

Fig. 113 (opposite page). French from Île de France, *Dormition of the Virgin*, 14th c., ivory

multiscene ivory was either the right leaf or the
uppermost leaf (Cust, p. 142). Another possibility
is that the artist may have depicted the Dormition
together with the Crucifixion of Christ, in order to
draw a parallel between these separate assumptions. That theory, however, still raises questions as
the Crucifixion, which is more central to the
Christian faith than the passing of the Virgin,
would have appeared on the left leaf.

JENNIFER SORRA PARK '01

NOTES

1. The museum has had the coating tested; it is insoluble and
cannot be safely removed. It was impossible to determine when
the coating was applied, or whether by the original artist or at a
later date.

2. The friars of the mendicant orders initiated this increase in
spirituality in the thirteenth century when they moved to urban
areas and became an important presence in the city.

BIBLIOGRAPHY

Cust, Anna Maria Elizabeth. *The Ivory Workers of the Middle Ages.*
London: G. Bell and Sons, 1902.

Randall, Richard H., Jr. *The Golden Age of Ivory: Gothic Carvings in
North American Collections.* New York: Hudson Hills Press,
1993.

CAT. NO. 4

A French, from Paris (produced for Nantes)

T *Officium Beatae Mariae Virginis* (Latin and
French Book of Hours, use of Nantes)

D 1400–10, with circa 1450 and circa 1470 additions

M manuscript with inks, glair, and gold leaf on
vellum, 197 folios with 3 full-page miniatures
and 11 half-page miniatures

X folios: 7 in. x 5 in. (180 mm x 127 mm)

I see checklist

C Wellesley College Library, Special Collections,
Guy Warren Walker, Jr. Collection, on deposit
from St. Mark's School, Southborough, Massachusetts
MS *81WM-1

The splendid *Book of Hours* (*Officium Beatae
Mariae Virginis*), illuminated in Paris around
1400–1410, is on long-term loan to Wellesley College from the Guy Warren Walker Collection of
St. Mark's School.[1] Containing fourteen miniatures (listed below) surrounded by exquisite foli-
ate borders and many other text pages with partial borders, the sumptuous Walker *Book of Hours*
is a type of prayer-book that has been called "*the
medieval best-seller*" (Wieck, p. 27). Books of
Hours evolved out of the Breviary, a book used to
celebrate the Divine Office, the cycle of daily
devotions recited by clerics at the eight canonical
hours of the liturgical day (Brown, pp. 23, 25–26,
50–51). Adapted for laypersons, the central text
of a Book of Hours is the Little Office of the
Blessed Virgin, or Hours of the Virgin, consisting
of eight short services corresponding to the
canonical hours: Matins (2:30 A.M.); Lauds (3:00
A.M.); Prime (6:00 A.M.); Terce (9:00 A.M.); Sext
(noon); Nones (3:00 P.M.); Vespers (6:00 P.M. or
sundown); and Compline (evening) (Backhouse;
Wieck).

The *Walker Hours* contains the Hours of the Virgin (fols. 13r-76v) and other texts that are also
standard components of a Book of Hours: a Calendar (fols. 1r-12v); the Hours of the Cross (fols.
76r-79v); the Hours of the Holy Spirit (fols. 80r-
83r); Gospel Sequences (fols. 83v-88v); prayers to
the Virgin (fols. 89r-99r); the Seven Penitential
Psalms and a litany (fols. 101r-127r); the Office of
the Dead (fols. 128r-174v); and other accessory
texts (fols. 174v-195v).

Normally illustrating the Hours of the Virgin are
events from the Life of the Virgin, and this pattern
is followed in the *Walker Hours*. Preceding Matins is

the *Annunciation* (fol. 13r), but Lauds and Prime
are not illustrated. The *Annunciation to the Shepherds*
(fol. 51r) precedes Terce; the *Adoration of the Magi*
(fol. 55r) appears before Sext; and the *Purification
of the Virgin* (also known as the *Presentation of the
Christ Child in the Temple*, fol. 59r) before Nones.
Normally Vespers follows the *Flight into Egypt* (fol.
70v) and the *Coronation of the Virgin* (fol. 63r) precedes Compline, but in the *Walker Hours* the position of these two scenes is reversed. Continuing a
traditional sequence for a Book of Hours, the *Crucifixion* (fol. 76r) is placed before the Hours of the
Cross; *Pentecost* (or the *Descent of the Holy Spirit*, fol.
80r) before the Hours of the Holy Spirit; *King
David in Prayer* (fol. 101r) before the Seven Penitential Psalms; *Chanting the Office of the Dead* (fol. 128r)
before the Office of the Dead; and *Christ Glorified*
(fol. 182r) before the Seven Requests to Our Lord
(Hadley, Appendix, pp. 1–2).

Margaret Hadley has firmly identified the
scenes noted above as Parisian work of circa
1400–10 (chapter 2, pp. 1–8). Many characteristic features of this style can be seen in the *Coronation of the Virgin* (fol. 63r) [fig 114]. The Virgin
and Christ are seated on a benchlike throne that
rests on a narrow strip of green flowered ground;
behind them is a flat blue background decorated
with geometric gold patterns. Christ, crowned
and wearing a bright orange robe lined with
ermine, carries an orb to symbolize his dominion
over the world. Simultaneously, he places a similar gold crown on the Virgin's head as she turns
to Christ, hands folded in a gesture of reverence.
The miniaturist has emphasized the silhouettes
and brilliant colors while the bodies remain unar-
ticulated. Faces are pale, enlivened only by dark
dots suggesting bright eyes. The effect is solemn
yet vivacious, effectively stressing the Virgin's role
as the Queen of Heaven, an aspect of Marian
devotion that was especially popular in twelfth- to
fourteenth-century France (Réau, pp. 621–26;
van Os).

The page layout sets the miniature above sev-

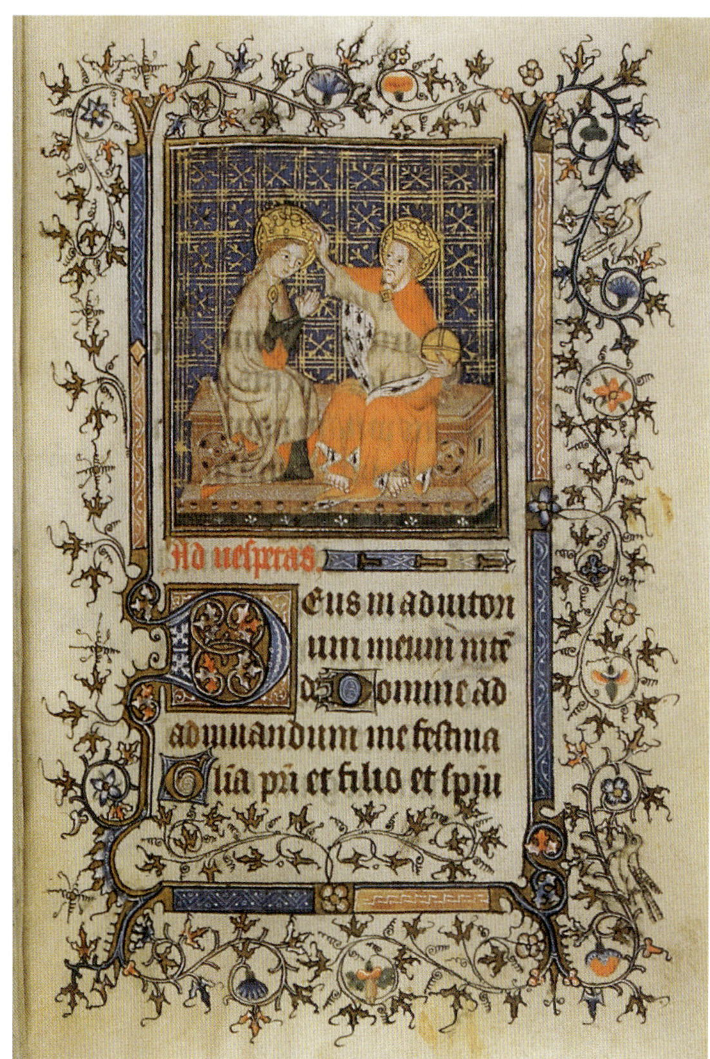

Fig. 114. *Coronation of
the Virgin*, half-page
illumination accompa-
nying Vespers, 2 7/8
in. x 2 3/8 in. (76 mm
x 60 mm), folio 63r

eral lines of text in Gothic script, initiated by a
large decorative initial, all surrounded by bars
(also called baguettes) of blue and pale red and a
border of ivy vines with gold leaves, blue and red
flowers, and an occasional bird, butterfly, or
dragon. The general features of the layout were
set in the early fourteenth century, but the choice
of colors, width, and density of the *Walker Hours*
borders coincides with Parisian manuscripts of
circa 1400. Hadley noted formal parallels between
the Walker miniatures and those in a Book of
Hours in the Walters Art Gallery Library, Baltimore (circa 1410) (MS W.232; Wieck, figs. 232,
pl. 32; Randall, No. 85, pp. 232–35, figs. 167–68,

pl. VIIb). To these should be added the iconographic and formal similarities between the Walker illuminations and MSS W.96, W.103, and W.101, all Books of Hours in the Walters Art Gallery Library dated and localized by Lilian Randall to Paris between 1400 and 1425 (1989, no. 76, pp. 205–09, figs. 153–55; no. 83, pp. 225–28, figs. 162–63; no. 91, pp. 254–57, figs. 175–76).

Various dioceses in medieval Europe adopted slightly different forms in their liturgical practices, known as "Uses." While the texts in most French Books of Hours follow the Use of Rome or the Use of Paris, the *Walker Hours* follows the Use of Nantes. Its western French destination is further supported not only by the names of saints especially venerated in Nantes that are inscribed in the Calendar, but also by a coat of arms (fol. 100r) identified as those of the Saint-Gilles family of Brittany (Hadley, ch. 2, p. 5). Several folios were inserted into the *Walker Hours* subsequent to its production; on these are *St. Catherine; and St. Sebastian* (fol. 99v) and *Dead Christ with an Angel and Symbols of the Passion; and a Dominican holding the Child; and the Saint-Gilles arms* (fol. 100r), rather crudely painted in a provincial French style of around 1450. Another miniature in the same inserted section is *St. Anne, the Virgin, and the Christ Child* (fol. 86r) which Hadley dates circa 1470 (Hadley, ch.2, pp. 4–8). Thus the *Walker Hours* not only exemplifies the elegant decorative style of Paris around 1400, but with its later additions provides fascinating evidence of commerce in illuminated manuscripts between Paris and other areas of France.

LILIAN ARMSTRONG

NOTE

1. Provenance history indicates this volume was formerly owned by the Saint-Gilles family of Brittany; and sold in Paris by the Librarie Auguste Fontaine to the Walker Collection. [Sale Catalogue, Item No. 16].

BIBLIOGRAPHY

Backhouse, Janet. *Books of Hours*. London: British Library, 1985.

Brown, Michelle. *Understanding Illuminated Manuscripts: A Guide to Technical Terms*. London: British Library, 1994.

Hadley, Margaret. "Five Late-Medieval Books of Hours at Wellesley: Issues of Style, Codicology, and Iconography." Senior honors thesis, Wellesley College, 1997.

Harthan, John. *Books of Hours*. London: Thames & Hudson, 1977.

van Os, H. W. "Kröning Mariens." *Lexikon der christlichen Ikonographie*, Engelbert Kirschbaum, ed., vol. 2. Rome: Herder, 1968, cols. 671–76.

Randall, Lilian M. C. *Medieval and Renaissance Manuscripts in the Walters Art Gallery*, vol. 1 (*France, 875–1420*). Baltimore: Walters Art Gallery, 1989.

Réau, Louis. *Iconographie de l'art chrétien*, vol. 2, part 2. Paris: Presses universitaires de France, 1957.

Wieck, Roger. *Time Sanctified: The Book of Hours in Medieval Art and Life*. New York: G. Braziller, 1988. Also published as *The Book of Hours in Medieval Art and Life*. London: Sotheby's, 1988.

CAT. NO. 5

According to the *Gospel of Pseudo Matthew* (an early medieval compilation of stories that embellish the biblical narrative of Mary, Joseph, and the young Jesus), when the Holy Family fled into Egypt, they stopped to rest at a place where a palm tree bent down to offer Mary its fruit (20:1). Schongauer's engraving shows Mary with Jesus in her arms—sitting on a donkey that has stopped, perhaps to graze—while angels bend down a palm tree so that Joseph can gather its fruit.

Schongauer carefully renders the botanical features of the date palm tree, of the thistle and mullein plants in the foreground, and of the "dragon tree" on the left. Indigenous to Africa and the Canary Islands, the dragon tree (*draco dragonis*) was a species that Schongauer was most likely familiar with only from another drawing (Koch, pp. 114–19).[1] The two trees in this print would have been identified with the trees that, according to the Book of Genesis, grew in the Garden of Eden: the tree of life and the tree of the knowledge of good and evil. By introducing the "trees of paradise" into this image of the Holy Family, the artist invokes a long-standing notion of Christ as the "new Adam" and Mary, the "new Eve" (Minott, pp. 15–16). Schongauer's attempt to render accurately

natural species that at the same time are bearers of symbolic meaning, places him in the company of those early Netherlandish painters of whom Erwin Panofsky wrote: "The more [they] rejoiced in the discovery and reproduction of the visible world, the more intensely did they feel the need to saturate all of its elements with meaning. Conversely, the more they strove to express new subtleties and complexities of thought, the more eagerly did they explore new areas of reality" (Panofsky, *Early Netherlandish Painting*, vol. 1, p. 115).

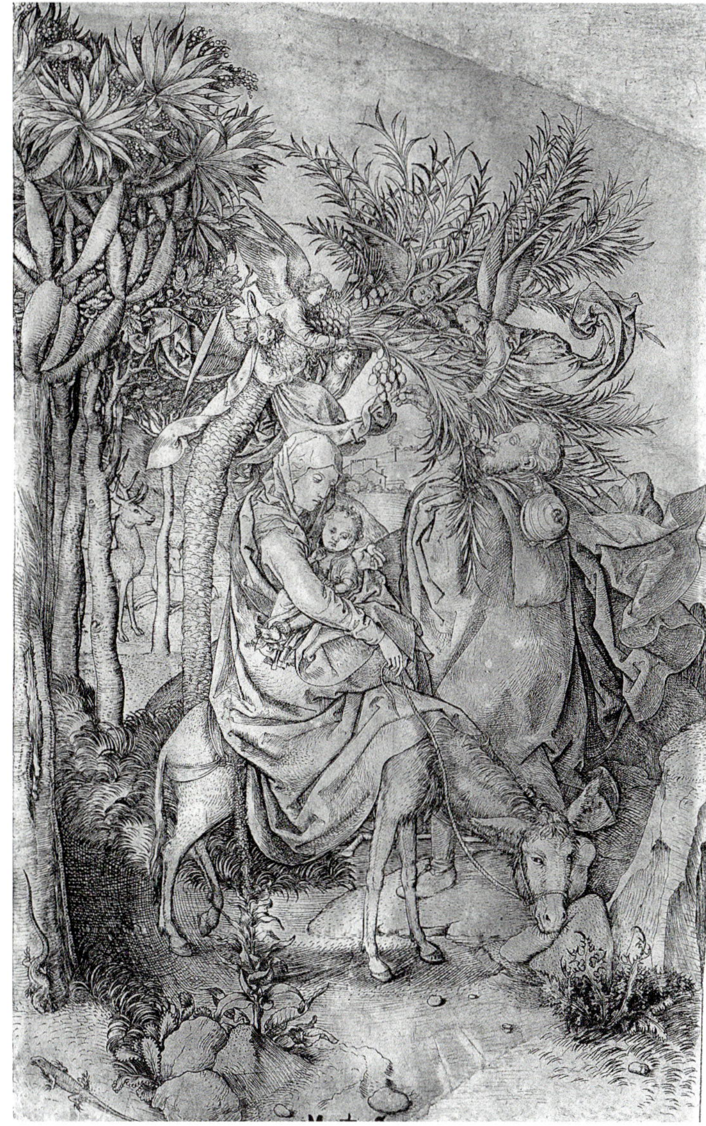

Fig. 115. Martin Schongauer, *Rest on the Flight into Egypt*, 3rd quarter 15th c., engraving

Like those early Netherlandish painters, Schongauer was also a technical innovator: in this case, in the medium of engraving (Panofsky, *Dürer*, p. 65; Landau and Parshal, pp. 50–51). Notwithstanding the worn condition of Wellesley's impression of Schongauer's engraving, the characteristic effect of his elegantly swelling and tapering burin lines is still notable. Schongauer organizes the curving lines used to render figures, animals, and vegetation into calligraphic patterns that infuse the composition with powerful, cursive energy.

MARGARET D. CARROLL

NOTES

1. Whereas the bark of the palm tree is accurately rendered, apparently that of the dragon tree is not. Jane Campbell Hutchison, *Early German Artists: Martin Schongauer, Ludwig Schongauer, and Copyists. The Illustrated Bartsch*, vol 8., *Commentary*, part 1. New York: Abaris, 1996, pp. 29–30, B.7.

BIBLIOGRAPHY

Koch, Robert A. "Martin Schongauer's Dragon Tree." *Print Review* 5 (1974), pp. 114–19.

Landau, David and Peter Parshal. *The Renaissance Print.* New Haven: Yale University Press, 1994.

Minott, Charles. "Albrecht Dürer: The Early Graphic Works." *Record of the Art Museum Princeton University*, vol. 30, 1971.

Panofsky Erwin. *Early Netherlandish Painting: Its Origins and Character* (1953), 2 vols. Princeton, NJ: Princeton University Press, 1971.

Panofsky, Erwin. *The Life and Art of Albrecht Dürer* (1st ed., 1943; 4th ed., 1955). Princeton, NJ: Princeton University Press, 1971.

CAT. NO. 6

A Circle of Willem Backer Van Vrelant
Utrecht, Netherlands, active circa 1449–81
Bruges, Flanders
active Bruges

T *Gebeden Boeck* (Dutch Book of Hours, use unknown)

D circa 1470

M manuscript with ink, gouache, gold leaf, and shell gold on vellum
117 folios, 6 full-page miniatures, and many decorative initials and borders in gold and colors

X folios: 6 15/16 in. x 4 13/16 in. (176 mm x 122 mm)

I see checklist

C Wellesley College Library, Special Collections, Gift of Bertha Mahony Miller
MS 27

A Book of Hours is a type of prayer-book that was commonly used by laypersons in fourteenth- through sixteenth-century Europe for daily recitation of religious devotions (see cat. no. 4 for a more detailed discussion). Bruges, located in the Duchy of Flanders (present-day Belgium), was an important center for the production of Books of Hours. Wellesley's MS 27 is a beautiful example from the circle of Willem Backer van Vrelant, active in Bruges from about 1450 to his death in 1481 (Proske-Van Heerdt). The texts of MS 27 include the normal components of a Book of Hours: Calendar (fols. 1r-6v); Hours of the Cross (fols. 8r-10v); Hours of the Holy Spirit (fols. 12r-14v); Mass of the Virgin (fols. 16r-22r); Hours of the Virgin (fols. 24r-64r); Suffrages of the Saints and other prayers (fols. 64r-81v); Seven Penitential Psalms (fols. 83r-92v); and the Office of the Dead (fols. 97r-118v). The entire text, except for a few titles (e.g., *Gloria in excelsis Deo*), is in Dutch, translated from the Latin by Geert Grote (died 1384). Grote was "a religious reformer involved in founding the *Devotio Moderna*, who sought a broadly based and personal brand of spirituality" (Hadley, Appendix, p. 5, following Marrow, p. 9).

The original illustrative program for MS 27 placed a miniature before each major division of the text. Each miniature, framed by illuminated borders, was painted on an inserted folio that was blank on one side. The six extant miniatures are the *Annunciation* (fol. 23v) before Matins of the Hours of the Virgin; the *Crucifixion* (fol. 7v); *Pentecost* (or the *Descent of the Holy Spirit*, fol. 11v); *Virgin and Child* (fol. 15v); the *Resurrection of the Dead* (fol. 82v); and a *Funeral Procession* (fol. 96v). A folio with a miniature preceding Lauds in the Hours of the Virgin may have been removed at an unknown early period. In addition, many pages also have illuminated, decorative borders similar to those surrounding the miniatures.

The miniatures proper occupy about three-quarters of a page; their format is rectangular except for an indented arch at the top. Scenes are separated from the decorative borders by thin gold frames. In the *Annunciation* [fig. 116], the Angel Gabriel floats in, announcing to the Virgin Mary that she will be the mother of Christ (Luke 1:26–38). The Virgin kneels near a prayer desk in a screened section of a gothic church, a setting more familiar to the fifteenth-century reader than any imagined building in Nazareth. Gabriel is dressed in a white robe under a brilliant red cloak edged with gold; he carries both a scepter and a banderole on which is inscribed his greeting: *Ave Maria gratia plena* (Hail Mary, full of grace). Mary acknowledges Gabriel with her slightly raised hand; her humility is signaled by her posture. Her deep blue dress and cloak are also edged in gold, and her reddish blonde hair escapes from the veil to straggle over her shoulders. The exquisite borders combine acanthus leaves, berries, flowers, and a bird, enhancing the delicate elegance of the miniature.

The iconography of two other miniatures is distinctive. The *Pentecost* is also set in a grey ecclesiastical interior with the dove of the Holy Spirit appearing in a golden halo in the window. The Virgin is prominently situated in the center of the asymmetrical composition, kneeling at a prayer-desk. A young apostle (St. John the Evangelist) kneels at the left, and a bearded apostle stands

behind the Virgin; the other apostles, however, are curiously crowded behind a waist-high barrier in the left middleground. Balancing St. John at the extreme right kneels a bareheaded young woman, like the Virgin dressed in dark blue. She presses her hands together in a gesture of devotion and may represent the contemporary Flemish patron.

Also clearly reflecting ordinary life in fifteenth-century Flanders is the miniature preceding the Office of the Dead (fol. 96v). A funeral procession moves out from a church: a small acolyte holding a cross leads both a cleric, wearing a blue cope and holding a book, and a tonsured Dominican

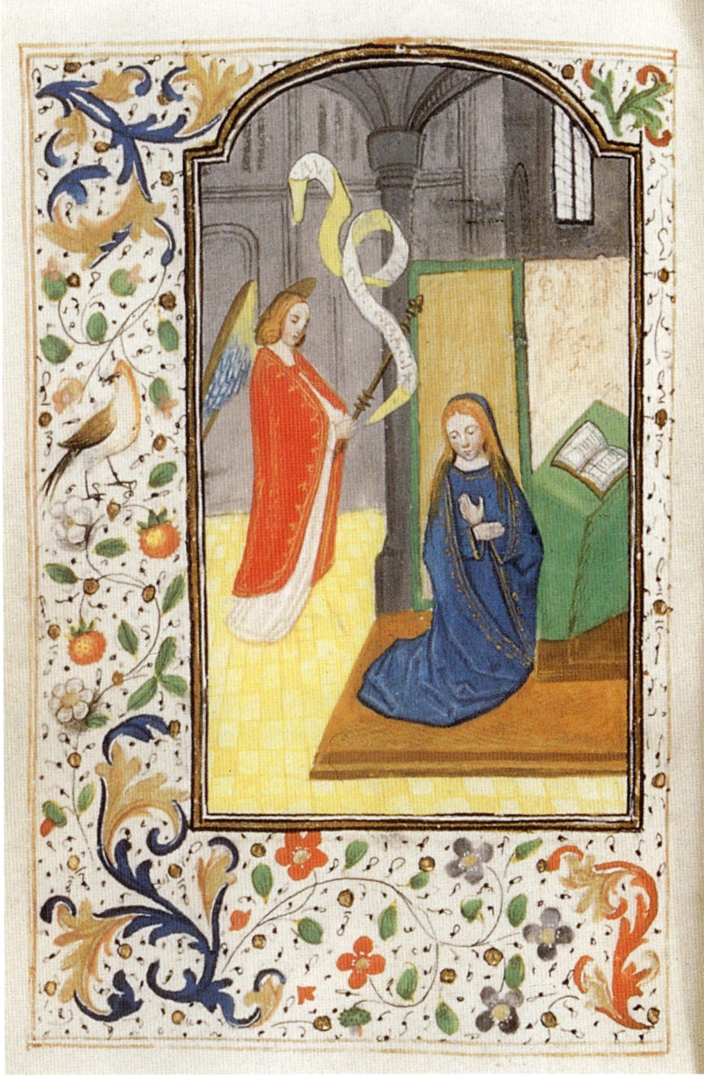

Fig. 116. Circle of Willem Backer van Vrelant, *Annunciation*, from a ca. 1470 Dutch Book of Hours, full-page illumination (4 5/16 in. x 2 1/8 in.) preceding the Hours of the Virgin, folio 23v

monk, carrying a gold asperge, or liturgical instrument for sprinkling holy water. Two mourners
dressed in yellow-brown robes emerge from a
church carrying a blue coffin on their shoulders.
Standing in an open grave is the gravedigger, who
turns to glare at the little procession, apparently
surprised by their early arrival.

Close formal and iconographic similarities exist
between Wellesley's MS 27 and a Book of Hours in
the Walters Art Gallery Library, Baltimore (MS
W.197), which has been attributed to Willem Vrelant or his circle and dated circa 1460 (Randall,
1997, no. 250, part I, pp. 251–62). The officiating
priest of the Walters *Burial Service* (Wieck, 1988, pl.
39) similarly appears at the entrance of a church
wearing a blue robe trimmed in gold. He asperges
the shrouded corpse as it is lowered into a grave,
observed by an acolyte. Green grass, a gray church,
touches of red in the workers' costumes are the
same hues found in the Wellesley miniature. In the
Walters manuscript, a *St. Genèvieve* (Randall, part 2,
pl. XXXVa) is frontally posed in a grey-walled interior very much like the Wellesley *Standing Virgin
and Child* (fol. 15v); both St. Genèvieve and the Virgin wear blue cloaks edged in gold over red
dresses; the shape of St. Genèvieve's head and her
long red-blonde hair recall the Wellesley Virgin
Annunciate (fol. 23v). The architecture and spatial
effects of the Walters *Circumcision* (Randall, fig.
507) can easily be seen as a precedent for the
Wellesley *Annunciation* and *Pentecost* scenes. The
borders, with delicate penwork scrolls, bright acanthus leaves, flowers and berries, form almost identical patterns in the two manuscripts. Similar borders, figure types, and the spatial effects are also
seen in another Book of Hours attributed to Vre-

lant, now in the Vatican Library, MS Barb. lat. 444
(Morello, p. 120, pl. XXXII) and in the closely
related Vatican MS Ross. 63 (Morello, p. 88, figs.
54, 78, 80). The compositions of Wellesley MS 27
are slightly less detailed and refined than the Walters miniatures, but there should be no hesitation
in attributing the former to the circle of William
Vrelant and in delighting in its charming evocation
of life and devotional practices in late fifteenth-
century Flanders.

LILIAN ARMSTRONG

BIBLIOGRAPHY

Bousmanne, Bernard. "Item à Guillaume Wyelant aussi enlu-
     mineur." *Willem Vrelant, un aspect de l'enluminenure dans les
     Pays-bas méridionaux sous le mécénat des ducs de Bourgogne
     Philippe le Bon et Charles le Téméraire.* Brussels: Brepols, 1997.

Hadley, Margaret. "Five Late-Medieval Books of Hours at Welles-
     ley: Issues of Style, Codicology, and Iconography." Senior
     honors thesis, Wellesley College, 1997.

Marrow, James H. "Introduction." In *The Golden Age of Dutch Man-
     uscript Painting,* ed. Henri L. M. Defoer, James H. Marrow,
     Anne S. Korteweg, and Wilhelmina C. M Wüstefeld. New
     York: G. Braziller, 1990.

Morello, Giovanni. *Libri d'Ore della Biblioteca Apostolica Vaticana.*
     Zurich: Belser Verlag, 1988.

Proske-Van Heerdt, D. "Vrelant, Willem Backer van." In *Dictio-
     nary of Art,* ed. Jane Turner. London: Grove, 1996, vol. 32,
     pp. 728–30.

Randall, Lilian M. C. *Medieval and Renaissance Manuscripts in the
     Walters Art Gallery,* vol. 3: *Belgium, 1250–1530,* 2 parts. Balti-
     more: Walters Art Gallery, 1997.

Wieck, Roger. *Time Sanctified: The Book of Hours in Medieval Art
     and Life.* New York: G. Braziller, 1988. Also published as *The
     Book of Hours in Medieval Art and Life.* London: Sotheby's,
     1988.

A Pedro González Berruguete
Paredes de Nava, Castile, Spain circa
1450/55–1503 Ávila
active Paredes de Nava, Toledo, and Ávila,
Spain; Urbino and Rome(?), Italy

T *Assumption of the Virgin* (central panel of a dispersed polyptych)

D circa 1485

M oil, shell gold, and gold leaf on panel

X 55 1/2 in. x 35 1/2 in. (141.0 cm x 90.2 cm)

C Gift of Mr. and Mrs. A. M. Adler
1965.52

The *Assumption of the Virgin* by Pedro Berruguete (1450/55–1503) is painted in the Hispano-Flemish style, a fusion of early Netherlandish attention to detail, and tense Spanish emotionalism. It was probably Berruguete's "eyckianismo" that appealed to his most important patron, Federigo de Montefeltro (1422–1482), duke of Urbino. Berruguete is now widely accepted as the "Pietro Spagnolo pittore" mentioned in a 1477 document (no longer extant) as being active at the ducal court in Urbino. In addition, a drawing has recently come to light that appears to confirm this link. Annotated in 1632 with the inscription "Petrus Hispanus pinxit," the drawing reproduces a painting from Urbino, the *Communion of the Apostles,* that is consistent with Berruguete's style.[1]

Berruguete's stay in at the ducal court in Urbino lasted about a decade, aproximately 1473 to 1482. While there, he collaborated with Joos van Gent (Joos van Wassenhove, active 1465–1475) in the decoration of the duke's *studiolo,* ringed with two tiers of *Portraits of Famous Men,* half of which remain in situ in Federigo's palace library, and the other half of which have been installed in a special gallery in the Louvre. (The *studiolo*'s famous intarsia *trompe l'oeuil* panels were simultaneously in production.) Berruguete must

have taken Federigo's death in 1482 as a signal that his Italian sojourn was at an end, for in 1483 he is documented at work in Toledo cathedral, and he remained in Spain until his death sometime before 6 January 1504.[2]

It is unlikely that Berruguete set out from Parades de Naves, a quiet north Castillian town twenty kilometers from the provincial capital of Palencia, for the great court of Urbino. Silva Maroto suggests quite plausibly that his first destination was Naples, a territory of the Aragonese crown that had passed to the united Spain following Fernando of Aragon's 1469 marriage to Isabel of Castile and Fernando's accession to the Aragonese throne in 1479. In Naples, Berruguete could have found work with Ferrante de Aragón, with whom Federigo de Montefeltro stayed in 1474. A *Portrait of Pope Sixtus IV,* attributed to Berruguete and now in the collection of the Cleveland Museum of Art, suggests a stay in Rome as well (Silva Maroto, pp. 75–78).

Wellesley's *Assumption of the Virgin* dates from after Pedro's return from Italy, around the time of his great Castillian altarpieces, the polyptych *retablos* for the churches of Santa María in Becerril de Campos (circa 1485–90) and Santa Eulalia in Paredes de Nava (circa 1490) [fig. 117]. Filled with a gravity of style, it shows little absorption of Italian Renaissance naturalism. Berruguete remained true to his Hispano-Flemish heritage, indicated by his crisp draperies, slender and expressive hands, and the lustrous wings of seven angels who surround the Virgin Mary, supporting her jeweled crown and silver-gilt sliver of moon, while guiding her heavenward. The copper-resinate glazing applied to the wings of three angels has oxidized over time to a semi-opaque brown; originally they would have been translucent green over gold. The Virgin's blue mantle and red robe, on the other hand, remain well preserved, the madder lakes glazes still deep red and sufficiently transparent to let the artist's underdrawn pleats show through.

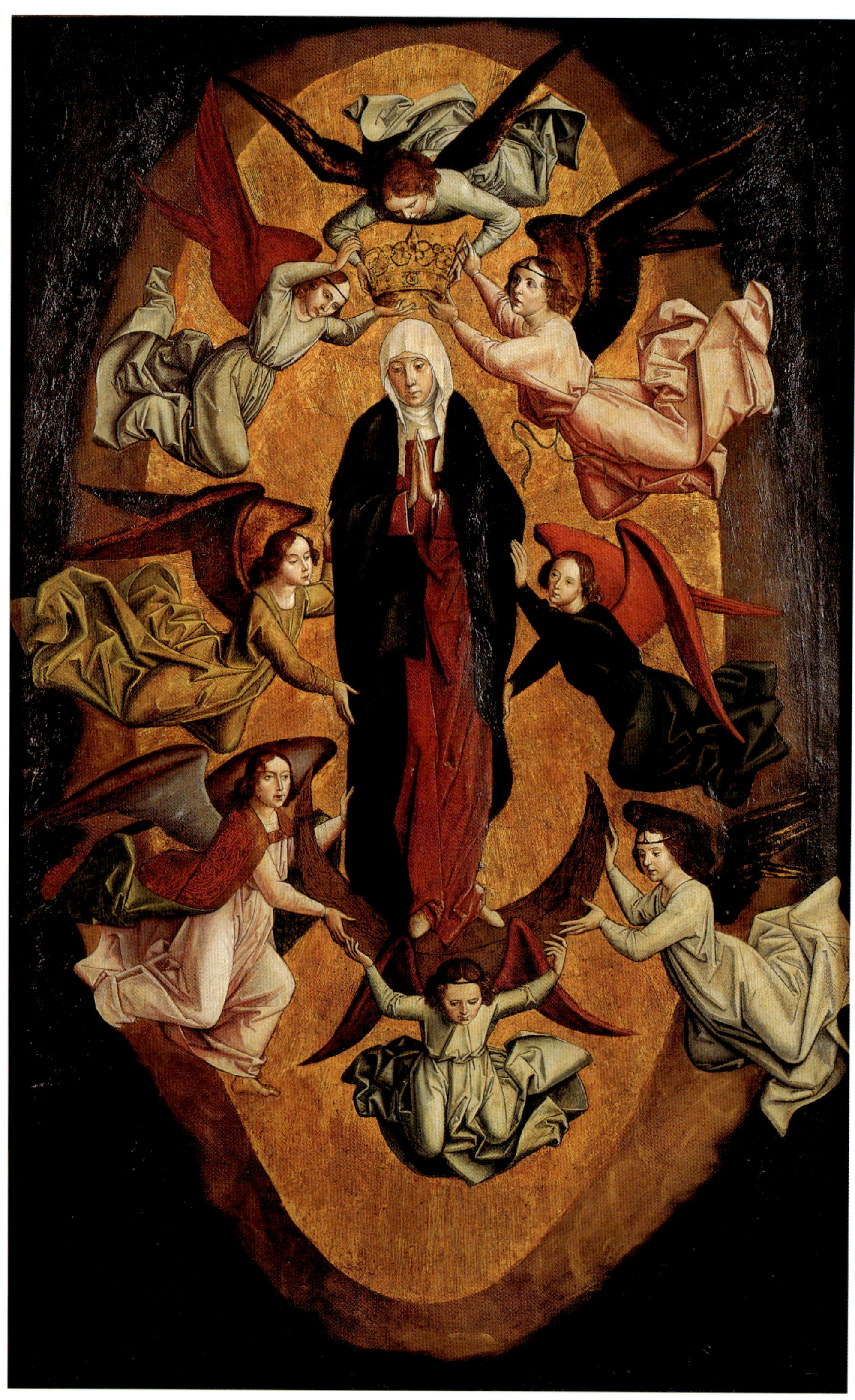

Fig. 117. Pedro Berruguete, *Assumption of the Virgin*, circa, 1485, oil on panel

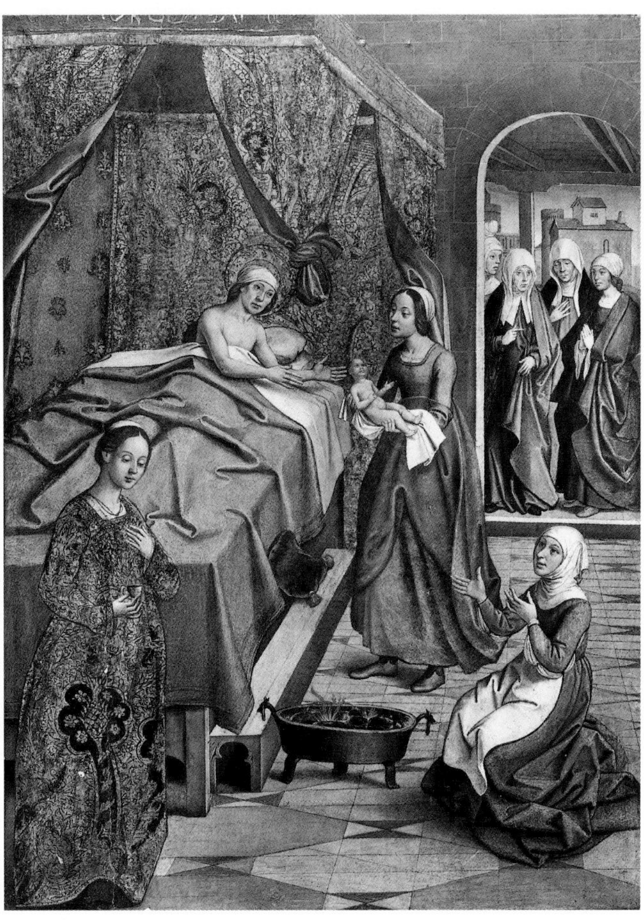 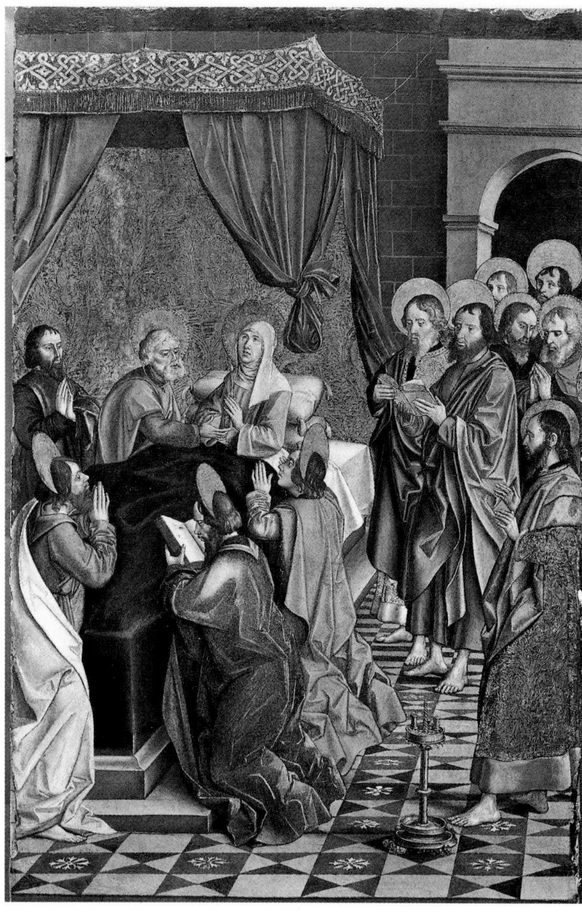

The *Assumption* originally formed part of a nine-panel polyptych, now disassembled and dispersed in 1925 when offered for sale in New York (Young, figs. 1–8).[3] Three of the large narrative panels—the *Birth of the Virgin* [fig. 118], the *Visitation*, and the *Death of the Virgin* [fig. 119]—are now in the collection of the Abbey and Sanctuary of Montserrat, near Barcelona, while the *Annunciation* panel is in the Museo de Pontevedra in northwest Spain, along with two of the four bottom panels featuring half-length prophets, *Isaiah* and *Jeremiah*. The remaining *banco* panels, *Solomon* and *David*, are in the collections of the Nassau County Museum, Long Island, New York, and the Bowdoin College Museum of Art, Brunswick, Maine (Silva Maroto, p. 253).

A *retablo* of this size—five main panels over a low *banco* composed of four panels—is small by Castillian standards and would have been destined for a side chapel rather than a main altar. The Santa Eulalia *retablo mayor* in Paredes de Nava—still in situ and comparable in date to the dispersed *retablo*—features a *banco* of six half-length prophets topped by six narrative panels divided by three tiers of polychromed sculpture surmounted by bas relief figures and a classical pediment (Sobré 1989, p. 198, fig. 129). The *retablo mayor* of Ávila cathedral, begun by Berruguete and completed after his death by Juan de Borgoña (active 1495–1536), features a *banco* of eight full-length prophets surmounted by ten large panels arranged in two tiers, with two vertical *entrecalles* formed of six narrow panels of saints, all enclosed in a housing of gilded tracery.

The *Assumption* panel, five inches wider than the lateral panels of the Virgin's *Birth* and *Death*,

Fig. 118 (left). Pedro Berruguete, *Birth of the Virgin* (panel from the same dispersed altarpiece as the *Assumption*), Abbey and Sanctuary of Montserrat

Fig. 119 (right). Pedro Berruguete, *Death of the Virgin* (also from the same dispersed altarpiece), Abbey and Sanctuary of Montserrat.

The Catalogue   167

Annunciation, and *Visitation*, probably stood at the
center of this altarpiece to the Virgin Mary. All
four lateral panels feature the high perspective
and deep recession characteristic of Berruguete's
larger works, while the museum's Virgin is silhou-
etted against a gold *mandorla* floating on a dark
sky. Most fifteenth-century Castillian altarpieces,
including the one at Paredes de Nava, featured a
polychromed wooden sculpture of a saint or the
Virgin at the center, and the *Assumption*'s simplified treatment may have been meant to simulate
the appearance of a sculpted figure against a dark
background.

Berruguete's other known *Assumption*, identified by Post as in a private collection in Barcelona
(vol. 11, fig. 193), similarly features Mary against a
plain background rising upward on a sickle moon
supported by angels; in the Barcelona painting,
however, God the Father, rather than a crown, hovers above. A related composition appears in
Berruguete's *Apparition of the Virgin to a Dominican
Community* from the disassembled Santo Domingo
retablo now in the Museo del Prado, Madrid. While
the lower half depicts monks assembled in prayer,
the upper half features a crowned Virgin silhouet-
ted against a gold-leafed circle ringed by attending
angels (Laínez Alcalá, p. 87, pl. 34).

MELISSA R. KATZ

NOTES

1. Juren, Vladimir. "Pietro Spagnolo et Juste de Gand: un dessin
inédit d'après le tableau d'autel du *Corpus Domini* à Urbin." *Revue
de l'Art*, no. 117 (1997), pp. 48–53. The anonymous drawing,
annotated by Gabriel Naudé (1600–1653) in 1632, is in the collection of the Bibliothèque Nationale, Paris. The *Communion of
the Apostles*, now in the Galleria Nazionale delle Marche in
Urbino, had until now been attributed to Joos van Gent.

2. This is the date of a document giving his eldest son, the sculptor Alonso Berruguete, custody of his five minor siblings and his
mother, Elvira González; Láinez Alcalá, p. 46. Because this date
falls in an active festive period, between Christmas (December
25th) and Epiphany (January 6th), and because in other better-
documented cases a lapse of weeks, if not months, occurs
between death and custodial transfer, it seems reasonable to
assume that Pedro died in late 1503, not early 1504.

3. The sale was held at the American Art Galleries on 9 December 1925, lots 739A-E; Young, p. 473. Raimondo Ruíz of Madrid
owned the *Birth of the Virgin*, *Visitation*, *Death of the Virgin*, and
Assumption panels, while his brother Luís Ruíz owned the *Annunciation* panel and the predella panels of *Solomon*, *Isaiah*, *Jeremiah*,
and *David*.

BIBLIOGRAPHY

Angulo Iniguez, Diego. *Pintura del Renacimiento: Ars Hispaniae*,
vol. 12. Madrid, Editorial Plus-Ultra, 1954.

Láinez Alcalá, Rafael. *Pedro Berruguete, Pintor de Castilla*. Madrid:
Espasa-Calpe, 1938.

Mateo Gómez, Isabel. "Berruguete, Pedro." In *Dictionary of Art*,
ed. Jane Turner. New York: Grove, 1996, vol. 3, pp. 844–45.

Post, Chandler R. *A History of Spanish Painting*. Cambridge, MA:
Harvard University Press, 1947, esp. vol. 9, part 1, pp.
114–17.

Silva Maroto, María Pilar. *Pedro Berruguete*. Valladolid: Junta de
Castilla y León, Conserjería de Educación y Cultura, 1998.

Sobré, Judith Berg. *Behind the Altar Table: The Development of the
Painted Retable in Spain, 1350–1500*. Columbia: University of
Missouri Press, 1989.

Sobré, Judith Berg. *The Artistic Splendors of the Spanish Kingdoms:
The Art of Fifteenth-Century Spain*. Boston: Isabella Stewart
Gardner Museum, 1996, cat. no. 10, pp. 46–48.

Young, Eric. "A Rediscovered Painting by Pedro Berruguete and
Its Companion Panels." *The Art Bulletin* 57, no. 4 (December
1975), pp. 473–75.

CAT. NO. 8

A Andrea Mantegna
Isola di Cartura, near Padua circa 1430–1506
Mantua
active Padua, Mantua

T *Entombment of Christ*

D circa 1470 or 1490

M engraving on greyish-white laid paper

X sheet and image: 12 in. x 17 11/16 in. (306 mm x 449 mm)

I see checklist

C Gift of Mr. and Mrs. Philip Hofer
1958.21

Andrea Mantegna's *Entombment* (Bartsch XIII.229,3) has always been praised for its powerful design, many times imitated and adapted by later artists such as Raphael and Rembrandt (Lincoln) [fig. 120]. Ten figures are arranged in a shallow, friezelike row in the foreground. Behind them opens a dark cavern in the craggy rocks, revealing the end of Christ's tomb on which is inscribed HVMANI GENERIS REDEMTORI. On the left, the limp but idealized body of Christ is carried on a sheet held by two men; the centrally situated man acts as a fulcrum, holding the shroud but also turning to the figures at the right. One mourning woman standing behind Christ helps to support his body while another throws her arms up in wild abandon. A young man covers his face in sorrow. The row of standing figures is interrupted by a group of women on the ground: the Virgin Mary has collapsed, and her head is cradled by an older woman as a third anxiously gazes at them. Finally, at the extreme right, St. John the Evangelist stands in profile clasping his hands together and crying out in anguish. A barren road twists up the hill of Golgotha on which the three crosses are outlined against the sky.

Mantegna's bodies are sculpturesque; draperies press against them revealing the limbs beneath.

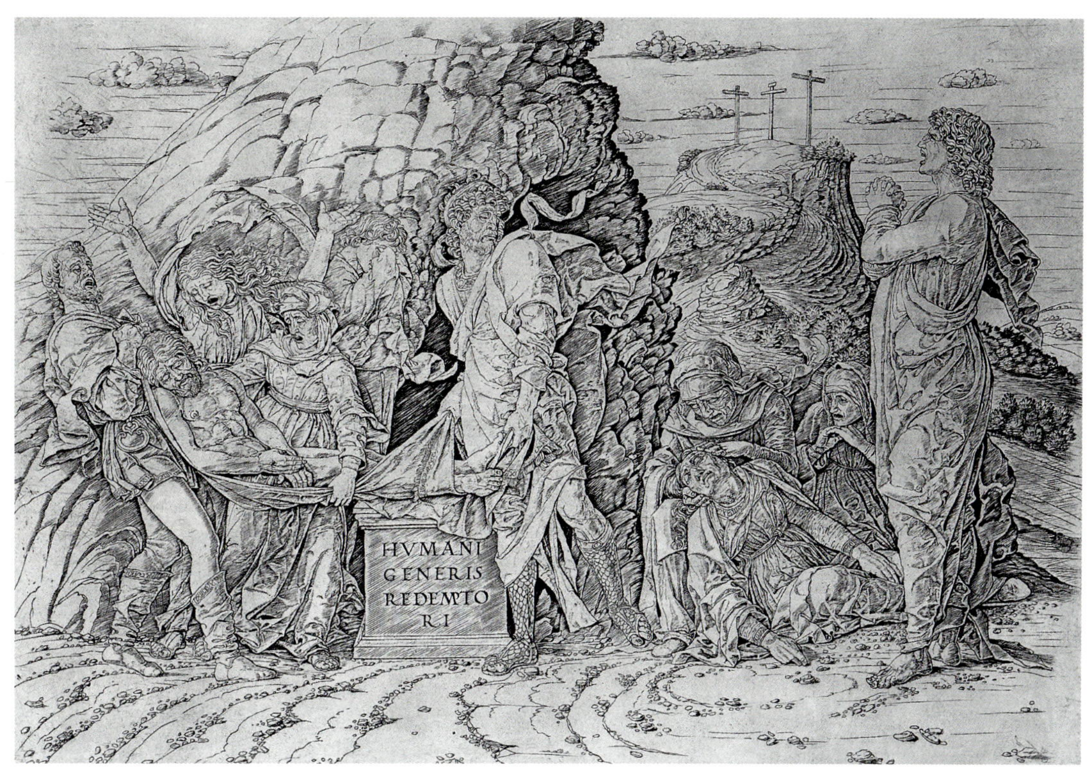

Fig. 120. Andrea Mantegna, *Entombment of Christ*, ca. 1470 or 1490, engraving

Deep-set eyes, wrinkled brows, and open crying mouths accentuate the intense grief of Christ's mother and followers. The Roman military boots and *contrapposto* pose of the central figure remind the viewer of Mantegna's deep commitment to the revival of Classical antiquity, as does the beautiful classical lettering of the inscribed tomb.

On Wellesley's impression of the *Entombment,* the outlines of the figures are strong and clear, but the fine parallel lines used to model the draperies and bodies are considerably fainter, indicating that the impression was made after the plate was worn. It quite closely resembles the impression from the National Gallery of Art, Washington, DC, which was noted as a "late impression" in the *Early Italian Engravings* exhibition of 1973 (Bartsch 8272; Levenson, Oberhuber, and Sheehan, no. 70, illus. p. 171). By comparison, an earlier impression also in the National Gallery shows a much richer range of blacks, creating a more dramatic *chiaroscuro* (Washington Patrons' Permanent Fund; Martineau, no. 39, illus. p. 202).

Many aspects of the engravings attributed to Andrea Mantegna remain controversial. As early as 1550, Giorgio Vasari in his *Vite de' più eccellenti pittori, scultori ed architettori* (*Lives of the Most Excellent Painters, Sculptors and Architects*) praised Mantegna for his engravings, citing the *Entombment* specifically among only a few others. Modern scholars have gradually come to the position that Mantegna both designed and engraved only seven prints, among them the *Entombment* (Kristeller; Hind; Levenson et al.; Zucker; Lightbown). They have also recognized that Mantegna designed a number of prints that were actually engraved by other professional engravers. For these scholars, the dating of the seven autograph prints poses a real problems. Kristeller and later Lightbown dated the *Entombment* around 1490, based on its technical and formal sophistication; both scholars relate it to the engraved *Risen Christ with Saints Andrew and Longinus* (Bartsch XII.231.6). On the other hand, Hind pointed to the close relation-

ship between the St. John the Evangelist and Mantegna's painted St. John in the *Crucifixion* of the San Zeno altarpiece *predella* of 1457–1459, and accordingly dated the print to this period. Both Levenson and Landau (1992), however, argued for a date around 1470, and certainly before 1475, the date of a letter in which one Simone de Ardizioni accused Mantegna of having him attacked. Simone claimed that he had been engraving plates for a painter named Zoan Andrea, and that this activity had unjustifiably enraged Mantegna; the episode at the very least demonstrated that Mantegna had a vested interest in the activity of engraving by 1475 (Christiansen, p. 612, Appendix).

A more complex issue is the question of whether Mantegna himself actually engraved plates or whether he only provided designs that were engraved by professional engravers. In her monograph of 1955, Erica Tietze-Conrat argued that Mantegna never himself engraved plates, but this view remained in the distinct minority until the great *Andrea Mantegna* exhibition of 1992. That exhibition's two curators of prints, David Landau and Suzanne Boorsch, arrived at diametrically opposed views of Mantegna as engraver. Landau praised his "astonishing number of technical innovations in printmaking—from using the burin alone to experimenting with drypoint, and then combining the two before returning to the burin—which resulted in a greatly increased tonal richness," concluding that Mantegna was the "greatest printmaker of the [fifteenth] century" (Landau, 1992, pp. 47, 54). At the other extreme, Boorsch determined that Mantegna did not himself engrave any plates: indeed, all of the "Mantegna engravings" were engraved by professional engravers other than the master himself (Boorsch, p. 64). Reviewers of the exhibition and its catalogue also divided over the conclusions—Patricia Emison, for example, leaning to Boorsch's position and Keith Christiansen siding with the more traditional view.

Yet other surprising evidence about Mantegna's

engravings has come to light recently. Much had been made of the softer *chiaroscuro* in an impression of the *Entombment* in the Albertina, Vienna, thought by Landau to have been the result of Mantegna's experimental use of drypoint on the plate. Following a high-tech photographic campaign, Shelley Fletcher in 1997 published the surprising conclusions that the softness of the Albertina *Entombment* and of a second highly praised Mantegna impression, the Albertina *Madonna and Child* (Bartsch: XIII, 232.8, State 1; Martineau, no. 48, illus. p. 220), was due to extensive overpainting with brush and ink rather than to the burr left by drypoint. The full implications of this downgrading of the Albertina impressions have not yet been explored.

Simultaneous with the Fletcher discoveries, a fascinating historical fact emerged about Mantegna's copper plates. Regardless of whether he or some member of his workshop engraved them, Mantegna certainly maintained possession of the plates throughout his lifetime. In a 1510 inventory of the possessions of Mantegna's son Lodovico are listed seven copper plates, some of which had images engraved on both sides for a total of twelve engravings. Included in the list is one plate with the *Entombment* (*"Christo nel monimento cum la Madonna e altre figure"*) on one side and the *Risen Christ with St. Andrew and St. Longinus* (*"Christo resusitato . . . et sancto Andrea e sancto Longino"*) on the other (Signorini, pp. 111–12). The inventory of 1510 affirms the acute observations of Landau and Boorsch, who had both hypothesized the pairings of exactly the same engravings.

Whatever the scholarly outcome of issues raised by Andrea Mantegna's engravings, it is a privilege for Wellesley to possess the *Entombment*, a famous print designed by one of the greatest artists of the Italian Renaissance. Its haunting beauty, emotional power, and fascinating technique make it one of Wellesley's prime treasures.

LILIAN ARMSTRONG

BIBLIOGRAPHY

N.B. The bibliography on Andrea Mantegna is vast, and every major monograph treats his engravings. The references listed below are selective and concentrate on Mantegna engravings, especially the *Entombment*.

Bartsch, Adam. *Le Peintre-Graveur*, vol. 13. Vienna, Austria: Degen: 1802–1821, repr. New York: Abaris Books, 1979.

Boorsch, Suzanne. "Mantegna and His Printmakers." In *Andrea Mantegna*, ed. Jane Martineau. New York: Harry N. Abrams, 1992, pp. 55–66, 199–202, nos. 38–3.

Christiansen, Keith. "The Case for Mantegna as Printmaker." *Burlington Magazine*, 135 (September 1993), pp. 604–12.

Emison, Patricia. "Andrea Mantegna, a Printmaker?! A Controversy." *Print Collector's Newsletter*, 23, no. 2 (May-June 1992), pp. 41–46.

Fletcher, Shelley. "A Re-evaluation of Two Mantegna Prints." *Print Quarterly*, 14 (1997), pp. 67–77.

Hind, Arthur M. *Early Italian Engraving*. 7 vols. London: B. Quaritch, 1938–1948, vol. 5, pp. 3–31, esp.10–12, no. 2. (Hind records the Wellesley *Entombment* then in Hofer Collection among known examples.)

Kristeller, Paul. *Andrea Mantegna*. London: Longmans, Green and Co., 1901, pp. 376–413 (esp. pp. 399–400, 445).

Landau, David. "Mantegna's Plates." *Print Quarterly*, 14 (1997), p. 81.

Landau, David. "Mantegna as Printmaker." In *Andrea Mantegna*, ed. Jane Martineu. New York: Harry N. Abrams, 1992, pp. 43–54.

Levenson, Jay A., Konrad Oberhuber, and Jacquelyn L. Sheehan. *Early Italian Engravings from the National Gallery of Art*. Washington, DC: National Gallery of Art Publications, 1973, pp. 165–232 (esp. pp. 170–75, no. 70).

Lightbown, Ronald W. *Mantegna: With a Complete Catalogue of Paintings, Drawings, and Prints*. Berkeley: University of California Press, 1986, pp. 233–41, 488–93 (esp. p. 489, no. 205).

Lincoln, Evelyn. "Mantegna's Culture of Line." *Art History*, 16 (1993), pp. 33–59.

Martineau, Jane, ed. *Andrea Mantegna*, exhibition catalogue, Royal Academy of Arts, London, and The Metropolitan Museum of Art, New York. New York: Harry N. Abrams, 1992.

Signorini, Rodolfo. "New Findings about Andrea Mantegna: His Son Lodovico's Post-Mortem Inventory (1510)," *Journal of the Warburg and Courtauld Institutes*, 59 (1996), pp. 103–18.

Tietze-Conrat, Erika. *Mantegna: Paintings, Drawings, Engraving.* New York: Phaidon, 1955, pp. 241–42.

Vasari, Giorgio. *Le Vite de' più eccellenti pittori, scultori ed architettori.* Florence: 1550, part 2, 2, pp. 222–23; 1568, part 3,1, p. 295.

Zucker, Mark J., ed. *Early Italian Masters. The Illustrated Bartsch,* vol. 25, *Commentary* (formerly vol. 13, part 2). New York: Abaris Books, 1980, pp. 73 ff (esp. pp. 79–85, no. 001 [B.3 (229)]).

CAT. NO. 9

A German, from Alsace

T *Virgin and Child*

D circa 1490

M polychromed wood, back hollowed out

X approx. 39 in. x 14 1/4 in. x 9 3/4 in. (99.1 cm x 36.2 cm x 24.8 cm)

I see checklist

C Gift in honor of Myrtilla Avery from her students 1957.1 (illustrated)

AND

A German, from Ulm

T *Virgin and Child*

D circa 1500–1515

M polychromed and gilded wood

X approx. 41 1/2 in. x 14 in. x 4 in. (105.4 cm x 35.6 cm x 10.2 cm)

C Museum purchase with help of Mrs. W. Taliaferro Thompson, Jr.
1965.26

The museum has two German Gothic wood Madonna figures carved about 1500. Although the *Avery Madonna* [fig. 121] and the *Virgin and Child* from Ulm [fig. 30] come from different regions, they reflect a similar stylistic attitude, one not confined to Germany but felt throughout Europe. Having originated in France, this style is known by the French term *Détente,* an unfortunate designation so far as it implies any lack of dynamic qualities or any artistic lassitude. Such negative evaluations overlook the positive attitude that made *Détente* artists react against the elaborate Late Gothic style of the preceding generation. They overlook also such positive qualities as the new monumentality of form, the new lyricism of feeling, and the new interest in accepting back into active practice some of the accomplishments of the art of earlier generations. In German sculpture, the Late Gothic (which Wilhelm Pinder revealingly termed "the first Late-Gothic Baroque") was the product of a generation of sculptors of exceptional quality and marked personal taste—Leinberger, Grasser, Pacher, Stoss, Notke, and others—who by torsion and movement expressed an intensity of feeling that already prophesies the shattering impact of the coming Reformation.

This generation of uneasy anticipation is followed by one that was temporarily able to resolve the tension and agitation. Only at this brief moment—already gone with the coming of the next "Late-Gothic Baroque" twenty years later—can one find the gentle grace so eloquently expressed by the two German Gothic Madonnas at Wellesley, a grace not gained at the expense of full assertion of the corporeal being.

The *Avery Madonna* is probably the earlier of the two. Her body is short and almost robust, but this is mitigated by the elegant diagonal of the curves of the edge of the mantle. Its deeply cut and fully rounded folds fall from both sides downward toward the middle. Loose abundant hair frames the face and hangs over the shoulders, half in front, half in back. The Child is held high and well out in front. All these are elements that point consistently toward Nikolaus Gerhaert and Martin Schongauer, two artists who, with the Master E. S., had made the region of Strasbourg and Colmar a center of art to which even the young Dürer was drawn and where Grünewald was soon to paint the greatest of all German religious pictures [the Isenheim altarpiece].

Works are found in this region that, while they do not give us the name of the master who made our Madonna, do indicate surely that this is where the figure must have been carved. A standing *Madonna* from nearby Niedermorschwihr, now in the Colmar Museum (no. U 128) has similar proportions and handling of drapery, hair, and facial features that, together with the fine quality of the work, suggest that the two were made by the same hand. Of more provincial character but still closely related is a *St. Margaret* in the Strasbourg Museum (no. 1037), and another *Virgin* there, originally from Mutzig (no. 1034). These Upper Rhenish work share with our Madonna or with other contemporaries, such as Riemenschneider or Gregor Erhart, a calm detachment, a quiet rhythm, and a new ideal of beauty. But they are distinguished from works of other regions by their sturdy proportions and the plastic rather than linear treatment of the folds. Finally, our Ulm and our Avery Madonnas differ from others in a most important way: their kinship to one another and their descent from the art of one of Germany's greatest sculptors of the mid-fifteenth century, Nikolaus Gerhaert.

CURTIS H. SHELL

Adapted from the *Catalogue of European and American Sculptures and Paintings at Wellesley College*, 1964 (2nd ed.), pp. 9–11.

BIBLIOGRAPHY

Baxandall, Michael. *The Limewood Sculptors of Renaissance Germany*. New Haven, CT: Yale University Press, 1980.

Gillerman, Dorothy. *Gothic Sculpture in America I: The New England Museums*. New York: Garland Publishing, 1989, cat. 200, pp. 256–57.

Harding, Annelise. *German Sculpture in New England Museums*. Boston: Goethe Institute, 1972, fig. 37, p. 34.

Pevsner, Nikolaus. "An Unknown Statue by Nikolaus Gerhaert." *Burlington Magazine*, 99, no. 647 (Feb. 1957), p. 40 and plates.

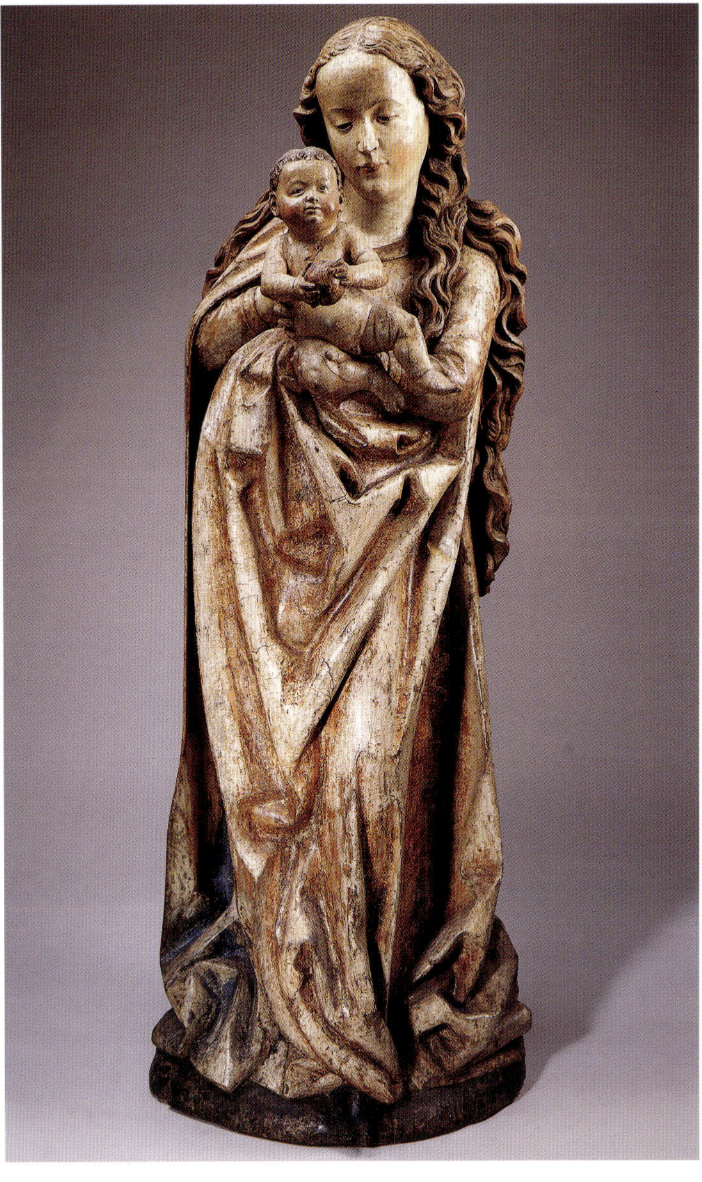

Fig. 121. German from Alsace, *Virgin and Child* (known as the Avery Madonna), ca. 1490, polychromed wood

A Bernardino di Betto di Biagio, called
il Pintoricchio
Perugia, Umbria ca. 1452–1513 Siena, Tuscany
active Perugia, Rome, Orvieto, Spoleto,
and Siena

T *Virgin and Child with the Infant Saint John the
Baptist and Saints Andrew and Jerome*

D 1495–1500

M oil, tempera, shell gold, and gold leaf on panel

X 24 3/8 in. diameter (61.9 cm), circular shape

I see checklist

C Museum purchase from the Dorothy Johnston
Towne (Class of 1923) Fund
1995.1

Pintoricchio's *Virgin and Child with the Infant St.
John the Baptist and Saints Andrew and Jerome* is
an exquisitely beautiful and well-conserved Italian
Renaissance devotional painting, probably destined for a secular palace rather than a church
[fig. 122]. In the era in which it was created, its
inspirational subject matter would have been
immediately comprehended by clerics and laypersons, and the painting would have been appreciated aesthetically for its harmonious composition,
brilliant colors, and material richness.

The Wellesley *Virgin and Saints* is a round panel
(called a *tondo*) instead of the more usual rectangular format. Five figures nearly fill its circular surface. The Virgin is seated in the center of the composition gently stabilizing the nude Christ Child
who sits on a golden cushion on her lap. With her
right hand she protectively holds the shoulder of
the infant St. John the Baptist, who looks out at
the viewer while pointing to the Christ Child. St.
John holds the lower portion of a slender gold
wand whose upper part is grasped by the Christ
Child just below its jeweled cross terminal. Simultaneously, the Christ Child raises his right hand to
bless St. John and, by implication, blesses the
believer who contemplates the painting. Behind

St. John stands St. Andrew who holds a partially
visible, large wooden cross; from his hand dangles
a fish. Balancing St. Andrew is St. Jerome, who is
clad only in a sleeveless tunic and who beats his
bloodied bare chest with a rock in an act of peni-
tence. Blue sky and small feathery trees are visible
between the heads of the Virgin and standing
saints.

Further unifying the densely packed composition are the rich colors and the somber facial
expressions of the saints. The Virgin Mary's dark
blue robe and red dress are edged in gold embroidery, as is the red cloak of the infant St. John. The
halos of all five figures consist of multiple dots of
gold, and more gold dots are used to model the
robes of St. Andrew and St. John. Even St.
Jerome's tunic and wreathlike belt are outlined
with fine gold lines. Played off against the dominant dark blue, red, and gold is the pale skin of
the Virgin and Child. The Virgin's delicately modeled face, her gently inclined head, lowered eyes
and wisps of blond hair ensure her lovely purity,
while the uniformly serious facial expressions
establish a mood of calm intensity.

The Christian messages of the painting are
explicit. The pointing gesture of St. John the Baptist signifies his words as he recognized the Messiah: "Behold the Lamb of God" (John 1:29).
John's own ascetic life is visualized by the penitential brown hair shirt he wears beneath his cloak.
Christ holds the cross indicating acceptance of his
death by crucifixion, yet its scepterlike gold and
jewels imply his future rule in heaven. Mary cher-
ishes and protects both children, her mood
sobered by foreknowledge of her son's destiny.
Indeed, the themes of dedication to Christ, of sacrifice, and of redemption are as intricately inter-
woven as is the pictorial composition. The martyrdom by crucifixion of the fisherman Andrew, who
was one of the first apostles to be called by Christ
(Mark 1:16–18), is symbolized by the wooden
cross. St. Jerome (ca. 341–420), one of the four
Church Fathers of the Western Church, spent time

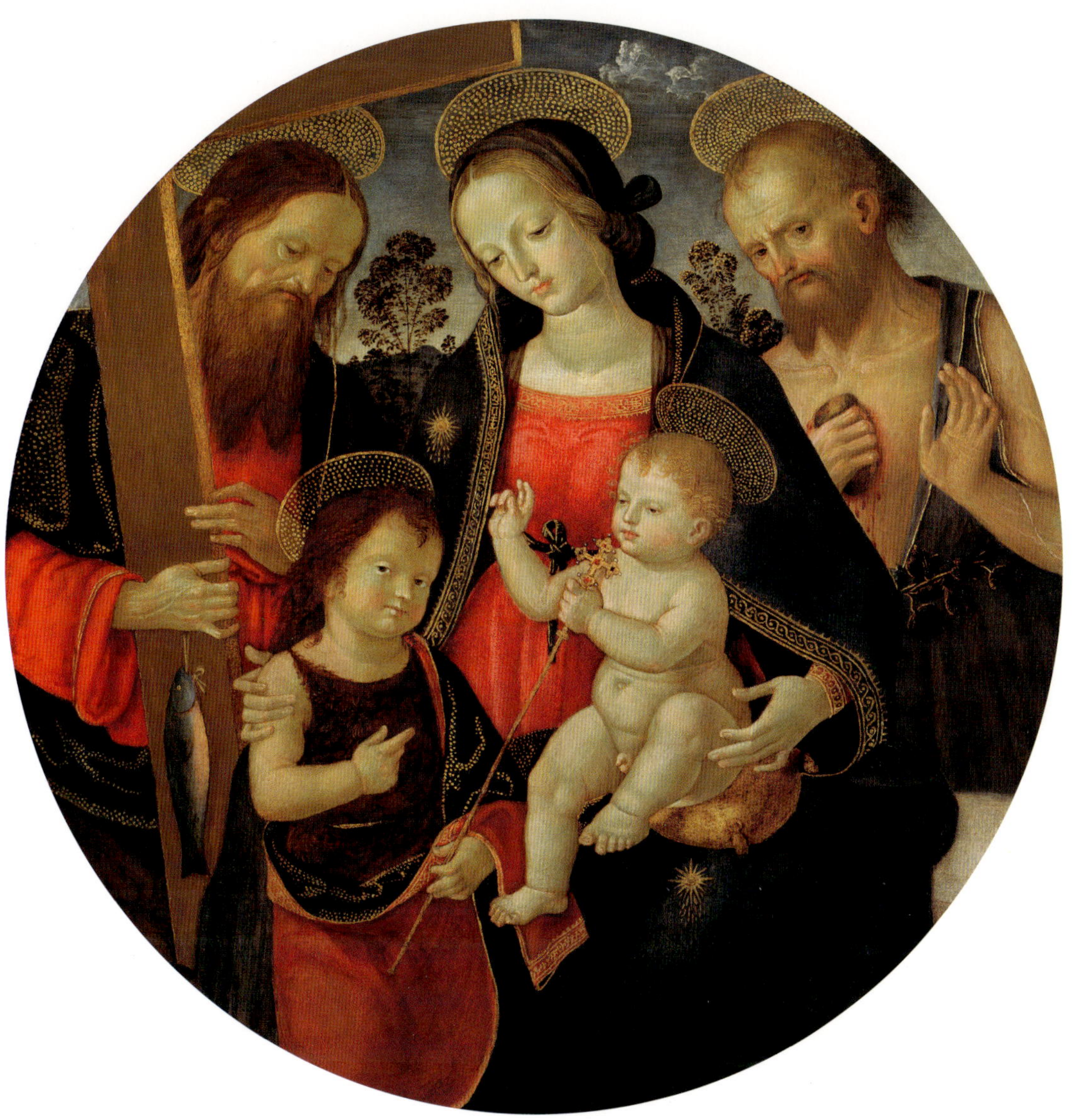

Fig. 122. Pintoric-
chio, *Virgin and
Child with Saints*,
1495-1500, oil on
panel

as a hermit repenting his early study of the Latin classics. In Rome between 382 and 385 CE, Jerome created a new translation of the Bible known as the Vulgate and eventually went to live a monastic life in Bethlehem, the birthplace of Christ.

The painter Benedetto di Betto di Biagio has always been known as Pintoricchio, or "Little Painter," according to Giorgio Vasari, because of his shortness in stature (Vasari). Born in Perugia in Umbria around 1452 (Scarpellini, p. 829), Pintoricchio enjoyed a highly successful career as a painter of panels and frescos and as an illuminator of manuscripts (Carli; Nucciarelli; Acidini Luchinat). In 1481 Pintoricchio entered the *Arte di San Luca* (Guild of Painters) in Perugia at a relatively mature age, but by 1482 he had already gone to Rome to work with Perugino on frescos in the Sistine Chapel for Pope Sixtus IV (Francesco della Rovere, r. 1471–84). Subsequent commissions in Rome included frescos in Santa Maria d'Aracoeli (1484–86) and in Santa Maria del Popolo (1488–90), panel and ceiling paintings in palaces belonging to the della Rovere family, and frescos in the Vatican Palace (1492–94) for Pope

Alexander IV (Rodrigo Borgia, r. 1492–1503). Having returned to Perugia by 1496, Pintoricchio spent several years in Umbria painting altarpieces and frescos. Probably the artist's most famous work is the fresco cycle depicting the life of Anenas Sylvius Piccolomini, Pope Pius II (r. 1458–64) in the Piccolomini Library of the Siena Cathedral (1502–07). After the completion of the Piccolomini cycle, Pintoricchio continued to live and work in Siena until his death in 1513.

The previously suggested date for the Wellesley *Virgin and Saints* was 1502–10 based on comparison with Pintoricchio's other major *tondo*, the *Holy Family with St. John the Baptist* now in the Pinocoteca Nazionale, Siena (*Sale Catalogue*, 11 January 1995). The Siena *tondo* was dated by Crowe and Cavalcaselle to the period of the Piccolomini frescoes (p. 410) but is now usually thought to have been painted even later (Carli, pp. 20–21; Scarpellini, p. 832; Acidini Luchinat, p. 73). After acquisition by Wellesley, the *Virgin and Saints* was conserved and the freshness of its original colors became more apparent. Based on observation of its present state and information provided by a recent study of *tondi*, the date of the Wellesley painting can reasonably be moved forward to Pintoricchio's prosperous years in Perugia from 1496 to 1500.

Many compositional elements relate the Wellesley panel to the artist's major commission of this Perugian period, the *Santa Maria dei Fossi Altarpiece* (1496–98) in the Galleria Nazionale dell'Umbria in Perugia (Accidini Luchinat, figs. 52–57). In the *Santa Maria dei Fossi Altarpiece*, Pintoricchio for the first time links Christ and the infant St. John the Baptist with a jeweled cross, almost a decade before Raphael's better-known versions of the motif in the *Madonna of the Meadow* (Vienna, 1505) and the *Alba Madonna* (Washington, circa 1511) (Jones and Penny, figs. 43, 95). The colors and decoration of the Wellesley Virgin's robe and dress follow that of the Umbrian altarpiece, and her head and hair arrangement closely resemble

the Virgin Annunciate in its upper panel. In the Wellesley panel, St. Jerome's balding head and sidelong glance echo the standing St. Jerome as Cardinal of the altarpiece, while his bared chest and hand gestures find counterparts in the predella panels.

Roberta Olson has shown that although painted *tondi* of the Virgin and Child are documented in Florence in the 1450s, it is not until the 1480s that the form became at all common. (Olson, 1993). The early examples are closely related to *deschi da parto*, circular or polygonal panels presented to new mothers, frequently depicting scenes related to childbirth (Musacchio). However, *tondi* with images of the Virgin and Child and often the infant St. John reached the height of their popularity only in the 1490s in the circle of Botticelli (Olson, 1993, p. 51). Documents indicate that the Florentine *tondi* were placed in domestic settings. Olson argues that they "flooded the Florentine market as part of the idealization of domestic life and the celebration of family relationships," and that they embody "the culture's obsession with women and children and the education of the latter" (Olson, 1993, p. 51).

Pintoricchio's frescoed *tondo* of a three-quarter length Virgin and Child in the Borgia Apartments of 1492–95 is one of the earliest painted *tondi* to appear outside of Florence (Olson, 1993, p. 47). Back in Perugia soon thereafter, it is likely that Pintoricchio wanted to demonstrate his mastery of the newly popular *tondo* format, an impulse resulting in the Wellesley painting. While there are formal similarities between Wellesley's *tondo* and Pintoricchio's Perugian works of the late 1490s, it can be easily distinguished from his *tondo* in Siena of circa 1508–09. For instance, the Siena *Holy Family* has a much less harmonious composition, with its asymmetrical arrangement of the figures and the whimsical placement of the two striding children. The Wellesley panel should thus be viewed as a painting executed at the height of Pintoricchio's

career, exhibiting the spiritual and aesthetic qualities that appealed strongly to wealthy patrons of
late *Quattrocento* central Italy.

LILIAN ARMSTRONG

BIBLIOGRAPHY

Acidini Luchinat, Cristina. *Pintoricchio.* Florence: Scala, 1999.

Carli, Enzo. *Il Pintoricchio.* Milan: Electra Editrice, 1960.

Christie's Auction House, New York. *Sales Catalogue.* Wednesday, 11 January 1995, lot 16, pp. 30–31.

Hauptmann, Moritz, *Der Tondo: Ursprung, Bedeutung und Geschichte des italienischen Rundbildes in Relief und Malerei.* Frankfurt am Main: V. Klostermann, 1936.

Jones, Roger, and Nicholas Penny. *Raphael.* New Haven, CT: Yale University Press, 1983.

Musacchio, Jacqueline M. *The Art and Ritual of Childbirth in Renaissance Italy.* New Haven, CT: Yale University Press, 1999.

Nucciarelli, Franco Ivan. *Studi sul Pinturicchio dalle prime prove alla Cappella Sistina.* Ellera Umbra, Perugia: Edizioni Era Nuova, 1998. Catalogued as "London, già Collezione privata, *Madonna con il Bambino e il piccolo S. Giovanni fra i SS. Andrea e Gerolamo penitente,*" vol. 1 (of 4), p. 289.

Olson, Roberta J. M. "Lost and Partially Found: The Tondo, a Significant Florentine Art Form, in Documents of the Renaissance." *Artibus et Historiae,* 14, no. 27 (1993), pp. 31–65.

Olson, Roberta J. M. *The Florentine Tondo.* New York: Oxford University Press, 2000, p. 261.

Scarpellini, P. "Pinturicchio [Pintoricchio]." In *Dictionary of Art,* ed. Jane Turner. London: Grove, 1996, vol. 4, pp. 829–32.

Todini, Filippo. *La Pittura Umbra dal Duecento al Primo Cinquecento.* (Milan: Longanesi, 1989), vol. 1 (of 2), p. 291 Catalogued as "già Londra, collezione privata. Tondo: *Madonna col Bambino e San Giovannino tra Sant'Andrea e San Girolamo penitente. Opera tarda,*" vol. 1, p. 291; vol. 2, p. 535, fig. 1238.

CAT. NO. 11

A Cristofano di Michele Martini, called il Robetta
Florence, Tuscany 1462–circa 1535 Florence
active Florence

T *Adoration of the Magi*

D 1496–1500

M engraving on medium-weight laid buff paper

X plate: 11 7/8 in. x 10 15/16 in. (301 mm x 277 mm)
sheet: 12 1/16 in. x 10 15/16 in. (307 mm x 278 mm)

S signed in plate, lower right: 'ROBETTA'

I see checklist

C Gift of Mr. and Mrs. Arthur Vershbow in memory of Harry B. Braude
1960.38

The *Adoration of the Magi* [fig. 123] is perhaps the most famous engraving by Cristofano Robetta, a goldsmith and engraver active in Florence from the 1490s into the 1530s (Collareta; Bellini). The engraving's composition is a free ver-
sion in reverse of Filippino Lippi's *Adoration of the Magi* (1496; Berti and Baldini, pl. on p. 209) for San Donato a Scopeto just outside of Florence, an altarpiece created as a substitution for Leondaro da Vinci's unfinished *Adoration of the Magi* of 1481–82 (Kemp, pl. 22), originally commissioned for the same monastery. Thus the engraving reflects one of the great icons of Renaissance devotional imagery and the artistic accomplishments of two famous Florentine painters of the late *Quattrocento.*

Central to all three compositions is the seated Virgin Mary holding the nude Christ Child in her lap. Joseph looks over her shoulder and before her kneel two of the three wise men who came to adore the newborn child (Matthew 2:1–12). In the engraving the youngest king stands to the right as an attendant removes his crown. Other members of the wise men's entourage crowd the foreground and middleground, while in the distance spreads a hilly landscape dotted with buildings and trees. In the lower right appears the engraver's signature: ROBETTA.

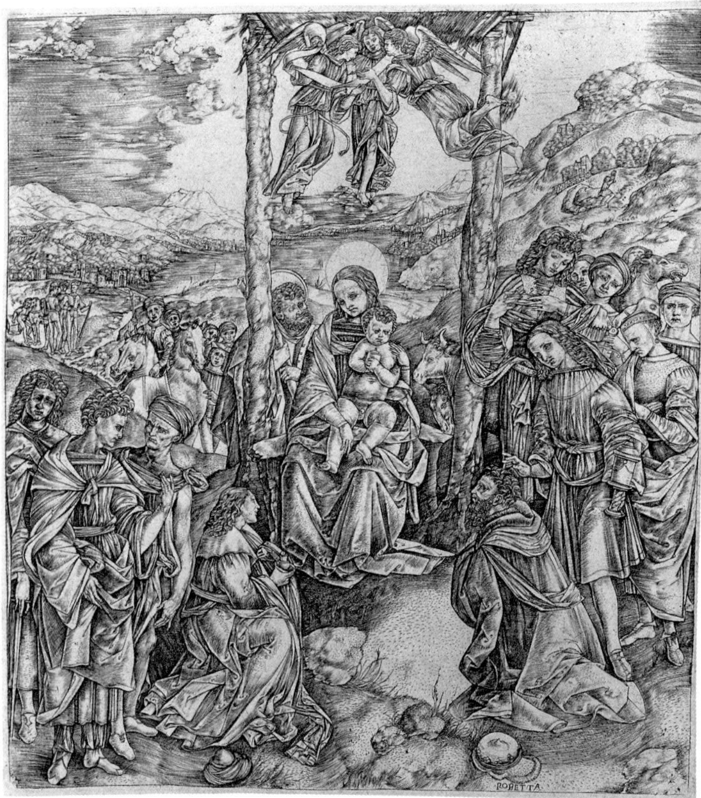

Fig. 123. Robetta, *Adoration of the Magi*, 1496-1500, engraving

Discussions of Robetta's engravings focus on their date, technique, artistic sources, and often enigmatic iconography. Seventeen of his over forty engravings are signed, but none are dated. The *Adoration of the Magi* must date after 1496, the date of Filippino Lippi's altarpiece; it is usually thought to be one of his earliest engravings, executed before 1500 (Levenson et al., Zucker). The rather stiff figures, complicated angular folds of the drapery, crowded foreground, and awkwardly placed horsemen in the left middleground suggest an early stage of artistic development, even though the *Adoration* is one of the largest and most ambitious of Robetta's prints.

Robetta's *Adoration* is a rare example of an Italian Renaissance engraving for which the original copper plate has survived, now in the British Museum, London; on its verso is Robetta's *Allegory of Love* (Hind, D.II.29). A. M. Hind cites the dimensions of the engraved area of the plate as

follows: 301 mm (right) to 305 mm (left) x 278 mm (below) to 283 mm (above), and he notes that "genuine impressions often show a difference of over half an inch in one direction and perhaps a quarter in the other, due to shrinkage of paper after damping" (Hind I, p. 201). The dimensions of the Wellesley impression cited above uphold this notion, as they are slightly smaller than the measurements cited by Hind.

Regarding his own technique, Robetta was dependent on the engravings of the German Martin Schongauer (1446–91) and adopts from him the fine dotting of the ground and modeling with short slightly curved lines. Almost as if acknowledging his artistic debt, Robetta copies the hat of a wise man from Schongauer's *Adoration of the Magi* (B.6; Shestack, fig. 8), and places it on the ground immediately above his signature. Robetta also shows his knowledge of Albrecht Dürer's prints in the composition of the distant landscape and in the representation of the sky (Hind, I, p. 201). The Wellesley impression is a fine one with typically strong outlines but with some fainter areas where the finer lines have worn slightly.

Unlike some of his later allegorical engravings, the iconography of Robetta's *Adoration of the Magi* is clear. Nevertheless, note that the subject of the *Adoration of the Magi* was particularly popular in Renaissance Florence. The feast of the Epiphany was celebrated with a great pageant on January 6th. Organizing the festivities was the Compagnia de' Magi, a lay confraternity that enjoyed the patronage of the Medici. The link between the Medici and the Magi is particularly apparent in Botticelli's *Adoration of the Magi* (1471–72) for the Chapel of the Magi in the Dominican Church of Santa Maria Novella; in this painting the three Magi are portraits of Cosimo, Piero, and Giovanni de' Medici while other Medici may be identified among the Magi's followers (Hatfield, 1976, fig. 1). Botticelli's innovative posing of the Virgin as the apex of a triangular composition was a model for Leonardo, and in turn for Lippi and Robetta.

As Rab Hatfield has observed of the Botticelli painting, "The Magi, all in the center of the picture, kneel before the Child as if performing a liturgical action. . . . Botticelli, it seems, has here depicted the Epiphany as the "figure" or prototype of a specifically eucharistic action, the sacramental oblation," the offering of the people (Hatfield, 1976, pp. 34–35). The echo of this Eucharistic offering persists in the Robetta engraving, subsuming the exotic richness of the Magi in its overall mood of quiet devotion.

LILIAN ARMSTRONG

BIBLIOGRAPHY

Bellini, Paolo. *Catalogo completo dell'opera grafica del Robetta* (Milan: Salamon e Agustoni, 1973), esp. pp. 34–35, no. 11.

Berti Luciano, and Umberto Baldini. *Filippino Lippi*. Florence: Edizioni d'arte il Fiorino, 1991.

Collareta, Marco. "Robetta [Cristofano di Michele Martini]." In *Dictionary of Art*, ed. Jane Turner. London: Grove, 1996, vol. 26, p. 469.

Hatfield, Rab. *Botticelli's Uffizi "Adoration": A Study in Pictorial Content*. Princeton, NJ: Princeton University Press, 1976.

Hind, A. M. *Early Italian Engraving*, 7 vols. London: B. Quaritch, 1938–1948, vol. 1, pp. 197–209, esp. 200–01, no. D.II.10.

Kemp, Martin. *Leonardo da Vinci: The Marvelous Works of Nature and Man*. London: Dent, 1981.

Levenson, Jay A., Konrad Oberhuber, and Jacquelyn L. Sheehan, *Early Italian Engravings from the National Gallery of Art*. Washington, DC: National Gallery 1973, pp. 289–305, esp. pp. 296–97, no. 118.

Shestack, Alan. *The Complete Engravings of Martin Schongauer*. New York: Dover, 1969.

Zucker, M. J., *Early Italian Masters (The Illustrated Bartsch, W. Strauss, ed., vol. 25, Commentary, formerly vol. 13, Part 2)*. New York: 1984, pp. 527–570, esp. p. 536, no. 010 [B.6 (396)].

CAT. NO. 12

A Silvestro di Giacomo da Sulmona dell'Aquila
Aquila 1471–1504 Aquila
active Aquila

T *Bust of the Virgin* (fragment of a seated figure with child)

D 1495–1500

M gilded and polychromed terra-cotta

X approx. 18 1/2 in. x 22 1/8 in. x 12 1/2 in. (47.0 cm x 56.2 cm x 31.7 cm)

C Gift of Mrs. John T. Pratt (Ruth S. Baker, Class of 1898)

1940.14

Shining surfaces dominate the first impression of Silvestro dell'Aquila's gilded terra-cotta bust of the *Virgin* [fig. 124]. The bust is lifesize, frontally posed, and truncated well below the shoulders. The Virgin's head is slightly inclined and her lowered eyes partially closed as she gazes downward. The cloak that covers her head and shoulders is entirely covered with dazzling gold leaf, now partially damaged and revealing reddish areas of bole and terra-cotta. Incised lines of gesso form eight-pointed gold stars that subtly pattern the cloak. Contrasting with the gold is the blue of the cloak's lining and the once-white veil that covers the Virgin's forehead and falls on each side of her neck. Her dress was originally a rich red, the color now muted because of paint losses. A large jeweled clasp rests on the Virgin's breast, its blue central stone surrounded by four smaller golden spheres. A distinctly rosy blush glows on the cheeks of the Virgin's otherwise pale skin; a fine straight nose, gently arching dark eyebrows, and red lips make up her other idealized features.

The damaged lower edges of the bust indicate that it is a fragment of a larger statue. In a definitive article of 1942, Laurine Mack Bongiorno argued that the Wellesley *Virgin* would originally have resembled Silvestro dell'Aquila's docu-

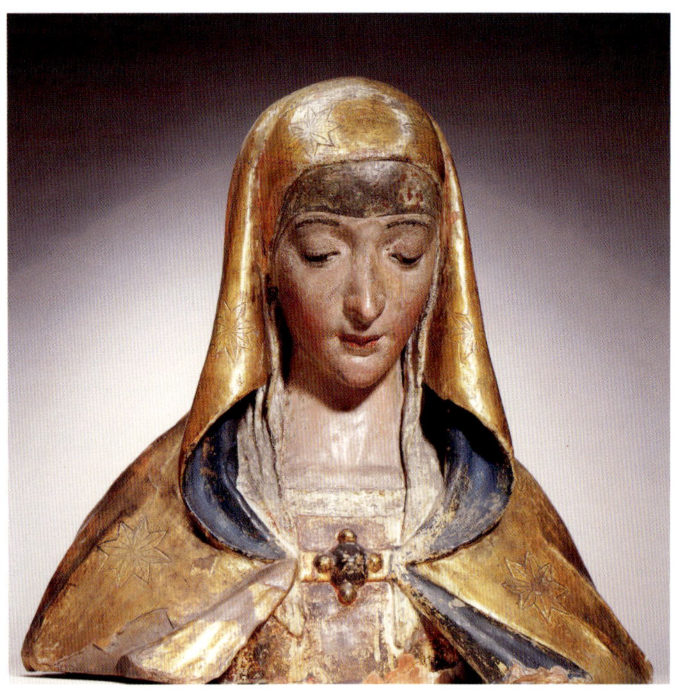

Fig. 124 (above). Silvestro dell'Aquila, *Bust of the Virgin* (fragment), 1495-1500, polychromed terra-cotta

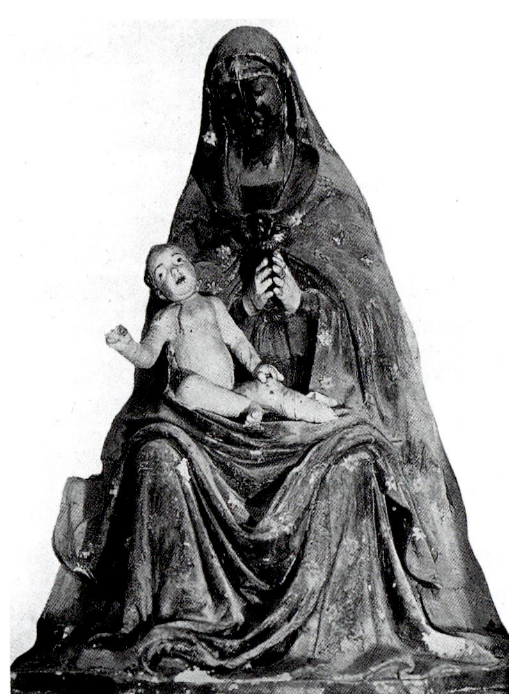

Fig. 125 (right). Silvestro dell'Aquila, *Virgin Adoning the Child* (circa 1494–1500) in the church of San Bernardino, Aquila

mented *Virgin Adoring the Child* (1494–1500), created for the prestigious burial church of San Bernardino of Siena in Aquila (Bongiorno) [fig. 125]. The San Bernardino *Virgin* is a life-size polychromed terra-cotta figure whose head is surrounded by a star-studded cloak and veil similar to that of the Wellesley *Virgin*. The head of a cherubim functions as a cloak fastener instead of the jeweled clasp of the Wellesley statue, but the extremely close resemblance of the two heads is undeniable. Seated in the lap of the San Bernardino *Virgin* is a nude Christ child, raising a hand to bless the viewer. This type of seated Virgin and Child became popular in the Abruzzi region at the end of the fifteenth century, mostly found in terra-cotta examples but also in stone (Bongiorno, 233–34).

From the 1470s until his death in 1504, Silvestro dell'Aquila was the leading sculptor in Aquila, the principal city of the Abruzzi region in central Italy. In the 1470s, Silvestro shared workshops there with other artists including a Florentine named Francesco Trugi. The apparent influence of Florentine sculptors on Silvestro's works has led to the suggestion that he may have trained in Florence in the late 1460s or early 1470s (Seymour, pp. 163, 274). Silvestro's major works in marble in Aquila are the *Tomb of Cardinal Bishop Amico Agnifili* (d. 1476), the *Shrine of Saint Bernardino* (1500), and the *Tomb of Maria Pereyra and Beatrice Camponeschi*, whose often repeated erroneous date of 1496 has recently been corrected to 1488–1490 in accord with the documentary evidence (Sulli). The sarcophagus of the Cardinal Agnifili tomb imitates Desiderio da Settignano's *Tomb of Carlo Marsuppini* (1455–58) in Santa Croce, Florence, while the seated putti of the Camponeschi tomb echo those of Antonio Rossellino's *Tomb of the Cardinal of Portugal* (1461–64) in San Miniato, confirming the strong impact of Florentine models (Seymour; Bongiorno; Sulli). Once again the close resemblance between the refined features of Maria Pereyra Camponeschi (Bongiorno, fig. 12) and the Wellesley *Virgin* confirms the latter's authorship by Silvestro.

If complete, Wellesley's *Virgin* by Silvestro dell' Aquila would have joined a monumentally draped figure with a more delicate idealized head, a combination found not only in provincial Aquila, but in such High Renaissance works as Michelangelo's *Pietà* in St. Peter's. Far from being a cheap substitute for marble, this kind of terra-cotta figure rightly gained popularity in the late *quattrocento* because of its appealing color and expressive possibilities. Positioned on an altar and probably surrounded by an architectural niche like that of the San Bernardino *Virgin Adoring the Child*, Wellesley's Virgin, with its size and gilded surfaces, would have been a dazzlingly impressive devotional object.

LILIAN ARMSTRONG

BIBLIOGRAPHY

Bongiorno, Laurine Mack. "Notes on the Art of Silvestro dell' Aquila." *Art Bulletin*, 24 (1942), pp. 232–43.

Shell, Curtis H., and John McAndrew. *Catalogue of European and American Sculpture and Paintings at Wellesley College.* Wellesley, MA: Jewett Art Center, 1958 (repr. 1964), p. 37 (with previous bibliography).

Seymour, Charles. *Sculpture in Italy: 1400–1500.* Harmondsworth, UK: Penguin, 1966, pp. 163, 274.

Sulli, Roberta. "Il monumento funebre Pereyra-Camponeschi: Contributo allo studio della cultura antiquariale a l'Aquila nel secondo quattrocento." *Bullettino della Deputazione abruzzese di storia patria*, 77 (1987), pp. 207–28.

"Silvestro (di Giacomo da Sulmona) dell'Aquila." In *Dictionary of Art*, ed. Jane Turner. London: Grove, 1996, vol. 28, pp. 744–45.

CAT. NO. 13

A French, from Paris

T *Annunciation*
detached folio from a printed *Horae Beatae Virginis Mariae* (Latin and French Book of Hours)

D circa 1507–15

M metalcut and typographic letters printed in ink on vellum, hand-illuminated with glair or gouache and shell gold

X image: 4 3/4 in. x 3 3/8 in. (120 mm x 80 mm)
folio: 7 7/8 in. x 5 1/8 in. (198 mm x 131 mm)

C Gift of Mrs. Toivo Laminan (Margaret Chamberlin, Class of 1929)
1962.22.2

The metalcut *Annunciation* is one of three prints on parchment folios in the Davis Museum and Cultural Center that were excised from Parisian *Books of Hours* (prayer-books for laypersons, also called *Horae* and *Heures*) printed in the early sixteenth century [fig. 126]. The *Annunciation*, given in tandem with a *David and Uriah* of the same dimensions, was similarly hand-illuminated after printing to resemble an illuminated manuscript. Another metalcut of *David and Uriah* was purchased by the museum in 1969. While it is of similar dimensions, it is not hand-illuminated but is surrounded by an architectural frame. All three prints have several lines of text printed under the image and full texts on the other side of the folio. The text below the *Annunciation* is in Latin; the text below both *David and Uriah* images is in French (with Latin text on their versos).

These metalcuts are aesthetically appealing works of art in their own right. In addition they demonstrate the enormous complexity of image production by sixteenth-century Parisian printers who specialized in Books of Hours, printing dozens of editions illustrated with woodcuts or metalcuts.

In both manuscript and printed Books of Hours, the Annunciation invariably illustrated the opening of Matins of the Hours of the Virgin (see cat. no. 4 for a detailed discussion). The black and white lines of the Wellesley *Annunciation* have been almost completely painted over in brilliant colors. Observation of the tiled floor shows that the illuminator has not followed the black and white pattern of the metalcut tiles but has superimposed red and green tiles in a different orientation; the paint also partially obscures a vase that is between the figures in the metalcut. Dominant blocks of red and blue transform the original black and white image. At the right, the monu-

mental dignity of the Virgin is enhanced by a red and blue canopy that blots out some architectural details of the underlying metalcut. The Virgin's piety is stressed by the book in her lap and by her hands pointed in prayer. Gabriel kneels on his right knee, wearing a red vestment over his long white tunic. He raises his left hand high in a gesture of salutation; above his hand hovers the Holy Spirit in the form of a white dove. Surrounding both the metalcut and the four-line Latin text below are architectural motifs, somewhat sloppily painted in shell gold and small areas of red and blue.

In both metalcuts of *David and Uriah*, David hands a letter to the kneeling Uriah intended for Joab, the general of his armies, directing Joab to send Uriah to the front of the battle so that he will be killed. This cruel act has resulted from David's involvement with Uriah's wife, Bathsheba, whom he has recently impregnated and plans to marry after Uriah's death (2 Samuel 11). Highlighting David's weaknesses and his need to repent, the scene of *David and Uriah* is commonly placed before the Seven Penitential Psalms in French Books of Hours. The *David and Uriah* that was given to Wellesley along with the *Annunciation* (1962.22.1) is also brightly painted and similarly surrounded by architectural motifs in shell gold.

The exact editions from which these three metalcuts were excised have not yet been identified, although some narrowing down of the possibilities can be made. It is certain that the metalcut of *David and Uriah* (1969.37) was in existence by around 1507 when it appeared in a Book of Hours printed by Guillaume Anabat for Gilles and Germain Hardouyn (Mortimer, no. 295: Harvard University, Houghton Library, Typ 515.07.261, fol. g7v). In the Hardouyn edition, however, there is no text below the image, and it is surrounded by a different architectural frame that incorporates Italianate cupids (illustrated in Mortimer, p. 380). The other *David and Uriah* (1962.22.1) is a reverse

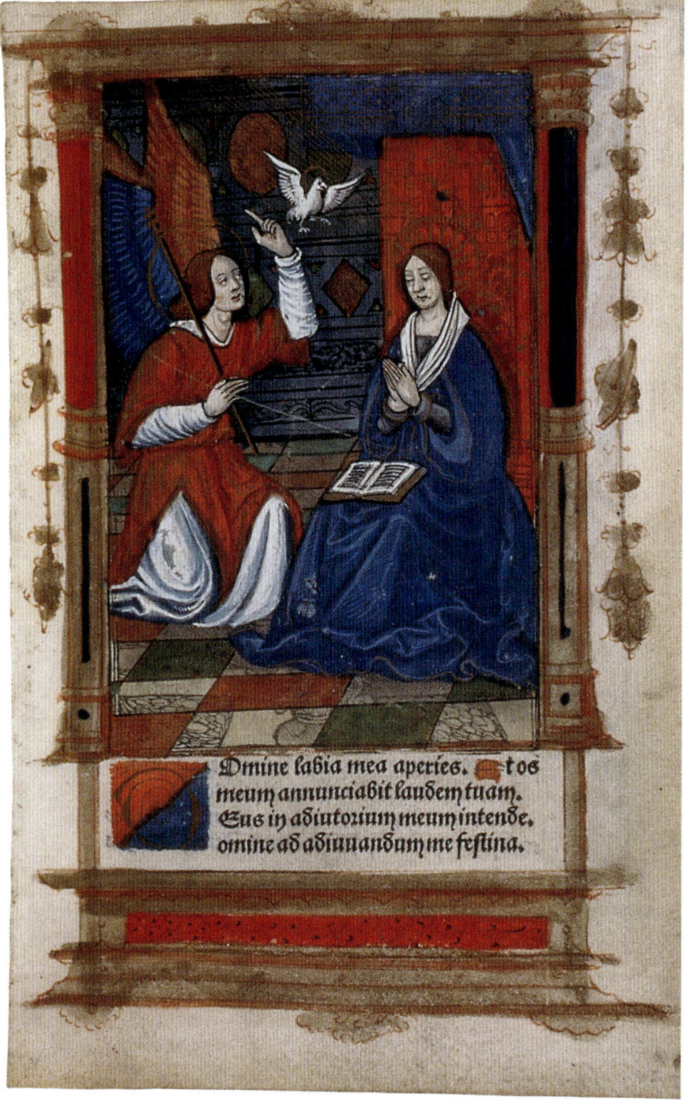

copy of a composition appearing in a Book of Hours printed for Simon Vostre (circa 1504) (Harvard University, Houghton Library, WKR 15.2.12, fol. i7r). In the Vostre edition, the three lines of text are in Latin, not French, and the scene is framed by columns; cupids hold the scroll on which the text appears to have been written.

Finally, the *Annunciation* is a close copy of a scene that also appears in the Hardouyn edition of 1507 (Mortimer no. 295). Comparison of the two scenes suggests the kind of error that was often incurred in copying. In Annunciation scenes, Gabriel normally salutes Mary with his right hand and carries a scepter or lily in his left. In the 1507 Hardouyn composition, Gabriel enters from the left and correctly salutes Mary with his right hand. In copying the composition, however, the designer of the Wellesley print has erroneously depicted Gabriel raising his left hand, a choice that is in fact more pleasing aesthetically but less appropriate iconographically. Further research into editions of Parisian Books of Hours that include both Latin and French texts may reveal exactly the origin of Wellesley's prints, but in the meantime they provide ample visual and intellectual stimulation.

Lilian Rmstrong

BIBLIOGRAPHY

Mortimer, Ruth, Harvard College Library Department of Printing and Graphic Arts. *Catalogue of Books and Manuscripts.* Part I: *French 16th Century Books*, vol. 2. Cambridge, MA: Belknap Press of Harvard University Press, 1964.

CAT. NO. 14

A Albrecht Dürer
Nuremberg, Franconia 1471–1528 Nuremberg
active Nuremberg, Venice, Strasbourg,
and Antwerp

T Fifteen prints from the *Life of the Virgin* series
1961.25; 1968.34.1–11; 1977.26; 3.1983; 1990.12
(see checklist for cataloguing)

ILLUSTRATED:

T *Christ Taking Leave of His Mother*
plate 17 (of 20) from the *Life of the Virgin* series

D circa 1504–1505, printed 1505–1540

M woodcut on medium-weight laid cream paper

X image: 11 3/4 in. x 8 1/4 in. (299 mm x 210 mm)
sheet: 11 7/8 in. x 8 3/8 in. (301 mm x 212 mm)

S monogrammed in block: '"AD"

I see checklist

C Gift of Mrs. Toivo Laminan (Margaret Chamberlin, Class of 1929) in memory of her mother, Anne B. Chamberlin (Class of 1898)
1968.34.10

The gifted German artist Albrecht Dürer executed his woodcut *Life of the Virgin* series between 1502 and 1511. The series consists of nineteen images, many issued as individual works, then published together with a frontispiece in 1511. Included was a Latin verse text by Benedict Schwalbe, known as Benedictus Chelidonius, who had also supplied the text for Dürer's *Large Passion* series. The full series consisted of 1. the title page featuring the Virgin Mary on a crescent; 2. the *Rejection of Joachim's Offer* (by the high priest in the Synagogue); 3. *Joachim and the Angel* (bringing news of Anna's pregnancy); 4. *Joachim and Anna Meet at the Golden Gate* [fig. 7 in the main essay]; 5. the *Birth of the Virgin* [fig. 59]; 6. the *Presentation of the Virgin in the Temple*; 7. the *Betrothal of the Virgin* [fig. 28]; 8. the *Annunciation* [fig. 22]; 9. the *Visitation* [fig. 25]; 10. the *Adoration of the Shepherds* [fig. 37]; 11. the *Circumcision*; 12. the *Adoration of the Magi*; 13. the *Presentation of Christ in the Temple*; 14. the *Flight into Egypt*; 15. the *Holy Family*

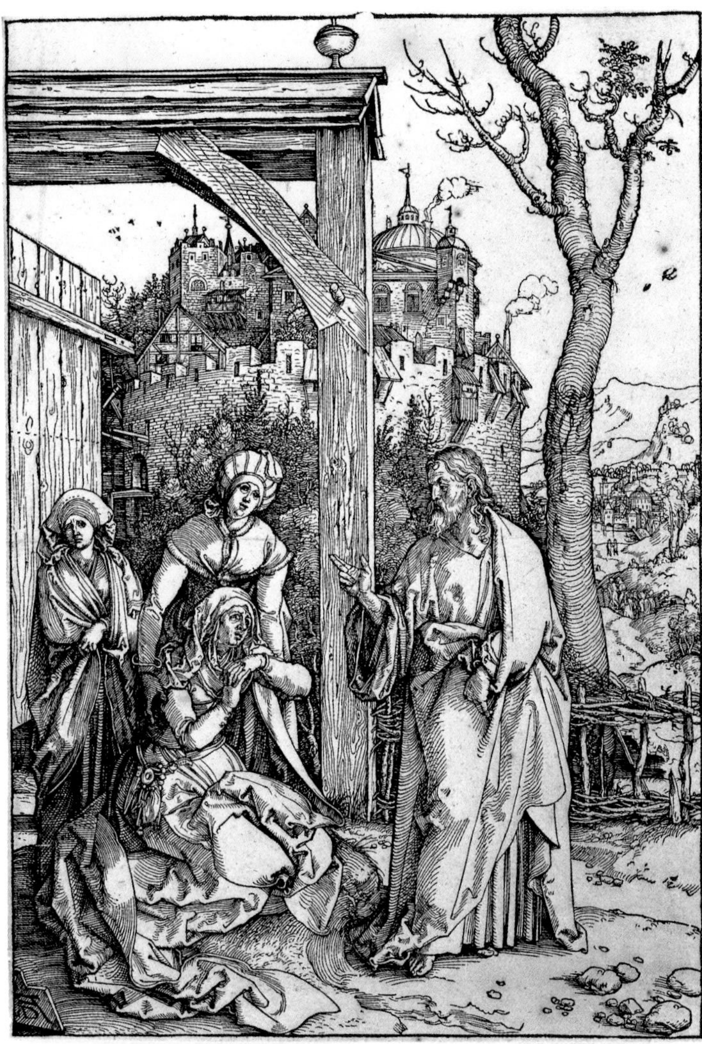

the Annunciation, Dürer has diminished any implications of "illegitimacy" regarding Mary's pregnancy. Note also that Dürer omitted a Nativity scene per se, the birth of Christ having been folded into the *Adoration of the Shepherds.*

Two works in the series, the *Glorification of the Virgin* and the *Holy Family in Egypt,* were conceived of independently and later integrated into the series. The former, in which saints Jerome, Paul, Augustine, Anthony, John the Baptist, Joseph, and Catherine of Alexandria surround the Virgin Mary in her bedchamber, is less an episode from Mary's life than a *sacra conversazione* between the Virgin and saints. The latter, a rarely depicted scene of the Holy Family's sojourn in Egypt rather than its dramatic flight from Herod's killers, has been interpreted as an homage to Dürer's own father, the goldsmith Albrecht Dürer the Elder, who died in 1502. It is also the first example of Dürer's signing his work with the familiar "AD" monogram placed on a modified writing tablet.

Although all but two of the works are undated, it is evident that seventeen images were completed by the time of Dürer's second journey to Venice, as copies of them were made by the Bolognese engraver Marcantonio Raimondi, who in 1510 moved to Rome where he reproduced many of the works of Raphael for circulation among other artists and collectors. Those woodcuts completed after the Venetian trip—the *Death of the Virgin* and *Assumption and Coronation of the Virgin* (both dated 1510)—reveal Dürer's advancement during the Venetian sojourn through their greater clarity and spatial organization. Due to the admiration of Dürer's work, both during and after his lifetime, the *Life of the Virgin* series continued to be reissued from Dürer's original woodblocks. In this particular case, it is possible to date both the original composition and the period in which the print was made by identifying the watermarks on the individual sheets of paper and comparing them with examples already catalogued and dated (see checklist, pages 270–72).

in Egypt [fig. 61]; 16. *Christ among the Doctors;* 17. *Christ Taking Leave of His Mother* [fig. 127]; 18. the *Death of the Virgin* [fig. 92]; 19. the *Assumption and Coronation of the Virgin;* and 20. the *Glorification of the Virgin.*

Note that Dürer placed the *Betrothal of the Virgin* before the *Annunciation,* providing Mary with matrimonial status prior to the moment she conceived her child. In selecting his order, Dürer followed the account in Matthew's Gospel, which refers to Mary as betrothed and Joseph as her husband.[1] In Dürer's time, most weddings consisted of two public ceremonies, betrothal followed by nuptials. By placing the marriage ceremony before

Dürer produced several print series of biblical
subjects that proved extremely popular with the
public and reasonably profitable for the artist. In
the *Life of the Virgin* series, he employed the device
of a framing arch to unite many of its scenes, while
also providing an architectural scale for the individual works and a means of drawing the viewer
into the scenes. Of the twenty scenes composing
the series, all but one treat joyful moments of
Mary's life. The one sorrowful subject, *Christ Taking Leave of His Mother,* is a stirring scene between a
mother who fears this parting may be their last
and a son determined to continue on to Jerusalem
[fig. 127]. It is a rare scene of intimacy between
two adults, rather than the familiar presentation of
mother and child, and more restrained in its grief
than scenes of Mary at the crucifixion and
entombment, but no less moving and powerful.

MELISSA R. KATZ

NOTE

1. Matthew also implies a solemnity to the betrothal ceremony
warranting divorce, should one not wish to proceed to nuptials.
The Gospel quote reads, "Now the birth of Jesus Christ took
place in this way. When his mother Mary had been betrothed to
Joseph, before they came together she was found to be with child
of the Holy Spirit; and her husband Joseph, being a just man and
unwilling to put her to shame, resolved to divorce her quietly"
(Matt. 1:18–19).

BIBLIOGRAPHY

Strauss, Walter L., ed. *Albrecht Dürer: Woodcuts and Woodblocks.*
New York: Abaris Books, 1980, cat. nos. 69–70, 74–79,
91–99, 146–47, and 156.

Talbot, Charles W. *Dürer in America: His Graphic Work.* Washington, DC: National Gallery of Art, 1971.

Waldmann, E. *Das Marienleben: Eine Holzschnittfolge.* Leipzig: Insel-
Verlag, 1921.

CAT. NO. 15

A Lucas Huygenszoon van Leyden
   Leiden, Netherlands 1494–1533 Leiden
   active Leiden

T *Virgin and Child in a Niche*

D 1518

M engraving on medium-weight laid dark cream
   paper

X sheet and plate: 4 5/8 in. x 2 7/8 in. (118 mm x
   74 mm)

S signed in plate: "Ł"

I see checklist

C Gift of Dr. Ruth Morris Bakwin (Class of 1919)
   1977.70

In *Virgin and Child in a Niche*, Dutch artist Lucas
van Leyden (1494–1533) used his untraditional
approach to engraving, his simplified composition, and his sense of humor to create an image of

the Madonna and Child appropriate for Martin
Luther's Netherlands. Probably trained in printmaking by his painter father Hugo Jacobsz. and by
Leiden artist Cornelis Engebrechtsz., Lucas began
his career at a young age. Unlike fellow printmakers such as Albrecht Dürer, Lucas would only
lightly incise engraving surfaces with painterly,
loose and shallow lines, to allow him to change his
compositions as they developed. Fewer quality
prints could be made from his works as a result.
The compositions of his engravings purposefully
highlight less familiar parts of a narrative—or
even the moment before its climax—depicting the
story anew from a witty perspective.

In *Virgin and Child in a Niche*, Lucas uncharac-
teristically stripped the composition of decorative
elements and complicated, panoramic backdrops,
leaving the viewer with a more intimate image of
Virgin and Child flanked only by two religious
symbols: the apple and the moon. The apple in

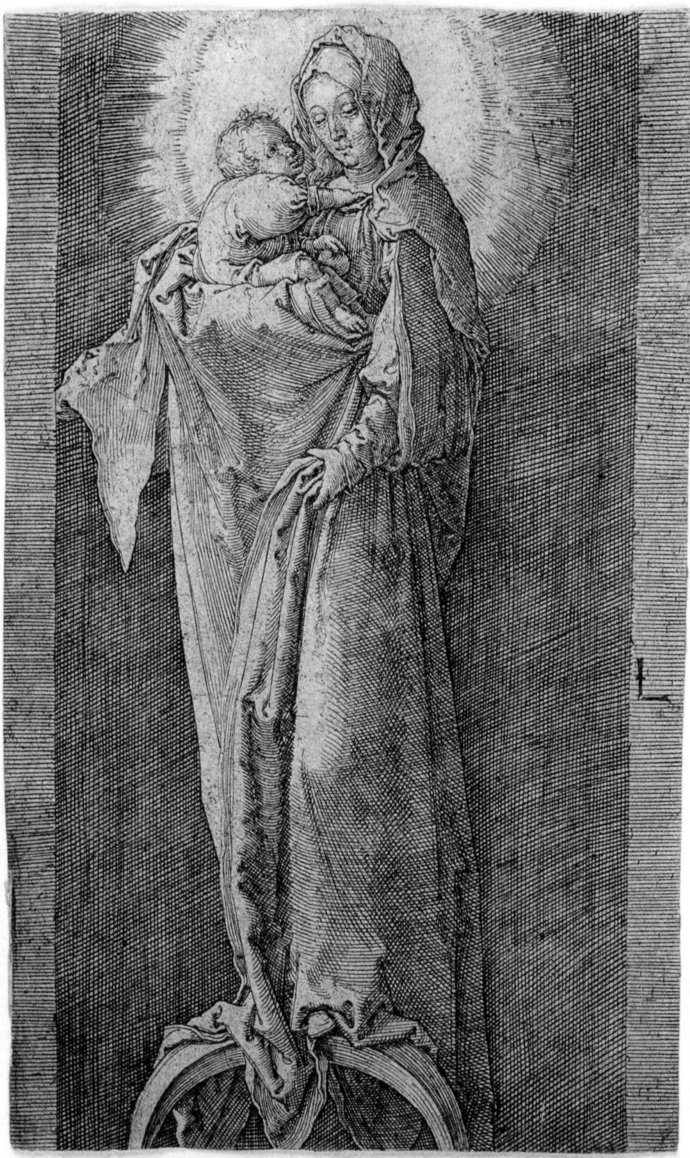

Fig. 128. Lucas van Leyden, *Virgin and Child in a Niche*, 1518, engraving

and Christ, as well as between the viewer and the holy pair.

While the long, lean form of the Virgin and the dramatic bunching of her robes reflect the Dutch painting style of the period, the stark background is an example of Lucas's originality. Unlike Lucas's print *Virgin and Child with Two Angels* [fig. 48 in the main essay] in which Madonna and Child are a part of a narrative, set in a complex landscape, flanked on one side by two angels, the holy pair in *Virgin and Child in a Niche* is the focus of the composition. Mary's maternal gaze is Lucas's emphasis, for her gaze sets an example for the viewer of soft deference to the Christ child.

The tenderness and reverence of *Virgin and Child in a Niche* reflect the solemn religious spirit of the Netherlands during the Reformation. Along with Martin Luther's emphasis on a simplified and individual faith without an intermediary, Lucas used a conspicuously unadorned setting for the Virgin and Child to emphasize the direct relationship between the viewer and the holy pair. Though religious imagery may appear to challenge Luther's belief in doctrine over iconography, the irony of offering an illustration of Luther's own doctrine makes the *Virgin and Child in a Niche* an example of both Lucas's clever commentary and an expression of his sincere veneration of the holy pair.

BLAIR A. BROOKS '02

BIBLIOGRAPHY

Filedt Kok, J. P. "Lucas van Leyden." In *Dictionary of Art*, ed. Jane Turner. New York: Grove, 1996, vol. 19, pp. 756–62.

Jacobowitz, Ellen S., and Stephanie Loeb Stepanek. *The Prints of Lucas van Leyden and His Contemporaries*. Washington, DC: National Gallery of Art, 1983.

Landau, David, and Peter Parshall. *The Renaissance Print 1470–1550*. New Haven, CT: Yale University Press, 1994.

Lucas van Leyden—Grafiek (1489 of 1494–1533): met een complete oeuvre-catalogus van zijn gravures, etsen en houtsneden. Amsterdam: Rijksmuseum, 1978.

the Christ child's hand serves as a reminder of the fall of man in Eden and foreshadows the Child's future resurrection, which would restore man to God's grace. Mary stands on the moon, which symbolizes the Catholic belief that she is the queen of heaven, although Lucas has omitted the crown of stars that are traditionally paired with the moon. The Virgin stands in a niche of evenly patterned incisions, subtly shaded with various hues of gray; this gives the print a serenity and richness of line that soften the connections between Madonna

A Marcantonio Raimondi
Argini (near Bologna), Papal States
1480/82–1527/34 Bologna
active Bologna, Venice, and Rome

T *Holy Family with the Infant Saint John the Baptist
(after Raphael)*
alternate title: *Madonna with the Long Thigh*

D circa 1520–25

M engraving on medium-weight laid buff paper

X sheet and plate: 15 11/16 in. x 10 5/8 in. (399 mm
x 270 mm)

S unsigned (tablet in lower left corner never
monogrammed)

I see checklist

C Museum purchase
1959.3

In Marcantonio Raimondi's treatment of the
Holy Family, the Virgin is seated on the ground,
with massive ancient ruins rising behind her. The
Christ child and the young Saint John the Baptist
gesture actively across her lap while she remains
serene and solid. Saint Joseph kneels humbly at the
left, watching the rest of the family group. An additional figure appears in the architecture of the
background at right, perhaps a shepherd, reminiscent of a more traditional Adoration scene. This
print probably dates from around 1520 and exemplifies the High Renaissance ideals of classicism
and careful structure. The composition is well balanced, with the Virgin and St. Joseph anchoring
both sides. The Virgin's leg provides a kind of
structural support across the picture plane, and,
consequently, the image is most commonly
referred to as the "Virgin with the Long Thigh."

Though Raimondi was perhaps the best-known
printmaker of the Renaissance era, his early life is
not well documented. He was born in Bologna
circa 1480 and is known to have moved to Venice
by 1506 and then on to Rome by 1511. His early
training was in the workshop of Francesco Francia,
a Bolognese goldsmith and painter. As a young
man, Marcantonio was well known as a master of
engraving, producing copies of prints by the German master Albrecht Dürer while in Venice; his
copies were so good, in fact, that Dürer himself
asked Marcantonio to stop copying his prints so
exactly—down to Dürer's trademark "AD" monogram! The most significant phase of Marcantonio's career began once he became associated
with the workshop of Raphael in Rome. The
engravings he produced that were based on
designs and compositions by Raphael and his stu-

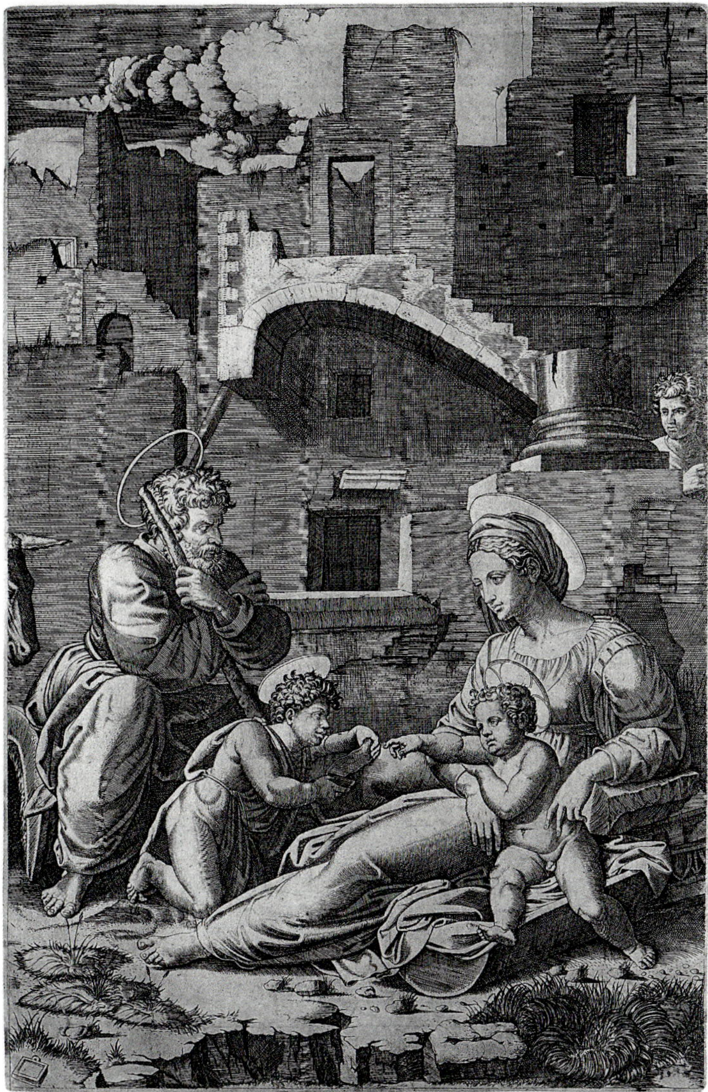

Fig. 129 . Marcanto-
nio Raimondi,
*Madonna with the
Long Thigh*, ca. 1520-
25, engraving

dents form the core of his *oeuvre*. Prints by Marcantonio were widely distributed throughout Europe and were a valuable resource for artists outside Italy. Indeed, painters who never traveled to Italy, such as Rembrandt, owned Marcantonio's prints and used them to become familiar with the techniques of the great Renaissance masters.

His prints, however, are not always slavish copies of other artists' compositions; when reproducing a painting, Marcantonio often made subtle adjustments to render the images more appropriate to the smaller print format. Many of his prints are based on original drawings, as opposed to the final painted versions of Raphael's compositions. Thus, Marcantonio's work records aspects of Raphael's painting process and provides glimpses of paintings that either have not survived or were never executed. This particular image of the holy pair has no known surviving original painting or drawing, but it has been linked to a group of paintings produced by Raphael's most important young workshop collaborator, Giulio Romano. The solid forms of the Virgin's head and leg, and the physiques of the children, reflect particular characteristics of Giulio's style in painting and drawing. The strange placement of the shepherd figure in the background suggests that the print may be based on a preliminary study for a painting that was never executed or that changed drastically after the early stages of its development.

LISA MCDERMOTT

BIBLIOGRAPHY

Landau, David, and Peter Parshall. *The Renaissance Print 1470–1550*. New Haven: Yale University Press, 1994, pp. 120–46.

Oberhuber, Konrad. *The Works of Marcantonio Raimondi and His School*. New York: Abaris Books, 1978, p. 65 listed as Bartsch 57.

Reed, Sue Welsh, and Richard W. Wallace. *Italian Etchers of the Renaissance and Baroque*. Boston: Museum of Fine Arts, 1989, pp. 234–43.

CAT. NO. 17

A Giorgio Vasari and workshop
Arezzo, Tuscany 1511–1574 Florence
active Arezzo, Florence, Bologna, Rome,
Venice, and Naples

T *Holy Family with the Infant Saint John the Baptist and Saint Francis*

D post-1544

M oil on panel

X 39 1/2 in. x 30 1/2 in. (100.3 cm x 77.5 cm)

C Museum purchase in honor of Nancy Angell Streeter (Class of 1950)
1974.10

The figure of the Virgin Mary dominates the *Holy Family with St. Francis and the Infant St. John the Baptist*, a painting designed by Giorgio Vasari and probably executed by a member of his workshop [fig. 130]. The Virgin reaches down to embrace the two children, the sleeping Christ who reclines on a drapery in front of her, and the toddler St. John the Baptist who reaches across to clasp hands with Christ while exchanging glances with Mary. Saints Joseph and Francis look on from behind Mary's shoulders.

Vasari's records indicate that a painting on this subject was commissioned in 1544 by a wealthy Florentine named Francesco Niccolo Vespucci (Cadogan). Two facts strengthen the case for this commission: St. Francis was the patron saint of Vespucci, and St. John the Baptist was the patron saint of Florence. A nearly identical version of Wellesley's painting, also recently attributed to Vasari's workshop, exists in the Musée des Beaux-Arts in Bordeaux (Habert; Cadogan; Corti), while a different version with a similar composition is now in a private collection. The painting's grace-

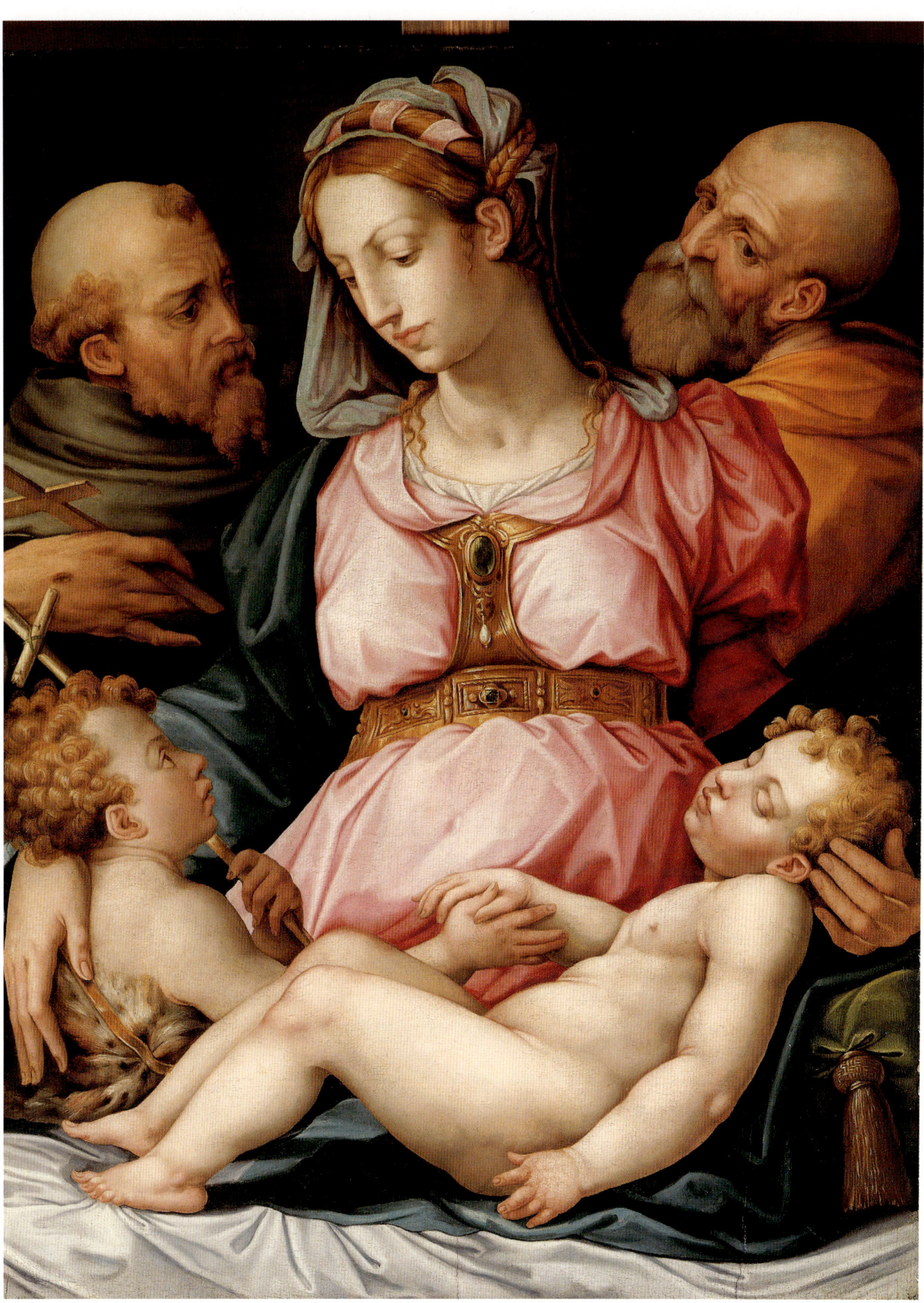

ful and harmonious composition undoubtedly made it a desirable work to copy.

Replicating much-admired compositions within the workshop of a master artist was a common practice during the Italian Renaissance; Leonardo da Vinci's two versions of the *Virgin of the Rocks* serve as well-known examples of such practices. In most cases, the artist himself would produce a cartoon, or precise model drawing, to which a closely supervised assistant would apply the paint. The master would then inspect the painting and even add finishing touches to ensure that its quality and style were up to his standards (Cadogan). The practices of workshop production explain both the existence of more than one example of a given composition and the difficulty of determining the original. Examination of the Wellesley *Holy Family* under infrared light reveals a detailed preparatory drawing beneath the paint surface. The existence of this underdrawing assures us that the painting is not a later copy, but from the Vasari workshop based on the master's cartoon.

In addition to his work as an artist, architect, and collector, Vasari is probably best known for his work as an art historian. In his book *Lives of the Most Excellent Painters, Sculptors, and Architects,* Vasari uses the biographies of artists to trace what he considered to be the progress of artistic achievement from its origins in classical antiquity to the pinnacle of perfection in the Italian High Renaissance (Shearman, pp. 172–73). The task of his generation of artists, he believed, was to master the technical advances of the High Renaissance in the use of the oil paint medium, perspective, and the modeling of figures and drapery in light and dark. By doing so, they would be able to create inventive and pleasing compositions in an increasingly sophisticated manner (Shearman, pp. 40).

In time, the goal of mid-sixteenth-century artists to surpass the perfection of the High Renaissance led to a self-conscious stylishness in their work, an extreme elegance that tended toward artificiality. This pursuit of beauty at the expense of naturalness became known as *maniera,* or Mannerism. It soon came under criticism by other artists and by the church; indeed, art historians looked down on Mannerist art until the twentieth century. Mannerist artists such as Vasari and those in his workshop were criticized for elevating issues of style above substance. They were overly concerned with aesthetic qualities and displays of technical virtuosity and less interested in depicting the subject in a clear and readable way (Shearman, pp. 52–53). Contributing to the criticism, the church found that these artists portrayed religious figures in an indecorous and inappropriate manner (Shearman, p. 166).

The characteristic qualities of Mannerist art, for which the style has been both criticized and praised, are exemplified in the Wellesley *Holy Family.* First, though the traditional iconography of the figures makes each easy to identify, the overall meaning of the scene remains unclear. Interpretation is made difficult by what appears to be a complex relationship among the figures. Rather than looking at her sleeping child, Mary gazes at St. John the Baptist, who looks expectantly up at her. St. Francis looks at Mary with a concerned air, while St. Joseph glances over his shoulder, the angle of his head echoing that of Christ, his gaze unresolved. There is nothing in the painting, no gesture or sign, to explain the meaning behind this series of gazes.

The depiction of Mary herself brings out even more ambiguities. Her elegant dress and ornate hairstyle seem out of place for a woman of humble origins, as does her jeweled gold belt. Furthermore, the strong light on the front of her body emphasizes her round breasts and belly; a dimple in her robe suggests her navel. By underlining Mary's corporeal nature and endowing her with a voluptuous quality, the artist defies the chaste, purely spiritual image of Christian tradition and gives her the physical attributes of womanliness and motherhood. While sensuality and grace were

certainly desirable qualities in contemporary portraiture, eventually they came to be considered
inappropriate in religious works. As a result, when
the Council of Trent in 1564 condemned "superfluous elegance" in church paintings, religious art
began to take on a more simple, sober character
(Shearman, pp. 168–70).

In addition to the disjuncture between style
and subject matter, critics have also objected to
the ambiguous settings and spatial relations in
Mannerist paintings. The Wellesley *Holy Family* is
no exception: its setting is not at all defined. It is
not clear whether Christ lies on a high bed, an
altar, or on Mary's lap; whether St. John the Baptist is beside him, or between him and Mary; and
how far behind Mary the Saints Francis and
Joseph are standing.

For Vasari and his contemporaries, providing
clear answers to these questions was less important
than creating an aesthetically sophisticated and
impressive work of art. Artists displayed their technical virtuosity in delicately modeled nudes such
as the softly rounded figure of Christ. Twisting
poses such as that of St. Joseph also gave them an
opportunity to show their knowledge of anatomy,
as well as their skill in foreshortening. Indeed,
when creating a composition that was innovative
and pleasing to the eye, artists considered spatial
realism to be of lesser importance. Vasari used
curving lines and round shapes to unify the group,
creating a sense of grace and harmony. The circular arrangement of the figures' heads mimics the
shapes of the heads themselves, while the curving
lines of limbs and drapery emphasize this roundness, smoothly connecting the figures. In keeping
with the sheer beauty of the composition, the figures' faces are of an extraordinary sweetness and
delicacy. Not only are Mary's features perfectly
regular and finely modeled, but even Saints Francis and Joseph are veritable porcelain doll versions
of old men. Elegant, refined dress rather than

coarse and simple clothing suited the tastes of the
day, if not the biblical personages depicted.

In creating private devotional pieces such as
the *Holy Family*, Vasari was responding to the aesthetic tastes of his cultured and artistically sophisticated patrons. In his *Holy Family*, he depicts the
Virgin with an elegance and sensuality perhaps
better suited to a portrait of one of his patrons
than to an historical, religious figure. Vasari's
interest in endowing her with the qualities of a
contemporary woman is an instance of the continued interplay between images of ordinary women
and images of the Madonna.

MARGARET A. SAMU DS '01

BIBLIOGRAPHY

DeGrazia, Diane. *The Age of Correggio and the Carracci: Emilian
Painting of the Sixteenth and Seventeenth Centuries*, exhibition
catalogue. Washington, DC: National Galley of Art, 1986.

Boase, T. S. R. *Giorgio Vasari: The Man and the Book*. Princeton, NJ:
Princeton University Press, 1979.

Cadogan, Jean K. "Giorgio Vasari's *Holy Family*: Master and Pupil
in a Renaissance Workshop." In *Wellesley College Museum: The
Centennial Year*. Wellesley, MA: Wellesley College Museum,
1989.

Corti, Laura. *Vasari: Catalogo completo dei dipinti*. Florence: Cantini, 1989, p. 50.

*Giorgio Vasari: Principi, letterati et artisti nelle carte di Giorgio Vasari.
Pittura vasariana dal 1532 al 1554*, exhibition catalogue.
Florence: EDAM, 1982.

Habert, Jean. *Bordeaux, Musée des Beaux-arts: Peinture italienne XVe-
XIXe siècles*. Paris: Editions de la Réunion des musées
nationaux, 1987, pp. 156–58.

Jacks, Philip, ed. *Vasari's Florence*. Cambridge, UK: Cambridge
University Press, 1998.

Kleinman, Julian. "Giorgio Vasari." In *Grove Dictionary of Art*, ed.
Jane Turner. London: Macmillan, 1996, vol. 32, pp. 10–25.

Shearman, John. *Mannerism*. New York: Penguin Books, 1990.

Warner, Marina. *Alone of All Her Sex: The Myth and the Cult of the
Virgin Mary*. New York: Vintage Books, 1983.

CAT. NO. 18

A Flemish

T *Judith with the Head of Holofernes*

D third quarter 16th century

M oil on panel

X 23 7/8 in. x 17 1/2 in.
(60.5 cm x 44.4 cm)

I inscribed in paint, verso: 'L.D. 24'

C Gift of Strafford Morss
in memory of his wife
Gabrielle Ladd Morss (Class of 1958)
1969.6

The painting illustrates an episode from the Book of Judith (an apocryphal book of the Old Testament that was still included in Christian bibles through the sixteenth century). Judith was a young widow of Bethulia, an Israelite city that was besieged by the Assyrian general, Holofernes. When Judith learned that the elders of Bethulia planned to surrender to the Assyrians, she reproached the elders and undertook to save the city herself. Exchanging her sackcloth for beautiful clothing and jewelry, Judith entered the camp of the enemy and offered herself as a slave to Holofernes. One evening Holofernes invited her into his tent and, "desirous of intimacy" with her, urged her to drink and be merry with him. That evening, Holofernes drank more wine "than he had ever drunk on any one day since he was born" (Judith 12:20). Before he could "commit any sin" with Judith, Holofernes fell asleep, whereupon Judith, using his scimitar, cut off his head in two strokes. She then summoned her maid, put the head in a sack, and returned with it to Bethulia. At Judith's command, the Israelites displayed the head of Holofernes on the battlements of their besieged city. Shortly thereafter, the Assyrian army fled in disarray (Judith ch. 7–15).

With the invention of the printing press (ca. 1455) and the subsequent publication of illus-

trated bibles and of other devotional texts in the late fifteenth century, printed images of Judith and Holofernes began to circulate widely in northern Europe.[1] In the early sixteenth century, half-length paintings of Judith with the head of Holofernes were popularized by Lucas Cranach the Elder in Germany, and by Jan Massys and Vincent Sellaer in the Netherlands. In the case of Cranach (1472–1553), the depictions of Judith were an occasion to depict a beautiful woman in the opulent attire worn by contemporary women of the German courts. In these works, if one is to be guided by texts written at the time, Judith is presented as an exemplary heroine who defended her people against tyranny, much as German Protestant princes were then claiming to do for their subjects against the Emperor (Straten).[2] Cranach's paintings of *Judith* may have also served to remind the viewer of the danger posed to men by a powerful woman (Smith, Dresen-Coenders).

In the case of the Antwerp painters, Jan Massys (circa 1509–73) and Vincent Sellaer (1500–89), their half-length depictions of Judith emphasize not the opulent clothing but the exposed flesh of Judith, who appears as a nude or semi-nude figure (Buijnsters-Smets, pp. 74–79).[3] Wellesley's painting is closest in design to a half-length composition attributed to Vincent Sellaer that depicts Judith and her servant in front of the tent of Holofernes, with a glimpse of the battle-tents and battlements in the distance on the right (*Siècle . . .*). Judith holds a sword in her right hand; with the left she lowers Holofernes' head into a bag held by her servant. In the background on the left one can decipher the decapitated torso of the Assyrian general inside his tent. Mannerist qualities in the treatment of the figures and the drapery in the Wellesley panel suggest a date no earlier than the second half of the sixteenth century—a time when the theme was gaining new currency in print cycles by Maarten van Heemskerck (1498–1571) and Philips Galle (1537–1612) (Dresen-Coenders).

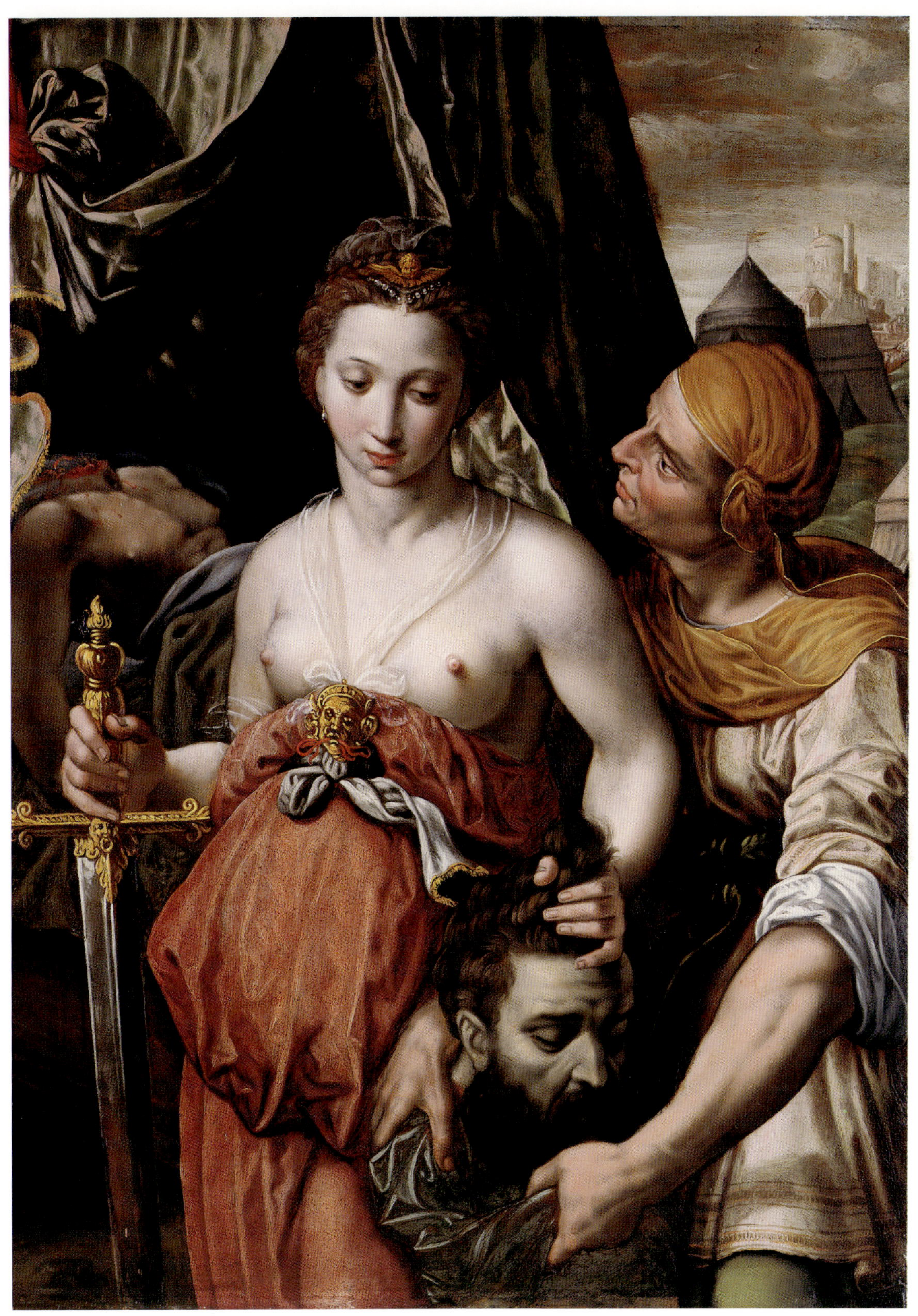

Like its predecessors, Wellesley's *Judith with the Head of Holofernes* offers a tantalizing mix of allusions to violence and beauty, to virtue and lust, and to patriotism and the power of women.

MARGARET D. CARROLL

NOTES

1. An extensive overview of Judith imagery through the early sixteenth century is offered in Schreyl, pp. 183–239.

2. Painting in Schloss Grünewald, Berlin (dated 1530), and in the Schlossmuseum in Gotha (dated 1531); see Dieter Koepplin and Tilman Falk, *Lukas Cranach* (Basel: Kirkhauser, 1974–76), vol. 1, pp. 413–20 and vol. 2, pp. 578–80.

3. Paintings of Judith by Massys are found in the Museum of Fine Arts, Boston (cat. no. 18, p. 172); the Louvre (cat. no. 19, pp. 173–74); and the Museeum voor Schone Kunsten, Antwerp (cat. no. 38, pp. 198–99). The Boston painting is signed and dated 1543. A painting of Judith attributed to Sellaer is in Bern (Buijnsters-Smets, pg. 78).

BIBLIOGRAPHY

Buijnsters-Smets, Leontine. *Jan Massys: een Antwerps schilder uit de zestiende eeuw.* Zwolle, Netherlands: Waanders, 1995.

Dresen-Coenders, Lene, et al. *Saints and She-Devils: Images of Women in the 15th and 16th Centuries.* London: Rubicon Press, 1987.

"Judith" in *The Apocrypha: an American Translation*, trans. Edgar J. Goodspeed. New York: Modern Library, 1959, pp. 143–64.

Schreyl, Karl Heinz. "Schäufeleins Judith-Wandbild im Nördlinger Rathaus," in *Hans Schäufelein: Vorträge, gehalten anlässich des Nördlinger Symposiums im Rahmen der 7. Rieser Kulturtage.* Nördlingen, Germany: Verein Rieser Kulturtage, 1990, pp. 183–239.

Le Siècle de Bruegel: la peinture en Belgique au XVIe siècle, exhibition catalogue. Brussels: Musées Royaux des Beaux-Arts de Belgique, 1963, cat. no. 216, p. 157; ill. 174.

Smith, Susan L. *"To Women's Wiles I Fell": The Power of Women Topos and the Development of Medieval Secular Art.* Ph.D. diss., University of Pennsylvania, 1978.

Straten, Adelheid. *Das Judith-Thema in Deutschland im 16. Jahrhundert: Studien zur Ikonographie—Materielen und Beiträge.* Munich: Minerva, 1983.

Though the quality of this painting may be recognizable, the name of its artist is not. Its style reflects that of northern European painters—particularly Flemish—influenced by contemporary southern European Mannerist painting. Many northern painters traveled to Italy in the mid-16th century, where they had direct contact with Italian masters and assimilated as much as they could of the admired style. Among the artists who have been suggested as possible authors of this work are the Flemish painters Vincent Sellaer, Michiel Coxie, and the Master of the Prodigal Son, and the Dutch artists Frans Floris, Willem Adriaensz. Key, Karel van Mander, and artists working in the circle of Hendrik Goltzius. Comparison of the Wellesley painting with the known works of these suggested artists has not yet provided a definitive attribution, although a stronger identification with the Flemish school has been observed.

Question of attribution can be aided by technical studies of an artist's working method. The person who painted *Judith with the Head of Holofernes* executed a detailed preliminary drawing directly on the gessoed surface of the wood panel support before beginning to paint [fig. 132]. The museum has been aware of the presence of this underdrawing for several years, and been able to view it using a special camera that reads light in the infrared spectrum range. This technique, known as infrared reflectography, allows non-carbon containing materials (such as the oil paint layers) to become transparent, while carbon-containing materials (such as the charcoal or graphite used by the artist to execute this drawing) remain visible. Thanks to advances in infrared imaging, and the capture and digital assembly of images by computer, it is now possible not only to view the preparatory drawing on screen but to obtain high quality reproductions of the image [fig. 133].

Working with the Straus Center for Conservation of the Harvard University Art Museums—pioneers in infrared research and capture—the museum has had an infrared reflectogram of this underdrawing assembled, which can now be circulated among experts to see if the drawing style can be identified as that of a particular artist.[4] Because drawing styles (like handwritings) are highly idiosyncratic, the chance of making an appropriate attribution is now greatly enhanced, but still not guaranteed. Finding a stylistic match depends on how many other underdrawings are available for comparison with that of *Judith with the Head of Holofernes*. As this technology becomes more widely available to museums, chances of making a successful attribution will improve. At present, however, it may not be possible to make a positive identification, but only to continue the process of elimination (of artists whom this painting is not by). Nevertheless, to be able to peer beneath the paint layers and appreciate the great care and skill with which this unknown artist prepared for the task of painting half a millennium ago is an achievement in its own right.

MELISSA R. KATZ

NOTE

4. Infrared-reflectograph captured and digitally assembled by Teri Hensick and Marc Giudicelli, Straus Center for Conservation, Harvard University Art Museums, February 2000.

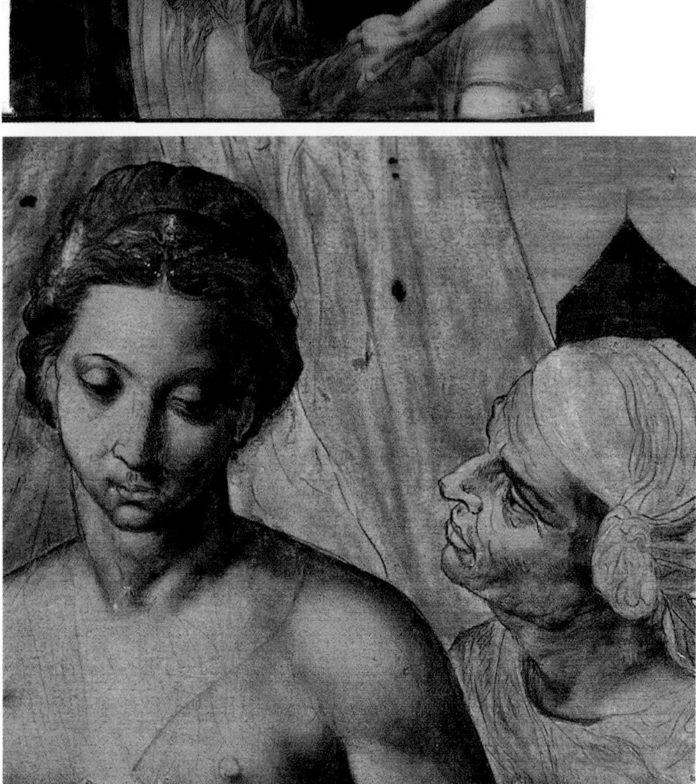

Fig. 132. Infrared-reflectograph of the artist's underdrawing; overall.

Fig. 133. Infrared-reflectograph of artist's underdrawing; detail of Judith's head.

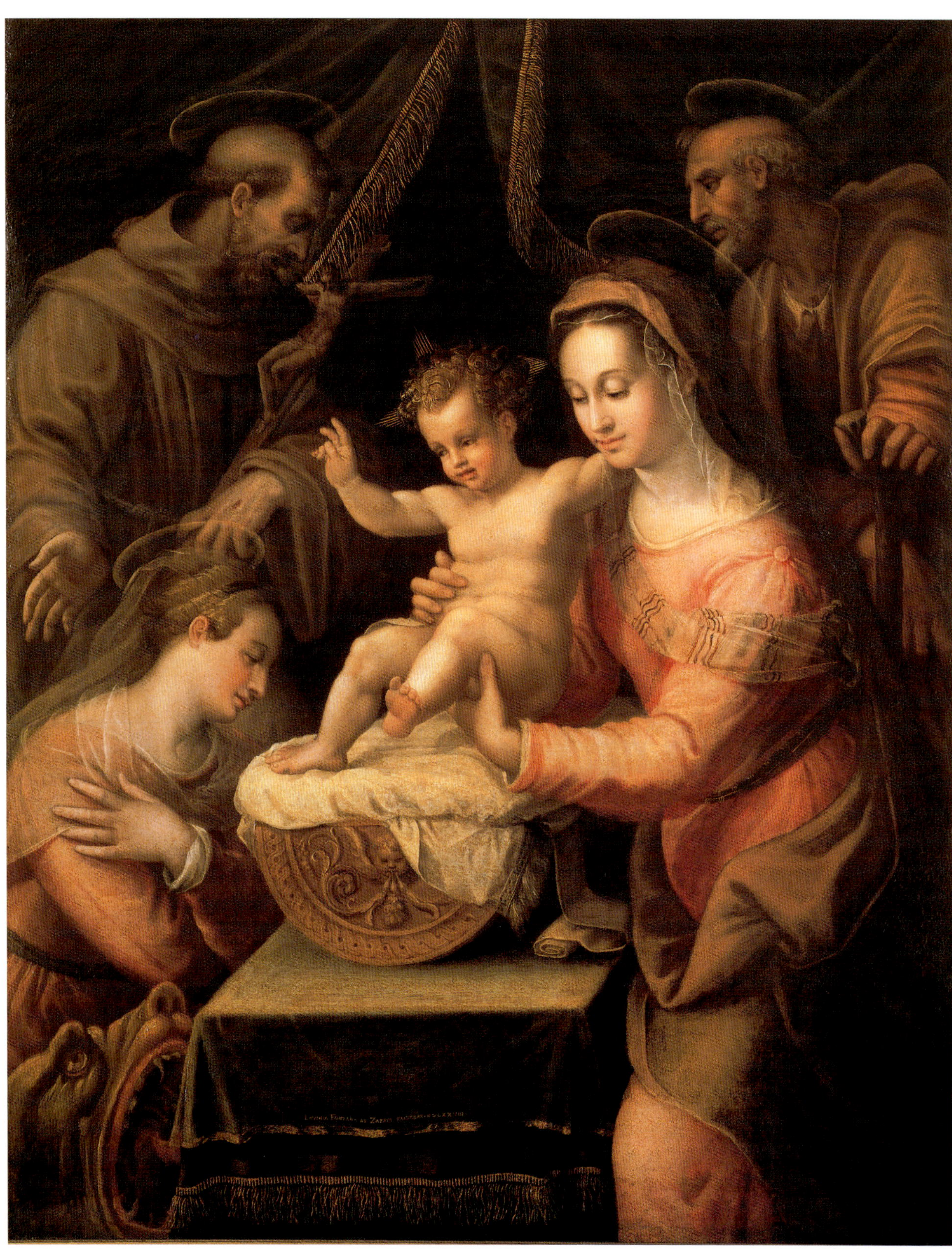
LAVINIA FONTANA DE ZAPPIS FACIEBAT M D LXXVIII

A Lavinia Fontana
Bologna, Papal States 1552–1614 Rome
active Bologna and Rome

T *Holy Family with Saints Margaret and Francis*

D 1578

M oil on canvas

X 50 in. x 41 in. (127.0 cm x 104.1 cm)

S signed and dated in paint (on tablecloth):
LAVINIA FONTANA DE ZAPPIS FACIEBAT
MDLXXVIII

C Extended loan from Mrs. Selma Postar
6.1983

In her *Holy Family with Saints*, Lavinia Fontana presents the Madonna in an intimate domestic scene. Mary tenderly places the infant Christ in a cradle as Joseph stands behind her; opposite them, Saints Margaret and Francis bow their heads in worship. At first glance, the painting appears to celebrate both Christ's divine birth and the human joy of motherhood, yet its iconographical elements speak also of Christ's death.

Fontana is widely considered to be the first professional woman artist, as she received numerous commissions for portraits and large-scale religious paintings and actually supported her family by her work (May, pp. 44–45). She painted the *Holy Family* just as her career was beginning to flourish. As an assertion of her arrival as an artist, the painting prominently bears her signature and the date: LAVINIA FONTANA DE ZAPPIS FACIEBAT MDLXXVIII. This signature not only allows us to date the painting with ease but also reveals something of the confidence of this artist, who signs her work like a master so early in her career. Unknown to Italian scholars before the 1990s, this painting has gained prominence in two recent exhibitions (Noone; Fortunati).

Like other artists of her period, Fontana responds to the artistic decrees of the Counter-Reformation by turning away from the excesses of the Mannerist style in which she had been trained. Instead, she uses linear perspective and foreshortening to create a realistic sense of spatial recession that clearly defines the setting. In addition, she gives her figures the modest dress and pious decorum that are appropriate to the painting's religious subject matter. By creating a balanced, nearly symmetrical composition with strong upward diagonals, she emphasizes the centrality of Christ to the devotional image. The linking of her figures by gazes and graceful gestures shows that, like other Bolognese artists, she was influenced by the work of the High Renaissance artist Correggio (DeGrazia). In order to succeed as a woman artist in a male-dominated art world, Fontana had to adhere scrupulously to the newly defined doctrines of the Church that arose out of the 1545–1563 Ecumenical Council of Trent (Fortunati, p. 13).

The artistic verisimilitude of the painting would have made its iconography all the easier for contemporary viewers to read. Saint Margaret is recognizable by her attribute, the dragon that accompanies her. According to legend, she became the patron saint of women in childbirth after using her cross to deliver herself unharmed from the belly of the dragon that had swallowed her as a test of her Christian faith; she then asked women to call upon her for the safe delivery of their children. Bathed in a beatific light, Mary and Saint Margaret are fully absorbed in the present moment, worshipping and caring for the child who raises his plump hand in a babyish sign of blessing. Standing in shadowy gloom, the male saints appear unaware of the scene of maternal bliss before them. Somberly contemplating the crucifix, they are occupied not with the present, the infant Christ, but with his coming death on the cross. To emphasize the point, Saint Francis reveals the stigmata on his hands, miraculous signs of his communion with Christ's suffering.

Yet the light and dark areas of the painting do not create an absolute division between present and future concerns. Saint Francis is also associ-

Fig. 134. (opposite) Lavinia Fontana, *Holy Family with Saints Margaret and Francis*, 1578, oil on canvas, Postar Collection

ated with Christ's birth: credited with creating the first Nativity scene in an Italian grotto in the thirteenth century, he cradles the tiny crucifix in his arm like a mother holding a child. Mary, on the other hand, does not cradle the child near her but places him in a sarcophagus-like crib on a sacrificial altar table. She lifts his body like a priest raising the Host—the transubstantiated body of Christ—in the celebration of the Holy Eucharist.

Fontana's inextricable merging of these signs of the birth, death, and resurrection of Christ may reflect her contemplation of the recent birth and subsequent death of her own first-born child in the year before she painted the *Holy Family* (Cheney 1984, 1998). As she depicts this theme of great personal significance, Fontana also establishes a connection between the divine and earthly planes: a holy subject takes on the real, everyday quality of a domestic scene, while an everyday scene of motherhood is lifted to a sacred level.

MARGARET A. SAMU DS '01

BIBLIOGRAPHY

Diane De Grazia, *The Age of Correggio and the Carracci: Emilian Painting of the Sixteenth and Seventeenth Centuries*, exhibition catalogue. Washington, DC: National Gallery of Art, 1986.

Cantaro, Maria Teresa. *Lavinia Fontana bolognese: "pittora singolare" 1552–1614*. Milan: Jandi Sapi, 1989.

Cheney, Liana. "Lavinia Fontana: Boston *Holy Family*." *Women's Art Journal* (Spring-Summer 1984), pp. 12–15.

Cheney, Liana. *"Holy Family with Saints, 1578."* In *Lavinia Fontana of Bologna 1552–1614*, ed. Vera Fortunati, exhibition catalogue, National Museum of Women in the Arts. Milan: Electa, 1998, cat. no. 3, pp. 54–55.

Fortunati, Vera. "Lavinia Fontana: A Woman Artist in the Age of the Counter-Reformation." In *Lavinia Fontana of Bologna 1552–1614*, ed. Vera Fortunati, exhibition catalogue, National Museum of Women in the Arts. Milan: Electa, 1998.

Hall, James. *Dictionary of Subjects and Symbols in Art*. New York: Harper & Row, 1979.

"Lavinia Fontana." In *Dictionary of Art*, ed. Jane Turner. New York: Grove, 1996, vol. 11, pp. 269–70.

May, Stephen. "Against All Odds." *Art and Antiques* (February 1998), pp. 44–51.

Noone, Andrew. "Lavinia Fontana." In *European Paintings from Private Collections of Friends of the Museum of Fine Arts, Boston*, ed. Peter Sutton, exhibition catalogue. Boston: Museum of Fine Arts, 1992, pp. 154–55.

Sandoval, Annette. *The Directory of Saints: A Concise Guide to Patron Saints*. New York: Dutton, 1996.

Tufts, Eleanor M. "A Successful 16th-century Portraitist: Ms. Lavinia Fontana from Bologna." *ARTnews* (February 1974), pp. 60–64.

Vertova, Luisa. "Lavinia versus Sofonisba." *Apollo*, 40 (January 1995), pp. 43–46.

Voragine, Jacobus de. *The Golden Legend; or Lives of the Saints*. William Caxton, trans. London: J. M. Dent, 1900.

Warner, Marina. *Alone of All Her Sex: The Myth and the Cult of the Virgin Mary*. New York: Vintage Books, 1983.

CAT. NO. 20

A Gregorio Martínez y Espinosa
Valladolid, Castile, Spain 1547–1598 San Millán de la Cogolla, La Rioja
active Valladolid, San Miguel de Él Escorial, Burgos, and Castile region

T *Lamentation with Saints Augustine and Nicholas of Tolentino*

D 1590s

M oil and shell gold on panel

X 9 in. x 11 1/4 in. (22.8 cm x 28.6 cm)

S monogrammed in ligature: 'MNTRZ'

I see checklist

C Museum purchase from the Class of 1947 Acquisition Fund in honor of José Rafael Moneo
1999.120

This intimate panel by Gregorio Martínez y Espinosa (1547–98) depicts a lamentation scene at the foot of the cross, with the Virgin Mary cradling her son's body [fig. 135]. At either end, Saints Augustine and Nicholas of Tolentino kneel and caress Christ's wounds. Halos shimmer on the blackened rocks behind them, giving way on the left to a lucent dawn. Composition and draughtsmanship reflect the artist's admiration for and familiarity with Italian Mannerist painting and sculpture, while its dramatic coloring and heightened emotions reveal his Spanish heritage. Attributed for at least a century to Sebastián Martínez (1599–1667), the painting was recently reascribed to Gregorio Martínez y Espinosa (1547–1598) by Alfonso E. Pérez Sanchéz, who recognized not only Gregorio's exquisite technique but also his signature at bottom right (correspondence 1 January 1999).

The gifted painter Gregorio Martínez was born and worked in Valladolid, largest city of the Castile region and de facto capital of Spain during much of the sixteenth century. Political power was divided between Toledo, seat of the church, and Valladolid, periodic residence of the royal court. Castillian Renaissance culture also centered around the two cities, with El Greco at work in Toledo, and Cervantes, Alonso Berruguete, and Juan de Juni, among others, based in Valladolid. Gregorio's lifetime coincided with the construction of the Él Escorial palace, and Philip II's move from his native Valladolid to his future capital Madrid.

Philip II (1556–1598) imported dozens of Italian artists to decorate San Lorenzo de Él Escorial, the royal palace and monastery complex Philip built in the mountains near Madrid. Documents confirm that Martínez received at least two palace commissions, one in 1580 from Pavia-born sculptor Pompeo Leoni (García Chico, p. 13), and one in 1589 to assist Bolognese painter Pellegrino Tibaldi (Zarco Cuevas, p. 185). In 1590 he returned to Él Escorial, this time as an agent of the Hieronymite congregation attached to the palace, to assess the value of frescos and oil paintings executed by the king's painter (Zarco Cuevas, p. 65). These Escorial residencies would have brought him into direct contact not only with Italian Mannerist painters but also with the magnificent works in the Spanish royal collection.

The *Lamentation with Saints Augustine and Nicholas of Tolentino* inventively combines a moment from the life of Christ—the lamentation of his mother following the deposition of his body from the cross—with a moment of reverence by saints Augustine of Hippo (354–430) and Nicholas of Tolentino (ca. 1246–1306). Augustine is shown at left with his attributes, a bishop's crozier and miter, and Nicholas at right in a black Augustinian habit studded with stars (in reference to a comet seen at his birth), near a plate of pigeons (which, according to legend, he restored to life when served to him roasted during an illness). Neither Mary nor the two male saints seem aware of any presence other than Christ's. Each is focused in deep reverence on the martyred body, an act of devotion presumably to be replicated by the painting's viewer(s).

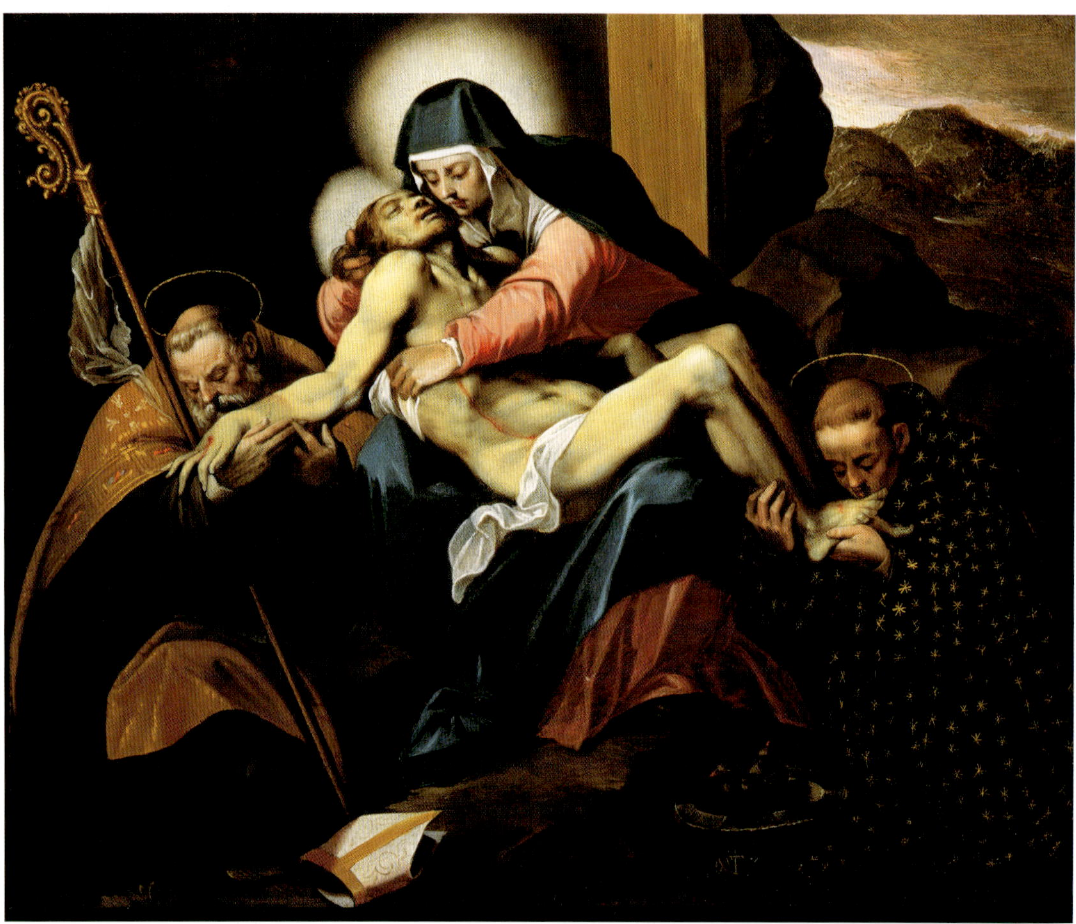

Fig. 135. Gregorio Martínez, *Lamentation with Saints Augustine and Nicholas of Tolentino*, 1590s, oil on panel

The placement of the two saints at the head and foot of Christ's limp body mimics the positions of Nicodemus and Joseph of Arimathæa in a traditional deposition scene, while the gesture of kissing Christ's wounds recalls the pose of Mary Magdalene in many lamentations. Yet by substituting familiar biblical personages with latter-day holy men, Martínez lifts his *Lamentation* into the realm of abstract time, facilitating the viewer's ability to enter into the scene and identify with its actions. A similar motive lies behind the inclusion of donor portraits within scenes of the life of Christ and the Virgin, although in Martínez's variant, the donor's presence is implied rather than portrayed.

Though rooted in the Castillian plains, Martínez drew upon Tuscan Mannerist painting for inspiration. The art of Rosso Fiorentino (1495–1540) provides precedents both for the deposed body placed within the Virgin's lap (*Deposition from the Cross*, Sansepolchro, circa 1525) and for Christ's back-flung head placed against his forward-flung shoulder (*Deposition from the Cross*, Volterra, 1521). Martínez probably knew Rosso's paintings and those of other European artists through widely circulated engravings of famous works. The fact that Christ's head and shoulder in Martínez's painting slope to the left and Rosso's to the right strengthens the argument that Martínez worked from a print, which would have reversed the original composition. Nor was Rosso's work the only source for the *Lamentation* composition. Inspiration for Christ's outstretched arm—one of the most dramatic and effective elements of this composition—can be found in a *Deposition from the Cross* by Giorgio Vasari (ex-Pisa, 1547). Vasari's painting, itself based on Rosso's work, incorporated both the splay of the Sansepolchro body and the conjoining of the Volterra head and shoulder, and added a kneeling Nicodemus holding Christ's arm. Vasari's *Deposition*, now lost, is known through an engraving by Enea Vico (1523–67), which Martínez may well have owned.

Yet no matter how extensive Gregorio Martínez's indebtedness to prints of Italian master paintings, elements of undeniable inspiration coexist within his *Lamentation* for which there are no Italian precedents. Vasari's replacement of Rosso's three Marys at the foot of the cross with Joseph and Nicodemus maintained a biblical setting time frame, while Martínez's substitution of Sts. Augustine and Nicholas removed the scene from its temporal grounding. Secondly, Vasari and Rosso portrayed the Virgin Mary upright, gazing into Christ's lifeless face but making no motion to approach it. Martínez's Virgin Mary actively embraces her son, inclining her head to his and drawing his body toward her, a gesture concordant with intense Spanish piety.

Without doubt Gregorio Martínez's *Lamentation* was designed for a Spanish audience seeking mystical experience stimulated by profoundly emotional art. His choice of saints (especially the rarely depicted Nicholas of Tolentino) suggests a connection with the Augustinian order, familiarly known as the Black Canons, who were active in Valladolid and its surrounding provinces. Alternatively, Martínez may have created this work for a private individual with Augustinian affinities.

Extant documents indicate Gregorio Martínez to have had one such client—Fabio Nelli, a Sienese banker resident in Valladolid. In 1596 Nelli commissioned Martínez to design the altarpiece for his family's funerary chapel in the church of Valladolid's Convent of San Agustín (Martí y Monsó, pp. 514–15). Nelli's contract does not mention a *Lamentation* scene, nor do the dimensions of the extant predella panels conform to those of Wellesley's painting. However, it does provide an Augustinian link in the last decade of Martínez's career, and access to a patron who could have commissioned a private devotional work as well as a large public altarpiece.

MELISSA R. KATZ

BIBLIOGRAPHY

García Chico, Esteban. *Documentos para el estudio de Arte en Castilla*, vol. 3 no. 1. Valladolid: Seminario de Arte y Arqueologia, 1946.

Martí y Monsó, José. *Estudios Historicos-Artísticos relativos principalment a Valladolid.* Valladolid: Impresión L. Miñón, 1898–1901, pp. 518–29.

Martín González, Juan José. "El pintor Gregorio Martínez." *Boletin del Seminario de estudios de Arte y Arqueologia, Valladolid,* vol. 21–22, 1954–56, pp. 81–91.

Pérez Sánchez, Alfonso E. "Una nueva pintura de Gregorio Martínez." *Boletín del Museo Nacional de Escultura,* no. 2, 1997/98, pp. 7–9.

Zarco Cuevas, Julián. *Pintores Españoles en San Lorenzo el Réal de Él Escorial (1566–1613).* Madrid: Instituto de Valencia de Don Juan, 1932.

CAT. NO. 21

A Pietro Faccini
Bologna, Papal States ca. 1562–1602 Bologna
active Bologna

T *Saint Francis Receiving the Christ Child in the Presence of the Virgin;* after an altarpiece by the artist for the Capuchin church, Bologna, now destroyed

D 1590s

M etching with engraving and stipple on medium-weight laid buff paper, state 1 of 1

X sheet: 14 1/4 in. x 9 3/4 in. (362 mm x 249 mm)
image: 13 3/8 in. x 9 5/8 in. (338 mm x 244 mm)

I see checklist

C Museum purchase
1986.3

The print of *Saint Francis of Assisi Receiving the Christ Child from the Virgin Mary* is an example of the influence of the Italian Baroque on printmaking styles and of the religious currents of the late sixteenth century on art in general. While the image is exemplary of fine prints of the period, the printmaker was exceptional. The versatile Faccini was a painter, draughtsman, and printmaker of the Emilian School and a *consigliere* of the *Compagnia dei pittori*. He began his career at a late age and apprenticed himself to Annibale Carracci. Unfortunately, Faccini's excellence as an imaginative and swift painter made his master jealous and he was forced to leave the Carracci Academy in Bologna (DeGrazia, p. 374).[1]

Such enviable mastery of composition and holy drama is displayed in *Saint Francis*, one of approximately eight prints attributed to Faccini.[2] St. Francis holds the infant Christ and looks up to his right, at the Virgin descending from heaven. Faccini boldly uses the freedom of the etched line to create a sketchy, ethereal image of the Virgin Mary, who appears as a vision to the more solidly rendered, down-to-earth saint. The artist highlights St. Francis by reserving cross-hatching for the texture of the saint's robe, which makes it stand out among the engraved parallel lines and loose, draughtsman's lines that create the rest of the composition. The sharp contrast of dark and light is probably influenced by Venetian art and, more specifically, by Tintoretto. There has been speculation about a visit in Venice that influenced Faccini (DeGrazia, p. 375). The sway and curve of St. Francis's seemingly ungrounded body, as if levitated by ecstatic emotion, precedes the extreme to which movement was taken during the Baroque period.

The composition is believed to record a painting made by Faccini as an altarpiece for the Church of the Cappuccini in Bologna in 1590. The painting had been removed from the church by the eighteenth century and is now thought to have been destroyed. Numerous preparatory drawings, in reverse of the etching, are known, although there is some debate as to whether they were studies for the print or the painting (Birke, p. 272, DeGrazia, p. 386). This print, like most of Faccini's work, is dated to the late sixteenth century, based on his one signed and dated painting, the *Martyrdom of Saint Lawrence* of 1590. Because Faccini did not begin studying art until he was approximately thirty years old, and died about age forty, it is likely that most of his work was created during the decade of the 1590s. This print is documented as having only one state, indicating that Faccini did not work the plate further and make changes beyond the initial printing.

Images with the motif of St. Francis receiving the Christ Child from Mary began to appear in Bolognese churches of the Capuchin order (a branch of the Franciscan order) in the 1590s, and most likely these monks were Faccini's patrons. Faccini's lost altarpiece of St. Francis coincided with the Capuchin's attempt to promote the emotional and mystical sides of Franciscan spirituality. No doubt the Capuchins were pleased with Faccini's vibrant and lively ecstatic vision. DeGrazia points out that the new iconography, possibly borrowed from that of St. Anthony of Padua, "stressed ecstatic visions of Franciscan saints. Chief among the new subjects was Saint Francis embracing and adoring the Infant, an event unknown in earlier biographies and the paintings of the Saint" (DeGrazia, p. 387).

> HILLARY L. ANDERSON '00
>
> and
>
> BLAIR A. BROOKS '02

NOTES

1. According to Garofoli, it was Faccini who became jealous of Annibale's success. Either way, the two men separated, and Faccini established a rival academy in Bologna.

2. The attribution of the other seven works rest on Faccini's connection to a 'PF' monogram; Birke, p. 271.

BIBLIOGRAPHY

Birke, Veronika, ed. *Italian Masters of the Sixteenth and Seventeenth Centuries: The Illustrated Bartsch*, vol. 40. New York: Abaris, 1982–1986, pp. 271–72.

DeGrazia, Diane. *Correggio and His Legacy: Sixteenth-Century Emilian Drawings*. Washington, DC: National Gallery of Art, 1984, pp. 374–88.

Garofoli, Marina. "Faccini, Pietro." In *Dictionary of Art*, ed. Jane Turner. New York: Grove, 1996.

Reed, Sue Welsh, and Richard W. Wallace. *Italian Etchers of the Renaissance and Baroque*. Boston: Museum of Fine Arts, 1989.

Cazort, Mimi, and Catherine Johnston. *Bolognese Drawings in North American Collections, 1500–1800*. Ottawa, ON: National Gallery of Canada, 1982.

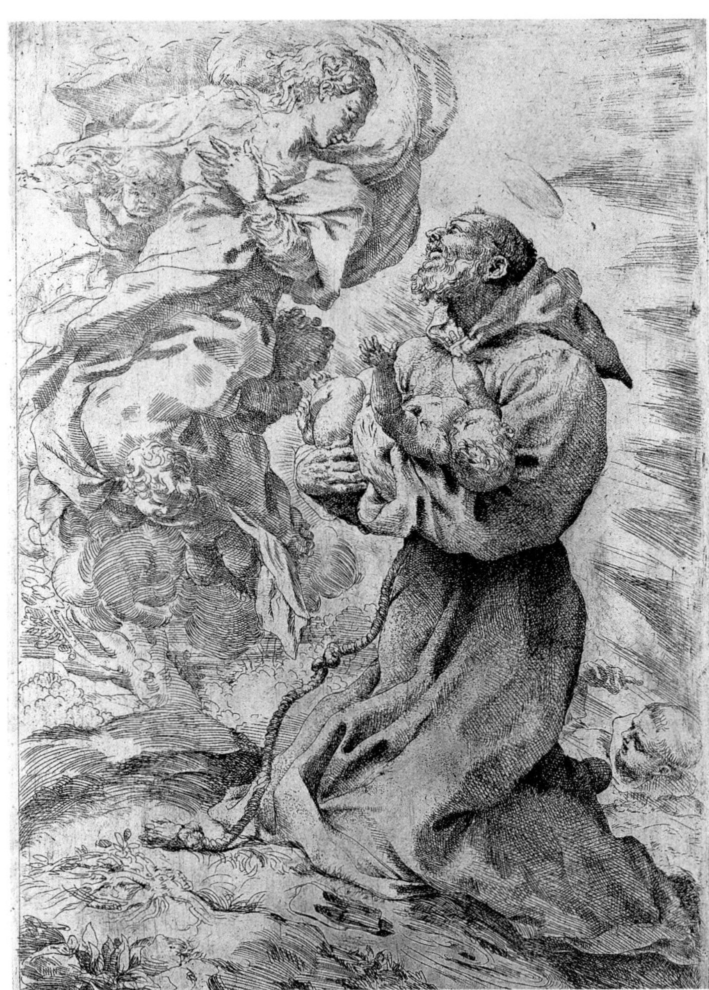

Fig. 136. Pietro Faccini, *St. Francis of Assisi Holding the Infant Christ in the Presence of the Virgin*, 1590s, etching with engraving

A Hendrik Goltzius
Mülbracht (now Bracht-am-Niederrhein), Westphalia 1558–1617 Haarlem, Netherlands
active Haarlem

T *Annunciation*
plate 1 (of 6) from the *Meesterstukjes* (*Little Masterpieces*) series; alternate title: the *Early Life of
the Virgin* series

D 1594

M engraving on medium-weight laid dark cream
paper, state 2 of 5

X sheet and image: 18 11/16 in. x 13 3/4 in. (475
mm x 350 mm)

S monogrammed and dated in plate: 'HG' in ligature above 'A. 1594'

I see checklist

C Museum purchase
1959.11

Though closely associated with the Haarlem
school of the Netherlands, Hendrick Goltzius
was born in Germany, the son of a stained glass
painter. In 1574 he apprenticed to Dirck Volkertsz. Coornhert (1522–90), an engraver in cop-
perplate, and followed him to Haarlem in 1577,
where he remained for the rest of his life. Though
he also worked at painting, his claim to fame is as
Europe's preeminent graphic artist, a reputation
he won through over 400 prints, most of which are
engravings. Before 1582, his work was published
by Philip Galle; but from 1582 onward Goltzius
published his own prints.

Goltzius's specialization in engraving was influenced by his own attempts, and those of fellow
artists, to distinguish art as an intellectual pursuit
and profession, as opposed to a craft activity. A tour
of Germany and Italy in 1590–91 made a significant impact on his work, which began to reflect
influences of the styles of Italian masters, especially
Raphael, Titian, Correggio, and Veronese.

The works that make up the *Early Life of the Vir-*

gin series are considered Goltzius's master engravings, his "*Meesterstukjes.*" Carried out after his
return from Italy, the series includes six plates—
the *Annunciation, Visitation, Adoration of the Shepherds, Adoration of the Magi, Circumcision,* and *Holy
Family with the Infant St. John*—and was dedicated
to Duke Wilhelm V of Bavaria. Wilhelm was a
Catholic and Goltzius's Marian iconography
reflects doctrines approved by the Council of
Trent. The *Annunciation,* although the first event
chronologically and the plate bearing the series's
dedicatory inscription, was the last of the five to be
engraved by Goltzius, in 1594.

Goltzius devised the series in part to display his
virtuosity in *teyckenconst,* the assimilation of the
styles of other masters. Each of the six plates imitates the style of another artist: Raphael, Parmigianino, Jacopo Bassano, Federico Barocci, Lucas
van Leyden, and Albrecht Dürer. These are not
mere copies, but works of Goltzius's own invention, created in the style of a renowned artist. The
dedication text, by Cornelieus Schongus, rector of
the Haarlem Latin school, compares Goltzius's
ability to mimic others to that of Proteus, a mythological deity famed for his powers of metamor-
phosis. The *Meesterstukjes' Annunciation* assimilates
the work of many Renaissance artists, including
Federigo Barrocci in the position of the angel
Gabriel, but Goltzius considered it his homage to
Raphael, particularly in the Madonna's sweetness
and grace.

Teyckenconst involved not only capturing the
style but also the burin-stroke or engraved line of
other artists—a very difficult feat. The seventeenth-century chronicler of Dutch art, Karel van
Mander, describes Goltzius playing a trick with
the two plates made after Dürer and Lucas van
Leyden:

With a heated burin [Goltzius] removed his
self-portrait and monogram [from the *Circumcision*], burnished the plate, and smoked several impressions, aging them as if they had

been in circulation for many years. This print
then traveled, disguised and in masquerade, to
Rome, Venice, Amsterdam, and elsewhere,
whereupon it was seen with astonishment and
delight by artists and knowledgeable collectors,
some of whom bought it at great cost, happy to
have gotten hold of a previously unknown work
by the Nuremberger [i.e., Dürer]. . . . The same
happened with the plate of the *Adoration of the
Magi* after Lucas. What was strangest was that
certain engravers, who thought themselves
expert at recognizing the rendering and burin-
stroke of the best masters, were themselves
deceived (Melion, p. 46).

Unlike other artists who strove to develop individual styles, Goltzius was most admired for his ability to
disguise rather than distinguish his enormous talent.

HILLARY L. ANDERSON '00

BIBLIOGRAPHY

Harcourt, Glenn, ed. *Hendrick Goltzius and the Classical Tradition*,
   exhibition catalogue. Los Angeles: Fisher Gallery, University
   of Southern California, 1992.

Melion, Walter S. *Shaping the Netherlandish Canon: Karel van Mander's Schilder-boeck*. Chicago: University of Chicago Press, 1991.

Reznicek, E. K. J. "Goltzius, Hendrick." In *Dictionary of Art*, ed.
   Jane Turner. New York: Grove, 1996, vol. 12, pp. 879–84.

Strauss, Walter L., ed. *Hendrik Goltzius 1558–1617: The Complete
   Engravings and Woodcuts*. New York: Abaris Books, 1977.

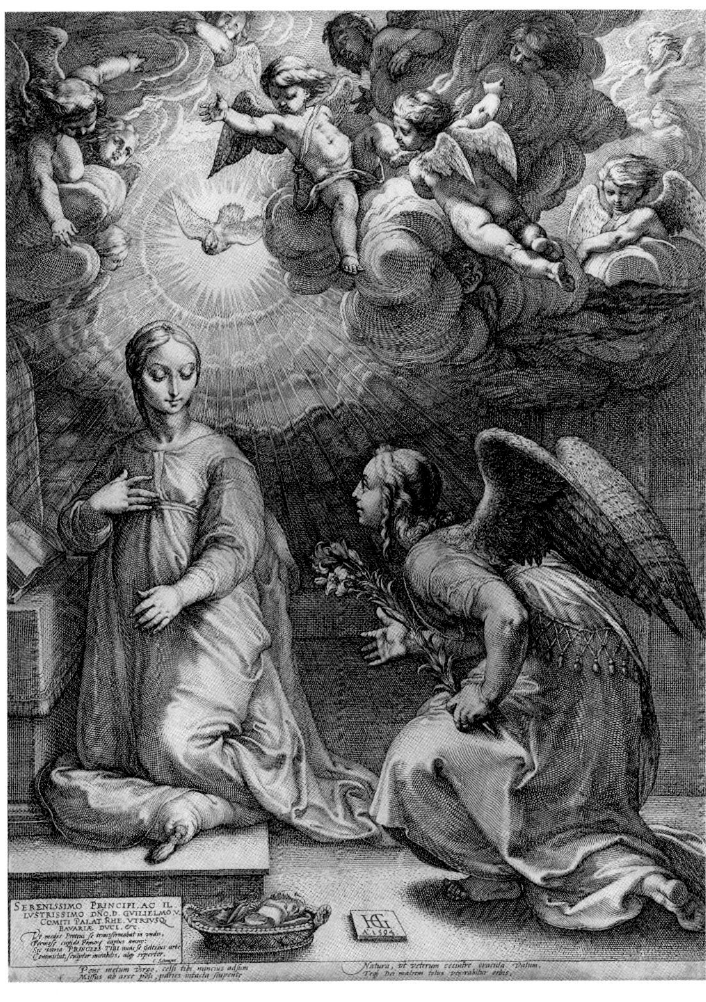

Fig. 137. Hendrik Goltzius, *Annunciation*, 1594, engraving

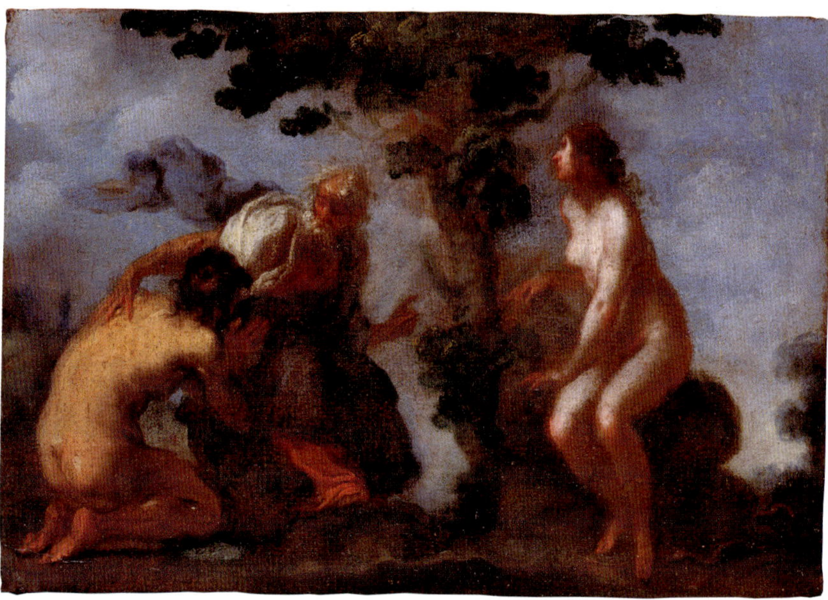

CAT. NO. 23

A Francesco Furini, called il Furino
Florence, Tuscany 1604–1646 Florence
active Florence and Rome

T *Adam and Eve*
sketch for an early 1630s painting now in the
Palazzo Pitti, Florence

D circa 1630

M oil on paper mounted to canvas

X 11 1/2 in. x 16 1/4 in. (29.2 cm x 41.3 cm)

C Anonymous gift
1938.2

Furini's interest in classical sculpture and admiration of the work of Michelangelo and Raphael are apparent in his work. Michelangelo he studied in the Medici collection in Florence, and Raphael he encountered in Rome, where he resided circa 1619 to 1624, after training with his father, Filippo Furini (called Pippo Sciamerone, active 1572–1514), and with Domenico Passignano (1559–1638) and Giovanni Bijlivert (1585–1644); the latter was part of a family of Dutch artists resident in Florence. Though in the 1630s Furini was ordained as a priest (serving by

1633 in a parish in the town of Mugello, just north of Florence), he continued his career as a painter and was considered one of Florence's leading interpreters of the female nude (Cappelletti, p. 846). Particularly admired are his 1630–1635 *Mary Magdalene* in Vienna's Kunsthistorisches Museum and his 1634 *Lot and His Daughters* in Madrid's Museo del Prado.

The museum's painting [fig. 138] is a sketch for one of Furini's best-known works, his *Adamo ed Eva nel Paradiso Terrestre* (*Adam and Eve in the Earthly Paradise*) dating from the early 1630s and now in the Galleria Palatina of the Palazzo Pitti [fig. 139].[1] Measuring over five feet tall and almost eight feet wide, the Pitti canvas reproduces on a grand scale this modest sketch. Furini's characteristic sensuality, highly refined painting style, and elegant treatment of figures are apparent in the Pitti work, whose Eve perches in anguish on a rock at left, excluded from the intimate union of Adam kneeling beside his creator, who extends a comforting arm. Between Eve and the hand of God the Father rests the tree that has been her downfall.

Executed in oil on paper (and later mounted to a canvas support), Wellesley's sketch has none

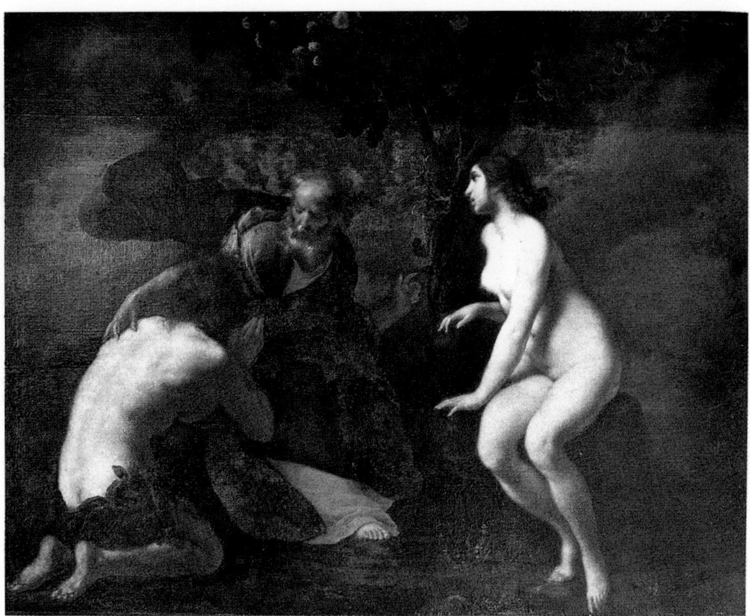

of the corporeality of Furini's finished composition, but it radiates a drama and sense of urgency lacking in the full-scale work. The two scenes are almost identical, indicating that the composition was well advanced in Furini's mind when he executed the preparatory sketch, but minute alterations between the two indicate much of Furini's thinking as he resolved a vigorous *bozzetto* into a subdued yet still moving scene of remorse and submission.

The angular flight of God the Father's flowing cape has been tamed into pliant circles, and the tendrils trimmed from Eve's hair, while Adam's naked form has been draped with a wreath of leaves.[2] God's forehead, once shaded by a thick thatch of hair, has receded to reveal a brow that conveys melancholy compassion for his fallen creatures. Above all, Furini tempered the blue background of the final painting to produce a filmy *sfumato* effect, while bathing Eve in a clear light that enhances her corporeality. The pale sapphire tones of the Wellesley sky, made all the more pure by a judicious cleaning on the occasion of this exhibition, weave in and out among the figures.[3] The daylight hope of the *bozzetto*, however, is balanced by the increased isolation of the figures,

particularly Eve, who looks with desolation across a gap—much wider than in the final rendition—at the Father who has forsaken her.

MELISSA R. KATZ

NOTES

1. The painting was produced for Bernardo Giunchi and acquired by the Grand Ducal collection in 1818; Gregori, p. 398. Furini is also represented in the Pitti by an allegorical cycle of frescos in the Sala degli Argenti.

2. Whether Adam has draped himself in shame at his newly discovered nudity, or has been aided in his modest intentions by the hand of a later restorer is uncertain. The leaves appear to be original.

3. Varnish thinned and replaced by Kate Olivier of the Straus Center for Conservation, Harvard University Art Museums, 2000.

BIBLIOGRAPHY

Cantelli, Giuseppe. *Repertorio della Pittura Fiorentina del Seicento.* Fiesole: Opus Libri, 1983, pp. 88–90, figs. 415–59.

Cappelletti, Francesca. "Furini, Francesco." In *Dictionary of Art,* ed. Jane Turner. New York: Grove, 1996, vol. 11, pp. 845–47.

Gregori, Mina. *Uffizi e Pitti: I Dipinte delle Gallerie Fiorentine.* Udine, Italy: Magnus Edizioni, 1994, p. 398, plate 572.

Gregori, Mina, and Erich Schleier, eds. *La Pittura in Italia: Il seicento.* Milan: 1989, vol. 1, pp. 315–16, and vol. 2, pp. 748–49.

Toesca, Elena. *Francesco Furini.* Rome: Tumminelli, 1950.

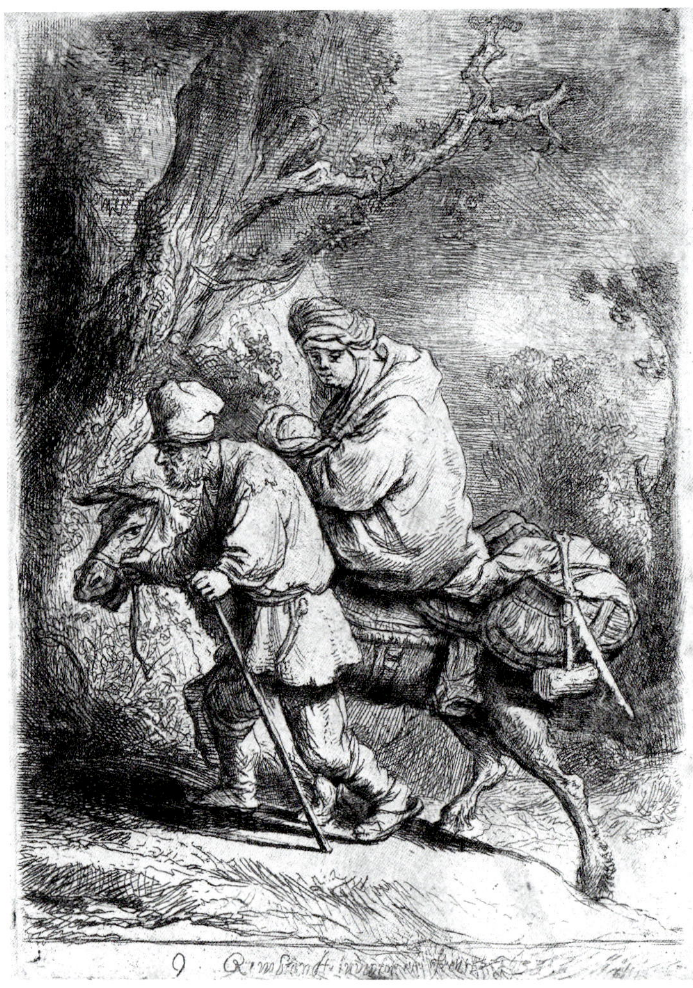

Fig. 140. Rembrandt, *Flight into Egypt (small plate)*, 1633, etching

CAT. NO. 24

A Rembrandt Harmenszoon Van Rijn
Leiden, Netherlands 1606–1669 Amsterdam
active Leiden and Amsterdam

T *Flight into Egypt (small plate)*

D 1633

M etching on medium-weight laid cream paper,
state 2 of 2

X plate: 3 1/2 in. x 2 1/2 in. (88 mm x 64 mm)
sheet: 3 11/16 in. x 2 11/16 in. (93 mm x 68 mm)

S signed and dated in plate: '9 Rembrandt·Inventor et fecit 1633'

C Gift of Mrs. Joseph Pendlebury (Katherine H. DeWolf, Class of 1922)
1984.21

Rembrandt's etching deals with the same biblical episode as Schongauer's engraving of the *Flight into Egypt* (cat. no. 5). In this print, however, the subject is stripped of its narrative and symbolic embellishments. The image conforms to the spare narrative offered in the Gospel of Matthew: after being warned by an angel to flee to Egypt to save the child from King Herod, Joseph "rose and took the child and his mother by night, and departed to Egypt" (Matt. 2:13–25). Rembrandt has chosen to depict the moment when the Holy Family seems just to be leaving the inn at Bethlehem, its light casting their shadows before them as they move into the darkness on the left.

Rather than presenting a scene of miraculous respite, as did Schongauer, Rembrandt conveys a sense of a dismal and arduous journey. Rembrandt deprives Mary and Joseph of stately grandeur, presenting them instead as poorly attired, misshapen "creatures of affliction." Even the donkey seems almost crushed by his heavy burden.

This vision of the Holy Family was in keeping with the Protestant emphasis on a literal interpretation of the Bible, which suggested the poverty and humbleness of Jesus and his earthly family. In Rembrandt's case, the roughness and inelegance in the appearance of the figures accords with a deliberate roughness and inelegance in pictorial form (Baldwin).[1] The scratched and scribbled lines of the etching needle are a far cry from the calligraphic gracefulness of Schongauer's carefully orchestrated strokes. Rembrandt's etched lines call to mind instead the graphic vocabulary he had developed in his early etchings of beggars and vagabonds. Still for all the "humbleness" of this etching, Rembrandt seems to have viewed it with some pride. One of the earliest works by the artist to bear his first name alone (in the tradition of Michelangelo), it is inscribed: "Rembrandt inventor et fecit. 1633" (White and Boon).[2]

MARGARET D. CARROLL

NOTES

1. The compatibility between Rembrandt's interpretation of the life of Christ and a Protestant tradition stressing Christ's lowliness has been widely recognized since at least the mid-nineteenth century.

2. White and Boon suggest that Rembrandt did not make the changes in the second state: "Background lightened by burnishing. Shading added in the upper background at the top of the tree. The Virgin's face and other places have been redrawn."

BIBLIOGRAPHY

Baldwin, Robert W. " 'On Earth we are as beggars, as Christ himself was.' The Protestant Background of Rembrandt's Imagery of Poverty, Disability, and Begging." *Konsthistorisk Tidskrift*, 54 (1985), pp. 122–35.

Hind, Arthur M. *A Catalogue of Rembrandt's Etchings, Chronologically Arranged and Completely Illustrated*, 2nd. ed. London: Methuen, 1923.

White, Christopher. *Rembrandt as an Etcher: A Study of the Artist at Work*. 2nd ed. New Haven, CT: Yale University Press, 1999.

White, Christopher, and Karel G. Boon. *Rembrandt's Etchings: An Illustrated Catalogue*, 2 vols. Amsterdam: Van Gendt, 1969.

CAT. NO. 25

A Circle of Bartholomeus Breenbergh
      Deventer, the Netherlands 1599–1659 Amsterdam
      active Rome and Amsterdam

T *Abraham Dismissing Hagar*

D 1630s

M oil on panel

X 15 in. x 12 5/16 in. (38.1 cm x 31.3 cm)

C Museum purchase with funds from bequest of
      Susan Pulitzer Freedberg (Class of 1953) and the
      New York Wellesley College Friends of Art
      1968.1

Hagar was the Egyptian maid of Sarai, wife of the biblical patriarch Abram, whose story is told in the Book of Genesis. After ten years of childless marriage, Sarai urges Abram to take Hagar, who eventually bears him Ishmael (Genesis 16, RSV). Thirteen years after the birth of Ishmael an angel appears and commands that he and his wife change their names to Abraham and Sarah; the angel also announces that Sarah will bear a son, Isaac (Gen. 17). After Isaac is born, Sarah demands that Abraham send Ishmael and Hagar away. Abraham is displeased, but God speaks to Abraham saying, "Be not displeased because of this . . . for through Isaac shall your descendants be named. And I will make a nation of the son of the slave woman also, because he is your offspring." Early the next morning, Abraham gives bread and water to Hagar and Ishmael and sends them away into the wilderness of Beersheba (Gen. 21:10–14).

The popularity of the story in seventeenth-century Dutch art may be explained on several grounds. In part, it had to do with the strong identification of the inhabitants of the newly created Dutch Republic—especially the 150,000 refugees who had recently resettled there from the Spanish Netherlands—with the "chosen people" of the Jewish Bible and the Christian Old Testament, who, guided by God, had journeyed to the Promised Land (Waal, pp. 22–23; Schama, pp. 93–125). This identification prompted requests for paintings that depicted episodes from the lives of the biblical patriarchs such as Abraham. The popularity of this particular story may have also been spurred by a demand for a new kind of religious painting, one less concerned with scenes of miracles and martyrdom (as adorned altars in Catholic churches) than with moments of psychological and moral complexity: scenes of family crisis, departure, separation, recognition, and reconciliation, which were suitable for displaying in Protestant homes (Tümpel, pp. 142–46).

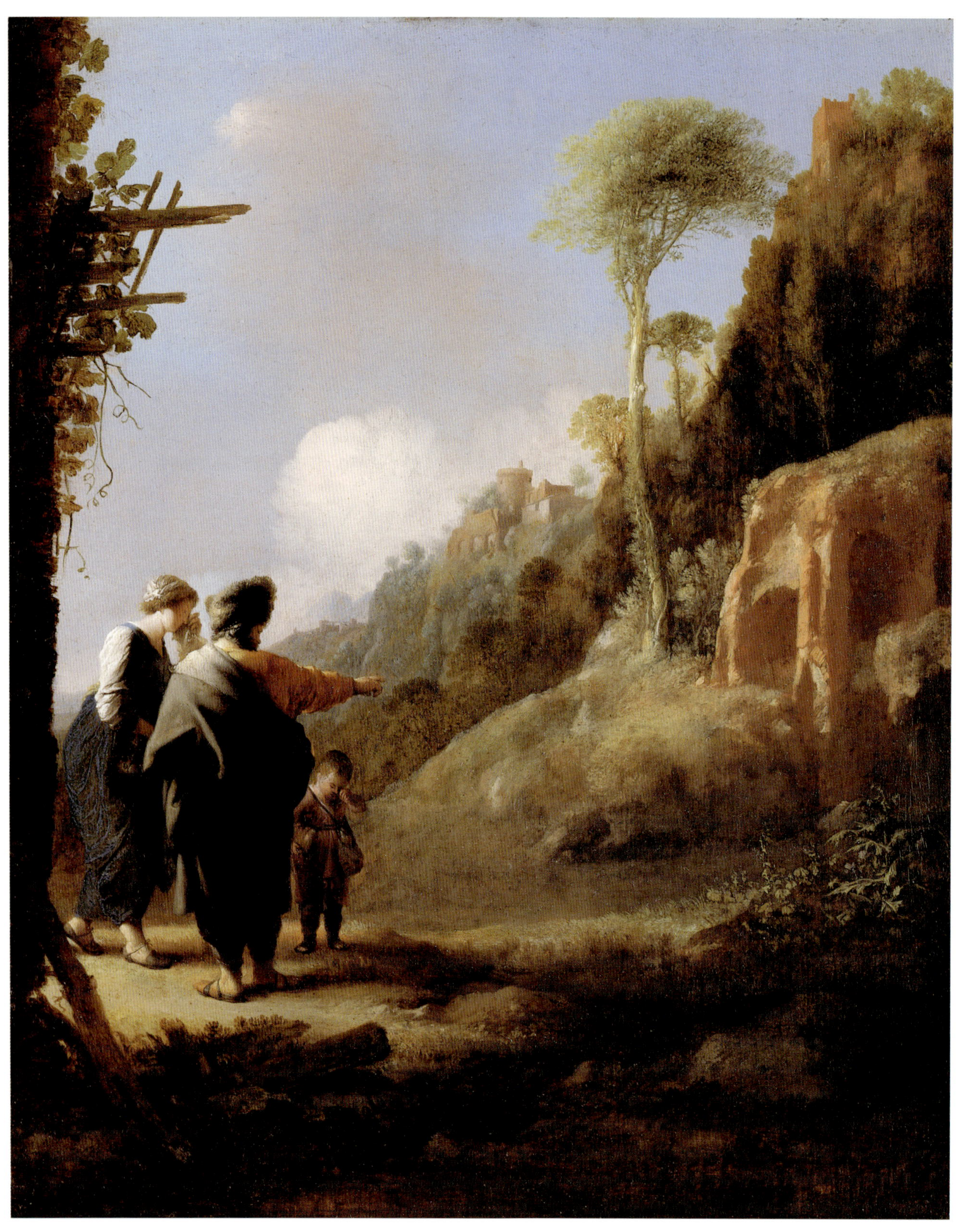

Breenbergh's subject might also have had specific appeal because it embodies themes that preoccupied seventeenth-century Dutch social and moral critics: the importance of the patriarchal family; and the need to distinguish between the rights of married and common-law wives, and between the rights of legitimate and illegitimate children.[1] In a country where many households included at least one maidservant, a recurrent theme in popular literature and the arts was the danger posed by maidservants to the well-being of the legitimate family. One need only think of the many genre paintings by Jan Steen of "unruly households" and of the figure of the flirtatious maid (Schama, pp. 455–60).[2]

Typically, depictions of Abraham dismissing Hagar engage the issue of the maidservant/mistress from a graver and more compassionate perspective. Works of art by Pieter Lastman (circa 1583–1633) and notably his pupil, Rembrandt (1609–69), draw attention to the human suffering that unfolds when the aging patriarch casts out his mistress and their son (Hamman, pp. 471–587). Wellesley's painting, possibly by a follower of the landscape painter, Bartholomeus Breenbergh (circa 1598/1600–57), draws upon that pictorial tradition; but this painting elicits a fresh interpretation of the story by underscoring the brutality of Abraham's action. Whereas Lastman and Rembrandt depict him in such a way that his face and gesture register his own suffering and feelings of attachment to the outcasts, this artist shows the shaded figure of Abraham from the back, with his arm outflung as he orders Hagar and the crying Ishmael to depart (Tümpel and Hecht, pp. 24–25).[3]

In the Wellesley panel the figures are set in front of a landscape with ruins, similar in style to the "Italianate" Dutch landscapes of Breenbergh and Cornelis Poelenbergh (1586 or 1596–1667). Though at the time of its acquisition in 1968, *Abraham Dismissing Hagar* was thought to have been painted by Breenbergh, its attribution has more recently been doubted (Blankert, p. 87; Roethlisberger, p. 103).[4] Unusual for Breenbergh is the upright format, the relatively large scale of the figures within the composition, and the way in which the figures block a view into the distant background.

MARGARET D. CARROLL

NOTES

1. On attitudes toward the family in the Dutch Republic, see Schama, pp. 398–480.

2. Maids made pregnant by their employers could be evicted from the house and were often forced into a life of prostitution; Schama, pp. 476–80.

3. Pieter Lastman, *Expulsion of Hagar*, 1612, oil on panel (Kunsthalle, Hamburg). Rembrandt, *Expulsion of Hagar*, etching, dated 1637 (Bartsch 30).

4. Blankert: "Attributed to Breenbergh, yet, especially in the figures, not entirely compatible with his style" [author's translation]. Roethlisberger: "Differs from Breenbergh in the composition, the figures, the soft, undulating ground and the handling."

BIBLIOGRAPHY

Blankert, Albert. *Nederlandse 17e eeuwse Italianiserende landschapschilders (Dutch 17th Century Italianate Landscape Painters)*. Soest, Netherlands: Davaco, 1978, no. 32.

Hamman, Richard. "Hagar's Abschied bei Rembrandt und im Rembrandt-Kreise." *Marburger Jahrbuch*, vol. 8–9, 1936.

Roethlisberger, Marcel. *Bartholomeus Breenbergh: The Paintings*. Berlin: De Gruyter, 1981, no. 316.

Schama, Simon. *The Embarassment of Riches: An Interpretation of Dutch Culture in the Golden Age*. New York: Knopf, 1987.

Tümpel, Astrid, and Peter Hecht. *Pieter Lastman: Leermeester van Rembrandt (Pieter Lastman: The Man Who Taught Rembrandt)*, exhibition catalogue, Rembrandthuis, Amsterdam. Zwolle, Netherlands: Waanders, 1991.

Tümpel, Christian. "The Iconography of the Pre-Rembrandtists." In *The Pre-Rembrandtists*, ed. Astrid Tümpel, exhibition catalogue. Sacramento, CA: E. B. Crocker Art Gallery, 1974.

Waal, Henri van de. *Drie eeuwen vaderlandsche geschied-uitbeelding 1500–1800: Een iconologische studie*, 2 vols. 'S-Gravenhage, Netherlands: M. Nijhoff, 1952.

Fig. 141. Circle of Bartholomeus Breenbergh, *Abraham Dismissing Hagar*, 1630s, oil on panel

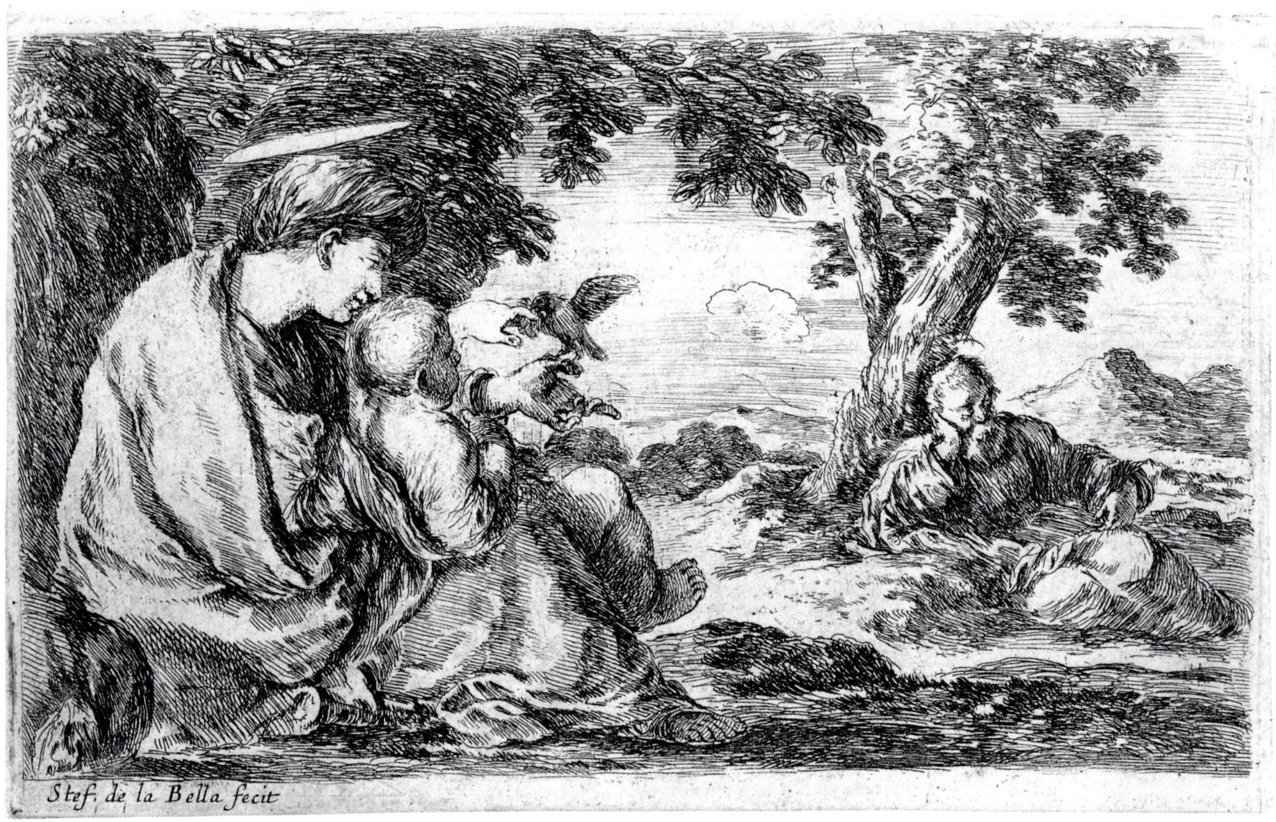

Fig. 142. Stefano
della Bella, *Rest on
the Flight into Egypt*,
pre-1642, etching

CAT. NO. 26

A Stefano della Bella
Florence, Tuscany 1610–64 Florence
active Florence, Rome, and Paris
printed in Paris by Pierre Mariette

T *Rest on the Flight into Egypt*

D before 1642

M etching on cream laid paper, state 1 of 4

X sheet and image: 3 1/4 in. x 5 3/8 in. (82 mm x
137 mm)
mount: 7 7/16 in. x 12 inches (189 mm x 304 mm)

S signed in plate: ' Stef de la Bella fecit'

C Gift of Mrs. Toivo Laminan (Margaret Chamberlin, Class of 1929)
1962.14.1 (illustrated)

and an additional etching of the *Flight into
Egypt*, 1981.76
(see checklist for cataloguing)

In Wellesley's two prints, Stefano della Bella uses
the popular subject of moments from the Holy
Family's flight into Egypt as a vehicle for experimenting with his interest in naturalistic landscape
studies. In the *Flight into Egypt*, he places the figure
group at the center of the composition, with St.
Joseph leading the donkey bearing the Virgin and
Child. They travel through a wooded landscape in
which the details of foliage are as carefully executed as the details of the costumes and facial
expressions. In the *Rest on the Flight into Egypt*, the
Virgin and Child are seated on the ground at the
left of the composition, playing with a small bird
that alights on the Virgin's outstretched hand; St.
Joseph relaxes with a book, lying beneath a tree in
the background at right [fig. 142].

Stefano was born in Florence in 1610 and studied first with a goldsmith; he was later sent to study
with a painter because of his demonstrated skill as
a draftsman. As a young artist he became attached

to the Medici court in Florence and then in Rome. While in Rome, rather than studying only antiquities and the work of older masters, he spent much of his time filling sketchbooks with on-the-spot studies from nature and everyday life. Stefano sketched out-of-doors, often in the Roman countryside, focusing his attention on the landscape and vignettes of peasants and travelers. He used bits and pieces of these sketchbook drawings in many of his later prints, such as these two scenes from the Flight into Egypt narrative.

Stefano traveled to Paris in the 1640s, where he continued to observe nature and perfect his craft as a printmaker, eventually returning to Florence. During his long career he was extremely prolific, producing hundreds of prints, large and small, for all markets, some of which depicted warriors and costumed figures—types he encountered in Paris and Rome, and in the prints of other well-known artists, like Rembrandt.

Perhaps because he was mainly interested in observing and recording the everyday world around him, Stefano produced relatively few prints of religious subjects. In his images of the Virgin and Child, he often presents the holy figures in a manner more like the peasants and gypsies he sketched on his travels. His figures are less idealized than those of the Renaissance masters who preceded him; they usually appear in casual poses, with naturalistic features, softly portrayed with delicately etched lines. In the *Flight into Egypt*, the Holy Family could be a band of traveling peasants in the countryside on the outskirts of Rome, a common subject for Stefano's sketchbooks. Indeed, the wooded landscape setting seems to have no relationship to the desert conditions of the Holy Land where St. Joseph received the warning from God's angel to leave Bethlehem to escape Herod's massacre of newborn children. In the *Rest on the Flight into Egypt*, the figures relax in a bucolic landscape, where the artist's interest seems to be more on the depiction of leaves, grass, and sunlight than on the drama of the surrounding events.

LISA MCDERMOTT

BIBLIOGRAPHY

Ballerini, Paola, et al. *Jacques Callot, Stefano Della Bella, dalle collezioni di stampe della Biblioteca degli Intronati di Sienna*, exhibition catalogue. Florence: Centro Di, 1976.

Massar, Phyllis Dearborn. *Presenting Stefano della Bella, Seventeenth-Century Printmaker*. New York: Metropolitan Museum of Art, 1971.

Reed, Sue Welsh, and Richard W. Wallace. *Italian Etchers of the Renaissance and Baroque*. Boston: Museum of Fine Arts, 1989, pp. 234–43.

CAT. NO. 27

A Carlo Antonio Sacchi
Pavia, Lombardy 1616/17–1707 Pavia
active Pavia, Rome, and Venice

T *Adoration of the Shepherds (after Tintoretto)*
copy of a 1579–81 painting by Tintoretto, now in the Scuola di San Rocco, Venice

D 1649

M etching strengthened with burin on medium-weight textured laid buff paper, state 1 of 1

X sheet and image: 20 3/16 in. x 15 3/16 in. (512 mm x 385 mm)

S signed in plate, lower right: 'Carolus Saccus Papiensis Scalp.'

I see Checklist

C Museum purchase
1988.2

Carlo Sacchi's etching, *Adoration of the Shepherds*, is a reverse reproduction of a painting by Tintoretto (Jacopo Robusti, 1519–94), which hangs in the Sala Grande of the Scuola di San Rocco in Venice. The composition is divided

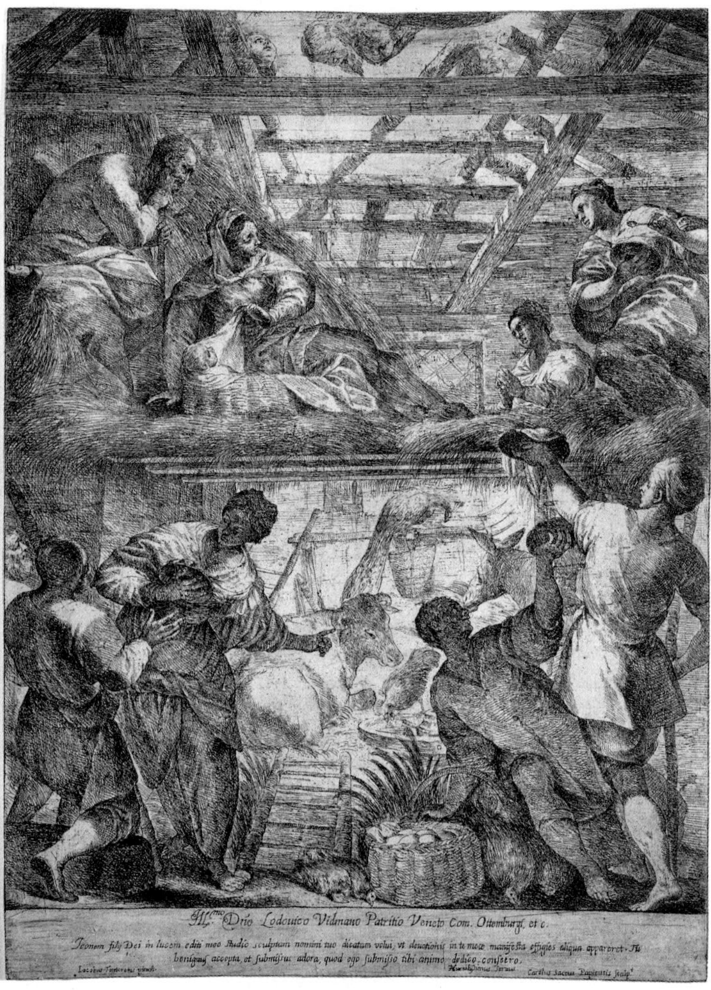

Fig. 143. Carlo Sacchi, *Adoration of the Shepherds* (after Tintoretto), 1649, etching with engraving

horizontally into two scenes. In the upper half, we find the holy family in a loft. Mary and Joseph, seated behind the sleeping Christ child, present him to the visitors who approach from the right. In the lower half, shepherds enter the stable and kneel down with their animals. Although biblically the annunciation of Christ's birth to the shepherds precedes the account of the nativity, artistic representations often combine the two scenes. After being startled by the angels' announcement, the shepherds travel to Bethlehem to find the Christ Child lying in a manger. The arrival of the shepherds parallels that of the three wise men and indicates Christ's recognition by men of high rank and humble stature.

Sacchi was trained by Carlo Antonio Rossi (circa 1581–1648), a Milanese painter working in Pavia's cathedral. Sacchi continued his studies during his travels to Venice and Rome. He is documented as being in Venice in 1649, the year in which this etching was made, and in Rome in 1664, though there may have been additional travels. Rather than developing a style of his own, Sacchi appears to have been heavily influenced by the work of other artists, particularly the Venetian painter Veronese (1528–88) and the Roman school. Sacchi was primarily a painter, and the majority of his career was spent in his native Pavia, where he painted primarily for churches. The Carmelites often commissioned his work for their churches.

Sacchi's total oeuvre of etchings comprises only ten prints. While in Venice he executed two large etchings, the *Adoration of the Shepherds* after Tintoretto and *Adoration of the Magi* after Veronese. These are the most widely circulated and best documented of his prints. It is presumed that the two were executed around the same time, and the date of the *Adoration of the Shepherds* is based on that of the *Adoration of the Magi* and the documentation about his stay in Venice. Sacchi's eight other known etchings depict scenes from Pavese history. They were most likely commissioned by Ottavio Ballada, an influential Pavese citizen who was known to request works of such subject matter.

HILLARY L. ANDERSON '00

BIBLIOGRAPHY

Bellini, Paolo, ed. *Italian Masters of the Seventeeth Century: The Illustrated Bartsch*, vol. 46, part 2. New York: Abaris, 1982–85, pp. 133–35.

Valsecchi, Marco. *Scuola di San Rocco: Tintoretto*. Novara, Italy: Istituto Geografico De Agostini, 1965.

Reed, Sue Welsh, and Richard W. Wallace. *Italian Etchers of the Renaissance and Baroque*. Boston: Museum of Fine Arts, 1989.

Thieme, Ulrich, and Felix Becker. "Carlo Sacchi." *Allgemeines Lexikon der bildenden Kunstler von der Antike bis zur Gegenwart*. Leipzig, Germany: W. Engelmann, 1907–50, vol. 29, p. 291.

A Salvator Rosa
Aranella (near Naples), Kingdom of the Two
Sicilies 1615–73 Rome
active Naples, Rome, and Florence

T *Three Marys at the Sepulchre*

D circa 1665

M oil on canvas

X 53 in. x 38 in. (134.6 cm x 96.5 cm)

C Gift of Dr. and Mrs. Arthur K. Solomon
1959.42

Salvator Rosa was born in Naples but spent most of his creative years in Rome, where he was a successful albeit highly individualistic participator in the flourishing artistic life of the papal city. He enjoyed considerable fame during his lifetime, but it was modest in comparison to his tremendous popularity with the romantics of the late eighteenth and early nineteenth centuries. His romantic admirers were overwhelmed by the dramatic power of his turbulent landscapes and unorthodox figure pictures and came to see Rosa as a symbol of free inspired creativity, "one who, in his flashing eye, mobile brow, and rapid movement—all fire, feeling, and perception—was the very personification of genius itself," to quote Lady Morgan's colorful biography of 1824. After this surge of intense popularity, his pictures and reputation suffered a long period of neglect. Only in recent years has an attempt has been made to restore him to his rightful position as a major figure in seventeenth-century art, especially landscape painting.

The Wellesley picture with its dramatic light effects, ominous and shadowy background cliff, and sunrise streaked sky is typical of Rosa's treatment of his larger figure compositions. As so often happens with seventeenth-century paintings, including several by Salvator Rosa, there is an exact replica of the Wellesley picture in the Ringling Museum, Sarasota, Florida. There can be no question that the basic conception of *The Three Marys at the Sepulchre* is Rosa's, since a splendid drawing for the composition by Salvator's own hand exists in the British Museum's collection of prints and drawings.

Both the Wellesley and Sarasota versions have suffered with time and show characteristic darkening and wear in the thinly painted dark areas, and indications of repainting in some of the better preserved passages. This necessarily makes the problems of connoisseurship considerably more difficult and suggest a flexible approach is the soundest one. Keeping this in mind, it seems rea-

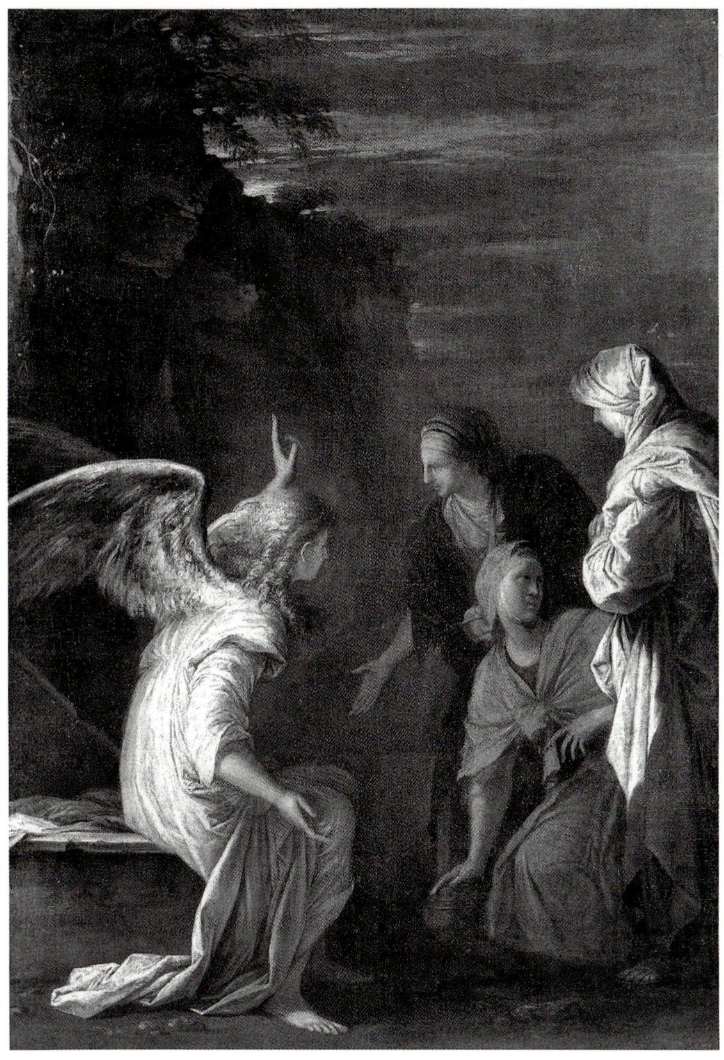

Fig. 144. Salvator Rosa, *Three Marys at the Sepulchre*, ca. 1665, oil on canvas

sonable to conclude that both the Sarasota and
Wellesley paintings are by Rosa himself.

RICHARD W. WALLACE

Reprinted from the *Catalogue of European and American Sculptures
and Paintings at Wellesley College*, 2nd ed., pp. 119–20.

BIBLIOGRAPHY

Morgan, Lady (Sydney). *The Life and Times of Salvator Rosa.* London: H. Colburn, 1824.

Scott, Jonathan. *Salvator Rosa: His Life and Times.* New Haven, CT:
Yale University Press, 1995.

Wallace, Richard W. "The Genius of Salvator Rosa." *Art Bulletin*,
47, no. 4 (December 1965).

Wallace, Richard W. *Salvator Rosa in America*, exhibition catalogue. Wellesley, MA: Wellesley College Museum, Jewett Arts
Center, 1979.

CAT. NO. 29

A Claudine Bouzonnet Stella
Lyons, France 1636–97 Paris
active Lyons and Paris

T *Calvary (after Poussin)*
copy of a circa 1645–46 painting by Nicolas
Poussin, now in the Wadsworth Atheneum,
Hartford, Connecticut

D 1674

M etching with engraving on two sheets (seamed
vertically) of medium-weight laid cream paper,
state 1 of 2

X image: 22 in. x 30 7/8 in. (556 mm x 781 mm)
sheet: 22 3/8 in. x 31 5/8 in. (571 mm x 803 mm)

I see checklist

C Museum purchase
1993.6

This engraving faithfully reproduces a painting by Nicolas Poussin (1594–1665), the
French classical painter who spent much of his
career in Rome. It was engraved by Claudine
Bouzonnet Stella, daughter of the goldsmith Eti-
enne Bouzonnet and niece of the great engraver
Jacques Stella (1596–1657). Claudine Bouzonnet
(1636–97) moved from her native Lyons to Paris
to study the art of engraving with her uncle, and
took his name in homage to his influence. Jacques
Stella was also a great friend of Poussin. *Le Calvaire (Calvary)* was commissioned in 1644 by
French president Jacques de Thou, but at some
point Poussin gave the painting to Jacques Stella
who subsequently bequeathed it to Claudine.
Once in her possession, Claudine refused to sell
the painting, even when offered five thousand
gold coins by a king. Poussin's original painting
now resides in the Wadsworth Atheneum, in Hartford, Connecticut.

Jacques Stella provided artistic training for all
four of his sister Madeleine Bouzonnet's children.
Claudine was trained as an engraver, and her siblings Antoine (1637–82), François (1638–
91/92), and Antoinette (1641–76) as painters.
Such cultivation of female talent was rare at the
time, as was the quality of work that Claudine
achieved in her etchings. Jacques's decision to
leave the contents of his studio to Claudine may
have indicated his approval of the skills she
acquired in etching and engraving under his
tutelage.

Although she never produced original compositions, Claudine's reproductions of her
uncle's and Poussins's work are admired for their
quality and exceptional craftsmanship. In the
technique of printmaking, whatever is drawn on
the metal plate appears reversed in the image
printed on paper. Traditionally, prints that reproduce paintings show the original image in
reverse. For example, Carlo Sacchi's *Adoration of
the Shepherds* (cat. no. 27) [fig. 143], is based on
a Tintoretto painting that depicted the Holy
Family on the right, not on the left as they
appear in Sacchi's print. Claudine Bouzonnet

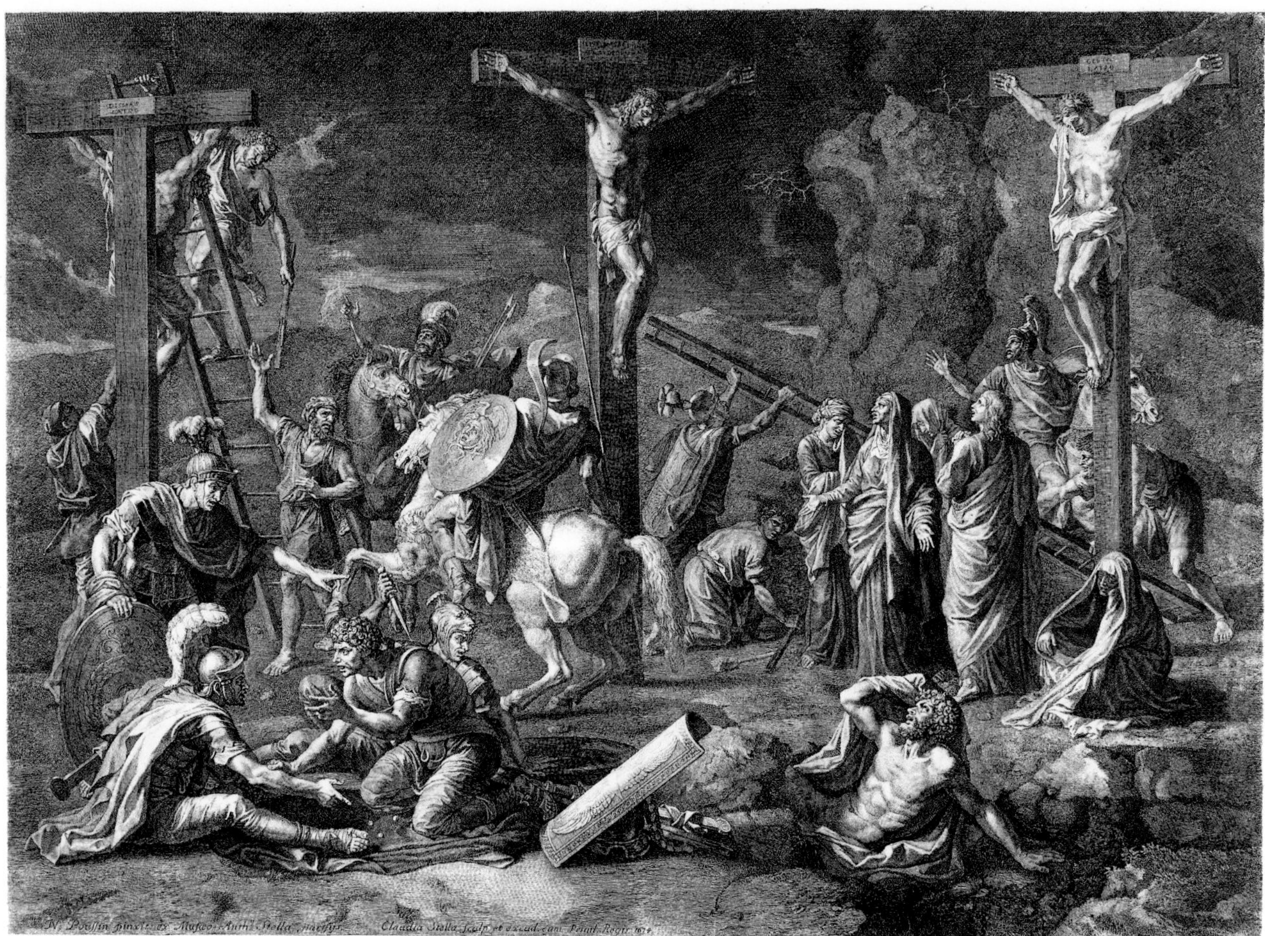

Stella, however, was one of few engravers to take on the challenge of reproducing a painting as it actually appeared, without reversing the image in the print.

The composition designed by Poussin and engraved by Bouzonnet Stella features a detailed scene of the crucifixion of Christ on the hill of Calvary on the outskirts of Jerusalem. It closely follows the description given in the Gospel of John 19:16–34, including the two thieves crucified alongside Jesus, the women weeping by the cross, the piercing of Christ's side with a lance, and the Roman soldiers casting dice to see who wins his garments. The description of a man rising out of the grave, in the foreground, however, comes from Matthew 27:52. He is often identified as Adam, the first man, who since early Christian times was thought to have been buried on the hill of Calvary.

Poussin's rendition of the crucifixion has been described as "devoid of all hope" (Verdi, p. 267). The Virgin Mary appears to the right of the center of the composition, within a circle of chaotic figures, horses, and soldiers, yet achieves prominence amidst the turmoil. The clouds overhead mimic her pose, Adam rises up at her feet, and the ground in front of her is left as open space, thus giving a spotlight to her figure. Her gaze of questioning pain, underscored by the diagonal of a ladder, connects the Virgin Mary to her crucified Son. The Hartford painting, due to problems with the original technique, has become significantly darker, and many elements are less legible. Thanks to Stella's engraving of *Le Calvaire*, viewers

Fig. 145 . Claudine Bouzonnet Stella, *Crucifixion* (after Poussin), 1674, etching with engraving

can fully encounter both the talent of a seventeenth-century female artist and the intricacies of
Mary's devastation within the tempestuous scene.

HILLARY L. ANDERSON '00

and

BLAIR A. BROOKS '02

BIBLIOGRAPHY

Blunt, Anthony. *Nicolas Poussin. The A. W. Mellon Lectures in the
Fine Arts, 7.* New York: Pantheon Books, 1967.

Kerspern, S. "Bouzonnet Stella." In *Allgemeines Künstler-Lexikon,*
ed. Gunter Meissner. Munich: K. G. Saur Verlag, 1996, vol.
13, pp. 422–23.

Verdi, Richard. *Nicolas Poussin 1594–1665,* exhibition catalogue.
London: Royal Academy of Arts, 1995, cat. no. 57, pp.
257–58.

Weigert, Roger-Armand. *Inventaire du fonds Français: Graveurs du
XVIIe siècle.* Bibliothèque Nationale Cabinet des Estampes.
Paris: Bibliothèque Nationale, 1939.

Wildenstein, Georges. "Les graveurs de Poussin au XVII siècle."
Gazette des Beaux Arts (Sept. 1955), no. 67, p. 192.

CAT. NO. 30

A Giuseppe Maria Crespi, called lo Spagnuolo
Bologna, Papal States 1665–1747 Bologna
active Bologna and Florence

T *Sacrament of Ordination*
sketch for one of a series of seven paintings
now in the Gemäldegalerie, Dresden

D before 1712

M oil on canvas

X 14 3/4 in. x 11 1/2 in. (37.5 cm x 29.2 cm)

C Museum purchase
1948.3

Although represented in paintings by Magnasco, Francesco de Mura, Marco Ricci, and
Trevisani, and in a dozen drawings, the art of
eighteenth-century Italy is best shown at Wellesley
by Crespi's only existing sketch for a major work.[1]
Crespi stood somewhat apart from the tradition of
his native Bologna, where the academic-classicizing
manner of the Carracci still ruled the High
Baroque and continued into the local Late
Baroque. He transformed the High Baroque
toward the Rococo in a way similar to what was
being done in Venice and Northern Europe. His
innate interest in pictorial drama and expression,
in contrast to the Carracci's emphasis on form,
made him turn to other sources, above all to the
Venetians. As early as the 1690s he made the Venetian coloristic vision his own. He studied not only
Titian and Veronese but also the work of two
adopted Venetians, Feti and Liss. Crespi soon
found even greater kinship and stimulus in the art
of a fellow Bolognese, Guercino, who two generations before had also taken a position slightly outside the main traditions of Bolognese painting.
Guercino had sought a more pictorial manner,
though not by the Venetian use of color so much as
by the use of light, defining his forms in a more
Caravaggesque way.

It is this selectively dramatized light and deep
shadow which has led some critics to link Crespi
with Rembrandt. Unlike that of the tonal painting
of Holland, however, Crespi's chiaroscuro is
largely meant to define forms in space. While his
near-monochrome might suggest analogies to
some Dutch seventeenth-century painting, the
sense of form remains as traditionally Italian as do
his gestures, facial expressions, and compositional
devices: all of these are far from Rembrandt.

The concentrated sensuous visual enjoyment
that is a major common denominator of the art of
the seventeenth and eighteenth centuries has dis-
turbed many laymen and some professional historians of art for several generations: some even now
feel their way into Baroque art barred by their dis-
trust of what is felt rather than thought. Yet it is

precisely the element of the sensuous that enabled Crespi—specifically in the great series of the Sacraments in Dresden—to represent for one of the last times in Western art a religious scene with full inner conviction and feeling. Shortly before the decisive break in Western thought that came in the later eighteenth century, Crespi presented religious dogma with a seriousness and intensity that carry conviction to the present day. Even the Soviet historian, Lasareff [*sic*], could write of the Dresden series, "Although most of the scenes are conceived as pure genre, the general style of execution is of such a serious character that they are raised to the level of true religious art, the roots of which lie deeply embedded in the human soul," and "this cycle of pictures marks the culminating point not only of Crespi's artistic development, but also of *seicento* painting as a whole" (Lazarev, pp. 92–95).

The translation to the larger size in the Dresden pictures gave a degree of formality that stresses even more the solemnity of the rite. The Wellesley sketch differs from the Dresden series not only in size, but also in choice of colors. Not only smaller, but limited to the smallest intervals between a range of olive-browns to tan and one of gray to silvery white, it compensates for these restrictions by a spontaneity of brushwork and a feeling of intimacy without loss of monumentality.

CURTIS H. SHELL

Reprinted from the *Catalogue of European and American Sculptures and Paintings at Wellesley College,* 2nd ed., pp. 46–48.

NOTE

1. Professor Shell's observation remains accurate to date. In the ensuing decades, paintings related to the the *Sacraments* series have come to light, including a *Sacrament of Ordination* catalogued as "Studio of Giovanni [*sic*] Maria Crespi" and auctioned at Sotheby's, London in the 14 March 1980 Old Master Paintings sale 4349 (lot 23). Small studies of five images from the Dresden series were auctioned at Christie's, London 22 April 1994, as studio works or studies after Crespi; these, however did not include a scene of the *Sacrament of Ordination.* In addition, a set of five French eighteenth-century copies after Crespi (including the *Sacrament of Ordination*) were auctioned at Christie's East, New York as lot 21 in the sale of 25 November 1988.

BIBLIOGRAPHY

Lazarev, Viktor Nikitich. "Studies on Giuseppe Maria Crespi." *Art in America,* 17 (1929), pp. 92–95.

Merriman, Mira Pajes. *Giuseppe Maria Crespi.* Milan: Rizzoli, 1980.

Spike, John T. *Giuseppe Maria Crespi and the Emergence of Genre Painting in Italy.* Fort Worth, TX: Kimbell Art Museum, 1986.

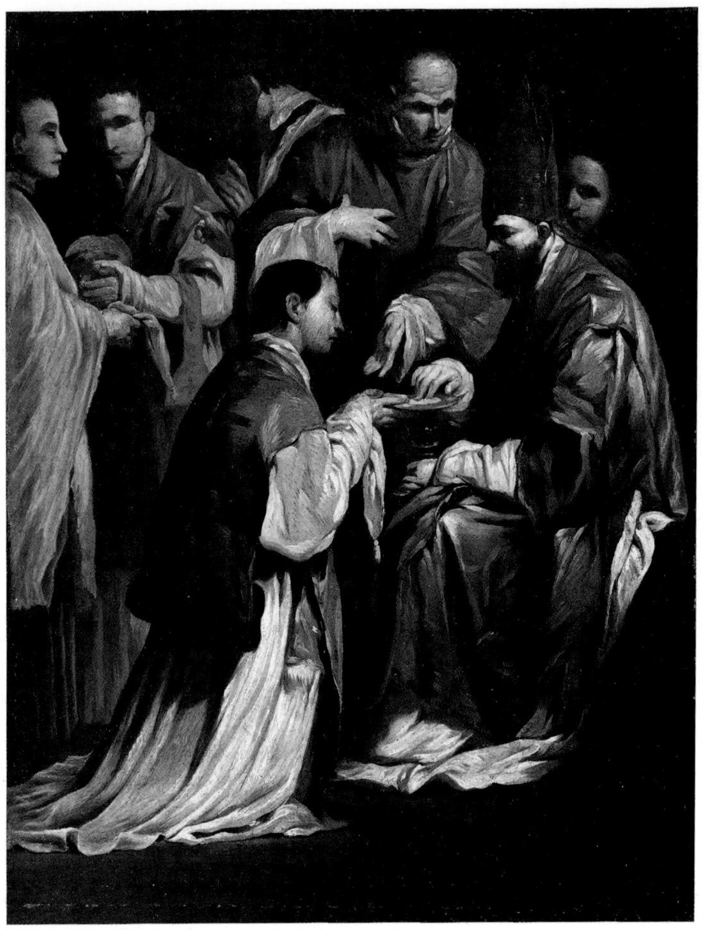

Fig. 146. Giuseppe Ma. Crespi, *Sacrament of Ordination,* pre-1712, oil on canvas

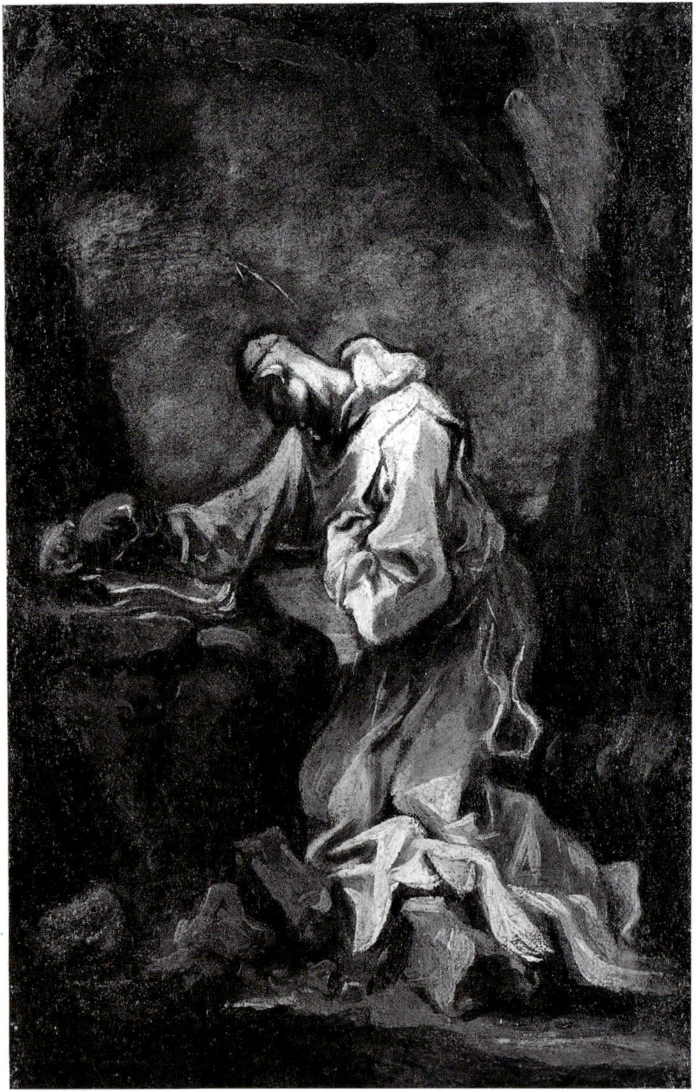

CAT. NO. 31

A Alessandro Magnasco, called il Lissandrino
Genoa, Republic of Genoa 1667–1749 Genoa
active Genoa, Florence, and Milan

T *Monastic Saint in Meditation*

D 1720s

M oil on canvas

X 16 15/16 in. x 10 15/16 in. (43.0 cm x 27.8 cm)

I see checklist

C Museum purchase
1949.14

In his scenes of popular life, pastorals, and encampments, his thieves', gypsies', and witches' dens, or his views of ruins and shipwrecks, Magnasco fills the air with a charged energy: sometimes the violence of nature and sometimes the violence of human character or condition. Even his religious pictures, more often showing the activities of monks or nuns than the usual sacred scenes, suggest violent physical and psychic activity. Little may actually be happening, but the glints of light and gashes of shadow of his brushstrokes make us sense activity even when none is specifically represented.

Magnasco painted many pictures of monks, often of a whole company of them scattered through a wild landscape in a sort of Baroque thebaid. A number of small pictures probably from the middle years of his career (ours, one in the Corsini Gallery in Rome, one in the Mauritshuis [the Hague], and one belonging to Sir Osbert Sitwell, for example) represent solitary white-robed monks in ecstatic meditation. (St. Ignatius had long ago given directions for achieving ecstasy by fixed staring at a skull or crucifix in a dim half-light.) St. Bruno is commonly shown in the white habit of a Carthusian contemplating a crucifix in a rocky landscape symbolic of the jagged wilderness where he founded the Grande Chartreuse. Our figure is robed in white and is in a rocky chasm, but as he contemplates a skull and not a crucifix, he must be some hermit saint, Carthusian or Camaldolesian, rather than St. Bruno. He is really contemplating the idea of death, tangibly represented by the skull.

The actual painting, as almost always with Magnasco, is extraordinarily skillful, even virtuoso. The highlights zigzag in a sort of crumpled ribbon of light charged with an uncanny potential energy. Transparent gleams and a vaporous sky contrast dramatically with the kinetic angular activity of the paint, which makes the light on the figure. As so often, very few pigments are used: only black, deep umber, white, and blue.

The rapid but sure sketchiness of the brush-work and its extraordinary evocation of forms, moving or about to move, give such pictures a "handwriting" that one would think easy to identify. Magnasco, however, was "lost"—like Vermeer and El Greco—for over a century, and his pictures were attributed to masters as varied as Callot, El Greco, Goya, Hals, Marco Ricci, Ribera, and Tiepolo. He was reconstituted as an artistic personality just before World War I, and attracted enthusiastic collectors with surprising speed: in London they even formed a *Magnasco Society.*

JOAN C. SIEGFRIED

Reprinted from the *Catalogue of European and American Sculptures and Paintings at Wellesley College,* 2nd ed., pp. 77–78.

BIBLIOGRAPHY

Bulletin of the Worcester Museum, 14, no. 4 (1924), pp. 91–96.

Durlacher Brothers. *A loan exhibition of Paintings by Alessandro Magnasco 1667–1749,* exhibition catalogue. New York: Durlacher, 1940, cat. no. 15, plate 40.

Geiger, Benno. *Magnasco.* Bergamo, Italy: Istituto Italiano d'arti Grafiche, 1949, pp. 153–54, plate 281. [Erroneously listed as Worcester Art Museum.]

Muti, Laura, and Daniele de Sarno Prignano. *Alessandro Magnasco.* Faenza, Italy: Edit Faenza, 1994, cat. no. 393, fig. 460, pp. 267 and 619. [Listed as Worcester Art Museum.]

CAT. NO. 32

A François Boucher
   Paris, France 1703–1770 Paris
   active Paris and Rome

T *Sacrifice of Isaac*

D 1720s

M black chalk with white chalk highlights on
   medium-weight laid buff paper

X sheet: 14 3/8 in. x 12 in. (365 mm x 305 mm)
   mount: 16 3/8 x 13 5/8 (340 mm x 346 mm)

I inscribed in pencil (not original): 'Boucher'

C Anonymous gift
   1969.13

At first glance, this chalk drawing of the *Sacrifice of Isaac* seems out of keeping with the work of François Boucher, celebrated rococo artist known for his delicate coqueteries and pastoral landscapes dotted with languid shepherds. A survey of his extensive drawings corpus, however, suggests this work is close in style and theme to other examples dating from Boucher's early career during the 1720s when he was studying at the Académie Royale and working for commercial print publishers. In 1723, Boucher won the Académie's coveted Prix de Rome. The award provided the student showing greatest promise with funding for three years of residence in the Italian capital at the French Academy. After some difficulty collecting his stipend, Boucher departed for Rome in 1728 at his own expense. Boucher was in Italy for only a brief sojourn but the experience was decisive in shaping his style and career aspirations.

Depictions of Old and New Testament themes were common among Boucher's earliest work. Religious themes were frequently assigned to academy students as exercises and competitions. Entrants submitted work on an assigned theme, and were then judged on both artistic merit, interpretation, and originality of composition. In 1720/21, Boucher entered a painting of a *Judgment of Susannah* (recently acquired by the National Gallery of Canada), and in 1723, he won first prize in an Académie competition whose theme was "Evilmerodach, son and successor to Nebuchadrezar" (whereabouts unknown). Boucher, like other Académie students, was known to have earned money supplying compositional drawings to Parisian engravers, principally Jean-François Cars. Many were Old Testament compositions of his own devising.

Executed in black and white chalks with the support (probably once a pale blue or grey, now faded to buff) serving as a middle tone, the drawing exhibits the fluid, attenuated strokes, delicate figures, and reinforced outlines that are found in Boucher's earliest works.[1] No painting related to this scene is known, nor is a competition on the subject of the "Sacrifice of Isaac" known to have taken place during the 1720s.[2] However, Aronoff records an undescribed drawing attributed to François Boucher representing a work on this subject as having passed through the salesroom in 1839.[3] The elegance of the composition, with its three interlocking figures, hints of the great artist Boucher was to become.

The three main figures, Abraham, Isaac, and the angel who halts the impending sacrifice, cluster to the center and left of the composition, with only the barest of indications at right of what would presumably become a landscape with the ram—to be sacrificed in Isaac's stead—trapped in a thicket. Isaac's hands and eyes are bound and he bends forward in submission, while his father stands, his arms fully extended, his back and neck arched as he confronts the hovering angel. The placement of the Isaac's legs are unresolved, and Abraham's stance appears awkward in spite of the graceful posture of his arms. Yet, a sculptural quality, evident in this rapid sketch, and dramatic arrangement of figures suggest that the composition would have been ultimately successful. Despite the indeterminate crossing of the angel's hand with respect to Abraham's upstretched arm, Boucher has captured the urgency with which the angel must arrest Abraham's motion and stay Isaac's execution. The composition and the drawing style speak of a talent not fully realized yet showing great potential. As a Boucher expert commented upon seeing the original, one may consider this either an immature work by an artist of quality, or a quality work by an immature artist. As so many further works attest, this artist fulfilled his early promise.

MELISSA R. KATZ

NOTE

1. I am indebted to Beverly Schreiber Jacoby for her observations regarding this drawing's attribution and her assistance with the preparation of this entry.

2. Alistair Laing notes that a later ink and wash drawing of *Le Sacrifice d'Abraham attributed to Boucher* was auctioned as lot 29 by Regnault-Delalande on 27 December 1793; correspondence 25 May 2000.

3. A. Aronoff, Sales Catalogue, 15 April 1839, p. 183, no. 690, coll. M. Lainé, Lausanne, 15 April 1939, no. 15.

BIBLIOGRAPHY

Bajou, Thierry. "Boucher, François." In *Dictionary of Art*, ed. Jane Turner. New York: Grove, 1996, vol. 4, pp. 511–20.

Brunel, Georges. *Boucher*. New York: Vendome Press, 1986.

Duclaux, Lise, et al. *Charles-Joseph Natoire: Nîmes, 1700–Castel Gandolfo, 1777: peintures, dessins, estampes et tapisseries des collections*

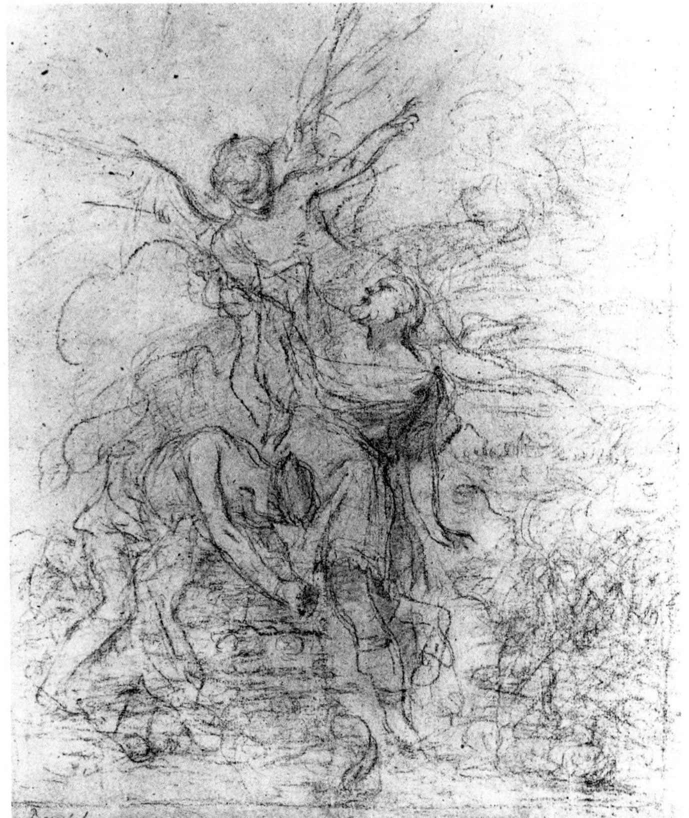

Fig. 148. François Boucher, *Sacrifice of Isaac*, 1720s, black and white chalk

publiques françaises, exhibition catalogue. Nantes, France: Imp. Chiffoleau, 1977.

Jacoby, Beverly S. *François Boucher's Early Development as a Draughtsman 1720–1734*. New York: Garland, 1986.

Laing, Jr., Alastair, J. Patrice Marendel, and Pierre Rosenberg et al. *François Boucher 1703–1770*, exhibition catalogue. New York: Metropolitan Museum of Art, 1986.

Slatkin, Regina Shoolman. *François Boucher: An Exhibition of Prints and Drawings*. New York: Charles E. Slatkin Galleries, 1957.

Ruch, J. E. "An Album of Early Drawings by François Boucher." *Burlington Magazine*, vol. 106 (1964), pp. 496–500.

CAT. NO. 33

A   John Baptist Jackson
Battersea, England 1701–circa 1780 Newcastle (?)
active London, Paris, Venice, Rome, and
Scotland

T   *Presentation of the Virgin in the Temple (after Titian)*
copy of a 1539 painting by Titian now in the Galleria dell'Accademia, Venice
right-hand plate of the *Presentation of the Virgin* triptych
one print of 24 from the *Venetian Paintings* series

D   1742, published 1745

M   chiaroscuro woodcut printed in brown and black ink in four blocks and heightened with embossing on two sheets of heavy-weight laid white paper, seamed horizontally

X   sheet and image: 22 5/16 in. x 17 5/16 in. (560 mm x 443 mm)

S   signed in block: 'J. B. Jackson'

I   see checklist

C   Bequest of Dr. Ruth Boschwitz Benedict (Class of 1935)
1994.43

The *Presentation of the Virgin* is a color woodcut in the chiaroscuro technique, designed originally in three adjoining panels. The museum's collection includes only the third (or far right) of these panels, in which the young Virgin approaches the High Priest with an outstretched hand on the temple steps. The two other panels (left and central) show a crowd gathering in a street that recedes back with a view of the hills beyond. Altogether the triptych measured over four feet long. A dedication box, which appeared in the left panel, gave the date of 1742 for the work and indicated that Jackson's *Presentation of the Virgin* was made in admiration of the work of Tiziano Vecelli, the celebrated Venetian painter who lived circa 1485–1576. Titian's original painting, made for the Scuola Grande of Santa Maria la Carità in 1539, can now be seen in the Galleria dell'Accademia in Venice.

This woodcut represents some of John Baptist Jackson's best and most impressive work done as a revival of the sixteenth-century technique of chiaroscuro woodcut. It was completed as part of a series of woodcuts based on Venetian paintings made by masters such as Titian, Bassano, Tintoretto, and Veronese. Jackson executed this series and published some other minor prints during his residency in Venice from 1738 to 1742. J. B. Pasquali published the 24 plates, which reproduced 17 paintings, as one bound volume in 1745. In 1746 Jackson returned to London, where he founded a wallpaper manufacturing company.

Early sources say lack of success led Jackson to leave his native London. First he settled in Paris, where he studied with the Parisian wood engraver Jean-Michel Papillon, the most celebrated book engraver of the time, before moving to Italy. Jackson's career reflects continual problems with money. From the beginning, the *Venetian Paintings* series was conceived with profit in mind. Joseph Smith, a British merchant Jackson met in Venice,

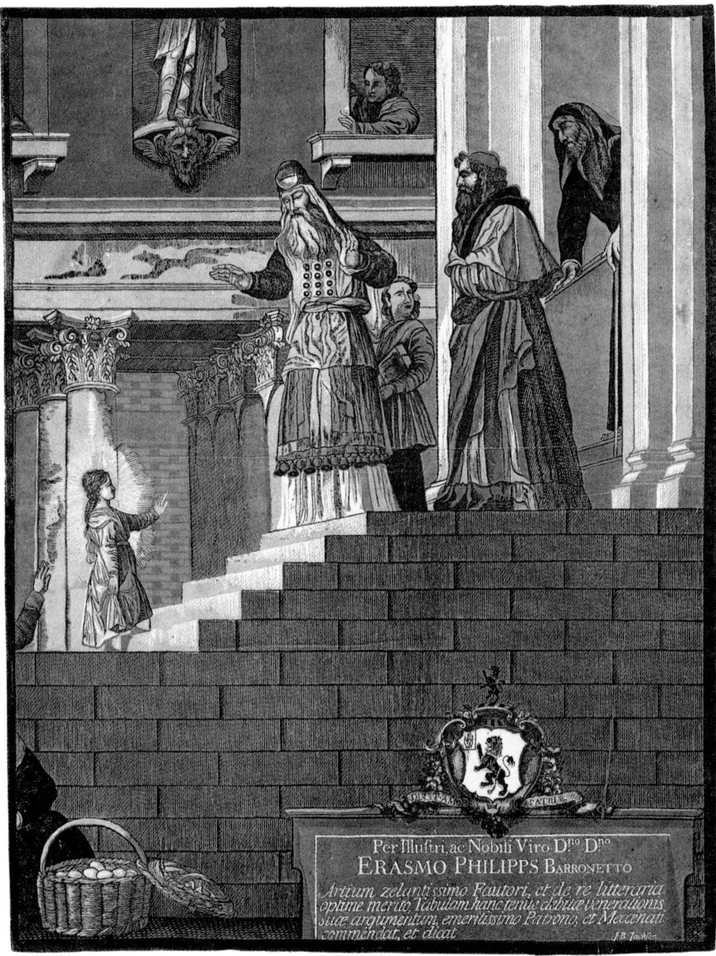

Fig. 149. John Baptist Jackson, *Presentation of the Virgin in the Temple* (after Titian), 1742, chiaroscuro woodcut

first proposed the idea of preparing a suite of reproductions of the works of Venetian Renaissance painters. With friends Charles Frederick and Smart Lethieullier, Jackson sold advance subscriptions to finance the creation and publication of the print series. The enthusiastic response of Englishmen visiting Italy to the work in progress helped sell further subscriptions to the yet-to-be-published series.

The chiaroscuro technique was considered very successful at capturing the visual characteristics of the original Old Masters. Jackson set out to reproduce the modeling effects of the paintings in woodcut by using a basic pattern of two to three tints—usually buff, ochers, or dull green—often with a broadly cut key block that printed many of the repeating outlines and inscriptions. Each

image took as many as seven individual blocks to print, each of which had to be planned, cut, and proofed. The blocks were then inked with oil-based color. When all the individual blocks were printed together, they gave the finished work a range of tones that earned them the Italian name *chiaroscuro*, light-and-dark. The entire series of 24 plates took Jackson 4-1/2 years to complete, and required the preparation of 94 separate woodblocks. Embossing was then employed to give added force to the impressions. Because the paper could not be pressed without weakening the embossing, it was often left with a scarred and buckled look that characterizes Jackson's Venetian chiaroscuros.

After leaving Venice in 1745 for England, Jackson did his best to continue working in this method. Although he continued to be highly praised for his skill, there was apparently little market for his chiaroscuro prints. He started a firm that produced specialized wallpaper, basing his designs on antique subjects and landscape painting by artists such as Claude Lorrain and Salvator Rosa. Finding it impossible to make a living creating art prints without patronage, the wallpaper venture allowed him to continue to exercise his creative abilities in a commercially viable medium. Jackon, however, was not a businessman, and the wallpaper printing also failed to earn him the status he desired and recognition he deserved. He died in obscurity, around 1777 to 1780, either in Newcastle or in Scotland, apparently in the employ of a minor Scottish nobleman, though little of his later life and death can be established.

According to traditional accounts of the Presentation of the Virgin, Mary mounted fifteen steps, one for each of the gradual Psalms. In Titian's painting, however, and therefore in Jackson's print, we only see thirteen-the first eight in the central sheet of the full composition and the next five in the right sheet. In addition, accounts in books such as the Infancy Gospel of James and *Golden Legend* of Jacobus da Voragine say Mary was three years old when she went to live in the Temple at Jerusalem. Here, however, she is presented as an older child, fully able to mount the steps on her own, unaided. Jackson's costumes, which are faithful to Titian's originals, show a mix of contemporary Renaissance dress, Roman togas, and representation of ancient Hebrew costumes. The cropped form of an old peasant woman selling eggs can be seen in the lower left corner. The high priest's jeweled breastplate and belled skirt come from descriptions in the Old Testament. The young Virgin Mary, however, is dressed in a simple, timeless tunic and is surrounded by a glowing halo of light that causes the powerful men awaiting her at the top of the temple stairs to gasp.

HILLARY L. ANDERSON '00

and

LISA MCDERMOTT

BIBLIOGRAPHY

Chatto, William Andrew. *A Treatise on Wood Engraving, Historical and Practical, with Upwards of Three Hundred Illustrations Engraved on Wood, by John Jackson. The Historical Portion by W. A. Chatto; 2nd ed. With a New Chapter on the Artists of the Present Day by Henry G. Bohn and 145 Additional Wood Engravings.* London: H. G. Bohn, 1861.

Clayton, Timothy. *The English Print 1688–1802.* New Haven, CT: Yale University Press, 1997.

Jacqué, Bernard. "Jackson, John Baptist [Jean-Baptiste]". In *Dictionary of Art*, ed. Jane Turner. New York: Grove, 1996, vol. 16, p. 820.

Kainen, Jacob. *John Baptist Jackson: 18th-century Master of the Color Woodcut*, bulletin 222. Washington, DC: United States National Museum, 1962.

Voragine, Jacobus de. *The Golden Legend: Readings on the Saints*, trans. William Granger Ryan. Princeton, NJ: Princeton University Press, 1993.

CAT. NO. 34

A Pierre Hubert Subleyras
Saint-Gilles-du-Gard, France 1699–1749 Rome, Italy
active Paris, Toulouse, Rome, and Naples

T *Pope Benedict XIV Presents Saint Catherine dei Ricci to the Virgin*
preparatory drawing for a painting now in the collection of the Marchese Sacchetti, Rome

D 1745

M ink, wash, and graphite with incising on medium-weight laid buff paper

X sheet: 9 5/8 in. x 11 3/16 in. (244 mm x 285 mm)

I see checklist

C Gift of James F. O'Gorman
1977.52

Pierre Subleyras was born in 1699 in Saint-Gilles-du-Gard, in the Languedoc region of southern France, but after brief periods in Toulouse and Paris, spent most of his career in Rome. In 1727 he won the Prix-de-Rome, and in 1728 arrived at the Académie de France in Rome and remained in Italy until his death in 1749. His serious, realistic approach was well-suited to Roman tastes in the 1730s and 1740s, as Neoclassicism was becoming the favored style. Most of his compositions, frequently executed in response to commissions by Pope Benedict XIV (1675–1758), either were portraits or treated religious subjects (Michel).

Subleyras's *Pope Benedict XIV Presents St. Catherine dei Ricci to the Virgin* is an ink drawing most likely related to a 1745 commission by the Dominican order of Rome on the occasion of Caterina dei Ricci's (1522–90) canonization in 1746. It differs in subject from the final painting, *The Mystic Marriage of St. Catherine dei Ricci*, which is currently in the collection of the Marchese Sac-

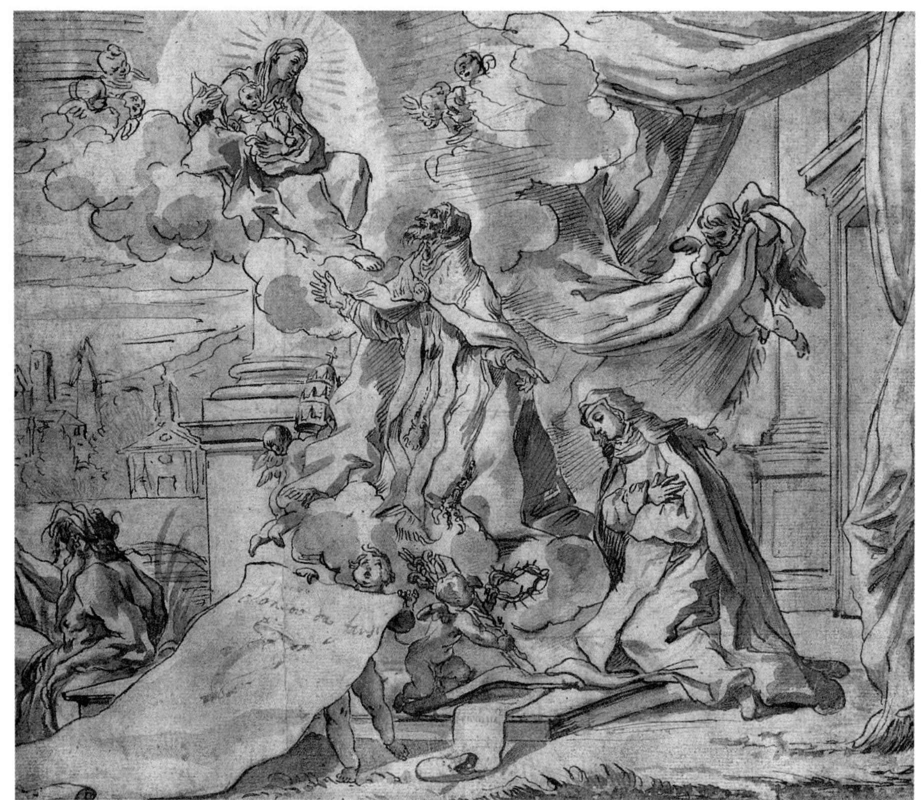

Fig. 150. Pierre Hubert Subleyras, *Pope Benedict XIV presents St. Catherine dei Ricci to the Virgin*, 1745, ink, wash, and graphite

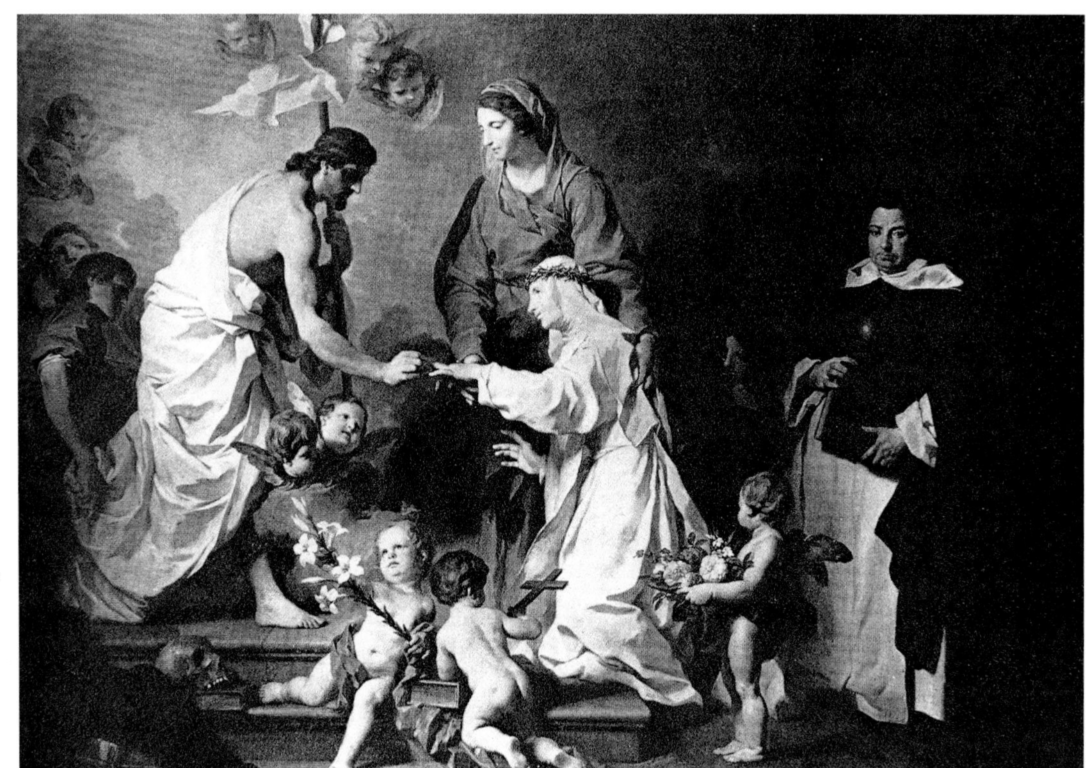

Fig. 151. Pierre Subleyras, *Mystic Marriage of St. Catherine dei Ricci*, 1746, oil on canvas, collection of the Marchese Giovanni Sacchetti, Rome

chetti in Rome [fig. 151]. A preliminary oil sketch, signed and dated 1746, now hangs in the Smith College Museum of Art in Northampton. It is similar in composition to the finished painting, which was presented by the Dominicans to Benedict XIV. It is not known who decided to change the painting's subject—the artist or the patrons—having the Virgin Mary present Catherine to Christ, and substituting the figure of the Dominican saint Thomas Aquinas for Pope Benedict. The revised theme does link the newly canonized saint more closely to her namesakes, saints Catherine of Alexandria and Catherine of Siena, who are also depicted as brides of Christ. During the same year, Subleyras was also at work on *St. Camillio de Lellis Saving the Sick of the Hospital of the Holy Spirit from the Floodwaters of the Tiber* (Palazzo Braschi, Rome), in honor of the founder of the Camillian order who was canonized at the same time as Catherine dei Ricci. He may have chosen the theme of saintly miracles as a more appropriate way to commemorate the pair (Michel and Rosenberg).

In the museum's drawing, Pope Benedict XIV stands with each arm extended, his right to the Virgin and Child, his left to St. Catherine dei Ricci. As he points to the kneeling St. Catherine on his left, he turns his face upward to the Virgin, who reclines on a cloud above him with the infant Christ in her arms. The three figures form a powerful diagonal through the composition. Surrounding these figures are several angels; some are simply sitting amid the clouds above, while others are more active: one is pulling open a curtain, another pulls a large scroll into the middle of the scene, and yet another carries a cross and a crown of thorns. Together, the angels form a more subtle, opposite diagonal, thus creating an intersection at the center of the composition where Pope Benedict stands.

Pope Benedict, the only contemporary figure in the scene, serves as a link between St. Catherine dei Ricci, a sixteenth-century Dominican nun of the Third Order, and her spiritual mother, the Virgin Mary. Benedict, who served as Pope from 1740 until his death in 1758, was considered conservative in most liturgical matters; he did not approve of recent changes to the Calendar of Saints and the introduction of new offices into the Breviary (Healy). Therefore his decision to canonize Catherine dei Ricci can be seen as part of his efforts to focus on older, more traditional orders, such as the Dominicans. This work serves both to commemorate St. Catherine and to promote the Dominican order.

Catherine dei Ricci was born Alessandra Lucrezia Romola in 1522 near Florence. After her mother's death, Alessandra decided to take the Virgin Mary as her mother, entering a convent at the age of six and taking the name Caterina. At the age of twenty, she began a twelve-year cycle of weekly ecstasies of the Passion from noon Thursday to 4:00 P.M. Friday. During these ecstasies, she would usually receive the wounds from the cross and crown of thorns and at the end of the cycle, an indent on her shoulder from the cross. Word soon spread of her experiences, and crowds began to gather every week to witness Catherine in ecstasy. It is said that skeptics and sinners were converted just by watching her. When, after several years, the crowds became too numerous and disruptive, the other sisters in the convent prayed for Catherine's wounds to become less visible; their prayer was apparently answered in 1554 (Capes).

Catherine was also said to have received an engagement ring from Christ in a vision, the scene depicted in Smith College's oil sketch and the Sacchetti painting. (Indeed, saints Catherine of Alexandria and Catherine of Siena also claimed to have undergone a similar mystical experience.) Beyond the stigmata and the ring, Catherine is noted for her supreme humility, which Subleyras depicts in this image: she kneels at the foot of Pope Benedict with arms clasped to her chest, her head bowed in the presence of the Virgin.

REBECCA MONGEON

BIBLIOGRAPHY

Capes. F. M. "St. Catherine de'Ricci." In *The Catholic Encyclopedia*, vol. 3. New York: Robert Appleton Company, 1907.

Healy, Patrick J. "Pope Benedict XIV (Prospero Lorenzo Lambertini." In *The Catholic Encyclopedia*, vol. 2. New York: Robert Appleton Company, 1907.

Michel, Olivier. "Pierre Subleyras." In *Dictionary of Art*, ed. Jane Turner. New York: Grove, 1996, vol. 29, pp. 886–89.

Michel, Olivier, and Pierre Rosenberg. *Subleyras: 1699–1749*, exhibition catalogue. *Le Mariage mystique de sainte Catherine de' Ricci.* pp. 317–24. Paris: Editorial de la Réunion des Musées nationaux, 1987.

Rosenthal, Donald A. *La grande manière: Historical and Religious Painting in France, 1700–1800.* Rochester, NY: Memorial Art Gallery of the University of Rochester, 1987, pp. 152–55.

Smith College Museum of Art. *A Guide to the Collections.* Northampton, MA: The Museum, 1986.

CAT. NO. 35

A Giovanni Domenico Tiepolo, called GianDomenico Tiepolo
Venice, Italy 1727–1804 Venice
active Venice and the Veneto, Milan, Würzburg, Madrid, and Aranjuez

T Four prints from the *Flight into Egypt* series
1957.26, 1973.18, 4.1983, 1984.22
(see checklist for cataloguing)

ILLUSTRATED

T *The Holy Family Leaving by a City Gate*
plate 7 of 27 from the *Flight into Egypt* series

D circa 1750–53, published 1753

M etching on white paper, state 1 of 1

X sheet and image: 7 3/16 in. x 9 1/2 in. (183 mm x 240 mm)

S signed in plate (twice): 'Doi Tiepolo fecit' and 'Doi Tiepolo in id fei'

C Museum purchase
1973.18

Giovanni Domenico Tiepolo (1727–1804), known as GianDomenico, collaborated for most of his career with his father, Giovanni Battista Tiepolo (GiamBattista, 1696–1770), a highly respected Venetian painter in fresco and oil, who also produced two famous series of etchings, the *Scherzi* and *Capricci*. GianDomenico's brother Lorenzo (1736–76) was also an accomplished painter and engraver. The Tiepolo family, father and sons, were in great demand throughout Europe, and commissions brought their work to Italy, Germany, and Spain. When GiamBattista died in Madrid in 1770, while at work for the royal family of Spain, his sons returned to their native Venice.

GianDomenico's *Flight into Egypt* series of 27 etchings were created from about 1750 until 1753 and published together in Würzburg in 1753 where the three Tiepolos were working on a fresco commission for the palace of the bishop-prince of Würzburg. Some elements of his fresco style were reflected in the prints created during this period. The ceiling painting features flowing lines and soft curves to create an ethereal and extensive vista of the heavens, a romantic style for which GianDomenico was most renowned. This style can be seen in the *Flight into Egypt* series in his portrayal of angels and floating clouds. Nevertheless, his great attention to detail and his use of chiaroscuro to create volumetric forms and suggest color creates decisively realistic images that depart from the illusionistic frescos.

As well as assisting his father in GiamBattista's many commisions, GianDomenico spent much of his career making reproductions of his father's paintings in the form of etchings. Of the 170 prints made by GianDomenico in his lifetime, 116 were after compositions by his father. This series, which GianDomenico called *Idee pittoresche sopra la Fugga in Egitto (Picturesque Ideas on the Theme of the Flight into Egypt)*, is often said to be the son's

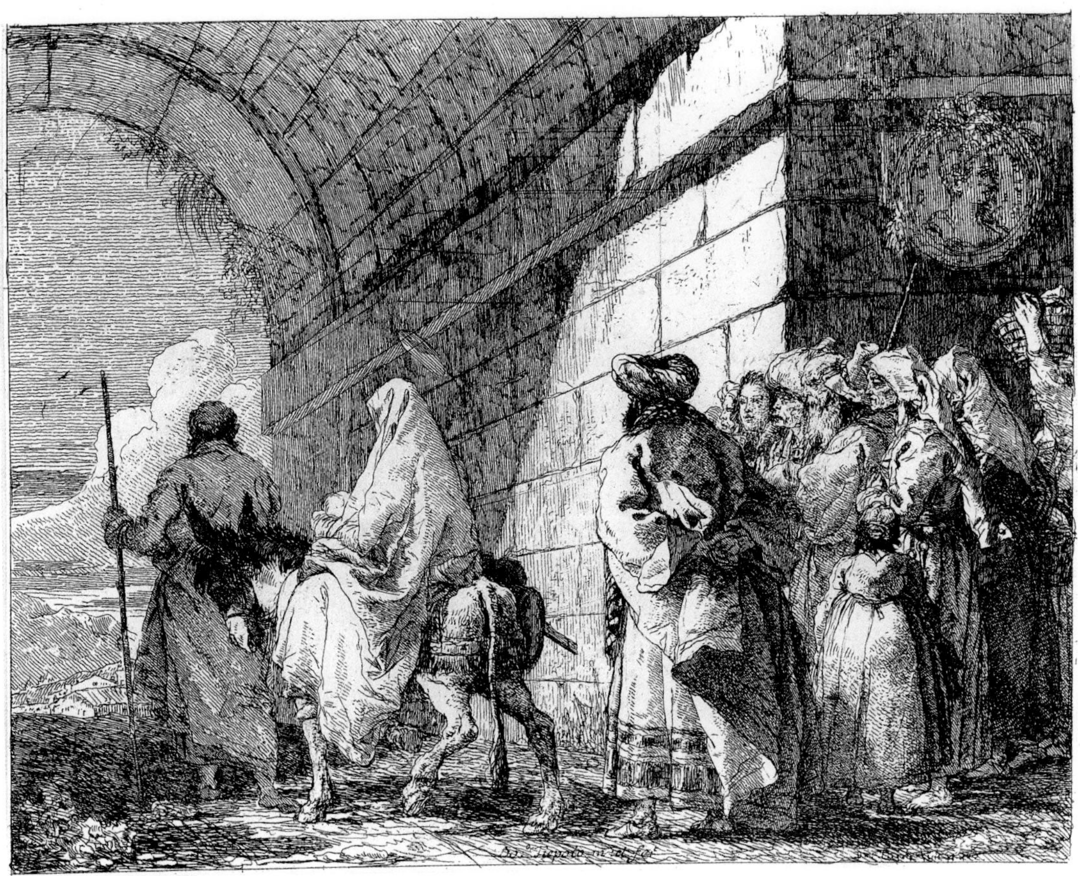

attempt to break loose from his father's example and showcase his own talent. Scholars disagree on whether the finished works actually demonstrated much originality. The final series consists of 24 images plus a title plate, a frontispiece, and a dedication page.

The *Flight into Egypt* series concentrates on the Holy Family, with Mary being central in all 24 scenes. Mary's holiness is emphasized by the halo around her head, the angels who attend her, and the artist's use of sharp lines to represent divine light surrounding her. GianDomenico's characterization of Mary also reveals two general trends throughout the series. Mary is portrayed as feminine with a soft and sensitive face (plate 6), or as a faceless, shrouded, abstract figure (plate 10, *Mary holding the Child in her Arms and Joseph with the Basket*) [fig. 54]. Occasionally elements of both are found in the same etching (plate 12, *Holy Family Escorted by an Angel*). Perhaps the feminine Mary resonated with the socially prescribed virtues of beauty and young motherhood, while the more substantial Mary testified to woman's strength as a bulwark of church and family. In plate 22 (*Episode of the Falling Idol*), for example, Mary, who lovingly gazes at her cradled baby, represents chaste beauty in the service of motherhood as opposed to the lascivious, seminude statue of a woman on the left. The statue's head falls to the ground as the holy family passes, thus validating Mary's triumph and warning those women who might ignore her example.

The portrayal of Joseph, who is featured prominently in the series, also varies among the images. Sometimes he seems to be a robust young father; at other times he is a feeble elderly man. Most of the time he is presented as old but still active, very much a patriarch yet quite elderly in comparison to the Virgin Mary. The artist also uses landscape

The Catalogue   229

as an expressive element of his compositions. Trees dominate the backgrounds in all but six of GianDomenico's *Flight into Egypt* etchings. The most striking of these trees are the palms; Gian-Domenico's skillful use of lines and curves creates their voluptuous and undulating forms. These tantalizing arboreal entities seem both mysterious and intensely sexual when juxtaposed with the sublime purity of the Virgin Mary. Although his rendering of the trees and the surroundings may seem fantastical today, GianDomenico's style is, arguably, suitable from the perspective of his day—one that imagined a locale such as Egypt to be utterly foreign and exotic.

The sensual palm trees underscore Mary's role as both mother and holy figure. The association of the palm tree with Egypt can be traced back to the worship of the goddess Isis, whose cult reached its greatest popularity in the mid-fourth century AD, just when the Church began to elevate the figure of the Virgin Mary. In contrast to Mary, who embodies the contradictory elements of maternity and purity, the pagan goddess embraced maternity's natural counterpart: sexuality. The palm tree has subsequently played a significant role in the Christian tradition. While the account of the flight to Egypt given by Matthew (2:13–18) fails to mention any vegetation at all, in the apocryphal tradition, according to the *Gospel of Pseudo-Matthew*, Mary is miraculously fed by her infant son Jesus with the fruit from the date palm under which they sit. Thus, palm trees, while offering an important contrast to Mary's purity, also accentuate her holiness as the mother of God.

ELIZABETH LOSADA '00

BIBLIOGRAPHY

Knox, George. *Etchings by the Tiepolos*. Ottawa, ON: National Gallery of Canada, 1976, pp. 10–23, 78–92.

McKenna, George L. "Prints: 1460–1995." *The Collections of the Nelson-Atkins Museum of Art*. Kansas City: Nelson Atkins Museum of Art, 1996, cat. no. 54. pp. 118–20.

Rizzi, Aldo. *The Etchings of the Tiepolos*. Lucia Wildt, trans. London: Phaidon Press, 1971.

Russell, H. Diane. *Rare Etchings by Giovanni Battista and Giovanni Domenico Tiepolo*. Washington, DC: National Gallery of Art, 1972.

Warner, Marina. *Alone of All Her Sex: The Myth and Cult of the Virgin Mary*. New York: Pocket Books, 1976, esp. pp. 208–09, 347–49.

Witt, R. E. *Isis in the Graeco-Roman World*. Ithaca, NY: Cornell University Press, 1971, pp. 31, 179, 237–40.

CAT. NO. 36

A Mexican, from Guanajuato state, possibly San Miguel de Allende

T *Ex-Voto Commissioned by José María Ramírez*

D 1798

M oil on canvas

X 27 1/2 in. H x 25 1/2 (70.0 cm x 64.8 cm)

S dated in paint, central cartouche: "10 de Abril de 1798 a°"

I inscriptions follow this entry

C Museum purchase from the Dorothy Johnston Towne (Class of 1923) Fund 1998.23

This rare early votive painting commemorates four miracles attributed to a dark-skinned Christ figure shown on an altar between light-skinned statues of the Virgin Mary (represented as *La Dolorosa*, Our Lady of Sorrows, with a sword piercing her heart) and St. John (?). Images and text recount how this wonder-working figure revived two girls believed to be deceased (upper and lower right), and saved men from robbers (upper left) and from a bad fall (lower left). Though the work is unsigned, a dedication indicates that it was commissioned by José María Ramírez in April 1798, while the accompanying text names towns in the north-central Mexican state of Guanajuato. Worshipping at the central altar are four indigenous Amerindians wearing feathered outfits that are appropriate neither for the time period nor the region, but rather reflect a generic concept of "Indian."

Miraculous black Christ figures can be found throughout Latin America and combine an imported European belief in the power of miraculous black Madonnas with an indigenous association of blackness and male power. The dark-skinned figure of this painting is identified as *El Señor Ecce Homo* (Our Lord Ecce Homo), an intriguing conflation of God the Father and Christ as the Man of Sorrows, and possibly unique to the region. His name refers to the biblical episode when Pontius Pilate presents Jesus to the crowd, after the flagellation, with the Latin words *ecce homo*, "behold the man." Often conflated with Christ as the Man of Sorrows, Renaissance *Ecce Homo* images usually show a half-length, naked Christ with bound hands, crown of thorns, a rope-encircled neck, and marks of scourging. The full-length figure depicted here, however, with his lavish blue-green robe, scepter, and gilded crown of thorns, more closely resembles imagery of God the Father and Christ the King.

This painting belongs to the vernacular form of ex-voto art, which combines text and image to give thanks for divine intervention. The name derives from the Latin *ex voto suscepto*—"from the vow made." An outgrowth of pagan worship, Christian votive paintings or objects—dedicated to Jesus, God, Mary, or a patron saint—can be found in churches, shrines, and pilgrimage sites in both South and Central America and Europe, particularly in traditionally Catholic countries and the Alpine region. Commissioned by donors from artists who, though professional, are usually anonymous, ex-votos reflect the popular continuation of high-art traditions of religious patronage enacted on a modest scale.

Small Mexican ex-votos painted on tin sheets are plentiful from the mid-nineteenth century onward and are often included in museum collections as folk art [fig. 154]. The Ramírez ex-voto is highly unusual, however, not only because of its early date, large size, and canvas support, but also because of its interracial and colonial references. At first glance, it appears to be directed to a native audience through the inclusion of a dark-skinned divinity. The incongruous costumes, on the other hand, require further interpretation. By 1798, both native-born and foreign-born Mexicans in Guanajuato wore standard Western clothing, and the outfits shown in the painting reflect more the garments of nomadic Comanche and Apache tribes of the North American plains (still Mexican territory in 1798) than the traditional dress of the Aztecs or other ancestral groups of the Guanajuato region. Even the indigenous inhabitants of central Mexico viewed these northern tribes as barbaric, and would not (wish to) see their identity reflected in such primitive—albeit Christianized—figures.

Both the date and the location of the work suggest another possible reason for the inclusion of mixed races and overt reference to indigenous, non-European populations. The French Revolution (1789–1795) had inspired emancipation movements throughout Europe and its colonies. Though the Mexican Revolution would not officially begin until 1810, Guanajuato would be the location of its first battle and the birthplace of its leader, Father Miguel Hidalgo y Costilla (1753–1811). During the years of tension leading up to open rebellion, issues of Mexican home rule, self-determination, and separation from colonial powers could very well have been embodied in an otherwise nonpolitical artwork intended for devotional purposes.

The resemblance between the deity and worshippers in the central scene reinforces the notion that the narrative is meant to be read positively, and the prevalence of white figures in the peripheral scenes does not detract from the approving manner in which the indigenous worshipers are

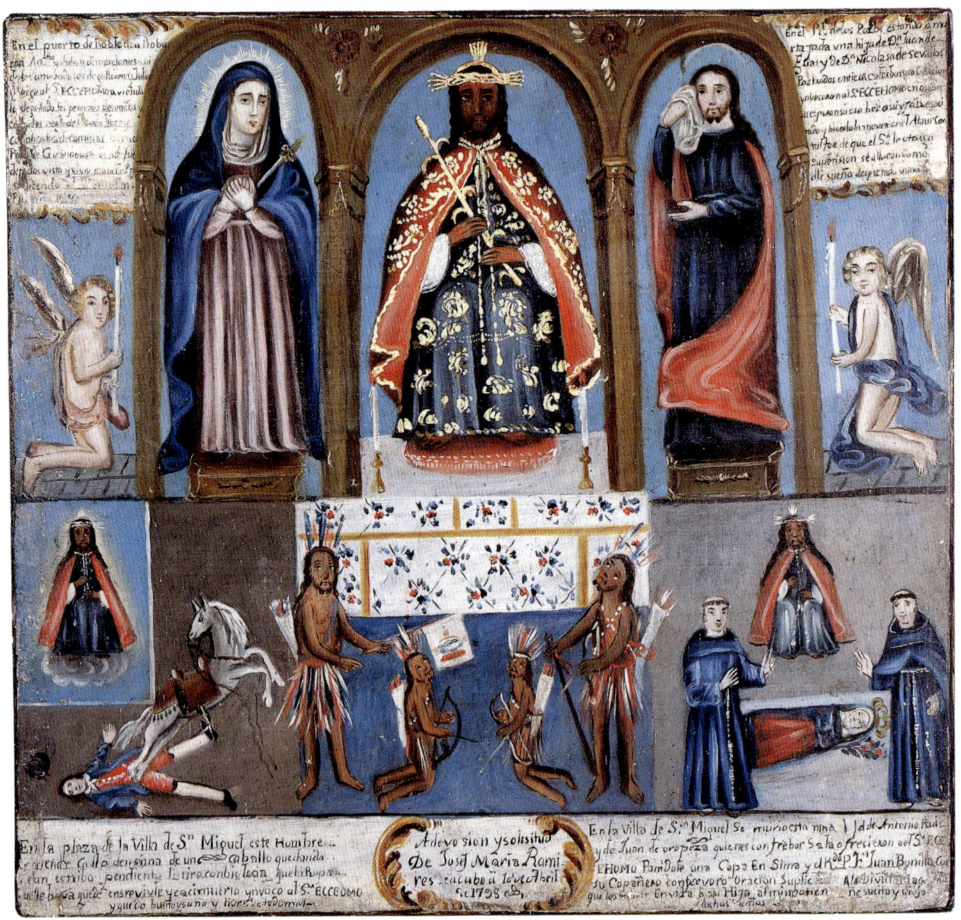

Fig. 153. Mexican, *Ex-Voto commissioned by José María Ramírez*, 1798, oil on canvas

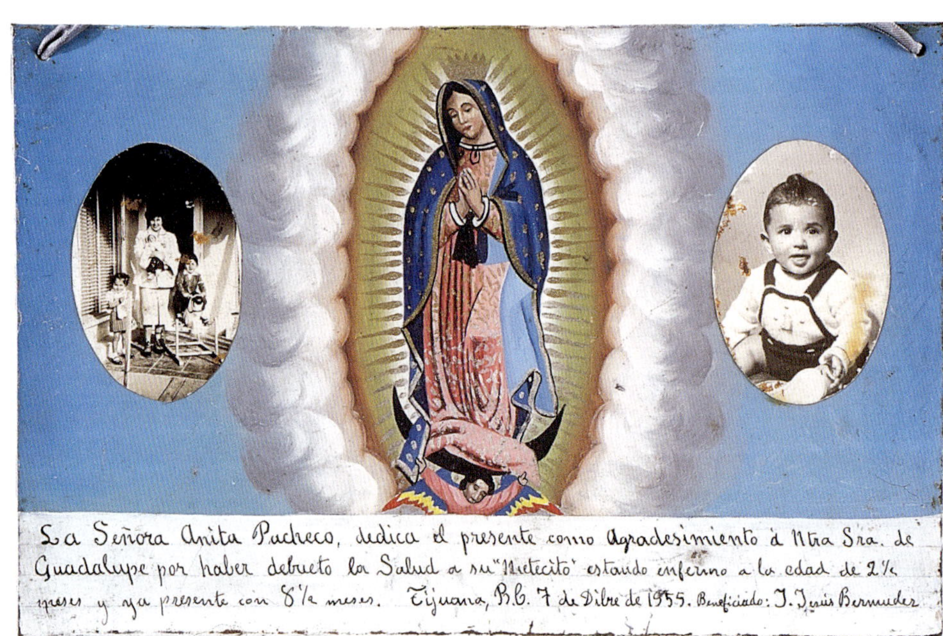

Fig. 154. Mexican, *Ex-Voto Commissioned by Anita Pacheco*, 1955 oil and photographs on tin, Collection of James Oles

presented. However, it is doubtful that the donors and/or eighteenth-century viewers of this work shared the ethnic heritage of the four men portrayed at the altar. More likely it was intended for a *criollo* audience—Mexican-born descendants of European settlers—who presumably felt anxiety at the prospect of Mexican statehood after three centuries of European domination. They may have wished to display their identification with darker-skinned non-European natives by demonstrating their support for the nationalist cause through a reference to Mexico's pre-Colonial identity. Nevertheless, the bounties of the Christian God—displayed to Amerindians, yet bestowed on Caucasians—reinforce the racial and class hierarchies of the colonial world.

MELISSA R. KATZ

BIBLIOGRAPHY

García-Noriega, Lucia, ed. *Imagenes Guadalupanas: Cuatro siglos.* Mexico City: Centro Cultural/Arte Contemporáneo, 1987.

Giffords, Gloria Fraser. *Mexican Folk Retablos.* Albuquerque: University of New Mexico Press, 1992.

In the two years since the DMCC acquired this painting, I have benefited from conversations with many colleagues, and am grateful to James Oles, Jeanette Favrot Peterson, Marion Oettinger, Jr., Jaime Lara, Carlos Ramos, Lorraine Roses, Nancy Hall, and Stephen Marini for their imaginative scholarship and aid with its interpretation.

Transcriptions of Text and English Translations:

Bottom Center:

A devosion y solisitud/De Josef Maria Rami-/res se acabo ã 10 de Abril/de 1798 a°

(For the devotion and solicitude of José María Ramírez[. This] was finished the tenth of April of the year 1798.)

Upper Left:

En el puerto de Robledal[?] Roba/ron An.ñ° y Julian Jemendan-tos abi/dãles amor[daz]ado Los degallaron y Julian/y[n]-boco al S.ʳ ECCEHOMO aviendo/le degollado los pescu[e]zos desunidos y/Cortados[?] se allo de la vida libre y/Con alientos de caminar hasta el/R[.ˡ S.ᵗᵒ] de Gua-naouato donde fue/ detodos visto y vivio muchos[?]/ años/saliendo el S.ʳ en su t[i]em/Po en el año de 1686 [1646?]

(At the city gate [outskirts] of Robledal[?], Antonio and Julian Jemendantos were robbed and gagged. Their throats were slit and Julian invoked [the help of our] Lord Ecce Homo having had his throat cut and his neck disunited and cut, he found himself still alive and with [enough] breath to [be able to] walk to the R[oyal settlement] of Guanajuato, where he was seen by all and lived many years, going unto the Lord in his [due] time in the year of 1686 [or 1646?])

Upper Right:

En el R.ˡ de los Pozos estando amo/rtajada vna hija de D.ⁿ Juan de/Elias[?] y de D.ª Nicolasa de Sevados [?]/Postrados entiera côterborose Oracion/ynvocaron al S.ʳ ECCEHOMO en quien/su esperansa era bera su yja B.esuci/tado y bien-dola mover en el Ataur Con/tal fee de que el S.ʳ le otoro[garon]/supetision se alloron Como[. . .]/dle sueña despertãdo viniera[?]

(In the Royal [settlement] of Los Pozos ["The Wells"] having been enshrouded [for burial] a daughter of Mr. Juan de Elias[?] and of Mrs. Nicolasa de Sevados[?] [and] throwing themselves on the ground in fervent prayer, they invoked [the help of our] Lord Ecce Homo in whom their hope was to see their daughter [well?] resuscitated. And seeing her move in the coffin, with such faith in that the Lord had answered their petition they found her as if [illegible] from a dream she was coming awake.)

Bottom Left:

En la plaza de la Villa de S.ⁿ Miguel este Hombre . . . /abiendo caido densima de un caballo quedando . . . /de un estribo pendiente le tiro conbi°lecia que la Ropa . . . /que llebava quedo ensrevivle y cacimuerto ynvoco al S.ʳ ECCEOMO/y quedo bueno y sano y livre de todo mal– –

(In the plaza of the town of San Miguel [de Allende] this man having fallen from on top of a horse remaining attached to a stirrup was thrown with [such] violence that the clothing he was wearing became unservable [i.e., useless] and almost dead he invoked [our] Lord Ecce Homo and remained well and healthy and free from all ills.)

Bottom Right:

En la villa de S.ⁿ Miguel Se murio esta niña yja de Antonio Ruis/y de Juan de oropeza quienes confrebor S a la

ofrecieron a el S.ᵳ ECC/EHOMO Pondole una Capa En
Sima y el R.ᵈᵒ P. F.ᶜᵒ Juan Bonilla Con[?]/su Copañero con-
fervoro Oracion Suplicã[do] A la Divinidad a
[illegible]ᴼ/que les diese[?] En vida a su Hija al mismo
tiem[po] resucito y vivia/muchos años.

(In the town of San Miguel [de Allende] this young girl died,
daughter of Antonio Ruis and of Juan de Oropeza [*sic*] who

with fervor offered her to our Lord Ecce Homo[,] putting a
cape over [her body]. And the Reverend Father Francisco
Juan Bonilla with[?] his companion, in fervent prayer [and]
supplication to the divinity [illegible] [asked] that he would
give to them their daughter alive[.] At the same time she
resuscitated and lived [on for] many years.)

CAT. NO. 37

A Julia Margaret Cameron
     Calcutta, India 1815–79 Kalutara, Ceylon
     active London, Kent, Surrey, Isle of Wight, and
     Ceylon (now Sri Lanka)

T *La Santa Julia (Portrait of Julia Prinsep Jackson)*

D 1867

M albumen silver print on original mount

X print: 11 1/8 in. x 9 1/4 in. (293 mm x 236 mm)
     mount: 16 7/8 in. x 14 in. (429 mm x 356 mm)

S inscribed in ink, on mount: 'From Life registered
     photograph copy right Julia Margaret Cameron
     1867/La Santa Julia'

C Given in honor of Eugenia Parry Janis by Profes-
     sor and Mrs. Hugo Munsterberg (Peggy Bowen,
     Class of 1943)
     1973.20

La Santa Julia shifts the image of the Madonna toward modernity. Julia Margaret Cameron used a new image technology to revitalize religious traditions and yet also to introduce the possibility of a secular Madonna.

The photograph is a portrait of Cameron's niece and godchild Julia Prinsep Jackson (1846–95), daughter of Cameron's sister Maria, called Mia. It was taken shortly before Julia Jackson's marriage to Herbert Duckworth. Julia Jackson was the model Cameron photographed most often. Cameron dearly valued all the portraits she made of her, especially *La Santa Julia.* In one surviving catalogue, at least, Cameron priced no photograph higher. *La Santa Julia* is both an excep-

tionally beautiful picture of an already beautiful woman, and a sign of momentous changes in the relationship between women's social roles and images of women.

Like all of Cameron's great portraits, *La Santa Julia* was inspired by its model. Cameron, herself a member of Britain's elite intellectual class, was attracted to what Julia Jackson's daughter Virginia Woolf (by her second husband Leslie Stephen) pithily called "Famous Men and Fair Women." Julia Jackson was renowned for her beauty in her time, and not only in her youth; she is the heroine Mrs. Ramsay of Woolf's great 1927 novel *To the Lighthouse.* While Cameron sought out female models for such gifts, as opposed to the accomplishments of her male models, she treated both women and men alike formally. Typically, Cameron emphasized faces by choosing simple settings, costume, and hairstyle. Subtly composing drapery, hair, focus, and light, as well as positioning the viewer close to, yet ever so slightly below her subject, Cameron created images that were both monumentally dignified and intimate. In *La Santa Julia*, for instance, Julia appears at once far away and close, gently inclining her head toward us, yet to our side, as if concentrating on some inner or otherworldly vision. The image is composed into a side of shining brightness and a side of more modulated shade. These effects are more striking when seeing the original print than when looking at a reproduction. Cameron chose a print format that would make her portraits almost mirror the scale and location of her viewers' faces when her photographs were framed and hung on walls according to the conventions of her time (and ours).

Cameron named *La Santa Julia* a divine saint and also a real human being: her niece Julia. In Cameron's time, Catholic imagery of the past was being given new meaning. Taking their distances from the original Catholic contexts in which images of saints and Madonnas had been created, nineteenth-century art critics and art lovers saw lessons for their own more secular age in Renaissance and Baroque religious images by claiming to have found universal truths. British and American women were especially active interpreters, seeing in older images sanctification of a new femininity. The Catholic Madonna, notably, came to be seen as the model for the mother of a nuclear, individualist, and capitalist family. Julia Jackson, for example, who inspired art, nursed many sick family members, and raised seven children, was obviously not a Catholic saint (with an Italian name) but rather saintly by the gender, political, and economic standards of Victorian Britain.

Just as Victorians made a transition from the past to their present ideologically through religious imagery, so they did technologically. By paying homage to Old Master paintings on a mass scale, copyists and adapters of religious imagery developed the new image technologies of industrial printing and of photography. Cameron was not the only one to remake the Madonna photographically. Yet few of her contemporaries were as able as she was to reveal the expressive possibilities specific to photography. And Cameron's formal understanding of purely aesthetic photographic light and its composition transformed her subject matter, beyond even the latest ideals of her time. By abstracting *La Santa Julia*, Cameron has given us a woman who might be named a saint, but who also escapes the limitations of any one role.

ANNE HIGONNET

BIBLIOGRAPHY

Cameron, Julia Margaret. *For My Best Beloved Sister Mia: An Album of Photographs by Julia Margaret Cameron.* Albuquerque: University of New Mexico Museum, 1994.

Gernsheim, Helmut. *Julia Margaret Cameron.* New York: Aperture, 1975.

Mavor, Carol. *Pleasures Taken: Performances of Sexuality and Loss in Victorian Photographs.* Durham, NC: Duke University Press, 1995.

Wolf, Sylvia, et al. *Julia Margaret Cameron's Women.* Chicago and New Haven: The Art Institute of Chicago and Yale University Press, 1998.

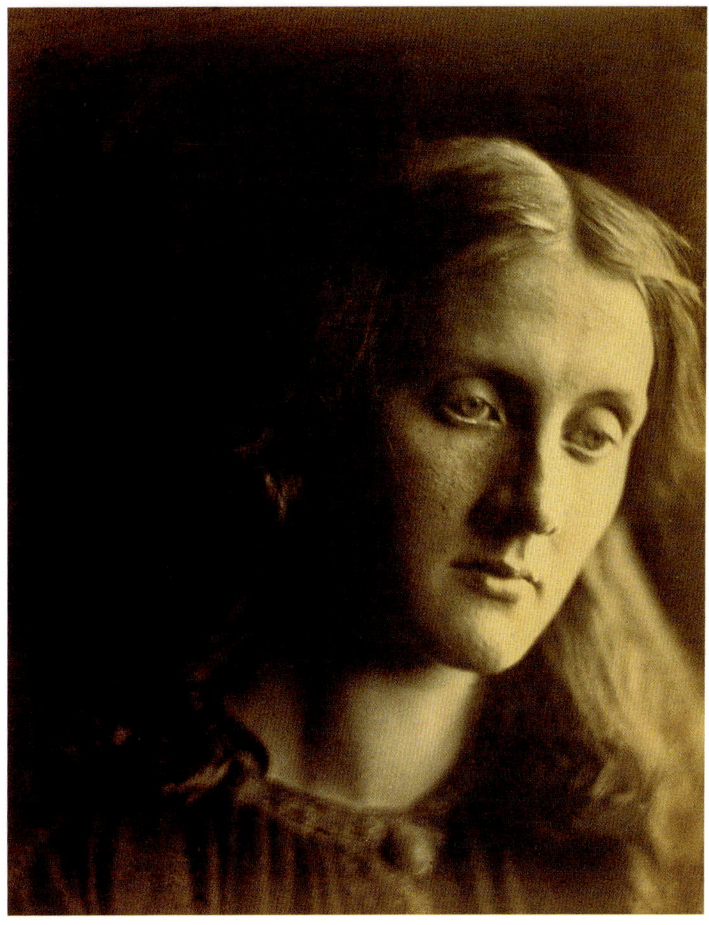

Fig. 155. Julia Margaret Cameron, *La Santa Julia*, 1867, albumen print

A Émile Bernard
Lille, France 1868–1941 Paris
active Paris, Venice, and Cairo

T *Confirmand's Procession*
alternate title: *Procession at Saint-Briac*

D 1891

M oil on canvas

X 21 in. x 28 1/2 in. (53.3 cm x 72.4 cm)

S signed and dated in red paint: "E.B. 1891"

I inscribed in paint, verso: 'Procession à St-Briac' and 'Deus est Magnus' (God is Great)

C gift of Chester D. Tripp in memory of his wife, Madeline Hanson Tripp (Class of 1907) 1966.15

The rural population of the French province of Brittany was of great interest to the Parisian intelligentsia of the later nineteenth century. Viewed as living embodiments of a "pure" rural past, Breton peasants were understood to carry the spirituality and mysticism of medieval France into the present. Among the intellectuals drawn to Brittany by this romantic ideal was Émile Bernard, a leading member of France's avant-garde in the 1880s and early 1890s. *Confirmand's Procession*, painted in 1891, is one of Bernard's numerous representations of Breton rituals that simultaneously enact sacred events and picturesque spectacles. Inscribing on its back the phrases "Procession à St-Briac" (Procession at Saint-Briac) and "Deus est Magnus" (God is Great), Bernard located the painting in place and sentiment: in the fishing village of Saint-Briac, where Bernard spent the summer of 1891, and at a moment when his latent spirituality began to intensify into the rigorous and deeply conservative Catholicism that propelled the rest of his career.

Rendered in a thinned oil medium, using sinuous red outlines to contain broad, unmodulated areas of color, *Confirmand's Procession* appears as a flat and artificial image rather than a reflection of the material world. In its cartoon-like use of line, nonnaturalistic jewel-like colors, and flat superimposed planes that represent spatial recession, the painting asserts its affiliation with the ideal, rather than corporal, world. The painting's high horizon line and flattened, overlapping forms are adapted from Japanese *Ukiyo-e* woodblock prints, circulating within the intellectual and artistic communities of Paris since the 1860s and avidly emulated by Bernard and his circle (see Welsh-Ovcharov). This use of media, in which conventional Western approaches to the representation of light, shadow, surface detail, and spatial relations are renounced, was one of Bernard's great innovations in the late 1880s. It was also one of the chief means by which artists of his generation articulated their affiliation with Symbolism, the mid-1880s Parisian literary movement that proclaimed the primacy of ideas over material reality (see Heller). Working side-by-side with Paul Gauguin in the village of Pont-Aven in the summer of 1888, Bernard helped to originate this approach to painting—a style that became known as "Synthetism" or pictorial Symbolism.

For Bernard, this mode of painting, bordering on abstraction, became the conduit for a new medieval piety:

> I would dream of creating a hieratic style looking beyond modernity and present-day reality for its methods and inspiration, I needed to go back to the Primitives: adopt a very abbreviated technique, use line solely in order to determine form and color, solely to determine each state. In other words, what I wanted to do was create a style for our age.[1]

Symbolism was also interpreted by Bernard to reconcile Catholicism with modernity, moving painting beyond the anecdotal to a transcendent sacred realm: "Symbolism led art back to the very reason for her existence: the expression of the ideal, the unreal. It reminded art of her origins and reinstated mysticism as the inspirer of the super-real."[2]

For Bernard, the Breton peasantry was a conduit for such renewal.

Confirmand's Procession represents a parade of young girls swathed in the white clothing signifying their participation in the sacrament of confirmation, the second stage of initiation (after baptism) into the Catholic church. The children seem transcendent as they file past Saint-Briac's old village church, followed by a male (presumably the priest) carrying a religious banner and a parade of women wearing traditional local lace caps: the girls' long, pale garments mask their feet and create the effect of suspending them above the delicate foliage beneath them. Like Gauguin, Bernard imagined Breton peasant life to straddle the barrier between the sacred and the secular, and to be pure of modern incursions. Gauguin had mused:

> There is something medieval looking about the peasants here in Brittany; they don't look as though they suspect for a moment that Paris exists. Their apparel, too, is little short of symbolic, influenced by the superstition of Catholicism. . . . Still fearful of the Lord and of the parish priest, Bretons hold their hats and tools as though they were in church.[3]

By the time Gauguin and Bernard established their Pont-Aven "School" in the late 1880s, however, Brittany had been a summer destination for artists from throughout Europe and North America for at least two decades. Breton rituals had been represented so frequently that they were avidly observed, photographed, sketched, and painted by artists and other tourists in the late 1880s. Moreover, the increasing cultivation of farm lands, the exploitation of the sea, and the growth of the Breton tourist industry itself had already transformed Brittany into a relatively prosperous member of

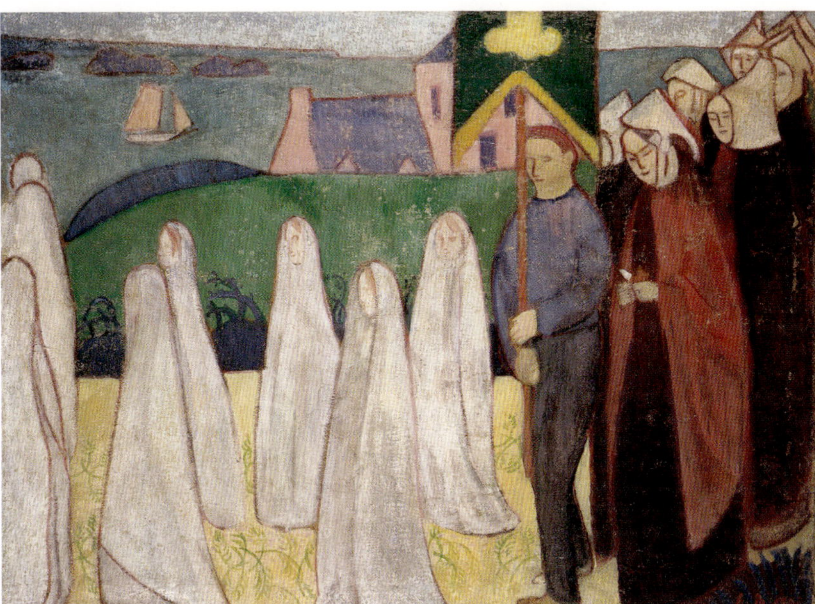

Fig. 156. Émile Bernard, *Confirmand's Procession*, 1891, oil on canvas

France's economy (Pollock and Orton). Bernard's confirmands, set against the harbor that secured the village's resources, processed before him as community ritual, as an invocation of the sacred, and as picturesque tourist motif.

Bernard, like Gauguin, ignored the modern material circumstances of Brittany in an attempt to find a timeless essence that would ignite his own creativity: "Atheist that I was, [Brittany] made of me a saint," wrote Bernard, "It was the Gothic Brittany which initiated me in art and God."[4] The summer of 1891 was decisive for Bernard. At that time, he had severed relations with Gauguin prior to the artist's departure for Tahiti and encountered Sãr Joséphin Péladan, the art theorist and founder of the Symbolist exhibition society *Rose+Croix Catholique* in Saint-Briac. Bernard was electrified by Péladan's promise of a renewed Catholic art that would restore ideal beauty and spiritualism to the industrialized present. This promise of a Catholic purpose to art finally came to dominate Bernard's theory after 1893: the once radical avant-gardist practiced a mode of representational painting firmly grounded in the old masters and authored reactionary criticism decrying modern art.

PATRICIA GRAY BERMAN

NOTES

1. Émile Bernard, "Chez les jeunes peintres," *Echo de Paris*, December 28, 1891, quoted in MaryAnne Stevens, "Introduction: Émile Bernard and His Artistic and Literary Context," in *Émile Bernard 1868–1941: A Pioneer of Modern Art*, exhibition catalogue, Städtische Kunsthalle, Mannheim (Zwolle, Netherlands: Waanders Verlag, 1990), p. 11.

2. Émile Bernard, in *Mercure de France*, 15 June 1936, p. 48, quoted in MaryAnne Stevens, "Bernard as Critic," in *Émile Bernard 1868–1941: A Pioneer of Modern Art*, p. 70.

3. Paul Gauguin, letter to Vincent Van Gogh, Le Pouldu, 20 October 1889, quoted in Françoise Cachin, *Gauguin: The Quest for Paradise* (New York: Abrams, 1992), p. 142.

4. Émile Bernard, quoted in *Post-Impressionism*, exhibition catalogue (London: Royal Academy of Arts, 1979), p. 41.

BIBLIOGRAPHY

Bernard, Émile. *Propos sur l'art*. Ed. Anne Rivière. 2 vols. Paris: Séguier, 1994.

Heller, Reinhold. "Concerning Symbolism and the Structure of Surface." *Art Journal*, 45, no. 2, Summer 1985.

Luthi, Jean-Jacques. *Émile Bernard: Catalogue raisonné de l'oeuvre peint*. Paris: Editions Side, 1982.

Pollock, Griselda, and Fred Orton. "Les Données bretonnantes: la prairie de la représentation." *Art History*, 3, no. 3, September 1980.

Stevens, MaryAnne, et al., eds. *Émile Bernard 1868–1941: A Pioneer of Modern Art*, exhibition catalogue, Städtische Kunsthalle, Mannheim, Germany. Zwolle, Netherlands: Waanders Verlag, 1990.

Welsh-Ovcharov, Bogomile. *Vincent van Gogh and the Birth of Cloisonism*, exhibition catalogue. Toronto: Art Gallery of Ontario, 1981.

CAT. NO. 39

A Edvard Munch
Løten, Norway 1863–1944 Oslo
active Kristiania (now Oslo), Paris, Berlin, and Kragerø

T *Madonna (Conception)*

D 1895, printed 1902

M color woodcut and lithograph on fine-weight Japanese-style buff paper, state 2 of 2

X image: 20 3/4 in. x 13 1/4 in. (527 mm x 336 mm)
sheet: 21 1/8 in. x 15 1/4 in. (831 mm x 600 mm)

C Gift of Mr. and Mrs. Robert Schwarz (Faith Lasser, Class of 1945)
1980.1

Madonna was one of the most audacious and troubling invocations of the Virgin Mary at the turn of the last century. Created by the Norwegian painter and graphic artist Edvard Munch in the mid-1890s, and reworked in 1902, the image seems to suggest, simultaneously, a highly sexualized woman viewed from the intimate perspective of her lover (Eggum 1990, p. 188) and the Christian sacred mother. The merging of religious and sexual themes in this image echoes one of Munch's objectives for his work of the 1890s: to examine procreative sexuality in its sacral dimensions, representing "only one of the thousands of sexual links tying one generation to another generation." He felt that "[p]eople should understand the sanctity, the grandeur of it, and should take off their hats as if in church" (Munch, p. 64). Viewed frontally and from a subtly lowered vantage point, the woman's face and torso are strongly lit so that they emerge dramatically from a dark, swirling background. The position of the figure's arms, raised and thrown back as though her hands are clasped behind her head, pushes her torso forward toward the viewer. The shadows that fall over the woman's face, creating dramatic hollows below her cheeks, in her eye sockets, and across her throat, suggest the merging of her features with their underlying skull. In its embodiment of death and sexuality, Munch's figure was immediately recognizable to his contemporary audiences as a *femme*

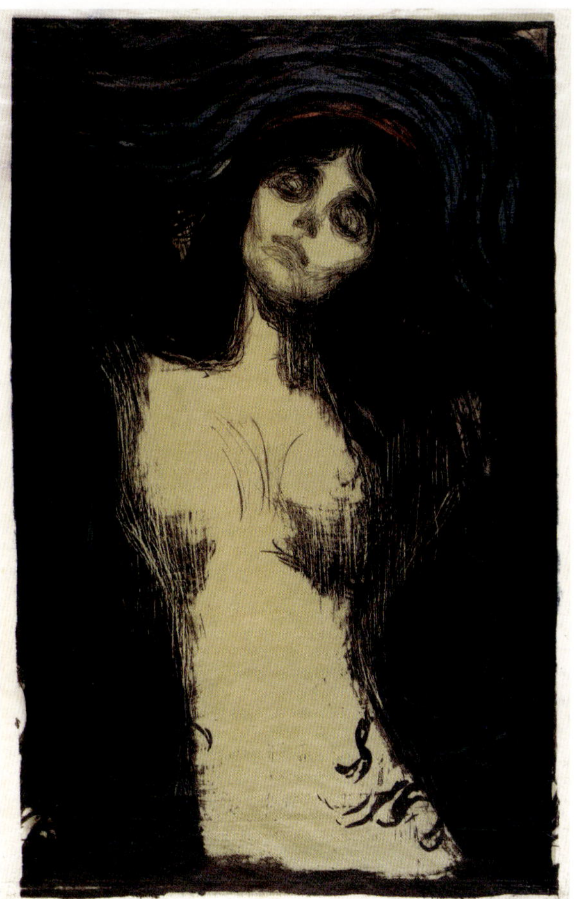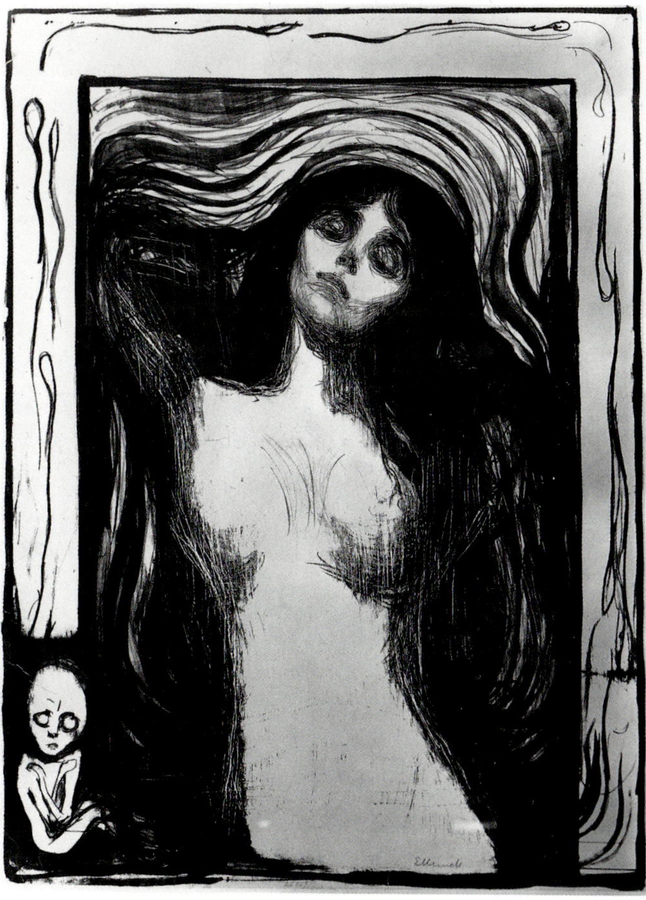

fatale, a fatal woman, an imagined social type that expressed Europeanwide male anxieties about women's unstable social roles at the turn of the century (see Berman and van Nimmen).

This print is one of numerous versions of the motif that Munch first explored in sketches dating to 1893 and in a painting exhibited in that year in Berlin. In one drawing of the motif (*Study for Madonna*, ca. 1893, Munch Museum, Oslo), the woman's head is surrounded by a large halo. In the various graphic versions, rendered in a complex combination of media (Prelinger and Parke-Taylor, pp. 99–104), the halo effect is achieved by a small red band that crowns the woman's head and the wavering lines of hair, and seemingly of physical or psychic energy, that radiate outward from her head and body. In several versions of the motif, created between 1893 and 1902, a decorative frieze surrounds the central image [fig. 158]. Comprised of a sickly, cowering embryo on the lower left and a ribbon of undulating spermatozoa, the border further articulates the woman's body as a vessel and the physical act of love as one of both cosmic beginnings and endings. A small fragmentary image of the embryo embedded in this border appears in the lower left corner of this print. It has been speculated that the border was conceived as an integral part of the motif. When the painted version was first exhibited, it was likely "furnished with a frame with painted or carved spermatozoa and embryos," which was later removed and lost (Eggum 1978, p. 49).

Because Munch developed this motif in connection with his literary milieu in Berlin, it has often been conjectured that the model for this image was Dagny Juel Przybyszewska, a Norwegian artist and poet who was a close colleague of the artist in the mid-1890s. Munch, however, discouraged this idea, instead claiming that the model simply bore a resemblance to her. Munch's cosmopolitan literary and artistic circle was preoccupied with cosmic questions of identity and existence, conscious of its historical place at the end of a century of material-ism and within a period of increasing scientific rationalism. Like intellectuals throughout the industrialized world at the turn of the century, Munch and his colleagues were particularly chal-lenged by the problem of reconciling spiritualism and religious mystery with the new positivist sci-ences. Working at the same time that Sigmund Freud began to formulate his theories of psychosex-uality, Munch proposed the idea that sexual instinct undergirded all of human consciousness. Providing a bridge between the seemingly oppositional sys-tems of religion and science, *Madonna*'s dual aspect of the sacred and the profane articulates the ways in which artists interrogated and recast historical, reli-gious identities at the *fin de siècle*.

PATRICIA GRAY BERMAN

BIBLIOGRAPHY

Berman, Patricia G., and Jane Van Nimmen. *Munch and Women: Image and Myth*, exhibition catalogue. Alexandria, VA: Art Services International, 1997.

Eggum, Arne. "Madonna." In *Edvard Munch: Symbols and Images*, exhibition catalogue. Washington, DC: National Gallery of Art, 1978.

Eggum, Arne. *Edvard Munch: Paintings, Sketches and Studies*. Oslo: J. M. Stenersens Forlag, 1984.

Eggum, Arne. *Edvard Munch: Livsfrisen fra Maleri til Grafikk*. Oslo: J. M. Stenersens Forlag, 1990.

Munch, Edvard. *Livsfrisens tilbrivelse*. Oslo: 1929. In *Munch: His Life and Work*, by Reinhold Heller. Chicago: University of Chicago Press, 1984.

Prelinger, Elizabeth, and Michael Parke-Taylor. *The Symbolist Prints of Edvard Munch*: The *Vivian and David Campbell Collec-tion*, exhibition catalogue, Art Gallery of Ontario, Toronto. New Haven: Yale University Press, 1997.

Stang, Ragna. *Edvard Munch: The Man and His Art*. Translated by Geoffrey Culverwell. New York: Abbeville Press, 1977.

CAT. NO. 40

A Gertrude Käsebier
Fort Des Moines, Iowa 1852–1934 New York, New York
active Brooklyn and Manhattan

T *Adoration*
alternate titles: *Mother and Child* and the *Vision*

D 1897

M gum bichromate print

X print: 11 1/2 in. x 6 3/8 in. (292 mm x 162 mm)

I inscribed in negative (fragment appears in print): 'MDCCCX'

C Museum purchase
1973.40

By 1897, when Käsebier made her lyrical pho-tograph *Mother and Child*, the secularized Madonna was at the height of her popularity. Only the gentlest reminders of religious imagery imbued Käsebier's image of the physical love between a real mother and child with a sacred aura. Käsebier's contemporary peers would all have instantly recognized her references to Madonna and child paintings. Any picture of a maternal woman with a baby would have triggered the label "Madonna"—above all, one of a mother with a naked baby who might be a boy.

But Käsebier composed and lit her subject in ways directly dependent on revered paintings by *quattrocento* and *cinquecento* painters like Raphael or Botticelli, and sculptors like Della Robbia or Verrochio. Like Italian Renaissance models, Käse-bier's mother presents her child's body to her audience. The mother, gracefully draped and in profile, holds up her child so that we see him (or her) frontally in a soft light that makes the child's body gently radiant. The echoing curves and folds at the embracing center of the image are emphasized by the image's shallow space, and by a background so flat it seems to have a date engraved on it in the style of many early modern European portraits. Above the variations in white of chair back, fabric, and lace, the mother's adoring head is tipped back in shadow, while the child's flashing eyes are raised heavenward.

All these connections to older Catholic paintings and sculptures would have been widely known because of the enormous prestige of those works in the late nineteenth and early twentieth centuries. Not only were Madonnas by artists such as Raphael, Botticelli, and Della Robbia the most prized items in the new art museums being founded throughout Europe and North America, but they were endlessly reproduced and hailed as the greatest masterpieces of all time. "The Raphael I *want* is a *Madonna*," wrote the museum founder Isabella Stewart Gardner.

In an increasingly secular society, the revered Madonna theme could appeal to an exponentially increased audience if its most obviously religious aspects disappeared. Halos, theological iconography like bunches of grapes and sheaves of wheat, companion saints, and the sexuality of Christ had to be replaced by discrete signs of middle-class affluence, incentives to maternal devotion, and the inclusion of girl children. This work was accomplished by women artists. Because women were assumed to feel a natural affinity for the subjects of maternity and childhood, they felt inclined, or were obliged, to specialize in them. Without exception, the most successful women commercial and fine artists at the turn of the century based their careers on pictures of mothers and children: Jessie Willcox Smith in commercial illustration, Bessie Potter Vonnoh in sculpture, Mary Cassatt in painting, and Käsebier in photography. (The fundamental conception of this particular Käsebier photograph, as well as its specific

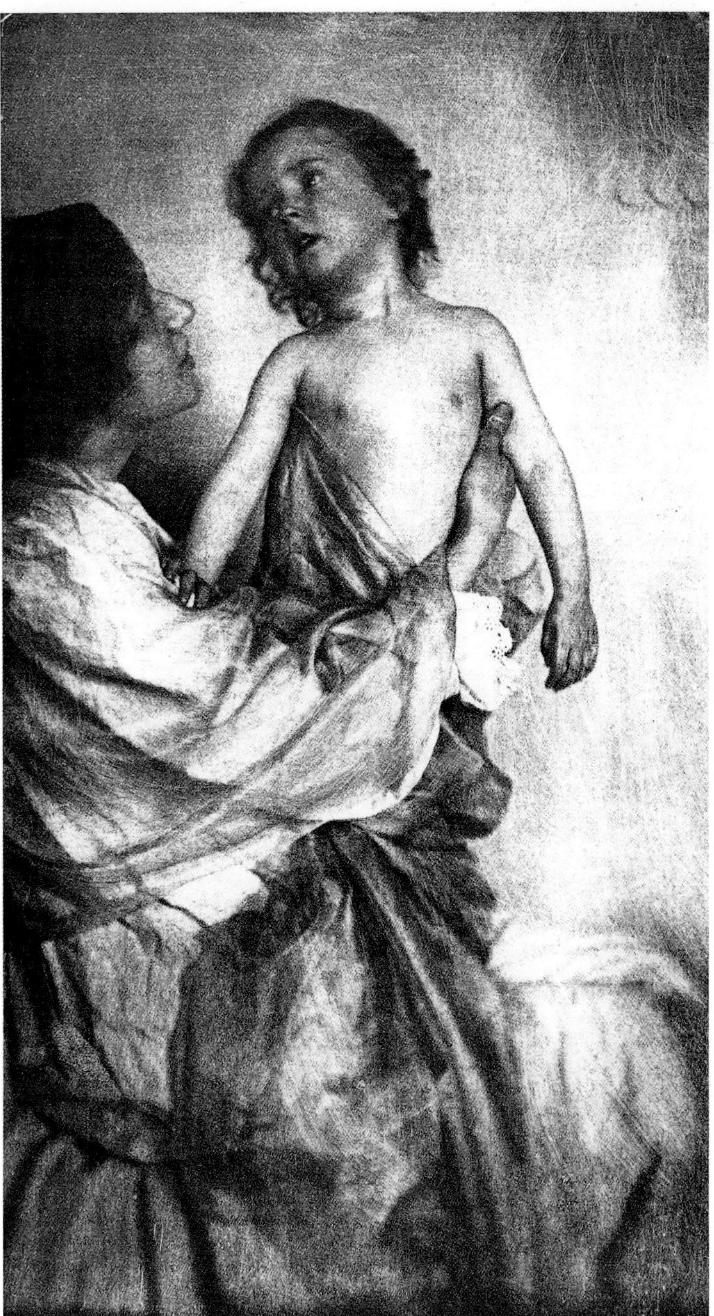

Fig. 159. Gertrude Käsebier, *Adoration (Mother and Child)*, 1897, gum bichromate print

composition, is in fact extremely similar to work by Smith, Vonnoh, and Cassatt.)

Even in the most self-consciously avant-garde circles, a gendered pattern held true: when Alfred Steiglitz published five of Käsebier's photographs in the April 1899 issue of the cutting edge *Camera Notes*, it was *Mother and Child* that was reproduced full-page. Käsebier's fellow pictorialist photographers also made images of children, yet somehow only Käsebier became famous for children represented with mothers. For F. Holland Day and Clarence White, notably, the body of the child was a sign of primordial sensuality, a figure to be rhymed with arcadian scenery and primitive worship.

Yet, in their own way, women artists like Käsebier, whose images of the Madonna seemed so chaste, were celebrating pleasure. If Käsebier's Madonna is not adoring her child because He is God, then she revels in her intimate love of a soft lithe little body. The child's flesh is what Käsebier's image is organized around. While the picture's space and light function as references to Old Master art, they also serve to isolate this Madonna from both the real world and the divine—thereby removing her and her child into a realm apart, in which they exist only for each other. Käsebier's idealization of maternity, at once innocent and passionate, still appeals to us almost a century later.

ANNE HIGONNET

BIBLIOGRAPHY

Berman, Patricia Gray. "F. Holland Day and His 'Classical' Models: Summer Camp." *History of Photography*, 18, no. 4 (1994), pp. 348–67.

Brown, David Alan. *Raphael in America*. Washington, DC: National Gallery of Art, 1983.

Higonnet, Anne. *Pictures of Innocence: The History and Crisis of Ideal Childhood*. London: Thames and Hudson, 1998.

Michaels, Barbara. *Gertrude Käsebier: The Photographer and Her Photographs*. New York: Harry N. Abrams, 1992.

Steinberg, Leo. *The Sexuality of Christ in Renaissance Art and in Modern Oblivion*, 2nd ed. Chicago: University of Chicago Press, 1996.

CAT. NO. 41

A Gertrude Käsebier
Fort Des Moines, Iowa 1852–1934 New York, New York
active Brooklyn and Manhattan

T *The Heritage of Motherhood*
alternate title: *Mrs. Lee Mourning her Child*

D 1904

M gum bichromate print on fine-weight laid paper mounted to long-fibered paper

X print: 9 15/16 in. x 11 15/16 in. (252 mm x 303 mm)
mount (original): 10 7/8 in. x 13 5/8 in. (275 mm x 358 mm)

S signed in white ink, on print: 'Gertrude Käsebier'

C Museum purchase
1973.41

And an additional print from the same negative 1973.42 [fig. 103] (see checklist for cataloguing)

Woman like a rock. Sorrow like forever. Light like darkness.

Before we know the title of Käsebier's photograph, its formal power already arrests us. The woman in the image is seated so close to us, and rises so majestically, that we must be at her feet. She is of the earth and above the earth, her skirt a lighter version of the hills behind her, her cloak a black mountain, her hands clasped as if crags. Her head dominates the sky though it is of the same shades as the sky, a sky whose looming weight is mystically conquered by her humanity and by the white streaks over the horizon.

The organic simplicity and broad rhythms of *The Heritage of Motherhood* were encouraged by the tenets of Pictorialism, a photography movement in its heyday at the turn of the twentieth century. Seeking to raise the artistic status of photography closer to that of painting, pictorialist photographers renounced the precision, focus, detail, and realism made possible by machinery and chem-

istry in favor of atmospheric effects, altered negatives, and allegorical subjects. *The Heritage of Motherhood*, for instance, is clearly not a candid scene
that happened to be captured by a camera, but
rather a vision staged for the camera, then
expressed through manipulations of the negative
and print, manipulations that include brushwork.
Most dramatically, Käsebier made at least one version of this image to which she added three
crosses on the horizon—an obvious reference to
the Christian crucifixion. Taken in tandem with
the image's title, the version with the three crosses
explicitly designates Käsebier's intention that the
image be understood as a modern Lamentation
(the standard Christian subject of Christ's mother
mourning his sacrificial death by crucifixion).

Käsebier tapped into the tradition of Lamentation paintings to create *The Heritage of Motherhood* and
also into a more recent Romantic tradition of self-
immersion in nature. From countless Depositions
(scenes of Christ being lowered from the cross, often
with his mother witnessing) and especially from
Pietàs (scenes of the Madonna holding the dead
body of her deposed son in her lap), Käsebier
derived her powerfully pyramidal composition as
well as her mood of deep mourning. Yet in Käsebier's image, that composition and mood is constituted only by the mother, and by the mother's solitary communion with a sweeping landscape. Käsebier's mother is an elemental force unto herself.

The Heritage of Motherhood attributes an
unprecedented power and grandeur to mourn-
ful maternity. Certainly Käsebier herself knew
what it felt like to struggle. A woman in a man's
artistic world, she had to work hard for a living,
let alone for fame and aesthetic recognition;
and the toll on her private life was of course
considerable. More pointedly, the model for
The Heritage of Motherhood had just experienced
terrible tragedy when the photograph was
made. Agnes Lee had recently suffered the
death of one child and the deafening of
another, as well as the collapse of her marriage.

She was apparently so absorbed in her thoughts
when Käsebier shot *The Heritage of Motherhood*, at
pictorialist photographer F. Holland Day's summer home in Maine, that she didn't notice the picture being taken. Perhaps only a convergence of
factors—the beliefs of an artistic movement; long,
rich painting traditions; an artist's circumstances;
and a model's—could produce an image so innovative and yet so primal.

ANNE HIGONNET

BIBLIOGRAPHY

Berman, Patricia Gray. "F. Holland Day and His 'Classical' Models: Summer Camp." *History of Photography*, 18, no. 4 (1994),
pp. 348–67.

Brown, David Alan. *Raphael in America.* Washington, DC: National
Gallery of Art, 1983.

Higonnet, Anne. *Pictures of Innocence: The History and Crisis of
Ideal Childhood.* London: Thames & Hudson, 1998.

Michaels, Barbara. *Gertrude Käsebier: The Photographer and Her Photographs.* New York: Harry N. Abrams, 1992.

Steinberg, Leo. *The Sexuality of Christ in Renaissance Art and in
Modern Oblivion*, 2nd ed. Chicago: University of Chicago
Press, 1996.

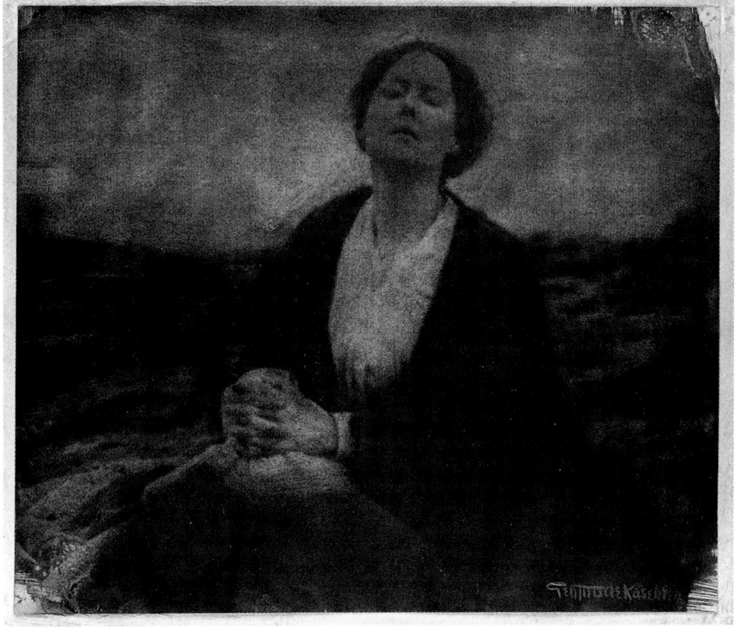

Fig. 160. Gertrude Käsebier, *Heritage of Motherhood*, 1904, gum bichromate print

CAT. NO. 42

A René-François-Auguste Rodin
Paris, France 1840–1917 Meudon
active Paris, Brussels, And Meudon

T *Eve (after the fall)*

D 1899

M marble

X approx. 30 3/4 In. X 8 In. X 11 In. (78.1 cm X 20.3
cm X 28.3 cm)

S signed on right side of base, rear: 'A. Rodin'

C Gift Of Mr. And Mrs. Dan Erskine Edgerton
(Phyllis Burke, Class of 1917) in memory of their
daughter Nancy Edgerton Johnson
1982.4

Rodin involves the viewer in his depiction of Eve's shame before God, using Eve's complete figure to display both her inner thoughts and immediate reactions to the Divine presence surrounding her. Rodin first carved *Eve after the Fall* in marble between 1883 and 1886, with eleven subsequent marble samples. Rodin had intended that it be placed in front of the *Gates of Hell,* his longest-running project, across from *Adam,* a composition that surfaced only posthumously. Stripped of these accompanying sculptures and setting, however, she has become simply *Eve.*

Rodin strove to recreate the movement, natural gestures, and soft flesh of his models in the typically static medium of marble. As a result, *Eve*'s form possesses a gentle fertility that Rodin witnessed in the changing physique of his model, Madame Abruzzezi, whom Rodin later discovered to be pregnant. Rodin even called *Eve* "unfinished" because he was not able to continue shaping *Eve* truthfully to Abruzzezi's growing form.

Rodin relied on the natural forms of his models rather than seek to idealize their figures. Current with the Symbolist movement of the time, he sought to convey the workings of the mind through mere depictions of movement. Rodin's interest in representing emotion with only the sur-face form of the body is partially due to his long-term study of Michelangelo's sculptures and paintings of the human figure.

Eve's forcefully submissive gesture is complete only when seen from all angles. Rodin involves the viewer in the tension of a simultaneous forward movement and surrender backward. From every side, as though in the middle of the scene, Eve's movement expresses a consciousness of the foreboding God who surrounds her. The classically influenced bend of the knee and coyly positioned left foot become symbols of Eve's shame and desire to retreat from her fate; Rodin partners these gestures with Eve's hunched posture and her arms' protective shielding of her cast-down face. As Eve reacts to God's imminence, Rodin involves the viewer in her movement and, thereby, in her torment. The struggle of the *Eve*'s contradictory gestures forces the viewer to actively participate—both physically and emotionally—in this "scene" between Eve and God.

Eve was commissioned directly from Rodin by Julia Richardson in 1899. Mrs. Richardson had the opportunity to visit Rodin in Paris several times during that year. Sculptor and patron also maintained a formal correspondence, reminiscing about their visits as well as about the artistry of *Eve;* one of Rodin's letters to Mrs. Richardson is preserved in the museum's archives [fig. 162].

BLAIR A. BROOKS '02

BIBLIOGRAPHY

Elsen, Albert E., ed. *Rodin Rediscovered*, exhibition catalogue. Washington, DC: National Gallery of Art, 1981.

Elsen, Albert E. *The Gates of Hell by Auguste Rodin.* Stanford, CA: Stanford University Press, 1985.

Goldscheider, Cecile. *Auguste Rodin: Catalogue raisonné de l'oeuvre sculpte.* Paris: Wildenstein Institute, 1989.

Russell, H. Diane. *Eva/Ave: Woman in Renaissance and Baroque Prints.* Washington, DC: National Gallery of Art, 1990.

Tancock, John L. *The Sculpture of Auguste Rodin.* Philadelphia: Philadelphia Museum of Art, 1976 [listed as Edgerton collection, Portland, Maine].

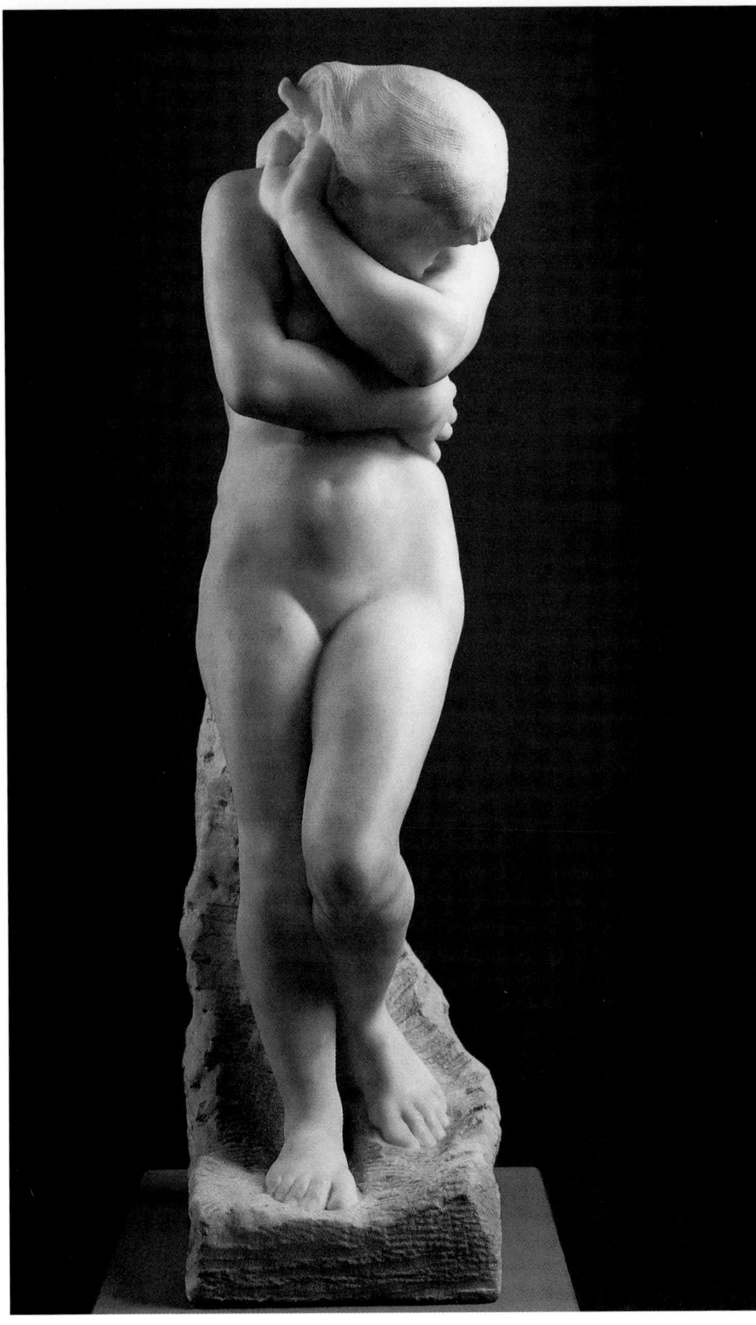

Fig. 161. Auguste
Rodin, *Eve (after the
Fall)*, 1899, marble

Fig. 162. Letter from
Auguste Rodin to Julia
Richardson, 6 October
1899 (front and back).

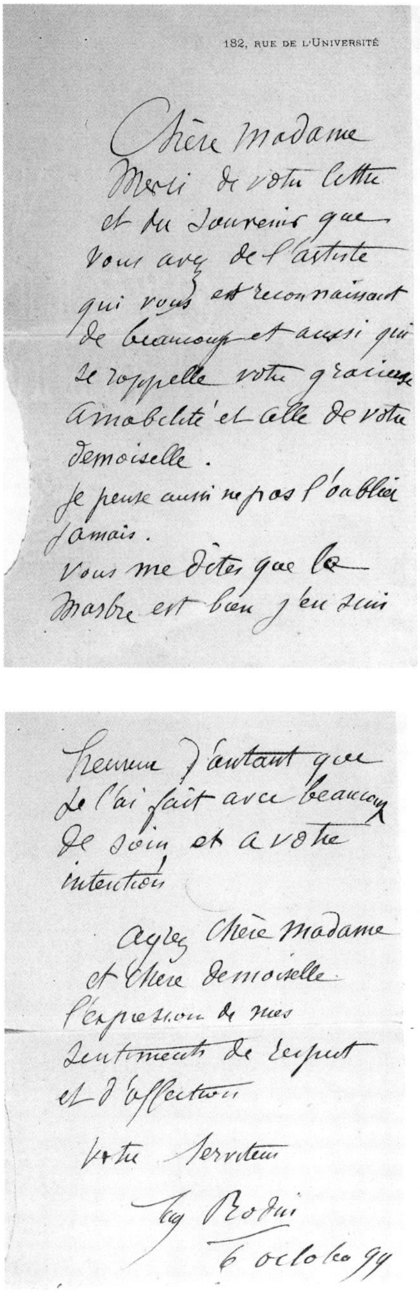

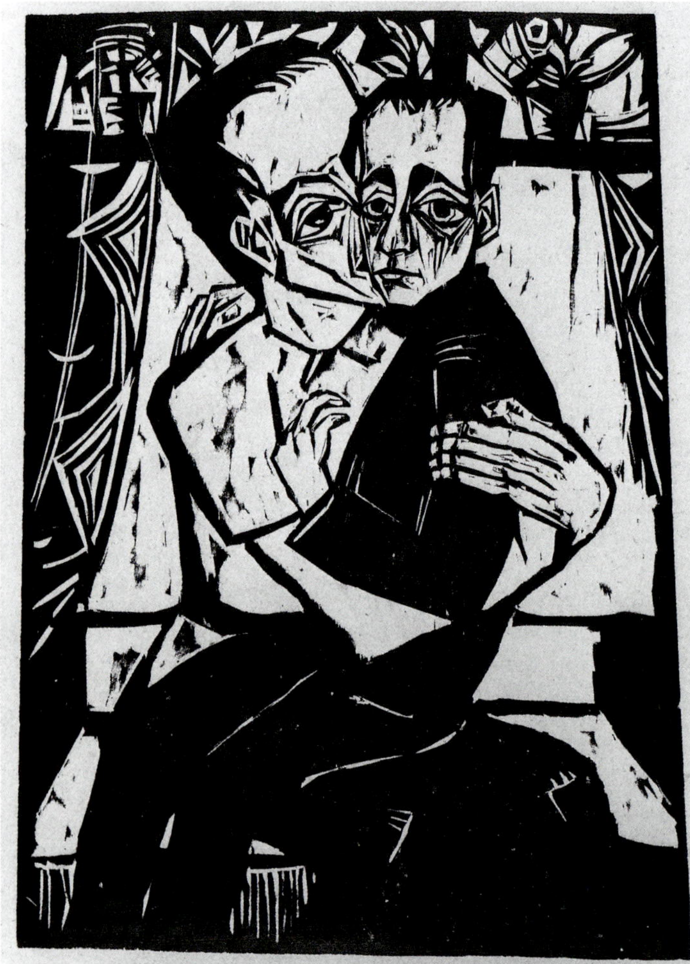

Fig. 163. Erich Heckel, *Geschwister (Siblings)*, 1913, woodcut

CAT. NO. 43

A Erich Heckel
Döbeln, Saxony 1883–1970 Radolfzell, Germany
active Dresden, Berlin, Hemmenhofen, and
Karlsruhe

T *Geschwister (Siblings)*
after a 1911 painting by the artist, now in the
Staatliche Kunsthalle, Karlsruhe

D 1913

M woodcut on Bütten paper (heavy-weight greyish-
white absorbent wove textured blotting paper)

X image: 16 1/4 in. x 11 5/16 in. (413 mm x 287
mm)
sheet: 25 3/4 in. x 19 11/16 in. (655 mm x 500
mm)

S signed and dated in pencil, recto: 'Erich Heckel
13'

I see checklist

C Gift of the Ferdinand Roten Gallery
1958.33

Organized in 1905, *Die Brücke* (*The Bridge*) was a rebel artist group established in Dresden, Germany by four young architecture students, including Erich Heckel. Together they defied the urge toward illusionism that had characterized Western art since the Renaissance and that had become the domain of repressive academic organizations. Marking the beginning of Expressionism in Germany, the group sought to form a bridge between the art of established academies and the art of the avant-garde. Together these artists created the earliest body of paintings, sculptures, drawings, and prints consistently representing German Expressionism, the major German contribution to modern art of the last century.

This brother-and-sister pair, whose identity is unknown, is also the subject of Heckel's 1911 painting bearing the same title. In both works the artist has set the figures in front of a window framed by curtains. The brother, whose youth is suggested only by his small size relative to that of his sister, gestures with his left hand while clinging to his older sibling. The sister holds her brother on her lap and wraps him in her arms; she is focused entirely on her brother as his gaze confronts the viewer, creating a psychological tension. Adding to the uneasiness of this image are the tensions produced by the strong black and white contrasts, the bold cutting, and the incongruities and distortions of the figures in compressed space, that narrows slightly at the top.

Though the composition foreshadows Heckel's woodcut *Ostende Madonna* (1916), a representation of the Virgin Mary holding Christ, the themes of youth and sibling relationships are, perhaps, as significant as these latent, religious references. The 1906 *Brücke Program* outlines "a belief in continuing the evolution [of modern art] and in a new generation of creators as well as appreciators," realized through the active participation of youth. Young people had long been thought to have an instinctively perceptive capacity to disregard the past and its institutions and to be enthusiastic partisans of a new future. This sibling portrait, undoubtedly informed by the value *Die Brücke* artists placed on youth, may therefore affirm these positive, youthful qualities. For these artists, the young embodied the process of change and were defined in terms of their potentiality as opposed to a restrictive past. Indeed, these qualities were central to the identity of *Brücke* artists themselves, who advocated in their art free-form individualism, creativity, spirituality, and independence from officially sponsored, established art organizations.

JEREMY J. FOWLER

BIBLIOGRAPHY

Buchheim, Lothar Günther. *Graphik des deutschen Expressionismus.* Feldafing, Germany: Buchheim Verlag, 1959.

Buchheim, Lothar Günther. *Die Kunstlergruppe Brücke und der deutsche Expressionismus: Sammlung Buchheim,* exhibition catalogue. Feldafing, Germany: Buchheim Verlag, 1973.

Dube-Heynig, Annemarie, and Wolf-Dieter Dube. *Erich Heckel: das graphische Werk.* New York: E. Rathenau, 1974.

Vogt, Paul. *Expressionismus: German painting 1905–1920,* Robert Erich Wolf, trans. New York, Harry N. Abrams, 1980.

Zigrosser, Carl. *The Expressionists: A Survey of their Graphic Art.* New York, G. Braziller, 1957.

CAT. NO. 44

A Gertrude H. Fiske
   Boston, Massachusetts 1878–1961 Weston, Massachusetts
   active Boston and Ogunquit, Maine

T *Mary*

D 1920

M oil on canvas

X 39 1/2 in. x 30 in. (100.3 cm x 76.2 cm)

S signed in black paint: 'Gertrude Fiske'

C Gift of Andrew F. Willis, Harold B. Willis, Jr. (husband of Artemis Pazianos, Class of 1951) and Mrs. Gilbert T. Wilkinson
   1969.46

In 1920 Gertrude Fiske (1878–1961) created this portrait of a teenage girl sitting solemnly with her hands clasped on her lap. The girl wears a red and blue checked pinafore over a loose, long-sleeved white blouse; her red hair is tied back in two braids that fall behind her shoulders. Her pose is controlled, yet tense, her expression guarded and ambivalent. Of the many portraits Fiske painted, the vast majority were of women and girls. In these works, she captured much more than her sitters' likenesses; she revealed their moods and personalities. The portrait of *Mary* is no exception.

Fiske attended the School of the Museum of Fine Arts, Boston from 1904 to 1912, studying with famous Boston painters such as Tarbell, Benson, Hale, and Paxton. After leaving school, she began working with Charles H. Woodbury in Ogunquit, Maine, where she set up a studio and spent summers. She also maintained studios in Boston and Weston, Massachusetts, throughout her career. During her lifetime, Fiske was considered a leading Boston painter—she was given over ten one-woman shows, won eighteen prestigious awards, and was made a member of the National Academy. Fiske received many commissions from prominent families in New England, but she also enjoyed painting portraits of people around her whom she found intriguing. The identity of this sitter is unknown, nor is it certain whether the portrait was commisioned. Its title, however, can be confimed by a December 1920 newspaper clipping that reads, "Miss Fiske had her nerve with her when she painted 'Mary'—the girl in the checked dress. It is mighty well done."

Fiske did not intend to present this Mary as the Virgin Mary, but because they share a name, the viewer begins to notice similarities. Images of the young Virgin Mary present her as innocent and demure, with her head lowered humbly, eyes downcast, and hands drawn to her chest. In Fiske's portrait, the girl's innocence is suggested by her youth. Though she may be a teenager, the braids in her hair and the pinafore she wears tie her to childhood. This Mary also slightly bows her head and modestly holds her hands close to her body. In addition, the Virgin's traditional colors, royal blue and blood red, appear in the long dress worn by Fiske's Mary. The Virgin's head is usually framed by a halo; in Fiske's portrait, a framed picture placed directly behind her Mary's head creates a haloing effect.

Nevertheless, distinctly secular aspects set Fiske's Mary apart from her sacred namesake. In this twentieth-century portrait, Fiske reveals more about the girl's psychological state than is attempted in most images of the Virgin Mary. The Virgin Mary is revered for her unquestioning obedience and is usually presented as tranquil and complacent. Although Fiske's Mary is certainly obedient as she sits still for her portrait, her expression reveals that her obedience is not unquestioning. It is difficult to tell what this girl is thinking, yet her steady gaze almost wills us to guess. Fiske has captured the moodiness of adolescence in this Mary, an emotion the Virgin Mary was never allowed to express. In this painting, Fiske puts the private emotions of a young girl on public display, yet it is the sitter, not the viewer, who remains in control of the exchange.

REBECCA MONGEON

BIBLIOGRAPHY

Gertrude Fiske (1878–1961): October 1 to December 31, 1987. Boston, MA: Vose Galleries of Boston, Inc., 1987.

Unsigned review. *Boston Post*. Wednesday, 22 December 1920.

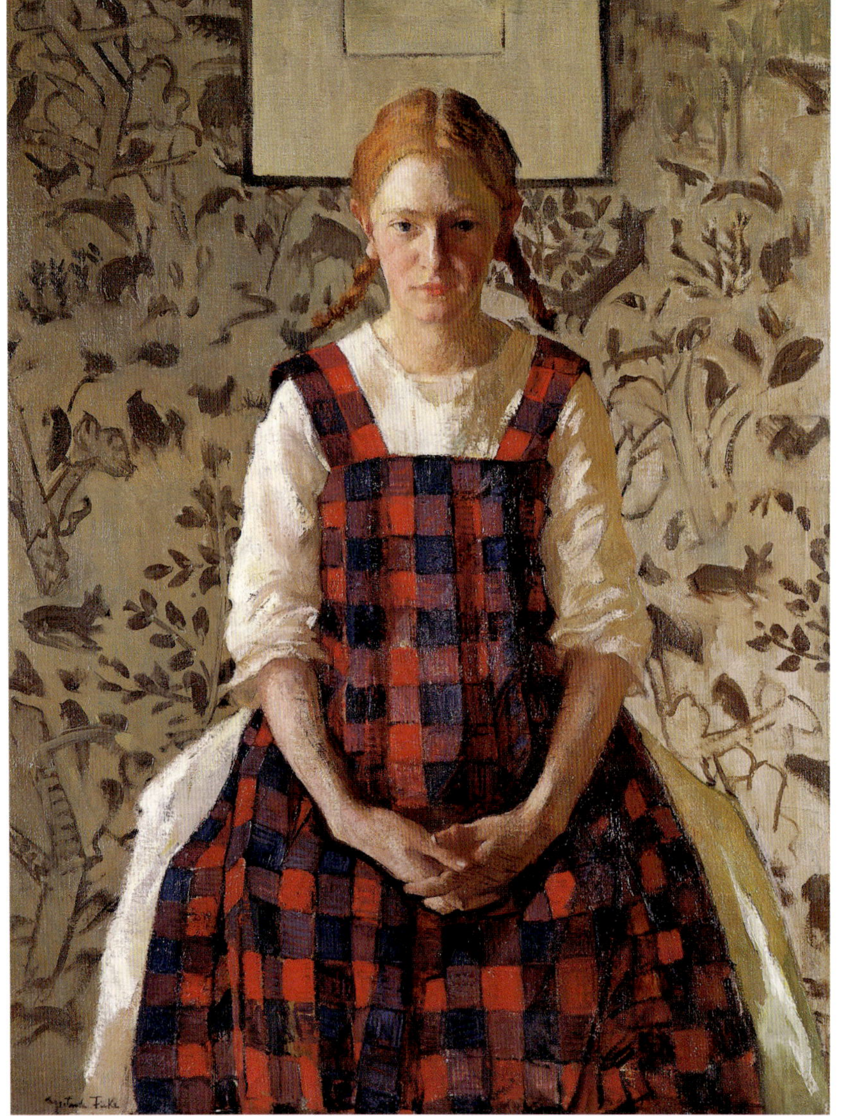

Fig. 164. Gertrude Fiske, *Mary*, 1920, oil on canvas

A Fernand Léger
Argentan, France 1881–1955 Gif-sur-Yvette
active Paris and New York

T *Woman and Child*

D 1921

M oil on canvas

X 25 5/8 in. x 21 1/4 in. (65.1 cm x 54.0 cm)

C Gift of Professor and Mrs. J. McAndrew in honor
of Alfred H. Barr, Jr.

1954.9

Created within the three years following the end of the Great War, this painting represents a kind of domestic Modernism, summarizing many of Léger's ideas and aspirations during the period of France's "return to order." Léger, a leading member of the Parisian vanguard in the prewar years, exhibited with the Cubists and other international Modernist circles. He had begun to explore a mechanical treatment of the human figure before the war, but when he reentered civilian life (he had enlisted in the army in August 1914), he committed himself to the "plastic possibilities of ordinary manufactured objects," the notion of the machine as a metaphor and avatar of modernity. In the years just after the war, Léger painted compositions celebrating the fragmentation and dissonance of the modern city and the rapidly expanding industrial and commercial advertising presence in its streets. After 1920, however, he began to integrate human figures more fully into machinelike environments and to concentrate on interior genre scenes, such as the monumental *Grand Dejeuner* (1921, Museum of Modern Art):

> I had broken down the human body, so I set about putting it together again and rediscovering the human face. . . . I wanted a rest, a breathing space. After the dynamism of the mechanical period, I felt a need for the staticity of larger figures. (Lanchner, p. 188)

Woman and Child, which Léger rendered in two versions in 1921 (Bauquier), suggests the balance between representation and abstraction that he sought in that period, and it articulates his grounding of a modernist industrial aesthetic in a scene of domestic intimacy.

In *Woman and Child*, a representation of a frontally oriented female figure—so large that it is cropped at the brow line by the top of the canvas and at the knees by the bottom—is placed within the pictorial scaffolding of a high modernist interior. A front-facing child, painted in steely grays, is held against this polychromatic figure's chest. Strong vertical elements, composed of black and white, and accented by horizontal lines and abrupt areas of bright color, structure the background. Equal attention seems to have been paid to both traditionally significant and insignificant details, so that patterns on what appear to be floor tiles vie for attention with the figures' inverted "L"-shaped faces. Although the two figures seem to be flattened against this insistent pictorial grid, the presence of a table displaying a still life that overlaps the woman's left elbow, and a second table supporting a house plant appearing behind her right elbow, map a recession into the room. The tension between this hint of palpable space and the overall flat geometric patterning is enhanced by the divergent treatments given to the figures and the setting. The organic presences—the woman, child, and plant—are painted in ovoid or rectangular areas of paint nuanced to suggest their roundness, while the architectural elements are rendered in flat areas of unmodulated pigment. At the compositional center, the woman's large, spatulate right hand shelters the child's chest. This gesture, like the eccentric geometry that radiates outward from it, articulates industrially inspired modernist design as a sanctuary for a new humanity.

Léger's professed fascination of the early 1920s was not with machines qua machines, but with human interaction with them. Having met Charles-Edouard Jeanneret (Le Corbusier) and Amédée

Ozenfant, founders of the art movement known as Purism, in 1920, Léger echoed their enthusiasm for a renewed, principled art based on mathematical systems, and he shared their belief in machines as the ultimate embodiments of human precision and rationality. At the same time, he was intent upon investing a historical sense of humanism into his compositions, and in the early 1920s, looked back to pre-Renaissance painters for inspiration. As Christopher Green has noted, the collections of the Musée de Cluny, reopened in 1920 after its wartime closure, may have provided fertile ground for Léger's musings (Green, pp. 230–31). Echoing the domestic rituals, both sacred and secular, represented in objects ranging from French fifteenth-century tapestries to devotional statuary, Léger's motifs of women and children in modernist domestic settings, created between 1920 and 1922, invest contemporary life with historical resonance. In light of his marriage to Jeanne Lohy in late 1919 and his commitment to the fusion between the "machine object . . . a polychrome absolute" (Léger, p. 62) and intimate daily ritual, *Woman and Child* expresses the optimism, and the sanctity, of daily experience in the early postwar years.

PATRICIA GRAY BERMAN

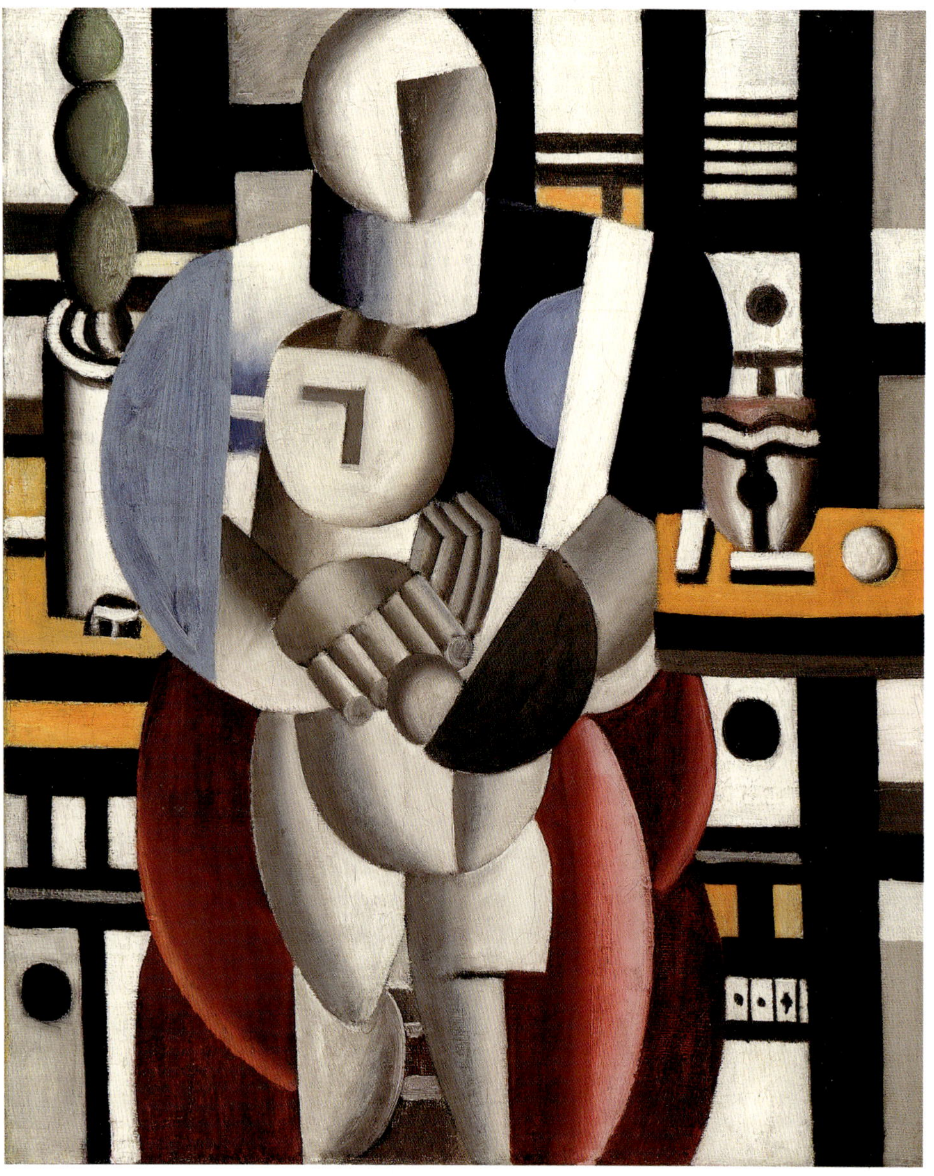

Fig. 165. Fernand Léger, *Woman and child,* 1921, oil on canvas

BIBLIOGRAPHY

Bauquier, Georges. *Fernand Léger: Catalogue raisonné*, vol. 2, 1920–1924, nos. 291 and 292. Paris: Adrien Maeght, 1992.

Golding, John, and Christopher Green. *Léger and Purist Paris*, exhibition catalogue. London: Tate Gallery, 1970.

Green, Christopher. *Léger and the Avant Garde.* New Haven: Yale University Press, 1976.

Lanchner, Carolyn, ed. *Fernand Léger*, exhibition catalogue, Museum of Modern Art. New York: Harry N. Abrams, 1998.

Léger, Fernand. *Propos d'artistes.* Paris: Le Renaissance du Livre, 1925. In *The Functions of Painting* by Fernand Léger, trans. Alexandra Anderson, ed. Edward F. Fry. New York: Viking Press, 1973.

A Otto Müller
Libau, Silesia, Prussia 1874–1930 Breslau, Silesia
active Dresden, Berlin, Eastern Europe, and
Breslau, Silesia (now Wroclaw, Poland)
printed at Breslau Academy by Lange

T *Zigeunermadonna (Gypsy Madonna)*
alternate title: *Ziguenerin mit kind vorm Wagen-rad (Gypsy Woman and Child in front of Wagon Wheel)*
after a 1920s painting by the artist, now in a private collection, Hannover, Germany
plate 5 (of 9) from the *Gypsy Portfolio*, edition of 60

D 1927

M color lithograph in black, brown, and gray ink, with green watercolor on fine-weight dark greenish-grey paper with lattice pattern

X sheet: 27 1/2 in. x 19 3/4 in. (699 mm x 502 mm)

I see checklist

C Gift of Elizabeth Prior Denis (Class of 1932) 1996.44

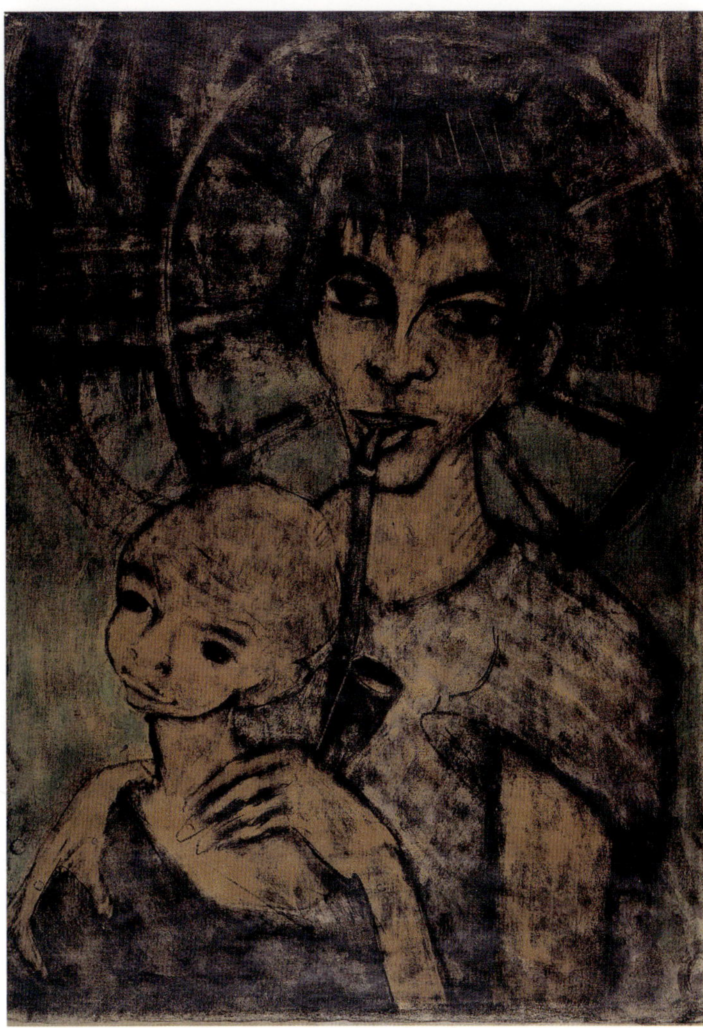

Fig. 166. Otto Müller, *Zigeunermadonna (Gypsy Madonna)*, 1927, hand-colored lithograph

Otto Müller, a highly skilled lithographer, was the only artist associated with *Die Brücke* group who received formal training. His work is informed by an emphasis on process and technical originality. In *Zigeunermadonna*, as with other examples, the artist experimented with the use of color plates. Often Müller hand-painted watercolor onto his lithographs after printing; a green tonality has been attained in this print via this method. Müller achieved strong contours by using a sharp point and soft values by sanding the surface of the litho stone.

The *Gypsy Portfolio* was published by Müller himself in 1927. Each print was made in an edition of sixty, though the artist was not satisfied with the results. As a result, he assembled only twenty complete, signed portfolios, some of which were overpainted by hand. The remaining prints were sold off partly as complete portfolios and partly as individual prints. Today only ten complete editions are known. In a series of nine color lithographs, Müller depicted the Romany people, with whom he had spent several weeks during his travels through Eastern Europe in the last years of his life. In particular, Szolnok, a small town near Budapest, Hungary, inspired many of the motifs that eventually found their way into his work. The entire *Gypsy Portfolio* reflects Müller's shifting understanding and sometimes stereotypical view of the cultural group. Not intended as ethnological documents, his portrayals of the Romany range from dissolute, alluring exotics to idealized wanderers in pursuit of a free and simple existence, and even, in this example, to religious icons.

Gypsy Madonna, a subject the artist also treats in painting, is perhaps the best known of Müller's work. A departure from traditional representations of the Virgin Mary and Christ, the swarthy, humbly clothed mother smoking a pipe and her bald, somewhat undernourished child are posed as if for a photograph, appearing more profane than sacred. While a woman smoking a cigarette might have been regarded as chic and cosmopolitan, a pipe-smoking mother would have been considered a provocative image in Weimar Germany. Furthermore, the title alludes to a visual pun: the wagon wheel encircles the mother's head like a halo, transforming her temporarily into the Mother of Christ.

JEREMY J. FOWLER

BIBLIOGRAPHY

Buchheim, Lothar Günther. *Die Kunstlergemeinschaft Brücke.* Feldafing, Germany: Buchheim Verlag, 1956.

Buchheim, Lothar Günther. *Graphik des deutschen Expressionismus.* Feldafing, Germany: Buchheim Verlag, 1959.

Müller, Otto. *Zigeunermappe.* Dresden: Verlag der Künst, 1958.

Otto Mueller zum hundertsten Geburtstag: das graphische Gesamtwerk: Holzschnitte, Radierungen, Lithographien, Farblithographien. Berlin: Galerie Nierendorf, 1974.

Waldemar, George. *Expressionism.* London: Thames & Hudson, 1960.

Zigrosser, Carl. *The Expressionists: A Survey of their Graphic Art.* New York, G. Braziller, 1957.

CAT. NO. 47

A Marc Chagall (born Moisei Zakharovich Segal) Vitebsk, Bellarus 1887–1985 Saint-Paul-de-Vence, France
active St. Petersburg, Paris, Berlin, Vitebsk, Moscow, New York, and Vence

T Twelve prints from the *Bible* series
1960.25, 1979.28 through 1979.38
(see checklist for cataloguing)

ILLUSTRATED:

T *Abraham Preparing to Sacrifice his Son, according to God's Command (Gen. 27:9–14)*
plate 10 (of 105) from the *Bible* series

D 1931–39, printed in 1956 by Tériade and hand-colored by artist

M watercolor over etching on heavy-weight textured wove discolored cream paper

X plate: 11 13/16 in. x 9 1/28 in. (300 mm x 240 mm)
sheet: 21 3/16 in. x 15 3/8 in. (538 mm x 390 mm)

S signed in pencil: 'M.Ch.'

I see checklist

C bequest of Mrs. Toivo Laminan (Margaret Chamberlin, Class of 1929)
1960.25

Marc Chagall, born on 7 July 1887, in Vitebsk, Bellarus, Russia, grew up in the midst of a strong Hasidic culture and was deeply influenced by the Jewish traditions of his Russian home. One of the most prolific modern artists, he made his first prints in Berlin at the age of 35, after he had been painting for fifteen years. His technique evolved from those beginning etchings, culminating finally with his monumental work on the Bible. In this later work, his Jewish background, technical expertise, and humanist interpretation of the Old Testament combine to form a positive translation of the traditional passages.

The original commission came from Ambroise Vollard, a famous art dealer and publisher in Paris. The project, to be entitled *Le Livre des Prophetes*, was to consist of five volumes: Genesis, Book of Kings, Book of Prophets, Song of Songs, and the Apocalypse. Initially, each book was to have forty illustrations; however, the more realistic number of 105 were planned and completed. When Vollard died suddenly in 1939, only months prior to the outbreak of World War II, 65 of the etchings had been completed and were in his possession, with 35 remaining to be finished. Vollard's brother announced that Chagall's *Bible* would be issued on 1 June 1940, but, as a result of the German invasion of France, the publication was never executed.

Not until 1948, when Chagall returned to France from exile in the United States, was he able to locate and complete the series. With the help of his daughter Ida, who also chose the biblical passages to match his images, Chagall reclaimed his distributed plates from Vollard's heirs and commenced printing. He printed the last three suites from 1952 to 1956 with Tériade, making sure to match the inks and papers with the prewar etchings. Chagall produced two volumes of the 105 etchings, issuing 275 sets signed and numbered by the artist on Montval paper. In addition, 100 albums on Velin d'Arches paper were signed, numbered, and hand-colored by Chagall.

Abraham Preparing Sacrificing to Sacrifice His Son [fig. 167] is one of the hundred hand-colored, signed images. In the etching, Chagall's subtly intricate treatment of the plates can be seen in the complex, textured surface and fine detail that gives substance to the expressive forms. The figures are rendered in an intimate tactile manner that accesses human emotion, with the artist working to portray them realistically by showing both their weakness and strength. Abraham stands poised over the vulnerable, bound body of Isaac, his hand resting tenderly on his son's leg, ready to sacrifice him to God. Above appears the angel to stop him, its wings echoing the form created by Abraham's arm and the menacing knife. Behind them, a ram emerges from the carefully etched thicket, to be sacrificed in Isaac's stead.

In this colored work, Chagall expresses human faith in God. This faith is reflected throughout the *Bible* etchings in a cycle of encounters between

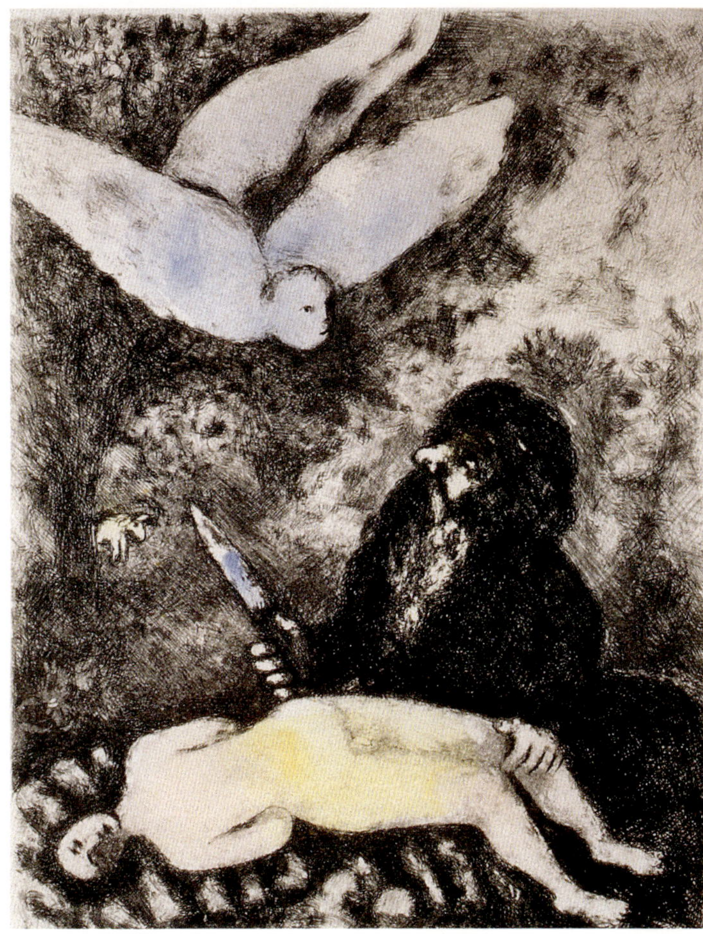

Fig. 167. Marc Chagall, *Abraham Sacrificing Isaac*, 1952, hand-colored etching from the *Bible* series

man and God that focuses on joy, grace, and the human element. This is not the first appearance of biblical themes, values, or ideals in Chagall's work and writings. He addressed scenes from the Old and New Testament in earlier pieces, handling the subjects in both direct and indirect ways. For example, Chagall explicitly utilized highly recognizable biblical figures in *Adam and Eve* (1910), but worked more subtly in *Jew in Green* (1914), with biblical text in Hebrew as its background.

Nor was Chagall's portrayal of biblical subjects his first venture into illustrated text. Chagall produced two other works for Vollard: Gogol's *Dead Souls* (1923–27) and La Fontaine's *Fables* (1928–31). Comparing these earlier illustrations to his later ones, we can see how his technique evolved and matured from crowded, linear compositions to the complex textures and painterly effects that characterize the sensuous, tactile surfaces of the biblical images. It is through these later etchings and selected texts that Chagall conveys the quiet modern spirituality inherent in his work.

MARLENE KUHN '00

BIBLIOGRAPHY

Musée National, Nice. *Musée National: Message Biblique Marc Chagall*, trans. C. de Chabannes. Paris: Editions des musées nationaux, 1976.

Rosensaft, Jean Bloch. *Chagall and the Bible*. New York: Universe Books, 1987.

CAT. NO. 48A

A   Lola Álvarez Bravo
     Lagos de Moreno, Mexico 1907–93 Mexico City
     active Mexico City

T   *La Patrona (The Patroness)*

D   1960s

M   gelatin silver print

X   print: 8 7/8 in. x 7 3/16 in. (225 mm x 183 mm)
     mount: 15 15/16 in. x 13 15/16 in. (405 mm x 354 mm)

S   signed in pencil, on mount: 'Lola Alvarez Bravo'

I   inscribed in pencil on mount, verso: La Patrona'

C   Museum purchase
     2000.12

CAT. NO. 48B

A   Danny Lyon
     born Brooklyn, New York, 1942
     active Chicago, Colombia, and New Mexico

T   *Showers, Diagnostic Unit, Texas*
     from *Conversations with the Dead* series
     reissued as no. 16 of 30 in Hyperion Press portfolio

D   1969–70, printed 1979

M   gelatin silver photograph

X   print: 13 3/8 in. x 9 in. (340 mm x 229 mm)
     sheet: 14 in. x 11 in. (356 mm x 279 mm)

S   signed in pencil, verso: 'Danny Lyon'

C   Extended loan from Mrs. Edith Davis Siegel

(Class of 1938)
44.1980

According to Catholic tradition, the Virgin of Guadalupe appeared to a recent Indian convert in Mexico City in 1531, only a decade after the Spanish conquest of the Aztec empire. When the indigenous witness was unable to convince authorities of the authenticity of the apparition, the Virgin appeared again, leaving an image of herself on the man's *tilma*, a rough cloak made of agave fiber, as indisputable proof. *Criollo* historians first recorded this apparition story in the 1630s. One account includes a woodcut illustration that shows divine light "penetrating" the Virgin and projecting her image onto the Indian's cloak. This probably reveals the artist's familiarity with the mysterious properties of the camera obscura, an optical device used to project an object onto a flat surface. The original image can thus be seen as a proto-photograph, "fixed" by God rather than by light-sensitive paper, which would not be invented until the nineteenth century (Casanova and Debroise, p. 10).

The "original" Virgin of Guadalupe hanging today in Mexico City's Basilica of Guadalupe may have in fact been painted in the sixteenth century by a indigenous artist known as Marcos (Poole, pp. 61–62). Nevertheless, it is still revered as the divine handiwork of the Virgin, and the Basilica has become the most important Catholic pilgrimage center in the Americas. The iconic, two-dimensional image, faithfully copied in thousands of colonial paintings, was adopted as a symbol of Mexican independence in the 1810s, and of Chicano identity in the 1960s; in both instances, the religious referent gave political movements renewed vigor.

Colonial renditions of the Virgin of Guadalupe frequently bear the inscription *"tocado con el original"* ("touched the original"), since actual physical contact not only implied the artist's faithfulness to the 1531 version but also suggested that his copy had absorbed some of its sacred power. Even as late as the early twentieth century, photographic reproductions of the Virgin, including postcards, asserted that they too had "touched the original." Distributors of these cheapest of copies thus sought to preserve the "aura" that Walter Benjamin would later declare lost in the age of mechanical reproduction. In these images by Mexican photographer Lola Álvarez Bravo (1907–93) and American photographer Danny Lyon (b. 1942), popular renditions of the Virgin of Guadalupe appear primarily as indicators of social and cultural identity, but, given the continuing iconic strength of the original, are also invested with an aura that elevates them above the mundane [figs. 168, 169].

Lola Álvarez Bravo's *La Patrona* (*The Patroness*) shows a pair of scarves bearing images of the Virgin of Guadalupe, hanging on display in a Mexican market. They are opened up (unlike the handkerchiefs and flowered scarves that flank them), exposing the holy image to possible buyers. As a fragment of a store name in the background suggests, the photograph is a miscellany of architectural, commercial, and human details, tied together by a subtle but rigid compositional grid. The central placement of the two Virgins further stabilizes the image. In many ways, *La Patrona* is also a study in the effects of light, especially as it passes through cloth. Light penetrates the images of the Virgin, and a gauzy band stretches horizontally across the lower section of the image, transforming the crisp forms of doorways and people into fuzzy, almost pictorialist shadows. Álvarez Bravo was certainly drawn to these scarves for their allusions to national and religious

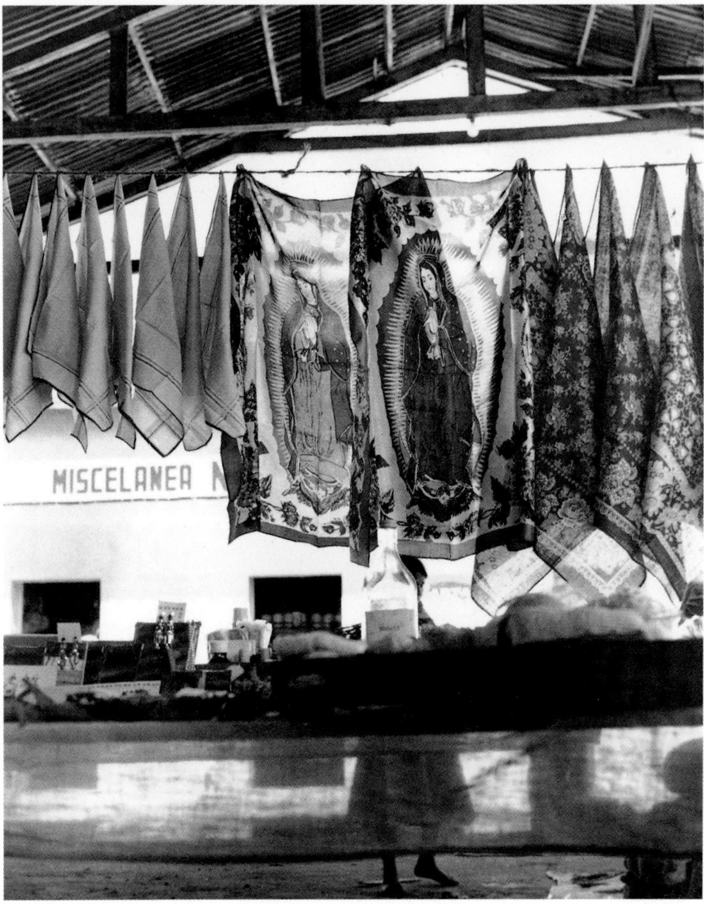

Fig. 168. Lola Álvarez Bravo, *La Patrona*, 1960s, gelatin silver print

values, but *La Patrona* is hardly didactic, maintaining the intimate yet respectful distance that typifies her most compelling photographs.

Danny Lyon's portrait of two men showering in a Texas prison is identified by an almost technical title that recalls less the poetic spirituality of Álvarez Bravo than the documentary tradition of the New Deal Farm Security Administration photographers. Lyon's close interaction with his subjects allows him access to private spaces and rituals, apparent in the frank intimacy of this particular scene. The image was taken during an extended and unrestricted project documenting convict life in Texas, which Lyon hoped would "emotionally convey the spirit of imprisonment shared by 250,000 men in the United States." The men bathe at a processing center for inmates at the beginning of their incarceration; occupying a tight, windowless space, stripped of free-

Fig. 169 . Danny Lyon, *Showers, Diagnostic Unit, Texas,* 1969/70, gelatin silver print from the *Conversations with the Dead* series

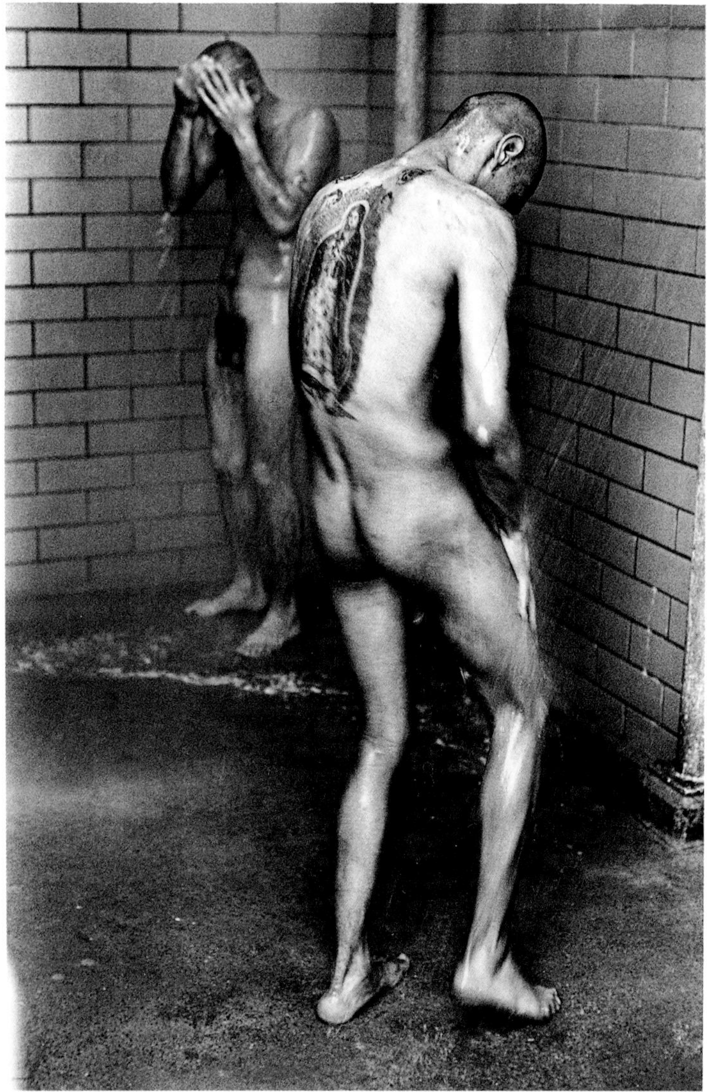

dom and clothing, the new prisoners seem trapped, even humiliated. Yet the Virgin of Guadalupe on one young inmate's back, a tattoo frequently seen in Mexican-American and Chicano communities, remains an indelible marker of individuality, and cultural and religious affiliation. As in *La Patrona,* the image of the Virgin stabilizes the image, ameliorating our rejection of the man as criminal, rooting him in a broader social context, and even deflating some of the image's erotic charge.

JAMES OLES

BIBLIOGRAPHY

Casanova, Rosa, and Olivier Debroise. *Sobre la superficie bruñida de un espejo: Fotografías del siglo XIX.* Mexico City: Fondo de Cultura Económica, 1989.

Conversations with the Dead by Danny Lyon, Photographs of Prison Life with the Letters and Drawings of Billy McCune #122054. New York: Holt, Rinehart and Winston, 1969.

Debroise, Olivier. *Lola Álvarez Bravo: In Her Own Light.* Tucson: Center for Creative Photography, 1994.

García-Noriega, Lucia, ed. *Lola Álvarez Bravo: Fotografías selectas, 1934–1984.* Mexico City: Centro Cultural/Arte Contemporáneo, Fundación Cultural Televisa, 1993.

García-Noriega, Lucia, ed. *Imagenes Guadalupanas: Cuatro siglos.* Mexico City: Centro Cultural/Arte Contemporáneo, 1987.

Poole, Stafford. *Our Lady of Guadalupe: The Origins and Sources of a Mexican National Symbol, 1531–1797.* Tucson: University of Arizona Press, 1995.

A Meg Henson Scales
   born Portland, Oregon 1953
   active Harlem, New York

T *Mary Loves Jesus Bartlet Prayers*

D 1997

M mixed media from a painting by the artist

X approx. 4 9/16 in. x 3 3/8 in. x 3 3/8 in. (11.7 cm x 8.5 cm x 8.5 cm)

S signed and editioned in blue ink, on label: 'Meg Henson Scales'

C Museum purchase
   2000.16.1–10

The "Mary Loves Jesus . . ." painting was the first I made on gessoed unstretched muslin, when I was in search of a more giving support a few years ago. I painted it in the style of the labels on fruit cans I saw as a small child in Oregon, in the late 1950s and early 1960s. The labels were beautifully vivid, and frequently depicted people of color, although the images were racially degenerate, typically of either deadpan Native American men or slavishly servile black and Native American women.

I read the Gnostic Gospels from the *Nag Hammadi Library* while painting "Mary Loves Jesus . . . ," and the Gospel of Mary [Magdalene] profoundly changed me. It tells of how she, unlike the male apostles, receives gnosis after witnessing Christ's resurrection. When Mary explains to the other apostles that she has seen Christ at the sepulcher, and that He has told her, among other things, "What binds me has been slain, and what turns me about has been overcome, and my desire has been ended, and my ignorance has died," she not only reveals Christ's message, but also, inadvertently, becomes Christ's true messenger.

When she speaks to the other apostles about her meditative vision of Christ—of Him having dropped His body, but not His soul—they first disbelieve, but then begin to lie, saying that they too have "seen" Him—not as spirit, but in the flesh. When we consider the insidious role gender bias has played in determining who should possess spiritual authority, this display of egocentric, one-upmanship was particularly egregious. By revising the nature of the Resurrection (!), the fathers of Christianity infer that gender supremacy was even more important to them than their doctrine. This type of bigotry is not rare in the church, of course, even today.

The injustices Mary Magdalene suffered resonate with the condition of many of us almost 2000 years later. I identify with this North African woman with nappy hair (the better to wash Christ's feet) and her life with its many obstacles. Mary was SO blackwoman, if we can use that raced term to describe her not only as an African

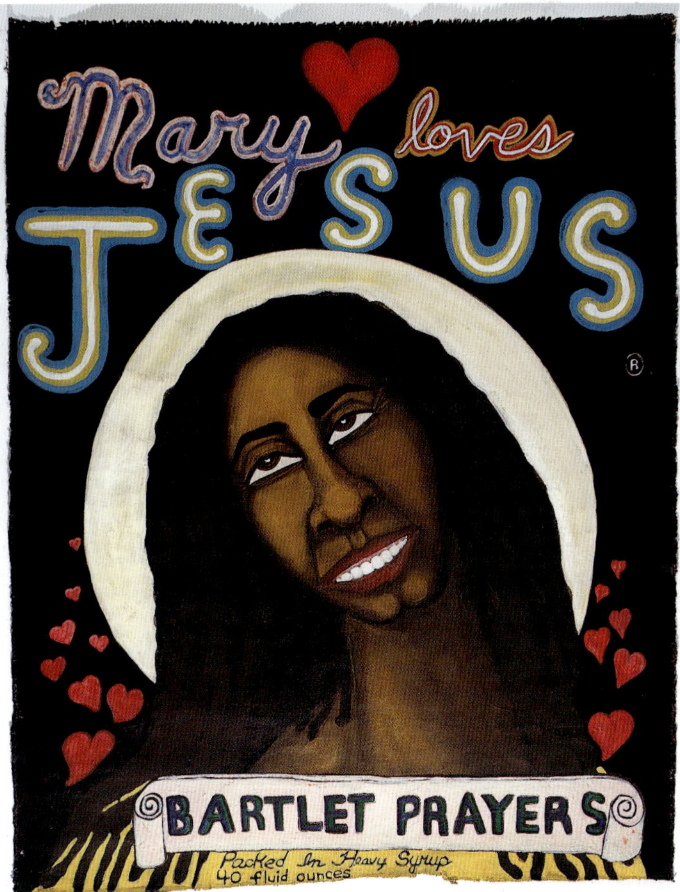

Fig. 170. Meg Henson Scales, *Mary Loves Jesus Bartlet Prayers*, 1997, mixed media

woman, but also as one who was deemed used, implausible, sub-male, and yet envied. Realized woman are typically accused of some heresy; and in Mary's case, she was deemed a whore and disparaged as a liar, even though she was not only Christ's best friend, but was obviously very gifted herself, spiritually. We can easily gather that reducing the significance of her to Christ was more important to most of the apostles than this truth. In our time and place, in black male popular culture, expressing hatred for women is not only popular but hugely profitable. The inference is the same—that invoking gender supremacy seems of far greater importance to these fans and dealers of misogynist pop culture than the truth of their own African American inequity.

When we compare the Virgin Mary with Mary Magdalene, we see two versions of the feminine ideal: one utterly unattainable, the other even too accessible. The concept of woman as chattel is explained within that paradox. Mary Magdalene as whore is but an irretrievable sexual experience away from the Virgin Mary—the two largely and mistakenly defined, as either a past and a future tense of where man has salaciously been. Although the planting of one's pole in newly explored territory as a declaration of ownership has functioned for men in the past, it is wholly inappropriate here. I have never been able to understand how carnal association with men renders one contaminated, while those who possess the contaminant (the penis) are deemed fundamentally superior; but this is nonetheless a popular, albeit disingenuous notion.

My cans were a natural offshoot of the painting, although the can was an enormous undertaking, compared with what I thought it would be. I buy the cans already sealed from a manufacturing plant in Canada, so as to leave room for my product (although it would have been much cheaper to buy them with fruit already in them). First, I paint the cans with several layers of gold and lavender, nontarnishing metallic paint. I then sign, number, and glue the labels, printed by a specialty printer in Manhattan, onto the cans by hand. Finally, I bag the cans and pack them in "Indestructo" boxes for shipping, with Certificates of Authenticity wrapped around them, which I print out on my PC.

My daughter and husband frequently help me assemble them, by gluing, boxing, bagging, and so on, but I alone fill the cans with prayers from different practices, by praying, chanting, meditating, circumambulating, among other techniques. I make about eleven cans at a time, and I record every transaction in an analog journal-ledger. The Mary Foundation, which is afforded by tithing from the gross proceeds, has awarded one grant thus far. I understood after a year of production that this was perhaps a lifelong project, and I even suspended production of them at one point, because I felt I wasn't in the proper spiritual state to fill the cans. Now, I make them when I am called to do so, and I look forward to the regimen of getting myself equal to filling them, for years to come.

In drawing upon the strength of Mary and Her Love for Christ, I felt the cans could both confer blessings upon the recipient and also challenge the hyper-sexualization and depravity of what has become black women's de facto cultural image. Since the advent of rap and negative hip hop, and in that context of the ongoing demonization of black women by (primarily) black men's music, video, and film, it becomes even clearer how the First Apostle-Mary Magdelene—could have been stigmatized a "ho" while in pursuit of her own good life.

However, my plan did not work. I did not change anyone's opinion about black women's imagery, nor about the exclusion of the Gospel of Mary from the canon. Instead, most of the people who have bought the cans are those who didn't need convincing of the humanity of other human beings but wished to give the cans to other people, as simple gifts of prayer. In some way, it was better

for me that they are of all races and every gender.
I believe that God can help us out of this radically
irrational set of circumstances, and I believe that
She will. In the interim, there will be some things
that never change, just like Mary's Love for Christ.
These are some of the things I am learning.

MEG HENSON SCALES

BIBLIOGRAPHY

"The Gospel of Mary." *The Nag Hammadi Library in English,* ed
James Robinson. San Francisco, CA: HarperCollins, 1990,
p. 526.

http://www.hensonscales.com/marycan.htm

CAT. NO. 50

A María Magdalena Campos-Pons
born Matanzas, Cuba, 1959
active Boston, Massachusetts

T *Sagrada Familia/Holy Family*

D 2000

M eight Polaroid photographs, mounted as a
triptych

X prints: each approx. 27 in. x 21 in. (1060 mm x
825 mm)
sheets: each approx. 33 1/2 in. x 22 in. (1320 mm
x 865 mm)

S signed and numbered in black marker, verso:
'Maria Magdalena Campos Pons'

I inscribed in black marker, verso: 'The Sacred
Family/La Sagrada Familia/20 x 24 Polaroid
New York Studio/2000'

C Museum purchase from the Dorothy Johnston
Towne (Class of 1923) Fund
2000.84.1–8

El tema de la familia ha sido de interés para mi
desde el inicio de mi carrera, la representación del concepto de familia como metáfora
y realidad sigue siendo fascinante.

De alguna manera la estructura de lo que con-
stituye familia ha establecido criterios de identidad, concepto de nacionalidad e idiosincrasia a
través de diferentes periodos y culturas. De que
forma diferentes poblaciones conviven y repro-
ducen establece normas y códigos que definen el
genero humano con sus prohibiciones y libertades.

La transgresión de barreras sociales, de clase,
de raza, de religión incluso nación, ha constitu-
ido una importante parte en la formación de culturas y modos de vida; el núcleo familiar ha sido
un vehículo en la realización de esas transac-
ciones espirituales, culturales, económicas
incluso políticas.

La Sagrada Familia comenta con lirismo y clari-
dad los complejos y al mismo tiempo simple aspec-
tos de la familia birracial, enfatizando en el tercer
componente de la trilogía "EL HIJO" la preciosa
prenda de esa negociación, con los delicados
detalles del laberinto de su identidad. Los padres
han sido reducido a una columna de sólido oscuro
fondo; desde la profundidad de ese espacio rico
en materia y textura, los brazos de la madre y el
padre se extienden creando una secuencia de
péquenos gestos que protegen y confortan, al
mismo tiempo EL HIJO emerge con los ricos tonos
de la unión de carnes prohibidas, su rostro suave-
mente iluminado expresa su regocijo y su incerti-
tud el elude y participa.

Esta obra es continuación de mi exploración de
las relaciones entre fotografía, pintura y *performance.* My intención era crear un retablo en el que
la tradición de la representación de la Madonna es
cuestionada en el contexto presente. Cuando
pense en realizar una pieza sobre La Sagrada
Familia la idea de comentar en este particular
"*interracial marriage*" apareció como imperativo, los
matrimonio interaciales, siguen siendo tabú en
América y el resto del planeta en periodos de con-
tinuo transculturación y globalismo. Sin embargo

esta nueva estructura de familia en una sociedad poscolonial establece conexiones en oposición de practicas del pasado.

Negro y blanco, claro oscuro, mestizaje. La Sagrada Familia 2000.

MARIA MAGADALENA CAMPOS-PONS

TRANSLATION

The subject of the family has been an interest of mine since the beginning of my career, and the representation of the concept of family as metaphor and reality continues to fascinate me.

In some ways, the structure of what constitutes a family has established its own criteria of identity, based on concepts of nationality and various historical and cultural idiosyncrasies. The manner in which different populations coexist and reproduce establishes the norms and systems that define humanity, its prohibitions, and its freedoms.

The transgression of social, class, racial, religious—and even national—boundaries has played an important part in the formation of cultures and lifestyles. The nuclear family has been a vehicle by which to achieve spiritual, cultural, and economic change, and political transitions as well.

The *Sagrada Familia/Holy Family* comments with lyricism and clarity on the at-once complex yet elemental aspects of biracial family life, emphasizing the third component of this trilogy, "the SON"—the precious token of that negotiation, whose own identity is a labyrinth of delicate details. The parents have been reduced to a solid, dark column of background, rich in material and texture, from the depths of which extend the arms of mother and father, creating a sequence of small gestures that both protect and comfort. At the same time, the SON emerges, his rich tones formed by the union of prohibited skins, his smoothly illuminated face expressing both amusement and doubt as he participates and withdraws.

This work continues my exploration of the relations between photography, painting, and performance. My intention was to create an altarpiece that questioned traditional representations of the Madonna from a contemporary context. When I thought about making a piece based on the Holy Family, the idea of commenting on this particular interracial marriage [my own] became obvious. Interracial marriage remains taboo in America and the rest of the planet despite periods of continuous transculturation and globalization. Nevertheless, this new family structure within postcolonial society has established connections that oppose the practices of the past.

Black and white, light and dark, blended. The Holy Family of 2000.

TRANSLATOR'S NOTE

In 1998, I contacted Maria Magdalena Campos-

Fig. 171. María Magdalena Campos-Pons, *Sagrada Familia/Holy Family*, 2000, Polaroid photographs

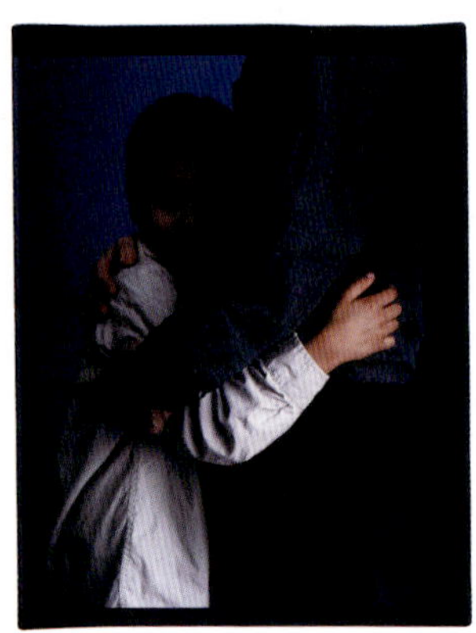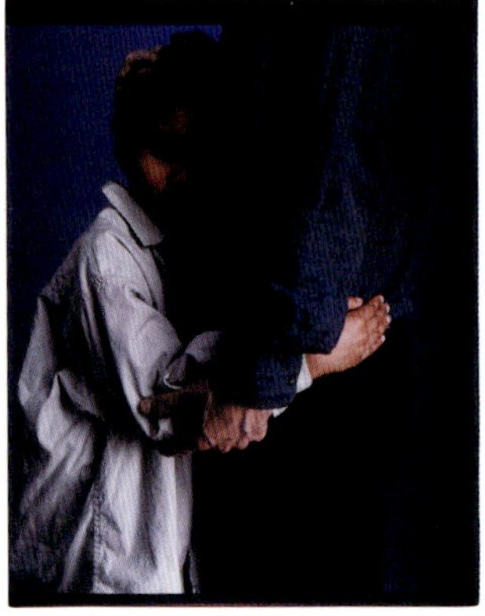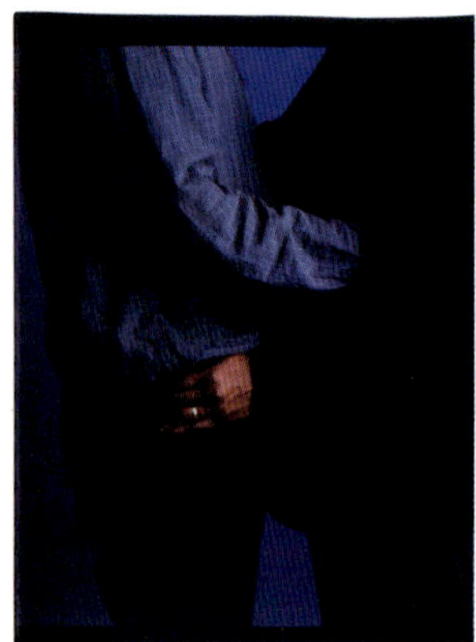

Pons and invited her to create a work of art specifically for the *Divine Mirrors* exhibition. Although we
had many conversations about the exhibition and
exchanged slides of the other works that would be
on view, I gave no specific guidelines, asking only
that she interpret her own identity as a woman
through traditional imagery of the Virgin Mary.
The result is truly gratifying; each viewing brings
to light greater nuances of meaning, as dark
masses resolve into soft layers of clothing, skin,
and touch. In addition, although the artist is flu-
ent in English, I asked her to contribute a statement in her native Spanish. Language adds one
more layer to the contrasts that mark her sacred
family and both isolate them and insulate them
from the wider community.

MELISSA R. KATZ

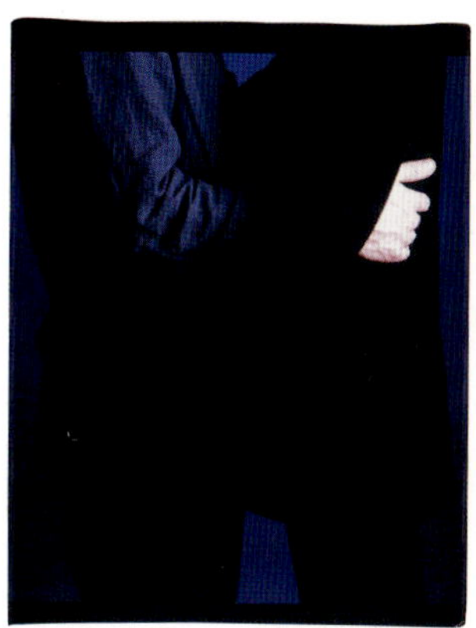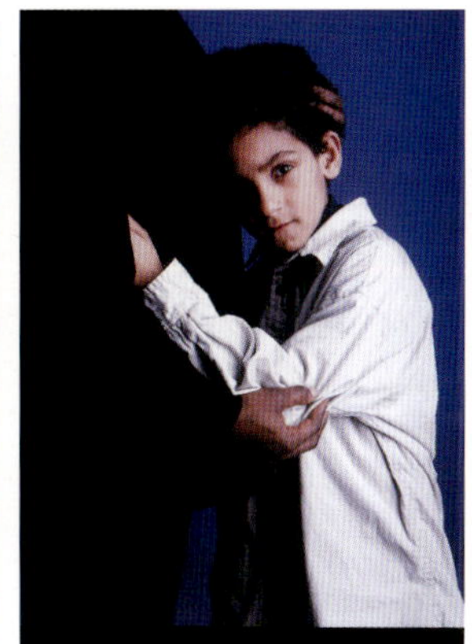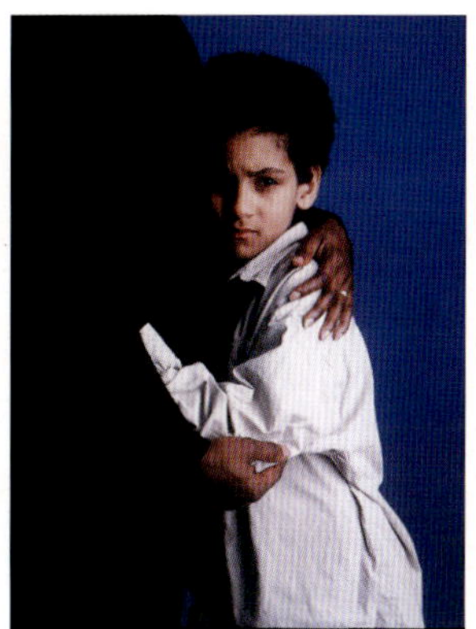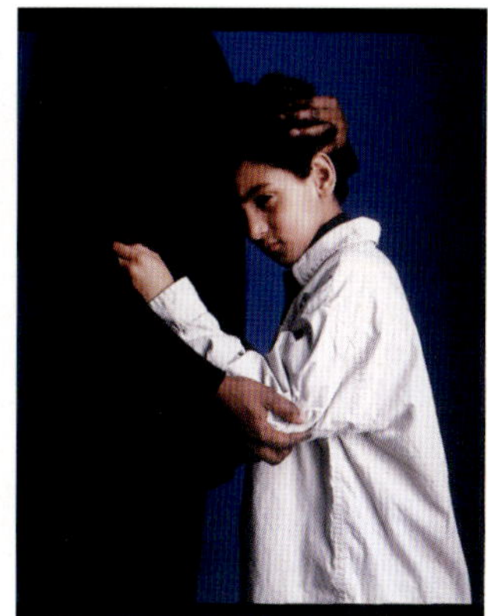

Part IV

Checklist

Works of Art with a Marian Theme in the Collection of the Davis Museum and Cultural Center, Wellesley College

Works are listed chronologically, with cataloguing information provided in the following order, and identified by the following symbols:

A ARTIST'S NAME
Place of birth/Year of birth–Year of death/Place of death
Place(s) of activity during the artist's career
T *Title of work*
D date of work (if known)
M medium and support
X dimensions (height x width x depth)
S signature (if present)
I inscriptions, collectors marks, stamps, labels, etc.
W watermark(s) (if present)
C credit line
Accession number (with figure and catalogue numbers, if applicable)

NOTES

A Birth name is listed if different from professional. name. If artist's name is unknown, national affiliation is listed.
Place listings record the name of country (or region) as it was known during artist's lifetime. If no country (or region) of death is listed, then it remains the same as for place of birth.

M Unless otherwise listed, all works on paper (prints and drawings) are on medium-weight hand-made laid paper. Paper color is described as it appears now, rather than when made.

X Dimensions for paintings are given in height followed by width, in inches and centimeters.
Dimensions for sculptures are given in height followed by width followed by depth, in inches and centimeters.
Dimensions for works on paper and photographs are given in height followed by width, in inches and millimeters. Drawings list full sheet size; prints list image size (plate or block) followed by sheet size. Book pages list folio size as equivalent of sheet size.

I All inscriptions, stamps, marks, etc. recorded for works on paper are on *recto* (front) side of sheet, unless *verso* (reverse) is specified.

W If no watermark is listed, none was found on the sheet.

C All works are from the permanent collection of the Davis Museum and Cultural Center, Wellesley College, unless otherwise specified. Wellesley alumnae are identified by class year. Accession numbers begin with the four digits of the year the work entered the permanent collection. Objects on loan to the museum end with the four-digit year the loan began.

Figures 1 through 6 accompany the essay "The Many names of the Mother of God." Figures 7 through 110 accompany the essay "Regarding Mary: Women's Lives Reflected in the Virgin's Image." Figures 111 through 171 accompany the catalogue entries.

Catalogue numbers refer to individual object entries.

Checklist compiled by Melissa R. Katz with the assistance of Hillary L. Anderson '00, Lisa Fagin Davis, Laura DeNormandie, Jeremy J. Fowler, Kate Heider '00, Lisa McDermott, Rebecca Mongeon, Anne Collins Smith, and Jennet Zerbe DS '98.

A attributed to HANS VON AACHEN
Cologne, Westphalia 1552–1615 Prague, Bohemia
active Cologne, Venice, Rome, Augsburg, Munich, and Prague
T *Crucifixion*
D late 16th/early 17th century
M ink and wash with gouache highlights on blue paper
X sheet: 16 1/6 in. x 10 7/8 in. (410 mm x 277 mm)
I inscribed in ink, verso: 'ROMA 15:91' (?) (and illegible)
green sealing wax, verso (no seal)
W watermark: encircled 4–pointed star surrounding a 6–pointed star
C Bequest of Mrs. Toivo Laminan (Margaret Chamberlin, Class of 1929)
1979.18   fig. 75

A AGNES ABBOT
Potsdam, Germany 1897–1992 Harvard, Massachusetts
active Wellesley, Massachusetts
T *Adoration of the Magi (after Botticelli)*
copy of detail of a painting by Botticelli, now in the Uffizi, Florence
D 20th century
M watercolor on paper
X sheet: 16 in. x 14 in. (406 mm x 356 mm)
C Gift of the Artist
1934.16

A LOLA ÁLVAREZ BRAVO
Lagos de Moreno, Mexico 1907–1993 Mexico City
active Mexico City
T *La Patrona (The Patroness)*
D 1960s
M gelatin silver print
X print: 8 7/8 in. x 7 3/16 in. (225 mm x 183 mm)
mount: 15 15/16 in. x 13 15/16 in. (405 mm x 354 mm)
S signed in pencil, on mount: 'Lola Alvarez Bravo'
I inscribed in pencil on mount, verso: 'La Patrona'
C Museum purchase
2000.12   fig.168, cat. no. 48a

A AMERICAN
T *Jesus Attached to the Cross*
D 19th century
M stereoptic card (double-mounted photographs)
X sheet: 3 3/8 in. x 7 in. (857 mm x 178 mm)
C Gift of Barbara Schinman Fields (Class of 1969)
1991.43.323

A JAMES ANDERSON (born Isaac Atkinson, also known as William Nugent Dunbar)
Blencarn, Cumbria 1813–1877 Rome, Italy
active Paris, Rome, Florence, and Greece
T Temple of Antonius and Faustina
D circa 1858
M albumen print
X print: 16 1/8 in. x 12 3/8 in. (410 mm x 315 mm)
mount (original): 24 1/2 in. x 18 3/8 in. (622 mm x 466 mm)
I inscribed in pencil, on mount: 'Trumpel den Antonius und das Faustina'
embossed seals, on mount: coat of arms and 'LIBRERIA TEDESCA/DI GIUS• SPITHOVER/ IN ROMA'
C Museum purchase
1989.9   fig. 15

A JOHN TAYLOR ARMS
Washington, DC 1887–1953 Fairfield, Connecticut
active Western Europe
T *Nativity*
D 20th century
M etching on cream paper
X sheet and image: 1 inch H x 1 inch W (24 mm x 25 mm)
I inscribed in plate around figures: 'Gloria in a*f*tisimmis Deo et in terra par et bona voluntas hominibus'
inscribed in pencil: 'Nativity' and '366'
C Bequest of Dorothy H. Fernald (Class of 1928)
1983.50.25

A AUSTRIAN
T recto: *Virgin and Child Appearing to a Saint*
verso: figure sketch
D 18th century
M black ink, brush, and wash, with graphite (or black chalk) and red chalk underdrawing on cream paper
X sheet: 5 3/4 in. x 3 1/4 in. (147 mm x 82 mm)
I inscribed in pencil, verso: 'EO' and '#5326'

C Anonymous gift
1969.8

A HANS SEBALD BEHAM
Nuremberg, Franconia 1500–1550 Frankfurt am Main, Holy Roman Empire
active Nuremberg, Munich, and Frankfurt
T *Virgin and Child with a Pear*
D 1520
M engraving on discolored buff paper
X sheet and image: 4 7/16 in. x 3 in. (112 mm x 75 mm)
S monogrammed and dated in plate: '1520' above 'HSP' in ligature
I inscribed in pencil, verso: 'M 9287/B.18'
C Gift of Mrs. Toivo Laminan (Margaret Chamberlin, Class of 1929)
1962.6.5   fig. 31

A STEFANO DELLA BELLA
Florence, Tuscany 1610–1664 Florence
active Florence, Rome, and Paris
T *Flight into Egypt*
D mid-17th century
M etching on cream paper
X image: 5 3/8 in. x 4 11/16 in. (136 mm x 119 mm)
sheet: 5 7/8 in. x 4 13/16 in. (149 mm x 122 mm)
S signed in plate: 'Ste*f*. de la Bella fecit'
C Gift of Mrs. Edythe Kumin Shulman (Class of 1932)
1981.76   cat. no. 26

A STEFANO DELLA BELLA
Florence, Tuscany 1610–1664 Florence

active Florence, Rome, and Paris

printed in Paris by Pierre Mariette

T   *Rest on the Flight into Egypt*

D   before 1642

M   etching on cream paper, state 1 of 4

X   sheet and image: 3 1/4 in. x 5 3/8 in. (82 mm x 137 mm)

mount: 7 7/16 in. x 12 inches (189 mm x 304 mm)

S   signed in plate: 'ʃteƒ. de la Bella fecit'

C   Gift of Mrs. Toivo Laminan (Margaret Chamberlin, Class of 1929)

1962.14.1   fig. 142, cat. no. 26

A   ÉMILE BERNARD

Lille, France 1868–1941 Paris

active Paris, Venice, and Cairo

T   *Confirmand's Procession*

Alternate title: *Procession à Saint-Briac*

D   1891

M   oil on canvas

X   21 in. x 28 1/2 in. (53.3 cm x 72.4 cm)

S   signed and dated in red paint: 'E.B. 1891'

I   inscribed in paint, verso: 'Procession à St-Briac' and 'Deus est Magnus' (God is Great)

C   Gift of Chester D. Tripp in memory of his wife, Madeline Hanson Tripp (Class of 1907)

1966.15   fig. 156, cat. no. 38

A   PEDRO GONZÁLEZ BERRUGUETE

Paredes de Nava, Castile, Spain ca. 1450/55–1503 Ávila

Active Paredes de Nava, Toledo, and Ávila, Spain; Urbino and Rome(?), Italy

T   *Assumption of the Virgin* (central panel of dispersed polyptych)

D   circa 1485

M   oil, shell gold, and gold leaf on panel

X   55 1/2 in. x 35 1/2 in. (141.0 cm x 90.2 cm)

C   Gift of Mr. and Mrs. A. M. Adler

1965.52   fig. 95, cat. no. 7

A   GIOVANNI Battista di Bernardino BONSIGNORI

Brescia, Lombardy 1493–ca. 1537 Brescia

active Brescia

T   *Madonna and Child with Two Male Saints*

D   16th century

M   oil on canvas

X   29 in. x 22 3/4 in. (73.7 cm x 57.8 cm)

C   Gift of Philip J. Gentner

1950.15

A   FRANÇOIS BOUCHER

Paris, France 1703–1770 Paris

active Paris and Rome

T   *Sacrifice of Isaac*

D   1720s

M   black chalk with white chalk highlights on buff paper

X   sheet: 14 3/8 in. x 12 in. (365 mm x 305 mm)

mount: 16 3/8 x 13 5/8 (340 mm x 346 mm)

I   inscribed in pencil (not original): 'Boucher'

W   fragment: 'CA[R]' above 'RE[X]' within crowned and draped oval (Churchill 298)

C   Anonymous gift

1969.13   fig. 148, cat. no. 32

A   JOSÉ BOVER BENNÀSSAR

born Palma de Mallorca, Spain 1921

active Mallorca, Barcelona, Felanitx, and the Baleares

T   *Deposition*

D   mid-20th century

M   pen, brush, and black India ink on mid-weight wove buff-brown paper

X   sheet: 13 11/16 in. x 19 11/16 in. (347 mm x 500 mm)

S   signed in ink: 'BENN'

I   inscribed in pencil, verso: 'Jose Bover Benasser'

stamped in violet ink, verso: 'GALERIAS COSTA'

C   Bequest of Virginia E. Lewis (Class of 1929)

1995.55

A   Circle of BARTHOLOMEUS BREENBERGH

Deventer, the Netherlands 1599–1659 Amsterdam

active Rome and Amsterdam

T   *Abraham Dismissing Hagar*

D   1630s

M   oil on panel

X   15 in. x 12 5/16 in. (38.1 cm x 31.3 cm)

C   Museum purchase with funds from bequest of Susan Pulitzer Freedberg (Class of 1953) and the New York Wellesley College Friends of Art

1968.1   fig. 10, cat. no. 25

A   DORIS PORTER CAESAR

Brooklyn, New York 1892–ca. 1971 New York

active New York

T   *Descent from the Cross*

D   1951

M   bronze

X   22 1/2 in. (57.2 cm)

C   Gift of Mrs. Helen H. Beebe (Helen Hulick, Class of 1931)

1953.4

A   JACQUES CALLOT

Nancy, Duchy of Lorraine 1592–1635 Nancy

active Nancy, Rome, and Florence

T   *Devotions of the Infant Saint John (Les Homages du petit Saint Jean)*

plate 3 (of 8) from untitled mid-17th-century series assembled by Israel Henriet for Alphonse de Rambervillers

D   1623–1628

M   etching and engraving with burin and stipple

on off-white paper

X   image: 3 5/8 in. x 2 11/16 in. (92 mm x 68 mm)

sheet: 4 in. x 2 13/16 in. (101 mm x 72 mm)

S   signed in plate: 'Callot fe'

I   inscribed in plate: 'maior ferinet manon Genes. 25 Le plus grand fera la feriteur de lantre. Ifrael ex cum priuil Reg.'

inscribed in pencil, verso: 'L-672 III/M-93 II/original'

C   Gift of Mrs. Edythe Kumin Shulman (Class of 1932)

1981.74

A   JULIA MARGARET CAMERON

Calcutta, India 1815–1879 Kalutara, Ceylon

active London, Kent, Surrey, Isle of Wight, and Ceylon (now Sri Lanka)

T   *La Santa Julia (Portrait of Julia Prinsep Jackson)*

D   1867

M   albumen silver print on original mount

X   print: 11 1/8 in. x 9 1/4 in. (293 mm x 236 mm)

mount: 16 7/8 in. x 14 in. (429 mm x 356 mm)

I   inscribed in ink, on mount: 'From Life registered photograph copy right Julia Margaret Cameron 1867/La Santa Julia'

C   Given in honor of Eugenia Parry Janis by Professor and Mrs. Hugo Munsterberg (Peggy Bowen, Class of 1943)

1973.20   fig. 102, cat. no. 37

A   MARÍA MAGDALENA CAMPOS-PONS

born Matanzas, Cuba 1959

active Boston, Massachusetts

T   *Sagrada Familia/Holy Family*

D   2000

M eight Polaroid photographs, mounted as a triptych
X prints: each approx. 27 in. x 21 in. (1060 mm x 825 mm)
sheets: each approx. 33 1/2 in. x 22 in. (1320 mm x 865 mm)
S Signed and numbered in black marker, verso: 'Maria Magdalena Campos Pons'
I inscribed in black marker, verso: 'The Sacred Family/La Sagrada Familia/20 x 24 Polaroid New York Studio/2000'
C Museum purchase from the Dorothy Johnston Towne (Class of 1923) Fund
2000.84.1–8 fig. 170, cat. no. 50

A CEBALLOS (first name unknown)
Mexican
active 20th century
T *Ex-Voto Commissioned by Bernardo Reyes Bravo*
D 1958
M oil on tin
X 7 1/8 in. x 9 15/16 in. (18.1 cm x 25.2 cm W)
S signed in white paint: 'Ceballos'
I inscribed in paint: 'El 20 de junio de 1957, estando camiando unas laminas de un jocalón en la Hda. de AMATITLANES, Una de las láminas, rozó al alambre de luz Eléctrica. que hizo contacto con dicha lámina, causando me graves quemadras y quedé inconciente de ahi me levantaron mis compañeros de trabajo. Hoy me encuentro luchando entre la vida la muerte./Es por eso que dedico el presente, a mi Madre Sma. de GUADALUPE, para que me mande el alivio./I. de Matamoros, Pue. Enero 5 de 1957/BERNARDO

REYES BRAVO'
('On June 20th, 1957, while replacing some metal plates on a shed on the Amatitlanes Hacienda (estate), one of the sheets grazed against an electric wire, making contact with the wire and causing me severe burns. I passed out and my workmates took me away from there. Today I am fighting between life and death. For this reason, I dedicate this to my Most Holy Mother of Guadalupe, that she may send me comfort. Bernardo Reyes Bravo')
C Extended loan from collection of James Oles
1. 2000

A GIUSEPPE CESARI, called il CAVALIERE D'ARPINO
Arpino, Roman Campagna 1568–1640 Rome
active Rome and Naples
T *Holy Family with a Male Saint*
D circa 1600
M red chalk with white highlights on deep buff paper
X sheet: 9 1/16 in. x 7 1/2 in. (230 mm x 191 mm)
I inscribed in pencil on mount, verso: 'Scant' collector's stamp in red ink: 'WM' in ligature within circle
C Gift of Mrs. Toivo Laminan (Margaret Chamberlin, Class of 1929)
1960.9 fig. 83

A MARC CHAGALL (born Moisei Zakharovich Segal)
Vitebsk, Bellarus 1887–1985 Saint-Paul-de-Vence, France
active St. Petersburg, Paris, Berlin, Vitebsk, Moscow, New York, and Vence
printed in France by Tériade and hand-colored by artist

T *Abraham Preparing to Sacrifice his Son, According to God's Command (Gen. 27:9–14)* plate 10 (of 105) from the *Bible* series
D 1931–39, printed in 1956
M watercolor over etching on heavy-weight textured wove discolored cream paper
X image: 11 13/16 in. x 9 1/28 in. (300 mm x 240 mm)
sheet: 21 3/16 in. x 15 3/8 in. (538 mm x 390 mm)
S signed in pencil: 'M.Ch.'
I editioned in pencil: '19/100'
inscribed pencil, verso: '10'
W 'ARCHES' (Velin d'Arches)
C Bequest of Mrs. Toivo Laminan (Margaret Chamberlin) Class of 1929
1960.25 fig. 167, cat. no. 47

A MARC CHAGALL (born Moisei Zakharovich Segal)
Vitebsk, Bellarus 1887–1985 Saint-Paul-de-Vence, France
active St. Petersburg, Paris, Berlin, Vitebsk, Moscow, New York, and Vence
Eleven etchings (of 105) from the *Bible* series
T *Abraham Preparing to Sacrifice his Son, According to God's Command (Gen. 27:9–14)*, plate 10
Abraham Weeping for Sarah (Gen. 23: 1), plate 11
Moses in the Desert Encounters his Brother Aaron, Sent to Meet him by God's Command (Exod. 4:27–8), plate 28
Moses Spreading Darkness over Egypt (Exod. 10:21–3), plate 31
Moses Dies in View of the Promised Land, which He was Never to Enter (Deut. 34:1–5), plate 41, fig. 11
*David, having Learned of

the Death of Jonathan, his Dearest Friend, Killed in Battle with the Philistines, Weeps and Sings a Funeral Dirge (2 Sam. 1:21–27)*, plate 66
The Eternal reveals himself to Elijah in the cave where he has taken refuge (1 Kings 19:9–12), plate 88
Peace and the Reign of Jerusalem According to the Prophesy of Isaiah (Isa. 2:1–5), plate 90
Jerusalem Freed from Babylon, According to the Prophesy of Isaiah (Isa. 14:1–7), plate 94
Jeremiah Receiving the Gift of Prophesy (Jer. 1:4–10), plate 100
The Taking of Jerusalem by Nebuchadrezzar, According to the Prophesy of Jeremiah (Jer. 21:4–7), plate 101
D 1931–39
M etchings on mid-weight textured wove cream paper
X images from: 11 5/8 in. x 8 7/8 in. (292 mm x 224 mm) to 12 7/8 in. x 10 in. (328 mm x 255 mm)
sheets from: 17 5/16 in. x 12 15/16 in. (440 mm x 328 mm) to 17 11/16 inches x 13 in. (449 mm x 330 mm)
S signed in plate: 'ChAgAll' (plate 10 unsigned)
I inscribed in pencil: number of plate in series (plate 90 also inscribed 'Laminan')
W plates 10, 11: nude woman holding crescent
W plates 28–101: stylized 'M' in circle with 'FRANCE' below (Montval)
C Bequests of Mrs. Toivo Laminan (Margaret Chamberlin, Class of 1929)
1979.28 through 1979.38 fig. 11, cat. no. 47

A WENZEL COEBERGHER (also known as Wences-

laus Koberger)
Antwerp, Flanders
1557/61–1634 Brussels
active Antwerp, Rome,
Naples, and Brussels

T *Holy Family with Saint Stephen*

D late 16th/early 17th century

M pen and wash with white highlights on brown paper (mounted at a later date to thin Japanese tissue)

X sheet: 9 5/16 in. x 6 9/16 in. (236 mm x 167 mm)

I collector's stamp in ink: 'IMG' (J. MacGowan, Lugt 1496)

C Gift of Mrs. Toivo Laminan (Margaret Chamberlin, Class of1929) 1960.8   fig. 60

A GIUSEPPE MARIA CRESPI, called lo Spagnuolo
Bologna, Papal States
1665–1747 Bologna
active Bologna and Florence

T *Sacrament of Ordination*
sketch for one of a series of seven paintings now in the Gemäldegalerie, Dresden

D before 1712

M oil on canvas

X 14 3/4 in. x 11 1/2 in. (37.5 cm x 29.2 cm)

C Museum purchase 1948.3   fig. 57, cat. no. 30

A DESIDERIO DA SETTIGNANO workshop
Settignano, near Florence, Tuscany
1429/32–64 Florence
active Florence

T *Madonna and Child*

D mid-15th century

M polychromed and gessoed terra-cotta

X 24 in. x 14 1/2 in. (61 cm x 36 cm)

C Extended loan 1.1972

A GUSTAVE DORÉ
Strasbourg, France
1832–83 Paris
active Paris

T *Christ at Calvary* (unfinished work)

D 1883

M oil on canvas

X 52 in. x 76 in. (132.1 cm x 193.1 cm)

S signed lower right, in red paint: 'ATELIER, G. Dore' in a circle

C Gift of Dr. and Mrs. Arthur K. Solomon 1977.58

A ALBRECHT DÜRER
Nuremberg, Franconia
1471–1528 Nuremberg
active Nuremberg, Venice, Strasbourg, and Antwerp

T *Lamentation*
plate 10 (of 11) from the *Large Passion* series

D circa 1498–99, printed before 1500

M woodcut on buff paper

X sheet and image: 15 1/4 in. x 11 in. (388 mm x 280 mm)

S monogrammed in block: 'AD'

I stamped in ink, verso: ALBERTINA VERÄUßERT
inscribed in pencil, verso: 'W4687 N'72/Me 122 Vordens text b/DT.9. 74 A8'
collector's stamp in ink, recto: 'M' surmounting 'C'

W bull's head with serpent or caduceus

C Anonymous extended loan 3.1983

A ALBRECHT DÜRER
Nuremberg, Franconia
1471–1528 Nuremberg
active Nuremberg, Venice, Strasbourg, and Antwerp

T recto: *Rejection of Joachim's Offer*
verso: printed Latin text (by Benedictus Chelidonius)
plate 2 (of 20) from the *Life of the Virgin* series

D circa 1504, printed circa 1504

· **M** woodcut with text on heavy-weight laid greyish-white paper

X sheet and image: 11 11/16 in. x 8 5/16 in. (297 mm x 211 mm)

S monogrammed in block: 'AD'

I inscribed in pencil, verso: '594'

W flower with triangle (Meder 127)

C Gift of Mrs. Toivo Laminan (Margaret Chamberlin, Class of 1929) in memory of her mother, Anne B. Chamberlin (Class of 1898) 1968.34.1   cat. no. 14

A ALBRECHT DÜRER
Nuremberg, Franconia
1471–1528 Nuremberg
active Nuremberg, Venice, Strasbourg, and Antwerp

T *Joachim and the Angel*
plate 3 (of 20) from the *Life of the Virgin* series

D circa 1504, printed post-1504

M woodcut on cream paper

X sheet and image: 11 13/16 in. x 8 1/4 in. (300 mm x 210 mm)

S monogrammed in block: 'AD'

I inscribed in ink, verso: 'F.D. 1339'

W triangle above lobed flower (not in Meder)

C Gift of Mrs. Toivo Laminan (Margaret Chamberlin, Class of 1929) in memory of her mother, Anne B. Chamberlin (Class of 1898) 1968.34.2   cat. no. 14

A ALBRECHT DÜRER
Nuremberg, Franconia
1471–1528 Nuremberg
active Nuremberg, Venice, Strasbourg, and Antwerp

T *Joachim and Saint Anne Meet at the Golden Gate*
plate 4 (of 20) from the *Life of the Virgin* series

D 1504, printed after 1511

M woodcut on white paper

X image: 11 13/16 in. x 8 1/4 in. (300 mm x 210 mm)
sheet: 11 7/8 in. x 8 3/8 in. (302 mm x 213 mm)

S monogrammed and dated in block: 'AD 1504'

I inscribed in ink, verso: 'G Storch a Milano 1797/Jn atʃ 360 Aʃ 19.'
inscribed in pencil, verso: '13,363'
stamped in ink, verso: 'FOGG ART MUSEUM/HARVARD UNIVERSITY/DUPLICATE' above 'THE WILLIAM HAYES FOGG/ART MUSEUM/HARVARD UNIVERSITY'

W fragment of escutcheon with diagonal beam (Meder 246)

C Gift of Mrs. Toivo Laminan (Margaret Chamberlin, Class of 1929) in memory of her mother, Anne B. Chamberlin (Class of 1898) 1968.34.3   fig. 7, cat. no. 14

A ALBRECHT DÜRER
Nuremberg, Franconia
1471–1528 Nuremberg
active Nuremberg, Venice, Strasbourg, and Antwerp

T *Birth of the Virgin*
plate 5 (of 20) from the *Life of the Virgin* series

D circa 1503–04, printed circa 1600

M woodcut on cream paper

X image: 11 3/4 in. x 8 5/16 in. (299 mm x 211 mm)
sheet: 11 7/8 in. x 8 1/2 in. (301 mm x 215 mm)

S monogrammed in block: 'AD'

I stamped in ink, verso: 'JOHN WITT RANDALL COLLECTION/HARVARD COLLEGE/NO.' above 'FOGG ART MUSEUM/HARVARD UNIVERSITY/DUPLICATE'
inscribed in pencil on blank line of stamp, verso: '851'

w escutcheon with diagonal beam and 'IB' countermark (Meder 246)
c Gift of Mrs. Toivo Laminan (Margaret Chamberlin, Class or 1929) in memory of her mother, Anne B. Chamberlin (Class of 1898) 1968.34.4 cat. no. 14

A ALBRECHT DÜRER Nuremberg, Franconia 1471–1528 Nuremberg active Nuremberg, Venice, Strasbourg, and Antwerp
T *Birth of the Virgin* plate 5 (of 20) from the *Life of the Virgin* series
D circa 1503–04, printed 1503–04
M woodcut on white paper
X image: 11 11/16 in. x 8 1/4 in. (297 mm x 210 mm) sheet: 11 13/16 in. x 8 1/4 in. (300 mm x 210 mm)
S monogrammed in block: 'AD'
I collector's stamp in ink: 'M' surmounting 'C'
W bull's head with serpent
C Gift of Mrs. William F. Stearns 1990.12 fig. 59, cat. no. 14

A ALBRECHT DÜRER Nuremberg, Franconia 1471–1528 Nuremberg Active Nuremberg, Venice, Strasbourg, and Antwerp
T *Betrothal of the Virgin* plate 7 (of 20) from the *Life of the Virgin* series
D circa 1504, printed circa 1504
M woodcut on discolored grey paper
X image: 11 3/4 in. x 8 in. (300 mm x 203 mm) sheet: 11 13/16 in. x 8 1/4 in. (300 mm x 210 mm)
S monogrammed in block: 'AD'
W high crown (Meder 20)
C Gift of Mrs. Edward A. Skinner (Jane Weissinger

Skinner, Class of 1937) in celebration of her 40th reunion 1977.26 fig. 28, cat. no. 14

A ALBRECHT DÜRER Nuremberg, Franconia 1471–1528 Nuremberg active Nuremberg, Venice, Strasbourg, and Antwerp
T *Annunciation* plate 8 (of 20) from the *Life of the Virgin* series
D circa 1503, printed circa 1503
M woodcut on discolored white paper
X sheet and image: 11 5/8 in. x 8 1/4 in. (295 mm x 210 mm)
S monogrammed in block: 'AD'
I collector's stamp in brown ink, verso: 'BR' or 'BL' in ligature
W high crown (Meder 20)
C Gift of Mrs. Toivo Laminan (Margaret Chamberlin, Class of 1929) in memory of her mother, Anne B. Chamberlin (Class of 1898) 1968.34.5 fig. 22, cat. no. 14

A ALBRECHT DÜRER Nuremberg, Franconia 1471–1528 Nuremberg active Nuremberg, Venice, Strasbourg, and Antwerp
T *Visitation* plate 9 (of 20) from the *Life of the Virgin* series
D circa 1504, printed circa 1600
M woodcut on cream paper
X image: 11 7/8 in. x 8 11/16 in. (301 mm x 221 mm) sheet: 12 1/16 in. x 8 3/4 in. (307 mm x 224 mm)
S monogrammed in block: 'AD'
I stamped in ink, verso: 'JOHN WITT RANDALL COLLECTION/HARVARD COLLEGE' above 'FOGG ART MUSEUM/HARVARD

UNIVERSITY/DUPLICATE'
w crest with fleur-de-lis (Meder 122)
c Gift of Mrs. Toivo Laminan (Margaret Chamberlin, Class of 1929) in memory of her mother Anne B. Chamberlin (Class of 1898) 1968.34.6 fig. 32, cat. no. 14

A ALBRECHT DÜRER Nuremberg, Franconia 1471–1528 Nuremberg active Nuremberg, Venice, Strasbourg, and Antwerp
T *Adoration of the Shepherds* plate 10 (of 20) from the *Life of the Virgin* series
D circa 1503, printed circa 1503
M woodcut on discolored cream paper
X sheet and image: 11 13/16 in. x 8 1/4 in. (300 mm x 210 mm)
S monogrammed in block: 'AD'
I stamped in ink, verso: 'JOHN WITT RANDALL COLLECTION/HARVARD COLLEGE' above 'FOGG ART MUSEUM/HARVARD UNIVERSITY/DUPLICATE'
W bull's head (Meder 62)
C Gift of Mrs. Toivo Laminan (Margaret Chamberlin, Class of 1929) in memory of her mother, Anne B. Chamberlin (Class of 1898) 1968.34.7 fig. 37, cat. no. 14

A ALBRECHT DÜRER Nuremberg, Franconia 1471–1528 Nuremberg active Nuremberg, Venice, Strasbourg, and Antwerp
T *Presentation of Christ in the Temple* plate 13 (of 20) from the *Life of the Virgin* series
D circa 1505, printed circa 1600
M woodcut on cream paper

x image: 11 5/8 in. x 8 5/16 in. (295 mm x 211 mm) sheet: 11 3/4 in. x 8 1/2 in. (298 mm x 214 mm)
s monogrammed in block: 'AD'
I stamped in ink, verso: 'FOGG ART MUSEUM/HARVARD UNIVERSITY/DUPLICATE' above 'THE WILLIAM HAYES FOGG/ART MUSEUM OF/HARVARD UNIVERSITY' inscribed in pencil: 'Proof impression without text/watermark shield with croſsbar. Hsm (?) Nº 46'
w escutcheon with diagonal beam and IB (Meder 246)
c Gift of Mrs. Toivo Laminan (Margaret Chamberlin, Class of 1929) in memory of her mother, Anne B. Chamberlin (Class of 1898) 1968.34.8 cat. no. 14

A ALBRECHT DÜRER Nuremberg, Franconia 1471–1528 Nuremberg active Nuremberg, Venice, Strasbourg, and Antwerp
T *Presentation of Christ in the Temple* plate 13 (of 20) from the *Life of the Virgin* series
D circa 1505, printed circa 1580
M woodcut on cream paper
X image: 11 9/16 in. x 8 5/16 in. (294 mm x 212 mm) sheet: 11 11/16 in. x 8 1/2 in. (297 mm x 217 mm)
S monogrammed in block: 'AD'
I collector's stamp in violet ink: two serifed 'G's in ligature within circle (A. G. Gerson of Vienna, d. 1904, Lugt suppl. 1156a)
w fish bladder and IM (Meder 309)
c Extended loan from Mrs. Phyllis Ingersoll

2.1974 cat. no. 14

A ALBRECHT DÜRER
Nuremberg, Franconia
1471–1528 Nuremberg
active Nuremberg,
Venice, Strasbourg, and
Antwerp

T *Holy Family in Egypt*
plate 15 (of 20) from the
Life of the Virgin series

D circa 1502, printed circa
1580

M woodcut on cream
paper

X image: 11 3/4 in. x 8 3/8
in. (299 mm x 212 mm)
sheet: 11 7/8 in. x 8 1/2
in. (302 mm x 216 mm)

S monogrammed in block:
'AD'

W fish bladder and 'IM'
countermark (Meder
309)

C Gift of Mrs. Toivo Laminan (Margaret Chamber-
lin, Class of 1929) in
memory of her mother,
Anne B. Chamberlin
(Class of 1898)
1968.34.9 fig. 61, cat.
no. 14

A ALBRECHT DÜRER
Nuremberg, Franconia
1471–1528 Nuremberg
active Nuremberg,
Venice, Strasbourg, and
Antwerp

T *Christ Taking Leave of His
Mother*
plate 17 (of 20) from the
Life of the Virgin series

D circa 1504–05, printed
1505–40

M woodcut on cream
paper

X image: 11 3/4 in. x 8 1/4
in. (299 mm x 210 mm)
sheet: 11 7/8 in. x 8 3/8
in. (301 mm x 212 mm)

S monogrammed in block:
'AD'

I stamped in ink on verso:
'THE WILLIAM HAYES
FOGG/ART MUSEUM
OF/HARVARD UNIVER-
SITY' above 'FOGG ART
MUSEUM/HARVARD UNI-
VERSITY/DUPLICATE'
pencil inscribed on

verso: 'Proof impression
before the text water-
mark and desc[ribed?] G.
Mar . . . [JMeder?]/(Nub.
N° 57)' above 'Indent[?]
[Imperial?] double eagle
in a shield'

W bishop's crest (Meder
39)

C Gift of Mrs. Toivo Laminan (Margaret Chamber-
lin, Class of 1929) in
memory of her mother,
Anne B. Chamberlin
(Class of 1898)
1968.34.10 fig. 128, cat.
no. 14

A ALBRECHT DÜRER
Nuremberg, Franconia
1471–1528 Nuremberg
active Nuremberg,
Venice, Strasbourg, and
Antwerp

T *Death of the Virgin*
plate 18 (of 20) from the
Life of the Virgin series

D 1510, printed circa 1580

M woodcut on cream paper

X sheet and image: 11 3/8
in. x 8 1/4 in. (290 mm x
210 mm)

S monogrammed and
dated in block: 'AD 1510'

I collector's stamp in
black ink: 'M' sur-
mounted by three
crosses in ligature
(Joseph Maberly of Sus-
sex 1783–1860, Lugt
1845)

W fish bladder and 'IM'
countermark (Meder
309)

C Museum purchase
1961.25 fig. 92, cat. no.
14

A ALBRECHT DÜRER
Nuremberg, Franconia
1471–1528 Nuremberg
active Nuremberg,
Venice, Strasbourg, and
Antwerp

T *Glorification of the Virgin
(with Saints Jerome, Paul,
Augustine, Anthony, John
the Baptist, Joseph, and
Catherine of Alexandria)*
plate 20 (of 20) from the
Life of the Virgin series

D circa 1502, printed
1502–45

M woodcut on dark cream
paper

X image: 11 3/4 in. x 8 5/16
in. (298 mm x 212 mm)
sheet: 11 3/4 inches H x
8 5/8 inches W (29.9 cm
H x 21.9 cm W)

S monogrammed in block:
'AD'

I stamped in ink, verso:
'JOHN WITT RANDALL
COLLECTION/HARVARD
COLLEGE' above 'FOGG
ART MUSEUM/HARVARD
UNIVERSITY/DUPLICATE'

W bishop's crest (Meder
39)

C Gift of Mrs. Toivo Laminan (Margaret Chamber-
lin, Class of 1929) in
memory of her mother,
Anne B. Chamberlin
(Class of 1898)
1968.34.11 cat. no. 14

A ALBRECHT DÜRER
Nuremberg, Franconia
1471–1528 Nuremberg
active Nuremberg,
Venice, Strasbourg, and
Antwerp

T *Madonna with a Pear*

D 1511

M engraving on paper

X sheet and image: 7 1/4
in. x 5 1/2 in. (184 mm x
140 mm)

S monogrammed and
dated: 'AD' '1511'

C Bequest of George H.
Webster
1934.14

A ALBRECHT DÜRER
Nuremberg, Franconia
1471–1528 Nuremberg
active Nuremberg,
Venice, Strasbourg, and
Antwerp

T *Crucifixion (round)*

D 1519

M engraving on fine-weight
laid cream paper, made
from a gold medallion

X sheet and plate: 1 9/16
in. diameter (40 mm),
circular shape

I inscribed above cross
(in reverse): 'INRI'

C Gift of Mrs. Dorothy S.
Villmont (Dorothy
Samuelson, Class of
1916)
1975.50 fig. 80

A after ALBRECHT DÜRER

T *Madonna with the Mon-
key*

D facsimile of a circa 1498
original

M mechanical reproduction of engraved original
on heavy-weight wove
discolored cream paper

X image: 7 1/4 in. H x 4
5/8 in. W (185 mm x 118
mm)
sheet: 16 7/8 in. H x 12
1/8 in. W (430 mm x 308
mm)

S monogrammed in block:
'AD'

I stamped in plate in
black ink: crowned 'BN'
in oval (Bibliothèque
National, France)

W watermark: 'M.B.M'

C Anonymous gift
1999.0.112

A MERLYN EVANS
Llandaff, near Cardiff,
Wales 1910–73 London,
England
active Glasgow; Durban,
South Africa; and Lon-
don

T *Mother and Child*

D 1933

M egg tempera on artist's
board

X 24 in. x 16 in. (61.0 cm x
40.6 cm)

C Gift of Mrs. Webster
Plass
1959.39

A PIETRO FACCINI
Bologna, Papal States
ca. 1562–1602 Bologna
active Bologna

T *Saint Francis Receiving
the Christ Child in the
Presence of the Virgin*
after an altarpiece by the
artist for the Capuchin
church, Bologna, now
destroyed

D 1590s

M etching with engraving

and stipple on buff
paper, state 1 of 1
x   sheet: 14 1/4 in. x 9 3/4
in. (362 mm x 249 mm)
image: 13 3/8 in. x 9 5/8
in. (338 mm x 244 mm)
I   inscribed in pencil,
verso: 'Carracci's skola,'
'Pietro Faccini bologna
1562–1602'
inscribed in green ink,
verso: 'Tone Lundh b.(?)
1896/Sweden'
c   Museum purchase
1986.3   fig. 136, cat. no.
21

A   GAUDENZIO FERRARI
Valduggia, near Vercelli,
Piedmont 1470–1546
Milan, Lombardy
active Varallo, Vercelli,
Milan, and Piedmont
region (Arona, Saranno,
Novara)
T   recto: *God the Father*
verso, upper half: rough
sketch of seated Roman
figures in togas
verso, lower half: rough
sketch of seated men
and child (or woman)
D   circa 1540
M   recto: brown ink with
black and white chalk on
buff paper
verso, top: brown ink
and wash with pencil
verso, bottom: in red
gouache (or chalk) and
brown ink
x   sheet: 7 7/8 in. x 10 1/2
in. (200 mm x 268 mm)
I   inscribed in pencil,
erased: 'Ferrari'
inscribed in ink, verso:
'Ferrari' and '229' above
B[illegible]'
inscribed in pencil,
verso: 'Ferrari Gott
Vater'
c   Bequest of Mrs. Toivo
Laminan (Margaret
Chamberlin, Class of
1929)
1979.53   fig. 41

A   GERTRUDE H. FISKE
Boston, Massachusetts
1878–1961 Weston,
Massachusetts

active Boston and Ogun-
quit, Maine
T   *Mary*
M   oil on canvas
x   39 1/2 in. x 30 in. (100.3
cm x 76.2 cm)
s   signed in black paint:
'Gertrude Fiske'
c   Gift of Andrew F. Willis,
Harold B. Willis, Jr. (husband of Artemis
Pazianos, Class of 1951)
and Mrs. Gilbert T.
Wilkinson
1969.46   fig. 163, cat.
no. 44

A   FLEMISH
T   *Annunciation*
D   16th century
M   woven fabric embroi-
dered with colored silk
and gold threads
x   18 3/4 in. x 17 1/4 in.
(47.6 cm x 43.8 cm),
shield-shaped
c   Gift of Mrs. Albert M.
Steinert
1964.30

A   FLEMISH, possibly MAS-
TER OF THE FEMALE
HALF-LENGTHS
T   *Triumph of Faith* (or *Alle-
gory of Patience as a
Christian Virtue*)
D   circa 1550
M   oil on canvas
x   22 1/2 in. x 20 3/4 in.
(57.2 cm x 52.7 cm)
I   inscribed on block: '(. . .
VS/T. PACIETICH.ALTITS/
DOR.DACHT ICH.'
(Patience is always supe-
rior)
c   Museum purchase
1948.4

A   FLEMISH
T   *Judith with the Head of
Holofernes*
D   3rd quarter 16th century
M   oil on panel
x   23 7/8 in. x 17 1/2 in.
(60.5 cm x 44.4 cm)
I   inscribed in paint, verso:
'L.D. 24'
c   Gift of Strafford Morss
in memory of his wife
Gabrielle Ladd Morss
(Class of 1958)

1969.6   fig. 130, cat.
no. 18
A   FLEMISH
T   *John and Mary* (lateral
figures from a crucifixion
scene)
D   17th century
M   boxwood figures
x   11 1/4 in. (28.6 cm) with
1 1/4 in. tenon
c   Museum purchase
1970.1.1–2

A   LAVINIA FONTANA
Bologna, Papal States
1552–1614 Rome
active Bologna and
Rome
T   *Holy Family with Saints
Margaret and Francis*
D   1578
M   oil on canvas
x   50 in. x 41 in. (127.0 cm x
104.1 cm)
s   signed and dated in
paint (on tablecloth):
'LAVINIA FONTANA DE
ZAPPIS FACIEBAT
MDLXXVIII'
c   Extended loan from Mrs.
Selma Postar
6.1983   fig. 134, cat. no.
19

A   FRENCH, from ÎLE DE
FRANCE
T   *Dormition of the Virgin*
(right wing of diptych)
D   14th century
M   ivory
x   3 3/8 in. x 2 1/2 in. (8.6
cm x 6.4 cm)
c   Museum purchase in
honor of Professor
Agnes A. Abbot
1964.35   fig. 94, cat.
no. 3

A   FRENCH, from LORRAINE
T   *Virgin and Child*
D   circa 1370
M   polychromed limestone
x   approx. 37 1/2 in. x 10
5/8 in. x 10 1/2 in. (95.3
cm x 27.0 cm x 26.7
cm)
c   Gift of Mr. and Mrs. Sid-
ney Wien, parents of
Joan Wien (Class of
1960) and Claire Wien

Morse (Class of 1957)
1959.15

A   FRENCH, from AMIENS
T   *Book of Hours* in Latin
and French (use of
Amiens) containing 36
illuminations and 240
folios
D   circa 1480
M   manuscript with rubricated text on vellum,
illuminated with glair or
gouache, shell gold,
and gold leaf on vellum
with
240 folios, with 60
miniatures, and initials
illuminated in colored
inks and gold
x   folios: 4 3/4 in. x 3 in.
(120 mm x 78 mm)
images: approx. 2 1/8 in.
x 1 1/2 in. (52 mm x 42
mm), arched tops
I   inscribed in pencil,
inside back cover: '12 ff
/223ff Eus 240 ff/36
12 ff E á'
collector's label, pasted
inside front cover: coat
of arms (crowned and
draped oval surrounding
five cockle shells
arranged in a cross, no
text)
c   Gift of Nancy Angell
Streeter (Class of 1950)
in honor of Lilian Arm-
strong (Class of 1958)
and Peter Fergusson
2000.23   figs. 9, 18, 27,
32, 38, 42, 44, 63, 89, 91
ILLUMINATIONS
i-xii. ZODIAC CALENDAR
AND LABORS OF THE
MONTH (24 miniatures)
GOSPEL SEQUENCE
1. folio 13r: *St. John on
Patmos (with an Eagle)*;
half-page illumination
accompanying reading
from John
2. folio 16r: *St. Luke
(with an Ox)*; half-page
illumination accompany-
ing reading from Luke,
fig. 9
3. folio 18v: *St. Matthew
(with an Angel)*; half-
page illumination

accompanying reading
from Matthew
4. folio 21r: *St. Mark
(with a Lion)*; half-page
illumination accompany-
ing reading from Mark
5. folio 23r: *Mary as the
Woman clothed with the
Sun*; half-page illumina-
tion accompanying
Obsecro Te, fig. 91
6. folio 29r: *Lamentation
with Sts. John and Mary
Magdalen*; half-page illumination accompanying
O intemerata, fig. 27
7. folio 35r: *Mass of St.
Gregory*; half-page illumination accompanying
Mass of St. Gregory
8. folio 41r: *Virgin and
Child enthroned*; half-
page illumination
accompanying *Stabat
mater dolorosa*, fig. 44
9. folio 45r: *Franciscan
Saint before Mary
enthroned with angel*;
half-page illumination
accompanying *Ave cuius
concepcio*, fig. 18
10. folio 47r: *Celebration
of the Mass*; half-page
illumination accompany-
ing *Ave te omnes anime
fideles*
11. folio 50r: *Bishop
Firmin of Amiens*; half-
page illumination
accompanying votive
prayer to St. Firmin of
Amiens

HOURS OF THE VIRGIN

12. folio 51r: *Annuncia-
tion*; half-page illumination accompanying
Matins
13. folio 65r: *Visitation*;
half-page illumination
accompanying Lauds,
fig. 32
14. folio 79r: *Nativity*;
half-page illumination
accompanying Prime,
fig. 38
15. folio 86v: *Annuncia-
tion to the Shepherds*;
half-page illumination
accompanying Terce, fig.
42
16. folio 92r: *Adoration of

the Magi*; half-page illumination accompanying
Sext
16. folio 92r: *Adoration of
the Magi*; half-page illumination accompanying
Sext
[MISSING: folio to
accompany Nones,
Hours of the Virgin]
17. folio 101r: *Flight into
Egypt*; half-page illumi-
nation accompanying
Vespers
18. folio 110r: *Coronation
of the Virgin*; half-page
illumination accompany-
ing Compline, fig. 89
19. folio 116v: *Crucifixion*;
half-page illumination
accompanying Hours of
the Cross
20. folio 121r: *Pentecost*;
half-page illumination
accompanying Hours of
the Holy Spirit, fig. 90

SUFFRAGES OF THE SAINTS

21. folio 125r: *St. Catherine of Alexandria*; half-
page illumination
accompanying Office of
St. Katherine
22. folio 130r: *St. Bar-
bara*; half-page illumination accompanying
Office of St. Barbara
23. folio 136r: *King David
at his Harp*; half-page
illumination accompany-
ing Penitential Psalms
and Litany
24. folio 160r: *Resurrection of Lazarus*; half-page
illumination accompany-
ing Office of the Dead
25. folio 226r: *Archangel
Michael*; half-page illu-
mination accompanying
votive prayer to St.
Michael
26. folio 227r: *St. John
the Baptist*; half-page
illumination accompany-
ing votive prayer to St.
John the Baptist
27. folio 228r: *St. Peter*;
half-page illumination
accompanying votive
prayer to St. Peter
28. folio 229r: *St. Sebastian*; half-page illumina-

tion accompanying
votive prayer to St.
Sebastian
29. folio 230r: *St.
Nicholas of Bari*; half-
page illumination
accompanying votive
prayer to St. Nicholas
30. folio 231: *St. Anthony
Abbott*; half-page illumination accompanying
votive prayer to St.
Anthony
31. folio 232r: *St. Christopher*; half-page illumination accompanying
votive prayer to St.
Christopher
32. folio 233r: *St. Mary
Magdalen*; half-page illumination accompanying
votive prayer to St. Mary
Magdalen
33. folio 234r: *Des V.
Sainctes Privilegies (Sts.
Christina, Catherine,
Martha, Margaret, Bar-
bara)*; half-page illumi-
nation accompanying
votive prayers to Sts.
Christina, Katherine,
Martha, Margaret, and
Barbara
34. folio 235v: *St. Bernard
of Clairvaux*; half-page
illumination accompany-
ing votive prayer to St.
Bernard
35. folio 238r: *Elevation of
the Host*; half-page illumination accompanying
prayer for the Elevation
of the Host, fig. 63
36. folio 240r: *Christ
before Pilate*; half-page
illumination accompany-
ing the *Passion According
to John* (John 19:1–35)

A   FRENCH, from PARIS
    printed in Paris
T   *Annunciation*
    half-page illumination
    probably accompanying
    Matins in the Hours of
    the Virgin
    detached folio from a
    printed *Horae Beatae
    Virginis Mariae* (Latin
    and French Book Hours)
D   circa 1507–15

M   metalcut and typo-
    graphic letters printed in
    ink on vellum, hand-illu-
    minated with glair or
    gouache and shell gold
X   image: 4 3/4 in. x 3 3/8
    in. (120 mm x 80 mm)
    folio: 7 7/8 in. x 5 1/8 in.
    (198 mm x 131 mm)
C   Gift of Mrs. Toivo Lami-
    nan (Margaret Chamber-
    lin, Class of 1929)
    1962.22.2   fig. 126, cat.
    no. 13

A   French or Italian,
    SCHOOL OF
    FONTAINEBLEAU
T   *Virgin and Child (or Holy
    Family) with Saints*
D   16th century
M   etching on cream paper
X   sheet and image: 8 7/8
    in. x 5 13/16 in. (225 mm
    x 148 mm)
I   inscribed in ink: 'Giorg.
    Va∫ariani'
    collectors mark,
    stamped in blue ink: 'G'
W   elaborate design (possi-
    bly fragment of a crest)
    with 'DI' countermark
C   Anonymous gift in
    honor of President Nan-
    nerl O. Keohane (Class
    of 1961)
    1986.67   fig. 29

A   FRENCH (?)
T   *Virgin and Child*
D   19th century in style of
    14th century
M   cast stone
X   approx. 37 1/2 in. H (95.3
    cm)
C   Museum purchase
    1953.7

A   FRANCESCO FURINI
    Florence, Tuscany
    1604–46 Florence
    active Florence and
    Rome
T   *Adam and Eve*
    sketch for an early 1630s
    painting now in the
    Palazzo Pitti, Florence
D   circa 1630
M   oil on paper mounted to
    canvas
X   11 1/2 in. x 16 1/4 in.

(29.2 cm x 41.3 cm)
C Anonymous gift
1938.2   fig. 39, cat. no. 23

A School of DOMENICO GAGGINI
Bissone, Ticino 1425/30–92 Palermo, Sicily
active Genoa, Naples, and Palermo
T *Madonna and Child*
D 15th century
M marble
X approx. 23 3/4 in. x 7 3/4 in. x 3 7/8 in. (70 cm x 20 cm x 10 cm)
C Gift of Michael de Havenon
1977.57

A UBALDO GANDOLFI
San Matteo della Decima (near Bologna) 1728–81 Ravenna, Romagna
active Bologna and Romagna region
T *Virgin, Child, and God the Father with Saint Joseph*
D circa 1775
M pen, ink, and wash with black chalk underdrawing on discolored cream paper
X sheet: 10 3/8 in. x 7 5/8 in. (263 mm x 194 mm)
I inscribed in pencil: '207.60 N23' and 'E/14' inscribed in ink, verso: 'F' and 'Ubaldo Sandolbi' inscribed in pencil, verso: '12/15', '3483' and '2'
W three arches surmounted by dove, within circle (del Marmol, 112)
C Gift of Mrs. Toivo Laminan (Margaret Chamberlin, Class of 1929)
1963.35   frontispiece, fig. 53

A GIOVITA GARAVAGLIA
Pavia, Lombardy 1790–1835 Florence, Italy
active Pavia, Milan, and Florence
T *Angels Adoring the Christ*

Child (in the manner of Carlo Maratti)
D early 19th century
M etching with burin and stipple on dark cream paper, state 1 of 2
X sheet and image: 10 1/h2 in. x 10 1/4 in. (269 mm x 261 mm)
I inscribed in plate: 'SPE-CIOSVS FORMA PRAE FIL-IIS HOMINVM Pfal 44 ADORATE EVM OMNES ANGELIEIVS Pfal 96/Car-olus Marattus Inuen.' inscribed in pencil, verso: 'avant l'ad-dresse/du Graveur'
W anchor within circle, indistinct countermark
C Gift of Madeline E. Almy (Class of 1919)
1950.19   fig. 82

A GERMAN, from the MID-DLE RHINELAND
T *Annunciation* (central panel of a triptych)
D circa 1460
M oil on panel
X 26 3/4 in. x 19 in. (67.9 cm x 48.3 cm)
C Museum purchase with funds from bequest of Laura E. Lockwood
1958.22   fig. 24

A GERMAN, from the MID-DLE RHINELAND
T *Saint Barbara* and *Saint Catherine of Alexandria* (left and right wings of a triptych)
D circa 1460
M oil and gold leaf on panel
X each 26 5/8 in. x 9 5/8 in. (67.6 cm x 24.4 cm)
C Gift of Dr. and Mrs. Arthur K. Solomon
1953.22.1–2   fig. 24

A GERMAN, from AUGS-BURG
printed in Augsburg by Johann Schönsperger and Thomas Rüger
T *Burial of the Virgin* detached folio (plate 67) from a printed German *Die Neue Ehe und das*

Passional von Jesu (The New Marriage and *Passion of Jesus)* containing 71 illustrations
D 1482
M watercolor or gouache over woodcut on cream paper
X image: 4 1/16 in. x 2 1/2 in. (104 mm x 63 mm)
I printed above image: 'Da kamê die zwolf=/boten zû dem grab ma=/rie' (Then came the bidden twelve to the grave of Mary)
C Bequest of Virginia E. Lewis (Class of 1929)
1995.85   fig. 93

A GERMAN, from STRAS-BOURG
printed in Strasbourg by Martin Schott
T *Pentecost* detached folio (plate 28) from printed German and Latin *Plenarium* Evangelary (compilation of epistle and evangeli-cal readers for the litur-gical year) containing 59 illustrations
D 1483
M gouache over woodcut on discolored buff paper with rubricated text
X image: 3 in. x 2 3/4 in. (78 mm x 70 mm) folio: 10 5/8 in. x 7 5/8 in. (269 mm x 193 mm)
I inscribed in block above plate: 'Dairun layſt vns Bidden zc/Evangelium' (Now let us pray, etc.) inscribed in block below plate: 'In illo tepore• Dixit jeſus di/fscipulis fins . . . Johânis xiiii'
C Gift of Mrs. Toivo Lami-nan (Margaret Chamber-lin, Class of 1929)
1962.21.2, folio 132v fig. 33

A GERMAN, from STRAS-BOURG
printed in Strasbourg by Johann Pruss

T *King Ortnit Christens the Heathens and the King Throws the Idols from the Altar* detached folio from *Das Heldenbuch (Book of Heroes)*
D 1483
M watercolor or gouache over woodcut on cream paper
X image: 3 7/8 in. x 4 7/8 in. (98 mm x 125 mm) folio: 10 1/2 in. x 71/4 in. (268 mm x 186 mm)
C Gift of Mrs. Toivo Lami-nan (Margaret Chamber-lin, Class of 1929)
1966.18.1   fig. 99

A GERMAN from STRAS-BOURG
printed in Strasbourg by Johann Pruss
T *Wolfdietreich Prays to God to Make Water Run out of a Stone to Baptize the Heathen* detached folio from *Das Heldenbuch (Book of Heroes)*
D 1483
M watercolor or gouache over woodcut on cream paper
X image: 3 7/8 in. x 5 in. (100 mm x 128 mm) folio: 10 1/2 in. x 7 3/16 in. (268 mm x 183 mm)
W cross above Gothic letter (indistinct)
C Gift of Mrs. Toivo Lami-nan (Margaret Chamber-lin, Class of 1929)
1966.18.2

A GERMAN, from ALSACE
T *Virgin and Child*
D circa 1490
M polychromed wood, back hollowed out
X approx. 39 in. x 14 1/4 in. x 9 3/4 in. (99.1 cm x 36.2 cm x 24.8 cm)
I printed circular label, pasted on back: 'MATH-IAS KOMOR/WORKS OF ART/NEW YORK' inscribed in ink on paper label: 'Q924/about 1480'
C Gift in honor of Myrtilla

Avery from her students

1957.1   fig. 35, cat. no. 9

A GERMAN, from ULM
T *Virgin and Child*
D circa 1500–15
M polychromed and gilded wood
X approx. 41 1/2 in. x 14 in. x 4 in. (105.4 cm x 35.6 cm x 10.2 cm)
C Museum purchase with help of Mrs. W. Taliaferro Thompson, Jr.

1965.26   fig. 30, cat. no. 9

A GERMAN
T *Pietà*
D 16th century
M polychromed lead
X 7 1/8 in. x 4 7/8 in. (18.1 cm x 12.4 cm)
C Gift of Wellesley College Friends of Art

1966.2   fig. 19

A GERMAN
T *Virgin and Child with Saints Hugh of Lincoln and Bridget of Sweden*
D late 17th century
M watercolor, gouache, ink, and shell gold on cream paper
X sheet: 9 1/4 in. x 5 in. (235 mm x 126 mm)
I inscribed in pencil, verso: '1594' and '39'
C Gift of Mrs. Brooks Thayer (Louise Govett, Class of 1956)

1966.25.2   fig. 87

A GERMAN, AUSTRIAN, or SWISS
T *Shepherdess Kneeling at a Rural Shrine*
D 19th century
M etching on cream paper
X sheet: 6 1/2 in. x 3 7/8 in. (165 mm x 86 mm)
I stamped in ink, verso: 'Duplum/veräussert' encircled by 'K. Sächsisches Küpferstich Kabinet'
inscribed in pencil, verso: 'Hoff 106 1896–765 J5120ƒ

C Anonymous gift

1999.0.1   fig. 84

A GERMAN, AUSTRIAN, or SWISS
T *Virgin and Child*
D 19th century in medieval style
M stained glass
X 10 3/8 in. diameter (26.4 cm), circular shape
C Gift of Agnes Abbot

1973.4

A HENDRIK GOLTZIUS
Mülbracht (now Bracht-am-Niederrhein), Westphalia 1558–1617 Haarlem, Netherlands
active Haarlem
T *Annunciation*
plate 1 (of 6) from the *Meesterstukjes* (*Little Masterpieces*) series
alternate title: the *Early Life of the Virgin* series
D 1594
M engraving on dark cream paper, state 2 of 5
X sheet and image: 18 11/16 in. x 13 3/4 in. (475 mm x 350 mm)
S monogrammed and dated in plate: 'HG' in ligature above 'A. 1594'
I inscribed in plate at left: SERENISSIMO PRINCIPI.AC IL-/ LVSTRISSIMO DÑO.D GVILIELMO.V./COMITI PALAT. RHE VTRIVSQ BAVARIÆ DVCI &C./vt medys Proteus ſe transſormabat in vndis./Formoſe cupido Pomone captus amore:/Sic varia PRINCEPS TIBI nunc le Goltzius arte/Commutat, ſculptor mirabilis, atqe rêpertor./C. schongus.'
inscribed in plate, across bottom: 'Pone metum Virgo, celſi tibi nuncius adlum/Miſſus ab arce poli, paries intacta ſtupente./Natura, vt veterum cecinêre oracula Vatum,/Teqé Dei matrem totus venerabitur orbis.'

W escutcheon with diagonal stripe and 'WR" appended, surmounted by fleur-de-lis (Briquet 995)
C Museum purchase

1959.11   fig. 23, cat. no. 22

A JEAN-BAPTISTE ARMAND GUILLAUMIN
Paris 1841–1927 Paris
Active Paris
T *Woman and Child in Landscape*
D circa 1892
M oil on canvas
X 13 1/2 in. x 16 1/2 in. (34.3 cm x 41.9 cm)
S signed in brown paint, lower left: 'Guillaumin'
C Gift of Charlotte Lazarus Witkind (Class of 1941); with Hattie Weiler Lazarus (Class of 1914), Babette Lazarus Sirak (Class of 1943), Jean Lazarus Hoffman (Class of 1947), Mary Kohn Lazarus (Class of 1950)

1991.45

A AXEL HERMAN HAIG (born Axel Herman Hägg)
Katthammarsvik, Gotland, Sweden 1835–1921 Southsea, England
active London and Glasgow
T *Church Interior with Worshippers at a Pietà*
D 1891
M etching on heavy-weight machine-made wove dark cream paper
X image: 25 7/8 in. x 19 3/8 in. (658 mm x 493 mm)
sheet: 26 in. x 19 3/4 in. (661 mm x 502 mm)
S signed and dated in plate: '18'. 'HA' in ligature within circle. '91'
I signed in pencil: 'Axel H. Haig'
C Anonymous gift

1999.0.3   fig. 73

A ERICH HECKEL
Döbeln, Saxony 1883–1970 Radolfzell, Germany
active Dresden, Berlin, Hemmenhofen, and Karlsruhe
T *Geschwister* (*Siblings*)
X after a 1911 painting by the artist, now in the Staatliche Kunsthalle, Karlsruhe
D 1913
M woodcut on Bütten paper (heavy-weight greyish-white absorbent wove textured blotting paper)
X image: 16 1/4 in. x 11 5/16 in. (413 mm x 287 mm)
sheet: 25 3/4 in. x 19 11/16 in. (655 mm x 500 mm)
S signed and dated in pencil, recto: 'Erich Heckel 13'
I editioned in pencil, verso: '46/47'
inscribed in pencil, verso: '53496'
C Gift of the Ferdinand Roten Gallery

1958.33   fig. 100, cat. no. 43

A ARTHUR WILLIAM HEINTZELMAN
Newark, New Jersey 1892–1965 Rockport, Massachusetts
active Marblehead, Massachusetts
T *Untitled (Mother and Child)*
D 20th century
M etching with drypoint on cream paper
X image: 8 1/2 in. x 6 1/2 in. (214 mm x 165 mm)
sheet: 17 11/16 in. x 12 5/8 in. (450 mm x 321 mm)
I inscribed in pencil: 'Ed. 70/Arthur Wm Heintzelman/P 1904/Maternity'
W fragment: [VAN GELD]ER ZONEN
C Gift of Lester and Ruth Erlich Werman (Class of 1936)

1983.7

A JOHANN FRANZ VAN HELMONT
Netherlands 1715–56
Germany
active Cologne and Munich
T *Study for an Altar of the Assumption*
D mid-18th century
M pen and ink with watercolor and incising on six sheets of discolored cream paper
X sheet overall: 27 7/16 in. x 15 15/16 in. (697 mm x 405 mm)
W stag's antlers encircled by four lobed flowers dividing letters 'A V L I T'; alternated with IHS moniker
C Museum purchase in memory of Professor Bernard Heyl
1967.12   fig. 65

A MEG HENSON SCALES
born Portland, Oregon 1953
active Harlem, New York
T *Mary Loves Jesus Bartlet Prayers*
D 1997
M mixed media from a painting by the artist
X approx. 4 9/16 in. x 3 3/8 in. x 3 3/8 in. (11.7 cm x 8.5 cm x 8.5 cm)
S signed and editioned in blue ink, on label: 'Meg Henson Scales'
C Museum purchase
2000.16.1–10   fig. 170, cat. no. 49

A ITALIAN, from UMBRIA or TUSCANY
T *Christ Mounting the Cross and the Funeral of Saint Clare* (central panel of an altarpiece)
D 1290s
M tempera and silver leaf on panel
X 31 1/4 in. x 20 3/8 in. (79.4 cm x 51.8 cm)
I inscribed in paint across center: '[Hic] est sepultura beatae clarae inquae sanctissim[us] papa [Innocentus] [a]s

[ti]tit cum cardinalibus [et] fratribus minoribus [et] sororibus hui[us] ordini[s] [q(ue)]. (Here is buried the Blessed Clare with the most holy Pope Innocent standing with cardinals and friars and sisters of the Order)
C Museum purchase from a fund given by President Caroline Hazard
1905.2   figs. 77, 88, cat. no. 1

A ITALIAN, from FLORENCE
T *Annunciation*
D circa 1400
M red woven fabric with design in green and white
X 10 7/8 x 5 5/8 without fringe (27.5 cm x 24.5 cm)
C James Jackson Jarves Collection
1875.J.164

A ITALIAN, from SIENA
T *Visitation, Adoration of the Magi, Flight into Egypt, Christ among the Doctors, and Raising of Lazarus*
I fragment of a stole(?) with scenes from the *Life of Christ*
D 15th century.
M woven fabric, embroidered and backed with green silk
X 47 1/2 in. x 7 1/2 in. (156.3 cm x 19.0 cm)
C James Jackson Jarves Collection
1875.J.398   fig. 20

A ITALIAN, from FLORENCE
T *Seated Madonna above Cherubim* (repeating pattern)
D 15th century
M faded red woven fabric with design in gold
X 19 3/8 in. x 9 1/2 in. (49.0 cm x 24.0 cm)
C James Jackson Jarves Collection
1875.J.189

A ITALIAN, from SIENA

T *Madonna and Child*
D style of 15th century
M oil on panel over ink with punchwork
X 19 3/4 in. x 10 3/8 in. (50.2 cm x 26.4 cm)
C Gift of Dr. William Stephen Serri
1970.4

A ITALIAN, from the NORTH
T *Antiphonal* with historiated initials of the *Purification of the Virgin* and *Palm Sunday*
D last third of 15th century
M manuscript (24 folios) with black ink and glair or gouache on vellum
X folio: 10 1/4 in. x 7 3/8 in. (260 mm x 188 mm)
I stamped in gold on front and back cover: (crucifix)
C Gift of Mr. and Mrs. Arthur Vershbow
1964.44, folios 1r and 11r

A ITALIAN, from FLORENCE
T *Annunciation*
D circa 1500
M gold woven fabric with design in color faded to rust
X 10 1/8 in. x 9 1/2 in. (25.8 cm x 24.0 cm)
C James Jackson Jarves Collection
1875.J.190

A ITALIAN, from FLORENCE
T *Annunciation*
D circa 1500
M woven fabric with design in gold
C James Jackson Jarves Collection
J.1875.190

A ITALIAN, from FLORENCE
T *Madonna and Child*
D 15th/16th century
M carta pesta bas relief on panel with engaged frame
X 24 5/8 in. x 24 in. (62.5 cm x 61 cm), octagonal shape
with frame: 33 5/8 in. x

32 7/8 in. (85.4 x 83.5 cm)
I inscribed around figures: 'Ave Maria Gratia Plena Dominvs Tecum' inscribed in chalk, verso: 'Kris/ex/Old Masters'
C Anonymous loan
2.1962

A ITALIAN
T *Lamentation* (used as a pax)
D mid-16th century
M brass, partially coated with silver
X 6 1/2 in. x 4 1/2 in. (16.5 cm x 11.4 cm)
C Gift of Mr. and Mrs. J.J. Klejman
1961.24   fig. 74

A ITALIAN, from LOMBARDY, EMILIA, or ROMAGNA
T *The Transfiguration* full-scale embroidery *modello* for hood of a cope, pricked for transfer along bottom edge
D circa 1575
M ink and wash with white gouache highlights on blue paper
X sheet: 18 1/8 in. x 14 1/2 in. (460 mm x 367 mm)
C Museum purchase
1964.53   fig. 68

A ITALIAN
T *Madonna and Child with the Infant Saint John the Baptist (after Raphael)* full-scale cartoon of Raphael's *Alba Madonna*, now in the National Gallery of Art, Washington, DC
D 16th or 17th century
M sepia, graphite, and white chalk on several irregular sheets of rag paper, mounted to linen affixed to panel
X sheet: 33 1/8 in. x 33 in. (841 mm x 838 mm)
C Gift of Janet and Drew Gillow in honor of their grandmother, Mary Jane Carrier MacLachlan Greve (Class of 1928)

and in memory of her beloved second husband, Clifford Greve
1998.15   fig. 58

A   ITALIAN
T   *Madonna and Child with Saint or Holy Family*
D   17th century
M   red chalk
X   sheet: 6 7/8 in. x 5 3/8 in. (175 mm x 135 mm)
I   inscribed in ink on mount: 'Biscaÿno No 164'
    inscribed in pencil on mount: 'Sainte Famille = Croquis a la Sanguine/ Ecole Italienne XVIo siecle/Collection Gault[?] Saint Germain/et Collections Baquin'
C   Gift of Dr. Ruth Morris Bakwin (Class of 1919) 1977.65

A   ITALIAN, from ROME
T   recto: *Half-length figure of the Virgin* (oval format)
    verso: sketch of arms
D   late 17th/18th century
M   red chalk and wash with white lead gouache highlights on discolored cream paper
X   sheet: 7 3/8 in. x 6 1/4 in. (185 mm x 158 mm)
I   inscribed in pencil, verso: '55'
    green sealing wax, verso (no seal)
W   outline of Greek cross
C   Gift of Mrs. Robert Soutter 1941.1.11   fig. 36

A   ITALIAN
T   *Assumption of the Virgin* (after Agostino Carracci)
    copy of the upper half of a 1592/93 painting by Agostino Carracci, now in the Pinacoteca Nazionale, Bologna
D   17th or 18th century
M   ink and wash with black chalk and incising on buff paper
X   sheet: 10 in. x 11 in. (255

mm x 279 mm), arched shape
I   inscribed in pencil, on mount: 'Guido Reni' collector's stamp in blue ink: ID in circle
C   Swetzoff Gallery in settlement of account 1964.54   fig. 96

A   ITALIAN
T   *Entombment*
D   18th century
M   pen and wash on cream paper
X   sheet: 7 1/4 in. x 6 3/4 in. (185 mm x 172 mm)
I   inscribed in pencil: 'Tableau Orig en Venice St. Polo G'
    inscribed in brown ink, on mount: 'Gio.Dom: Tiepolo : del'
C   Gift of Mrs. Brooks Thayer (Louise Govett, Class of 1956) 1966.25.10

A   ITALIAN or ENGLISH
T   *Virgin and the Dead Christ*
D   18th or 19th century
M   pencil and wash
X   sheet: 12 13/16 in. x 10 3/16 in. (325 mm x 258 mm)
C   Gift of Mrs. Brooks Thayer (Louise Govett 1956) 1966.25.9

A   ITALIAN or FRENCH
T   recto: *Annunciation*
    verso: *Nativity* and *Annunciation to the Shepherds*
    cover for hand-illuminated 14th century Italian ferial psalter consisting of 132 folios
D   19th century
M   partially gilded bas-relief silver applied to red velvet binding
X   image: 6 3/4 in. x 4 3/4 in. (17.0 cm x 12.0 cm)
    binding: 6 7/8 in. x 5 1/4 in. (17.4 cm x 12.8 cm)
C   Gift of Mr. and Mrs. Arthur Vershbow 1965.58

A   JOHN BAPTIST JACKSON
    Battersea, England 1701–80 Newcastle (?)
    active London, Paris, Venice, Rome and Scotland
T   *Presentation of the Virgin in the Temple* (after Titian)
    copy of a 1539 painting by Titian now in the Galleria dell'Accademia, Venice
    right-hand plate of the *Presentation of the Virgin* triptych
    one plate of 24 from the *Venetian Painting* series
D   1742, published 1745
M   chiaroscuro woodcut printed in brown and black ink in four blocks and heightened with embossing on two sheets of heavy-weight laid white paper, seamed horizontally
X   sheet and image: 22 5/16 in. x 17 5/16 in. (560 mm x 443 mm)
S   signed in block: 'J. B. Jackſon'
I   inscribed in block: 'Per Illuftri, ac Nobili Viro Dnᵒ.Dnᵒ. ERASMO PHILIPPS BARRONETTO Artium zelantissimo Fautori, et de re litteraria/optime merito, Tabulam hanc tenue debitæ venerationis suæ argumentum, emeritissimo Patrono, et Mecænati commendat, et dicat/J.B. Jackson.'
    inscribed in crest: 'DUCIT AMOR PATRIÆ'
W   top sheet: fleur-de-lis
C   Bequest of Dr. Ruth Boschwitz Benedict (Class of 1935) 1994.43   fig. 8, cat. no. 33

A   GERTRUDE KÄSEBIER
    Fort Des Moines, Iowa 1852–1934 New York, New York
    active Brooklyn and Manhattan
T   *Adoration*

alternate titles: *Mother and Child* and the *Vision*
D   1897
M   gum bichromate print
X   print: 11 1/2 in. x 6 3/8 in. (292 mm x 162 mm)
I   inscribed in negative (fragment appears in print): 'MDCCCX'
C   Museum purchase 1973.40   fig. 159, cat. no. 40

A   GERTRUDE KÄSEBIER
    Fort Des Moines, Iowa 1852–1934 New York, New York
    active Brooklyn and Manhattan
T   *The Heritage of Motherhood*
    alternate title: *Mrs. Lee Mourning Her Child*
D   1904
M   gum bichromate print on fine-weight laid paper mounted to long-fibered paper
X   print: 9 15/16 in. x 11 15/16 in. (252 mm x 303 mm)
    mount (original): 10 7/8 in. x 13 5/8 in. (275 mm x 358 mm)
S   signed in white ink, on print: 'Gertrude Käsebier'
C   Museum purchase 1973.41   fig. 160, cat. no. 41

A   GERTRUDE KÄSEBIER
    Fort Des Moines, Iowa 1852–1934 New York, New York
    active Brooklyn and Manhattan
T   *The Heritage of Motherhood*
    alternate title: *Mrs. Lee Mourning Her Child*
D   1904
M   gum bichromate print on smooth heavy-weight paper
X   print: 9 3/4 in. x 12 7/16 in. (235 mm x 316 mm)
C   Museum purchase 1973.42   fig. 103, cat. no. 41

A THIELMAN KERVER
Holy Roman Empire 15th
century–1522/31 Paris
active Paris
T recto, top to bottom:
*Creation of Adam and
Eve; Piercing of Christ's
side; The Antichrist;
Prophets*
verso, top to bottom:
*Crowned King; Lamenta-
tion; Descent from the
Cross; Prophets*
detached folio from
printed *Horae Beatae
Virginis Mariae* (Latin
Book of Hours)
D 1505
M metalcut on vellum with
rubricated text and capi-
tals highlighted with
watercolor
X folio: 6 11/16 in. x 4 in.
(169 mm x 101 mm)
C Gift of Mrs. Toivo Laminan (Margaret Chamber-
lin, Class of 1929)
1962.21.1

A FERNAND LÉGER
Argentan, France
1881–1955 Gif-sur-Yvette
active Paris and New
York
T *Woman and Child*
D 1921
M oil on canvas
X 25 5/8 in. x 21 1/4 in.
(65.1 cm x 54.0 cm)
C Gift of Professor and
Mrs. J. McAndrew in
honor of Alfred H. Barr,
Jr.
1954.9   fig. 164, cat.
no. 45

A LUCAS Huygenszoon
VAN LEYDEN
Leiden, Netherlands
1494–1533 Leiden
active Leiden
T *Virgin and Child in a
Niche*
D 1518
M engraving on dark cream
paper
X sheet and image: 4 5/8
in. x 2 7/8 in. (118 mm x
74 mm)
S signed in plate: 'L'
I inscribed in pencil,

verso: 'dubbel' and '83'
stamped in violet ink,
verso: 'RM (in rectan-
gle)/DUBBEL/R.P.K'
C Gift of Dr. Ruth Morris
Bakwin (Class of 1919)
1977.70   fig. 127, cat.
no. 15

A LUCAS Huygenszoon
VAN LEYDEN
Leiden, Netherlands
1494–1533 Leiden
active Leiden
T *Virgin and Child with Two
Angels*
D 1523
M engraving on cream
paper, state 1 of 2
X sheet and image: 5 3/4
in. x 3 15/16 in. (146 mm
x 100 mm)
S signed and dated in
plate: 'L 1523'
W Gothic-script 'P'
C Gift to College Library
from Heirs of the Estate
of Susan Minns
1941.11   fig. 42, cat. no.
15

A LUCAS Huygenszoon
VAN LEYDEN
Leiden, Netherlands
1494–1533 Leiden
active Leiden
T copper plate for *Adora-
tion of the Magi*
D 16th century
M engraved copper
X 12 1/4 in. x 17 3/4 in.
(31.1 cm x 45.1 cm)
C Gift of Grazia and Flo-
rence Avitabile
1979.9.2

A LUCAS Huygenszoon
VAN LEYDEN
Leiden, Netherlands
1494–1533 Leiden
active Leiden
T *Adoration of the Magi*
D modern restrike of 1513
original
M engraving on mid-weight
wove white paper
X image: 12 1/4 in. x 17 3/4
in. (310 mm x 447 mm)
sheet: 17 1/2 in. x 22
9/16 in. (445 mm x 573
mm)

S signed and dated in
plate: 'L/1513'
W 'BFK RIVES/FRANCE'
C Gift of Grazia and Florence Avitabile
1979.9.1

A Attributed to BENEDETTO
LUTI
Florence, Tuscany
1666–1724 Rome
active Rome
T *Madonna and Child*
D circa 1700
M black chalk with white
highlights on prepared
warm grey-brown paper
X sheet: 7 in. x 5 7/8 in.
(177 mm x 149 mm)
I inscribed in pencil,
verso: '56'
C Gift of Mrs. Robert Soutter
1941.1.6

A DANNY LYON
born Brooklyn, New York
1942
active Chicago, Colom-
bia, and New Mexico
T *Showers, Diagnostic Unit,
Texas*
from *Conversations with
the Dead* series
reissued as no. 16 of 30 in
Hyperion Press portfolio
D 1969–70, printed 1979
M gelatin silver photograph
X print: 13 3/8 in. x 9 in.
(340 mm x 229 mm)
sheet: 14 in. x 11 in. (356
mm x 279 mm)
S signed in pencil, verso:
'Danny Lyon'
C Extended loan from Mrs.
Edith Davis Siegel (Class
of 1938)
44.1980   fig. 108, cat.
no. 48b

A ALESSANDRO
MAGNASCO, called il Lis-
sandrino
Genoa, Republic of
Genoa 1667–1749
Genoa
active Genoa, Florence,
and Milan
T *Monastic Saint in Medi-
tation*

D 1720s
M oil on canvas
X 16 15/16 in. x 10 15/16 in.
(43.0 cm x 27.8 cm)
I printed on first label
attached to stretcher:
'Wadsworth Atheneum/
art museum'
printed on second label
attached to stretcher:
'Chenue French Packer'
inscribed on second
label: 'Sackville
Gallery/East St. Andrews
St./Shaftesbury
Ave./London WC2'
C Museum purchase
1949.14   fig. 72, cat.
no. 31

A ANDREA MANTEGNA
Isola di Cartura, near
Padua ca. 1430–1506
Mantua
active Padua, Mantua
T *Entombment of Christ*
D circa 1470 or 1490
M engraving on greyish-
white paper
X sheet and image: 12 in. x
17 11/16 in. (306 mm x
449 mm)
I inscribed in plate, on
tomb: 'HVMANI GENERIS
REDEMPTORI'
inscribed in pencil,
verso: '13485/PZ'
C Gift of Mr. and Mrs.
Philip Hofer
1958.21   fig. 120, cat.
no. 8

A MARCEL-LENOIR (born
Jules Oury)
Montauban, France
1872–1931 Montricoux
active Montauban,
Paris, and Toulouse
T *Invocation a la Madonne
d'Onyx Vert (Invocation
to the Onyx-Green
Madonna)*
alternate title: *La
Madonne aux yeux
d'Onyx Vert (Madonna
with Green Onyx Eyes)*
D circa 1897
M color lithograph on
smooth heavy-weight
wove discolored white
paper

x image: 13 3/4 in. x 9 7/16
in. (351 mm x 240 mm)
sheet: 15 in. x 10 5/8 in.
(380 mm x 269 mm)
mount (original): 15 3/4
in. x 12 inches (400 cm x
306 cm)

s signed in plate, gothic
lettering: 'Mᴀʀᴄᴇʟ
Lᴇɴᴏɪʀ' within rectangle

ɪ chopmark, embossed
and stamped in brown
ink: youth's head in pro-
file
inscribed in pencil,
recto: 'Lenoir ɪɴᴠᴏᴄᴀ-
ᴛɪᴏɴ' and '45'

c Museum purchase
1968.71   fig. 105

A ɢʀᴇɢᴏʀɪᴏ ᴍᴀʀᴛíɴᴇᴢ y
Espinosa
Valladolid, Castile, Spain
1547–98 San Millán de la
Cogolla, La Rioja
active Valladolid, San
Miguel de Él Escorial,
Burgos, and Castile
region

т *Lamentation with Saints
Augustine and Nicholas of
Tolentino*

D 1590s

M oil and shell gold on
panel

x 9 in. x 11 1/4 in. (22.8 cm
x 28.6 cm)

s monogrammed in ligature: 'ᴍɴᴛʀᴢ'

ɪ inscribed in black ink,
verso: 'Sebastian Mar-
tinez.'
printed in black ink on
first paper label, verso:
'Dr. Th Engelmann,
Basel.'
inscribed in black ink on
first paper label, verso:
'gute aller E[. . .] B[. . .]
—/S. Martinez/Oel-
gemälde auf Holz x 24.5
Br 30/Der Leichnam
[. . .] Christ in den
Armen des/Maria
E[. . .] i Bischof ihr
A[. . .] G[. . .]e/zu fuhr
Christi K[. . .]rend. Vor
der Halle mit/2 Tarten[?]
bezeichnet S.MARZ
(*f*n c22)/*f*1.05'
inscribed in black ink on

second paper label,
verso: 'The dead Christ
embraced/by the Virgin
with two Saints/in
devout adoration—
by/Sebastien
Martinez/Jaen 1602–67
(Madr[id)]/"Un des plus
grands/peintres de
l'ecole de/Seville; tra-
vaille pour/les convents
de Cordove/et pour les
Églises de la/méme ville,
nominé en/1660, par
Philippe IV peintre/du
roi. Bon dessin—colo-
rie/plein de gràce et
d'aramonie"/Siret. Dic.
His des Peintres.'

c Museum purchase from
the Class of 1947 Acqui-
sition Fund in honor of
José Rafael Moneo
1999.120   fig. 71, cat.
no. 20

A Mexican, from ɢᴜᴀɴᴀ-
ᴊᴜᴀᴛᴏ state
possibly San Miguel de
Allende

т *Ex-Voto Commissioned by
José María Ramírez*

D 1798

M oil on canvas

x 25 3/4 in. x 27 3/4 in
(65.4 cm x 70.5)

s dated in paint, central
cartouche: '10 de Abril
de 1798 aᵒ'

ɪ inscribed in paint, upper
left and right quadrants
and across bottom: see
catalogue entry no. 36

c Museum purchase from
the Dorothy Johnston
Towne (Class of 1923)
Fund
1998.23   fig. 69, cat.
no. 36

A ᴏᴛᴛᴏ ᴍüʟʟᴇʀ
Libau, Silesia, Prussia
1874–1930 Breslau, Sile-
sia
active Dresden, Berlin,
Eastern Europe, and
Breslau, Silesia (now
Wroclaw, Poland)
printed at Breslau Acad-
emy by Lange

т *Zigeunermadonna (Gypsy*

Madonna)
alternate title: *Zigeunerin
mit kind vorm Wagenrad
(Gypsy Woman and Child
in front of Wagon Wheel)*
after a 1920s painting by
the artist, now in a pri-
vate collection in Han-
nover, Germany
plate 5 (of 9) from the
Gypsy Portfolio, edition
of 60

D 1927

M color lithograph in black,
brown, and grey ink,
with green watercolor on
fine-weight dark green-
ish-grey paper with lat-
tice pattern

x sheet: 27 1/2 in. x 19 3/4
in. (699 mm x 502 mm)

ɪ stamped in red ink
(twice): script '*O.M.*'
above 'Nachless/Prof.
Otto Mueller/Breslaw'
inscribed in pencil: √
24/'

c Gift of Elizabeth Prior
Denis (Class of 1932)
1996.44   fig. 101, cat.
no. 46

A ᴇᴅᴠᴀʀᴅ ᴍᴜɴᴄʜ
Løten, Norway
1863–1944 Oslo
active Kristiania (now
Oslo), Paris, Berlin, and
Kragerø, Norway

т *Madonna (Conception)*
after a painting by the
artist now in the Nasjon-
algalleriet, Oslo

D 1895, printed 1902

M color woodcut and lithograph on fine-weight
Japanese-style buff
paper, state 2 of 2

x image: 20 3/4 in. x 13 1/4
in. (527 mm x 336 mm)
sheet: 21 1/8 in. x 15 1/4
in. (831 mm x 600 mm)

c Gift of Mr. and Mrs.
Robert Schwarz (Faith
Lasser, Class of 1945)
1980.1   fig. 157, cat. no.
39

A ɢɪᴜsᴇᴘᴘᴇ Nicola ɴᴀsɪɴɪ
Castel del Piano, near
Siena, Tuscany
1657–1736 Siena

active Siena, Venice, Florence, Rome, and Tus-
cany

т *Apotheosis of a Male
Saint(?)*
study for a fresco lunette

D late 17th/18th century

M ink and wash with black
chalk underdrawing and
white lead gouache high-
lights on textured grey
paper

x sheet: 6 1/2 in. x 13 1/8
in. (165 mm x 333 mm),
arched shape

ɪ typed label, affixed to
verso: 'Giufeppe Nafini'
inscribed in pencil,
verso: 'Cortone'
inscribed in ink, verso:
'N 3105'

c Bequest of Mrs. Toivo
Laminan (Margaret
Chamberlin, Class of
1929)
1979.73   fig. 98

A ᴘɪᴇᴛᴇʀ ɴᴇᴇғs the
Younger
(with possible collabora-
tion of ғʀᴀɴs ғʀᴀɴᴄᴋᴇɴ
II the younger)
Antwerp, Flanders
1620–1675 Antwerp
active Antwerp

т *Interior of Antwerp Cathedral*

D 1657

M oil on canvas

x 24 3/8 in. x 34 in. (61.9
cm x 86.4 cm)

c Extended loan from a
private collection
28.1995   fig. 16

A Girolamo Francesco
Maria Mazzola, called il
ᴘᴀʀᴍɪɢɪᴀɴɪɴᴏ
Parma, Lombardy
1503–1540 Casalmag-
giore, Cremona
active Parma, Rome,
Bologna, and Casalmag-
giore

т *Nativity*

D early 16th century

M engraving on dark cream
paper

x image: 4 3/4 in. x 3 in.
(120 mm x 78 mm)
sheet: 5 3/8 in. x 3 7/16

in. (137 mm x 88 mm)
I inscribed in pencil, verso: 'Gebort Christi/ 1503–1540/Mazzuoli/Par migianino'
C Bequest of Merrill Millar Lake (Class of 1936) 1980.48

A GEORG PENCZ Nuremberg, Franconia 1500–1550 Leipzig or Breslau, Holy Roman Empire active Nuremberg, Krakow, and Königsberg
T Three Marys at the Tomb plate 18 of 26 from the Life of Christ series
D early 16th century
M engraving on dark cream paper
X sheet and image: 1 9/16 in. x 2 3/8 in. (40 mm x 60 mm)
S monogrammed in plate: 'PG' in ligature
C Gift of Margaret C. Laminan (Margaret Chamberlin, Class of 1929) 1962.7.2

A Bernardino di Betto di Biagio, called il PINTORICCHIO Perugia, Umbria ca. 1452–1513 Siena, Tuscany active Perugia, Rome, Orvieto, Spoleto, and Siena
T Virgin and Child with the Infant Saint John the Baptist and Saints Andrew and Jerome
D 1495–1500
M oil, tempera, shell gold, and gold leaf on panel
X 24 3/8 in. diameter (61.9 cm), circular shape
I inscribed in ink on octagonal paper label, pasted to verso: 'Fairfield Esq./Nr. 3' stenciled in black ink, verso: '1 F Y/939 GH/85 NA' inscribed in chalk, verso: 'Nov 13 36' red wax seal, verso (impression illegible)

C Museum purchase from the Dorothy Johnston Towne (Class of 1923) Fund 1995.1 front cover, fig. 45, cat. no. 10

A GIULIO CESARE PROCACCINI Bologna, Papal States 1574–1625 Milan, Lombardy active Cremona, Parma, Genoa, and Milan
T Holy Family with an Angel
D late 16th/early 17th century
M etching on greyish-white paper
X sheet and image: 6 3/8 in. x 4 13/16 in. (162 mm x 123 mm)
I inscribed in pencil, verso: 'D7M1021x B2 48' collector's stamp in ink: serifed 'GW'
C Museum purchase 1983.34

A MARCANTONIO RAIMONDI Argini (near Bologna), Papal States 1480/82–1527/34 Bologna active Bologna, Venice, and Rome
T Holy Family with the Infant Saint John the Baptist (after Raphael) alternate title: Madonna with the Long Thigh
D circa 1520–1525
M engraving on buff paper
X sheet and image: 15 11/16 in. x 10 5/8 in. (399 mm x 270 mm)
S unsigned (tablet in lower left corner never monogrammed
I inscribed in pencil, verso: 'Coll von Nagler m. Kgl Kupferſtich cabj' stamped in black ink, verso: 'KUPFERSTICH= SAMMLUNG DER KONIGL. MUSEEN' within oval and 'TILGUNGS . . . IMPER K.I.C.' within octagon

collector's stamp in blue ink, verso: 'vN.' in circle (K.F.F. von Nagler of Berlin 1770–1846, Lugt 2529)
W escutcheon with grape-filled chalice (Briquet 2118)
C Museum purchase 1959.3 fig. 129, cat. no. 16

A after MARCANTONIO RAIMONDI Argini (near Bologna), Papal States 1480/82–1527/34 Bologna active Bologna, Venice, and Rome
T Lamentation of the Virgin (after Raphael)
D early copy of a 16th-century original
M engraving on fine-weight laid buff paper
X image: 11 3/4 in. x 8 1/4 in (298 mm x 210 mm) sheet: 11 7/8 in. x 8 3/8 in. (302 mm x 213 mm)
I inscribed in plate: 'Ovos omnes, qui tranlitis per viam/Attendite, & videte, si elt dolor/sicut dolor meus/Huc me meus impulit amor'
C Gift of Mrs. Toivo Laminan (Margaret Chamberlin, Class of 1929) 1963.49

A REMBRANDT Harmenszoon van Rijn Leiden, Netherlands 1606–1669 Amsterdam active Leiden and Amsterdam
T Flight into Egypt (small plate)
D 1633
M etching on cream paper, state 2 of 2
X image: 3 1/2 in. x 2 1/2 in. (88 mm x 64 mm) sheet: 3 11/16 in. x 2 11/16 in. (93 mm x 68 mm)
S signed and dated in plate: '9 Rembrandt•Inventor et fecit 1633'

C Gift of Mrs. Joseph Pendlebury (Katherine H. DeWolf, Class of 1922) 1984.21 fig. 140, cat. no. 24

A REMBRANDT Harmenszoon van Rijn Leiden, Netherlands 1606–1669 Amsterdam active Leiden and Amsterdam
T Jews in the Synagogue alternate title: Pharisees in the Temple
D 1648
M etching on cream paper, state 2 of 3
X image: 2 13/16 in. x 5 1/8 in. (72 mm x 131 mm) sheet: 3 1/4 in. x 5 1/2 in. (82 mm x 140 mm)
I inscribed in pencil, verso: 'A 9041 B126 M198 a.11427 GT inscribed in pencil, verso: AD Nº 122' (Alcide Donnadieu of Paris, 1791–1861, Lugt 97) inscribed in black ink, verso: 'FL 9021' collector's stamp in red ink, verso: 'JWB' (Jane Whitman Bradley [Mrs. Charles Bradley] of Providence, 1849–1937, not in Lugt) collector's stamp in violet ink, verso: 'FL' in ligature (F. Lehman of Berlin, d. 1885, Lugt 1024)
C Bequest of Mrs. Toivo Laminan (Margaret Chamberlin, Class of 1929) 1979.82 fig. 12

A REMBRANDT Harmenszoon van Rijn Leiden, Netherlands 1606–1669 Amsterdam active Leiden and Amsterdam
T Star of Kings: A Night Piece
D circa 1652/54 (possibly later restrike)
M etching on cream paper, state 1 of 1

x image: 3 11/16 in. x 5 5/8
in. (93 mm x 142 mm)
sheet 4 1/16 in. x 6 1/8
in. (103 mm x 155 mm)

c Bequest of Mrs. Toivo
Laminan (Margaret
Chamberlin, Class of
1929)
1979.84

A DIEGO RIVERA (born
Diego María de la Con-
cepción Juan Nepomu-
ceno Estanislao de la
Rivera y Barrientos
Acosta y Rodríguez)
Guanajuato, Mexico
1886–1957 Mexico City,
Mexico
active Mexico City,
Spain, Paris, Soviet
Union, Cuernavaca, San
Francisco, Detroit, New
York

T *Mother and Child*

D 1944

M brush and black ink on
lightweight textured
cream Japanese paper

x 15 1/4 in. x 15 in. (387
mm x 279 mm)

s signed and dated in ink:
'Diego Rivera 44'

c The Dorothy Braude
Edinburg (Class of 1942)
Collection
1961.32

A Cristofano di Michele
Martini, called il
ROBETTA
Florence, Tuscany
1462–ca. 1535 Florence
active Florence

T *Adoration of the Magi*

D 1496–1500

M engraving on buff paper

x image: 11 7/8 in. x 10
15/16 in. (301 mm x 277
mm)
sheet: 12 1/16 in. x 10
15/16 in. (307 mm x 278
mm)

s signed in plate, lower
right: 'ROBETTA'

I inscribed in pencil,
verso: '600'

w large Latin cross ending
in P[X?]

c Gift of Mr. and Mrs.
Arthur Vershbow in

memory of Harry B.
Braude
1960.38   fig. 47, cat.
no. 11

A René-François-AUGUSTE
RODIN
Paris, France 1840–1917
Meudon
active Paris, Brussels,
and Meudon

T *Eve (after the Fall)*

D 1899

M marble

x approx. 30 3/4 in. x 8 in.
x 11 in. (78.1 cm x 20.3
cm x 28.3 cm)

s signed on right side of
base, rear: 'A. Rodin'

c Gift of Mr. and Mrs. Dan
Erskine Edgerton (Phyl-
lis Burke, Class of 1917)
in memory of their
daughter Nancy Edger-
ton Johnson
1982.4   fig. 40, cat. no.
42

A SALVATOR ROSA
Aranella (near Naples),
Kingdom of the two
Sicilies 1615–1673 Rome
active Naples, Rome,
and Florence

T *Three Marys at the Sepulchre*

D circa 1665

M oil on canvas

x 53 in. x 38 in. (134.6 cm x
96.5 cm)

c Gift of Dr. and Mrs.
Arthur K. Solomon
1959.42   fig. 144, cat.
no. 28

A CARLO Antonio SACCHI
Pavia, Lombardy
1616/17–1707 Pavia
active Pavia, Rome, and
Venice

T *Adoration of the Shepherds (after Tintoretto)*
copy of a 1579–1581
painting by Tintoretto,
now in the Scuola di San
Rocco, Venice

D 1649

M etching strengthened
with burin on textured
buff paper, state 1 of 1

x sheet and image: 20

3/16 in. x 15 3/16 in. (512
mm x 385 mm)

s signed in plate, lower
right: 'Carolus Saccus
Papíensis Scalp.t'

I inscribed in plate, bottom edge: 'Ill.mo Dño
Lodouico Vidmano Patri-
tio Veneto Com. Ottem-
burgí et c./Iconem Filij
Dei in lucem editi meo
studio sculptam nomini
tuo dicatum volui, vt
deuotíonís in te meæ
manifesta effigies
alíqua appareret.
Tu/benignuſ accepta, et
ſubmiſsus adora, quod
ego ſubmiſſo tibi animo
dedico conſecro./
Iacobus Tentoretus
pinxit/Humiliſsimus
Servus/Carolus Saccus
Papiensis Scalp.t'
inscribed in pencil,
verso: 'C. Saccus:
Geburt Christi: Original-
radierung von (illegible)
(illegible) Maler'
[collector's stamp in
blue ink: serifed 'BB'
(Cabinet Brentano-Birck-
enstock of Vienna and
Frankfurt, collection
formed 18th c., Lugt 345)

w indistinct

c Museum purchase
1988.2   fig. 143, cat. no.
27

A attributed to Jacopo
d'Antonio Sansovino
Tatti, called il SANSO-
VINO
Florence, Tuscany
1486–1570 Venice,
Republic of Venice
active Florence, Rome,
and Venice

T *Madonna and Child*

D circa 1540

M polychromed terra-
cotta

x approx. 36 1/2 in. x 13
3/4 in. x 8 1/4 in. (92.7
cm x 34.5 in. x 21.0 in.)

c Anonymous Gift in
honor of Mrs. George C.
Lee, Sr.
1953.1

A Circle of Giovanni Bat-
tista Salvi, called il SAS-
SOFERATTO
Sassoferrato, Papal
States 1609–1685 Rome
active Sassoferrato,
Naples, Umbria, and
Rome

T *Madonna and Child with
the Infant Saint John
(after Raphael)*
copy of a painting by
Raphael known as the
Aldobrandini Madonna
(or *Garvagh Madonna*),
now in the National
Gallery, London

D late 17th century

M oil on canvas

x 17 1/2 in. x 13 3/4 in.
(44.5 cm x 34.9 cm)

c Bequest of Marie A.
Phillips Steinert
1968.38

A MARTIN SCHONGAUER
Colmar, Alsace
1446–1491 Breisach am
Rhein, near Freiburg,
Holy Roman Empire
active Leipzig, Cologne,
and Breisach

T *Rest on the Flight into
Egypt*

D third quarter of 15th century

M engraving on medium-
weight laid brown paper

x sheet and plate: 9 13/16
in. x 6 1/4 in. (250 mm x
158 mm)

s monogrammed in plate,
bottom center: 'M + S'

I inscribed in pencil:
'xx/JG'
inscribed in ink:
'VI.123.7'
inscribed in crayon: 'R'
collector's stamp in
black ink: 'JG' in ligature,
encircled (J. F. Gigoux of
Paris, 1806–1894, Lugt
1164)

c Gift of Dr. and Mrs.
Lester S. King (Marjorie
Meehan, Class of 1929)
1976.32   fig. 115, cat.
no. 5

A CORNELIS SCHUT
Antwerp, Flanders

1597–1655 Antwerp
active Antwerp and Florence
printed in Antwerp by J. Haest
T *Holy Family with the Infant Saint John*
D 17th century
M etching on cream paper
X 7 7/8 in. x 6 1/2 in. (200 mm x 165 mm)
I inscribed in plate: 'C. Schut cum privileg' and 'Anvers chez J. Haest'
W 'cn Loone'
C Anonymous gift
1999.0.2

A SILVESTRO di Giacomo da Sulmona dell'Aquila
Aquila, Abruzzi 1471–1504 Aquila
active Aquila, Abruzzi region
T *Bust of the Madonna*
fragment (once part of a seated figure with child)
D 1495–1500
M gilded and polychromed terra-cotta
X approx. 18 1/2 in. x 22 1/8 in. x 12 1/2 in. (47.0 cm x 56.2 cm x 31.7 cm)
C Gift of Mrs. John T. Pratt (Ruth S. Baker, Class of 1898)
1940.14   fig. 124, cat. no. 12

A CLAUDINE BOUZONNET STELLA
Lyons, France 1636–1697 Paris
active Lyons and Paris
T *Calvary (after Poussin)*
copy of a ca. 1645/46 painting by Nicolas Poussin, now in the Wadsworth Atheneum, Hartford, Connecticut
D 1674
M etching with engraving on two sheets (seamed vertically) cream paper, state 1 of 2
X image: 22 in. x 30 7/8 in. (556 mm x 781 mm)
sheet: 22 3/8 in. x 31 5/8 in. (571 mm x 803 mm)
I inscribed in plate, lower

left: 'N. Pouʃʃin pinxit ex Mufæo Anth.º ʃtella pariʃijs. Claudia Stella ʃculp. et ex cud. cum Priuil. Regis. 1674'
inscribed in pencil, verso: 'ex. 427 71 71' (and illegible)
C Museum purchase
1993.6   fig. 69, cat. no. 29

A PIERRE HUBERT SUBLEYRAS
Saint-Gilles-du-Gard, France 1699–1749 Rome, Italy
active Paris, Toulouse, Rome, and Naples
T *Pope Benedict XIV Presents Saint Catherine dei Ricci to the Virgin*
preparatory drawing for a painting now in the collection of the Marchese Sacchetti, Rome
D 1745
M pen, wash, and graphite with incising, on buff paper
X sheet: 9 5/8 in. x 11 3/16 in. (244 mm x 285 mm)
I inscribed in pencil, mount: 'Juedwin 11/61' and '351 Cab Fr Boucher' inscribed in brown ink, on mount: '20/Cabt. Boucher'
C Gift of James F. O'Gorman
1977.52   fig. 66, cat. no. 34

A Giovanni Domenico Tiepolo, called GIANDOMENICO TIEPOLO
Venice, Italy 1727–1804 Venice
active Venice and the Veneto, Milan, Würzburg, Madrid, and Aranjuez
T *The Holy Family under a Palm Tree*, plate 6 (of 27) in the *Flight into Egypt* series
D circa 1750–1753 published 1753
M etching on greyish white paper, proof state (before the number)

X sheet and image: 7 in. x 9 1/2 in. (179 mm x 241 mm)
I inscribed in brown ink, verso: '11/16' above '3495'
inscribed in pencil, verso: 'GD Tiepolo' and 'Dupl'
C Gift of Mrs. Joseph Pendlebury (Katherine H. DeWolf, Class of 1922)
1984.22   cat. no. 35

A Giovanni Domenico Tiepolo, called GIANDOMENICO TIEPOLO
Venice, Italy 1727–1804 Venice
active Venice and the Veneto, Milan, Würzburg, Madrid, and Aranjuez
T *The Holy Family Leaving by a City Gate*
plate 7 (of 27) from The *Flight into Egypt* series
D circa 1750–1753, published 1753
M etching on white paper, state 1 of 1
X sheet and image: 7 3/16 in. x 9 1/2 in. (183 mm x 240 mm)
S signed in plate (twice): 'Doi Tiepolo fecit' and 'Doi Tiepolo in id fei'
C Museum purchase
1973.18   fig. 152, cat. no. 35

A Giovanni Domenico Tiepolo, called GIANDOMENICO TIEPOLO
Venice, Italy 1727–1804 Venice
active Venice and the Veneto, Milan, Würzburg, Madrid, and Aranjuez
T *Mary Holding the Child in Her Arms and Joseph with the Basket*
alternate title: *The Flight, with the Holy Family at the Left*
plate 10 (of 27) from the *Flight into Egypt* series
D circa 1750–1753, published 1753

M etching on textured white paper, state 2 of 2
X image: 7 1/2 in. x 9 7/8 in. (190 mm x 250 mm)
sheet: 8 in. x 10 7/16 in. (204 mm x 265 mm)
S signed in plate: 'Do: Tiepolo' and '10'
I collector's stamp in ink, verso: serifed 'BB' (Cabinet Brentano-Birckenstock of Vienna and Frankfurt, collection formed 18th century, Lugt 345)
C Gift of Professor and Mrs. John McAndrew
1957.26   fig. 54, cat. no. 35

A Giovanni Domenico Tiepolo, called GIANDOMENICO TIEPOLO
Venice, Italy 1727–1804 Venice
active Venice and the Veneto, Milan, Würzburg, Madrid, and Aranjuez
T *Episode of the Falling Idol*
alternate title: *The Holy Family Passing a Statue, the Head of Which Falls to the Ground*
plate 22 (of 27) from the *Flight into Egypt* series
D circa 1750–1753, published 1753
M etching on white paper, state 2 of 2
X sheet and image: 7 1/8 in. x 9 5/16 in. (181 mm x 238 mm)
S signed in plate, bottom left: 'TIEPOLO'; bottom center: '22'
I collector's stamp in blue ink, recto: 'M' surmounting 'C'
verso in pencil, center: old script 'Tipoli'
C Anonymous loan
4.1983   cat. no. 35

A Giralomo di Tommaso Pennacchi called GIRALAMO DA TREVISO the Younger
Treviso, Republic of Venice 1497–1544 Boulogne-sur-Mer, Eng-

lish-occupied France
active Bologna, Faenza,
Ravenna, and Boulogne-
sur-Mer

T *Raising of the Cross*

D circa 1530

M oil on panel transferred
to canvas

X 14 7/16 in. x 12 3/4 in.
(36.7 cm x 32.4 cm)

C Museum purchase with
funds given by Wellesley
College Friends of Art
1980.122

A FRANCESCO TREVISANI
Capodistria, Republic of
Venice (now Slovenia)
1656–1746 Rome
active Venice and Rome

T *Deposition (Descent from
the Cross)*

D circa 1698

M oil on canvas

X 22 1/16 in. x 16 1/16 in.
(56.0 cm x 40.8 cm)

C Gift of Professor and
Mrs. John McAndrew
1956.45   fig. 76

A GIORGIO VASARI and
workshop
Arezzo, Tuscany
1511–1574 Florence
active Arezzo, Florence,
Bologna, Rome, Venice,
and Naples

T *Holy Family with the
Infant Saint John the
Baptist and Saint Francis*

D post-1544

M oil on panel

X 39 1/2 in. x 30 1/2 in.
(100.3 cm x 77.5 cm)

C Museum Purchase in
honor of Nancy Angell
Streeter (Class of 1950)
1974.10   fig. 62, cat.
no. 17

A Bonifazio di Pitati, called
BONIFAZIO VERONESE
Verona, Republic of
Venice 1528–1588 Venice
active Verona, Rome,
Maser (near Treviso),
and Venice

T *Adoration of the Shepherds*

D mid-16th century

M oil on canvas

X 67 1/2 in. x 82 1/2 in.
(171.5 cm x 209.6 cm)

C Gift of Dr. and Mrs.
Arthur K. Solomon
1965.51   fig. 43

A JACOPO VIGNALI
Pratovecchio, Tuscany
1592–1664 Florence
active Florence

T *Abraham Entertaining
the Three Angels*

D circa 1620

M oil on canvas

X 45 1/4 in. x 57 1/4 in.
(114.9 cm x 145.4 cm)

C Gift of Nancy Jackson
Seiberling (Class of
1939) in memory of
Rebecca C. J. Shepherd
1991.48   fig. 21

A ANTONIE WIERIX the
Younger
Antwerp, Flanders
1555/59–1605 Antwerp
active Antwerp

T *The Garden (after
Hieronymus Wierix)*
plate 22 of 32 from the
*Vita Deiparæ Virginis
Mariæ (Life of the Virgin
Mary)* series

D late 16th century

M engraving on cream
paper, state 2a of 3

X image: 4 in. x 2 1/2 in.
(104 mm x 67 mm)
sheet: 6 7/8 in. x 5 in.
(175 mm x 127 mm)

S signed in plate, left of
center: 'AN.W sculp.'

I inscribed in plate:
'Hieronymus Wierx inu.
et excud. Cum Gratia et
Priuilegio. Piermans.'
and 'Carpe mater, carpe
flores/Verni temporis
honores, Carpe pater lil-
ium./Floris honor hic
vileſ cit,/Dum cæleſ tis
horti creſ cit/Puer hic
delicium.'
inscribed in pencil,
verso: 'Wierix/A.430'

W fragment: foolscap above
'4' surmounting orb

C Gift of Mrs. Samuel W.
Anderson (Lorraine
Combs, Class of 1923)
1982.29   fig. 56

A EMANUEL DE WITTE
Alkmaar, Netherlands
1617–1691/92 Amster-
dam
active Delft, Alkmaar,
Rotterdam, and Amster-
dam

T *Interior of a Renaissance
Church*

D 1660s

M oil on canvas

X 39 3/4 in. x 31 3/4 in.
(101.0 cm x 80.7 cm)

C Anonymous gift
1954.18   fig. 62

A MICHAEL WOHLGEMUT
Nuremberg, Franconia
1434/37–1519 Nurem-
berg
active Nuremberg
printed in Nuremberg by
Anton Koberger

T recto: *Circumcision*
verso: *Baptism*
detached folio from
Stephan Fridolin's
*Schatzbehalter der
wahren Reichtümer des
Heils (Treasure Box of the
True Riches of Salvation)*

D 1491

M double-sided woodcut
on discolored grey paper
with rubricated text

X images: 9 7/8 in. x 6 7/8
in. (250 mm x 175 mm)
folio: 13 in. x 8 1/2 in.
(330 W x 215 mm)

I inscribed above block,
recto: 'Die
∂reyund treiſ igiſt figur'
(the 33rd figure)
inscribed above block,
verso: 'Die
vierund treiſ igiſt figur'
(the 34th figure)

W fragment: flower lobe

C Gift of Mrs. Toivo Laminan (Margaret Chamber-
lin, Class of 1929)
1962.3.1   fig. 52

SUPPLEMENTAL
CHECKLIST

The following is a list of works
from outside collections
included in the exhibition
and/or reproduced in this catalogue.

A AUSTRIAN, from TYROL
region

T *Madonna and Child*

D circa 1430

M polychromed and gilded
wood

X 61 in. x 18 7/8 in. x 12 1/4
in. (155 cm x 48 cm x 31
cm) including pedestal

C Courtesy of the Busch-
Reisinger Museum, Har-
vard University Art
Museums, Antonia
Paepcke DuBrul Fund
BR63.2   fig. 78

A AUSTRIAN

A *Pietà*

D circa 1420

M polychromed poplar
wood

X 36 1/4 in. x 28 3/8 in. x 11
1/2 in. (93.1 cm x 72.0
cm x 29.2 cm)

C Courtesy of the Busch-
Reisinger Museum, Har-
vard University Art
Museums, Purchase in
memory of Eda K. Loeb
BR59.95   fig. 79

A PEDRO González
BERRUGUETE
Paredes de Nava,
Castile, Spain ca.
1450/55–1503 Ávila
active Paredes de Nava,
Toledo, and Ávila, Spain;
Urbino and Rome(?),
Italy

T *Nacimiento de la Virgen
(Birth of the Virgin)* (lateral panel of dispersed
polyptych)

D circa 1485

M oil, shell gold, and gold
leaf on panel

X 50 3/8 in. x 37 3/8 in.
(128.0 cm x 95.0 cm)

C Abadia y Santuario de
Montserrat, Spain
fig. 118, cat. no. 7

A PEDRO González
BERRUGUETE
Paredes de Nava,
Castile, Spain ca.
1450/55–1503 Ávila
active Paredes de Nava,
Toledo, and Ávila, Spain;

Urbino and Rome(?),
Italy

T   *Muerte de la Virgen
(Death of the Virgin)* (lateral panel of dispersed
polyptych)

D   circa 1485

M   oil, shell gold, and gold
leaf on panel
50 3/8 in. x 37 3/8 in.
(128.0 cm x 95.0 cm)
Abadia y Santuario de
Montserrat, Spain
fig. 119, cat. no. 7

A   ETHIOPIAN, from
GONDAR

T   *Mary Enthroned with
Christ*
folio from the *Miracles of
Mary (Taamera Maryam)*

D   second half of 17th century

M   parchment, wood end
boards

C   Dabra Warq, Gojjam,
Ethiopia
Courtesy, Institute of
Ethiopian Studies, Addis
Ababa
folio 125r   fig. 110

A   FRENCH, from PARIS or
NORTHEASTERN FRANCE

T   *Historiated initials*
From Richard de Saint-
Laurent's *De laudibus
beatae virginis mariae (In
Praise of the Blessed Virgin Mary)* containing 11
illuminations and 503
folios

D   circa 1290–1300

M   manuscript with black,
red, and blue inks, glair,
and gold leaf on vellum

X   folios: 11 3/4 in. x 8 1/4
in. (300 mm x 200 mm)

I   inscribed in ink, folio 2r:
'Auctor eſt ſsr Orðinis
Præðicatorum erraſ si
Sic putaſ'

C   Wellesley College Library,
Special Collections, Gift
of Caroline Hazard
MS 19   figs. 46, 50, 81,
82, cat. no. 2

ILLUMINATIONS
Preface, folio 1r: *Vision of
the Virgin to a Dominican
Friar*

Book I, folio 2v: *Three
Divine Salutations
(Annunciation, Visitation,
after Resurrection)*
Book II, folio 36v: *Quare
Mariae serviend[um]* . . .
(*On the Ways of Serving
the Virgin*); Mary pres-
ents the infant Jesus to
the Men and Women
who serve her with
Devotion, fig. 46
Book III, folio 90v: *De
privilegiis Mariae (Twelve
Privileges of Mary)*; Mary
as the apocalyptic
woman
Book IV, folio 102r: *De
virtutibum Mariae (On
the Innumerable Virtues
of Mary)*
Book V, folio 161v: *De
puchritudine (On the
Beauty of Mary)*
Book VI, folio 192r: *De
appellationibus (On the
Names of Mary)*;

I   inscribed around the let-
ter 'M': MATER, AMICA,
SOROR, SPONSA, FILIA,
VIRGO, ANCILLA, MIN-
ISURA, fig. 81
Book VII, folio 216r:
*Mariae c[a]elum, Mariae
firmamentum, Maria sol,
Maria luna* . . . (*Mary as
the Sun, Moon, and Stars*)
Book VIII, folio 239r:
*Maria terra (Mary as the
Earth)*, fig. 112
Book IX, folio 251v:
*Maria mare, Maria fons,
Maria flumen (Mary as
every kind of water)*
Book X, folio 264r: *Maria
archa (Mary as the Ark)*
Book XI, folio 319r:
*Maria ciuitas dei (Mary
as the City of God)*, fig.
50
Book XII, folio 358r:
*Maria ortus conclusis
(Mary as the Closed Gar-
den)*; 15th century Italian
addition

A   FRENCH, from PARIS
(produced for NANTES)

T   *Officium Beatae Mariae
Virginis* (Latin and
French Book of Hours,

use of Nantes)

D   1400–1410, with addi-
tions ca. 1450 and ca.
1470

M   manuscript with inks,
glair, and gold leaf on
vellum
197 folios, 3 full-page
miniatures, and 11 half-
page miniatures

X   folios: 7 in. x 5 in. (177
mm x 125 mm)

I   inscribed in faded ink on
final folio, 195v: (illegible)
stamped in gold on 17th
century leather binding:
'JEANNE' (front cover),
'GOVRO' (back cover)
collectors' labels, pasted
inside front cover:
'HENRI' LAMBERT/AVO-
CAT./VERSAILLES'; and
'Auguste/FONTAINE/E.
RONDEAU/Successeur/
35 Passage des Panora-
mas/PARIS'; and 'SAINT
MARK'S SCHOOL/Guy
Warren Walker, Jr./Col-
lection'

C   Wellesley College Library,
Special Collections, Guy
Warren Walker, Jr. Collec-
tion, on deposit from St.
Mark's School, South-
borough, Massachusetts
MS *81WM-1, folio 63r
fig. 114, cat. no. 4

A   FRENCH and/or FLEMISH

T   *Visitation*
half-page illumination
accompanying Lauds in
the Hours of the Virgin
from a French and Latin
Book of Hours (use of
"Vomine") containing 6
miniatures and 121
folios

D   circa 1450

M   inks, glair, and gold leaf
on vellum

X   folio: 7 1/4 in. x 5 3/16 in.
(184 mm x 132 mm)

C   Wellesley College Library,
Special Collections
MS 28, folio 49r   fig. 26

A   FRENCH, from BRITTANY

T   *Saint Anne Enthroned
with the Virgin and Child*
half-page illumination

accompanying devo-
tional prayer
from a printed *Officium
Beatae Mariae Virginis*
(Latin and French Book
of Hours, use of Nantes)
containing 14 miniatures
and 195 folios

D   circa 1470

M   inks, glair, and gold leaf
on vellum with printed
borders

X   image: 2 5/8 in. x 2 3/8
in. (76 mm x 60 mm)
folio: 7 in. x 5 in. (177
mm x 125 mm)

C   Wellesley College Library,
Special Collections, Guy
Warren Walker, Jr. Collec-
tion, on deposit from St.
Mark's School, South-
borough, Massachusetts
MS *81WM-1, folio 89r
fig. 34, cat. no. 4

A   FRANCESCO FURINI
Florence, Tuscany
1604–1646 Florence
active Florence and
Rome

T   *Adamo ed Eva nel Paradiso Terrestre (Adam
and Eve in the Earthly
Paradise)*

D   early 1630s

M   oil on canvas

X   76 in. x 95 1/4 in. (193.0
cm x 242.0 cm)

C   Palazzo Pitti, Galleria
Palatina
inv. Pal. 426   fig. 138,
cat. no. 23

A   GERTRUDE KÄSEBIER
Fort Des Moines, Iowa
1852–1934 New York,
New York
active Brooklyn and
Manhattan

T   *The Heritage of Motherhood*

D   1900/1904

M   platinum print with
some additions by hand

X   9 1/8 in. x 12 7/16 in.
(232 mm x 315 mm)

C   Detroit Institute of Art,
Founders Society Pur-
chase, Henry E. and
Consuelo S. Wenger
Foundation Fund and

John S. Newberry Fund
F1987.3   fig. 104

A   Master of the TUCHER
ALTARPIECE
active Nuremberg, Fran-
conia, ca. 1430–1450
T   Circumcision
D   circa 1450
M   oil on panel
X   39 3/4 in. x 35 7/16 in.
(101 cm x 90 cm)
C   Suermondt-Ludwig-
Museum, Aachen
Inv. nr. GK0312   fig. 51

A   MEXICAN
T   La Inmaculada (Immacu-
late Conception)
D   1870
M   oil on canvas
X   16 1/8 in. x 12 7/8 in.
(41.0 cm x 32.7 cm
S   dated in paint: 'año de
1870'
C   The Robert K. Winn Col-
lection, San Antonio
Museum of Art
85.1.706   fig. 97

A   MEXICAN
T   Ex-Voto Commissioned by
Anita Pacheco
D   1955
M   oil and photographs on
tin
X   7 3/4 in. x 12 1/4 in. (19.7
cm x 31.2 cm)
S   dated in paint: 1955
I   inscribed in paint: 'La
Señora Anita Pacheco,
dedica el presente como
Agradesimiento [sic] a
Ntra Sra. de Guadalupe
por haber debueto [sic] la
Salud a su "Nietecito"
estando enfermo a la
edad de 2 1/2 meses y ya
presente con 8 1/2
meses. Tijuana, B.C. 7
de Dibre de 1955. Benefi-
ciado: J. Jesús
Bermudez'
(Mrs. Anita Pacheco
dedicates this in thanks-
giving to Our Lady of
Guadalupe for having
restored the health of
her little grandson who
became ill at the age of 2
1/2 months old and is

now 8 1/2 months old.
Tijuana, B[aja] C[alifor-
nia], December 7th,
1955. Beneficiary: J. Jesús
Bermúdez)
C   Collection of James Oles
2.2000   fig. 153,

A   EDVARD MUNCH
Løten, Norway
1863–1944 Ekely
active Kristiania (now
Oslo), Paris, Berlin, and
Kragerø, Norway
T   Madonna
from "The Mirror"
D   1895
M   lithograph with crayon,
tusche, and needle on
blue wove paper
X   sheet: 23 1/4 in. x 17
1/8 in. (592 mm x 436
mm)
S   signed and dated in pen-
cil on mount: 'Edv.
Munch 1895'
C   Courtesy of the Fogg Art
Museum, Harvard Uni-
versity Art Museums,
Through the generosity
of Lynn and Philip A.
Straus, class of 1937
M20227   fig. 158, cat.
no. 39

A   ROMAN
T   Orant Virgin and Child
wall painting from the
Coementerium Maius
catacomb
D   4th century
M   fresco on plaster
C   Courtesy Foto Mar-
burg/Art Resource New
York
fig. 13

A   ROMAN
T   Virgin and Child with
Prophet (Proto-Annuncia-
tion)
ceiling painting from the
Catacomb of Priscilla
D   early 3rd century (?)
M   fresco on plaster
C   Courtesy Alinari/Art
Resource NY
fig. 14

A   FERÊ SEYON (?)

active Central Ethiopia,
15th century
T   Our Lady Mary with her
Beloved Son, the Ancient
of days, Prophets, Apos-
tles, and Saints (triptych)
D   1445–1480
M   tempera on gesso-cov-
ered wood panels
X   24 13/16 in. x 40 3/16 in.
(63.0 cm x 102.0 cm)
open
C   Institute of Ethiopian
Studies, Addis Ababa
no. 4186   fig. 49

A   SILVESTRO dell'Aquila
T   Virgin Adoring the Child
D   1494–1500
M   polychromed and gilded
terra-cotta
C   Church of San
Francesco, Aquila, Italy
fig. 125, cat. no. 12

A   SPANISH
T   Como o bona dona rogou
o monge que lli trouxesse
da c[. . .] una omagen de
Santa Maria (How a
good woman asked a
monk to bring her an
image of Saint Mary)
Miniature from Alfonso
X el Sabio's Cantigas de
Loor de Sancta Maria,
Escurialense manuscript
D   circa 1280
M   glair on vellum
C   Biblioteca del Monaste-
rio de San Lorenzo de Él
Escorial
Ms T.I., cantiga 9, folio
17,   fig. 17

A   SPANISH
T   Como un pintor pintava a
omagen de Sancta Maria
muy fremosa e a do demo
muy fea (How a painter
painted a beautiful image
of St. Mary and an ugly
one of the devil)
miniature from Alfonso
X el Sabio's Cantigas de
Loor de Sancta Maria,
Escurialense manuscript
D   circa 1280
M   glair on vellum
C   Biblioteca del Monasterio de San Lorenzo de Él

Escorial
Ms T.I. cantiga 74, folio
109 vignette
fig. 85

A   SPANISH
T   Our Lady of Montserrat
D   final third of the 12th
century
M   polychromed and gilded
wood
X   37 1/2 in. x 13 5/8 in. x 15
in. (95.0 cm x 34.5 cm x
38.0 cm)
C   Abadia y Santuario de
Montserrat
100.001   fig. 86

A   PIERRE HUBERT SUB-
LEYRAS
Saint-Gilles-du-Gard,
France 1699–1749
Rome, Italy
active Paris, Toulouse,
Rome, and Naples
T   Mystic Marriage of Saint
Catherine dei Ricci
D   1746
M   oil on canvas
X   69 in. x 98 1/2 in. (175.0
cm x 250.0 cm)
S   signed and dated
C   Collection of the March-
ese Giovanni Sacchetti,
Rome
fig. 151, cat. no. 34

A   Circle of WILLEM BACKER
VAN VRELANT
Utrecht, Netherlands
active ca. 1449–1481
Bruges, Flanders
active Bruges
T   Gebeden Boeck (Dutch
Book of Hours, use
unknown)
D   circa 1470
M   manuscript with ink,
glair or gouache, gold
leaf, and shell gold on
vellum
117 folios, 6 full-page
miniatures, and many
decorative initials and
borders in gold and col-
ors
X   folios: 6 15/16 in. x 4
13/16 in. (68 mm x 110
mm), arched top
folio: 6 15/16 in. x 4 13/16
in. (176 mm x 122 mm)

I inscribed on the angel's banner: 'ÆVE/MA/RIA/GRACIA' stamped in gold on spine: 'GEBEDEN BOECK' label pasted inside cover: coat of arms above 'Le Comte D. Boutourlin' collector's stamp on end-paper: gothic letter 'O' within trapezoid

C Wellesley College Library, Special Collections, Gift of Bertha Mahony Miller
MS 27   fig. 116, cat. no. 6

A J. MICHAEL WALKER
born Little Rock, Arkansas 1952
active Los Angeles, California, and the Sierra Tarahumara, Chihuahua state, Mexico

T *Planchando, Pensando (Ironing, Thinking)*
no. 2 of an ongoing series of the *Daily Life of the Virgin of Guadalupe*

D 1995

M color pencil on heavyweight wove white paper

X sheet: 54 in. x 32 in. (1372 mm x 813 mm)

C Collection of Henry and Patricia Schwarz
fig. 109

A MICHAEL WOHLGEMUT
(with possible collaboration of WILHELM PLEYDENWURFF)
Nuremberg, Franconia 1434/37–1519 Nuremberg
active Nuremberg
printed in Nuremberg by Anton Koberger

T *Holy Kinship*
from Hartmann Schedel's *Fasciculum temperum*, known as the *Liber chronicarum (Nuremberg Chronicle)*

D 1493

M woodcut on paper with printed text

X image: 10 1/8 inches x 8 7/8 inches (258 mm x 226 mm)
folio: 18 1/4 inches x 12 3/8 inches (463 x 313 mm)

S colophon, final page: '. .
. Michaele Wolgemut et Wilhemo Pleydenwurft 1493'

I collector's stamp in blue ink, title page: IHS moniker with cross above and anchor below surrounded by text within oval, 'SOCIETATIS JESU * SEMINAR. VALSENS'

W lobed latin cross alternating with crown

C Wellesley College, Special Collections, Guy Warren Walker Jr. Collection, on deposit from St. Mark's School, Southborough, Massachusetts
MS *81W-2a, folio 95r
fig. 55

INDEX

Aachen, Hans von, *Crucifixion,* 79, 80
Abortion conflict, 9
Abraham Dismissing Hagar (Breenbergh), 24, 209–11
Abraham Entertaining the Three Angels (Vignali), 36
Abraham/Ibrahim, 24, 209–11
Abraham Preparing to Sacrifice his Son, according to God's Command (Chagall), 252–54
Abruzzezi, Madame, 244
Acts, Book of, Mary noted in, 94
Adam and Eve (Chagall), 253
Adam and Eve (Furini), 50, 206–07
Adam and Eve story, 50–51
Adams, Henry, vii, xx
Adoration (Käsebier), 103, 240–42
Adoration of the Magi, 21
    art of, 53–60
    continents, Magi and, 57–59
    social strata in, 56–57
Adoration of the Magi (after Veronese) (Sacchi), 214
Adoration of the Magi (Botticelli), 178–79
Adoration of the Magi (da Vinci), 177
Adoration of the Magi (Italian), 36
Adoration of the Magi (Lippi), 177, 178
Adoration of the Magi (Robetta), 55, 177–79
Adoration of the Magi (Schongauer), 178
Adoration of the Shepherds (after Tintoretto) (Sacchi), 213–14, 216
Adoration of the Shepherds (Dürer), 49, 53
Adoration of the Shepherds (Veronese), 53
Africa
    Biafra, 143
    early missionaries in, 58
    Mary in, 58, 109, 142–44
    primitivism in artifacts, 5
Agony in the Garden, 36
Akita, Japan apparition, 110
Alba Madonna (Italian, after Raphael), 64
Albert the Great, saint
    on beauty of Mary, 44
    on reproduction and women, 52, 53
Alexander IV, pope, 176
Alfonso X (Castile), 88
Allegory of Love (Robetta), 178
Alone of All Her Sex: The Myth and Cult of the Virgin Mary (Warner), xix
Alpheus, 62
Altarpieces in Middle Ages, 34
Álvarez Bravo, Lola, 109
    La Patrona (The Patroness), 254–56
Ambiguous Marys, 20. *See also* Three Marys
Ambrose of Milan, saint 62, 84
American Catholics, 9–10
    in Cold War years, 14
American Protestants, 10
    as art collectors, 81
Americas, Our Lady of the, 11. *See also* Guadalupe, Our Lady of, Mexico
Anabat, Guillaume, 182
Andachtsbilder, 32
Anderson, Hillary L., 203, 205, 214, 218, 225
Anderson, James, *Temple of Antonius and Faustina,* 30
Andrea, Zoan, 170
Andrew, saint, 174–77

Angels, Our Lady of the, Costa Rica, 89
Angels Adoring the Christ Child (Garavaglia), 87
Ani, Nigerian deity, 143–44
Anne, saint, 21
    annunciation to, 37
    in Counter-Reformation, 70
    iconography of, 41
    marriages of, 62
    in Protevangelium of James, 136–37
Annual feast days, 11, 12, 69, 78
Annunciation, 20, 24
    art of, 37–41
    in early Christian art, 38
    in Gospels, 21
    interaction between Mary and Gabriel, 40
    mental activity of Mary, 39–40
    physical posture of Mary, 38
    in Qur'an, 23
Annunciation (Berruguete), 97
Annunciation (Dürer), 37
Annunciation (Dutch Book of Hours), 162–64
Annunciation (French, from Paris), 181–83
Annunciation (Goltzius), 20, 38, 204–05
Annunciation (Martini), 40
Annunciation (Vrelant), 39, 41
Annunciation to the Shepherds, 21, 53
Annunciation to the Shepherds (French, from Amiens), 52
Annunciation with Sts. Barbara and Catherine of Alexandria, 35, 39
Anti-Catholicism, 10–11
Anti-Semitism
    in circumcision scenes, 60
    Crusades and, 59–60
Antwerp cathedral, 30, 75
Apocrypha, 22
Apolito, Paolo, 8
Apotheosis of a Male Saint (Nasini), 99
Apostle's Creed, 33
Apparel of Magi, 56–57
Apparitions of Mary, 7–8
    Christian tradition and, 137
    in nineteenth century, 105–07
    in twentieth century, 110
Arab populations, 58
Aristotle, 51, 52, 53
Ark of the Covenant, 38
Armstrong, Lilian, 152, 155, 160, 164, 171, 177, 179, 181, 183
Aronoff, A., 222
Arpino, Cavaliere d', *Holy Family,* 87
El Arte de la pintura (Art of Painting) (Pacheco), 98
Artemis of Ephesus, 133, 134
Assumption, 71. *See also* Coronation of the Virgin of Mary, 97
Assumption of the Virgin (Berruguete), 97, 165–68
Assumption of the Virgin (Carracci), 97, 98
Athena, 133, 134
Augustine of Hippo, saint, 76, 199–201
    on nativity, 49
    on virginal conception, 42–43
Augustinian order, 32, 201
Austern, Linda Phyllis, 140
Ave Maria, 33
Avery Madonna, 172–73

Avioth, Our Lady of, France, 89
Avril, François, 155

Balaam, 27
Balbi, Giovanni, 29–30
Ballada, Ottavio, 214
Balthasar, magus, 57
Banneaux, Belgium apparition, 106
Barbara, saint, 71
Barletta, Gabriele de, 43–44
Barocci, Federico, 204
Baroque
    Counter-Reformation and, 70
    Crespi, Giuseppe and, 218–19
    Italian Baroque, 202
Bartsch, Adam, 169, 170
Basilica, National Shrine of the Immaculate Conception, Washington, DC, 9–10
Basque apparition, 8
Bassano, Jacopo, 204
Bathsheba, 182
Bauquier, Georges, 249
Bayside, Queens, New York apparition, 110
Beata communities, 82
Beauraing, Belgium apparition, 106
Beauty of Mary, 43–44
Becon, Thomas, 51
Beguine order, 82
Beham, Hans Sebald, *Virgin and Child with a Pear,* 46
Bella, Stefano della, *Rest on the Flight into Egypt,* 212–13
Benedictine order, 32
Benedict of Nursia, saint, 63
Benedictus Chelidonius, 183
Benedict XIV, pope, 225–28
Benjamin, Walter, 255
Benson, Frank W., 247
Berber settlers, 58
Berceo, Gonzalo de, 88
Berman, Patricia Gray, 237, 239, 240, 250
Bernadette, saint, 6
Bernard, Émile, 104
    Confirmand's Procession, 236–38
Bernardino di Betto. *See* Pintoricchio
Bernardino of Siena, saint, 85, 88
Bernard of Clairvaux, saint, 42, 50, 57, 106
Bernardone, Giovanni Francesco da, 32. *See also* Francis of Assisi
Berruguete, Alonso, 199
Berruguete, Pedro
    Assumption of the Virgin, 165–68
    Assumption panels, 97–98
    Birth of the Virgin, 97, 167
    Death of the Virgin, 97, 167
Betrothal ceremonies, 44
Betrothal of the Virgin (Dürer), 44
Betto di Biagio, Bernardino di. *See* Pintoricchio
Biafra, 143
Bible. *See* Hebrew Bible
Bibles of the poor, 35
Biblia pauperum, 35
Bijlivert, Giovanni, 206
Birgitta, saint, 48, 106
    Revelations, 84
Birth of Jesus, Liberius dating, 29
Birth of Mary, 22
Birth of Mary (Berruguete), 97

Birth of the Virgin (Berruguete), 167
Birth of the Virgin Mary (Dürer), 65
Black Canons, 32, 201
Black Madonnas/Christs, 11, 72–73
Blondeness of Mary, 47
Boccaccio, Giovanni, 40
Bodenstein von Karlstadt, Andreas, 32
Bonaventura, 64
Bonaventure, saint, 81–82
Bongiorno, Laurine Mack, 179–81
Book of Hours (Officium Beatae Mariae Virginis) (Walker), 158–60
Book of Hours (use of Amiens), 46, 49
  hair of Mary, 45
  youth of Mary, 43
Book of Revelations, 95
Books
  in annunciation scene, 39, 40–41
  illustrated books, 35
Books of Hours, 35. *See also* specific
    books
  Hardouyn *Book of Hours*, 182–83
  literacy and, 40–41
  passion cycle, 80
  Rouen *Book of Hours*, 48
  Vostre, Simon, *Book of Hours*, 183
  Vrelant, Willem Backer van, 162–64
  Walker *Book of Hours*, 158–60
  Walters *Book of Hours*, 164
Boorsch, Suzanne, 170
Borgia, Rodrigo, 176
Borgoña, Juan de, 167
Botticelli, Sandro, 176
  Adoration of the Magi, 178–79
  Madonnas by, 240, 241
Boucher, François, *Sacrifice of Isaac*,
    221–23
Boulogne, Our Lady of, France, 89
Bouzonnet family, 216
Bouzonnet Stella, Claudine, *Calvary (after
    Poussin)*, 79–80, 216–18
Breastfeeding
  Maria lactans, 139, 143
  Milk-Giving icons, 29
  Protestants on, 86–87
  scenes of, 85–86
  wet nurses, 85
Breenbergh, Bartholomeus, *Abraham Dis-
    missing Hagar,* 24, 209
Brethren of the Common Life, 34, 86, 93
  women's education, 41
Breviary, 227
Bridget, saint. *See* Birgitta, saint
Brooklyn Museum, *Sensation: Young
    British Artists from the Saatchi Col-
    lection,* xx, 13
Brooks, Blair A., 203, 218, 244
Bruno, saint, 220
Burial of the Virgin (German, from Augs-
    burg), 95
Burin-stroke, 204–05
Bust of the Virgin, (Silvestro dell'Aquila),
    179–81
Byzantine church, 48

Caesarius of Heisterbach, 59
Calendar of Saints, 227
Calvary (after Poussin) (Bouzonnet Stella),
    79–80, 216–18
Calvin, Jean, 32, 88
  on importance of Mary, 53
Camera Notes (Steiglitz), 241
Cameron, Julia Margaret, *La Santa Julia
    (Portrait of Julia Prinsep Jackson),*
    103, 234–35
Cameroon apparition, 110

Camillian order, 227
Campos-Pons, Maria Magdalena, *Sagrada
    Familia/Holy Family,* 259–61
Cana, wedding feast at, 23
Cantigas de loor de Sancta Maria (Alfonso
    X), 88
Capitalizations, 20
Cappelletti, Francesca, 206
Capricci (Tiepolo), 228
Capuchin order, 202
  on Franciscan spirituality, 71
Caracciolo da Lecce, Fra Roberto, 40
Caravaggio, Michelangelo Merisi da,
    77–78
Caridad, La (Our Lady of Charity), 11
Carmelite order, 214
Carracci, Agostino, 218
  Assumption of the Virgin, 97, 98
Carracci, Annibale, 202
Carroll, Margaret D., 162, 194, 208, 211
Cars, Jean-François, 221–22
Cassatt, Mary, 241
Castrati, 140
Catacomb of Priscilla, 27, 28, 133
  breastfeeding Mary, 86
Catacombs, art in, 26, 27
Catalan Atlas, 1375-1385, 56
Catherine dei Ricci, saint, 71, 91, 92,
    225–28
Catherine of Alexandria, saint, 227
  cult of, 71
Catherine of Bologna, saint, 71
Catherine of Siena, saint, 64, 71, 227
Catholic, derivation of, 57
Catholicon (Balbi), 29–30
Cavalcaselle, G.B., 176
Ceres, 133
Cervantes, Miguel de Saavedra,199
Cesari, Giuseppe, *Holy Family,* 87
Chagall, Ida, 253
Chagall, Marc
  Abraham Preparing to Sacrifice his Son,
    252–54
  Adam and Eve, 253
  Jew in Green, 255
  Moses dies in view of the Promised Land,
    25
Chanukah, 22
Chapi, Our Lady of, Peru, 89
Chartres Cathedral, 88
Chiaroscuro
  of Crespi, Giuseppe, 218
  in *Entombment of Christ* (Mantegna),
    171
  woodcuts of Jackson, John Baptist,
    223–24
Chicanos
  gang members, 15
  identity, 254
Childbirth
  Luther, Martin on, 66
  role of Mary, 64–66
Child mortality, 85–87
Children
  of Mary, 8
  parents, care for, 83
  in Renaissance, 67
  status of, 66–67
China, twelfth century, 57–58
Christ. *See* Jesus Christ
Christ among the Doctors (Italian), 36
Christ before Pilate, 37
Christ Carrying the Cross, 37
Christiansen, Keith, 170
Christmas
  crèche, 65

  guilds and confraternities celebrat-
    ing, 48
  music of, 139
*Christ Mounting the Cross and the Funeral of
    St. Clare,* 81, 151–52
Christ's Ascension, feast of, 96
Christ Taking Leave of His Mother (Dürer),
    183–85
Church attendance, 78, 79
Church Interior with Worshipers at a Pietà
    (Haig), 78
Church Interior (de Witte), 84
Church of England, *Homily on Matrimony,*
    44–45
Circumcision of Jesus, 21, 59–60
Circumcision (Master of the Tucher altar-
    piece), 60
Circumcision (Wohlgemut), 60
Civil marriage, 63
Clare of Assisi, saint, 79, 92–93
  *Christ Mounting the Cross and the
    Funeral of St. Clare,* 151–52
Claude Lorrain, 224
Clearwater, Florida apparition, 7
Clermont-Ferrand, shrine of Mary, 59
Cleveland Museum of Art, 102
Cleves, Count of, 155
Coebergher, Wenzel
  Virgin and Child with St. Stephen, 66
Coemeterium Maius, 27
Coinci, Gautier de, 59
  Les miracles de Notre Dame, 88
Commissioned art, 35, 104
Commonweal, 14
Communion, 78. *See also* Eucharist
Communion of the Apostles (Berruguete),
    165
Compassionate Virgin, 28–29
Compline, 93–94
Conceptio Christi, 28
Concerning Widows (Ambrose of Milan),
    84
Concordance to the Old and New Testa-
    ments (Cruden), 20
Confession, 78
Confirmand's Procession (Bernard), 104,
    236–38
Confraternities
  commissioned art, 35
  widows, care for, 83
Congress of Vienna, 105
Constantine, 100
  Edicts of Tolerance, 28
Convents, 91–92
  life in, 92–93
  Protestants closing, 101
  scholarships for, 93
Conyers, Georgia apparition, 110
Coornhert, Dirck Volkertsz., 204
Coptic Christians, 58
Cordero, Gil, 89
Co-redemptrix, 109
Coronation of the Virgin, 12, 94–101
  in early Christian art, 94
Coronation of the Virgin (French, from
    Amiens), 94, 158–60
Corpus Christi, 48
Correggio, Antonio Allegri da, 197, 204
Council of Chalcedon, 26
Council of Constance, 66
Council of Constantinople, 26
Council of Ephesus, 26
  Mother of God, Mary as, 28
Council of Florence, 58
Council of Nicaea, 26, 157
  ideal woman, Mary as, 48

Second Council of
Nicaea, 30–31
Council of Trent
on devotional art, 70, 197
on elegance in religious
art, 191
Goltzius' iconography
and, 240
Immaculate Conception
controversy, 99
marriage ceremonies, 44
modern worship and, 78
sacraments defined by, 63
Counter-Reformation, 70
Fontana, Lavinia and,
197
Francis of Assisi, saint
and, 71
Mary's place in art, 70–71
in Spain, 76–77
spirituality, 76
Covenant of Mercy, 109–10
Coxie, Michiel, 194
Cranach, Lucas, 31–32, 75
Judith and Holofernes
depictions, 192
Crashaw, William, 86
Crèche, Christmas, 65
Crespi, Giuseppe Maria,
*Sacrament of Ordina-
tion,* 63, 218–19
Cresques, Abraham, 56
Crowe, J.A., 17
Crowning Mary. *See* Queen-
ship of Mary
Crowning with Thorns, 37
Crucifixion, 36, 37
John's Gospel, 23
pax and, 78
in Protestant art, 74–75
Crucifixion (von Aachen), 79,
80
Crucifixion (Dürer), 82
Crucifixion (Dutch Book of
Hours), 163
Cruden, Alexander, 20
Crusades, 49, 59, 100
anti-Semitism and, 59–60
Cubism, 249
Cuius regio, eius religio, 100
Cult of Mary
adoration and, 56
as sorrowing mother, 82
Cult of Montserrat, 90
Cults of saints, 71
Cultural figure, Mary as, 7–8
Cybele, 134
Czestochowa, Our Lady of,
11

*Daily Life of the Virgin of
Guadalupe* series
(Walker), 107
Daniel in the Lion's Den, 27
Dante on beauty of Mary, 44
Darwin, Charles, 105
David and Uriah, 181, 182–83
Day, F. Holland, 242, 243
Dead Souls (Gogol), 253
Death of Mary, 94–96. *See also*
Deposition
immortality and, 134
Death of the Virgin
(Berruguete), 97,
167
Death of the Virgin (Dürer), 95

Deborah, 24
Decameron (Boccaccio), 40
DeGrazia, Diane, 202
*De institutione foeminae chris-
tianae* (Education of a
Christian Woman)
(Vives), 84
Delacroix, Eugène, 102
*De laudibus beatae virginis
Mariae* (In Praise of the
Blessed Virgin Mary)
(Richard de Saint-
Laurent), 153–56
della Robbia, Madonnas by,
240, 241
della Rovere, Francesco, 175
Demeter, 133, 134
Deposition, 37, 243
Book of Hours on, 80
Deposition from the Cross
(Rosso), 200
Deposition from the Cross
(Vasari), 200–01
Deposition (Trevisani), 79, 80
Descent of the Holy Spirit
(Dutch Book of
Hours), 163
Desiderio da Settignano,
*Tomb of Carlo Marsup-
pini,* 180
Détente style, 172
Deutero-Canonical books, 22
Devotio moderna movement,
33, 34, 73–74, 76, 163
Devotional experience, 5
Devotional images, 30
in Middle Ages, 32–35
Dialogus miraculorum (Caesar-
ius of Heisterbach),
59
Die Brücke (*The Bridge*),
246–47, 251
Diego, Juan, 6, 107, 137
Discipulus (Herold,
Johannes), 88
Diseases of Women (Trotula of
Salerno), 52
Doctrine of Mary, 8
Dolorosa, La (Our Lady of
Sorrow), 230. *See also*
Mater dolorosa
Dome of the Rock mosque,
99
Dominic, saint, 32
Dominican order, 32
on assumption of Mary,
99
outreach programs, 63
Subleyras, Pierre and,
225
Doré, Gustave, 102
Dormition, 96
Pius XII, pope on, 137
Dormition of the Virgin
(French, from Île de
France), 34, 95–96,
157–58
Dowries, 44
to convents, 93
Dresden series (Crespi), 219
Duckworth, Herbert, 103, 234
Duecento painting, 29
Durandus, William, 29, 33
Dürer, Albrecht, 75
Adoration of the Shepherds,
49, 53

Annunciation, 37
Betrothal of the Virgin, 44
Birth of the Virgin Mary, 65
*Christ Taking Leave of His
Mother,* 183–85
on Church of Our Lady
at Antwerp, 30
Crucifixion, 83
Death of the Virgin, 95
Goltzius in style of,
204–05
on hair of Mary, 44
Holy Family in Egypt, 67
*Joachim and St. Anne Meet
at the Golden Gate,* 21
Judith, bust of, 84
Life of the Virgin series,
183–85
Lutheran doctrine and
art, 32
Marcantonio Raimondi
and, 187
Robetta and, 179
in Strasbourg and Col-
mar region, 173
Visitation, 42
Dürer the Elder, Albrecht, 184

Early church art, 26–29
Early history of Mary, 21
Early Life of the Virgin series
(Goltzius), 204
Easter
guilds and confraterni-
ties celebrating, 48
music of, 139
Eastern Orthodox churches,
23
Ecumenical Council of Eph-
esus, 137
Edicts of Tolerance, 28
Egypt
Coptic Christians, 58
Isis, 134
Einsiedeln, Our Lady of,
Switzerland, 90
Eleousa, 28–29
Elevation of the Host (French,
from Amiens), 69
El Greco (Domenico Theoto-
copuli), 199
Elijah, ascension of, 99
Elisabeth of Schönau, saint,
96
Elizabeth, saint 13, 41–42
in Gospels, 21
Magnificat, 22
matronly appearance of,
43
Elkins, Sharon, 21, 136–38
Emilian School, 202
Emison, Patricia, 170–71
Engebrechtsz., Cornelis,
185–86
Enoch, ascension of, 99
Entombment, 37
Book of Hours on, 81
Entombment of Christ (Man-
tegna), 169–72
Erasmus of Rotterdam, 86
Erhart, Gregor, 173
Escorial, San Lorenzo de Él,
199
Esther, 22, 24
Ethiopian Christians, 58, 109
Ethnic Madonnas, 11–12

Eucharist, 78–79
fish symbol, 26
Eve, 50–51
antithesis, Mary as, 134
defenses of, 51
Eve (after the Fall) (Rodin), 50,
244–45
Expressionism, 101, 246
Expression of Mary, 47
*Ex-Voto Commissioned by José
María Ramírez* (Mex-
ico), 72, 230–34
Ex-Votos, Mexico, 72, 230–34
Eyck, Jan van, 39
Ezekiel on devotional art, 33

Fables (La Fontaine), 253
Faccini, Pietro, *St. Francis
Receiving the Christ
Child in the Presence of
the Virgin,* 71–72,
202–03
Faith, Our Lady of, Namur,
France, 89
False doctrine, prohibition
on, 70
Farel, Guillaume, 32
Fátima, Our Lady of, Portu-
gal, 8, 106, 137
Feast of Assumption, 96
Feast of the Circumcision,
59–60
Federigo de Montefeltro,
duke of Urbino, 98,
165
Felicity, saint, 91
Fernando of Aragon, 165
Ferrante de Aragón, 165
Ferrari, Gaudenzio, 87
God the Father, 52
Fertility goddesses, 25
Feti, Domenico 218
Fish symbol, 26
Fiske, Gertrude H., *Mary,*
247–48
Flagellation, 37
Fletcher, Shelley, 171
Flight into Egypt, 21
art of, 60–62
Flight into Egypt (Italian), 36
Flight into Egypt (Rembrandt),
208–09
Flight into Egypt series
(Tiepolo), 228–30
Flores, Our Lady of, Indone-
sia, 89
Floris, Frans, 194
Fontana, Lavinia, *Holy Family
with Sts. Margaret and
Francis,* 65, 196–98
Fontijn-Harris, Claire, 70,
139–41
Fourth Crusade, 29
Fowler, Jeremy J., 252
Francia, Francesco, 187
Franciscan order, 32, 93. *See
also* Clare of Assisi,
saint
on assumption of Mary, 99
outreach programs, 63
*Franciscan Saint before seated
Virgin,* 33
Francis de Sales, saint, 76
Introduction a la Vie Dévoté
(Introduction to the
Devout Life), 84

Francis of Assisi, saint, 32, 91–93, 197–98, 202. *See also* Franciscan order
on convent sisters, 82
cult of, 71
Frauenkirche altarpiece, 60
Frederick, Charles, 224
Freedberg, David, 4, 5
Free will, 24
French Book of Hours
hair of Mary, 46
youth of Mary, 43
French Revolution, 101, 231
Freud, Sigmund, 105, 240
Funeral of St. Clare (Italian, from Umbria), 92
Funeral Procession (Dutch Book of Hours), 163, 164
Furini, Filippo (Pippo Sciarmerone), 206
Furini, Francesco
Adam and Eve, 50, 206–07
Lot and His Daughters, 206
Mary Magdalene, 206

Gabriel, archangel, 20
in annunciation art, 38
Balaam and, 27
interaction with Mary, 40
Muhammad and, 23
Galaktotrophousa, 29
Galen of Pergamos, 51, 52
Galle, Philip, 192, 204
Gandolfi, Ubaldo, *Holy Family with God the Father*, 61
Garabandal, Spain apparition, 110
Garavaglia, Giovita, *Angels Adoring the Christ Child*, 86–87
The Garden (Wierex), 62–63
Gardner, Isabella Stewart, 241
Gaspar, magus, 57
Gates of Hell (Rodin), 244
Gauguin, Paul, 236, 237
Gender bias, 257–58
Generation of Animals (Aristotle), 52
Genesis, Book of, 50
Geneviéve, saint, 164
Gent, Joos van, 165
George, saint, 71
Gerhaert, Nikolaus, 172–73
German Expressionism, 246
Gerson, Jean, 66, 86
Geschwister (Siblings) (Heckel), 102, 246–47
GianDomenico. *See* GianDomenico Tiepolo
Gibbons, James Cardinal, 10
Giulio Romano, 188
Glorious Mysteries, 12–13
Glykophilousa, 29
Gnostic Gospels, 257
Goddesses, 133–35
Mary compared, 133–34
God the Father (Ferrari), 52
Gogol, *Dead Souls*, 253
Goltzius, Hendrik, 194
The Annunciation, 20, 38, 204–05
Good Shepherd figure, 26–27
Gospel of Mary [Magdalene], 257
Gospel of Pseudo-Matthew, 161, 230
Gospels, 20–23. *See also* specific Gospels
on coronation of the Virgin, 94–95
on nativity, 48
Grand Dejeuner (Léger), 249
Grande Chartreuse, 220
Grasser, Erasmus, 172
Gratian (Master Honoré), 155
Greek myth, 133

Green, Christopher, 250
Gregory the Great, pope, 29, 89
on devotional art, 33
Gregory "the Wonder-Worker," saint, 106
Gregory XIII, pope, 65
Grote, Geert, 34, 41, 162–63
on convents, 93
Grünewald, Matthias, 173
Guadalupe, Our Lady of, Mexico, 11, 14–15, 73, 107, 137
Daily Life of the Virgin of Guadalupe series (Walker), 107
images of, 6
La Patrona (The Patroness) (Álvarez Bravo), 254–56
Guadalupe, Our Lady of, Spain, 89
Guercino, il, 218
Guido da Siena, 151, 152
Guilds and widows, 83
Gúzman, Domingo de (Saint Dominic), 32
Gypsy Madonna (Müller), 102, 103, 251–52
Gypsy Portfolio (Müller), 251

Haarlem school, 204
Hadley, Margaret, 159, 160, 163
Hagar, 24, 209–11
Haig, Axel Herman, *Church Interior with Worshipers at a Pietà*, 78
Hail Mary prayer, 33
Hair of Mary, 44–47
Haitian Vodou, 4
Hale, Philip Leslie 247
Half Length figure of the Virgin (Italian, from Rome), 47
Halos, 241
Hannah, 42
Hardouyn, Gilles and Germain, Book of Hours, 182–83
Hatfield, Rab, 178, 179
Hawkins, Henry, 140
Hazard, Caroline, 153
Healy, Patrick J., 227
Hebrew Bible, 23–26, 24
ascension in, 99
leaders, women as, 24
Mary in, 24
in Protestant art, 74
Hebrew canon, 22
Hecht, Peter, 209, 211
Heckel, Erich
Geschwister (Siblings), 102, 246–47
Ostende Madonna, 246
Heemskerck, Maarten van, 192
Helmont, Johann Franz van, *Study for an altarpiece of the Assumption*, 70
Henson Scales, Meg, *Mary Loves Jesus Bartlet Prayers*, 257–259
Henry VI, England, 94
Henry VIII, England, 41
Hera, 133
The Heritage of Motherhood (Käsebier), 103–04, 242–43
Herod, 21, 60
Herolt, Johannes, 88
Hidalgo y Costilla, Father Miguel, 73, 231
High Renaissance, 190
Higonnet, Anne, 235, 242, 243
Hillier, Mary, 103
Hind, Arthur M., 171, 179
Hippocrates, 51, 52
Holbein, Hans, 75
Holofernes, Judith and, 84, 192–95
Holy family, art of, 60–69
Holy Family (d'Arpino), 87

Holy Family in Egypt (Dürer), 67
Holy Family with God the Father (Gandolfi), 61
Holy Family with Sts. Margaret and Francis (Fontana), 65, 196–98
Holy Family with Saints (School of Fontainebleau), 45
Holy Family with the Infant St. John the Baptist and Sts. Andrew and Francis (Pintoricchio), xix–xx, 34, 47, 54, 55, 174–77
Holy Family with the Infant St. John the Baptist (after Raphael) (Marcantonio Raimondi), 187–88
Holy Family with the Infant St. John the Baptist and St. Francis (Vasari), 67–69, 188–91
Holy kinship, 41
art of, 61–69
Holy Kinship (Wohlgemut), 62
Holy Roman empire, 100
Holy Virgin Mary (Ofili), 13
Holy Week, music of, 139
Homily on Matrimony, Church of England, 44–45
Horus, 25
Hours of the Cross, 35, 36
Hours of the Holy Spirit, 35
Hours of the Virgin, 35, 36
compline, 93–94
Walker *Book of Hours*, 158–59
Humanity of Mary, 25, 134
Humilitati community, 82
Humility of Mary, 24
Hyperdouleia, 55
Hypostatic union, 56

Iberian peninsula, Arab settlers, 59
Ichthys, 25
Iconodules, 30
Iconography
of Anne/Anna, 41
Council of Trent on Goltzius, 240
of Mary, 4
Icons, veneration of, 30–31
Iconum Biblicarum (Biblical Illustrations) (Merian), 75
Idolatry, 30, 55
Igbos, Nigeria, 142–44
Ignatius of Loyola, saint, 76, 220
Illustrated books, 35
Il Pintoricchio. *See* Pintoricchio
Images of Mary, 4–5
Immaculate Conception, 26, 71
formal definition of, 97–99
mendicant orders on, 99
Immaculate Conception, Feast of, 99
Immigrant Madonnas, 11–12
Immortality of Mary, 134
Impressionism, 101
Imran/Joachim. *See* Joachim/Imran
Indulgences, 100
Infancy Gospel of James, 22
Infancy Gospel of Thomas, 22
Infancy of Mary, 36
Infrared reflectography, *Judith with the Head of Holofernes* and, 194–95
Innocent IV, pope, 92
The Inquisition, 70
Interior of Antwerp Cathedral (Neefs), 31
Interior of a Renaissance Church (Witte), 69, 70
Ireland apparition, 8
Isaac, 24, 209
Isabel of Castile, 165
Isaiah, 27

ascension of, 99
Book of Isaiah, 39
Ishmael, 24, 209
Isis, 25–26, 134
  palm trees and, 230
Islam. *See* Muslim tradition
Italian Baroque, 202
Italy
  duecento painting, 29
  Madonna del Carmine, 11
  Oliveto Citra, 8, 9, 15
  song, seventeenth century, 139–41
  Weeping Madonna of Siracusa, 9
Ivory, *Dormition of the Virgin*, 34, 157

Jackson, John Baptist, 21
  *Presentation of the Virgin in the Temple
    (after Titian)*, 22, 223–25
Jackson, Julia Prinsep, 103, 234–35
James, apostle, 62. *See also* Protevan-
    gelium of James
  Cleophas, 20
  Infancy Gospel of James, 22
James Alpheus, 62
Japan
  Namban studios, 58
  Ukiyo-e woodblock prints, 236
Jeanneret, Charles-Edouard, 250
Jerome, saint, 174–77
  on marriage, 62
Jerusalem
  Crusades, capture in, 59
  apparition of Mary, 110
Jesuit order
  in Asia, 58
  on convents, 92
  Ignatius of Loyola, 87
Jesus Christ
  Carrying the Cross, 37
  corporeality of, 55–56
  dual natures of, 53
  in early Christian art, 28
  in Luke's Gospel, 22
  as Man of Sorrows, 231
  in Matthew's Gospel, 23
  before Pilate, 37
  in Qur'an, 23
  siblings of, 61–62
Jew in Green (Chagall), 253
Jews in the Synagogue (Rembrandt), 25
Joab, 182
*Joachim and St. Anne Meet at the Golden
  Gate* (Dürer), 21
Joachim/Imran, 21, 24
  annunciation to, 37
  in Counter-Reformation, 70
  in Protevangelium of James, 136–37
Joan of Arc, 78–79
John, Gospel of, 21, 22
  crucifixion, presence of Mary,
    82–83
  fish symbol, 26
John Lateran, saint, 88
John of Damascus, saint, 55
John (son of Mary Cleophas), 62
John the Baptist, saint, 21, 174–77
  announcement of birth of, 37
Jonah, 24
Joseph, saint, 14
Joseph of Arimathaea, 76, 200
Joseph of Nazareth, 24
  annunciation to, 37
  Cleophas, 20
  in *Flight into Egypt* series (Tiepolo),
    229–30
  images of, 66

Protevangelium of James on, 137
  in Qur'an, 24
Joseph (son of Mary Salome), 62
Joyful Mysteries, 12–13
Judaism. *See also* Anti-Semitism
  Crusades and, 59–60
  Mary in, 24–25
  Protevangelium of James depicting,
    137
Judas' betrayal, 36–37
Jude, 62
Judgment of Susannah (Boucher), 221
Judith, 24, 84
Judith, Book of, 22, 192–95
Judith with the Head of Holofernes (Flem-
  ish), 192–95
Juni, Juan de, 199
Juno, 133

Käsebier, Gertrude
  Adoration, 103, 240–242
  The Heritage of Motherhood, 103–04,
    105, 242–43
Katz, Melissa R., 12, 19–129, 185, 195,
    201, 207, 222, 230–34, 261
Key, Willem Adriaensz., 194
Kibeho, Rwanda apparition, 110
King Ortnit Christens the Heathens (Ger-
  man, from Strasbourg), 100
Kiss of peace, 78
Knock, Ireland apparition, 106
Koch, Robert A., 161
Koimesis, 95
Koran. *See* Qu'ran
Kristeller, Paul, 171
Kuhn, Marlene, 254

Labouré, Catherine, 106–107
La Caridad, 11
La Dolorosa, 230. *See also* Mater dolorosa
La Fontaine, *Fables*, 253
La Inmaculada (Immaculate Conception)
  (Mexican), 98
Laity
  in spiritual communities, 33–34
  spiritual needs of, 63
La Madonne aux yeux d'Onyx Vert (Marcel-
  Lenoir), 104, 106
Lamentation. *See* Entombment
Lamentation (French, from Amiens), 43
Lamentation (Italian), 79
*Lamentation with Sts. Augustine and
  Nicholas of Tolentino* (Martínez),
    35, 76–77, 199–201
La Morenita. *See* Guadalupe, Our Lady
  of, Mexico
Landau, David, 162, 170, 171
Languages of Mary, 8
Lanyer, Aemilia, 51
La Patrona (The Patroness) (Alvarez
  Bravo), 254–56
La Salette apparition, 106
*La Santa Julia (Portrait of Julia Prinsep Jack-
  son)* (Cameron), 103, 234–35
Lasso, Orlando di, 140
Lastman, Pieter, 211
Last Supper in Protestant art, 74–75
Late-Gothic Baroque, 172
Latin America
  black Christs in, 72–73
  Counter-Reformation Spanish piety
    and, 76–77
Latinos. *See* Chicanos
Lazarev, Viktor Nikitich, 219
Leandro, saint, 89
Le Corbusier, 250

Lee, Agnes, 243
Lefkowitz, Mary R., 25, 133–35
Legacy of Mary, 101–10
Legenda aurea (Golden Legend) (Voragine),
    49, 62, 91, 224
Léger, Fernand, 102
  Grand Dejeuner, 249
  Woman and Child, 249–50
Le Goff, Jacques, 66–67
Leiden, Netherlands, 100
Leinberger, Hans, 172
Leonardo da Vinci
  Adoration of the Magi, 177
  Virgin of the Rocks, 190
Leoni, Pompeo, 199
Les Miracles de Notre Dame (Coinci), 59, 88
Lethieullier, Smart, 224
Levenson, Jay A., 170
Liber chronicarum (Nuremberg Chronicle)
  (Schedel), 63
Liberius, pope, 29
Life of the Virgin series (Dürer), 183–85
Lightbown, Ronald W., 171
Lipa, Philippines apparition, 110
Lippi, Filippino, *Adoration of the Magi*,
    177, 178–79
Lips of Mary, 47
Liss, Johann, 218
Lissandrino, *Monastic Saint in Meditation*,
    220–21
Little Office of the Virgin Mary, 42
*Lives of the Most Excellent Painters, Sculptors,
  and Architects* (Vasari), 190
Lohy, Jeanne, 250
Lord's Prayer, 33, 42
Loreto, shrine of, 88
Losada, Elizabeth, 230
Lot and His Daughters (Furini), 206
Lourdes, Our Lady of, 11, 106, 137
Lourdes grotto, University of Notre
  Dame, 5–6
Louvre, Musée de, 105
Loving icons, 29
Lucas van Leyden
  father Hugo Jacobsz., 185
  Goltzius in style of, 204–05
  Virgin and Child in a Niche, 185–86
  Virgin and Child with Two Angels, 56
Luini, Bernardino, 87
Luján, Our Lady of, Argentina, 89
Luke, Gospel of, 21–22
  on adoration, 55
  on annunciation, 37
  Elizabeth, Mary's visit with, 42
  fish symbol, 26
  on nativity, 48
Luke, saint, 89–90
Luther, Martin, 31–32, 73, 75. *See also*
  Reformation
  on childbirth, 66
  Feast of Assumption, removal of, 96
  on veneration of Mary, 56
  widows, role of, 84
Lyon, Danny, 109, 110
  Showers, Diagnostic Unit, Texas, 15,
    108, 225–56

McAndrew, John, 151
Maccabees, 22
McDermott, Lisa, 188, 213, 225
Madonna and Child (Man Ray), 102
Madonna and Child (Tyrolese), 82
*Madonna and Child with the Infant St. John
  the Baptist and Sts. Andrew and
  Jerome* (Pintoricchio), xix–xx, 54,
    174–77

Madonna (Conception) (Munch), 104,
    238–40
Madonna del Carmine, 11
Madonna della Sedia (Raphael), 87
Madonna del Parto (Sansovino), 5
Madonna (Niedermorschwihr), 173
Magi, 50-60. *See also* Adoration of the
    Magi
    in Catacomb of Priscilla, 28
Magnasco, Alessandro, 218
    Monastic Saint in Meditation, 78,
        220–21
Magnificat, 22, 42, 56
Magnus, Albertus. *See* Albert the Great,
    saint
Malmaritate women, 93
Manasseh, 84
Mander, Karel van, 194, 204–05
Mandorla, 95
    in *Assumption* (Berruguete), 97
Manet, Edouard, 102
Maniera, 190
Mannerism, 190
    Judith with the Head of Holofernes, 192,
        194
    Martínez, Gregorio, 200
Man Ray, *Madonna and Child*, 102
Mansa Musa, 57
Mantegna, Andrea, *Entombment of Christ*,
    169–72
    Albertina *Madonna* and *Entombment*,
        171
Mantegna, Lodovico, 171
Mantellati community, 82
Maphorion, 25
Maratti, Carlo, *Angels Adoring the Christ
    Child*, 87
Marcantonio Raimondi, 184
    *Holy Family with the Infant St. John the
        Baptist (after Raphael)*, 187–88
Marcel-Lenoir, *La Madonne aux yeux
    d'Onyx Vert*, 105, 106
Marcos, 254
Marenzio, Luca, 140
Margaret of Anjou, England, 94
Margaret of Antioch, saint, 65, 71, 197
Maria lactans, 139, 143
Mariolatry, 56, 90
Mark, Gospel of, 21, 22
Marriage
    of Mary, 62–63
    premodern marriages, 63–64
    purpose of, 64
    Reformation and, 101
    as sacrament, 63
Martínez, Gregorio, 76–77
    *Lamentation with Sts. Augustine and
        Nicholas of Tolentino*, 34, 76–77,
        199–201
Martínez, Sebastián, 199
Martini, Simone, *Annunciation*, 40
Martyrdom of Saint Lawrence (Faccini), 202
Martyrs, cults of, 71
Mary, (daughter of Henry VIII), 41
Mary as the City of God (French, North-
    eastern), 59
Mary as the Woman Clothed with the Sun
    (French, from Amiens), 94
Mary Cleophas, 20, 62
Mary Enthroned with Christ (Ethiopian), 109
Mary (Fiske), 247–48
Mary Foundation, 258
Mary holding the Child in her Arms
    (Tiepolo), 61
Mary Loves Jesus Bartlet Prayers (Henson
    Scales), 257–59

Mary Magdalene, 20, 257–259
    assumption of, 99
    Gospel of Mary, 22
Mary Magdalene (Furini), 206
Mary of Bethany, 20
Mary of Magdala, 20
*Mary presents the infant Jesus to the Men and
    Women who Serve Her* (French,
    Northeastern), 54
Mary Salome, 62
*Mary through the Centuries: Her Place in
    the History of Culture* (Pelikan),
    xix
Massacre of the innocents. *See* Flight into
    Egypt
Massys, Jan, 192
Master E.S., 1972-73
Master Honoré, 155
Master of the Tucher altarpiece, *(Circum-
    cision)*, 60
Mater dolorosa, 82, 139, 143. *See also* La
    Dolorosa
Matthew, Gospel of, 21, 23
    on adoration, 55
    on annunciation, 37
    on flight into Egypt, 60
Maximilian, emperor, 83
Meanings of Mary, 3–4
Medici, Cosimo de', 178
Medici, Giovanni de', 178
Medici, Piero de', 178
Medici court, 179
    Stefano della Bella and, 213
Medieval Woman's Guide to Health, 52
Meditations on Mary (Thomas à Kempis),
    87–88
Meditations on the Life of Christ (Bonaven-
    ture), 81–82
Medjugorje, Herzegovina apparition, 110
Melchior, magus, 57
Memorare, 12
Menkiti, Ifeanyi Anthony, 142–44
Mense, 93
Merian, Matthaus, *This is My Dear Son,
    Whom You Shall Hear!*, 75
Metalcuts, 181–183
Mexico. *See also* Guadalupe, Our Lady of,
    Mexico
    Black Christ, Guanajuato, 73
    Ramírez ex-voto, 230–34
    Revolution, 231
Michelangelo
    Furini, Francesco and, 206
    Pietà, 181
Michele Martini, Cristofano di (Robetta).
    See Robetta, Cristofano
Middle Ages
    commissioned art, 35
    devotional images in, 32–35
    literacy of women, 40–41
    nativity, celebration of, 49
    reproduction, understanding of,
        51–52
Migrant Madonnas, 11–12
Milagros de Nuestra Señora (Berceo), 88
Milk-Giving icons, 29
Minerva, 29
The Miracle (Rossellini), 14
Miracles of Mary, 88–90
Miracula sancte dei genitricis Virginis Marie
    (Nigel of Canterbury), 88
Miraculis beate Marie virginis (Herolt), 88
"Miraculous Medal of Paris," 106, 107
Mithras, 29
Modernism, 101, 240
Monastery of El Éscorial, 199

Monastic orders. *See also* Convents
    as ecclesiastical elite, 63
    in Middle Ages, 32
    third orders, 34
Monastic Saint in Meditation (Magnasco),
    78, 220–21
Mongeon, Rebecca, 227, 248
Mongol empire, 58
Monk Purchasing a Painting, 32
Monte Corvino, Giovanni da, 57–58
Monte-Croce, Ricoldo da, 59
Montefeltro, Federigo da, 97
Montichiari, Italy apparition, 110
Montserrat, Our Lady of, 55, 89–90
Moon, Magdalena, 100
Morgan, David, 4
Morgan, Lady (Sydney), 215
Moses, 24
    ascension of, 99
    on devotional art, 33
    Striking the Rock, 27
Moses dies in view of the Promised Land
    (Chagall), 25
Motherhood, reverence for, 64
Mount Aigu, Our Lady of, Belgium, 89
Mouth of Mary, 47
Muhammad, 23
    ascension of, 99
Müller, Otto, *Zigeunermadonna (Gypsy
    Madonna)*, 103, 251–52
Munch, Edvard
    Madonna (Conception), 104, 238–40
    Study for Madonna, 239
Mura, Francesco de, 218
Music
    in African education, 142–43
    in Post-Reformation era, 70
    seventeenth century Italian song,
        139–41
Muslim tradition. *See also* Qu'ran
    Biafra, 143
    parents of Mary in, 21
Mysteries, 12–13
Mysticism
    as artistic subject, 77–78
    in sixteenth century, 76
*The Mystic Marriage of St. Catherine dei
    Ricci* (Subleyras), 225–28

Namban studios, 58
Names for Mary, 12, 20
Napoleon Bonaparte, 105
Nasini, Giuseppe, *Apotheosis of a Male
    Saint*, 99
National Gallery of Art, Washington
    D.C., 170
    Eyck, Jean van, panel by, 39
Nationality and religion, 100
National Shrine of the Immaculate Con-
    ception, Basilica, Washington
    DC, 9–10
Native American artifacts, 5
Nativity, 35–36
    art of, 48–53
Nativity (French, from Amiens), 49
Nazarenes, 102
Necedah, Wisconsin apparition, 110
Neefs, Pieter, 75
    Interior of Antwerp Cathedral, 30, 31
Nelli, Fabio, 201
Neoclassicism, 225
Nestorian Christians in China, 57–58
Nestorius, 57
New Deal Farm Security Administration
    photographers, 255
New Eve, Mary as, 50, 137

The New Mother (Erasmus of Rotterdam), 86
New Testament. *See also* Gospels
    early art, 26
New World colonies, 10, 72–73, 97–98, 107, 230–34
Nicholas of Tolentino, saint, 76, 199–201
Nicodemus, saint, 76, 90, 200
Nigel of Canterbury, *Miracula sancte dei genitricis Virginis Marie*, 88
Nigeria, 142–44
    Civil War, 143
Nineteenth century, Mary in, 105–06
95 theses (Luther), 31
Noah, 24
Noah's Ark, 27
Notke, Bernt, 172
Nuestra Señora Santa María de Guadalupe. See Guadalupe, Our Lady of, Mexico
Nuns. *See* Convents
Nuremberg, Germany, 45, 60, 69
Nuremberg Chronicle (Schedel), 63

Office of Crowning, 44
Office of the Dead, 35
Ofili, Chris, *Holy Virgin Mary*, 13
Old Testament. *See also* Hebrew Bible
    annunciation, precedent for, 38
    illustrations, 27
Oles, James, 256
Oliveto Citra, Italy, 8, 9, 15
Olson, Roberta J.M., 176
On the Apparel of Women (Tertullian), 51
On the Imitation of Christ (Thomas à Kempis), 34
On the Nature of the Child (Hippocrates), 52
Orants, 26
Orant Virgin and Child, 27
Origen, 57
Orsi, Robert A., xix, 3–18
Orthodox church, 22, 23, 87, 99
    dormition, 96
    on perpetual virginity, 43
    wedding ceremonies, 44
Osiris, 134
Ostende Madonna (Heckel), 246
Our Lady Mary with her Beloved Son (Seyon), 58
Our Lady of Guadalupe spray, 109
Our Lady of Montserrat (Spanish), 90
Outrage for Mary, 13–14
Ozenfant, Amédée, 250

Pacheco, Anita, 232
Pacheco, Francisco, 70, 98, 106
Pacher, Michael, 172
Pagan religion
    comparison of Mary, 134
    coronation of the virgin, 94
    goddesses, 25–26
Palm Sunday, 79
Palm tree symbol, 79, 230
Papillon, Jean-Michel, 223
Paris, apparition of Mary in, 106
Parisian Book of Hours, 46
Annunciation (French, from Paris), 181–83
Park, Jennifer Sorra, 158
Parmigianino, 204
Parthenia sacra, 140
Parthenon, 134
Pasquali, J. B., 223
Passignano, Domenico Cresti il, 206
Passion, 36
    art of, 79–87

Patron saints, 91
Pax, 78
Paxton, William, 247
Peace of Augsburg, 100
Péladan, Sâr Joséphin, 237
Pelikan, Jaroslav, xix
Penitential Convent of Mary Magdalene, 93
Pentecost, 95
    hair of Mary, 45
Pentecost (Dutch Book of Hours), 163
Pentecost (French, from Amiens), 94
Pentecost (German, from Strasbourg), 46
Pérez Sanchéz, Alfonso E., 199
Perpetua, saint, 91
Perpetual Help, Our Lady of, 11
Perpetual virginity, 26, 43, 134
    hair of Mary and, 46
Perugino, Pietro Vanucci il, 175
Peter, saint, 62
    fish symbol, 26
    Gospel of, 22
Petitioners to Mary, 4
Philanthropy, representation of, 27
Philip II, Spain, 199
Photography. *See also* Käsebier, Gertrude
    La Santa Julia (Portrait of Julia Prinsep Jackson) (Cameron), 103, 234–35
    New Deal Farm Security Administration photographers, 255
    religious subjects in, 102–03
    Victorian photography, 102–05
Phylactery, 39–40
Piccolomini Library, Siena Cathedral, 176
Pictorialism, 242–243
Pictorial Symbolism, 236
Pietà, 80–81
    German *Pietà*, 34
    women commissioning, 82
Pietà (Austrian), 82
Pietà (Michelangelo), 181
Pilgrimage, 4, 12, 100
    in the Americas, 231, 254
    Montserrat as site of, 88–90
    revival in France, 106
Pinder, Wilhelm, 172
Pintoricchio
    Holy Family with St. John the Baptist, 176
    Madonna and Child with the Infant St. John the Baptist and Sts. Andrew and Jerome, xix–xx, 34, 47, 54, 55, 174–77
Pippo Sciamerone (Furini, Filippo), 206
Pisan, Christine de, 48
Pius II, pope, 176
Pius XII, pope, 137
Plague of 1348-1351, 67
Planchando, Pensando (Ironing, Thinking) (Walker), 107
Poelenbergh, Cornelis, 211
Poetry in Middle Ages, 40
Poitou Cathedral, 88
Pontius Pilate, 231
Pontmain apparition, 105
Pope Benedict XIV Presents St. Catherine dei Ricci to the Virgin (Subleyras), 71, 225–28
The Pope Fleeces His Sheep broadside, 100
Portugal, apparition in, 8, 106, 137
Post, Chandler R., 168
Postpartum virginity, 43
Poussin, Nicolas, 216–18
    Calvary, 79
The Power of Images: Studies in the History

and Theory of Response (Freedberg), 4
Prayer
    devotional art and, 32–33
    Hail Mary (*Ave Maria*) prayer, 33
    Lord's Prayer, 33, 42
    Magnificat, 22, 42, 56
    Memorare, 12
Prebend, 93
Pregnancy and Mary, 64–66
Pre-Raphaelites, 102
Presence of Mary, 8
Presentation of the Virgin in the Temple (after Titian) (Jackson), 22, 223–25
Primitivism, 5
Priscilla. *See* Catacomb of Priscilla
Profane aspects of Mary, 240
Prostitutes, convent for, 92
Protestants. *See also* Reformation
    American Protestants, 10, 81
    art of, 69–70
    Books of Hours and, 35
    breastfeeding issues, 86–87
    coronation of Mary, 96
    on cult of Mary, 56
    Last Supper in art, 74–75
    Mariolatry, 90
    perpetual virginity, 26, 43
    on role of Mary, 53
    in sixteenth century, 73–75
    widows, role of, 84
    women and, 101
Protevangelium of James
    annunciations, 37
    birth of Mary, 22
    on perpetual virginity, 43, 134
    prints illustrating, 136–37
    on siblings of Jesus, 61
Prybyszewska, Dagney Juel, 239–40
Psychological effect of Mary, 506
Purification, feast of, 96
Purim, 22
Purism, 250
Putti, 67
    ascension, escorting, 99

Queenship of Mary, 12, 92, 100, 109, 155. *See also* Coronation of the Virgin
    as empress, 27, 134, 137
    opposition to, 86, 100
    secular monarchy and, 94
Qur'an, 23–26
    chapter on Mary, 24
    on nativity, 49

Raimondi, Marcantonio. *See* Marcantonio Raimondi
Raising of Lazarus (Italian), 36
Ramírez, José María, 72, 230–31
Randall, Lilian M.C., 160
Raphael Sanzio, 87, 169 214
    Furini, Francesco and, 206
    Goltzius in style of, 204
    Madonnas by, 240, 241
    Marcantonio Raimondi and, 187–88
Raymond of Peñafort, saint, 64
Reading, teaching of, 40–41
Realism, 101
Reformation. *See also* Luther, Martin; Protestants
    art during, 31–32
    effect of, 69–70
    Immaculate Conception in Catholic art, 97–98
    women and, 100–101
Relationships with Mary, 7

Relics of Mary, 88
Remarriage of widows, 83–84
Rembrandt van Rijn, 169
    Abraham and Hagar depictions, 211
    Flight into Egypt, 208–09
    Jews in the Synagogue, 25
Renaissance
    children in, 67
    High Renaissance, 190
    putti, 67
    reproduction, understanding of,
        51–52
    women's education, 41
Reni, Guido 87
Reproduction
    understanding of, 51–52
    women's involvement in, 53
Rest on the Flight into Egypt (Schongauer),
    161–62
Rest on the Flight into Egypt (Stefano della
    Bella), 212–13
Resurrection, 258
Resurrection of the Dead (Dutch Book of
    Hours), 163
Revelations (Birgitta), 48, 84
Ricci, Marco, 218
Richard de Saint-Laurent, *De laudibus
    beatae virginis Mariae (In Praise of
    the Blessed Virgin Mary),* 153–56
Richardson, Julia, 244, 245
Riemenschneider, Tilman, 173
Robetta, Cristofano
    Adoration of the Magi, 55, 177–79
    Allegory of Love, 178
Robusti, Jacopo. *See* Tintoretto
Rococo, 218
    Boucher, François, 221
Rodin, René-François-Auguste, *Eve (after
    the Fall),* 50, 244–45
Role of Mary, 136–38
Romano, Giulio, 188
Romola, Alessandra Lucrezia (Catherine
    dei Ricci), 71, 90, 92, 225–28
Rosa, Salvator, 224
    Three Marys at the Sepulchre, 215–16
Rosaries, 5
    in abortion conflict, 9
Rose+Croix Catholique, 237
Rossellini, Roberto, 14
Rossellino, Antonio, *Tomb of the Cardinal
    of Portugal,* 180
Rosso Fiorentino, 200
Rossi, Carlo Antonio, 214
Rostock, Germany, 100
Rouen Book of Hours, 48
Ruiz, Estella, 11
Ruíz, Luís and Raimondo, 168
Rule of Saint Clare, 78–79
"Rules for Thinking with the Church"
    (Ignatius of Loyola), 76

Saarland apparition of Mary, 8
Sacchetti, Marchese, 225, 227
Sacchi, Carlo Antonio, *Adoration of the
    Shepherds (after Tintoretto),* 213–14,
    216
Sacrament of Ordination (Crespi), 63,
    218–19
Sacrifice of Isaac (Boucher), 221–23
Sagrada Familia/Holy Family (Campos-
    Pons), 259–61
*St. Camillo de Lellis Saving the Sick of the
    Hospital of the Holy Spirit from the
    Floodwaters of the Tiber* (Sub-
    leyras), 227
St. Margaret (Strasbourg Museum), 173

*St. Francis Receiving the Christ Child in the
    Presence of the Virgin* (Faccini),
    71–72, 202–03
St. Luke the Evangelist, 23
Samu, Margaret A., 191, 198
San Bernardino of Siena church, Aquila,
    180
Sanctity of Mary. *See* Veneration of Mary
Sand, Our Lady of the, Roemond, Hol-
    land, 89
San Lorenzo in Miranda church, Rome,
    29
San Lorenzo de El Éscorial monastery,
    Spain, 199
Sansovino, Jacopo
    Madonna del Parto, 5
Santa Eulalia chuch, Paredes de Nava,
    165, 167, 168
Santa María church, Becerril de Campos,
    165
Santa Maria d'Aracoeli church, Rome,
    175
Santa Maria del Popolo church, Rome,
    175
Santa Maria Maggiore church, Rome, 28
Santa Maria sopra Minerva, church, 29,
    88
Saracens, 58
Sarah/Sarai (wife of Abraham), 24, 42,
    209
Scales, Meg Henson, *Mary Loves Jesus
    Bartlet Prayers,* 257–59
Scandinavian tribes, 57
Schedel, Hartmann, *Liber chronicarum
    (Nuremberg Chronicle),* 63
Scherzi (Tiepolo), 228
Schmerzenmutter, 80–81
Schönemadonna, 80–81
Schongauer, Martin, 172–73, 208
    Adoration of the Magi, 178
    Rest on the Flight into Egypt, 161–62
    Robetta and, 178
Schongus, Cornelieus, 204
Schwalbe, Benedict, 183
Secondary relics, 88
Second Council of Nicaea, 30–31
Second Eve, Mary as, 50
Sede Sapientiae (Throne of Wisdom), 29
The Seed (Hippocrates), 52
Sellaer, Vincent, 192, 194
*Sensation: Young British Artists from the
    Saatchi Collection* (Brooklyn
    Museum), xx, 13
Seth, 134
Seymour, Charles, 180
Seyon, Ferê, *Our Lady Mary with her
    Beloved Son,* 58
Sfumato effect, 207
Shell, Curtis H., 173, 219
Shepherdess Kneeling at a Rural Shrine (Ger-
    man), 88
Shestack, Alan, 178
Showers, Diagnostic Unit, Texas (Lyon), 15,
    108, 225–56
Shrine of Saint Bernardino (Silvestro del-
    l'Aquila), 180
Siblings of Jesus, 61–62
Siegfried, Joan C., 221
Siena Cathedral, Piccolomini Library,
    176
Sievers, Ann, 153
Apparitions of Mary. *See* Apparitions of
    Mary
Silva Maroto, María Pilar, 165
Silvestro dell'Aquila
    Bust of the Virgin, 179–81

Virgin adoring the Child, 180
Simone de Ardizioni, 170
Simon Peter, 62
    fish symbol, 26
    Gospel of, 22
Simonsdr, Kenau Hasselaar, 100
Sins
    confession, 78
    women and, 50–51
Sitwell, Osbert, 220
Sixtus IV, pope, 175
Smith, Jessie Willcox, 241
Society of Jesus. *See* Jesuit order
Soldier, Mary as, 59
Song of Solomon, 39
    marriage and, 63
Sophia, 134
Soprano voice, 140
Soranus of Ephesus, 52, 85
Sorrowful Mother, 11
Sorrowful Mysteries, 12–13
Soul of Mary, 95–96
Souvenirs, 6
Sowernam, Ester, 51
Spellman, Francis, 14
Spiritual Exercises (Ignatius of Loyola), 76
Status of Mary, 90–91
Steen, Jan, 211
Stefano della Bella, *Rest on the Flight into
    Egypt,* 212–13
    Flight into Egypt, 212-13
Steiglitz, Alfred, 241–42
Stella, Jacques, 79, 216
Stella, Claudine Bouzonnet. *See* Bouzon-
    net Stella
Stephen, Leslie, 234
Stephen, saint, 90
Stewart, Susan, 6
Stigmata of Catherine dei Ricci, saint,
    227
Stoss, Veit, 172
Straten, Adelheid, 192
Study for an altarpiece of the Assumption
    (Helmont), 70
Study for Madonna (Munch), 239
Subleyras, Pierre Hubert
    *The Mystic Marriage of St. Catherine dei
    Ricci,* 225–28
    *Pope Benedict XIV Presents St. Catherine
    dei Ricci to the Virgin,* 71, 225–28
Susannah and the Elders, 22
Symbolist movement, 102, 236–37. *See
    also* Pictorialism
    Rodin, Auguste and, 244
Synthetism movement, 236

Tarbell, Edmund Charles, 247
Tattoos, 109
Telgte, Our Lady of, Germany, 89
Temple of Antonius and Faustina (Ander-
    son), 29, 30
Ten Commandments, 26
Teresa of Ávila, saint, 76
Tériade (Eleftheriades, Efstratios), 253
Tertullian, 51
    Magi, identification of, 57
Teyckenconst, 204
Thaumaturgus, Gregory, 106
Theotokos, 26, 137
Theotokos Hodegetria, 28–29
Third orders, 34
This is My Dear Son, Whom You Shall Hear!
    (Merian), 75
Thomas à Kempis, 34
    Meditations on Mary, 87–88
Thomas Aquinas, saint, 227

on Immaculate Conception, 99
veneration, categories of, 55
on women, 51
Thou, Jacques de, 216
Three Marys, 20, 62, 215-16
Three Marys at the Sepulchre (Rosa),
    215–16
Throne of Wisdom, 29
Tibaldi, Pellegrino, 199
Tiepolo, GianDomenico
    Flight into Egypt series, 228–30
    Mary holding the Child in her Arms, 61
Tiepolo, Giovanni Battista, 228
Tiepolo, Lorenzo, 228
Tietze-Conrat, Erica, 170
Time magazine, 110
Tintoretto, 48, 213, 216
Titian, 87, 218, 223
    Presentation of The Virgin at the Temple,
        21
Tobias and the Angel, 22
Tomb of Cardinal Bishop Amico (Silvestro
    dell'Aquila), 180
Tomb of Carlo Marsuppini (Desiderio), 180
*Tomb of Maria Pereyra and Beatrice Cam-
    poneschi* (Silvestro dell'Aquila),
    180
Tomb of the Cardinal of Portugal
    (Rossellino), 180
Tondo (Pintoricchio), xix–xx, 34, 47, 54,
    55, 174–77
To the Lighthouse (Woolf), 234
Tower of David, Mary as, 59
Transfiguration (Italian, North), 73
Transitus Mariae (Transition of Mary), 95
Transubstantiation, 69
Trevisani, Francesco, 218
    Depositions, 79, 80
Trevor, Emily, 153
Trotula of Salerno, 52, 85
Trugi, Francesco, 180
Twelfth century, veneration of Mary in,
    57–58
Twentieth century, Mary in, 107–10

Ukiyo-e woodblock prints, 236
United States. *See also* American Catholics
    nineteenth century, 106–07
    Protestants, 10
University of Notre Dame, Lourdes
    grotto, 5–6
Urban II, pope, 59
Uriah, 182
Uses in Books of Hours, 160

Varazze, Jacopo da, 49, 62
Vasari, Giorgio, 47
    Deposition from the Cross, 200–10
    *Holy Family with the Infant St. John the
        Baptist and St. Francis*, 67-69,
        188–91
    on Mantegna, Andrea, 171
    on Pintoricchio, 175
Vatican II, 33

reforms, 78
Vatican Palace, 175
Vecelli, Tiziano. *See* Titian
Velásquez, Diego, 70
Veneration of Mary, 87–93
    categories of, 55
Venetian Paintings series (Jackson),
    223–24
Vernacular prayer, 33
Vernacular texts, 35
Veronese, Bonifazio, *Adoration of the Shep-
    herds*, 53
Veronese, Paolo, 204, 214, 218, 223
Vesperbild, 80
Vespers, 80–81
Vespucci, Francesco Niccolo, 188
Vico, Enea, 201
Victorian photography, 102–05
Vignali, Jacopo, *Abraham Entertaining the
    Three Angels*, 36
Villani, Giovanni, 41
Virgencita. See Guadalupe, Our Lady of,
    Mexico
Virgin, Child, and St. Anne (French, from
    Brittany), 46
Virgin adoring the Child, (Silvestro del-
    l'Aquila), 180
Virgin and Child (Dutch Book of Hours),
    163
Virgin and Child Enthroned (French, from
    Amiens), 54
Virgin and Child (German, from Alsace),
    47, 172–73
Virgin and Child (German, from Ulm),
    45, 172
Virgin and Child in a Niche (Lucas van Ley-
    den), 185–86
Virgin and Child with a Pear (Beham), 46
Virgin and Child with Prophet (Catacomb
    of Priscilla), 28
*Virgin and Child with Sts. Hugh of Lincoln
    and Bridget of Sweden* (German),
    91
Virgin and Child with St. Stephen
    (Coebergher), 66
Virgin and Child with Two Angels (Lucas
    van Leyden), 56
Virgin birth, 25–26, 36
    in Qur'an, 23
Virginity. *See also* Perpetual virginity
    of saints, 91–92
Virgin of the Rocks (da Vinci), 190
Virgin Rescuing a Painter from the Devil
    (Spanish), 89
Virgo lactans, 85, 86
Virgo Lactans (French, Northeastern), 85
Vision of the Virgin to a Dominican Friar, 154
Visitation
    art of, 41–48
    feast of, 96
    in Gospels, 21
Visitation (Berruguete), 97
Visitation (Dürer), 42
Visitation (French, from Amiens), 43

Visitation (French from Amiens), 46
Visitation (Italian), 36
Vives, Juan Luís, 41, 84
Vodou, Haitian, 4
Voice of Mary, 140
Vollard, Ambroise, 252–53
Vonnoh, Bessie Potter, 241
Voragine, Jacobus de, 49, 91, 224
    holy kinship legend, 62
Vostre, Simon, Book of Hours, 183
Vrelant, Willem Backer van, 39, 41,
    162–64

Walker, Guy Warren, Jr., 158
Walker, J. Michael, *Planchando, Pensando
    (Ironing, Thinking)*, 107
Walker *Book of Hours*, 158–60
Wallace, Richard W., 215
Walters *Book of Hours*, 164
Warner, Marina, xix, 20, 134
Wassenhove, Joos van, 165
Wedding customs, 44
Weeping Madaonna of Siracusa, Italy, 9
Weimar, Germany, 252
Western Rule, 63
Wet nurses, 85–86
White, Clarence, 242
Whitsun, 48. *See also* Pentecost
Widdowes Mite, 53
Widows in sixteenth century, 83–84
Wierix, Anton, *The Garden*, 62–63
Wilhelm V, Bavaria, 204
Window symbolism, 42–43
Wireker, Nigellus, 88
Witchcraft, 84
Witte, Emmanuel de, 75
    Church Interior, 84
    Interior of a Renaissance Church, 69, 70
Wohlgemut, Michael
    Circumcision, 60
    Holy Kinship, 62
Woman and Child (Léger), 249–50
Woman Clothed with the Sun, 94, 95
Women. *See also* Convents
    as guild members, 83–84
    literacy and, 40–41
    in Reformation period, 100–101
    in sixteenth century, 83–84
    widows, care for, 83
Woodbury, Charles H., 247
Woolf, Virginia, 234
World War I, 107
Würzburg Cathedral, 40

Youth of Mary, 43–44

Zar'a Ya'eqob, Ethiopia, 58
Zebedee, 62
Zechariah, 21, 37
Zeitoun, Egypt apparition, 110
Zigeunermadonna (Gypsy Madonna)
    (Müller), 102, 103, 251–52
Zwingli, Huldrych, 32, 75

PHOTOGRAPHIC CREDITS

Alinari/Art Resource, NY: fig. 14

Biblioteca del Monasterio de San Lorenzo de Él Escorial, Spain: figs. 17, 85

Steve Briggs: figs. 7, 8, 9, 12, 16, 18, 20, 25, 27, 28, 29, 31, 32, 33, 36, 37, 38, 39, 44, 45, 47, 48, 52, 54, 55, 56, 59, 61, 63, 66, 67, 68, 70, 73, 74, 82, 84, 88, 90, 91, 92, 93, 96, 98, 101, 103, 105, 106, 108, 109, 120, 121, 123, 125, 127, 129, 131, 136, 142, 149, 151, 153, 154, 156, 157, 160, 166, 168, 169, 171

Barney Burstein: figs. 40, 64, 161

David Caras: figs. 95, 117

Archives, Catholic University of America: fig. 106

Tony Cunha: fig. 107

Detroit Institute of Art: fig. 104

Herbert Edelstein: fig. 53

Foto Marburg/Art Resource, NY: fig. 13

Deborah Hardy: figs. 26, 34, 42, 89, 114, 116

Photographic Services, Harvard University Art Museums: figs. 78, 79, 158

Greg Heins: figs. 69, 145

Meg Henson Scales: fig. 170

Santiago Hernandez: figs. 5, 46, 50, 81, 112

Abadia y Santuario de Montserrat, Spain: figs. 86, 118, 119

Museum of Modern Art: fig. 6

Ned Rothstein: frontispiece, figs. 53, 58, 83, 87, 99, 102

Robert Sawchuck: cover, fig. 122

Dan A. Soper: fig. 21

Galleria Palatina, Palazzo Pitti, Italy: fig. 139

David Stansbury: figs. 10, 22, 23, 57, 60, 62, 72, 75, 76, 77, 94, 100, 111, 113, 130, 137, 141, 143, 147, 163, 164, 165

Straus Center for Conservation, Harvard University Art Museums: figs. 132, 133

Suermondt-Ludwig-Museum, Aachen, Germany: fig. 51

Malcolm Varon: figs. 49, 110

Herbert P. Vose: figs. 65, 152

Mary Lou White: fig. 24

Guss Wilder III: fig. 2

George Zimberg: fig. 19

REPRODUCTION RIGHTS COURTESY

We are grateful to the following entities for permission to reproduce works in this publication:

Abadia y Santuario de Montserrat: Our Lady of Montserrat (fig. 86), Pedro Berruguete (figs. 118, 119)

Alinari/Art Resource: fig. 14

© 2001 Artists Rights Society (ARS), New York/ADAGP, Paris: Émile Bernard (fig. 156), Marc Chagall (figs. 11, 167), Fernand Léger (fig. 165)

© 2001 Artists Rights Society (ARS), New York/VG Bild-Kunst, Bonn: Erich Heckel (figs. 100, 163)

© Basilica of the National Shrine of the Immaculate Conception, Washington, DC/Photo used with permission. All rights reserved: fig. 4.

© 1995 Center for Creative Photography, The University of Arizona Foundation: Lola Álvarez Bravo (fig. 168)

© 2000 Courtesy, Detroit Institute of Art: Gertrude Käsebier (fig. 104)

Foto Marburg/Art Resource: fig. 13

© 2000 The Gale Group, from the New Catholic Encyclopedia by Catholic University of America, vol. ix (McGraw-Hill, 1967): fig. 106

© President and Fellows of Harvard College, Harvard University: figs. 78, 79, 158

© 1997 Meg Henson Scales: fig. 170

Courtesy, Institute of Ethiopian Studies, Addis Ababa: figs. 49, 110

Monfort Fathers, Bay Shore, New York: fig. 3

© 2001 The Munch Museum/The Munch-Ellingsen Group/Artists Rights Society (ARS), New York: figs. 157, 158

© Patrimonio Nacional, Madrid, Spain: figs. 17, 85

Courtesy, San Antonio Museum of Art, Texas: fig. 91

Sopritendenza peri Beni Artistici e Storici di Firenze, Pistoia e Prato, Italy: fig. 133

© 2000 Malcolm Varon, NY: figs. 49, 110)

© 2000 Guss Wilder: fig. 2

STAFF LIST

Sincere thanks to the staff of the Davis Museum and Cultural Center, Wellesley College for their contributions to this publication; and to our collaborators at Oxford University Press.

Publication designer: Adam B. Bohannon

Copy editors: Lucy Flint-Gohlke, Patterson Lamb, Ruth Mannes

Project interns: Hillary L. Anderson, Rielly Andrews, Colleen Baik, Alina C. Bankowski, Eugenia Beh, Blair A. Brooks, Shine Choi, Jennifer Kirchmyer Dobe, Jennifer Erin Hughes, Juno Park, Amy Reed, Alyssa Wright, Jennet Zerbe

Checklist research: Hillary L. Anderson, Laura DeNormandie, Kate Heider, Melissa R. Katz, Lisa McDermott, Rebecca Mongeon, Jennet Zerbe

Photography coordinators: Sandra Petrie Hachey, John L. Rossetti

Photographer: Steve Briggs

Rights and reproduction research: Rebecca Mongeon

Conservation coordinator: John L. Rossetti

Conservators: Elizabeth Coombs, Marc Giudicelli, Teri Hensick, Elizabeth Fulton Leto, Rika Smith McNally, Kate Olivier, Joan Wright, Martina Yamin

Budget coordinator: Janet E. Saad

Funding and donor relations: Nancy Gunn, Melissa R. Katz, Lisa Mary Priest, Gwen Pratt, Alexandra Ziegel

Media and public relations coordinator: Nina J. Berger

Indexing: Katherine V. Stimson